School, Family, and Community Partnerships

SCHOOL, FAMILY,

AND

COMMUNITY PARTNERSHIPS

Preparing Educators and Improving Schools

SECOND EDITION

JOYCE L. EPSTEIN

Center on School, Family, and Community Partnerships
Johns Hopkins University

WESTVIEW
PRESS

A Member of the Perseus Books Group

Find us on the World Wide Web at www.westviewpress.com.

Westview Press books are available at special discounts for bulk purchases in the
United States by corporations, institutions, and other organizations. For more information, please contact the Special Markets Department at the Perseus Books
Group, 2300 Chestnut Street, Suite 200, Philadelphia, PA 19103, or call (800) 810-
4145, ext. 5000, or e-mail special.markets@perseusbooks.com.

Type set in 10 point Sabon by the Perseus Books Group.

Library of Congress Cataloging-in-Publication Data

Epstein, Joyce Levy.
  School, family, and community partnerships : preparing educators and improving
schools / Joyce L. Epstein. — Rev. ed.
      p. cm.
  Includes bibliographical references and index.
  ISBN 978-0-8133-4447-8 (alk. paper)
  1. Community and school—United States. 2. Home and school—United States.
3. School improvement programs—United States. I. Title.
  LC221.E68 2010
  371.190973—dc22

                                                                        2010023427

                              10 9 8 7 6 5 4 3 2 1

This book is dedicated to the memory of Mollie C. and Edward P. Levy, whose love and support helped three sisters set and reach their goals, and to Paul Jerrold Epstein, who turned my research on school, family, and community partnerships into treasured real-life experiences.

Contents

Part One
Understanding School, Family, and Community Partnerships

Tables and Figures

TABLES

FIGURES

Preface and Acknowledgments

THIRTY YEARS SOUNDS LIKE A LONG TIME to work on a topic, but it is not very long to build a field of study on school, family, and community partnerships. My colleagues and I began our research on parental involvement in elementary schools in 1981. We followed with studies of involvement in the middle grades in 1987 and in high schools in 1990. Since that time, we conducted research and development activities with state and district leaders, and we continue this work with educators at all policy levels.

In 1996, with useful results from many studies, I established the National Network of Partnership Schools (NNPS) at Johns Hopkins University. NNPS guides schools, districts, states, and organizations to use research-based approaches to build goal-oriented partnership programs that contribute to student success. Members of NNPS not only develop programs and improve practices of family and community involvement, but also identify new questions and challenges that influence our research. These connections—research that improves practice and practices that extend research—are often discussed in academic circles but rarely accomplished. NNPS is showing how these connections can be organized and conducted to benefit all partners.

Funding and Collegial Support

My work at Johns Hopkins University has been funded over the years by various governmental agencies, including the Office of Educational Research and Improvement (OERI) and its predecessor, the National Institute of Education (NIE) in the U.S. Department of Education, and by a recent five-year grant from the National Institute of Child Health and Human Development (NICHD). At Johns Hopkins, my program on family and community involvement has been housed at the Center for Social Organization of Schools (CSOS) in centers that changed names with each new governmental grant, including the Center for Research on Elementary and Middle Schools (CREMS); Center for Research on Effective Schooling for Disadvantaged Students (CDS); Center on Families, Communities, Schools, and Children's Learning; and Center for Research on the Education of Students Placed at Risk (CRESPAR). To give research on partnerships a permanent home, I established the Center on School, Family, and Community Partnerships within CSOS in 1995.

Grants from the Lilly Endowment, Edna McConnell Clark Foundation, Leon Lowenstein Foundation, National Endowment of the Arts, Disney Learning Partnership, Wallace–Reader's Digest Funds, and MetLife Foundation also supported my research and development projects. Over the years, many funders became colleagues in helping me think about needed directions for school, family, and community partnerships. They included Oliver Moles and Ron Pedone at OERI; Joan Lipsitz, Gayle Dorman, and Kent McGuire at Lilly; John Van Gorder at Lowenstein; Hayes Mizell at the Clark Foundation; Jane Quinn and Catherine Pino at Wallace–Reader's Digest Funds; Laurie Lang, Tony Jackson, and Pamela Rubin at Disney Learning Partnership; and Rick Love at MetLife Foundation. I value their ideas and support.

Special thanks are due to educational leaders in Baltimore who supported, assisted, and inspired me for many years. They included Jerry Baum, who directed the Fund for Educational Excellence and who was a partner in fieldwork for nearly 10 years; Lucretia Coates, the first facilitator for school, family, and community partnerships in the Baltimore City Public Schools (BCPS), whose deep knowledge about schools and families continues to influence this work; and Vivian Jackson, who assisted middle schools for several years in implementing interactive homework. Other talented facilitators for school, family, and community partnerships worked with more than 160 elementary, middle, and high schools in Baltimore City to learn how leadership on partnerships could, in fact, be organized in a large, urban school district and how all schools in nine areas could organize teams of educators, family members, and community partners to plan and implement effective partnership programs. They included (by history of participation) Marsha Powell-Johnson, Paula Williams, Brenda G. Thomas, Joyce Bowyer, Marsha Greenfeld, Patricia Kidd-Ryce, Joann E. Brown, Sandra E. Morgan, and Anjali Patel. Their knowledge and talents helped many schools turn research into action and helped me learn about the real world of district leadership and school-based program development.

Other district leaders in Baltimore supported the work of their facilitators and schools in developing programs of partnership. They included (by history of participation) Gary L. Thrift, Clifton Ball, Cynthia Janssen, Christolyne Buie, Charlene Cooper Boston, Sandra L. Wighton, Ellen D. Gonzales, Anne Carusi, Jeffrey Grotsky, Barry Williams, Patricia E. Abernathy, Cecil Ramsey, Irby Miller, and Carole Seubert. These area superintendents and other administrators taught me valuable lessons about how different district leadership styles contributed to improving schools' connections with families and communities.

Several local foundations in Baltimore also supported fieldwork conducted with my community-based partner, the Fund for Educational Excellence. I owe a great debt to the Fund and to BCPS for making it possible to systematically gather ideas and data from countless teachers, principals, parents, other family members, and students. Baltimore was a "learning laboratory" for school, family, and community partnerships for more than a decade and helped identify the challenges and possibilities for organizing district programs of school, family, and community partnerships in elementary, middle, and high schools. Knowledge gained in BCPS contributed to the development of NNPS and underlies many of the processes that are used, now, in districts and schools across the country.

At this writing, the National Network of Partnership Schools (NNPS) at Johns Hopkins University has grown to include about 1,200 schools and 150 school districts located in more than 35 states, as well as 21 state departments of education and over 50 organizations that work with schools and districts on partnerships. I am grateful to thousands of teachers, administrators, parents, and students who have worked with me and my colleagues over the years. They showed that with skill and will it is possible to develop programs that engage all families in ways that help students succeed in school. Their trials, tribulations, and triumphs contributed to the practical approaches that are included in this volume.

Many colleagues and students at Johns Hopkins University worked with me on studies in this volume and on countless other publications that are referenced here. I am indebted to all of them, especially Henry Jay Becker, who met the challenge in 1981 to start our research program with a survey of educators and parents. His creative work and collaborative spirit helped generate many questions for the studies that followed. Other valued research partners at Hopkins included Susan L. Dauber, Susan C. Herrick, Seyong Lee, Lori Connors-Tadros, and many other helpful graduate and undergraduate students.

Colleagues who worked with me from 1990 to 1995 in the Center on Families, Communities, Schools, and Children's Learning included codirector Don Davies and researchers Carole Ames, Josephine Bright, Melvin Delgado, Larry Dolan, Charles Glenn, Nitza Hidalgo, Vivian Johnson, Sharon Lynn Kagan, Colleen Morisset, Saundra Nettles, Diane Scott Jones, Sau-Fong Siu, and the late Susan M. Swap. These researchers conducted many studies that deepened an understanding of the scope of school, family, and community partnerships from birth through high school. Their work and that of many other researchers cited throughout this volume influenced my thinking about the content of courses to prepare teachers, administrators, social workers, school psychologists, sociologists of education, and other education professionals to understand and conduct school, family, and community partnerships.

Ongoing Research and Development

Special thanks are due to my colleagues at the Center on School, Family, and Community Partnerships, currently including researchers Mavis G. Sanders, Steven B. Sheldon, and Frances Van Voorhis; facilitators Marsha Greenfeld, Darcy Hutchins, Brenda Thomas, and Jenn Ganss; and, in recent years, Claudia Galindo, Natalie Rodriguez Jansorn, Cecelia S. Martin, Mary G. Nesbitt, Karen Clark Salinas, Beth S. Simon, and Kenyatta Williams. The work we did together influenced the topics, discussions, and activities in chapters throughout this volume and new research underway.

Other longtime colleagues and valued friends at Johns Hopkins University supported and encouraged my work for many years, including James M. McPartland, Edward L. McDill, and the late John H. Hollifield. All of the researchers and facilitators at CSOS are working to show that social and educational research can help educators improve schools for all students and benefit families and communities.

I am convinced that researchers learn most about schools by collaborating with educators, parents, students, and others who implement programs, evaluate their efforts, and report their results. All that we know or ever will learn about school, family, and community partnerships depends on researchers, educators, families, students, and others sharing the role of expert. All of my projects, publications, presentations, and collaborations with other researchers, educators, parents, and others have been a true delight, making thirty years seem like a very short time indeed.

My family's interest in my work has been most appreciated, including my late parents' unconditional support and my sisters' ongoing encouragement. My son Paul's experiences in school literally brought my theories and research to life. He showed how important it was for his mom and dad to be positively involved in his education and how crucial it is for every child—all students—to be the focus of school, family, and community partnerships. Now Paul and daughter-in-law Adrienn continue to support my work that is built on family history.

What Is New in the Second Edition?

A direction-shaping survey that Mavis Sanders and I conducted asked over 160 deans and other leaders in colleges of education across the country how well their institutions prepared future teachers and administrators to involve families and communities in children's education. Their responses revealed a dramatic gap between their belief that family and community involvement is a very important topic for future teachers and administrators to master and their honest reports that their graduates were unprepared to conduct effective programs of school, family, and community partnerships. Those data inspired the completion of the first edition of this book as one way to help new teachers and administrators begin their professional lives with a better understanding of useful approaches to family and community involvement.

Some progress has been made since the publication of the first edition of this book. Research on partnerships has improved each year, as more and better studies using ever more rigorous methods are completed. Inservice education has increased to help practicing educators improve their plans and partnership programs. And there are more preservice and advanced education courses on partnership program development—*but not enough*. Most new teachers and administrators are inadequately prepared to work effectively with all students' families in communities across the country.

At the end of the first edition of this book, published in 2001, I noted: "Today's students are tomorrow's parents. They are witnessing and experiencing how their schools treat their families and how their families treat the schools. They are learning by example how parents are involved at school and at home in their education."

Some who were middle and high school students in 2001 now are reading this book—preparing to be teachers! They need to know how to engage their future students' families and communities in productive ways. In this edition, some readings, comments, and activities were retained from the first edition to ensure that future teachers, administrators, and researchers of school, family, and community partnerships understand the history and development of this field of study. Other sections are "new and improved" to share the progress that has been made in research, policies, and practical programs of family and community involvement.

- New readings include a literature review that discusses new directions for partnership program development; a summary of research on homework; and new approaches to district-level leadership, state-level leadership, and policies on family and community involvement.
- Comments, discussion topics, activities, references, and projects were added and updated to enable future teachers and administrators to "think new" about and delve deeper into many aspects of school, family, and community partnerships.

The new edition of this book aims to encourage more professors of education, sociology, psychology, and related fields to incorporate topics covered across chapters in required courses that will prepare the next generation of education professionals to understand and implement programs and practices of family and community involvement to increase student success in school.

Joyce Levy Epstein
Baltimore, October 2010

Understanding School, Family, and Community Partnerships

Introduction

WHOSE DREAMS ARE THESE? Children will like school; work hard; do the best they can; graduate from high school; continue their education; gain employment; and become good citizens, friends, and members of their families. Countless surveys and projects with thousands of educators, families, and students reveal that these are common goals and dreams. Too often, though, these ideals are unattained by this nation's children. How can more students be helped to meet these goals?

To answer questions about goals, we must ask questions about roles: What should families do, what should schools and communities do, and what should students do to reach their common objectives for children's success in school and in the future? These questions are the reasons for studying, implementing, and improving school, family, and community partnerships.

MATCHING RHETORIC WITH PRACTICE

No topic about school improvement has created more rhetoric than parental involvement. Everyone says that it is important. In study after study, teachers, parents, administrators, and even students from elementary through high school say that parental involvement benefits students, improves schools, assists teachers, and strengthens families. There are basic beliefs and agreements about the importance of families and the benefits of parental involvement.

There also are some clearly expressed hopes and wishes for parental involvement. Teachers would like families to assist, guide, and influence their children to do their schoolwork. Families want teachers to let them know how to help their children at home. Students wish their families were knowledgeable about their schools and helpful to them on school matters at home. These desires are expressed in numerous studies with diverse samples, in varied communities, and at all grade levels.

There is some confusion and disagreement, however, about *which* practices of involvement are important and *how* to obtain high participation from all families.

Some educators expect parents to become involved in their children's education on their own. If they do, they are "good" parents. If not, they are irresponsible, uninterested, or "bad" parents. Some educators and parents expect the school to "tell parents what to do" and that parents will simply respond. Neither of these approaches—waiting for involvement or dictating it—is effective for informing or involving all families.

Research shows that *partnership* is a better approach. In partnership, educators, families, and community members work together to share information, guide students, solve problems, and celebrate successes. Partnerships recognize the shared responsibilities of home, school, and community for children's learning and development. Students are central to successful partnerships. They are active learners in all three contexts—at home, at school, and in the community. They link members of these groups to each other. Students are not bystanders but contributors to and actors in the communications, activities, investments, decisions, and other connections that schools, families, and communities conduct to promote children's learning.

What should programs of partnership look like? How can they be developed and sustained? How could teachers, administrators, parents, other family members, and others in communities be prepared to initiate and maintain productive relationships in their work to benefit students? How would teachers, administrators, and others who work with children and families put the best knowledge and practices to work? How must practices change over time as students proceed through the grades? How can research address these questions to continue to increase knowledge and improve practices? These are the questions this book will address. Research, to date, informs the answers; new research will enrich, confirm, or redirect practice.

THE NEED

All teachers and administrators have one thing in common, whether they are in Maine or California; work with students in grade 1 or grade 12; teach Anglo, Latino, African American, Asian American, Native American, or other students; or have advanced or struggling students: All teachers' students have families.

Students' families, however, are not all the same. Some students live with two parents, and others have only one parent at home. Some parents are employed, and some are unemployed; some speak English, and some speak other languages at home. Students come from many different family structures. Indeed, there are important variations in the characteristics and situations of students, families, schools, and communities.

However configured, however constrained, families come with their children to school. Even when they do not come in person, families come in children's minds and hearts and in their hopes and dreams. They come with the children's problems and promise. Without exception, teachers and administrators have explicit or implicit contact with their students' families every day.

All students and their families live in communities, whether close to or distant from schools, that are diverse in geography and history and in economic and social characteristics. Wherever they are located, all communities include individuals, groups, and organizations that care about children; share responsibility for children's futures; and are potentially valuable resources for children, families, and schools. Children, families, and schools also are valuable resources for their communities.

Educators need to understand the contexts in which students live, work, and play. Without that understanding, educators work alone, not in partnership with other important people in students' lives. Without partnerships, educators segment students into the school child and the home child, ignoring the whole child. This parceling reduces or eliminates guidance, support, and encouragement for children's learning from parents, relatives, neighbors, peers, business partners, religious leaders, and other adults in the community.

THE GAP

Teachers learn to teach reading, math, science, and other specialties. They learn to teach students in kindergarten and in all other grade levels. Administrators learn how to manage the school as an organization, create schedules, and supervise many tasks and many people. Most teachers and administrators, however, are presently unprepared to work positively and productively with one of the constants of life in school—their students' families.

Consequently, many educators enter schools without adequately understanding the backgrounds, languages, religions, cultures, histories, structures, races, social classes, and other characteristics and goals of their students and families. Without such information, it is impossible for educators to communicate effectively with the people who matter most to the children in their schools, classrooms, and communities (Bryk and Schneider, 2002).

Few educators enter their profession with an understanding of how they and their colleagues can develop and maintain partnership programs that inform and involve all families every year that children are in school. Without such programs, it is impossible for all families to remain active in their children's education and development.

Few educators are prepared to work with businesses, agencies, and institutions in their students' communities to promote student success in school and beyond. Without these connections, students are underserved and disconnected from opportunities that enrich their schoolwork and prepare them for the future.

An early survey conducted in the southwest region in 1980 found that only 4 to 15 percent of teacher educators taught a full course or part of a course on parent involvement, and only 37 percent of the teacher educators included even one class period on the topic. In the same region, just about all of the practicing teachers and administrators who were surveyed agreed that teachers needed to be better prepared to understand and work with families. And over 70 percent thought that there should be a *required* course on the topic in undergraduate education (Chavkin and Williams, 1988).

Another early study of elementary school teachers in Maryland indicated that few attributed their practices of partnership to their formal education. Most teachers who had even one class on the topic of parental involvement specialized in early childhood or special education or took administrative or other courses as part of an advanced degree. Sometimes the topic was limited to families' legal rights and responsibilities to make specific decisions about children with special needs (Becker and Epstein, 1982; see Reading 3.1).

Little change occurred in the 1980s and 1990s in preparing educators to understand and work with families and communities to support their children's education, despite considerable progress in research, policy, and practice. An informal survey of six campuses of the University of California that prepared teachers found that few courses or even classes-within-courses were offered on family and school partnerships (Ammon, 1990). In Minnesota, more than half of the 27 colleges and universities with degree-granting undergraduate education programs offered no course related to parent involvement for prospective teachers of kindergarten through grade 12, and only one had a required course on the topic (Hinz, Clarke, and Nathan, 1992). Most courses that were offered were for future teachers in early childhood education or special education. Only 6 of 1,300 course listings focused on comprehensive programs of school, family, and community partnerships.

A companion study of the 50 states indicated that no state required an entire course in family involvement for the certification or licensing of teachers. According to these reports, nine states required coverage of the topic in some course, with a few more specifying that requirement for teachers of early childhood (11 states) and special education (15 states). Approximately one-quarter of the states identified the need for elementary educators to show competence (however attained) in school, family, and community partnerships. Fewer states expected middle or high school educators to have competence in family involvement. Only seven states required principals or central office administrators to study parent involvement or demonstrate proficiency in promoting parent involvement in their schools. No state included this competency in recertification or renewal of certification, thereby reducing the likelihood that practicing educators will update their family and community involvement skills (Radcliffe, Malone, and Nathan, 1994).

A study of official certification materials from all states in 1992 found similar patterns and concluded that parental involvement was not a high priority in state certification (Shartrand, Weiss, Kreider, and Lopez, 1997). The researchers conducted follow-up inquiries with leaders of about 60 teacher education programs in 22 states that mentioned family involvement in their certification requirements. The results indicated that teacher education programs responded to state policies by teaching topics of parental involvement in some courses. Only nine of the universities in that sample reported having a required course on family involvement, usually for teachers of young children.

At the start of the new decade, a study of 161 deans and chairpersons in schools, colleges, and departments of education in the United States examined courses offered to prospective educators and leaders' perspectives of the need for change (Epstein and Sanders, 2006). About 70 percent of the leaders strongly agreed that future teachers, administrators, and counselors needed partnership skills, but only 7.2 percent strongly agreed that the new teachers who graduated from their programs were prepared to work with all students' families and communities. Slightly higher percentages believed that future principals (19 percent) and counselors (27 percent) were prepared to work effectively with families. About 60 percent of the leaders of the sampled institutions—more than in past surveys—reported offering a full course on partnerships, mainly to graduate students or, as noted historically, to specialists in early childhood and special education. Most (92 percent) noted that courses at their colleges covered the topic of partnerships in at least *one class*. Even today—even with some progress—most colleges and universities are not adequately preparing new professional educators to work with students' families and communities.

The education leaders' reports were confirmed in a national survey of education school alumni in which 62 percent reported they were not well prepared for the realities of the classroom (Levine, 2006). This includes a lack of skills to work with diverse students and parents in ways that support student learning. Some might say this reflects poorly on the teacher candidates, but the statistic really reflects the poor quality of teacher education programs to help future teachers gain the skills they need—immediately and in every classroom—to work with all students and their families on students' attitudes, efforts, achievements, and progress.

EVIDENCE OF CHANGE

There is evidence that change is possible. In 1989, deans of education and other curriculum leaders at California campuses attended a conference on the need to add school, family, and community partnerships to teacher education. Some took action quickly. Within one year, five of the eight campuses represented at the conference reported making a few changes in the content of courses and assignments in required and elective courses for prospective teachers and administrators. The changes included adding readings about parent involvement to existing courses, professional development, or supervised teaching seminars. One campus added the topic of partnerships to an induction program for first-year teachers who had graduated from the university the prior year (Ammon, 1990). These examples showed that small changes, such as adding readings or discussions about school, family, and community partnerships to existing courses, could be made quickly.

Other changes take longer if they require formal university approval, such as creating a new required or elective course on school, family, and community partnerships for all future teachers or designing a certificate program to develop educational leaders on partnerships. One example of this is a certificate program at the School of Education at Johns Hopkins University. This five-course, 15-credit certificate at the graduate student level, Leadership for School, Family, and Community Collaboration, developed by Dr. Mavis Sanders and her colleagues, required approval from the department and the school's academic review council (Graduate Division of Education, 2003).

In the past few years, more textbooks for various courses on teaching practice, classroom management, and administrative leadership added topics on family and community involvement (Cox-Peterson, 2011; Cunningham and Cordeiro, 2003; Weinstein, 2006; Weinstein and Mignano, 2006; Santrock, 2008; Woolfolk, 2004).

Positive actions also have been taken by individual professors at various colleges and universities who designed and taught courses on school, family, and community partnerships or added readings to existing courses in education, leadership and cultural foundations, sociology, psychology, and social work (Chavkin, 2005; deAcosta, 1996; Kaplan, 1992; Katz and Bauch, 1999; Kirschenbaum, 2001; Riehl, 2004; Van Wyk, 1998). For example, Bermudez and Padron (1988) designed a graduate-level course that included classwork and fieldwork to help educators learn to communicate better with families who spoke Spanish at home. Evans-Shilling (1996) initiated a responsive field-based course that provided educators with experiences in family-school relations. Allexsaht-Snider and others designed a required course for educators preparing for early childhood education to increase understanding of family-school relations; it included fieldwork with families in school, at home, and in the community (Allexsaht-Snider, Phtiaka, and Gonzalez, 1996). She and her colleagues at the University of Georgia also infused these topics into elementary education, field experiences, and other programs to prepare educators. For several years, Mapp (2009) offered future teachers and policy analysts a full-semester course on family and community involvement at the Harvard Graduate School of Education. And the Harvard Family Research Project's Family Involvement Network of Educators (FINE) conducts projects and maintains a website (www.finenetwork.org) to engage professors of education on topics of family and community involvement.

Over the past two decades, these and other professors have worked to help future educators understand the important roles that families and communities play in students' education. A few studies examined the impact of coursework about family and community involvement on future teachers' knowledge, skills, and attitudes about partnerships. Morris and her colleagues at the University of Memphis found positive effects of a four-semester school and community relations course on students' understanding of partnerships, attitudes toward parents, confidence about working with families, and feelings of comfort and competence in planning family involvement activities and programs (Morris and Taylor, 1998; Morris, Taylor, and Knight, 1998).

Studies also show that teachers who feel more competent about their own skills were more likely to implement activities to involve families, raising important questions about the need to improve coursework to increase teachers' efficacy on partnerships (Garcia, 2004). Other professors have reported that coursework increased their undergraduate and/or graduate students' understanding of partnerships as one of the essential components of school and classroom organization and as a major influence on student learning and development (Albert, 2008; deAcosta, 1996; Deslandes, Fournier, and Morin, 2008; Katz and Bauch, 1999; Shartrand et al., 1997; Shumow, 2004; Weiss, Kreider, Lopez, and Chatman-Nelson, 2010).

The American Association of Colleges of Teacher Education (AACTE) partnered with MetLife Foundation to fund five innovative projects to increase attention to family and community involvement in their preservice programs for teachers (AACTE, 2002). These included field experiences for future teachers at the University of Texas at El Paso working with Latino parents in one school's community and trials of Teachers as Faculty and Families as Faculty workshops to give future teachers at the University of South Florida and the University of North Florida, respectively, a chance to hear from local teachers and family members about desired collaborations. Northern Illinois University's project embedded partnership topics throughout the curriculum for preservice teachers, and the University of North Texas designed online components that professors in various courses could use to provide future teachers with new knowledge about family and community involvement. More support of this kind would greatly advance innovative attention to teacher training on aspects of school, family, and community partnerships. More research is needed to learn if and how courses with different designs and requirements affect teachers' and administrators' daily practice.

These examples and the results of the survey of deans suggest that leaders in colleges and universities may be more ready than in the past to add the topic of school, family, and community partnerships to their curricula. Readiness for change also has been influenced by federal policies (e.g., recently by No Child Left Behind [NCLB], with continued influence of Head Start, Even Start, and other programs that require family and community involvement; see Reading 4.3). More college and university professors have read research on school, family, and community partnerships that accumulated in the past two decades, and more professors have graduate students at the master's and doctoral degree levels who are choosing topics on family and community involvement for their dissertations (Epstein and Sanders, 2006).

POLICIES ENCOURAGE PREPARATION ON PARTNERSHIPS

States are beginning to include school, family, and community connections in their qualifications for the certification of teachers, administrators, counselors, and other educators. For example, California's Education Code and Commission on Teaching Credentialing, Ohio's Standards Revisions Teacher Education and Certification, Illinois's General Supervisory Endorsement, Minnesota's Higher Education Coordination Board, Virginia's student teaching requirements, and other legislation refer to the importance of school practices to involve families and communities.

Some states require teachers, administrators, counselors, and other educators to demonstrate knowledge and skills on partnerships to qualify for state certification and reflect the standards for licensure of collaborating organizations. The Education Commission of the States (2005) reported that of the 50 states, 17 directed all districts and schools to implement parental involvement policies while 15 others "urge" these programs. In the past few years, other states reported that, in addition to requiring schools and districts to comply with federal requirements for parental involvement policies and programs, state leaders provided professional development on partnerships, awarded grants for innovative partnership practices, and recommended (rather than required) schools conduct programs that involve all families in their children's education (Moles, 2008). Many states are reluctant to issue detailed mandates and requirements for all districts and all schools to take the same actions, but most states have issued clear recommendations and other documents that support parental involvement as an essential organizational component for effective schools and successful students.

National organizations for college and university program accreditation—including the National Council for Accreditation of Teacher Education (NCATE, 2002), the Interstate New Teacher Assessment and Support Consortium (INTASC, 1992), and the Interstate School Leaders Licensure Consortium (ISLLC)—have standards for teacher and administrator education that explicitly include preparation and competence in working with families and communities (Council of Chief State School Officers, 1996). For example, NCATE specifies that teacher candidates should understand principles and strategies for school, family, and community partnerships to support students' learning. INTASC and ISLLC stipulate competencies that all teachers and administrators should master, including fostering relationships with families and community groups to support student learning and well-being. National teacher examinations for new teachers and national assessments for highly accomplished teachers include questions and require skills on parent and community involvement (National Board for Professional Teaching Standards, 1994).

Still, all state and credentialing requirements about competencies on partnerships tend to be general and aspirational, rather than specific about course content and required credits. It takes time for state laws and accreditation standards to affect college and university courses for future teachers and administrators.

MORE IS NEEDED

Despite some progress in the past ten years, the picture is still bleak. Most teachers and administrators are not prepared to understand—much less design, implement, and evaluate—new approaches for developing programs of family and community involvement that increase the success of all students in school. Most administrators are not prepared with new strategies to guide and lead their staffs to develop strong school programs and classroom practices that inform and involve all families about their children's learning, development, and educational plans for the future. The problem is serious for all educators and is particularly urgent for educators teaching in public and charter schools that serve diverse families. It is still the case that rising teachers and administrators need a repertory of research-based approaches to work with all families, especially in economically distressed communities.

Even big changes that were made in the past few years have had limited impact. Relatively few new teachers or administrators graduate from any one college or university. The fact is that many more colleges and university programs need to improve their programs to enable all future teachers and administrators to gain basic knowledge and skills on partnership program development. It will be necessary to scale up the number of professors and programs of teacher education, educational administration, and other courses in order to prepare all educators to engage all families in positive ways in their children's education at all grade levels.

It is time to advance undergraduate and graduate education by ensuring that future teachers and administrators have the required courses with the newest content coverage on school, family, and community partnerships. Simultaneously, it is important to encourage state education leaders to improve certification standards for teachers, administrators, and counselors by specifying course requirements and competencies that educators must have to support general statements about the importance of family and community involvement.

THE GOALS

Just as teachers are prepared to teach subject matter and administrators are prepared to direct and manage schools and programs, all educators also must be prepared to draw on all of the resources that will help students succeed in school, including families and communities. This volume aims to:

- add an understanding of school, family, and community partnerships to the education and training of teachers, administrators, counselors, and professionals in related fields;
- include this knowledge in the definition of what it means to be professional;
- promote respect, trust, appreciation, and collaboration between and among all adults who influence children's lives and learning;
- enable educators to apply their knowledge to develop effective programs of partnership in their schools and classrooms;
- support the integration of school, family, and community partnerships in broader programs of school improvement, giving explicit attention to improving practices of involvement; and
- encourage research on the simultaneous influences of home, school, and community contexts on children's learning and development.

The professional preparation of educators must include the information they need to understand, conduct, and maintain school, family, and community partnerships. Without this information, teachers and administrators are restricted in the resources they have to help students do their best. Also, families are then limited in the influence they may have on their children's learning and development for at least 12 years of school life. In turn, many children miss the support, encouragement, and understanding they might have from their families and communities. In the end, if educators lack knowledge and skills in organizing and implementing effective partnerships with all students' families, fewer students succeed in school.

The research base of the first edition of this book has been strengthened by advances in research, policy, and practice over the past ten years. It is now possible to enable prospective and practicing educators to gain the knowledge, tools, and examples they need to mobilize families and communities to assist children's learning and development from preschool through high school.

ACHIEVING THE GOALS

To recognize the need, fill the gap, and achieve the goals stated above, we must change some of the requirements, options, and content of higher education courses. Courses must be revised and expanded to include a solid base of information to prepare teachers and administrators to understand and involve families in their children's education.

Ideally, there should be at least one comprehensive required course on school, family, and community partnerships in every preparatory program. Because every teacher and administrator works with children's families (in person or unseen) every day of their professional lives, this requirement is as important as a course in teaching reading, math, or another subject in the preparation of school teachers, and as important as any major required course in educational administration or other educational specialties.

A less meritorious policy decision that still improves most preparatory programs is to organize and offer elective courses on the topic of partnerships at the undergraduate and graduate levels. There also should be a formal plan for how readings on school, family, and community partnerships will be integrated in other required and elective courses to ensure that all who are preparing for professions in education have had substantial exposure to and experience with the theory, research, and implementation of these partnerships.

The call for required, elective, and/or integrated courses is offered with a mix of urgency and understanding. It is urgent that educators better understand families' roles in children's education and how to implement programs of school, family, and community partnerships. It is understood that change in higher education must be discussed and planned to alter long-standing practices in order to offer students these options. Leaders in higher education must be change agents and take steps to ensure that the educational professionals who are prepared in their courses, programs, departments, colleges, and universities are, in fact, well-qualified to teach children and work with families and communities as partners in education.

In colleges and universities, courses also should be enhanced to prepare researchers in sociology, psychology, education, and related disciplines to understand the questions, methods, and problems of studying multiple contexts—home, school, and community—and the interactions of individuals in these contexts. We must prepare the next generation of education researchers to study the overlapping spheres of influence on children's learning and development, just as we must prepare the next generation of teachers and administrators to work effectively with families and communities.

USING THIS VOLUME

This book is about school, family, and community partnerships: how to think about them, talk about them, study and understand them, act on them, and improve them. It includes selected readings and excerpts of readings on the theory, research, policy, and practice of school, family, and community partnerships to provide a solid base of information on the development, directions, problems, and possibilities of these connections.

The readings and accompanying comments, discussions, and activities can be used as the basis for a full course or as supplementary materials in courses such as foundations of education, methods of teaching, contemporary issues in education, education policy studies, educational administration, counseling, sociology of education, sociology of family, educational psychology, school social work, and related courses. Following are suggestions for using this volume as a text for a full course or for supplementary readings.

A Comprehensive Required or Elective Course

A comprehensive course on partnerships must cover the major topics that educators need to study to proceed thoughtfully in their work with children, families, and communities. This includes theoretical perspectives; results of research on particular approaches; effective policies and practices that teachers and administrators should understand and be able to use to engage all families, involve the community, and best serve students; and organizational strategies to help educators and families work together to design and implement sustainable programs of partnership. Other texts or readings, activities, and projects may supplement this volume in a full course.

Supplementary Readings in Other Required or Elective Courses in Education and the Social Sciences

Readings on family, school, and community connections are important for fully understanding the sociology of education, sociology of the family, social foundations of education, school administration and management, political science, political action and organizations, social policy, school psychology, human development, social work, community services, group processes, urban policy, and related fields. Individual chapters, articles, and activities in this volume may be selected to bring the topic of partnerships to courses in these specialties.

Presently, many courses focus on families without paying attention to children's schools; focus on schools without attending to their connections with families and communities; or instruct about communities without considering the connections and investments of community groups and organizations with educators, families, and children. The readings in this volume will broaden the background and understanding of undergraduate and graduate students about the important connections among home, school, and community for the purposes of assisting students, strengthening families, and renewing communities.

Selections from this volume also may be woven into thematic courses. For example, a course in education, sociology of education, or related fields may take a historical perspective, addressing the question: How have research, policy, and practice on school, family, and community connections changed over the past half century? Family and school connections have changed from rather superficial, peripheral activities to theory-driven and research-based frameworks that guide basic and applied research and school program development. Research on "community" has changed from using mainly demographic data that rank locations as high or low on social or economic variables to studying the people, processes, and resources in any community that can assist student learning. More and different themes would emerge in a course covering the organization and effects of connections among children, families, schools, and communities over the past two centuries.

Another elective course might address comparisons of school, family, and community connections across nations with comparative readings that explore common and distinct international themes, policies, and school-based programs of family and community involvement. A third thematic course might focus on social-psychological perspectives of the interconnections and interrelationships of individuals that influence student development. This might include research on social networks of educators, parents, parents-and-educators, and student-peers-and-parents, and the two-way, three-way, and many-way connections between and among schools, families, students, peer groups, and communities.

Linkages to Courses on the Methods of Teaching
Specific School Subjects and Practice Teaching

Readings on school, family, and community connections should be included in methods of teaching courses that prepare educators to teach specific subjects. That is, teachers of every subject and grade level need to understand, design, select, conduct, and evaluate appropriate connections with their students' families about the curriculum in specific subjects, homework policies, attendance and behavioral expectations, children's grades, challenges, and progress, and about academic decisions such as course choices and the selection of enrichment programs. Teachers of all subjects and grade levels need to understand, design, select, conduct, and evaluate connections with individuals and groups in communities to maximize learning opportunities in reading, math, writing, science, computer skills, art, music, family life, physical education, and other subjects.

Important theoretical issues to study and discuss include whether and how sharing power with parents increases or decreases teachers' power and professional standing. Also, teachers need to learn specific skills, such as how to design homework that enables children to share skills and ideas at home, how to inform families about what their children should know and do each year in each subject, and how to inform families about children's progress and involve families in the assessment of students' work. Teachers of all subjects also should understand the community near the school; the home communities of their students; and the connections with businesses, groups, and individuals in the surrounding community that may help enrich and extend their teaching and students' learning.

Educators who are being prepared to teach, administer, or work in the schools of the twenty-first century should learn about the scope and expansion of research and practice in the field of school, family, and community partnerships. This information will help them develop their own perspectives, understand the pros and cons and the strengths and weaknesses of various approaches, and thoughtfully select or design strategies to communicate with and involve families and communities in children's education.

Other Information

Even if a required course covered all of the topics in this volume, undergraduate and graduate students still would need other information about families, schools, and communities to be prepared for their professions. For example, students need to read about the family as a social organization, the influence parents have on their children at various age levels, diversity in family backgrounds and cultures, and trends in family life. Similarly, professionals who work with families and children need to know about school and classroom organizations to understand basic school structures, functions, staffing, and alternative curricular and instructional approaches for educating students. Educators need to build their knowledge about community structures, processes, and services. The readings in this volume address these topics only as they affect the design and conduct of school, family, and community partnerships. The fields of parent education and parent leadership are also related to topics of family and community involvement (Bornstein, 2002).

No single course or class in higher education will provide all the information and examples that professionals need to make decisions about which practices to use in every school in which they work. Nevertheless, a basic, comprehensive, required course or substantial coverage in several courses should increase awareness and understanding of the topic, alert educators that collaborating with families is part of their professional responsibility, and provide many ideas and examples to help teachers and administrators "tailor" programs and practices of partnership to their particular school, family, and community settings.

Links to Inservice Education

The vast majority of practicing educators, social workers, school psychologists, and others who work with families and children have had no prior formal education in school, family, and community partnerships. Thus, there is and will continue to be a great need for inservice education for practitioners in preschools; in elementary, middle, and high schools; and at the district and state leadership levels to meet new laws and requirements for effective programs of family and community involvement linked to student achievement and success in school.

Most inservice programs, presently, are limited to a few hours' duration and may introduce teachers and administrators to one or two new practices of partnerships.

A companion volume—*School, family, and community partnerships: Your handbook for action* (Epstein et al., 2009)—is a comprehensive inservice guidebook that enables educators and parent leaders in schools, districts, and states to organize, improve, and maintain effective programs of partnerships in their own locations.

SETTING A COURSE

This volume brings together a set of basic readings, with comments on new issues; topics for class discussions; questions and activities for classwork, homework, field experiences, and suggested projects; and other material for use in undergraduate and graduate courses in education, psychology, sociology, and other disciplines. The content, based on my work with colleagues, educators, and parents connects child development, socialization, and education with the institutions of school, family, and community and the individuals within them. The collection of readings and activities stresses the importance of developing and maintaining *programs* of partnerships at the school, district, and state levels—not only what one teacher or one principal or one parent might do on their own.

Some chapters should be particularly useful for improving the actions and activities of prospective teachers, administrators, and others who plan to work with schools and families. Other chapters aim to encourage research on new and needed questions to advance the field of school, family, and community partnerships. The readings include literature reviews, original research, policy issues, and activities for practice teaching and subject specialization. The final chapter serves as a bridge to the practical, inservice education and program development that must be customized for and conducted in all schools. The chapters cover the following topics:

Chapter 2: Theory and Overview. Two readings provide a broad perspective on school, family, and community partnerships to introduce a theory of *overlapping spheres of influence* and to provide an understanding of new directions for research, policy, and practice. Theories of authority and decision making and their applications at the school, district, and state levels are explored and may be expanded.

Chapter 3: Research. Several original research studies are presented with data collected from teachers, parents, and students on the nature and extent of involvement, relationships among partners in children's education, and effects of partnership practices. The readings help students examine research methods, interpret results, and consider implications for school practice or for new studies to extend the field. The involvement of parents in one- and two-parent homes is discussed to focus on what schools may do to involve all parents, not just those who usually become involved on their own. This chapter also introduces research on homework to study connections of the classroom curriculum, family involvement, and student attitudes and achievements.

Chapter 4: Policy. Several readings summarize issues and advances in state, district, school, and federal policies of partnership and the connections of policies to leadership actions. These include research on NCLB, guidelines for policy development, and examples of state and district policies on family and community involvement. The readings and activities show how research influences policy, how policy sparks improvements in practice, and, coming full circle, how new policies and practice open opportunities for more and better research. These topics and a discussion of funding partnership programs make this chapter of particular interest in educational administration courses.

Chapter 5: Practical Framework. This chapter connects research and policy with practice. The reading and activities focus on my *framework of six types of involvement*, sample practices of partnerships, the challenges that must be met in excellent programs, and results that can be expected if practices for each type of involvement are well designed and well implemented. By applying knowledge and information to real-world situations, future educators will gain an understanding of the basic components for building goal-linked, school-based partnership programs.

Chapter 6: Practical Applications. Particularly targeted to courses on methods of teaching specific subjects and practice teaching, this chapter summarizes research on a practical method for improving connections with families about students' homework. It discusses and illustrates how to organize and conduct feasible family and community connections connected to the curriculum at home and at school by (1) designing interactive homework for students to discuss with their families at home (Type 4 in the framework of six types of involvement) and (2) organizing volunteers who present interdisciplinary discussions of art and social studies (Type 3 in the framework). Both practical applications demonstrate ways to organize family and community involvement to increase student learning. These topics should be of interest in courses for curricular specialists, students in methods of teaching classes, and student teachers.

Chapter 7: Strategies for Action in Practice, Policy, and Research. This chapter describes an action-team approach for implementing comprehensive programs of school, family, and community partnerships. *Teamwork* is key for organizing and sustaining programs and practices of partnerships. As a team, educators, parents, and community members can work together to plan and implement effective practices that involve all families and promote children's success in school. Essential program elements—leadership, teamwork, written plans, funding, internal and external collegial support, action to implement plans, evaluations, and continuous improvement—must be organized to sustain excellent partnership programs just as these factors are needed for effective reading, math, testing, and other school programs. This chapter also summarizes the volume's central themes and major conclusions about school, family, and community partnerships.

FEATURED TOPICS FOR DISCUSSION

Each chapter introduces provocative and useful terms that change the way we think about school, family, and community partnerships. For example, readings in Chapter 2 describe *school-like families* and *family-like schools* to contrast collaborative actions with previous narrow views of the different goals and missions of these institutions. This chapter also asks readers to consider how the *multiplication of labor* may describe how educators and families help students learn better than the *division of labor* that was emphasized in prior studies of organizations. Finally, the chapter discusses seven ways to "think new" about partnerships in research, policy, and practice.

Chapter 3 presents original research that provided a base on which studies of school, family, and community partnerships continue to build. The readings illustrate and emphasize the importance of multiple reporters and multiple measures of partnerships in research on partnerships. One reading identifies ten purposes of homework and discusses the need for improving the design of homework to ensure higher quality assignments before simply assigning more homework.

Chapter 4 emphasizes the need for *side-by-side* policies to balance top-down and bottom-up approaches in states, districts, and schools. Readings and discussions in this chapter also show how to translate legislated requirements for family involvement into measures to study how federal (and other) legislation is implemented. Comments in this chapter discuss *food-for-thought stamps* to support and expand extracurricular, after-school, and summer enrichment activities for economically distressed students and families.

Chapter 5 suggests *redefinitions* for each of the six types of involvement that will bring school, family, and community partnerships into alignment with family factors in the twenty-first century. For example, a new definition states that workshops for parents are not only meetings at school but also the content of those meetings disseminated to all who could not come, thereby enabling parents to attend workshops in different ways.

Chapter 6 shows that homework is not always completed by the student alone but can be purposely *interactive* with a parent or family partner. The chapter also demonstrates how volunteers in the middle grades can make real contributions to student learning.

Chapter 7 explains how concepts of trust and mutual respect are central to the success of all partnerships and how seemingly contradictory concepts of equity and diversity in partnerships must coexist. The chapter describes *goal-oriented* and *process-oriented* approaches that educators may use to plan, implement, and evaluate their programs of family and community involvement.

The readings and discussions in several chapters contrast *what is* versus *what might be* in school, family, and community partnerships to encourage fuller interpretations of research results, new directions for research, and the application of research for school improvement.

ACTIVITIES AND EXERCISES

Each chapter includes comments and key concepts that extend and update the readings, topics for informal classroom discussions, classroom activities, written assignments, and field activities that encourage students to reflect on the readings, debate ideas, describe related experiences, and conduct short-term and long-term projects. Activities include classroom discussions; written comments; interviews with parents, teachers, administrators, community members, and students; panel presentations; role plays; school visits; and other activities. Questions are provided for students to use in their interviews, and students are asked to compose some of their own questions. Some interviews with educators, parents, or others may be assigned to all students to be completed individually, or interviewees may be invited to the class for group interviews. Field activities and other tasks also may be assigned to individuals, pairs, or groups.

Selection of assignments. There are more questions and activities in each chapter than students in most classes can address in one semester. Professors are encouraged to select and balance assignments so that students engage in a mix of reflective writing, interviews, research, discussions, and other activities. The assignments should reflect course themes and meet the needs of undergraduate or graduate students in teaching, administration, research, and other fields.

Answers to questions. Most of the discussion topics and questions have many correct answers, not one right answer. Some questions first ask students to "identify a school level (preschool, elementary, middle, or high) or grade level that interests you." Thus, students will select different settings on which to base their answers. Students should contribute ideas and written work using information from the readings as well as their own perspectives and experiences. They should be asked to justify their responses based on data or summaries provided in the chapter or refute ideas with specific examples. Professors need to encourage well-argued discussions and debates based on the content of the readings, other research, data collected by students for homework or projects, and students' experiences.

Many students come into education, sociology, psychology, and other courses with stereotypic views of families from backgrounds that differ from their own (Graue and Brown, 2003). The discussion topics and activities in this volume are designed to challenge stereotypes and strengthen future teachers' and administrators' understanding of the *variations* that define students and families in all groups.

Follow-up. Some assignments may be followed up in class by sharing ideas, discussing issues, and pooling data to create larger and more representative samples for additional discussions. For example, if each student interviewed two parents for an assignment, a class of twenty students would produce a combined sample of 40 parents to better understand parents' ideas, goals, or problems. As another example, if each student in a class identifies an exemplary product, the collection of good ideas may be compiled as a computerized resource file for future reference.

Adaptation. Professors are encouraged to adapt or expand the exercises to match the emphases of particular courses and classes. For example, topics and questions about home-school connections at the school level can be adapted and redirected to focus on district, state, or community issues to meet the needs of students in educational administration or community studies. Professors may increase the difficulty or length of assignments by requiring students to complete more readings, conduct and report activities marked "optional," provide more examples, or complete other related activities. Similarly, professors may reduce the difficulty or length of assignments by assigning parts or sections of activities that are provided in each chapter.

Elaboration. The questions in each chapter may spark ideas for term papers, master's or doctoral theses, or other research projects.

SUMMARY

This book offers a clear perspective on the importance of theory-driven and research-based approaches to programs of school, family, and community partnerships. To think about, talk about, and take action to improve home, school, and community connections that support students' education and school improvement, educators must have a foundation on which to build. It is not acceptable to base ideas and future actions only on personal, limited, or selected experiences or outdated stereotypes. It is necessary to understand the basic and complex aspects of a field of study to decide whether, when, why, and how to apply research in practice or to select important questions for new research.

The volume supports six facts and one urgently needed action:

- **Fact:** All students have families. All students and families live in communities. Families and communities are important in children's lives and, along with schools, influence students' learning.
- **Fact:** Teachers and administrators have direct or indirect contact with students' families every day of their professional careers.
- **Fact:** Few teachers or administrators are prepared to work with families and communities as partners in children's education.
- **Fact:** There is widespread agreement and accumulating evidence that well-designed programs and practices of school, family, and community partnerships benefit students, families, and schools.

- **Fact:** Ever more rigorous research and evaluations are needed to continually improve knowledge about family and community involvement and the effectiveness of state, district, and school programs and practices.
- **Fact:** Although there is more to learn, we know enough now to implement research-based, goal-linked programs of school, family, and community partnerships that engage all families and help all students succeed to their full potential.
- **Action Needed:** There must be immediate and dramatic changes in the preservice and advanced education of teachers, administrators, counselors, and others who work with schools, families, and students. Changes are needed in coursework and field experiences to prepare professionals to understand, respect, and collaborate with parents, other family members, and individuals, groups, and organizations in communities that can help students succeed.

This book will help. The readings and references provide a history of the field and a window on how research and programs of school, family, and community partnerships developed over time and must continue to develop. The comments, questions, and activities in each chapter introduce topics that should be discussed, debated, and studied. Whether used to organize a full course or to supplement other courses in education and social science, this volume introduces new directions for improving school, family, and community partnerships and will generate new ideas for research, policy, and practice.

REFERENCES

American Association of Colleges for Teacher Education (AACTE). (2002). *Partners for student success 2002: National summit on parent involvement in teachers education: Proceedings document.* Washington, DC: AACTE.

Albert, M. (2008). Personal communication about "Literacy," a family/school/community collaborations course. State University of New York, Potsdam.

Allexsaht-Snider, M., H. Phtiaka, and R. M. Gonzalez. (1996, November). *International perspectives: Preparing teachers for partnership.* Paper presented at the Education Is Partnership conference, Copenhagen, Denmark.

Ammon, M. S. (1990). *University of California project on teacher preparation for parent involvement. Report I: April 1989 conference and initial followup.* Berkeley: University of California. Mimeographed.

Becker, H. J., and J. L. Epstein. (1982). Parent involvement: A study of teacher practices. *Elementary School Journal* 83: 85–102. (Reading 3.1).

Bermudez, A. B., and Y. N. Padron. (1988). University-school collaboration that increases minority parent involvement. *Educational Horizons* 66: 83–86.

Bornstein, M., ed. (2002). *Handbook of parenting* (2nd ed.). Mahwah, NJ: Lawrence Erlbaum.

Bryk, A. S., and B. Schneider. (2002). *Trust in schools: A core resource for improvement.* New York: Russell Sage Foundation.

Chavkin, N. F. (2005). Preparing educators for school-family-community partnerships: Challenges and opportunities. In E. N. Patrikakou, R. P. Weissberg, S. Redding, and H. J. Walberg (Eds.), *School-family partnerships: Fostering children's school success* (pp. 164–180). New York: Teachers College Press.

Chavkin, N. F., and D. L. Williams. (1988). Critical issues in teacher training for parent involvement. *Educational Horizons* 66: 87–89.

Council of Chief State School Officers. (1996). *Interstate school leaders licensure consortium: Standards for school leaders*. Washington, D.C.: Author.

Cox-Peterson, A. (2011). *Educational partnerships: Connecting schools, families, and the community*. Thousand Oaks, CA: Sage.

Cunningham, W. G., and P. A. Cordeiro. (2003). *Educational leadership: A problem-based approach* (2nd ed.). Boston: Allyn and Bacon.

deAcosta, M. (1996). A foundational approach to preparing teachers for family and community involvement in children's education. *Journal of Teacher Education* 47: 9–15.

Deslandes, R., H. Fournier, and L. Morin. (2008). Evaluation of a school, family, and community partnerships program for preservice teachers in Quebec, Canada. *Journal of Educational Thought* 42: 27–52.

Education Commission of the States. (2005). *Parental involvement in education*. Denver: Author.

Epstein, J. L., et al. (2009). *School, family, and community partnerships: Your handbook for action* (3rd ed.). Thousand Oaks, CA: Corwin.

Epstein, J. L., and M. G. Sanders. (2006). Prospects for change: Preparing educators for school, family, and community partnerships. *Peabody Journal of Education* 81: 81–120.

Evans-Shilling, D. (1996). Preparing educators for family involvement: Reflection, research, and renewal. *Forum of Education* 51: 35–46.

Garcia, D. C. (2004). Exploring connections between the construct of teacher efficacy and family involvement practices. *Urban Education* 39: 290–315.

Graduate Division of Education. (2003). Announcement of graduate certificate program: Leadership for School, Family, Community Collaboration. Baltimore: Johns Hopkins University.

Graue, E., and C. P. Brown. (2003). Preservice teachers' notions of families and schooling. *Teaching and Teacher Education* 19: 719–735.

Hinz, L., J. Clarke, and J. Nathan. (1992). *A survey of parent involvement course offerings in Minnesota's undergraduate preparation programs*. Minneapolis: Center for School Change, Humphrey Institute of Public Affairs, University of Minnesota.

Interstate New Teacher Assessment and Support Consortium (INTASC). (1992). *Model standards for beginning teacher licensing and development: A resource for state dialogue*. Washington, DC: Council of Chief State School Officers.

Kaplan, L. (1992). Parent education in home, school, and society: A course description. In L. Kaplan (Ed.), *Education and the family* (pp. 273–277). Needham Heights, MA: Allyn and Bacon.

Katz, L., and J. P. Bauch. (1999). The Peabody family involvement initiative: Preparing preservice teachers for family/school collaboration. *The School Community Journal* 9: 49–69.

Kirschenbaum, H. (2001). Educating professionals for school, family and community partnerships. In D. Hiatt-Michael (Ed.), *Promising practices in school, family and community partnerships* (pp. 185–208). Greenwich, CT: Information Age Publishers.

Levine, A. (2006). *Educating school teachers*. New York: Teachers College, Columbia University.

Mapp, K. (2009). Personal communication.

Moles, O. (2008). *State requirements for parent involvement activities*. Rockville, MD: Author.

Morris, V. G., and S. I. Taylor. (1998). Alleviating barriers to family involvement in education: The role of teacher education. *Teaching and Teacher Education* 14: 219–231.

Morris, V. G., S. I. Taylor, and J. Knight. (1998, April). *Are beginning teachers prepared to involve families in education?* Paper presented at the annual meeting of the American Educational Research Association, San Diego.

National Board for Professional Teaching Standards (NBPTS). (1994). *What teachers should know and be able to do.* Washington, DC: NBPTS. (See standards for specific certificates, e.g., family partnerships in early adolescence/generalist standards.)

National Council for Accreditation of Teacher Education (NCATE). (2002). *Professional standards for the accreditation of schools, colleges, and departments of education.* Washington, DC: Author.

Public Law 107–110. (2002). *No Child Left Behind Act of 2001.* Washington, DC: Congressional Record, 115 STAT. 1501–1505, January 8, 2002.

Radcliffe, B., M. Malone, and J. Nathan. (1994). *Training for parent partnership: Much more should be done.* Minneapolis: Center for School Change, Hubert H. Humphrey Institute of Public Affairs, University of Minnesota.

Riehl, C. (2004, April). Personal communication.

Santrock, J. W. (2008). *Educational psychology* (3rd ed.). Boston: McGraw Hill.

Shartrand, A. M., H. B. Weiss, H. M. Kreider, and M. E. Lopez. (1997). *New skills for new schools: Preparing teachers in family involvement.* Cambridge, MA: Harvard Family Research Project.

Shumow, L. (2004, April). *An integrated partnership model preparing teachers for parental engagement.* Paper presented at the Twelfth International Roundtable on School, Family, and Community Partnerships, San Diego.

Van Wyk, J. N. (Ed.). (1998). *Home-school relations study guide.* Pretoria: University of South Africa.

Weinstein, C. S. (2006). *Middle and secondary classroom management* (3rd ed.). Boston: McGraw Hill.

Weinstein, C. S. and A. J. Mignano. (2006). *Elementary classroom management* (4th ed.). Boston: McGraw Hill.

Weiss, H. B., H. Kreider, M. E. Lopez, and C. M. Chatman-Nelson. (2010). *Preparing educators to involve families: From theory to practice* (2nd ed.). Thousand Oaks, CA: Sage Publications.

Woolfolk, A. (2004). *Educational psychology* (9th ed.). Boston: Pearson.

Theory and Overview

T HE FIRST READING IN THIS CHAPTER examines theories of family and school connections, discusses how data support or refute different theoretical perspectives, and presents a new theoretical model—*overlapping spheres of influence*—to explain and guide research on school, family, and community partnerships. The article explains the organizational and interpersonal components of the theory of overlapping spheres of influence and how this perspective extends previous theoretical models.

The second reading is a review of the literature that identifies seven principles that ask researchers across disciplines to think in new ways about how to study the structures, processes, and results of family and community involvement in education. The new directions also guide educators at all school levels to develop more powerful and effective partnership programs.

Together, the two readings in this chapter guide future educators and researchers in how to think about, talk about, and study school, family, and community partnerships.

Toward a Theory of Family-School Connections: Teacher Practices and Parent Involvement*

THREE PERSPECTIVES ON FAMILY-SCHOOL RELATIONS

Three perspectives currently guide researchers and practitioners in their thinking about family and school relations:

1. Separate responsibilities of families and schools
2. Shared responsibilities of families and schools
3. Sequential responsibilities of families and schools.

These perspectives are profoundly different. Assumptions based on the *separate responsibilities* of institutions stress the inherent incompatibility, competition, and conflict between families and schools. This perspective assumes that school bureaucracies and family organizations are directed, respectively, by educators and parents whose different goals, roles, and responsibilities are best fulfilled independently. It asserts that the distinct goals of the two institutions are achieved most efficiently and effectively when teachers maintain their professional, universalistic standards and judgments about the children in their classrooms and when parents maintain their personal attention and particularistic standards and judgments about their children at home (Parsons, 1959; Waller, 1932; Weber, 1947).

The opposing assumptions, based on *shared responsibilities* of institutions, emphasize the coordination, cooperation, and complementarity of schools and families and encourage communication and collaboration between the two institutions. This perspective assumes that schools and families share responsibilities for the socialization and education of the child. Teachers and parents are believed to share common goals for their children, which can be achieved most effectively when teachers and parents work together. These assumptions are based on models of inter-institutional interactions and ecological designs that emphasize the natural, nested, and necessary connections between individuals and their groups and organizations (Bronfenbrenner, 1979; Leichter, 1974; Litwak and Meyer, 1974).

The third perspective, *sequential responsibilities* of institutions, emphasizes the critical stages of parents' and teachers' contributions to child development. This approach is based on the belief that the early years of a child's life are critical for later success, and that by age five or six, when the child enters formal schooling in kindergarten or first grade, the child's personality and attitudes toward learning are well established. Parents teach their young children needed skills, arrange educational

---

* By Joyce L. Epstein. Originally published in K. Hurrelmann, F. Kaufmann, and F. Losel, eds., *Social Intervention: Potential and Constraints* (New York: de Gruyter, 1987), 121–136. Reprinted with permission.

programs and experiences, and are guided or supported by social and educational agencies (e.g., pediatricians, preschool teachers, and the media) to prepare their children for school. At the time of children's formal entry into school, the teacher assumes the major responsibility for educating them (Bloom, 1964; Freud, 1937; Piaget and Inhelder, 1969).

Understanding the Contrasting Theories: Mechanisms Producing Family-School Relations

In addition to the three major theoretical distinctions between separate, shared, and sequential responsibilities, there are other theories that help explain the *mechanisms* for building family and school relations and the resulting variations in the connections between institutions and their members. Among the most useful are symbolic interactionism and reference group theories. *Symbolic interactionism* (Mead, 1934) assumes that self-concept, personality, values, and beliefs are products of our interactions with others. The theory suggests that we learn how others perceive and anticipate our goals and behaviors, and that we fashion our behavior to fulfill the expectations of others and to receive their recognition. In terms of family and school connections, if teachers do not interact with parents, they cannot be informed about or understand the parents' expectations for their children and the teachers. They cannot shape their teaching behavior to be responsive to those expectations. If parents avoid teachers, they cannot be informed about or understand the schools' expectations for their children or the parents. They cannot shape their behavior to provide useful assistance to the students and teachers.

Reference group theory (Merton, 1968) makes other important connections between esteem and interaction. A reference group is a collectivity or an individual who is taken into consideration by another group or individual to influence their attitudes and behaviors. This happens when one group or individual recognizes the importance of the other or admires the positions and actions of the other. For example, if, in planning children's educational programs, a teacher considers the roles parents can play, it may be because the teacher considers parents an important reference group. If, in planning their family activities, parents take the teachers' or schools' goals and actions into account, it may be because they consider teachers an important reference group. Sometimes only the higher-status group influences the behavior of the other in an unreciprocated pattern. Teachers may take parents into account without parents reciprocating the consideration, as in some communities where parents have strong control of educational politics and policies. Or parents may consider teachers an important reference group without the teachers reciprocating, as when parents try to help their children with schoolwork even if the teacher has not given them encouragement or ideas about how to help at home.

The three main theories explain the basic differences in philosophies and approaches of teachers and parents that produce more or fewer, shallow or deep family-school connections. The other theories explain the motivations to remove or reinforce boundaries between schools and families.

Understanding the Contrasting Theories: Changing Patterns in Family-School Relations

There have been important changes in the patterns of partnerships between the home and school over time. In the early 19th century, parents and the community greatly controlled the actions of the schools. The home, church, and school supported the same goals for learning and for the integration of the student into the adult community (Prentice and Houston, 1975). The community, including parents and church representatives, hired and fired the teachers, determined the school calendar, and influenced the curriculum. When the students were not in school, the families and others in the community taught their children important skills and knowledge needed for success in adulthood.

In the late 19th and early 20th centuries, a different pattern of family and school relations emerged. Increasingly, the school began to distance itself from the home by emphasizing the teachers' special knowledge of subject matter and pedagogy. Teachers began to teach subjects that were not familiar to parents, using methods and approaches that were not part of the parents' experiences. The family was asked to teach children good behavior and attitudes to prepare them for school and to take responsibility for teaching children about their ethnicity, religion, and family origins. These family responsibilities were separate from the schools' goal to teach a common curriculum to children from all ethnic, religious, social, and economic groups.

During the 1980s and 1990s, family-school relations changed again in response to increased demands from the public for better, more accountable schools. Both better-educated and less educated parents want a good education for their children and are requesting or requiring schools to keep them informed about and involved in their children's education.

AN INTEGRATED THEORY OF FAMILY-SCHOOL RELATIONS

Changing times require changing theories. School and family relationships have been different at different times in history. It is not surprising, then, to see a restructuring of theories, from inter-institutional separation in the 1930s–1950s to cooperation between schools and families in the 1970s–1980s to accommodate the social changes affecting these organizations. But we do not yet have a model of family-school relations that accounts for the variation and process of change that will continue to influence the interactions of families and schools. The existing theories omit attention to history, student development, and the influence families and schools have on each other.

A life-course perspective (Elder, 1984) enables us to integrate useful strands from the different theories of family and school relations to correct the weaknesses of the separate theories. This perspective requires that we pay attention to three characteristics in family-school relationships: history, developmental patterns, and change.

History

Four recent trends help to explain why changes are needed in our theories of family and school relations:

1. **More mothers with a college education and bachelor's degree.** Over the past 40 years there has been a dramatic increase in the number of U.S. high school students, especially women, who attend and graduate from college. Whereas fewer than 20 percent of bachelor's degrees were earned by women prior to 1950 (mostly in the field of education), fully half of the earned bachelor's degrees were awarded to women in 1980 in many fields (Bureau of the Census, 1984). The education of mothers affects their interactions with teachers. Whereas most mothers were once less educated than college-trained teachers, most mothers are now attending some college and have near, equal, or higher educational status than their children's teachers. There is still great variation in the education of women, but the proportion of educated mothers has made a difference in how parents view teachers, how teachers view parents, and whether and how mothers become involved in their children's education.

2. **Baby and child care.** Dr. Spock's (1950) influential and popular book increased the number of parents who became knowledgeable about and involved in the education of their infants and toddlers. The book offers sensible information to all parents about the importance of home environments for children's learning, information that had previously been known to only a few parents. Although Spock's book is not very useful in its discussions of older children and has little to say about school, it increased parents' awareness of and experience with their children as young learners. Spock's book, other child care books, and private and public health care programs continue to prime new generations of parents of infants and toddlers for the next phase of their children's lives: school.

3. **Federal regulations and funding for parent involvement.** In the 1960s, Head Start and other federally sponsored programs for disadvantaged preschoolers recognized that parents needed the help of educators to prepare their preschool children for regular school to break the cycle of school failure that threatened their children. More important, the preschools recognized that, despite the lack of advanced education of many mothers, the schools and the children needed the mothers' involvement to be successful. Mothers of children in Head Start were required on advisory councils and often were involved in classrooms as volunteers and paid aides, and at home as tutors.

During the same decade, Follow-Through programs required schools to recognize the continued importance of parents as educators beyond the preschool years (Gordon, Olmsted, Rubin, and True, 1979). The Education for All Handicapped Children Act (Public Law 94–172) of 1975 brought teachers and parents together to discuss the educational program of each child. The federal programs and their official recognition of the importance of parents put parent involvement on the agendas of the local schools (Hobson, 1979; Keesling and Melaragno, 1983; Valentine and Stark,

1979). Schools could not easily limit parent involvement to the parents of children in federally sponsored programs, and so more parents at all grade levels, regardless of education or economic background, became involved with their children's schools and teachers.

4. Changing family structures. In the past decade, two key changes in family structure have dramatically affected family and school relations. These are the increase in the number of single parents and in the number of mothers working outside the home. Mothers who work outside the home need to manage the care and schooling of their children with more exactitude than do mothers who work at home. They must arrange for their children's care before and after school, on school holidays, and during illnesses. Attention to the needs of the children has increased the concern of working mothers about the quality of day care, school, and after-school programs.

Single mothers are even more likely than other mothers to work outside the home and are especially sensitive about their responsibilities to their children. They have accentuated the need of all parents for information from teachers to help them use their limited time at home more productively in the interest of their children. Although [employed] mothers and single parents do not volunteer to help at the school building as much as other mothers, research shows that they are just as interested as other mothers in their children's education and spend as much or more time helping their children at home (Epstein, 1984 [Reading 3.5]).

Increasingly, schools have had to replace traditional images of family life and patterns of communication with mothers at home with new images and new patterns of communication to accommodate different types of families. Some schools have made these adjustments to help all families, however structured, to interact successfully with the school. Other schools have not changed their expectations for or communications with families, despite the changes in families.

These four trends, over the last 40 to 50 years of the 20th century, changed family-school connections in the United States. These changes, singly and in combination, involved more parents in their children's education beyond preschool, officially and publicly recognized parents as "teachers," and increased the need for better communication between the home and school.

Developmental Patterns

Schools' and families' interactions need to fit the age, grade level, and level of social and cognitive development of the children. Schools are more like families for young students, with closer ties between teachers and parents of preschool and early elementary students. Schools may become increasingly impersonal in the secondary grades, with the aim of preparing students for interactions in adulthood with other formal organizations in government, work, and society. But through high school, schools vary in the extent to which they communicate with, inform, and involve parents in their children's education. We do not know the type, degree, or optimal mix of personal and impersonal relations across the grades that lead to maximum learning and successful preparation for adulthood. But our model of family-school relations must be based on a developmental framework to account for the continuity of school and family actions and interactions across the school years and the changes in forms and purposes of parent involvement at different student ages and stages of development.

Change

Families and schools are ever-changing. Families change as the members mature, developing new skills, knowledge, contacts, and patterns of social interaction. A family builds a changing, cumulative history of relationships with the school for each child in attendance. Interactions with one school affect the family's knowledge and attitudes in dealing with new schools that their children enter.

Schools change as the members come and go. New students enter the school each year, new combinations of students enter classes, and new teachers and administrators join the staff. The talents, perspectives, and leadership of the school change with the maturity and stability of the staff's abilities to consider complex educational issues, practices, and goals. They may be more open to parents' requests and to parental involvement. Schools can build a changing, cumulative history of relationships with families as the students proceed through the grades.

A MODEL OF OVERLAPPING FAMILY AND SCHOOL SPHERES

Figures 2.1 and 2.2 introduce a model of family and school relations that accounts for history, development, and changing experiences of parents, teachers, and students.

External Structure

The external structure of the model consists of overlapping or nonoverlapping spheres representing the family, school, and community. The degree of overlap is controlled by three forces: time, experience in families, and experience in schools.

Force A represents a developmental time and history line for students, families, and schools. Time refers to individual and historical time: the age and grade level of the child and the social conditions of the period during which the child is in school. For example, in infancy the spheres in our model may be separate. The child first "attends" home, and the family provides the main educating environment. Parents and teachers do not initially interact directly about the child's learning. Even in infancy, however, the spheres may overlap. For example, if an infant is physically, mentally, or emotionally handicapped, parents and special teachers may begin a highly organized cooperative program to benefit the child. For all children, the family and school spheres may overlap to some extent in infancy and early childhood, as parents apply knowledge of child rearing and school readiness from books, their own school experiences, and information from pediatricians, educators, and others.

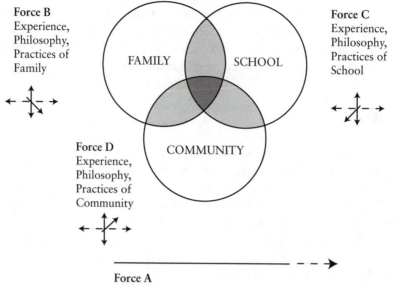

FIGURE 2.1 Overlapping Spheres of Influence of Family, School, and Community on Children's Learning (External Structure of Theoretical Model)

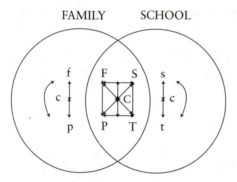

KEY: Intra-institutional interactions (lowercase)
Inter-institutional interactions (uppercase)

f/F = Family   c/C = Child
s/S = School   p/P = Parent
                      t/T = Teacher

Note: In the full model the internal structure is
      extended, using the same KEY to include:
      co/CO = Community
      a/A   = Agent from community/business

FIGURE 2.2 Overlapping Spheres of Influence of Family, School, and Community on Children's Learning (Internal Structure of Theoretical Model)

Later, in a regular pattern, the spheres overlap when the child "attends" home, school, and the community.

There will be a "typical" or expected pattern of separation or overlap at different times based on the age of the child, the level of school, and the historical period when the child is in school. Up to now, the greatest overlap of family and school spheres for most children has occurred during the preschool and early elementary grades. But there has also been great overlap for some children at all grade levels because of the varying philosophies, policies, practices, and pressures of parents, teachers, or both, as represented by Forces B and C.

Force B and Force C represent the experiences of and pressures on family and school organizations and their members that need to be accounted for to study, understand, or change family-school relations. These forces push together or pull apart the spheres to produce more or less overlap of family and school actions, interactions, and influence all along the time line. When parents maintain or increase interest and involvement in their children's schooling (Force B), they create greater overlap of the family and school spheres than would be expected on the average. When teachers make parents part of their regular teaching practice (Force C), they create greater overlap than would typically be expected.

After the child enters school there will be some overlap of the two organizations at every grade level. This is true as long as there are family members (or surrogates) with whom the child and school interact. Even in seemingly separate situations such as private, elite boarding schools or state boarding schools for delinquent youngsters, there are family and school contacts about contracts, payments, rules, visits, evaluations, and so forth that define the "minimum" overlap of the two spheres over the school years. The "maximum" overlap occurs when schools and families operate as true "partners," with frequent cooperative efforts and clear, close communication between parents and teachers in a comprehensive program of many important types of parent involvement (Epstein, 1986 [Reading 3.4]; Gordon, 1979; Seeley, 1981). But there is never "total" overlap because the family maintains some functions and practices that are independent of the schools' or teachers' programs, and the school maintains some functions and practices that are independent of families.

Children are connected to the same families but to different teachers over the course of their school years. Each new teacher (Force C) and each family's continuing or new involvement (Force B) create dynamic patterns of family-school relationships. There is continual adjustment in the overlap or separation of the two spheres.

Time alone (Force A), or the increasing age of the child, does not make parents more knowledgeable about how to help their children with particular school problems. Indeed, our research shows that it currently works the other way. The older the child (after grade 1), the less overlap there is in the two environments, and the less the parent feels able to help the child in school (Epstein, 1986). Thus, in Figure 2.1, if we included only Force A, we would see, for most families and schools, quite separate spheres in infancy, increasing overlap during the preschool years and grade 1, and decreasing overlap from grades 2 or 3 on.

By adding Forces B and C we recognize that the parents' and teachers' practices and the pressures they put on each other alter the typical patterns to create more or less overlap for families and schools at every grade level. For example, some teachers of older students increase their interactions with the parents of their upper elementary and secondary school students to keep the families involved in their children's education. For children in these teachers' classes, there will be greater overlap of family and school goals and interactions than for children whose teachers ignore the role of parents in their teaching practice.

Internal Structure

The internal structure of the model in Figure 2.2 shows the interpersonal relationships and influence patterns of primary importance. Two types of interactions and influence are shown: within organization (lowercase letters) and between organizations (capital letters). Two levels of interaction are also shown: standard, organizational communications (family and school) and specific, individual communications (parent and teacher). Family (f) and parent (p) [interactions] and school (s) and teacher (t) interactions are those that occur separately [within the organization in separate spheres of influence] as parents, offspring, or other relatives conduct their family life and personal relationships, or as teachers, principals, and other school staff create school policies or conduct school or individual activities. By contrast, Family (F) and School (S) [interactions] and Parent (P) and Teacher (T) interactions are those that occur as members of the two organizations interact in standard, organizationally directed communications (F and S), or in unique, individually directed communications (P and T) [in the overlapping spheres of influence].

Family (F) and School (S) connections refer to the interactions between family members and school staff that concern all families and the general school staff or school programs. These include, for example, communications to all parents about school policies; workshops available to all parents on child rearing or child development; programs for all parents to become involved at the school as parent volunteers; or family actions that may affect the schools, such as activities of parent-teacher organizations, parent advisory councils, or citizen advocacy groups in the community. These types of involvement establish common structures for communications and interactions between families and schools as organizations.

Parent (P) and Teacher (T) connections refer to specific interactions between parents and teachers about an individual child. These may include, for example, parent-teacher conferences about the child's progress; parents' notes or phone calls to teachers about the child's academic, social, or personal problems or needs; or the teacher's specific suggestions to parents about how they can help their own child with learning activities at home.

The Child (C) has the central place in all of the patterns of interaction and influence in this model. We assume that the child's welfare and interests are the parents' and teachers' reasons for interacting. For the child, the school and family policies, parent and teacher interactions, and the child's understanding and reactions to these connections influence academic learning and social development. The multidirectional arrows in the model show that children interact with, influence, and are influenced by their families and especially parents, and by changes in their families and parental behavior that result from the actions of the schools. Children interact with, influence, and are influenced by their schools and especially teachers, and by the changes in schools' and teachers' practices that result from the actions of families.

The external and internal structures of the model are, of course, intimately related. The internal organizational and individual relationships are influenced simultaneously by the age and grade level of the student and the common practices of the time period (Force A) and by the actions, attitudes, experiences, and decisions of teachers and parents (Forces B and C). The degree of overlap of family and school organizations and their goals and practices affects the social and psychological distance between the family and school members, their patterns of communication, and the results or outcomes of more or less interaction. Each of the components of the model can be translated into well-specified measures to study the effects of parent involvement (e.g., teachers' practices of parent involvement, parents' initiatives or responses to teachers' requests) on student achievement, attitudes, and other student, parent, and teacher outcomes.

The model recognizes the interlocking histories of the institutions and the individuals in each, and the continuing, causal connections between organizations and individuals. The model energizes an integrated theory of family and school relations by acknowledging the continuous change that occurs in families and schools; the accumulated knowledge and experiences of parents, teachers, and students; and the influence of these different patterns on student motivations, attitudes, and achievement.

SCHOOL-LIKE FAMILIES AND FAMILY-LIKE SCHOOLS

The proposed model of overlapping spheres assumes that there are mutual interests and influences of families and schools that can be more or less successfully promoted by the policies and programs of the organizations and the actions and attitudes of the individuals in those organizations. Although there are important differences between schools and families (Dreeben, 1968), we need to recognize also the important similarities, overlap in goals, responsibilities, and mutual influence of the two major environments that simultaneously affect children's learning and development.

Earlier theories asserted that schools treat students equally, judging them by universal standards and rewarding students for what they do (achievements) and not for who they are (ascriptions). In contrast, families are said to treat children individually, judging them by personal standards and special relationships, basing rewards and affection on the children's individual growth and improvement or on their membership in the family and not on achievements relative to other children. These "pure" images of different institutional approaches and functions are not very accurate portrayals of how schools or families actually work to motivate students toward success in school. The distinction between universalistic and particularistic treatments has been blurred in families that are more aware of the importance of schooling and its components and in schools with more personal and individualized environments. These are *school-like families* and *family-like schools*.

School-Like Families

Some parents run "school-like" homes. They know how to help their children in schoolwork and take appropriate opportunities to do so. School-like families often have persistent and consistent academic schedules of learning for their children from infancy on, with books on colors, shapes and sizes, and music and art as part of their early "school-like" curricula. Before the children enter school, these families are directed by "absentee" or remembered teachers or by contemporary educational sources and resources. During the early years the family teaches the young child, but in fact it may be that images of school or teachers in absentia influence the family in how and what to teach the child.

Some families operate very much like schools. They not only create school-like tasks for their children and reward them for success but also match tasks to each child's level of ability and involve the children in active learning rather than passive listening. These families not only translate the curriculum of the school into home tasks, but also put into practice principles of organizational effectiveness (Rich and Jones, 1977) and use the same structures (i.e., the task, authority, reward, grouping, evaluation, and time or TARGET structures) that guide effective classroom instruction (Epstein, 1988).

Although most parents accept and love their children for their unique qualities and lineal connections, many families reward their children for real and objective accomplishments, as teachers do. Many families judge their children on standard criteria and reward their children as they learn the "basic skills" (from learning to walk to learning to read) and as they acquire social skills and advanced academic skills or other talents. School-like families place more emphasis than other families on their children's place in a status hierarchy.

Family-Like Schools

Teachers vary in their recognition and use of the overlap between family and school spheres of influence. Some schools make their students feel part of a "school family" that looks out for their interests and provides unique experiences for each child. Schools may relax and de-standardize their rules, vary the students' roles, and alter the reward system to be more responsive to the student and to be more like a family.

Although schools impose some uniform standards on all students (e.g., attendance regulations, graduation requirements, formal codes for dress or conduct), these may not be as important as student-teacher relationships and personal, individual attention for influencing and improving student motivation and progress. Presently, brighter students often are given various opportunities to interact on friendly and preferential terms with teachers. Slower students often experience less personal, less family-like treatment, which may further reduce their motivation to come to school to learn.

Schools vary in how much they emphasize uniform or special standards. Some schools recognize and reward only students who are in the top groups or tracks or who get the highest grades. Other schools reward students for individual progress and improvement in achievement, as parents do. They place less emphasis on the students' place in a status hierarchy. Particularistic treatment, associated with family relations, implies a degree of favoritism or special attention to the unique and endearing qualities of individuals. This kind of treatment occurs at some schools, also, with some students receiving family-like treatment, attention, and even affection from teachers.

Time in Family and School Environments

The child is either in or out of school. Some count the hours that students spend in school (e.g., Rutter, Maughan, Mortimore, and Ouston, 1979). Others cite the time that students are not in school and are under the influence of the family, community, media, churches, camps, day care programs, peer groups, or part-time employers (Csikszentmihalyi and Larson, 1984). At least 16 hours per school day plus weekends and vacations are out-of-school time. The seemingly clear dichotomy of time in or out of school is obscured by the degree of overlap in the two environments. For example, when the student is in school, the family's influence may still be at work. A student knows whether a parent knows what is happening in school, what the student is learning, and how he or she is expected to behave. Homework activities may affect the student's attention in class and readiness for new and more difficult work. Similarly, when the student is at home, the school's influence may be still at work. At home, a student may consider how a teacher wants homework to be completed and may use school skills and information to discuss ideas and solve problems.

Time in and out of school, then, is not "pure" school or family time. Time in school may be influenced by the family; time out of school may be influenced by teachers and other school programs and experiences. The degree of overlap in the two environments on matters of schoolwork and on the recognition and support of students' unique, individual talents influences the students' attention, motivation, and learning in and out of school.

EXPLORING THE THEORY: EFFECTS OF FAMILY-SCHOOL OVERLAP ON PARENTS, STUDENTS, AND TEACHING PRACTICE

From research completed over the past several years, we have some evidence of how teachers' practices reflect the three current theories of family and school relations and how the degree of overlap in family and school spheres influences parents' attitudes and behaviors and student attitudes and achievements.

Variation in Overlap in Teaching Practice

As stated previously, the philosophies and practices of teachers reflect the three theories of school and family relations: separate, sequential, and shared spheres of family and school responsibilities and influence. For example, some teachers believe that they can be effective only if they obtain parental cooperation and assistance on learning activities at home. In their classrooms, cooperation is high. These teachers make frequent requests for parental assistance in reinforcing or improving students' skills. They orchestrate actions to increase the overlap in family and school spheres of influence.

Other teachers believe that their professional status is in jeopardy if parents are involved in activities that are typically the teachers' responsibilities. In their classrooms, inter-institutional cooperation is low. These teachers make few overtures to parents and rarely request them to help their children with learning activities at home. They maintain more separate spheres of influence for the school and the family (Becker and Epstein, 1982 [Reading 3.1]; Epstein and Becker, 1982 [Reading 3.2]). Teachers' present practices also illustrate assumptions of sequential patterns in family-school relations. More teachers of young children (grade 1) than of older children (grades 3 and 5) are frequent users of parent involvement techniques. In a clear, linear pattern, most teachers of young children assist parents to become involved in their children's education, but most teachers of older children ignore or discourage parental involvement. Along the time line, then, there is increasingly less overlap of family and school spheres.

Benefits from Greater Overlap

Our surveys of teachers, principals, parents, and students show that:

- Teachers control the flow of information to parents. By limiting or reducing communications and collaborative activities, teachers reinforce the boundaries that separate the two institutions. By increasing communications, teachers acknowledge and build connections between institutions to focus on the common concerns of teachers and parents: a child who is also a student (Becker and Epstein, 1982).
- Parents do not report deep conflict or incompatibility between schools and families. Rather, parents of children at all grade levels respond favorably to teachers' practices that stress the cooperation and overlap of schools and families. Frequent use by teachers of parent involvement leads parents to report that they receive more ideas about how to help their children at home and that they know more about the instructional programs than they did in the previous year (Epstein, 1986).
- Teachers who include the family in the children's education are recognized by parents for their efforts. They are rated higher by parents than are other teachers on interpersonal and teaching skills, and they

are rated higher in overall teaching ability by their principals (Epstein, 1985, 1986).

- Students' test scores suggest that schools are more effective when families and schools work together with the student on basic skills. Students whose teachers use frequent practices of parent involvement gain more than other students in reading skills from fall to spring (Epstein, 1991 [Reading 3.7]). And fifth-grade students recognize and benefit from cooperation between their teachers and parents (Epstein, 1982 [Reading 3.9]).

The results of our research show that although teaching practice reflects all three of the major theoretical positions, parents, students, and teachers benefit most from practices that increase the overlap in school and family spheres of influence all along the developmental time line.

CONCLUSION

Over the last few decades of the 20th century, ideas about family-school relations changed as other social conditions affected schools and families. Theories moved away from the separation of family and school and toward greater teacher-parent cooperation and communication. Our model of family-school relations integrates the discrete, extant theories and reflects the fact that at any time, in any school, and in any family, parent involvement is a variable that can be increased or decreased by the practices of teachers, administrators, parents, and students. Programs and practices can be designed, revised, and evaluated to learn which variations produce greater school and family effectiveness and student success. The members of the school and family organizations can act and interact with others in ways that include or exclude parents from their children's education and that include or exclude teachers as influences on the family. These actions push the spheres of family and school influence together or apart in a continuous, dynamic pattern, and influence student learning and development.

Schools and families vary on the dimensions that are supposed to distinguish family and school treatments and attention to children. There are family-like schools and school-like families, as well as schools and families that are distinct in their approaches to education and socialization. Some have suggested that schools and families have different goals for their children (Lightfoot, 1978), but our research suggests that although parents' educational backgrounds differ, both more- and less-educated parents have similar goals to those of the school for their children's education (Epstein, 1986).

The main differences among parents are their knowledge of how to help their children at home, their belief that teachers want them to assist their children at home, and the degree of information and guidance from their children's teachers in how to help their children at home. These factors create more or less school-like families.

The main differences among teachers are their ability to put principles of child and adolescent development and organizational effectiveness into practice in instruction and classroom management, their ability to communicate with students as individuals, their beliefs about the importance of parents' involvement and parents' receptivity to guidance from the school, and their ability to communicate with parents as partners in the children's education. These factors create more or less family-like schools.

The theoretical model of overlapping spheres of influence, its underlying assumptions, and research on the effects on parents and students of teachers' practices of parent involvement aim to:

- extend studies of families by intensifying attention to the interplay of family and school environments during that part of the parents' and children's lives when the children are in school or are preparing for school, from infancy through the high school grades; and
- extend studies of school organization and effects by intensifying attention to the total educational environment of children including the home, and by examining the implications of this extension for teachers' roles and student learning and development.

REFERENCES

Becker, H. J., and J. L. Epstein. (1982). Parent involvement: A study of teacher practices. *Elementary School Journal* 83: 85–102. (Reading 3.1).

Bloom, B. S. (1964). *Stability and change in human characteristics.* New York: Wiley.

Bronfenbrenner, U. (1979). *The ecology of human development.* Cambridge, MA: Harvard University Press.

Bureau of the Census. (1984). *Statistical abstract of the United States, 1985.* Washington, DC: Government Printing Office.

Csikszentmihalyi, M., and R. Larson. (1984). *Being adolescent: Conflict and growth in the teenage years.* New York: Basic Books.

Dreeben, R. (1968). *On what is learned in school.* Reading, MA: Addison-Wesley.

Elder, G. H., Jr. (1984). Families, kin, and the life course: A sociological perspective. In R. Parke (Ed.), *Review of child development research,* Vol. 7 (pp. 80–135). Chicago: University of Chicago Press.

Epstein, J. L. (1982). *Student reactions to teacher practices of parent involvement.* Paper presented at the annual meeting of the American Educational Research Association, New York. (Reading 3.9).

———. (1984). *Single parents and the schools: The effect of marital status on parent and teacher evaluations.* Report 353. Baltimore: The Johns Hopkins University Center for Social Organization of Schools. (Reading 3.5).

———. (1985). A question of merit: Principals' and parents' evaluations of teachers. *Educational Researcher* 14: 3–10.

———. (1986). Parents' reactions to teacher practices of parent involvement. *Elementary School Journal* 86: 277–294. (Reading 3.4).

———. (1988). Effective schools or effective students? Dealing with diversity. In R. Haskins and D. MacRae (Eds.), *Policies for America's public schools: Teachers, equity, and indicators* (pp. 89–126). Norwood, NJ: Ablex.

———. (1989). Family structures and student motivation. In C. Ames and R. Ames (Eds.), *Research on motivation in education, Vol. 3* (pp. 259–295). New York: Academic Press.

———. (1991). Effects on student achievement of teachers' practices of parent involvement. In S. Silvern (Ed.), *Advances in reading/language research, Vol. 5: Literacy through family, community, and school interactions* (pp. 261–276). Greenwich, CT: JAI. (Reading 3.7).

Epstein, J. L., and H. J. Becker. (1982). Teacher practices of parent involvement: Problems and possibilities. *Elementary School Journal* 83: 103–113. (Reading 3.2).

Freud, A. (1937). *The ego and mechanisms of defense.* London: Hogarth.

Gordon, I. J. (1979). The effects of parent involvement in schooling. In R. S. Brandt (Ed.), *Partners: Parents and schools* (pp. 4–25). Alexandria, VA: Association for Supervision and Curriculum Development.

Gordon, I. J., P. J. Olmsted, R. I. Rubin, and J. H. True. (1979). How has Follow-Through promoted parent involvement? *Young Children* 34: 49–53.

Hobson, P. J. (1979). The partnership with Title I parents. In R. S. Brandt (Ed.), *Partners: Parents and schools* (pp. 41–46). Alexandria, VA: Association for Supervision and Curriculum Development.

Keesling, J. W., and R. Melaragno. (1983). Parent participation in federal education programs: Findings from the federal programs surveys phase of the study of parent involvement. In R. Haskins (Ed.), *Parent education and public policy* (pp. 230–256). Norwood, NJ: Ablex.

Leichter, H. J. (Ed.). (1974). *The family as educator.* New York: Teachers College Press.

Lightfoot, S. L. (1978). *Worlds apart: Relationships between families and schools.* New York: Basic Books.

Litwak, E., and H. J. Meyer. (1974). *School, family, and neighborhood: The theory and practice of school-community relations.* New York: Columbia University Press.

Mead, G. H. (1934). *Mind, self, and society from the standpoint of a social behaviorist.* Chicago: University of Chicago Press.

Merton, R. K. (1968). *Social theory and social structure* (Enl. ed.). New York: Free Press.

Parsons, T. (1959). The school class as a social system: Some of its functions in American society. *Harvard Educational Review* 29: 297–318.

Piaget, J., and B. Inhelder. (1969). *The psychology of the child* (H. Weaver, Trans.). New York: Basic Books.

Prentice, A. R., and S. E. Houston. (1975). *Family, school, and society.* Toronto: Oxford University Press.

Rich, D., and C. Jones. (1977). *A family affair: Education.* Washington, DC: Home and School Institute.

Rutter, M., B. Maughan, P. Mortimore, and J. Ouston. (1979). *Fifteen thousand hours: Secondary schools and their effects on children.* Cambridge, MA: Harvard University Press.

Seeley, D. (1981). *Education through partnership: Mediating structures and education.* Cambridge, MA: Ballinger.

Spock, B. (1950). *The pocket book of baby and child care.* New York: Pocket Books.

Valentine, J., and E. Stark. (1979). The social context of parent involvement in Head Start. In E. Zigler and J. Valentine (Eds.), *Project Head Start: A legacy of the war on poverty* (pp. 291–314). New York: Free Press.

Waller, W. (1932). *The sociology of teaching.* New York: Wiley.

Weber, M. (1947). *The theory of social and economic organization.* New York: Oxford University Press.

Moving Forward: Ideas for Research on School, Family, and Community Partnerships*

It is a social fact that children learn and grow at home, at school, and in the community. People in these three contexts affect children's learning and development, for better or for worse, from infancy through the school years and beyond. This important reality often is ignored by researchers who study only schools or only families. Educators, too, may focus only on the school curriculum, instruction, or testing, without giving attention to students' families and communities, as if students were not also children, friends, and neighbors.

Increasingly, research and exemplary practice reveal that it is all but impossible to separate the interests and influences of educators, parents, and other educational partners on student achievement, attitudes, and behaviors. Although it is, admittedly, harder to study more than one setting at a time, it is critical for researchers to recognize the simultaneous and cumulative effects of home, school, and community on student development. It is, therefore, imperative that we "think new" about research on school, family, and community partnerships.

The field of school, family, and community partnerships is a young field of study, compared to other educational research topics. Knowledge has grown over the past twenty-five years with sharper theory, expanded research questions, improved methods of analyses, and with the interest and efforts of educators and policy leaders. Advances have been made by researchers across disciplines and across countries using varied methodologies to study the nature and effects of school programs and family involvement at different grade levels and in diverse communities. Many publications have summarized the results of research, documented progress in programs and in policies of parental involvement, and pressed for more and better studies (Booth and Dunn, 1996; Boethel, 2003; Castelli, Mendel, and Ravn, 2003; Chavkin, 1993; Christenson and Conoley, 1992; Davies and Johnson, 1996; Edwards, 2004; Epstein, 2001; Fagnano and Werber, 1994; Fruchter, Galletta, and White, 1992; Henderson and Mapp, 2002; Hiatt-Michaels, 2001; Patrikakou, Weissberg, Redding, and Walberg, 2005; Ryan, Adams, Gullotta, Weissberg, and Hampton, 1995; Sanders and Epstein, 1998a, 1998b; Schneider and Coleman, 1993; Smit, Van der Wolf, and Sleegers, 2001; Swap, 1993; and see extensive, annual bibliographies compiled by the Harvard Family Research Project, 2004, at www.gse.harvard.edu). Collectively, these and many other publications have shaped the field and, literally, speak volumes about topics that need more attention in future research.

In one overview of the field, Epstein and Sanders (2000) discussed several topics that needed more research, including partnerships at times of student transitions; the organization of school-community connections; students' roles in school, family,

---

* By Joyce L. Epstein and Steven B. Sheldon. Originally published in C. F. Conrad and R. Serlin, eds., *SAGE Handbook for Research in Education: Engaging Ideas and Enriching Inquiry* (Thousand Oaks, CA: Sage, 2006), 117–137. Reprinted with permission.

and community partnerships; results of school, family, and community connections; fathers' involvement in children's education; the impact of federal, state, and local policies; the effects of preservice and advanced education on partnerships for future teachers and administrators; and more. These topics, scarcely studied a few years ago, still need attention.

SEVEN PRINCIPLES TO HELP RESEARCHERS THINK IN NEW WAYS

The many thoughtful overviews and summaries of research on partnerships make it unnecessary to re-review the literature. In this chapter, we look in a different direction and identify seven principles that have emerged from prior studies and from exemplary practice that should help researchers across disciplines think in new ways about how to study the structures, processes, and results of family and community involvement in education. These principles require researchers to think in new ways to (1) broaden the familiar term of *parental involvement* to *school, family, and community partnerships* to recognize the shared responsibilities of educators, parents, and others for children's development and learning; (2) understand the multidimensional nature of involvement; (3) view the structure of partnerships as a component of school and classroom organization; (4) recognize multilevel leadership for involvement at the school, district, and state levels; (5) focus involvement on student success; (6) acknowledge the importance of increasing the equity of involvement of parents to promote more successful students; and to (7) advance knowledge and improve practice with more and better studies. We discuss the importance of these defining principles for researchers, educators, families, and others who have a stake in improving schools and in increasing student success.

1. *School, family, and community partnerships* is a better term than *parental involvement* to recognize that parents, educators, and others in the community share responsibility for students' learning and development.

The development of a theory on partnerships opened new ways to think about the involvement of parents in children's education. The theory of *overlapping spheres of influence* posits that students learn more when parents, educators, and others in the community work together to guide and support student learning and development (Epstein, 1987, 2001). In this model, three contexts—home, school, and community—overlap with unique and combined influences on children through the interactions of parents, educators, community partners, and students across contexts. Each context "moves" closer or farther from the others as a result of external forces and internal actions.

The external structure of the model of overlapping spheres of influence shows that, by design, the three contexts can be pulled together or pushed apart by important forces (i.e., the backgrounds, philosophies, and actions of families, schools, and communities and the developmental characteristics of students). The internal structure of the model identifies the institutional and individual lines of communication and social interactions of parents, teachers, students, and community members with students and each other.

Classic sociological theories suggested that school and family organizations are most efficient and effective when they had separate goals, roles, and responsibilities (Waller, 1932; Weber, 1947). However, data on student learning indicated that students did better in school when the important people in their lives at home, at school, and in the community had common goals and played collaborative, complementary, and supportive roles (Epstein, 2001).

The theory of overlapping spheres of influence integrates and extends ecological, educational, psychological, and sociological theories and perspectives on social organization and relationships (e.g., Bronfenbrenner, 1979, 1986; Comer, 1980; Elder, 1997; Leichter, 1974; Lightfoot, 1978; Litwak and Meyer, 1974; Seeley, 1981). Based on concepts of symbolic interactionism, social exchange, reference group, and ecological theories, the theory of overlapping spheres of influence recognizes the interdisciplinary nature of school, family, and community partnerships. It emphasizes the need for reciprocal interactions of parents, educators, and community partners to understand each others' views, to identify common goals for students, and to appreciate each others' contributions to student development. For example, as the theory translates to practice, we see that teachers who hold parents as a reference group are more likely to design and conduct interactions and activities that account for the roles parents play in their children's education. Similarly, parents who understand teachers' work and school goals for their children communicate with the school and organize home activities that support their children as students (Epstein, 1987).

Concepts of social capital (Coleman, 1988; Lin, 2000) also are relevant to the theory of overlapping spheres of influence. Through their interactions, parents, educators, and community partners establish social ties and exchange information that accumulates as social capital, and that may be used to improve children's schools and learning experiences.

The theory of overlapping spheres of influence has been tested in two ways. Most often it has been applied to study school and district programs of family and community involvement and to learn whether and how well educators, parents, and community partners interact to help students succeed in school (Sanders, 1999; Sanders and Simon, 2002; Sheldon and Van Voorhis, 2004). The theory also has served as a lens through which to examine how future teachers and administrators are prepared to understand shared leadership in schools, including educators' shared responsibilities with families and communities to maximize student learning (Chavkin, 2005; Epstein, 2001, 2005a; Epstein and Sanders, 2006). For example, teachers who believe that they, alone, are responsible for student learning may teach differently from teachers who believe that they share responsibilities with parents and others for student success (Blackwell, Futrell, and Imig, 2003; Epstein, 2001). Administrators who believe that they and their teachers form a "professional community" may manage their schools differently from administrators who view schools as full "learning communities," including educators, students, parents, and community partners (Epstein,

2001; Epstein and Salinas, 2004; Price, 2005). By focusing family and community involvement broadly on how students learn and grow, we may improve the education of future educators as well as the policies and practices in schools.

Other useful theories and extensive research on parent involvement focus mainly on parents' motivations and actions, largely absent the school context. Hoover-Dempsey and Sandler's (1997) theory of why parents get involved in their children's education, for example, emphasize the role of parental beliefs and feelings of competence as chief determinants of parental behavior. Also, Grolnick and Slowiaczek (1994) created a multidimensional model of parental involvement that stresses the phenomenological experiences of children resulting from parent-child interactions related to schooling. In contrast, the theory of overlapping spheres of influence focuses on school-family-community interactions and the design and development of school programs and practices that affect parental behavior and student success in school. Taken together, the varied theories support research on different aspects of the complex work of parenting, teaching, and learning, and contribute to a fuller understanding of education and the roles of home, school, and community in child development.

The theory of overlapping spheres of influence should help researchers across disciplines "think new" about family and community involvement in children's education. Research may focus on school-level activities that affect all families (such as all teachers' interactions with all families about all children at a school open-house night) and individual-level communications that affect one family at a time (such as one teacher's meetings or phone calls with one parent about one child). With attention to contexts and social relations, the theory of overlapping spheres of influence changes the narrow focus of "parental involvement" from what an individual parent does to a broader, more realistic representation of how students move, continuously, in and out of several contexts and how the influential people in those contexts may work together contribute to students' education and development.

Researchers may conduct studies of the social forces that affect the external structure of the theoretical model, including how federal, state, and local policies influence the implementation of programs and actions to strengthen families, improve schools, and increase student achievement. The theory also grounds studies of the internal structure of the model by recognizing that there are many paths to partnerships in the interactions between and among teachers, administrators, counselors, parents, community partners, students, and others. For example, Sanders (1998) explored how family, school, and church affiliation supported African-American teens' achievement levels and identified positive effects across contexts. Catsambis and Beveridge (2001) studied family, school, and neighborhood factors that affected high school students' math achievement and found that negative neighborhood influences may be offset by positive family involvement. Additional research is needed on whether and how each and all connections are affected by the design and implementation of partnership programs and practices. Questions may be asked, for example, about how much overlap of home, school, and community is necessary for students' optimal achievement at each grade level.

2. School, family, and community partnerships is a multidimensional concept.

In many early studies, definitions of parental involvement were unclear, incomplete, or confounded. It was hard to know how to categorize and measure the ways that parents were involved in their children's education. Terms such as *parents as teachers* and *parents as learners* were not useful because they defined roles that were part and parcel of the same types of involvement. A parent could be both a teacher and a learner when working as a school volunteer and when helping students with homework, even though these are two very different activities. The early terms used to classify involvement were neither theoretically grounded nor research-based, but grew out of Head Start and Chapter 1 program descriptions that focused on parents, not on students, and not on actions that could be taken at home, at school, and in the community to promote student success.

A series of studies in elementary, middle, and high schools conducted from 1981 to 1991 generated a framework of six types of involvement: *parenting, communicating, volunteering, learning at home, decision making,* and *collaborating with the community* (Epstein, 1995, 2001). The framework identifies broad, separable categories of practices that involve parents with teachers, students, and community partners in different locations and for specific purposes, all contributing to student learning and success. The six types of involvement are represented by many different practices, raise specific challenges, and are responsible for producing varied results for students, families, and educators (Epstein et al., 2009). The framework has proven useful in research, policy, and practice across school levels and in diverse communities (Catsambis, 2002; Lee, 1994; Simon, 2004; Epstein and Lee, 1995; Salinas and Jansorn, 2004; Sanders, 1999; and see practical examples for the National Network of Partnership Schools, 2005, on the website www.partnership schools.org).

In brief, the six types of involvement are:

Type 1: Parenting—helping all families understand child and adolescent development and establishing home environments that support children as students

Type 2: Communicating—designing and conducting effective forms of two-way communications about school programs and children's progress

Type 3: Volunteering—recruiting and organizing help and support at school, home, or in other locations to support the school and students' activities

Type 4: Learning at Home—providing information and ideas to families about how to help students with homework and curriculum-related activities and decisions

Type 5: Decision Making—having parents from all backgrounds serve as representatives and leaders on school committees and obtaining input from all parents on school decisions

Type 6: Collaborating with the Community—identifying and integrating resources and services from the community to strengthen and support

schools, students, and their families, and organizing activities to benefit
the community and increase students' learning opportunities.

Schools may choose among hundreds of practices for each type of involvement
to guide and encourage purposeful interactions of parents, educators, students,
and others in the community. For example, there are many ways to use common
and advanced technologies for teachers and parents to communicate with each other
(Type 2); many ways to organize volunteers to assist educators, students, and families (Type 3); and so on. Each type of involvement requires two-way communications, so that educators and families exchange information and ideas with each
other and recognize and honor their shared responsibilities for children's education.

Each type of involvement poses clear challenges that must be addressed to reach
all families (Epstein et al., 2009). For example, schools may be faced with the challenge of involving parents who cannot speak or read English. Teams of educators
and parents may work together to provide information in words and forms the families understand and to implement activities that ensure that these parents, like all
others, have easy access to channels of communication with teachers and administrators, and opportunities for input to school decisions. Other challenges include
getting information to families who cannot attend school meetings; sending parents
positive communications about their children's work and accomplishments so that
connections are not only about students' problems; providing ways for parents and
teachers to communicate so that information about students flows from school to
home and from home to school; providing opportunities for many parents to volunteer at school and in other locations; preparing teachers to guide families to monitor and interact with their children about homework; ensuring that families from
diverse neighborhoods are represented in the decision making process and on school
committees; and identifying and using community resources to help meet school improvement goals (Epstein et al., 2009). By addressing these and other challenges,
schools can reach out to involve parents across racial, educational, and socioeconomic
groups so that they can actively support their children's education.

The framework of six types of involvement was adopted by the National PTA
(2004) as its "standards" for all schools to inform and involve parents and community partners in the schools and in children's education. Further, the No Child Left
Behind Act (Public Law 107-110, 2002) outlines activities for the six types of involvement in its guidelines for schools' programs for family involvement.

Researchers who are ready to think in new ways about the nature of school, family, and community partnerships may use the framework of six types of involvement
in full or in part to address questions about programs, activities, and results of involvement. Research is sorely needed on the design and effects of contrasting approaches to resolve the countless challenges that arise for each type of involvement.
The challenges must be solved to help all families feel welcome at school and ready
and able to support their children (Epstein, 2001; Epstein et al., 2009). For example,
many studies in diverse communities will be needed to solve questions about the
design of effective parent-teacher conferences with parents who do not speak English, and to identify other effective formats for two-way communications with all

families throughout the school year. Because the vast majority of parents work full or part time during the school day, today's schools must schedule meetings at varied times and have many different ways for parents to become and remain informed and involved with their children at home and in the community. It no longer is enough to require "bodies in the school building" as the only evidence of parents' interest and involvement in their children's education. (See Chapter 5, Reading 5.1, for a complete overview and activities on the six types of involvement.)

These kinds of "nitty-gritty" questions must be addressed to provide a stronger research base for educators' decisions about the design and content of partnership programs. The framework should help researchers focus studies on the challenges associated with particular types of involvement, increase understanding of what schools may do to involve families in different ways, and provide parents with realistic and productive options for their involvement. Researchers also may focus on complex questions about the connections between and among the six types of involvement and the sequence or mix of types of involvement that helps schools build comprehensive and high-quality programs. The framework of six types of involvement provides an efficient way to categorize activities and to accumulate and synthesize results of studies so that knowledge grows and so the results of research can be used by educators to improve practice.

3. A program of school, family, and community partnerships is an essential component of school and classroom organization.

The theory of overlapping spheres of influence and framework of six types of involvement promote the view that school, family, and community partnerships should operate as an organized *program* of structures, processes, and collaborative activities to help students succeed in every school, not as a set of fragmented activities for parents. A planned program of partnership with activities linked to school improvement goals establishes family involvement as a component of school improvement, part of the professional work of educators, just as the curriculum, instruction, and assessments are understood as essential school organizational components. The difference is that programs of partnership require educators to interact and collaborate with parents, other family members, and community partners, and not only with other educators.

A series of studies identified eight "essential elements" for effective school programs of school, family, and community partnerships: *leadership, teamwork, action plans, implementation of plans, funding, collegial support, evaluation,* and *networking.* Specifically, in longitudinal studies of over 500 schools, Sheldon and Van Voorhis found that schools whose Action Teams for Partnerships received technical assistance and support from district leaders and from external partners were more likely to form committees, write plans, adjust for changes in principals, reach out to more families, evaluate their efforts, and sustain their programs. These schools also addressed more challenges to involve "hard-to-reach" parents and reported that more families were involved in their children's education (Sheldon, 2003; Sheldon and Van Voorhis, 2003). By implementing the essential program elements, elementary, middle, and high schools improved the scope and quality of activities for several types of involvement (Epstein, 2001; Sanders, 1999, 2001; Sanders and Harvey, 2002; Sanders and Simon, 2002; Sheldon and Van Voorhis, 2004).

Longitudinal studies confirmed the connections of essential program elements with increased outreach and involvement (Epstein, 2005b; Sheldon, 2005, 2007; Sheldon and Van Voorhis, 2004). Specifically, schools that improved their programs over time increased the involvement of more and different parents as volunteers and in decision making at school. These schools also increased outreach by teachers, including greater use of homework designed to encourage parent-child interactions (Sheldon 2003; Sheldon and Van Voorhis, 2004). The studies show, repeatedly, that more can be done to involve more families if educators, parents, and others work as a school team to plan their partnership programs, schedule activities, share leadership for activities, evaluate progress, and continually improve the quality of activities and outreach.

In schools, the word *plan* often raises concerns among educators. Presently, most schools have an annual school improvement plan that outlines major goals for students and for improving the school climate. Pressed for time, most educators are not eager to write additional, different, or extra plans for family and community involvement. Yet studies of partnership program development show that educators and parents do more together when they work as a team and write annual, detailed schedules of partnership activities.

One of the most helpful new directions for applying research on partnerships in practice has been for educators to link detailed written action plans for family and community involvement to their annual school improvement plans. For example, in Buffalo, plans for partnership are appended to the Comprehensive School Education Plan (CSEP); in Maryland to the School Improvement Plan (SIP); in Los Angeles to a Single School Plan. Each school, then, has only one major plan with stated improvement goals, accompanied by a detailed schedule and assigned responsibilities for family and community involvement activities. In this way, a formal program of partnerships is linked to school goals for which educators and students are held accountable, bringing parents and community partners to the central purpose of schools and schooling, and not treated as an extra burden or afterthought.

Several studies also suggest that it was necessary, but not sufficient, for schools to establish "the basics" of a partnership program, such as organizing a team, writing a plan, or even implementing planned activities. To measurably affect program quality, parents' responses, and results for students, schools also had to address key challenges to reach all families (Sheldon, 2003, 2005, 2007).

Researchers who are ready to think in new ways about school, family, and community partnerships may conduct studies on the design and development of any or all of the eight essential elements to extend an understanding of the formation and qualities of programs of family and community involvement. The result is not a "parent program," which, by its very label excuses educators from participating, but a "student success program"—part of school organization—which requires teachers, parents, students, and other critical partners to organize their interactions, efficiently and effectively to support children's education. Two basic questions for researchers and for educators are: How can family and community involvement programs be organized systematically as a regular part of every school's work? Which structures, processes, and activities best help principals, teachers, parents, and others plan, implement, and sustain partnership programs that help boost student achievement and success?

4. Programs of school, family, and community partnerships require multilevel leadership.

Family and community involvement activities focus mainly on the school level because that is where students and their families are located every day. Nevertheless, district and state leaders have important roles to play in guiding and motivating superintendents, principals, and school teams to develop and implement policies and plans for good partnerships (Epstein, 2001; Epstein et al., 2009).

Multilevel leadership supports the view that family and community involvement is part of school organization, as district leaders help coordinate and facilitate the smooth operation of all schools within a district. District leaders for partnerships may, for example, develop clear policies for all schools' partnership programs, organize and offer professional development workshops to school teams, help teams write plans for goal-oriented partnership programs, share best practices, evaluate their programs, and improve from year to year.

Analyses of longitudinal data from about 80 school districts indicated that these functions and activities improved the quality of district leadership on partnerships, increased direct connections with schools, and helped schools improve their school-based programs, as discussed above (Epstein and Williams, 2003; Epstein, Williams, and Lewis, 2002; Epstein, Williams, and Jansorn, 2004). The quality of district partnership programs was affected by the leaders' years of experience and time spent on partnerships, use of NNPS (National Network of Partnership Schools) planning and evaluation tools, and the extent to which district leaders directly assisted their schools.

Compared to their counterparts in other districts, experienced district leaders were more likely to write annual district-level leadership plans, identify a budget for partnerships, conduct training workshops for school teams and other colleagues, offer grants or other funding to schools, recognize excellence in school programs, help schools share best practices, and conduct other leadership actions. District leaders who evaluated their own and their schools' programs were more likely to visit their schools more often to provide support and assistance (Epstein and Williams, 2003). Regardless of their initial practices in the prior school year, district leaders who used NNPS tools and services for program development, planning, and evaluation increased the number of activities they conducted at the district level to organize their own work, facilitated their schools to address challenges to reach more families, conducted program evaluations, and increased the overall quality of their own and their schools' programs (Epstein and Williams, 2003; Epstein et al., 2004). It may be that by using planning and evaluation tools, district leaders were more serious about their work on partnerships and, therefore, guided schools to take more actions in developing their programs.

Historically, the earliest federal policies concerning Chapter 1 and Title I called for district advisory councils. These were almost always symbolic committees that enabled a few parents to have input to district policies, but that did little to increase the involvement of all families in all schools. District advisory councils still are useful, but district-level professional leaders also are needed to assist schools to understand the importance of teamwork and how to develop their programs of family and community involvement.

State leaders for partnerships, too, have shown that clear policies and professional development activities can increase districts' attention to their work on partnerships with their schools (Epstein, 2001; Epstein and Williams, 2003; and see National Network of Partnership Schools, 2005, for summaries of Wisconsin's and Connecticut's policies and programs on the website www.partnershipschools.org in the section "Success Stories"). The importance of active multilevel leadership on partnerships is recognized and codified in the requirements for family involvement in the No Child Left Behind Act (NCLB) (Public Law 107–110, 2002), which redirects state and district leaders away from monitoring sites for compliance to actively helping schools improve the quality and results of partnership programs.

Researchers who are ready to think in new ways about school, family, and community partnerships may ask questions about the effects of contrasting district and state leadership structures and processes. The fifty states and nearly 15,000 districts in the United States will respond in varied ways to NCLB requirements for parental involvement. Researchers have a rare opportunity to conduct multilevel studies to identify the most effective ways that states and districts organize their leadership on partnerships and the impact of their policies and actions for their schools. (See Chapter 4 on district and state leadership and links to policy development.)

5. Programs of school, family, and community partnerships must include a focus on increasing student learning and development.

The most common question from researchers, reporters, and educators about school, family, and community partnerships is: What are the effects of family and community involvement on student achievement? The question is on the right track with its focus on students. The theory of overlapping spheres of influence places students at the center of the internal structure of the model, as the main reason for interactions among educators, parents, and others in the community. The theory, then, supports the intense interest in how schools' practices to involve families affect student outcomes. But the question, as typically posed, is far too narrow, as family and community involvement affects not only student achievement, but also student health, attitudes, and behaviors (Epstein 2001; Hill and Craft, 2003; Patrikakou et al., 2005; Reynolds, Temple, Robertson, and Mann, 2002).

Attention to results for students is fueled by present policies and practice. For example, NCLB and most state and local policies specify that parental involvement should be designed to help increase student achievement and success in school. In practice, numerous innovative ideas are emerging of how to involve families with students on reading, math, and other subjects and on how to design involvement activities that are linked to other school goals (such as good attendance and behavior) that contribute to student success (Salinas and Jansorn, 2004).

For more than a decade, research has been strengthening its base of evidence on results of family involvement for students. Many studies at the elementary, middle, and high school levels confirmed that students had higher achievements, better attendance, more course credits earned, better preparation for class, and other indicators of success in school, if families were involved in their education (Catsambis, 2002; Epstein, 2001; Lee, 1994; Muller, 1993; and see summaries of studies in Henderson and Mapp, 2002).

Types of involvement. Researchers have extended their studies from general questions about involvement to pointed questions about how the six types of involvement affected student outcomes. For example, Simon (2001, 2004) found that when high schools conducted specific activities to increase parents' attention to teens' high school work and postsecondary planning, parents responded by conducting more interactions with their teens about those subjects. Catsambis and Beveridge (2001) pressed further, using hierarchical linear modeling (HLM) analyses to study how school, family, and neighborhood factors independently affected students' math achievement. Specifically, they showed that students in neighborhoods with high concentrations of poverty had had lower math achievement test scores, but this effect was ameliorated by ongoing parental involvement in high school. These studies, conducted with large national sample surveys of parents and students at the middle and high school levels in the National Educational Longitudinal (NELS) data set, indicated that it is never too late to initiate programs of family and community involvement. Students benefited from their parents' interest, interactions, and guidance through high school.

Subject-specific goals for students. New studies are contributing to an understanding of the importance of goal-linked family involvement to help students produce specific results. Studies of family involvement in reading have been most numerous and offer some pertinent lessons for future research.

A review of research on family involvement interventions in schools reported that these programs had mixed results on student achievement in reading and other subjects (Mattingly, Prislin, McKenzie, Rodriguez, and Kayzar, 2002). That review, however, examined diverse partnership programs with varied goals, without giving separate attention to whether or how parents or other family members were encouraged or guided to support their children's learning in targeted, goal-linked ways.

Of the 41 studies reviewed by Mattingly et al. (2002), 16 (with a sample size of more than 2 students) guided parents to become involved with their children on reading and language arts activities. Fifteen of these targeted "reading" programs were reported to produce significant gains on students' reading or language arts achievement test scores and, where measured, differences between intervention versus comparison groups on reading or language arts skills and scores. Interventions that were not closely linked to intended results (such as general communications with teachers or about school programs, improving student attendance, or improving students' skills asking questions) did not produce gains in students' reading skills.

Another review of research conducted from 1997 to about 2000 strengthened the importance of measuring subject-specific involvement for results in specific subjects (Henderson and Mapp, 2002). Of 51 studies, 7 examined the impact of family involvement interventions that guided parents to participate in reading-related activities. All 7 studies indicated that targeted, reading-related family involvement was associated with increased students' reading and language arts skills in case and control groups or as participants in the interventions over time.

These and earlier reviews (Miller, 1986; Silvern, 1985; Tizard, 1982) and additional studies (Cairney, 1995; Epstein, 2001) support the position that when family involvement is focused on reading and literacy activities at home, including reading aloud and discussing stories, students' reading achievement increased. The results should help researchers think in new ways about which interventions to increase parental involvement are most likely to affect specific results for student learning.

Many schools already are implementing subject-specific involvement activities to engage families in productive ways to help students reach specific goals. Schools may strengthen their partnership programs by including various activities for all six types of involvement for specific goals for students, including improving reading (Epstein et al., 2009). For example, a school may conduct workshops for parents to help them understand reading standards and parent-teacher conferences that focus only on reading progress and next steps, recruit reading volunteers to help students improve reading, assign reading homework to increase students' reading time and discussions of books at home, and implement other activities that emphasize the importance of the school's reading goals and parents' opportunities to talk with their children about reading. A review of literature on family involvement with students on reading, indicated that, across the grades, subject-specific interventions to involve families in reading and related language arts positively affected students' reading skills and scores (Sheldon and Epstein, 2005b).

A series of school-level studies, titled *Focus on Results*, examined whether schools that implemented family and community involvement activities to address other learning and behavioral goals for students showed measurable changes on student outcomes over one year. On achievement outcomes, schools that focused family involvement with students on math, particularly through math homework that required parent-child interactions and math materials for families to take home, increased the percentages of students who were proficient in math on state tests from one year to the next (Sheldon and Epstein, 2005a).

Family involvement also affected students' non-achievement outcomes. In schools where educators communicated well with families about attendance, schools' rates of average daily attendance increased, and chronic absence decreased from one year to the next (Epstein and Sheldon, 2002; Sheldon and Epstein, 2004). These results were reinforced by another study using longitudinal data from Ohio, which showed that schools in NNPS improved attendance rates compared to a matched sample of schools that did not receive guidance on partnership program development (Sheldon, 2007). Similarly, when educators communicated effectively and involved family and community members in activities focused on student behavior and school safety, schools reported fewer disciplinary actions with students from one year to the next (Sanders, 1996; Sheldon and Epstein, 2002).

Other researchers explored the effects of family involvement with children on homework at the individual student level (Epstein and Van Voorhis, 2001). They found significant results of subject-specific family involvement for students' writing skills (Epstein, Simon, and Salinas, 1997) on science report card grades and homework completion (Van Voorhis, 2003, 2004).

The range of studies described above shows the potential for researchers to conduct many more studies of the effects of subject-specific and goal-linked activities for family and community involvement on linked student outcomes. The extant studies also revealed several difficulties that must be addressed in conducting research on the results of involvement for student outcomes. Here we discuss three challenges that make effects studies difficult.

The challenge of conducting studies of interventions. Studies of the effects of particular practices of involvement require intensive and extensive cooperation and collaboration between researchers and educators. And there are no shortcuts for the time and care needed from all participants. For example, the studies discussed above of family involvement with students on homework required teachers to connect with students' families in targeted, well-designed, subject-specific assignments for an extended period of time, up to one year.

The quality of the implementation of a program or practice must be measured *before* it is possible to measure results related to the intervention. For example, a three-year study of the Partnership Schools Comprehensive School Reform (CSR) Model (Epstein, 2005b) demonstrated that a Title I elementary school could organize whole-school change that combined changes in instruction with improvements in family and community involvement focused on reading, writing, and math. Over three years, the CSR school improved its state achievement test scores in these subjects compared to matched schools. The CSR school also closed the gap in test scores with the district as a whole, despite the fact that the district included several schools in more affluent neighborhoods with higher test scores in the base year. The school also increased the number of families involved in students' education at school and at home.

To build on present knowledge, studies of the effects of parental involvement on student outcomes must be longitudinal with data on families' prior involvement and students' prior scores on the selected outcomes, the nature and quality of schools' involvement activities, the families' responses to those activities, and the students' present outcomes. With these rich data, researchers will be able to address the basic question: How do school practices to involve families affect parents' behaviors *and* the change or continuity of student achievements and behaviors? Without the full complement of longitudinal measures, studies simply document that successful students tend to have parents who are involved.

The challenge of isolating effects of partnerships. In practice, when educators develop programs to involve families with students on specific subjects or on other goals, they may report positive results, overall, for children's achievement. For example, an Action Team for Partnerships in an elementary school serving mainly

Latino and Hmong families in Saint Paul, MN, wrote annual plans with many activities for the six types of involvement that focused on student learning. This school reported gains in 2004 on students' test scores of 13 percent in reading and 10 percent in math, which they attributed, in part, to the hard work of their teachers and students and to family involvement and support (see National Network of Partnership Schools, 2005, and the awards summaries on the website www.partnership schools.org in the section "Success Stories").

The example illustrates an inescapable problem for research on comprehensive partnership programs. It is difficult to isolate the effects of one program component from the effects of all other school improvement activities that are occurring simultaneously. In the school example, teachers were working with students on more demanding reading and writing standards and curricula, and more parents were involved with students on reading and writing tasks. The problem plagues all studies of school reform and can only be resolved by applying increasingly reliable measures of the nature and quality of specific practices, and by using increasingly rigorous methods, including longitudinal data to account for starting points on key independent and dependent variables.

The challenge of explaining negative results. Among the most provocative and least studied patterns of results of school, family, and community partnerships are the negative associations of certain types of involvement with some measures of student achievement and behavior (Desimone, 1999; Lee, 1994; Muller, 1993; Simon, 2000). Several studies, particularly in middle and high schools, indicate that more parents communicate with teachers if their students have low achievement and poor behavior in school. By contrast, in the same schools, more parents volunteer and participate in school decision making if their students have high achievement and better behavior.

These contradictory correlations must be put in context. Without well-developed partnership programs, teachers and parents contact each other mainly when students have academic and behavior problems. If a school is not conducting some positive interactions with all families, then the number of communications between teachers and parents will be correlated with low achievement or poor behavior (Epstein, 2001; Epstein and Lee, 1995; Lee, 1994; Catsambis, 2002). This intriguing pattern of effects shows why researchers need to understand the different types of involvement and the contexts in which communications among teachers, parents, and students are conducted. Studies are sorely needed that delve deeper into the results of parent-teacher-student communications to solve students' academic and behavioral problems over time.

Despite real progress in research on results of family and community involvement for student learning and development, this remains the most important topic for new and better studies. Researchers who are ready to think in new ways may study whether and which family and community involvement activities affect specific academic, attitudinal, behavioral, health, and other outcomes at all school and grade levels for diverse groups of students. Research is needed on whether parent-teacher communications about poor achievement and behavior have different effects at different grade levels and as a function of the roles that students' play in the process.

The agenda is all but limitless because there is a long list of student outcomes that are of interest and importance in school studies (Epstein, 2001; Gerne and Epstein, 2004; Patrikakou et al., 2005). These include *academic outcomes* such as readiness for school, participation in class, completion of homework, report card grades, test scores, course credits, high school completion, and enrollment in post-secondary education; *social and emotional outcomes* for students' personal development, such as motivation to learn, attitudes toward schoolwork, dimensions of self esteem, positive relationships with teachers, peers, friends, and other adults in school, attendance, good behavior, perseverance on tasks, postsecondary planning; *health-related outcomes* for student growth and development, such as nutrition, weight management, physical strength, exercise, sex education, prevention of the use of drugs, alcohol, and tobacco, and other health topics; and other indicators of citizenship, good character, and academic commitment. The varied outcomes may, in turn, affect student achievement and vice versa, yielding a vast agenda for studies of results of family and community involvement on student development.

Research on the effects of family involvement on student outcomes is, presently, a mile wide and an inch deep. Studies have identified numerous types of involvement and an array of academic, attitudinal, behavioral, and health outcomes for students. But only a few studies have been conducted on any single outcome, at certain grade levels, and in selected communities. Few studies are based on appropriate longitudinal data or other rigorous methods. We still need to know: Which involvement activities produce measurable results for students, and under what conditions? Thus, the topic of whether, which, and how family and community involvement affects results for students needs many new contributions to improve the topography of the field.

6. All programs of school, family, and community partnerships are about equity.

Parental involvement programs must include all families, not only those who are presently involved or easiest to reach. This requirement, written into federal law in the No Child Left Behind Act (NCLB), also is stipulated in just about all state education policies and district mission statements. For example, NCLB's Section 1118 requires educators to communicate with all parents in languages that they will understand about their own child's achievement test scores, trends in test scores for all schools in a district and major subgroups of students, and other indicators (e.g., attendance, graduation rates, teachers' qualifications). Schools also are required to provide clear information and options to parents to transfer their children to a more successful school if their own school underperforms for two consecutive years, and information for selecting supplemental education services for eligible children.

The emphasis in federal policy on well-designed partnership programs that involve all families has important implications for research on school, family, and community partnerships. Many studies show that although most parents report that they want to be partners with educators, only some parents, particularly those with more formal education, higher incomes, and familiarity with schools remain involved in their children's education across the grades (Baker and Stevenson, 1986; Dauber and Epstein, 1993; Lareau, 1989; Useem, 1991, 1992). The well-documented inequalities raise new questions about producing greater equity of family and community involvement in order to promote more success of students.

Typical distributions of involved and uninvolved parents can be changed with well-designed partnership programs. Studies conducted with elementary, middle, and high schools are accumulating that indicate that *when* schools conduct high-quality partnership programs, parents respond. This includes parents with less formal education or lower incomes who might not become involved on their own. Program quality and the actions taken at home are as important as or more important than family background variables such as race, ethnicity, social class, marital status, mother's education or work status, or language spoken at home for determining whether, how, and which parents become involved in their children's education and how students progress and succeed in school (Cairney and Munsie, 1995; Comer and Haynes, 1991; Dauber and Epstein, 1993; Epstein, 2001; Henderson and Mapp, 2002; Sanders and Epstein, 2000; Simon, 2004). These results are also represented in exemplary practice (Salinas and Jansorn, 2004).

Some research and practical reports like to discuss over-involved and under-involved parents (Gibbs, 2005). In fact, both groups may be assisted by well-planned partnership programs. In surveys of parents, highly involved and hard-to-reach parents report that they need more and better information from their children's schools to know how to use their limited available time to best assist their children (Dauber and Epstein, 1993). Without good guidance, the under-involved wait for information and the over-involved set their own agendas, whether their actions benefit their children or not.

Several decades of studies of family involvement with children about reading show how this works in practice. Many studies in this and other countries confirm that children do better in reading and other literacy skills if their families support reading at home with more books and reading experiences (Binkley, Rust, and Williams, 1996; Donahue, Finnegan, Lutkus, Allen, and Campbell, 2001; Sheldon and Epstein, 2005b). Although more educated families and those with more disposable income have more books at home, schools can create more equity in involvement about reading by implementing activities that help all parents understand their children's reading programs and encourage reading at home. Schools also may work with local businesses to provide children with books to take home, thereby making home reading environments more equitable (National Network of Partnership Schools, 2005; Salinas and Jansorn, 2004).

As another example, district leaders in the Seattle Public Schools are helping schools develop partnership programs that increase the equity of involvement for highly diverse families. District leaders from several departments worked together to develop presentations, website communications, handbooks, and other publications for parents in 10 languages. The Superintendent noted that these programs helped educators "align parent involvement practices with academic goals, contributing to real systemic change in school buildings." In the past year, the district tracked over 260 activities for the six types of involvement attended by over 18,360 parents, with translated materials provided at over 60 percent of the activities. The work in Seattle is demonstrating that, with committed district leaders, even schools in challenging communities can increase the equity of parental involvement to support students' success in school (National Network of Partnership Schools, 2005, and see these and other examples of programs and practices at www.partnership schools.org in the section "Success Stories").

It no longer is enough to identify inequalities in parental involvement. Researchers who are ready to think in new ways about family involvement may conduct studies designed to produce greater equity of involvement for all parents. Because families are important for students' success in school, it is important to learn how more families—ideally, all families—become involved in ways that positively support their children's success in school. This requires researchers to go beyond questions of whether families are involved or not, to test alternative strategies that help families and educators build trust and respect for one another and that enable all parents to guide their children to do their best in school. Researchers may study the processes and technologies needed to involve parents who are typically hard to reach, including parents who have less formal education, speak languages other than English at home, and typically would not become involved on their own.

At its core, education is about providing equal opportunities to learn. Because it is well documented that students benefit from goal-linked family and community involvement, researchers may conduct studies that yield more and better information on which partnership approaches help resolve the past and present inequalities in levels of involvement among diverse families.

7. Methods of research on school, family, and community partnerships must continue to improve.

The young field of school, family, and community partnerships will continue to grow if researchers ask new and pointed questions about the implementation and results of involvement activities. Knowledge will grow, too, with better measures, larger and more diverse samples, and the use of various methods of data collection, including surveys, case studies, experimental or quasi-experimental designs, longitudinal studies, field tests, program evaluations, and policy analyses. Researchers who are ready to think in new ways about school, family, and community partnerships will contribute new knowledge on partnerships by using the most rigorous methods of analyses that are appropriate for their questions.

After more than two decades of research on family involvement that framed the field, researchers should be ready to move from exploratory and descriptive studies to confirmatory studies and targeted evaluations about how full programs and specific practices of school, family, and community partnerships develop and affect families and students. Here, we discuss a few ways that researchers may move forward with various methods of analyses.

Experiments and matched samples. Experimental and quasi-experimental research is needed to compare schools that are implementing specific partnership programs or practices with similar schools that are not (Boethel, 2003; Henderson and Mapp,

2002; Mattingly et al., 2002). Experimental and quasi-experimental methods are best suited for studying well-defined, tightly controlled interventions. For example, Van Voorhis (2001, 2003) built on early studies of the feasibility of the Teachers Involve Parents in Schoolwork (TIPS) interactive homework process (Epstein et al., 1997) by conducting a quasi-experimental study of case and control classrooms to better understand the impact of student-parent interactions about science homework. The study revealed that parents were much more involved when children led conversations and experiments with family partners at home on science, and students benefited in report card grades and homework completion, compared to parents and students in matched classrooms that had the same homework without a family involvement component. She also showed that parental involvement for case and control classes did not differ in English and math—subjects that did not use the TIPS method.

Experimental designs with strict comparisons of partnership versus non-partnership schools are difficult, given widespread support for parent involvement and far-reaching federal, state, and local policies that require all schools to have programs of family and community involvement (Kessler-Sklar and Baker, 2000). When experimental or quasi-experimental conditions are not possible, researchers can improve studies of the effects of family and community involvement on student achievement and other indicators of success by using longitudinal data with well-specified effects models, and closely matched samples of schools and/or students.

Well-specified multivariate models. Researchers can advance knowledge by identifying the paths that connect school activities to family responses and to results for students. For example, Sheldon (2005) employed Structural Equation Modeling (SEM) techniques to identify the connections of key program structures with the extent of schools' outreach to involve more families and with the resulting family involvement. He showed that program plans, district support, and collegial support at the school contributed to better program outreach to more families. In turn, outreach promoted greater family involvement. The processes occur simultaneously, as the program grows and as plans and activities are implemented.

Notable research on other aspects of parental involvement using SEM has been conducted by Hill and her colleagues, on the mechanisms by which parent-child interactions may translate into various student outcomes and how these processes vary across ethnic and socioeconomic groups (Hill et al., 2004; Hill and Craft, 2003). SEM holds promise for testing different theoretical models of school, home, and community connections and for identifying simultaneously occurring effects such as parents' responses to school practices of involvement and results for students.

Multilevel analyses. Researchers who are ready to think in new ways about school, family, and community partnerships can advance knowledge by studying the multi-level effects of state policies and actions on district leadership and school programs to reach all families. Multilevel analyses using Hierarchical Linear Modeling (HLM) will be useful in separating the independent effects of policies and leadership actions that occur with a nested system (e.g., families within schools, schools within districts, districts within states). Because federal policies require state, district, and schools to have coordinated activities for partnership program development, multilevel methods such as HLM are particularly appropriate for studying the connections and influences that occur across policy levels (Bryk and Raudenbush, 1992).

Researchers may be helped in framing new studies of family and community involvement and effects using SEM and HLM methods, by tapping national data sets, such as the Early Childhood Longitudinal Study (ECLS-K), starting with a kindergarten cohort in the fall of 1998, and ECLS-B, starting with a birth cohort in 2000. The large-scale surveys included surveys of teachers, parents, and students and may encourage model testing and studies of multilevel effects of family and community involvement in schools and in neighborhoods. Still, large national surveys have strengths and weaknesses. The number of items on school, family, and community partnerships may be limited, and items may be unrelated to theoretical or practical concerns. Researchers ready to think in new ways about family and community involvement still may benefit from well-designed local, regional, and state surveys, case studies, experimental studies, and action research that can delve deeply into the implementation and effects of specific practices of family involvement.

Small, in-depth studies. Although large and methodologically sophisticated studies are needed, as noted above, there still are times, in a young field of study, that small, in-depth quantitative and qualitative studies are appropriate. For example, over the past twenty years, most research has focused on school-family connections. Therefore, initial studies on school-community connections had to be conducted from the ground up. By using survey data from schools in many parts of the country and intensive inquiries in one elementary school, Sanders (2001) developed a useful catalogue of school-community connections and their targeted participants (i.e., community connections to assist parents, students, teachers) (Sanders, 2003; Sanders and Harvey, 2002). A series of studies of three high schools in urban, suburban, and rural communities revealed how high schools can organize school-community connections to benefit all partners in education (Sanders, 2005; Sanders and Lewis, 2005). Now, there is a much stronger base on which to build future studies of the effects of school-community partnerships on student learning and development.

Other topics that have not been studied much (e.g., the involvement of parents in nontraditional families such as foster parents, gay and lesbian parents, and noncustodial parents; involvement at transition points; involvement to influence students' postsecondary plans; involvement to improve students' health outcomes; and other topics that researchers identify) may benefit from small, exploratory studies that help define terms, identify activities, develop measures, and establish other parameters. By contrast, topics that have been studied extensively (e.g., teachers' and parents' attitudes about involvement and all effects studies) may be revisited, but require researchers to ask more detailed questions and use more advanced methods than in prior studies in order to make original contributions to the field.

More rigorous research on school, family, and community partnerships, using diverse methods and valid and reliable measures, should increase knowledge on the factors that produce the most effective programs and on the processes and paths that strengthen (1) leadership for partnerships, (2) the quality of program plans, (3) outreach to involve more families, (4) responses by families and community partners, and (5) the impact on student achievement and other indicators of success in school.

CONCLUSION

If family involvement is important for student success, as decades of research indicates, then we must address the fruitful question: *How can more families—indeed all families—become involved in their children's education in ways that will contribute to student success?*

Studies of parental involvement over the past twenty-five years have set a firm base on which new research can build to increase understanding of programs and practices of school, family, and community partnerships. The early work yielded a useful theory and framework of six types of involvement that have guided research, policy, and practice. Studies to date have identified and explored many aspects of the involvement of parents, teachers, administrators, and students. Researchers have begun to inspect, dissect, and identify components and effects of partnership programs in schools and school districts. By framing the field, the early work also shows that much is left to learn.

Despite the challenges of studying schools, families, and communities simultaneously, it is necessary to "think new" about how students learn and develop as they progress from preschool through high school. Well-documented problems with student achievement, motivation, attitudes about education, school behavior, and future plans are partly due to "old think" that separated school and students from home and community, leaving teachers to work on their own, isolated from other influential people in children's lives.

The seven principles featured in this chapter should help researchers think in new ways about the structures and processes of family and community involvement that will help educators, parents, and community partners work more systematically, organizationally, and collaboratively to support student success. The sixth principle—that involvement is all about equity—is pivotal, as it requires attention to all of the other principles. That is, to study how to produce more equal opportunities for family involvement and for student success, it is imperative for researchers to understand that parents, educators, and others at home, in school, and in the community share an interest in and responsibilities for students' education and development.

It is necessary for researchers to recognize the difference between asking or rebuking each parent, individually, to become involved versus enabling every school to organize effective programs that encourage the productive involvement of all families. It is important for researchers to explore whether and how district and state leaders may work in concert with schools to establish and continually improve effective partnership programs that reach all families. Because schools are being held accountable for improving academic and other results for students, researchers must conduct studies that go beyond process outcomes for parents to study the effects of school, family, and community partnerships on academic and behavioral outcomes for students. If researchers think in these new ways, they will move the field forward with studies that go beyond documenting inequities to explore and identify programs and practices that promote greater equity in the involvement of diverse families and the effects of involvement on indicators of success for students in elementary, middle, and high schools.

All seven changes in thinking are needed to study the design and development of comprehensive partnership programs, outreach to involve all families, family and community responses, and results for students. By thinking in new ways about school, family, and community partnerships, researchers not only will extend the knowledge base, but also help educators improve policy and practice.

NOTE

This research was supported by a grant from NICHD. The opinions expressed are the authors' and may not represent the policies or positions of the funding agency.

REFERENCES

Baker D. P., and D. L. Stevenson. (1986). Mothers' strategies for children's school achievement: Managing the transition to high school. *Sociology of Education* 59: 156–166.

Binkley, M., K. Rust, and T. Williams. (1996). *Reading literacy in an international perspective* (NCES 97-875). Washington, DC: U.S. Department of Education/National Center for Education Statistics.

Blackwell, P. J., M. H. Futrell, and D. G. Imig. (2003). Burnt water paradoxes of schools of education. *Phi Delta Kappan* 84: 356–361.

Boethel, M. (2003). *Diversity: School, family, and community connections.* Austin: Southwest Educational Development Laboratory.

Booth, A., and J. Dunn, eds. (1996). *Family-school links: How do they affect educational outcomes.* Hillside, NJ: Lawrence Erlbaum Associates.

Bronfenbrenner, U. (1979). *The ecology of human development: Experiment by nature and design.* Cambridge: Harvard University Press.

———. (1986). Ecology of the family as a context for human development: Research perspectives. *Developmental Psychology* 22: 723–742.

Bryk, A. S., and S. W. Raudenbush. (1992). *Hierarchical linear modeling: Applications and data analysis methods.* Newbury Park, CA: Sage.

Cairney, T. H. (1995). Developing parent partnerships in secondary literacy learning. *Journal of Reading* 38: 520–26.

Cairney, T. H., and L. Munsie. (1995). Parent participation in literacy learning. *Reading Teacher* 48: 392–403.

Castelli, S., M. Mendel, and B. Ravn, eds. (2003). *School, family, and community partnership in a world of differences and change.* Proceedings of the ERNAPE conference on school, family, and community partnerships. Gdansk, Poland: University of Gdansk.

Catsambis, S. (2002). Expanding knowledge of parental involvement in children's secondary education: Connections with high school seniors' academic success. *Social Psychology of Education*: 5: 149–177.

Catsambis, S., and A. A. Beveridge. (2001). Does neighborhood matter? Family, neighborhood, and school influences on eighth grade mathematics achievement. *Sociological Focus* 34: 435–457.

Chavkin, N., ed. (1993). *Families and schools in a pluralistic society.* Albany NY: SUNY Press.

————. (2005). Preparing educators for school-family partnerships: Challenges and opportunities. In E. N. Patrikakou, R. P. Weissberg, S. Redding, and H. J. Walberg (Eds.), *School-family partnerships: Fostering children's school success* (pp. 164–180). New York: Teachers College Press.

Christenson, S., and J. Conoley, eds. (1992). *Home and school collaborations: Enhancing children's academic and social competence.* Colesville, MD: National Association of School Psychologists NASP.

Coleman, J. S. (1988). Social capital in the creation of human capital. *American Journal of Sociology* 94: 95–120.

Comer, J. P. (1980). *School power: Implications of an intervention program.* New York: Free Press.

Comer, J. P., and N. Haynes. (1991). Parent involvement in schools: An ecological approach. *Elementary School Journal* 91: 271–277.

Dauber, S. L., and J. L. Epstein. (1993). Parents' attitudes and practices of involvement in inner-city elementary and middle schools. In N. Chavkin (Ed.), *Families and schools in a pluralistic society* (pp. 53–71). Albany NY: SUNY Press.

Davies, D., and V. R. Johnson, eds. (1996). Crossing boundaries: Family, community, and school partnerships. *International Journal of Educational Research*, 25(1), Special Issue.

Desimone, L. (1999). Linking parent involvement with student achievement: Do race and income matter? *Journal of Educational Research* 93: 11–30.

Donahue, P.L., R. J. Finnegan, A. D. Lutkus, N. L. Allen, and J. R. Campbell. (2001). *The Nation's Report Card: Fourth-grade reading 2002* (NCES 2001-499). Washington, DC: Office of Educational Research and Improvement, National Center for Education Statistics.

Edwards, P. (2004). *Children's literacy development: Making it happen through school, family, and community involvement.* Boston: Allyn and Bacon.

Elder, G. H., Jr. (1997). The life course and human development. In R. M. Lerner (Ed.), *Handbook of child psychology, volume 1: Theoretical models of human development* (pp. 939–991). New York: Wiley.

Epstein, J. L. (1987). Toward a theory of family-school connections: Teacher practices and parent involvement. In K. Hurrelman, F. Kaufmann, and F. Losel (Eds.), *Social intervention: Potential and constraints* (pp. 121–136). New York: DeGruyter.

————. (1995). School/family/community partnerships: Caring for the children we share. *Phi Delta Kappan,* 76: 701–712.

————. (2001). *School, family, and community partnerships: Preparing educators and improving schools.* Boulder: Westview.

————. (2005a). Links in a professional development chain: Preservice and inservice education for effective programs of school, family, and community partnerships. *New Educator* 1: 125–141.

————. (2005b). Results of the Partnership Schools-CSR model for student achievement over three years. *Elementary School Journal* 106: 151–170.

Epstein, J. L., and S. Lee. (1995). National patterns of school and family connections in the middle grades. In B. A. Ryan, G. R. Adams, T. P. Cullota, R. P. Weisberg, and R. L. Hampton (Eds.), *The family-school connection* (pp. 108–154). Thousand Oaks, CA: Sage.

Epstein, J. L., and K. C. Salinas. (2004). Partnering with families and communities. *Educational Leadership* 61: 12–18.

Epstein, J. L., and M. G. Sanders. (2000). Connecting home, school, and community: New directions for social research. In M. Hallinan (Ed.), *Handbook of sociology of education* (pp. 285–306). New York: Plenum.

————. (2006). Prospects for change: Preparing educators for school, family, and community partnerships. *Peabody Journal of Education* 81: 81–120.

Epstein, J. L., and S. B. Sheldon. (2002). Present and accounted for: Improving student attendance through family and community involvement. *Journal of Educational Research* 95: 308–318.

Epstein, J. L., et al. (2009). *School, family, and community partnerships: Your handbook for action* (3rd ed.). Thousand Oaks, CA: Corwin.

Epstein, J. L., B. S. Simon, and K. C. Salinas. (1997, September). Effects of Teachers Involve Parents in Schoolwork (TIPS) language arts interactive homework in the middle grades. *Research Bulletin* 18. Bloomington, IN: Phi Delta Kappa, CEDR.

Epstein, J. L., and F. L. Van Voorhis. (2001). More than minutes: Teachers' roles in designing homework. *Educational Psychologist* 36: 181–194.

Epstein, J. L., and K. J. Williams. (2003). *Does professional development for state and district leaders affect how they assist schools to implement programs of partnership?* Paper presented at the annual meeting of the American Educational Research Association, Chicago.

Epstein, J. L., K. J. Williams, and N. R. Jansorn. (2004). *Does policy prompt partnerships? Effects of NCLB on district leadership for family involvement.* Paper presented at the annual meeting of the American Educational Research Association, San Diego.

Epstein, J. L., K. J. Williams, and K. C. Lewis. (2002). *Five-year study: Key components of effective partnership programs in states and school districts.* Paper presented at the annual meeting of the American Educational Research Association, New Orleans.

Fagnano, C. L., and B. Z. Werber. (1994). *School, family, and community interaction: A view from the firing lines.* Boulder: Westview.

Fruchter, N., A. Galletta, and J. L. White. (1992). *New directions in parent involvement.* Washington, DC: Academy for Educational Development.

Gerne, K. M., and J. L. Epstein. (2004). The power of partnerships: School, family, and community collaboration to improve children's health. *RMC Health Educator* 4(2): 1–2, 4–6.

Gibbs, N. (2005, February 21). Parents behaving badly. *Time* 165 (8).

Grolnick, W. S., and M. L. Slowiaczek. (1994). Parents' involvement in children's schooling: A multi-dimensional conceptualization and motivational model. *Child Development* 65: 237–252.

Harvard Family Research Project. (2004). Bibliographies of published work on school, family, and community partnerships. www.gse.harvard.edu/hfrp/projects/fine/resources/bibliography/family-involvement-2004.html.

Henderson, A., and K. L. Mapp. (2002). *A new wave of evidence: The impact of school, family, and community connections on student achievement.* Austin: Southwest Educational Development Laboratory.

Hiatt-Michaels, D., ed. (2001). *Promising practices for family involvement in schools.* Greenwich, CT: Information Age Publishing.

Hill, N. E., D. R. Castellina, J. E. Lansford, P. Nowlin, K. A. Dodge, J. E. Bates, and G. S. Pettit. (2004). Parent academic involvement as related to school behavior, achievement, and aspirations: Demographic variations across adolescence. *Child Development* 75: 1491–1509.

Hill, N. E., and S. A. Craft. (2003). Parent-school involvement and school performance: Mediated pathways among socioeconomically comparable African-American and Euro-American families. *Journal of Educational Psychology* 95: 934–959.

Hoover-Dempsey, K. V., and H. M. Sandler. (1997). Why do parents become involved in their children's education? *Review of Educational Research* 67: 3–42.

Kessler-Sklar, S. L., and A. J. L. Baker. (2000). School district parent involvement policies and programs. *Elementary School Journal* 101: 101–118.

Lareau, A. (1989). *Home advantage: Social class and parental intervention in elementary education.* Philadelphia: Falmer.

Lee, S. (1994). *Family-school connections and students' education: Continuity and change of family involvement from the middle grades to high school.* Unpublished doctoral dissertation, Johns Hopkins University.

Leichter, H. J. (Ed.). (1974). *The family as educator.* New York: Teachers College Press.

Lightfoot, S. L. (1978). *Worlds apart: Relationships between families and schools.* New York: Basic Books.

Lin, N. (2000). *Social capital: Theory of structure and action.* Cambridge: Cambridge University Press.

Litwak, E., and H. J. Meyer (1974). *School, family, and neighborhood: The theory and practice of school-community relations.* New York: Columbia University Press.

Mattingly, D. J., R. Prislin, T. L. McKenzie, J. L. Rodriguez, and B. Kayzar (2002). Evaluating evaluations: The case of parent involvement programs. *Review of Educational Research* 72: 549–576.

Miller, B. I. (1986). *Parental involvement effects on reading achievement of first, second, and third graders.* South Bend: Indiana University Exit Project (EDRS ED 279 997).

Muller, C. (1993). Parent involvement and academic achievement: An analysis of family resources available to the child. In B. Schneider and J. Coleman (Eds.), *Parents, their children, and schools* (pp. 77–113). Boulder: Westview.

National Network of Partnership Schools. (2005). Summaries of promising partnership practices and Partnership Award winning programs. www.partnershipschools.org.

National PTA. (2004). *National standards for parent/family involvement programs.* Chicago: Author.

Patrikakou, E. N., R. P. Weissberg, S. Redding, H. J. Walberg. (Eds.). (2005). *School-family partnerships: Fostering children's school success.* New York: Teachers College Press.

Price, H. B. (2005, January 19). Winning hearts and minds. *Education Week* 24 (19): 47, 35.

Public Law 107–110. (2002, January 8). *No Child Left Behind Act of 2001.* Washington, DC: Congressional Record, 115 STAT. 1501–1505.

Reynolds, A. J., J. A. Temple, D. L. Robertson, and E. A. Mann. (2002). Age 21 cost-benefit analysis of the Title I Chicago child-parent centers. *Educational Evaluation and Policy Analysis* 24: 267–303.

Ryan, B. A, G. R. Adams, T. P. Gullotta, R. P. Weissberg, and R. L. Hampton. (Eds.). (1995). *The family-school connection.* Thousand Oaks, CA: Sage.

Salinas, K. C., and N. R. Jansorn. (2004). *Promising partnership practices 2004.* Baltimore: Center on School, Family, and Community Partnerships.

Sanders, M. G. (1996). School-family-community partnerships focused on school safety. *Journal of Negro Education* 65(3): 369–374.

———. (1998). The effects of school, family, and community support on the academic achievement of African-American adolescents. *Urban Education* 33: 385–410.

———. (1999). Schools' programs and progress in the National Network of Partnership Schools. *Journal of Educational Research* 92(4): 220–229.

———. (2001). A study of the role of "community" in comprehensive school, family and community partnership programs. *The Elementary School Journal* 102: 19–34.

———. (2003). Community involvement in schools: From concept to practice. *Education and Urban Society* 35(2): 161–181.

———. (2005). *Building school-community partnerships: Collaboration for student success.* Thousand Oaks, CA: Corwin.

Sanders, M. G., and J. L. Epstein. (Eds.). (1998a). International perspectives on school, family and community partnerships. *Childhood Education* 74 (International Focus Issue).

———. (1998b). School-family-community partnerships and educational change: International perspectives. In A. Hargreaves, A. Lieberman, M. Fullan, and D. Hopkins (Eds.), *International handbook of educational change* (pp. 482–502). Hingham, MA: Kluwer.

———. (2000). Building school, family and community partnerships in secondary schools. In M. G. Sanders (Ed.), *Schooling students placed at risk: Research, policy and practice in the education of poor and minority adolescents* (pp. 339–362). Mahwah, NJ: Lawrence Erlbaum Associates.

Sanders, M. G., and A. Harvey. (2002). Beyond the school walls: A case study of principal leadership for school-community collaboration. *Teachers College Record* 104: 1345–1368.

Sanders, M. G., and K. C. Lewis. (2005). Building bridges toward excellence: Community involvement in high school. *High School Journal* 88 (3): 1–9.

Sanders, M. G., and B. S. Simon. (2002). A comparison of program development at elementary, middle, and high schools in the National Network of Partnership Schools. *School Community Journal* 12: 7–27.

Schneider, B., and J. S. Coleman. (Eds.). (1993). *Parents, their children, and schools.* Boulder: Westview.

Seeley, D. S. (1981). *Education through partnership: Mediating structures and education.* Cambridge, MA: Ballinger.

Sheldon, S. B. (2002). Parents' social networks and beliefs as predictors of parent involvement. *Elementary School Journal* 102: 301–316.

———. (2003). Linking school-family-community partnerships in urban elementary schools to student achievement on state tests. *Urban Review* 35: 149–165.

———. (2005). Testing a structural equations model of partnership program implementation and parent involvement. *Elementary School Journal* 106: 171–187.

———. (2007). Improving student attendance with a school-wide approach to school-family-community partnerships. *Journal of Educational Research* 100: 267–275.

Sheldon, S. B., and J. L. Epstein. (2002). Improving student behavior and discipline with family and community involvement. *Education in Urban Society* 35: 4–26.

———. (2004). Getting students to school: Using family and community involvement to reduce chronic absenteeism. *School Community Journal* 4: 39–56.

———. (2005a). Involvement counts: Family and community partnerships and math achievement. *Journal of Educational Research* 98: 196–206.

———. (2005b). School programs of family and community involvement to support children's reading and literacy development across the grades. In J. Flood and P. Anders (Eds.), *Literacy Development of Students in Urban Schools: Research and Policy* (pp. 107–138). Newark, DE: International Reading Association (IRA).

Sheldon, S. B., and F. Van Voorhis. (2003). *Professional development and the implementation of partnership programs in schools.* Paper presented at the annual meeting of the American Educational Research Association, Chicago.

———. (2004). Partnership programs in U.S. schools: Their development and relationship to family involvement outcomes. *School Effectiveness and School Improvement* 15: 125–148.

Silvern, S. (1985). Parent involvement and reading achievement: A review of research and implications for practice. *Childhood Education* 62: 44–49.

Simon, B. S. (2000). *Predictors of high school and family partnerships and the influence of partnerships on student success.* Unpublished doctoral dissertation. Johns Hopkins University.

———. (2001). Family involvement in high school: Predictors and effects. *NASSP Bulletin* 85(627): 8–19.

———. (2004). High school outreach and family involvement. *Social Psychology of Education* 7: 185–209.

Smit, F., K. Van der Wolf, and P. Sleegers. (Eds.). (2001). *A bridge to the future.* Proceedings of the ERNAPE conference on school, family, and community partnerships. Netherlands: ITS.

Swap, S. M. (1993). *Developing home-school partnerships: From concepts to practice.* New York: Teachers College Press.

Tizard, J., et al. (1982). Collaborating between teachers and parents in assisting children's reading. *British Journal of Educational Psychology* 52: 1–15.

Useem, E. L. (1991). Student selection into course selection sequences in mathematics: The impact of parent involvement and school policies. *Journal of Research on Adolescence* 1: 231–250.

———. (1992). Middle school and math groups: Parents' involvement in children's placement. *Sociology of Education* 65: 263–279.

Van Voorhis, F. L. (2001). Interactive science homework: An experiment in home and school connections. *NASSP Bulletin* 85(627): 20–32.

———. (2003). Interactive homework in middle school: Effects on family involvement and students' science achievement. *Journal of Educational Research* 96: 323–339.

———. (2004). Reflecting on the homework ritual: Assignments and designs. *Theory Into Practice* 43: 205–212.

Van Voorhis, F. L., and S. B. Sheldon. (2004). Principals' roles in the development of U.S. programs of school, family, and community partnerships. *International Journal of Educational Research* 41: 55–70.

Waller, W. (1932). *The sociology of teaching.* New York: Wiley.

Weber, M. (1947). *The theory of social and economic organization.* New York: Oxford University Press.

DISCUSSION AND ACTIVITIES

The comments in this section extend and update the content of the two readings in this chapter. Main concepts are listed that summarize what you should know after reading the articles. Questions and activities are provided for class discussions and homework assignments. They may suggest field activities, research projects, or other exercises.

COMMENT

Emerging Theory

New theories develop or emerge in several ways. One way—the "out-of-the-clear-blue-sky" process—is to think about an unexplained phenomenon and devise an explanation. Then the explanation must be tested to determine whether the theory is correct. Usually, a puzzle of this sort is solved little by little, as evidence accumulates to prove or disprove a theory.

Another way that new theories emerge—the "wait-a-minute-what-was-that again?" process—is to conduct studies based on an established theory and be forced by the results to question, challenge, and reformulate existing ideas. When results repeatedly disprove a prevailing theory or parts of it, new or integrated theories are needed.

The latter example explains why I developed the theory of overlapping spheres of influence to explain the effects of families, schools, and communities on students' learning and development. Early sociological theory suggested that organizations are most efficient and effective if they have separate missions and operate independently. Data from my own and many other studies revealed repeated evidence that educators who worked in partnership with families and communities were more effective than those who worked in isolation in improving school climate, teachers' professional behavior, parents' confidence, and students' success in school. The model of overlapping spheres of influence more completely and accurately depicts and explains the simultaneous influence of schools, families, and communities on students' learning and development and on improving school programs and family support.

A new, revised, or expanded theory encourages researchers to redraw models, recast hypotheses, reexamine patterns in data, consider alternative explanations, and decide whether the theories operate as complementary or competing perspectives. The old and new theories of school, family, and community partnerships are complementary because the overlapping spheres of influence model acknowledges that families, schools, and community organizations conduct some activities separately and others jointly.

Research supports the theory. At different grade levels, with various data sets, in diverse communities, and with different involvement and outcome measures, studies show that students do better when their teachers, parents, and other important adults in their lives work together to help the students succeed in school. Researchers have reported results of family and community involvement on *attendance* (Chang and Romero, 2008; Epstein and Sheldon, 2002; Sheldon, 2007); *behavior* (Davalos, Chavez, and Guardiola, 2005; Noguera, 1995; Sheldon and Epstein, 2002; Taylor and Adelman, 2000); *homework attitudes and achievements* (Epstein and Van Voorhis, 2001; see Readings 3.8 and 6.1); *reading* (Lonigan and Whitehurst, 1998; Sénéchal and LeFevre, 2002; Sheldon and Epstein, 2005b; see Reading 3.7); *math* (Catsambis and Beveridge, 2001; Desimone, 1999; Friedel, Cortina, Turner, and Midgley, 2007; Hong and Ho, 2005; Sheldon and Epstein, 2005a; Sheldon, Epstein, and Galindo, 2010; Valadez, 2002; Yan and Lin, 2005); and *other subjects and outcomes* (Sheldon, 2009).

The results to date are important, but researchers and practitioners should conduct new studies to learn if and how the theory works in their locations with their students and families. Additional tests of the theory of overlapping spheres of influence will improve knowledge, particularly in studies that use robust and reliable measures and longitudinal data on outcomes to control for students' starting points.

COMMENT

Connecting Literature with Theory

Reading 2.2 reviews research on and draws conclusions about knowledge gained on school, family, and community partnerships nearly 25 years after the theoretical model was first introduced. Periodically, it is important to review how a field is growing, what has been learned, and where it needs to go. Many comprehensive literature reviews have been conducted over the years, including Booth and Dunn (1996), Fan and Chen (2001), Henderson and Mapp (2002), Jeynes (2003), Jordan, Orozco, and Averett (2001), Ryan et al. (1995), Weiss, Bouffard, Bridglall, and Gordon (2009), and others. The reviews document and organize the work of many researchers who conducted studies to increase knowledge on partnerships. Literature reviews also help other researchers, graduate and undergraduate students, and practitioners learn which topics have been covered and what questions need to be addressed to strengthen the field, clarify confusing or contradictory findings, and apply results in policy and practice.

In this chapter, the two readings are linked because the literature review (Reading 2.2) draws from the studies that tested and confirmed the theoretical model. The principles drawn from the literature also inform policy leaders and educators about new directions that will produce more successful programs than in the past.

MAIN CONCEPTS

From the two readings in this chapter and the comments and activities that follow, you should have a good understanding of the following concepts and terms:

- overlapping spheres of influence
- external and internal structures of the model of overlapping spheres of influence
- separate versus shared responsibilities of families, schools, and communities
- importance of historic events and trends for changing theories of school, family, and community relationships
- family-like schools and school-like families
- central role of the child in partnerships for education
- *school, family, and community partnerships* as a term that includes and also extends *parent involvement*
- multilevel leadership, including district support and guidance to enable each school to develop its goal-linked partnership program
- the importance of focusing on *equity* in developing partnership programs to change the historic pattern from some families becoming involved some of the time to all families being involved in their children's education at all grade levels
- a research-based framework of six types of involvement that can be studied systematically by researchers and can guide educators in developing comprehensive programs of partnerships

These concepts and terms are discussed in the following comments, questions, and activities.

COMMENT

"Overlap" in Spheres of Influence

In the model of overlapping spheres of influence, shared responsibilities of home, school, and community are identified and developed. Families, educators, and community members and organizations also conduct activities independently. The boundaries of home, school, and community are flexible and permeable in this model. That is, the extent of overlap is affected by the backgrounds, philosophies, and accumulated actions and experiences of families, educators, and community members. These factors lead to more or fewer practices of school, family, and community partnership and, thereby, more or less overlap of the spheres of influence on student learning and development.

QUESTIONS TO DISCUSS

1. a. How might overlapping spheres of influence of home, school, and community create *less efficient* but *more effective* organizations than are created by separate spheres of influence? Could overlapping

spheres of influence of home, school, and community ever create *more efficient* organizations? *less effective* ones? Explain your ideas.

   b. Which organizational feature—efficiency or effectiveness—would you choose for a school attended by your child, and why? When might you trade one for the other?

   c. Discuss how boundaries between and among schools, families, and communities can be fixed and rigid or flexible and permeable. What different effects might permeable and impenetrable home-school-community boundaries have on student attitudes, behavior, and learning?

2. a. What statements or actions have you heard or seen that showed that *parents* were operating within a model of separate spheres of influence or within a model of overlapping spheres of influence?

   b. What statements or actions have you heard or seen that showed that *teachers* were operating within a model of separate spheres of influence or within a model of overlapping spheres of influence?

   c. How would a student describe schoolwork and homework within these two models?

3. Suppose you wanted to know which theory—separate spheres or overlapping spheres of influence—better explains changes in students' writing skills or classroom behavior. Remember, changes in students' writing skills and classroom behavior may be positive or negative over time.

   a. Write a hypothesis to test one of these theories.

   b. Briefly describe a study that would address your hypothesis and that could be conducted in one year or less.

ACTIVITY

External Structure of the Model

Figure 2.1 (page 32) represents the *external* structure of the model of the theory of overlapping spheres of influence of family, school, and community on children's learning and development.

   A. Draw or photocopy the diagram. Write the title of one activity that you think belongs in one of the nonoverlapping sections. This would be an activity that is exclusively or mainly the family's responsibility, the school's responsibility, or the community's responsibility. Under the diagram, write a sentence or two to explain why you placed the activity in that particular nonoverlapping area.

   B. Write the title of one activity that you would place in overlapping sections. The activity may be one that represents shared responsibilities by the school and family, by the family and community, or by any two or three of the contexts. Under the diagram, write a sentence or two to explain why you placed the activity in those overlapping areas.

C. Share your diagram and ideas with an educator, parent, or student. Identify whom you worked with. Ask the interviewee the following questions:

1. Do you agree or disagree that the activity in A (above) is exclusively or mainly the separate responsibility of home or school or community? Explain your ideas.

2. Do you agree or disagree that that the activity in B (above) requires shared, cooperative, or overlapping responsibilities of home and school or any two or three contexts? Explain your ideas.

3. Record the responses you receive. Do you want to revise your examples, or were they confirmed in your interview? Explain.

ACTIVITY

Internal Structure of the Model

At the core or inner structure of the model of overlapping spheres of influence are the interactions that occur between and among the people in the major contexts—parents, teachers, community members, and students—as individuals and in groups. Figure 2.2 (page 32) shows one part of the internal structure of the model of overlapping spheres of influence. It illustrates the institutional and individual interactions of individuals at school and at home, with the student as the center of the interactions.

A. Examine Figure 2.2. In the chart below, provide one positive and one negative example of an interaction that might occur for each two-way connection that is listed here.

Connection ⟷	A positive interaction might be . . .	A negative interaction might be . . .
1. A parent (p) and a teacher (t)		
2. All Families (F) and all teachers and staff at School (S)		

B. Identify one more set of two-way arrows in the diagram that interests you. List one positive and one negative interaction that might occur for the connection you selected.

C. Figure 2.2 on p. 32 depicts the interactions at the individual and institutional levels among people in schools and families. Draw the same diagram showing the institutional and individual interactions for the overlapping spheres of influence of *family and community* or *school and community* contexts. Describe one positive and one negative example of an interaction for one set of two-way arrows in your diagram that interests you.

Forces That Activate the Model

Four "forces" are shown in the model of school, family, and community partnerships that press for more or less overlap of the spheres of influence: (1) family background characteristics, philosophy, and practices; (2) school characteristics, philosophy/policy, and practices; (3) community characteristics, policies, and practices; and (4) time (age of student) and history. These multifaceted forces move the external structure, creating more or less overlap, and activate the interactions and communications in the internal structure that create new interactions and exchanges.

The various forces push or pull the spheres of influence from within, based on the activities for the six types of involvement that are selected, implemented, and improved over time. In simple terms, if there is greater overlap, there will be room for more and different kinds of connections, communications, and collaborations between and among students, parents, teachers, community members, or others involved in students' learning and development at home, at school, or in the community.

QUESTIONS TO DISCUSS

1. a. Select one of the "forces" that pushes the spheres together or pulls them apart: school, family, or community backgrounds; philosophies/policies; practices; or time/history.
   b. How do you think the force that you selected might increase or decrease the shared responsibilities of families and schools? What about that force would make educators and parents have more or less contact with each other about students' work, attitudes, behavior, health, or other indicators of student success in school?
2. List three variables representing the force you selected that could be measured to study their influences on school, family, and community partnerships. Explain why each variable would be a useful measure of the force that you selected. For example, grade level is one variable that represents the force of time or history. This variable can be easily measured and used to study whether connections between home, school, and community increase or decrease as students move through the grades.

School-Like Families and Family-Like Schools

When educators and families recognize their shared responsibilities and interests in children's success in school, the activities and attitudes in both environments tend to change. Teachers and administrators create more *family-like schools*. A *family-like school* recognizes each child's individuality and uniqueness, and, like a family, it makes each child feel special and included. Families create *school-like families* through their attitudes and practices. A *school-like family* recognizes each child as a student, and, like a school, it reinforces the importance of school, homework, and activities that build students' skills, talents, and feelings of success. These constructions and the resulting actions at school and at home help more children define themselves as students, as well as sons or daughters.

A teacher may say, "I know when a student is having a bad day, and how to approach the situation. We're like a family here." A parent may say, "I keep after my daughter to let her know that homework comes first—before TV," or, "My son's first job at home is to finish his schoolwork." A student slips and calls a teacher "Mom" and then laughs with a mixture of embarrassment and happiness about the error.

As soon as you hear these concepts you will remember examples of schools, teachers, and classes that were "like a family" to you and activities or events at home that were "just like school" that supported your work as a student. You may think of how a teacher paid individual attention to you, recognized your uniqueness, and praised you for your own progress, just as a parent would. You may recall that parents, siblings, and other family members engaged in and enjoyed some educational activities with you and took pride in the good schoolwork or homework that you did, just as a teacher would. You begin to hear, see, and read about family-like schools and school-like families in newspapers or magazines, on television, and from children in your family.

There also are school-like and family-like community groups and organizations. A local zoo or botanical gardens may be "just like school"—a place to learn. A local library that welcomes, works with, and cares for students, families, and educators may feel "like a family."

QUESTIONS TO DISCUSS

1. Describe and discuss one example of a *school-like family* and one example of a *family-like school* that you have experienced, read, or heard about.
2. a. Give one example of how a school-like family and how a family-like school may be positive forces for children.
   b. Give one example of how these could be negative influences.
   c. What information might a school give families to help keep their connections positive?
   d. What information might a family give a teacher to help keep their connections positive?

3. A community also may be family-like and school-like. The statement, "We're like a family here," is often used in community groups, organizations, and businesses. Some communities, however, are more active than others in supporting the needs and goals of schools, students, and families.

   a. Give one example of an activity that you have read or heard about that illustrates a *family-like community* that cares for children as a family should.

   b. Give one example of an activity that you have read or heard about that illustrates a *school-like community* that gives children messages about the importance of school, learning, citizenship, or other issues that match the messages of home and school.

ACTIVITY

Reading for Understanding

Explore the concepts and terms that other researchers have used for school-like families or families whose actions at home help their children define themselves as "students." Terms such as *cultural capital*, *social capital*, *funds of knowledge*, and *management skills* have focused attention on how families gather and use resources and skills to help their children succeed in school.

A. Read one of the following articles or books by other researchers that contribute in important ways to the literature on school, family, and community partnerships.

CULTURAL CAPITAL

Lareau, A. (1987). Social class differences in family-school relationships: The importance of cultural capital. *Sociology of Education* 60: 73–85.
———. (1989). *Home advantage*. Philadelphia: Falmer.
———. (2003). *Unequal childhoods: Class, race, and family life.* Berkeley: University of California Press.

SOCIAL CAPITAL

Coleman, J. S. (1987). Families and schools. *Educational Researcher* 16: 32–38.
Lin, N. (2000). *Social capital: theory of structure and action.* Cambridge: Cambridge University Press.

FUNDS OF KNOWLEDGE

Moll, L. C., C. Amanti, D. Neff, and N. Gonzalez. (1992). Funds of knowledge for teaching: Using a qualitative approach to connect homes and classrooms. *Theory into Practice* 31: 132–141.

Gonzalez, N., L. C. Moll, and C. Amanti. (Eds.). (2005). *Funds of knowledge: Theorizing practices in households, communities, and classrooms.* Mahwah, NJ: Erlbaum.

MANAGEMENT SKILLS

Baker, D. P., and D. L. Stevenson. (1986). Mothers' strategies for children's school achievement: Managing the transition to high school. *Sociology of Education* 59: 156–166.

Useem, E. L. (1992). Middle schools and math groups: Parents' involvement in children's placement. *Sociology of Education* 65: 263–279.

ASSETS

Benson, P. (1997). *Creating healthy communities for children and adolescents.* San Francisco: Jossey-Bass.

Benson, P. L., P. C. Scales, S. F. Hamilton, and A. Sesma Jr. (2006). Positive youth development: Theory, research, and application. In W. W. Damon and R. M. Lerner (Eds.), *Handbook of Child Psychology, Volume 1* (pp. 894–941). New York: John Wiley.

INTEGRATED COMMUNITY SERVICES

Dryfoos, J. (1994). *Full-service schools.* San Francisco: Jossey-Bass.

Dryfoos, J., and S. Maquire. (2002). *Inside full-service community schools.* Thousand Oaks, CA: Corwin.

COMPLEMENTARY AND SUPPLEMENTARY LEARNING

Gordon, E. W., B. L. Bridglall, and A. S. Meroe. (2004). *Supplementary education: The hidden curriculum of high academic achievement.* Lanham, MD: Rowman and Littlefield.

Weiss, H. B., S. M. Bouffard, B. L., Bridglall, and E. W. Gordon. (2009). *Reframing family involvement in education: Supporting families to support educational equity.* Equity Matters: Research Review No. 5. New York: The Campaign for Educational Equity, Teachers College, Columbia University.

B. 1. Give the full reference for the article, book, or chapter you read, and write a short summary of the main ideas on family support for children's education.

   2. Explain whether and how the main ideas correspond to, complement, or contradict the theory of overlapping spheres of influence.

   3. Discuss how the author's concepts match, contribute to, or differ from *school-like families, family-like schools, family-like communities,* or *school-like communities.*

Central Role of the Child in School, Family, and Community Partnerships

The theory of overlapping spheres of influence sets the child at the center of the internal structure of the model. The assumption is that students are the main actors in their own education and the primary reason for communications between school and home. The students must do the work to learn to read, write, calculate, master other skills, and develop personal talents.

Not only are students responsible for learning, they also are responsible for whether most communications between school and home have the desired effects. Studies show that students are often the main source (sometimes the only source) of information for parents about school and community activities. In strong programs of school, family, and community partnerships, teachers prepare and encourage students to help conduct traditional communications such as delivering memos or report cards, and new communications such as interactive homework and student-led parent-teacher-student conferences.

The central role of students in school, family, and community partnerships is supported by research in this and other countries. For example, early on, Swiss researchers Montandon and Perrenoud (1987) described the child as a "go-between" who was both the messenger and the message between family and school.

Teachers and parents know that students serve as messengers to transmit information from school to home and from home to school. Students also communicate nonverbally. Their attitudes, facial expressions, and body language tell teachers, parents, coaches, and others a great deal about students' experiences at home, at school, and in the community. At different times and in many ways, students speak for themselves, for their teachers, and for their parents.

QUESTIONS TO DISCUSS

1. How do or how should students' roles in school and family partnerships change from one grade level to the next?
   a. Give one example of a *typical* activity and one example of an *ideal* activity that students conduct to connect home and school at each school level:

School Level	*Typical* Activity Students Conduct to Connect School and Home	*Ideal* Activity Students Could Conduct to Connect School and Home
(1) Preschool		
(2) Elementary School		
(3) Middle School		
(4) High School		

2. Students can be guided to be more effective messengers, communicators, discussants, interactors, demonstrators, and celebrators of new skills.
   a. Select a grade level that interests you.
   b. Discuss one way in which a teacher at that grade level might inform students about their roles and responsibilities in school, family, and community partnerships.
   c. Discuss one way in which parents might encourage their children at that grade level to communicate with them about school and classroom activities.

COMMENT

Understanding Authority in Theories of Partnership

Underlying the contrasting theories of school, family, and community connections are questions of *who* has responsibility and authority for children's education. What do parents do? What do teachers do? What does the community do? Where? When? How well? With what goals? These are questions of control and the division of labor. By contrast, the model of overlapping spheres requires the *multiplication of labor*.

Control

Principals, teachers, and district and state leaders may fully control the school organization or share control and leadership with parents, students, and others in the community. Principals can make decisions about the school and students' education with or without allowing or encouraging teachers, parents, and students to participate. Teachers can direct student learning with or without allowing or encouraging parents to assist.

On their own, some parents become and stay involved in their children's education at home, at school, and in the community, regardless of whether the school shares control with them. School policies and decisions about control make a difference, however, in whether there is broad involvement by all parents or limited involvement by a few parents who are able to obtain information and organize their own activities and participation.

Division of Labor

Teachers and administrators may stress the separate skills and contributions of teachers and parents, emphasizing the specialization in their work at school and at home. Specialization requires expertise in a few well-defined tasks. Teachers who have been advised to stick to the basics restrict their attention to teaching academic skills. They may emphasize the tests they give students to show how teachers' work differs from that of families.

Teachers who separate school from home may say, "If the family would just do its job, I could do mine. I could teach these kids." Families who separate home from school may say, "I get my child to school each day; then it's the school's job to teach him." This division of labor reflects early social organizational theory that schools, families, and other organizations are more efficient and effective if they have separate goals and responsibilities to influence different behaviors. The *division of labor* reflects a model of *separate spheres of influence*.

Multiplication of Labor

By contrast, educators and families may stress the combination of skills of teachers and parents, emphasizing the generalization of their efforts to educate students at school and at home. When they teach the "whole child," teachers teach academic skills *and* increase their attention to the child's self-concept, aspirations, social skills, and talents—some of the traditional responsibilities of parents. When involved in their children's education, parents increase their attention to their children's abilities and mastery of skills, how they get along with other children and adults, and their future plans for education and work—some of the traditional responsibilities of teachers.

Shared responsibilities multiply the messages that children receive about the importance of the work they do as students. The *multiplication of labor* reflects a model of *overlapping spheres of influence* and the view that schools, families, and other community organizations will be more effective, if not always as efficient, when they work together to promote student success.

Thus, schools can be characterized by sole or shared control with families, by a strict division and separation of labor, or by the multiplication and "overlap" of labor concerning students' learning. These are not mutually exclusive concepts, and both are pictured in the model of overlapping spheres of influence.

QUESTIONS TO DISCUSS

1. Why is it important for children to receive common messages about the importance of school from their teachers, their families, and their communities? In addition to giving common messages, what is one other way in which schools, families, and communities might multiply their resources to assist students?
2. When might it be important to maintain a *division of labor* between school and home? Give one example of when it would be good for children to hear a unique message from home or from school.
3. Which groups or organizations in a community do you think are most

likely to demonstrate a *multiplication of labor* to assist students' learning and development?

Mutual Respect of Teachers and Parents

All discussions about school, family, and community partnerships begin with a call for mutual respect between teachers and parents, teachers and other family members, students and teachers, business partners and educators. A perceived lack of respect is often given as the reason for the lack of communication and interactions among the home, school, and community. This becomes a self-fulfilling prophecy, making the history of poor communication the reason for perpetuating separate spheres of influence. Parents' and teachers' respect, appreciation, recognition, and admiration for each other and for the work they do separately and together with children are represented in the structure and processes of the model of overlapping spheres of influence.

Parents and teachers establish respect for each other in different ways when they work in separate or overlapping spheres of influence on children's learning. In organizations that maintain separate spheres of influence, parents may receive respect for their home training and child raising. Depending on one's perspective, a "good mother" may have a well-behaved or creative child or a child who is both. Teachers are respected for their school lessons and educational programs. A "good teacher" may make tough demands on students or conduct highly engaging classes or do both.

Traditionally, teachers' expertise is based on professional training; parents' expertise is based on successful home management. When the emphasis is on the efficiency of separate organizations, respect for teachers and parents is *site specific*, based on the role of the adults in each setting and the distinct jobs they do.

In organizations that support overlapping spheres of influence, respect is extended to parents and teachers who work well together and who fulfill shared responsibilities for the education and socialization of children across the school years. In overlapping spheres of influence, parents and teachers require information about each other's goals to be knowledgeable partners and responsive to student needs. When the emphasis is on overlapping influence, respect for teachers and parents is *student specific*, based on the combined interests and efforts of teachers, parents, students, and others across settings to support and encourage learning and development.

QUESTIONS TO DISCUSS

1. Why do you think the concept of respect is so powerful as the basis for school, family, and community partnerships? Which do you think comes first, respect or partnership? Explain your answer.

2. Give examples from your reading or experience of:
   a. Respect by teachers and parents for the *separate* work of families and schools.
   b. Respect by teachers and parents for the *shared* or *overlapping* work of families and schools.
3. How do the theories of social behavior (e.g., symbolic interactionism or reference group theory) described in Reading 2.1 help to explain how respect is developed in school, family, and community partnerships?
   a. Select and identify one social or behavioral theory discussed in Reading 2.1.
   b. Describe two ways in which the assumptions of the theory you selected increase or decrease mutual respect between teachers and parents or between teachers and citizens of the community.

COMMENT

Shared Responsibilities: Who Teaches What? What Families Do, but Schools Do Too

Families are responsible for teaching children about their cultural background, values, religious beliefs, manners, and other important aspects of life. Many families also take responsibility for developing their children's talents. They reward their children's successes and redirect failures. Increasingly, schools share some of these responsibilities. Programs and intergroup processes in many schools nurture students' self-respect and increase their knowledge, tolerance, and appreciation of other students' cultural backgrounds and values. Some teachers and some school and community programs help students develop self-confidence, manners, sportsmanship, and talents as much as or more than some families.

Parents are expected to act as advocates, liaisons, and buffers for their children, protecting and advancing their children's rights to participate in school programs and to receive needed social, health, and educational services. Some families fulfill these responsibilities easily, whereas other families need information and assistance to fulfill them. Increasingly, schools provide these protections and share information with families so that they become more knowledgeable about how to work with the school, school system, and community on behalf of their children.

What Schools Do, but Families Do Too

Schools have a major responsibility for helping students develop *independence* and *self-reliance* because teachers cannot give all students instant individual attention. By their practices, however, some schools foster children's *dependence* on the teacher. For example, some teachers give students few opportunities to design and conduct projects, answer questions that have more than one right answer, or develop their individual talents. Some families at all economic levels influence their children's development of independence as much as or more than some schools.

Schools are responsible for helping students learn school subjects and gain academic and intellectual skills. Teachers' daily, focused, and challenging lessons increase students' abilities to read, write, compute, think, and apply their knowledge in useful and creative ways. In partnership with schools, some families at all economic levels boost their children's knowledge and skills with numerous learning activities at home in reading, writing, computing, thinking, and solving problems.

Some schools and teachers guide all or most parents to conduct activities and interactions at home that support and enhance children's learning. In some cases, the creative and useful activities at home increase student learning as much as or more than the activities at some schools.

These and many other examples illustrate why it is hard to determine "Whose job is it?" to help students develop knowledge, skills, attitudes, values, and talents. For students, learning is not limited in time or place but occurs in school, at home, and in the community. These complex factors underlie the concept and model of overlapping spheres of influence.

QUESTIONS TO DISCUSS

1. Describe two traditional "teachings" of families that are aided by the actions of schools.
2. Describe two traditional "teachings" of schools that are aided by the actions of families.
3. Describe two traditional "teachings" of communities that are aided by the actions of families and/or schools.
4. Think about how children learn. Discuss your views on these questions:
   a. Is it possible for children to separate what is learned at home from what is learned at school or in the community? Give one example to support your view.
   b. Identify one school subject that is likely to be strongly influenced (1) by school, (2) by home, and (3) by the community. Are any of your examples solely influenced by one context? Explain.
   c. How might your ideas on A and B affect the development of programs of school, family, and community partnerships?

COMMENT

Partnerships Subsume Parental Involvement

When educators talk about *parental involvement*, they often put all of the responsibility on parents to connect with teachers and administrators and to become involved with their children at home. By contrast, the term *school, family, and community partnerships* assigns responsibilities to schools, to families, and to communities to share information, ideas, activities, and services with each other about schools and children's education.

Some researchers, educators, and others use terms like *parent engagement* or *parent participation*. These terms still focus on the actions and efforts by parents but hide the requirement for schools and communities to take responsibility for organizing programs that make it possible for all parents to become involved in their children's education in productive ways. When the focus is only on *parents*, we lose sight of the importance of school programs that assist parents and engage community partners in exciting and important goal-linked activities that support student learning and development.

Developing *programs* of school, family, and community partnerships in schools and districts gives all families more equal opportunities to become involved in their children's education and development, rather than just a few. The broader term also makes room for students as key members of the partnership because they are influenced by all three contexts—home, school, and community—and recognizes that students are the main actors in their education. Swap (1992) contrasted programs that separate and isolate parents with those that build good partnerships, and showed clearly that educators' philosophies about involvement affect the actions they take.

As noted in Reading 2.2, the broader, better term *school, family, and community partnerships* is necessary to increase equity of involvement. Equity aims for equal opportunities for parents to become involved in their children's education, equal feelings of welcome at a school, equal evidence of respect from schools for parents' roles, and, in two-way communications, equal respect from parents for teachers' efforts in promoting students' success.

QUESTIONS TO DISCUSS

As noted in Reading 2.2, the term *partnership* for programs that involve families and communities in education has been chosen with care. It has a history of meanings, connections, and examples in other fields, particularly in business, that strengthen the meaning of partnerships in education. The term will not go out of favor as a whim or fad in education. It stands for some important interactions.

1. a. Do you think that *school, family, and community partnerships* is a better term than *parent involvement* for studying the connections of teachers, parents, and others and for developing practical programs in elementary, middle, and high schools? Why or why not?
   b. List other terms that you have seen, heard, or read that refer to family and community involvement (e.g., home-school relations, caring community). Select one term on your list, and compare its usefulness to the term *school, family, and community partnerships*.
2. How many similarities and differences can you think of in comparing the concepts of partnerships in business and in home, school, and community connections? Following are two examples:

Concept of Partnerships	Partners in Education and in Business
• shared responsibilities	Recognize their responsibilities to each other, to the "product," and to the public
• shared investments	Put in the necessary time to reach their goals in business

    a. Give two more examples of *similarities* between partnerships in business and school, family, and community partnerships in education. State the concept, and explain the similarities in intent or actions.

    b. Give two examples of *differences* between partnerships in business and school, family, and community partnerships in education. State the concept, and explain the differences in intent or actions.

3. a. How might the following terms guide teachers, parents, and community members to work as partners to increase children's success in school?

To ensure this quality:	Teachers, parents, and community partners could take this action:
(1) Unity	
(2) Commitment	
(3) Trust	
(4) Obligation	
(5) Assurance	

COMMENT

The Influence of History on Theory

Reading 2.1 argues that changing times require changing theories. The concept of overlapping spheres of influence reflects social changes that have affected families, schools, and communities over the past half century. Four trends were discussed that altered the relationships of schools, families, and communities, reducing their separate responsibilities and increasing shared responsibilities:

1. More mothers have higher education and are prepared to work on an equal status with teachers.
2. Baby and child care books and media guide families through the infant, toddler, and early childhood years and prepare them to seek information and advice as their children continue to grow through later childhood, early adolescence, and adolescence.

3. Federal regulations and federal, state, and local policies reinforce the importance of the involvement of all families in their children's education, including economically disadvantaged families and families that speak languages other than English at home. Over time, starting in the 1960s, federal, state, and district policies have directed schools to conduct programs that will increase family and community involvement in ways that support student achievement and success in school.

4. Changes in family structure (including more mothers working, more single parents, and more diverse family groups, such as blended families, same-gender parents, and families in transition) require educators to understand the diversity among family forms and to provide all families with good information so they can make productive use of limited time together. Employed parents, homeless families, and other critical conditions require schools and communities to provide services to assist families with the supervision of children before and after school, during the summer, and in major vacation periods.

The demands on schools have increased educators' awareness that they cannot do the job of educating children alone. Educators have learned that they need families and communities as partners in children's education. Similarly, the complexities and demands in family life have increased parents' awareness that they need their schools and communities as partners to increase their children's chances for success.

QUESTIONS TO DISCUSS

1. Select one historic trend listed above that interests you.
   a. Give one example of how the trend you selected might promote successful partnerships with families.
   b. Give one example of how the trend you selected might create problems for schools or for families. Explain how that problem might be solved.
2. Parents with more formal education *and* those with less formal education are increasingly interested and involved in their children's education. Discuss why you think these simultaneous (and seemingly contradictory) trends are important for the design and implementation of programs of school, family, and community partnerships.

COMMENT

Changing the Question

Family environments and activities influence student learning and success in school. From the 1960s to today, studies in sociology, psychology, and education have been conducted on whether and how families and home environments influence children's achievement and which family practices affect children's development, learning, and success. I call these "first-generation" studies of home and school connections. The results of almost all such studies show that children do better in school on many measures *if* their parents support and encourage school activities. This is a social fact in children's education and development.

There still are many questions to ask about family influences on children at all grade levels and in diverse cultural, linguistic, and community contexts. However, the consistent and confirmatory results on the importance of families in children's lives prompted me to ask a new question that changed the way that I think about and study school, family, and community partnerships: *IF families are so important, HOW can schools and communities help more families become and stay involved in their children's education—especially parents who would not, typically, become involved on their own?*

You will read studies in this book and in other books and journals that ask what educators, parents, and others can do to develop effective programs to involve all families and communities in children's education and in schools. I call these "second-generation" studies of home, school, and community partnerships, because they change researchers' attention from questions about the importance of families to a harder question about the structures and processes in schools' *programs* that may increase the *equity* of outreach to all families and their involvement in their children's education at all grade levels. Because surveys of parents from all backgrounds and cultures show that they want to be able to guide and assist their children at all grade levels, new studies should focus on the nature of programs and practices that help all parents—particularly those who would not otherwise become involved on their own—to support their children's learning and development through high school graduation and beyond.

QUESTIONS TO DISCUSS

1. In your view, what is the difference between the two lines of research that explore (1) if and how families are important for student success (first-generation studies) and (2) if and how schools can develop programs to involve all families in their children's education (second-generation studies)? Discuss your ideas about why each focus is important for understanding students' success in school.

2. Read these two sentences:
   a. It is important for all children to be ready for school.
   b. It is important for all schools to be ready for children and their families.
      (1) How are the two sentences linked in meaning?
      (2) How do these two sentences differ in meaning?
      (3) Give one idea of how each of these sentences is informed by first-generation studies of family involvement and by second-generation studies of school, family, and community partnerships.

Does Family Involvement in a Specific Subject Generalize to Help Students Succeed in Other Subjects?

It is important to learn whether and how specific practices of involvement produce particular results for students in the short term and over the long term. As Reading 2.2 suggests, family involvement with children in reading at home may lead students, first, to be motivated to read and to pay greater attention to instruction in reading class. This may help students gain reading skills in the short term and, if their motivation is sustained, in the long term.

Over time, involvement in reading may lead to family discussions and interactions with children about other subjects. Also, after learning how to involve families in reading, teachers may, over time, improve the quality of the information they give to families about how to interact with their children in other subjects.

Subject-specific interactions at home may help children see that their families are interested in all aspects of their education. Initial support from families in reading, then, may translate into more serious work by students in many school subjects and activities. This line of events and effects may progress at different rates, depending on how much the school informs and involves families about their children's education.

In surveys of students, most students report that their families believe education is important (MetLife, 2008). But not all of these students succeed in reading, math, and other subjects. Not all students who say that their families value education graduate from high school on time. Indeed, most families who *believe* education is important are not presently involved in school-related learning activities at home unless their children's teachers guide these interactions.

There are many unanswered questions about the paths between parents' beliefs about education, activities initiated by teachers to reach out to families, families' responses, students' motivation to learn, students' work in school, and students' achievement in specific subjects and overall success in school.

QUESTIONS TO DISCUSS

1. Draw and label a diagram with paths that show how family involvement in one activity (e.g., involvement in reading aloud or listening to a child read) might lead to family involvement in other subjects.
2. Draw and label a diagram with paths that show how the effects of family involvement on student learning might "travel" from family involvement in a specific subject (e.g., reading) to improved student achievement in that subject, other subjects, and success in school overall.

Next Questions

Many topics need more attention in research on whether and how school programs and practices can effectively involve all families in supporting, guiding, and encouraging students to do their best in school. Here are six topics that need more and better studies:

Transitions. Which practices of school, family, and community partnerships are needed at important points of transitions when children move from elementary to middle to high school, or from one grade level to the next, or at unexpected times when students change schools or change teachers?

Results of Family and Community Involvement. What are the results of specific types and practices of school, family, and community partnership for students, parents, teachers, and the school community?

Community Connections. How can we better understand and activate the resources in communities that contribute to comprehensive programs of school, family, and community partnerships and to results for students?

Students' Roles. What active roles must students play at all grade levels in programs of school, family, and community partnerships?

Involving Fathers. What practices to involve all who "parent" children (mothers, fathers, grandparents, foster parents, and others) are most effective in engaging fathers and father figures, who have typically been less actively involved with the schools and in their children's education?

Collaborations in Research. How can researchers, policy leaders, and educators most effectively collaborate in developing, maintaining, and evaluating programs of school, family, and community partnerships that make a difference for student success?

Many topics and many issues are embedded in these six questions.

1. Select one of the six topics/questions listed above that interests you.
2. a. From the readings in this chapter, summarize two results from prior research that you believe are "basic" for understanding the topic you selected and that would benefit from more and better studies in the future.
   b. Write one clear question that you believe would extend knowledge on the topic that you selected. Explain in a few sentences why you think your new question is important.

Interview to Discover How Theory Works in Practice

There are some things that families do on their own (nonoverlapping spheres of influence) and some things that families do with information and support from or in collaboration with schools, other families, and the community (overlapping spheres of influence). Interview two parents individually who have different socioeconomic situations or who live in different neighborhoods.

A. Briefly describe the two parents you interviewed and the features of their economic conditions or neighborhoods.

B. Ask each one the following questions, and record their responses.

What is one topic, problem, or decision concerning your child's development or education that you discuss as a family with:

1. little or no information or influence from the school, community, or other families?

Parent 1 _____

Parent 2 _____

2. some or most information or influence from the school?

Parent 1 _____

Parent 2 _____

3. some or most information or influence from the community?

Parent 1 _____

Parent 2 _____

4. some or most information or influence from other families?

Parent 1 _____

Parent 2 _____

C. How did the responses from the two parents differ? How were their responses similar? What surprised you in their responses? Summarize your views on how the two families make decisions or resolve problems about child raising, independently or with school, family, and community connections.

D. Compare summaries in class to determine how other families in different socioeconomic situations work within the nonoverlapping and overlapping spheres of influence in raising children.

REFERENCES

Booth, A., and J. F. Dunn. (Eds.). (1996). *Family-school links: How do they affect educational outcomes?* Mahwah, NJ: Lawrence Erlbaum Associates.

Catsambis, S., and A. A. Beveridge. (2001). Does neighborhood matter? Family, neighborhood, and school influences on eighth grade mathematics achievement. *Sociological Focus* 34: 435–457.

Chang, H. N., and M. Romero. (2008). *Present, engaged, and accounted for: The critical importance of addressing chronic absence in the early grades*. New York: National Center for Children in Poverty, Columbia University.

Davalos, D., E. Chavez, and R. Guardiola. (2005). Effects of perceived parental school support and family communication on delinquent behaviors in Latino and White non-Latinos. *Cultural Diversity and Ethnic Minority Psychology* 11: 57–68.

Desimone, L. (1999). Linking parent involvement with student achievement: Do race and income matter? *Journal of Educational Research* 93: 11–30.

Epstein, J. L., and S. B. Sheldon. (2002). Present and accounted for: Improving student attendance through family and community involvement. *Journal of Educational Research* 95: 308–318.

Epstein, J. L., and F. L. Van Voorhis. (2001). More than minutes: Teachers' roles in designing homework. *Educational Psychologist* 36: 181–193.

Fan, X., and M. Chen. (2001). Parental involvement and students' academic achievement: A meta-analysis. *Educational Psychology Review* 13: 1–22.

Friedel, J. M., K. S. Cortina, J. C. Turner, and C. Midgley. (2007). Achievement goals, efficacy beliefs and coping strategies in mathematics: The roles of perceived parent and teacher goal emphases. *Contemporary Educational Psychology* 32: 434–458.

Henderson, A. T., and K. L. Mapp. (2002). *A new wave of evidence: The impact of school, family, and community connections on student achievement*. Austin: Southwest Educational Development Laboratory.

Hong, S., and H. Ho. (2005). Direct and indirect longitudinal effects of parental involvement on student achievement: Second-order latent growth modeling across ethnic groups. *Journal of Educational Psychology* 97: 32–42.

Jeynes, W. H. (2003). A meta-analysis: The effects of parental involvement on minority children's academic achievement. *Education and Urban Society* 35: 202–218.

Jordan, C., E. Orozco, and A. Averett. (2001). *Emerging issues in school, family, and community connections*. Austin: Southwest Educational Development Laboratory.

Lonigan, C. J., and G. J. Whitehurst. (1998). Relative efficacy of parent and teacher involvement in a shared-reading intervention for preschool children from low-income backgrounds. *Early Childhood Research Quarterly* 13: 263–290.

MetLife. (2008). *The MetLife survey of the American teacher: Past, present, and future*. New York: MetLife, Inc.

Montandon, C., and P. Perrenoud. (1987). *Entre parents et ensignants: Un dialogue impossible?* [Between parents and teachers: An impossible dialogue?] Berne: Lang.

Noguera, P. A. (1995). Preventing and producing violence: A critical analysis of responses to school violence. *Harvard Educational Review* 65: 189–212.

Ryan, B. A., et al., eds. (1995). *The family-school connection: Theory, research and practice*. Newbury Park, CA: Sage.

Sénéchal, M., and J. LeFevre. (2002). Parental involvement in the development of children's reading skill: A five-year longitudinal study. *Child Development* 73: 455–460.

Sheldon, S. B. (2003). Linking school-family-community partnerships in urban elementary schools to student achievement on state tests. *Urban Review* 35: 149–165.

———. (2007). Improving student attendance with a school-wide approach to school-family-community partnerships. *Journal of Educational Research* 100: 267–275.

———. (2009). Improving student outcomes with school, family, and community partnerships: A research review. In J. Epstein et al. (Eds.), *School, family, and community partnerships: Your handbook for action* (3rd ed.; pp. 40–56). Thousand Oaks, CA: Corwin.

Sheldon, S. B., and J. L. Epstein. (2002). Improving student behavior and discipline with family and community involvement. *Education in Urban Society* 35: 4–26.

———. (2004). Getting students to school: Using family and community involvement to reduce chronic absenteeism. *School and Community Journal* 4(2): 39–56.

———. (2005a). Involvement counts: Family and community partnerships and math achievement. *Journal of Educational Research* 98: 196–206.

————. (2005b). School programs of family and community involvement to support children's reading and literacy development across the grades. In J. Flood and P. Anders (Eds.), *Literacy development of students in urban schools: Research and policy* (pp. 107–138). Newark, DE: International Reading Association (IRA).

Sheldon, S. B., J. L. Epstein, and C. L. Galindo. (2010). Not just numbers: Creating a partnership climate to improve math proficiency in schools. *Leadership and Policy in Schools* 9: 27–48.

Swap, S. M. (1992). *Developing home-school partnerships: From concepts to practice.* New York: Teachers College Press.

Taylor, L., and H. S. Adelman. (2000). Connecting schools, families, and communities. *Professional School Counseling* 3: 298–307.

Valadez, J. R. (2002). The influence of social capital on mathematics course selection by Latino high school students. *Hispanic Journal of Behavioral Sciences* 24: 319–339.

Weiss, H. B., S. M. Bouffard, B. L. Bridglall, and E. W. Gordon. (2009). *Reframing family involvement in education: Supporting families to support educational equity.* Equity Matters: Research Review No. 5. New York: The Campaign for Educational Equity, Teachers College, Columbia University.

Yan, W., and Q. Lin. (2005). Parent involvement and mathematics achievement: Contrast across racial and ethnic groups. *Journal of Educational Research* 99: 116–127.

3

Research

STARTING WITH A STATEWIDE STUDY of teachers, parents, students, and administrators in six hundred elementary schools in Maryland in 1980 and 1981, my colleagues and I began to learn about practices of partnership that were used by teachers, guided by principals and district leaders, aligned with state and district policy, desired by families, and responsive to students. We examined how often and in what ways teachers and their schools involved parents, whether and how parents' social class and marital status affected their involvement, and how elementary school students understood and reacted to connections between their families and teachers. We studied the results of partnerships on the attitudes and practices of teachers, the actions and behaviors of parents, and the attitudes and achievements of students.

The early studies provided systematic, quantitative analyses of the nature and extent of family involvement in the elementary grades. The data raised many questions about existing theories of effective school organizations and effective families and communities and led to the development of the theory of overlapping spheres of influence (see Chapter 2, Reading 2.1).

In 1987, we began field studies with educators, families, and students in urban elementary and middle schools. This research—a collaborative effort with the Baltimore City Public Schools and a community organization, the Fund for Educational Excellence, in Baltimore—increased understanding of how involvement changes across the grades, by teachers of different subjects, for parents from various racial and cultural groups, and in schools that are guided to systematically organize their programs of partnership with families and communities.

In 1991, we started a series of field studies to learn how to define, organize, and study school, family, and community partnerships at the high school level. This research in urban, suburban, and rural settings identified how to expand the language and actions of partnership for educators, parents, and students through the twelfth grade. These studies reinforced and extended our understanding of the important roles students play in school, family, and community partnerships.

The early studies and the research that continues today aim to improve knowledge about whether and how family, school, and community connections improve school organization and assist student learning and development across the grades, from preschool through high school.

This chapter presents data from teachers, parents, and students on the nature and results of school-based partnership programs. See Chapter 4 for research, policy, and program development at the district and state levels.

DATA FROM TEACHERS

Readings 3.1 and 3.2 report results of a survey of nearly 3,700 teachers in about six hundred elementary schools in the state of Maryland. The survey, conducted in 1980, was one of the first large-scale studies of teacher attitudes and practices of involvement that also included data from administrators, parents, and students in the same schools and classrooms. In addition to the survey data, we analyzed teachers' written comments and concerns about school and family connections. Their reports revealed that some teachers were farther along on this agenda than others. That is, some teachers knew how to reach parents whom other teachers did not reach. We learned many things from these teacher-leaders that subsequently helped us help other educators to develop their programs of school, family, and community partnerships.

In 1987, we collected data from teachers and parents in the elementary and middle grades in Baltimore City. With these data, we tested the theory of overlapping spheres of influence and explored and extended research on the major types of involvement. Reading 3.3 reports the attitudes and practices of teachers in urban elementary and middle schools that served a majority of African American students and families in economically distressed neighborhoods.

The data show that teachers' ideas and behaviors are more positive if they believe that their school as a whole is working to involve families. Some teachers communicate effectively with families regardless of parents' race, formal education, neighborhood, or school context. These teachers' efforts and successes suggest that other teachers could do the same if they were helped to use similar strategies for developing partnerships, particularly if they are supported by the administrators and other teachers in the school. Data from teachers and reports from parents in the same schools (see Reading 3.6) document changes in the practices of partnerships that typically occur from the elementary to the middle grades in schools that have not started to organize partnership programs.

DATA FROM PARENTS

Three readings present results of research on parents' reactions to and involvement in their children's education, with data from families who are in the same schools as the teachers described above. Reading 3.4 presents data from a survey of parents of students in six hundred elementary schools in Maryland. Reading 3.5 takes a closer look at these data to explore patterns of participation of single and married parents in their children's education.

These data help explain why earlier ideas about parental involvement were limited by their inattention to whether schools and teachers were conducting practices to involve all parents. Omitting measures of what schools and teachers do to encourage and increase the involvement of all families distorts an understanding of the involvement of single parents, those with less formal education or low income, and mothers who work outside the home. Many of these families rely on information and guidance from schools to help them organize their admittedly limited time and to enable them to remain involved in their children's education at each grade level.

Reading 3.6 reports data from parents of elementary and middle school students in urban schools that were beginning to plan and implement practices of partnership. Conventional wisdom is that low-income families, racial minorities, single parents, and parents with less formal education are not and do not want to be involved in their children's education. Presently, in many schools, this belief is partly true. These families tend not to be as involved as other families. But the statement also is partly false. These families *want* to be involved. Indeed, in all of the surveys we conducted since 1980, just about all parents report that they try to remain involved at home in their children's schooling, but they need more and better information to know what to do that will help their child each year.

In schools that are actively working to develop partnership programs that reach out to and involve all families, the conventional wisdom is completely false. In these schools, just about all parents are informed and involved in their children's education in important ways each year (Epstein et al., 2009; see also the section "Success Stories" at www.partnershipschools.org).

DATA FROM STUDENTS

The last three readings in this chapter are based on data from elementary school students who were in the classrooms of teachers who varied in their practices of involving families in their children's education. Reading 3.7 reports the effects on student achievement of school programs that involve families in learning activities at home. This study reveals an important subject-specific connection. Involvement by parents in a particular subject at home—here, in reading—leads to gains in student achievement in that subject.

Reading 3.8 explores how homework creates three-way connections among student, teacher, and family. Reading 3.9 uses data from a survey of fifth-grade students to better understand their views about homework and parent involvement and their attitudes toward school. We wanted to learn whether teachers' practices to involve families affected students' perceptions of the congruency between home and school and whether students' homework habits were affected by teachers' practices to involve families. We also wanted to see if reports from teachers, principals, and students about parent involvement produced similar results on these measures.

The results of these analyses influenced a new line of research and development to help teachers design new forms of interactive homework to involve families in various school subjects to boost student achievement (see Chapter 6 on practical approaches to homework design).

SUMMARY

One of the most consistent results in the various surveys that we and other researchers have conducted in the United States and other countries is that teachers have very different views of parents than parents have of themselves. Most teachers do not know parents' hopes and dreams for their children or their questions about parenting children at different age and grade levels, nor do they understand what parents presently do at home to help their children.

Similarly, neither parents nor teachers fully understand what students think about school, family, and community partnerships. Indeed, most adults believe that students want to avoid or minimize family involvement in their education. Data from students from the elementary grades through high school suggest the opposite. Students want families to be knowledgeable partners with their schools in their education and available as helpful sources of information and assistance at home.

Although the readings in this chapter and other studies show that there are connections between family involvement and student achievement, there is still much to learn about *which practices* produce positive results for student learning. We need to learn how, when, for whom, and why particular practices increase students' skills and scores in specific subjects. The readings, discussion topics, and activities in this chapter raise new questions for research on the effects of school, family, and community partnerships on student learning and development.

Data from teachers, parents, and students can be gathered with various research methods, including surveys, experimental and quasi-experimental studies, interviews, focus or discussion groups, and other strategies. Whichever study designs and methods of inquiry are used, one group's perspective—educators, parents, or students—alone will not provide an accurate base on which to plan better programs or practices of partnerships.

The readings in this chapter illustrate why it is important to measure and account for teachers', parents', and students' views to identify gaps in knowledge that each has about the other. These studies also illuminate the common interests of teachers, parents, and students in developing better communications between home and school. This chapter should give you a good understanding of the early, basic research on school, family, and community partnerships and the results of initial studies of teachers, parents, and students. The early studies and the comments, discussion topics, and activities in this chapter suggest many new questions that can be studied now with rigorous methods to advance the field.

REFERENCE

Epstein, et al. (2009). *School, family, and community partnerships: Your handbook for action* (3rd ed.). Thousand Oaks, CA: Corwin.

*Parent Involvement: A Survey of Teacher Practices**

Teachers approach their instructional tasks with a variety of perspectives and strategies that emphasize certain aspects of teaching and de-emphasize others. For example, some teachers teach language skills using organized games, whereas other teachers teach the same skills by direct instruction. Teachers adopt different approaches to the same subject matter partly because their teaching situations differ. Their students may have different learning problems, or their classrooms may have varied resources and facilities. Even in the same teaching situation, however, teachers may vary the instructional techniques they use depending on the particular skills and talents they have for using various materials and forms of instruction or the influences of their college training, supervisors, or colleagues. In a particular situation, for a certain type of student, which is the most effective teaching strategy? That is the most difficult question in the world of education and research.

One general approach that some teachers have found useful is to involve parents in learning activities with their children at home. This type of parent involvement is distinctly different from the parent involvement that brings parents into the classroom to assist the teacher or the parent involvement that includes parents as participants in decisions on school governance. Parent involvement in learning activities is a strategy for increasing the educational effectiveness of the time that parents and children spend with one another at home.

As with most educational strategies, there are different opinions about the likely effectiveness of teacher efforts to get parents to be more active in learning-related activities at home. Some educators believe that widespread parent interest in the academic progress of their children constitutes an immensely underutilized teaching resource, requiring only general guidance and modest effort to bring results in many cases. Pointing out the major competing time commitments of parents and teachers and the highly variable instructional skills of parents, others have suggested that all teaching of academic skills should be left to the teacher in the classroom. They suggest that little if any effort should be made by educators to influence parent-child academic-related interaction patterns at home.

There is very little information to support or refute either position. Research that systematically relates teachers' efforts to stimulate parent involvement in learning activities at home to the effects of this strategy on students and their families has not been conducted. Up to now, there has been very little research even to indicate how much teachers focus their activities in this direction. However, there are several studies showing that parents can influence student achievement and social development (Leichter, 1974; Lightfoot, 1978; Marjoribanks, 1979).

* By Henry Jay Becker and Joyce L. Epstein. We gratefully acknowledge the contributions of the teachers and administrators in Maryland for their time and interest in this study. The research was supported by the National Institute of Education, Grant NIE-G-80-0113. No official endorsement of the authors' opinions by the NIE should be inferred. Reprinted with permission from *Elementary School Journal* 83 (1982): 85–102.

To measure how elementary school teachers feel about parent involvement in home learning as a teaching strategy and to see how widespread this teaching strategy is, we conducted a formal survey of first-, third-, and fifth-grade school teachers in most of the public schools in the state of Maryland in spring 1980. This survey was the first phase of an ongoing study that will give teachers and administrators information about the effects of these parent involvement strategies on the educators who use them and on the parents and students who are affected by them.

SURVEY RESPONDENTS

The survey's results describe the teaching practices and professional attitudes of approximately 3,700 public elementary school teachers in more than 600 schools in 16 of the 24 school districts in Maryland. In the 15 districts that offered full cooperation with the project, the response rate was 73 percent of the teachers selected as participants in the study. In the remaining district, where access to teachers was limited, the response rate was only 35 percent. The study also includes information from more than 600 elementary school principals in the state who responded to a brief questionnaire on parent involvement programs in the school.

Table 3.1 describes the characteristics of the 3,698 teacher respondents. Approximately 28 percent of the survey respondents are first-grade teachers, 30 percent teach third grade, 29 percent teach fifth grade, and 13 percent are either reading or math specialists or others whom the principal designated as important contacts for a study of parent involvement (e.g., parent involvement coordinators).

Approximately 90 percent of elementary teachers are female; of the male teachers, about 70 percent teach the fifth grade. About 20 percent of the sample is black, and more than 60 percent of the black teachers are in a major central city district. The teachers range in age from their early twenties to their seventies, with most teachers (38 percent) in their thirties, born between 1940 and 1949. Approximately half of the teachers have taught for more than 10 years, and of the rest, most have taught at least 5 years. Nearly half have graduate school degrees. Although a majority of teachers teach a single class of children both reading and mathematics, team teaching and departmentalization of instruction are common. For example, among fifth-grade teachers, 75 percent report some form of nontraditional teaching arrangement.

The responding teachers are representative of their profession in the state, and they reflect the broad range of geographic and socioeconomic variation in their student populations. The state's large metropolitan population and several smaller urban and rural areas are represented in the statistics in Table 3.1, as is the range of parents that are college educated, high school educated, and less educated.

The questionnaire for teachers requested information on what teachers think about parent involvement strategies and how they practice them. The survey focused on 14 specific techniques that teachers may employ to encourage parents' participation in learning activities with their children.

TABLE 3.1   Characteristics of Teachers in Survey*

Teacher Characteristics	Respondents (%)
Grade level:	
Grade 1	28
Grade 3	30
Grade 5	29
Other reading, math, parent involvement specialists	13
Sex:	
Female	91
Male	9
Race:	
White	78
Black	21
Other	1
Education:	
Bachelor's	12
B.A. or B.A. plus credits	40
Master's	26
Master's and credits or doctorate	21
Experience:	
1–5 years teaching	17
6–10 years teaching	32
Over 10 years	51
Class assignments:	
Teach single class all day	55
Teach several classes during day	45
Location of school district:	
Rural/small town/small city	32
Suburban ring of metropolitan area	49
Central city of metropolitan area	19
Students' parents' education (teachers' estimates)	
Majority did not complete high school	25
Majority are high school but not college graduates	52
Majority are college graduates	23

* N = 3,698.

Overall, the survey results indicate a very positive view of parent-oriented teaching strategies and widespread, although not intensive, use of these 14 teaching techniques. The next sections describe teachers' attitudes about parent involvement, reported practices, and some of the differences in opinions and practices among teachers who responded to the survey.

TRADITIONAL TEACHER-PARENT COMMUNICATIONS

Some forms of communication and contact between parents and teachers are nearly universal. Virtually all teachers (over 95 percent of the respondents) report that they talk with children's parents, send notices home, and interact with parents on open-school nights. Approximately 90 percent of the teachers ask parents to check and sign students' homework. These standard parent-teacher communications have become accepted ways of bridging the information gap and the sense of distance felt by teachers and parents who may be strangers to one another but who share common interests in the same children. Based on their questionnaire responses and the comments initiated on the survey form, teachers clearly support the use of these standard patterns of interaction with parents.

However, the survey shows considerable variation in the ways that teachers conduct these standard interactions with parents and in the topics teachers emphasize in these discussions. For example, 65 percent of the teachers report that they discuss "with each parent" what they can do at home with their children; the other 35 percent discuss this topic "as the need arises," which may mean once, twice, or never. Similarly, most teachers discuss with all parents how they teach reading and math in their classrooms, but some do this only with a few parents. More significantly, many teachers who discuss their own teaching methods with parents do not talk about parents' responsibilities with homework, and many who discuss helping with homework do not discuss their own teaching methods.

Only a minority of teachers initiate interactions with parents that go beyond what is traditionally expected of them. Although nearly 80 percent of the teachers conduct more than three parent conferences in a school year, only 7 percent initiate three or more group meetings or workshops for parents apart from school-sponsored parents' nights. Generally, teachers who conduct workshops for parents are the ones who most actively emphasize the teaching role of parents at home.

Principals of the schools in which teachers were surveyed reported near-universal support of traditional parent-teacher communications. Approximately 95 percent of the principals report that they have a PTA or PTO, and about half report an active parents' advisory council associated with Title I or other programs. These standard organizations for parent participation usually have a core of active parents; approximately half of the principals report that more than 20 parents are actively involved in meetings and activities each month. Of course, even 20 parents active in developing schoolwide and school-community activities is only a small fraction of the parents who may become involved in activities that concern their own children.

Like the teachers, principals generally support the concept of parent involvement. Most of the principals have strong opinions in favor of parent volunteers in the classroom, and nearly three out of five report that they have held staff meetings or workshops during the school year that focused on methods for helping parents work with their children at home.

THE FEASIBILITY OF PARENT INVOLVEMENT

The teachers' responses to the questionnaire suggest that many teachers believe parent involvement at home could be an important contributor toward achieving the goals they have set for themselves and their students. At the same time, many teachers do not know how to initiate and accomplish the programs of parent involvement that would help them most. This dilemma is suggested by responses to six statements in the questionnaire about the value of parent involvement strategies. Figure 3.1 contains the wording of these items and graphs of the teachers' responses.

On two of the six items, there was a good deal of agreement. Most teachers feel that parent involvement is an important factor in solving the problems faced by schools and that parent involvement in the classroom is useful for increasing parent

Can Parent Involvement Work?   Maryland elementary school teachers . . .

In this country, parent involvement is not an answer to the major problems of the schools—the schools must solve their problems on their own.

Teachers can only provide parents with ideas about how to help with their children's schoolwork—teachers cannot influence parents to use these ideas.

Most parents—although they can teach their children to sew, use tools, or play a sport—do not have enough training to teach their children to read or to solve math problems.

Realistically, it is too much to ask parents to spend a full hour per day working with their children on basic skills or academic achievement.

If parents regularly spend time in the classroom, one result is that they usually make a greater effort to help their children at home.

Many parents want more information sent home about the curriculum than most teachers provide.

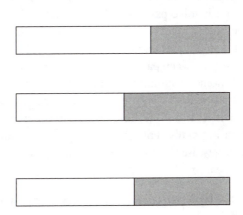

FIGURE 3.1   Opinions of Maryland Teachers about Parent Involvement

learning assistance at home. On the other four items, teacher opinion was divided concerning whether teachers can actually influence parents to help their children at home, whether most parents have sufficient skills to teach their children to read or solve math problems, whether it is fair to ask parents to spend an hour each evening working with their children on school-related activities, and whether parents want to know more about the school curriculum than they are usually told.

Although almost three-quarters of the teachers agreed that the general idea of parent involvement is a good one, approximately half of the teachers had serious doubts about the success of practical efforts to involve parents in learning activities at home. This should not come as a surprise. Teachers have not been educated in the management of parent involvement, the teachers' and parents' time is finite, teachers and the parents have different skills and often diverse goals for the children, and teachers and parents may have many children (and other family obligations) that require a share of their time and interest. Despite these real difficulties, some teachers have developed procedures that enable them to select and manage parent involvement programs.

FOURTEEN TECHNIQUES TO INVOLVE PARENTS

Teachers were asked several questions about each of 14 specific teaching techniques that involve parents in learning activities at home with their children. These techniques, as well as others added by the teachers, can be grouped into five categories: (1) techniques that involve reading and books; (2) techniques that encourage discussions between parent and child; (3) techniques that specify certain informal activities at home to stimulate learning; (4) contracts between teacher and parents that specify a particular role for parents in connection with their children's school lessons or activities; and (5) techniques that develop parents' tutoring, helping, teaching, or evaluation skills. The graphs in Figure 3.2 summarize how often the teachers in our survey use the 14 techniques, grouped according to these five categories.

Techniques Involving Reading and Books

One of the most frequently mentioned home-learning activities for parents to conduct with preschool and elementary school children is reading. It is not surprising that the teachers in our survey reported that parent-child reading is their most used parent involvement technique. Two-thirds of the teachers said they frequently ask parents to read to their children or listen to the children read, and more than one-fifth named this activity as the most valuable parent involvement technique in their own teaching practices. Parent involvement in reading activities is a more prevalent teaching practice among teachers of younger children. For example, only one-third of the fifth-grade teachers make active use of this technique in their practice, whereas seven out of eight first-grade teachers do so. The decline in use of this technique may be because teachers of older students see less need for assigning read-aloud

Evaluation
Categories:

☐ Unrealistic to expect parent cooperation
  □ Parents do not have sufficient skills
  ▨ Workable, but did not use this year
  ▦ Used a few times this year
  ▩ Used MANY TIMES this year
  ■ The MOST SATISFYING parent involvement techniques

"no support"

"passive support"

"active support"

ACTIVITIES EMPHASIZING READING

Ask parents to read to their child regularly or to listen to the child read aloud.

Loan books, workbooks, etc., to parents to keep at home for short periods as extra learning material.

Ask parents to take their child to the library.

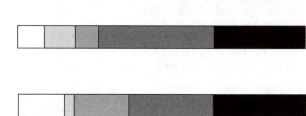

LEARNING THROUGH DISCUSSION

Ask parents to get their child to talk about what he or she did that day in your classroom.

Give an assignment that requires the children to ask their parents questions, for example, the children write their parents' experience.

Ask parents (one or more) to watch a specific television program with their child and to discuss the show afterwards.

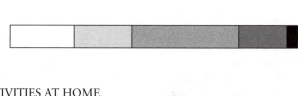

INFORMAL LEARNING ACTIVITIES AT HOME

Suggest ways for parents to incorporate their child into their own activities at home that would be educationally enriching.

Send home suggestions for game or group activities related to the child's schoolwork that can be played by parent and child.

Suggest how parents might use the home environment (materials and activities of daily life) to stimulate their child's interest in reading, math, etc.

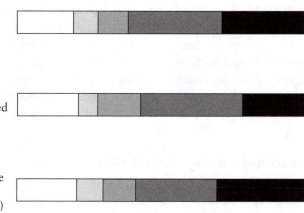

(continues)

FIGURE 3.2   Fourteen Techniques for Involving Parents in Teaching Activities at Home (Evaluations by Maryland Teachers)

FIGURE 3.2 *(continued)*

CONTRACTS BETWEEN TEACHER AND PARENT

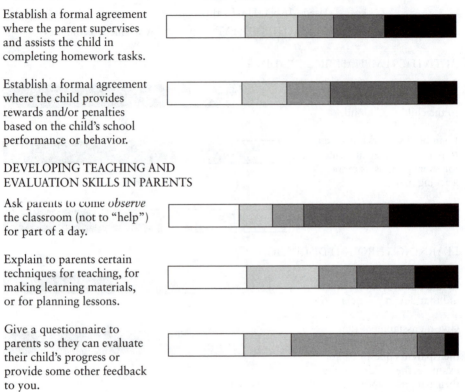

Establish a formal agreement where the parent supervises and assists the child in completing homework tasks.

Establish a formal agreement where the child provides rewards and/or penalties based on the child's school performance or behavior.

DEVELOPING TEACHING AND EVALUATION SKILLS IN PARENTS

Ask parents to come *observe* the classroom (not to "help") for part of a day.

Explain to parents certain techniques for teaching, for making learning materials, or for planning lessons.

Give a questionnaire to parents so they can evaluate their child's progress or provide some other feedback to you.

activities or because they believe parents are less able to organize instruction for fifth graders.

Teachers in the survey were asked about two other parent involvement techniques directly related to reading and written material: asking parents to take their child to the public library and loaning books and teaching materials to parents on a short-term basis. The majority of teachers believed these to be useful techniques.

As a group, the three techniques involving reading and books elicited more support from teachers than any of the other categories of parent involvement. Reading-related techniques have broad support across all teaching situations but are most often chosen as the most important method by first-grade teachers and by teachers with a large proportion of children who have difficulty learning.

Learning through Discussion

Schooling is more than learning the mechanics of reading. Many teachers place importance on the development of students' ability to express themselves orally. Even if families do not usually spend much time reading together, they can provide opportunities for students to learn from conversations and discussions.

The teachers in the survey were asked about three techniques that structure parent-child conversation in ways that might be educationally useful. One of these asks parents to view a particular television program with their child and to discuss the program afterward. When this technique is employed, it may be a mild suggestion to parents or it may include a set of discussion questions prepared by the teacher for the parents prior to the evening of a specific telecast. To use this technique intensively, the teacher would have to have advanced access to, or knowledge of, the content of the television program.

The systematic assignment of discussion about television programs was one of the least frequently used parent involvement techniques in the survey. Approximately one-third of the teachers said that parents would not cooperate with a request to participate or that they would be unable to handle such discussions in ways that would be educational. Only about 2 percent of the teachers reported that they used this technique frequently. However, there was more "passive" support for this technique than for any other on the survey. Most teachers said that this was a way of involving parents that could work in their teaching practices, even though they had not used it.

Two other methods of involving parents in discussions are (1) family exchanges about daily school activities and (2) homework assignments that require children to interview parents to obtain biographical or other information. Parent-child discussions about school were frequently mentioned by teachers as a technique they request or require of parents, but student interviews of parents were infrequently assigned. Most teachers felt that students could profit from assignments that required them to ask parents questions, but only 15 percent made active use of the method. As expected, the older the children the more likely they were to be assigned homework that involved asking parents questions. There is a large amount of "passive support" among teachers for this method of parent involvement in school activities. It may be that the procedures necessary to implement these techniques are not established well enough to permit wide adoption by teachers.

Informal Learning Activities at Home

The "parent as tutor" is one model of structuring parent-child teaching and learning activities at home. This model involves efforts to have parents read to the child, supervise and review the child's homework, or give practice tests or math drills using teacher-distributed flash cards. The parents' role is to supplement the formal school curriculum to ensure greater mastery of basic skills by their child.

The "parent as role model" is another way of structuring parent-child learning activities. This model is based on the idea that the parent is a natural teacher of varied skills and serves as a role model. The child may learn different skills at home from those taught in schools and may imitate the parents or adopt the parents' values about what kinds of skills are important, interesting, or fun. A number of those who propose more intensive parent involvement in learning activities at home suggest that parents can be most effective when they informally introduce their children to skills different from those emphasized at school (Rich, 1980). The question is whether and how teachers can motivate parents who would not normally do so to take time to provide informal learning opportunities at home.

The teachers in the survey were asked about three techniques that involve parents and their children in informal educational activities: suggesting educationally enriching ways for parents to involve their child in their own activities at home; sending home suggestions for game or group activities related to the child's schoolwork that can be played by parent and child; and suggesting how parents might use the home environment (common materials and activities of daily life) to stimulate their child's interest in reading, math, and other subjects.

Each of these three techniques, as shown in Figure 3.2, elicited a similar pattern of responses from the teachers. Approximately 30 percent of the teachers rejected these techniques either because of insufficient parent cooperation or because they felt the activities would be too difficult for parents to conduct. Another 40 percent supported the use of these methods in theory but only infrequently used the techniques in their teaching practice. Finally, about 30 percent of the teachers actively supported and used these methods in their teaching practice. Approximately 10 percent chose one of the three items in this category as the parent involvement method they found most useful and satisfactory.

Many of the parent involvement techniques presented to the teachers in our survey were employed as extensively by teachers just starting their careers as by teachers who had had many years of experience in the classroom. However, all three techniques in this category were used most extensively by experienced teachers. For example, only 16 percent of the teachers in their first or second year of teaching said they frequently sent home ideas for parent-child learning games and activities, whereas 25 percent of the teachers with more than 10 years of classroom experience said they did so. Eighteen percent of new teachers often suggested ways for parents to involve their child in their own activities, but 30 percent of the experienced teachers did so. It is interesting that many of the new teachers who used these activities reported that these were their most satisfying parent involvement techniques. These techniques tended to be preferred by reading and math specialists, teachers of low-achieving students, teachers of students from highly educated families, and teachers in rural or small-town areas.

Contracts between Teachers and Parents

The techniques presented to the teachers in the survey included two that involve the use of "contracts." This term implies a formal agreement to conduct and complete an activity or set of activities. The two techniques are distinguished by the kinds of behavior requested of the parents. In one case, the parent is asked to provide or withhold privileges or punishments to the child for school performance and behavior patterns, based on rules determined jointly by the parent, teacher, and student. The parent does not engage in any direct instructional activity in this type of contract, but assists the teacher in shaping productive school behavior.

The second "contract" technique requires parents to supervise or assist with the student's homework or other projects. This may or may not involve some instruction or clarification by the parents but always involves the structuring of the home environment to support the student's school responsibilities. This kind of activity is often informally organized by teachers and parents, but we were interested in those instances where a formal contract for parental responsibilities was arranged by the teacher, parent, and child.

Teachers expressed less consensus about the value of both types of parent-teacher contracts than about most of the other parent involvement techniques. Approximately 40 percent of the teachers felt that these techniques were not worth pursuing because they would not increase learning or because of insufficient parental cooperation or skills. On the other hand, 20 percent of the teachers felt that contracts for parental supervision of homework and projects were valuable enough to use "many times" during the year or were the most important parent involvement technique in their practices. Fewer teachers gave active support to formal contracts involving parental rewards for school behavior, but many of those who used the technique believed it was the most useful one they employed.

There were some important differences in the use of contracts by teachers at different grade levels. In contrast to many other parent involvement techniques supported mainly by teachers in the lower grades, contracts were used equally across the grades. They were preferred as the most satisfying techniques by twice as many fifth-grade teachers as first-grade teachers. Teachers used contracts with parents of students at all achievement levels but were more apt to use them with students of more educated parents. Teachers in suburban districts used contracts more frequently, and younger teachers were more likely than older teachers to classify contracts as their most satisfying parent involvement technique.

Helping Parents to Teach

The list of 14 parent involvement techniques contained three activities for teachers to use to equip parents with observational and instructional skills: (1) instruction for parents in teaching and in making learning materials that could be used at home to supplement the teacher's work at school, (2) classroom observations to see how teaching proceeds in school and how the children respond to particular lessons and methods of teaching, and (3) parent responses to teachers' questionnaires to evaluate their own child's progress or problems in school. The latter activity may assist the teacher more directly than it assists the parent. However, evaluation forms are often useful sensitizers, and thus may help parents to conduct activities at home with the child. Of these three activities, more teachers use classroom observation by parents than the other choices; very few of the teachers reported frequent use of evaluation forms from parents. Classroom observations and teaching parents about teaching and evaluation were encouraged by teachers of young children. Urban teachers and experienced teachers used these techniques more than teachers in suburban and rural areas and new teachers.

TABLE 3.2   Correspondence of Principals' Active Encouragement and Teachers' Active Use of Selected Techniques of Parent Involvement

Techniques	Principals Who Encourage (%)	Teachers Who Use Actively (%)
Read aloud or listen to reading	76	66
Informal games at home	45	24
Contract with parents on students' projects	33	25
Loan books to parents	31	41
Teach parents techniques for tutoring and evaluation	24	21
Parent contracts to reward or punish behavior	12	13
Parent-led discussion of TV shows	12	2

Techniques Encouraged by Principals

The reports from principals show the same selective emphasis on reading as the reports from teachers. As Table 3.2 indicates, 76 percent of the principals say they have personally encouraged many teachers to adopt the technique of asking parents to read to their children or listen to their children read. The principals placed least emphasis on the same two techniques that were given least emphasis by the teachers: parent-led discussion of television programs and contracts with parents to systematically reward or punish student behaviors.

Although teachers and principals, as groups, seem to make similar judgments about the usefulness of different parent involvement techniques, direct influence from the principal on the teacher's practice is difficult to measure with the data available. Only one teacher in six indicates that the source of his or her most valuable parent involvement technique is a "principal or other administrator." Teachers who actively use a particular parent technique are only slightly more likely than other teachers to have a principal who encourages teachers to adopt that same technique.

HOW MUCH EMPHASIS ON THE 14 TECHNIQUES?

Most teachers understand that parent involvement is a complex process and make only tentative requests for such involvement. Regardless of which technique they use, only 9 percent of the teachers "require" parental cooperation; the rest "suggest" the technique. This means that teachers' control over the technique and the response from parents are limited. Indeed, approximately 40 percent of the teachers report that none, fewer than half, or an unknown proportion of the parents carried out their requests to conduct certain activities. These conditions may explain why nearly 60 percent of the teachers say they can provide ideas for learning activities at home but they cannot influence the parents to use them.

Teachers estimated how many parents would attend meetings or workshops on learning activities at home. As the table on the next page shows, only one-third of the teachers believe they could attract a good number of parents to the meetings, and then only if they were conducted in the evening. Thus, it would require extra or voluntary effort by teachers for even a small percentage of parents to become teaching partners through workshops conducted at school.

Estimated Attendance of Parents	Few or None (% of Teachers)	Many or Most (% of Teachers)
At morning meeting	87	13
At evening meeting	66	34

Teachers report having the most contact with parents of children with learning and discipline problems and with parents who are already active in the school. For example, one-third as many contacts with parents are reported for "average" students as for students with problems. Most teachers report that they ask only some parents (not parents of all students in the class) to conduct particular learning activities at home.

Actions that are requested rather than required and carried out with little or unknown frequency, meetings attended by small groups of parents rather than all parents, and selected use of parent involvement techniques with only certain parents are all indications that, for the average teacher, parent involvement at home is not indispensable to satisfactory teaching.

DIFFERENCES IN TEACHERS' USES OF PARENT INVOLVEMENT

In this section, teachers' opinions and practices are reported for different grade levels and for various educational levels of students' parents. Results are then summarized for the pattern of home visits, the use of parent involvement with different school subjects, and the relationship between parent involvement at home and parent assistance in the classroom. Finally, we discuss the use of techniques by teachers in schools where all teachers practice parent involvement and where few teachers do so.

Grade Level of Students

Most researchers who have studied parent involvement in learning activities, as well as those who have developed programs for parent involvement, have viewed the parents of preschoolers and early elementary-aged children as their primary targets. In the 1960s and 1970s, various Head Start and Follow-Through programs systematically incorporated specific functions for parents as part of their organizational arrangements. Many of these programs were found to increase student learning of school-readiness skills more than programs used as alternate "control" treatments. Much of the emphasis on early childhood has been due to a belief that parents of young children are more willing and more able to perform useful functions in an educational program than are parents of older children. It may be, however, that procedures and tasks for useful parent participation for older children simply have not been worked out.

Figure 3.3 shows that most of the 14 parent involvement techniques in our survey were more likely to be used by teachers of younger students. However, in only a few cases were the differences of large magnitude. Parent and child reading activities had the most pronounced decline with increasing grade level. The three "informal" learning activities included in the list also declined with increasing grade level, as did efforts to teach parents techniques for teaching their children. On the other hand, the techniques of contracts and assignments that required children to ask their parents questions and the limited use of television-based family discussions and parent-evaluation forms were as often used with older children as with younger. Some teachers at all grade levels used each of the techniques in the survey.

Educational Level of Parents

Many of the written comments of teachers reinforced common stereotypes of parents: "pushy" upper-middle-class parents, "helpful" middle-class parents, and "incapable" lower-class parents. However, the statistics on the techniques teachers use successfully with different groups of parents tell a different story. Teachers who deal with college-educated parents, those who work with parents with average schooling, and those whose students' parents have very little schooling are about equally likely to be active users of parent involvement strategies. However, teachers who do not actively use parent involvement techniques respond differently to questions about the likely success of these techniques according to the educational levels of their students' parents. Teachers who are not active users and who teach children with highly educated parents report that the parent involvement techniques would work but that they do not choose to use them. Teachers who are not active users and who teach children with less-educated parents are more apt to report that the parents would not be able or willing to carry out activities related to the child's schoolwork at home.

Figure 3.4 illustrates the differences in the pattern of use of several of the techniques with parents of different educational levels. For each technique, bar graphs are shown for three groups of teachers—those whose students' parents were mainly college graduates, those whose students' parents were mainly high school graduates, and those whose students' parents nearly all lacked a high school diploma. Each bar graph shows the proportion of teachers who make active use of the technique, the proportion who believe it could work but are not frequent users, and the proportion who do not feel that their students' parents could or would participate effectively.

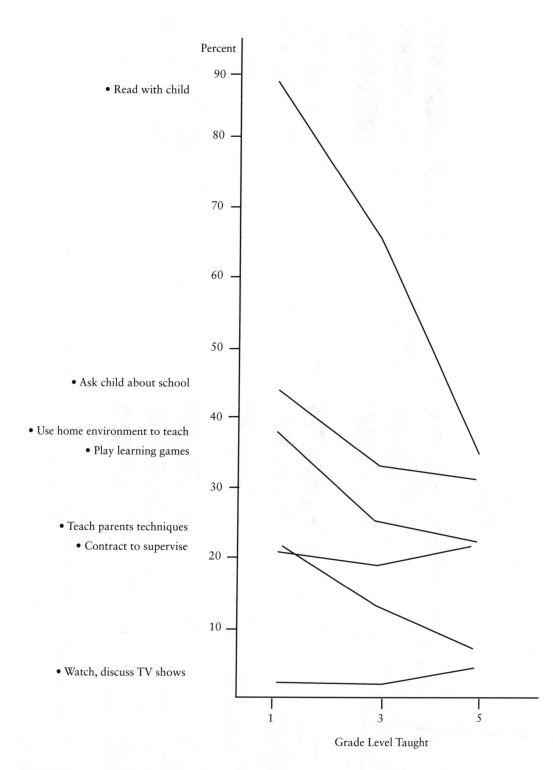

FIGURE 3.3   Active Use of Parent Involvement Techniques by Grade Level

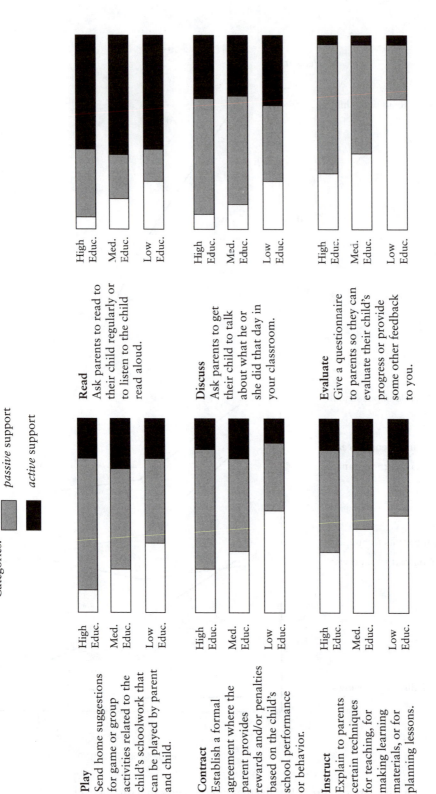

Play
Send home suggestions for game or group activities related to the child's schoolwork that can be played by parent and child.

Contract
Establish a formal agreement where the parent provides rewards and/or penalties based on the child's school performance or behavior.

Instruct
Explain to parents certain techniques for teaching, for making learning materials, or for planning lessons.

Read
Ask parents to read to their child regularly or to listen to the child read aloud.

Discuss
Ask parents to get their child to talk about what he or she did that day in your classroom.

Evaluate
Give a questionnaire to parents so they can evaluate their child's progress or provide some other feedback to you.

Evaluation
Categories:

☐ *no* support

▨ *passive* support

■ *active* support

FIGURE 3.4   Levels of Support for Some Techniques by Estimated Formal Education of Parents

To summarize Figure 3.4, let us consider two examples. The upper-right panel of the figure shows that techniques that involve parent and child reading activities are used by a majority of teachers with students whose parents are from all educational backgrounds. The solid black segments indicate that approximately 60 percent of the teachers made active use of this technique at every parent-education level. Of the remaining teachers, those whose students' parents had little education were more apt to attribute their lack of use to the absence of parental cooperation or skills, whereas teachers of students whose parents had more education claimed the technique could work but that it was not currently part of their teaching practice. Thus, whether parents with little schooling are viewed by the teacher as "capable" of assisting their children in reading at home may depend on whether the teacher has worked out procedures and communication patterns that would enable parents with little schooling to assist.

The middle-right panel of the figure shows that approximately 30 percent of the teachers surveyed make active use of techniques that involve parent-child discussions at home with parents at all educational levels, with slightly more teachers actively using the technique with low-educated parents. Teachers who were not active users offered contradictory explanations for lack of use in relation to their students' family social class. Those who reported that their students' parents had little schooling said that using discussions could not work, whereas those whose students had better-educated parents said the techniques could work but that they were not being used.

The pattern for all of the techniques in Figure 3.4 (and the others not listed there) is fairly uniform. It seems clear that some teachers of students from families with less formal education have developed techniques that enable these parents to participate in the schooling of their children and to successfully cooperate with the school. How do they do this? Are the teachers' techniques generalizable so that other teachers with similar populations can use them? Do the efforts of the teachers and the parents benefit the students, the teachers, or the parents?

Home Visits

Most contacts between teachers and parents are in the form of notes and memos transmitted by the child. Yet personal contacts between parent and teacher may be vitally important to develop the commitment of parents to participation in a program of learning reinforcement at home. Teachers make personal contact most often by brief conversations before and after school, by parent conferences on "parent night" or by special appointment, and by telephone conversations with parents.

One infrequently used method for developing personal relationships is home visits by the teacher. Fewer than one-quarter of the teachers in the survey indicated that they had made any home visits during the school year, and only 2 percent said they had visited more than a handful of children's homes. The teachers who visited children's homes were more likely to be favorable toward parent involvement techniques. In particular, they were most likely to be active users of techniques that emphasized oral exchanges between parent and child: having parents discuss TV programs, having parents ask children about school, and having children interview parents. Also, teachers who visited several homes made more use of parent evaluations and parent classroom-observation methods than did other teachers.

School Subjects for Parent Involvement at Home

Teachers reported the academic subjects in which they used their favorite parent involvement techniques. Their responses indicate the popularity of reading as an activity parents can conduct successfully. Over 80 percent of the teachers listed one or more reading-related subjects as the focus of their most successful technique for parent involvement. In contrast, only 20 percent of the teachers emphasized parent involvement in science activities, and approximately one-half used their favorite techniques in math-related home-learning activities. Especially in the early elementary grades, teachers ask parents to supplement the teachers' emphasis on basic skills rather than enrich or extend students' experiences with other subjects such as arts, sciences, or home and hobby skills.

Parents in School

Some teachers report having many parents who are active at school and willing volunteers in their classrooms. Others report almost no parent activity in the school building and no use of classroom volunteers. Approximately half the teachers have at least some parental assistance in the classroom, ranging from a few days per month to every day. Most parents who assist are selectively recruited, although some teachers send out general requests for parental help.

Most teachers (84 percent) agree that if parents spend time at school, "they usually make a greater effort to help their children learn at home." Observing a teacher's techniques for presenting material, handling questions, and analyzing mistakes may help parents to be more effective in conducting school-related learning activities at home. This helps to explain why teachers invite parents to observe their classes. If watching the class can aid the parent at home, it is a rather effortless way for teachers to help parents to assist in learning activities at home.

Not surprisingly, teachers who report more parent involvement in the school also are more favorable to using techniques that involve parents in learning activities at home. Support for each one of the 14 parent involvement techniques was positively correlated with the proportion of parents who were active at school and the frequency with which the teacher made use of parent volunteers in the classroom. Teachers who reported the most active parents in the school and in the classroom were especially supportive of the techniques that use informal activities at home and that teach parents tutoring and evaluation skills. For example, of the teachers who often suggested how parents might use materials and activities at home to stimulate their child's interest in school subjects, about 60 percent had parent help in the classroom, mostly on a weekly basis. Of those who "passively" supported this technique, fewer than 50 percent had parent classroom volunteers. Only 30 percent of the teachers who were pessimistic about this kind of at-home parent activity had parents' help during the school day.

School Support for Parent Involvement

Do teachers develop attitudes about parent involvement and related teaching practices as a consequence of their observations of, and conversations with, other teachers at the same school? This question is of interest because it is useful to know whether a "group effort" across an entire school is necessary for successful parent involvement programs or whether individual teachers develop personal programs regardless of the activities of other teachers in their schools.

For all types of parent involvement techniques except the activities involving reading and books, there was a small but positive association between an individual teacher's support for a technique and a measure of overall parent involvement orientation for all teachers in the school. It appears that some teachers are encouraged to use some techniques when their school climate supports parent involvement, but there are many examples of individual successes without support from other teachers in the school.

CONTINUING STUDIES OF PARENT INVOLVEMENT

We have documented teachers' reports of different practices in parent involvement across the state of Maryland. We discuss the teachers' comments on major issues of parent involvement in Reading 3.2. In other research we are collecting more detailed information from a small sample of teachers and principals who participated in the survey. We need to know why teachers use particular techniques, how they implement them, and why they reject other techniques. We are surveying parents and students to obtain reports of teachers', parents', and students' experiences with parent involvement and the effects of family involvement on student achievement and attitudes. (See Readings 3.3 through 3.9 and Reading 4.3.) This information will enable more teachers to make reasoned choices and decisions about implementation, adoption, or adaptations of parent involvement techniques for particular settings and students.

What do the differences in teachers' practices mean in terms of student learning, the quality of education for students, and the quality of the school environment for teachers and for parents? It may be that parent involvement helps to improve student learning or improves the process by which teachers and parents provide education. It may also be that other teaching strategies are equally or more effective and efficient. Although proponents and opponents of parent involvement in learning activities have their opinions about the answers to these questions, the facts are not yet known.

REFERENCES

Leichter, H. J. (1974). *The family as educator.* New York: Teachers College Press.

Lightfoot, S. L. (1978). *Worlds apart: Relationships between families and schools.* New York: Basic Books.

Marjoribanks, K. (1979). *Families and their learning environments: An empirical analysis.* London: Routledge & Kegan Paul.

Rich, D. (1980). *Families learning together.* Washington, DC: Home and School Institute.

Teachers' Reported Practices of Parent Involvement: Problems and Possibilities*

DEBATABLE ISSUES OF PARENT INVOLVEMENT

Several major issues related to parent involvement were discussed in the comments added by over 1,000 teachers to a survey of teachers' practices. Results of the survey of 3,700 teachers in approximately 600 schools in Maryland are described in Reading 3.1. The teachers' comments reflect the variation in years of experience and in the number and types of contacts individual teachers have had with parents. Each theme can be viewed from two perspectives: There are potential advantages, but there are also potential problems, with any parent involvement technique. Teachers' comments reveal their contrasting opinions on the benefits expected from parent assistance at home and on the organizational structures used to conduct parent involvement activities. Some teachers are very positive about parent involvement; others have been discouraged by their attempts to communicate and work with parents.

Teachers' Time

Many teachers commented on the amount of time needed to prepare projects, workshops, and/or directions for parents to use and supervise at home. The crucial questions are whether the time required by the teacher is worth the trouble and whether teachers should volunteer their time without knowing the likely effects of their efforts.

Some teachers telephone parents frequently to give positive messages about a child's progress in school or special skills or abilities observed as well as to discuss problems. If a teacher telephones 30 parents and talks for 10 minutes to each, the teacher spends 5 hours voluntarily on the telephone with parents. The teacher may do this in addition to preparing lessons, grading papers, preparing report cards, working with parents, and preparing parent involvement activities. How much time can teachers give to parent-related activities? How often? With what effect? These are not trivial questions.

Several teachers offered positive statements that indicated that the job of teaching cannot be accomplished without programs that involve parents. For example:

* By Joyce L. Epstein and Henry Jay Becker. We gratefully acknowledge the efforts of the teachers who contributed comments to the survey. Research was conducted at the Johns Hopkins R and D Center for Social Organization of Schools and was supported by the National Institute of Education, Grant NIE-G-80-0113. No official endorsement of the authors' opinions by the NIE should be inferred. Reprinted with permission from *Elementary School Journal* 83 (1982): 103–113.

I really rely on parent help. Long ago I realized that only with parent help can my job be performed adequately.

Other comments indicated that the time needed to develop learning activities for parents to use at home or in schools is just not available to teachers or not worth the trouble:

You completely omitted from your questionnaire any items regarding the additional time and effort required of the busy teacher in parent involvement activities.

I believe both parents and students can benefit from parent involvement. However, I also know that it takes a great deal of training and explaining and coordinating to have a good program. I've spent many hours doing just this. Frankly, I no longer feel like giving the many hours of extra time required to do this. We are not provided with time to do this type of training. It's all our own time. I no longer feel like giving my time without compensation.

Parents' Time

The teachers acknowledged that parents' time at home is limited by the responsibilities of children, spouse, and/or other family members; cooking and chores; and a general need for relaxation. Many teachers wondered whether parents should be asked to spend at least a short time with each child on academic activities, whether parents' time at home (and how much time) should be spent developing their children's nonacademic skills and responsibilities, or whether teachers have any justification in requesting or requiring parent assistance in academic or social development.

Some teachers suggested that short periods of time spent on learning activities at home can be beneficial to the students if the time is well planned:

Parents have so little "prime" time to spend with their child or children. It is essential that we give these people some very practical and meaningful tips on how to spend quality time with their children.

In my memo to parents I ask them to spend just 10 minutes a night going over the child's word cards. This way neither the child nor the parent feels over worked.

I have also experienced that parents are more than willing to help children in assignments that are short, reinforcement-type work, on which the child (and therefore the parent) can be successful. Parents love to hear their children read.

Others stressed that the "learning activities at home" should not be on school lessons but on general socialization and development:

I find it far more profitable for the child to get "home training" at home, since today's children do not seem to display the sense of responsibility needed to do their best. . . .

Self-reliance, responsibility, and a good self-concept learned at home contribute to improved academics at school. Then there would be less need for parental involvement in teaching the academics.

I feel it is my job to teach and that parents may become impatient and frustrated when working on skills at home. Some reinforcement at home is quite helpful as long as it is kept to a minimum amount of time and done consistently. An hour a day is unrealistic, and unfair to parent and child. I feel that children spend a large part of their day in school (hopefully learning) and at home need to be released for relaxation, play, and pursuing interests (hopefully, not all television). Parenting is in itself a demanding job.

Students' Time and Feelings

Many teachers focused their comments on the benefits or problems for the students of parent involvement in learning activities at home. Some believed academic activities should be kept to a minimum so children could follow interests in their out-of-school time. Many stressed with deep conviction that students' time at home should be mainly the time to play, participate in activities of special interest, or relax. Others expressed concern that academic tasks at home can cause parents and children psychological stress as the pressure to perform vies with the child's need for help and the parents' desire to help. Others believe the child's time at home should reflect parents' teaching of home-related skills and responsibilities.

Several teachers expressed concern that the complex relationships between parents and children can be affected by the kinds of activities assigned for work at home by teachers:

Most parents are very willing to assist at home and welcome ideas, but I stress working for short periods of time and only when both parties are not becoming upset. Some parents tell me they want to help, but they lose their patience. On the other hand, children often feel embarrassed when they don't think they are performing as well as they want to for their parents.

Care must be taken in "home help" situations so that pressure on the child is not increased by emotional or unenlightened parental involvement when the goal is to help the child and thereby lighten pressure placed upon him.

Teachers had varied opinions on whether they should try to maximize the potential advantages of parent assistance for some children, even if other children may not be assisted. Some teachers believe parent activities are valuable even if only some parents complete them; other teachers believe no parent-conducted learning activities should be assigned unless all parents agree to cooperate. They charge that children of parents who do not do their part are put at a disadvantage through no fault of the students. Compare the two points of view:

Although many of my students come from homes where support of schools is great, there are also a good number of students who come from homes where support is minimal and parent involvement is very low. This makes it difficult to give the class an assignment involving parents when only some of the students have parents who would bother to help.

Most parents talk a good story, but rarely follow through on any involvement. Then there are some who, given prodding, guidance, and a great deal of specific directions on what to do, will try consistently to help their child. It pays off, even if the results are minimal. It is for these few that it is worth doing what we can to get them involved—because it's ultimately for the children.

The teachers', parents', and students' time, commitment, and reactions were repeatedly discussed by the teachers. There were legitimate differences of opinion. Should some of the parents' and students' time at home be spent on lessons and school assignments, or should the time be spent on new experiences and diverse skills that build on parents' special abilities? The answers to such questions may depend on such factors as children's ages, the types of learning problems that might be involved, the parents' education, the subject matter being studied, and the existing relationship between the parents and the child.

Expected Benefits

There are few rewards, other than internal ones, to encourage a teacher to spend time working toward the potential benefits of parent involvement. Some teachers lamented the lack of support from their principals or other teachers. Others recounted the psychological obstacles that prevent teachers from trying some activities or from trying more than once. In spite of some real problems, many teachers described benefits they perceived or expected for their students and for the parents from parent involvement: better basic skills, and greater retention of skills over the summer because of work conducted at home during the vacation; better behavior of students in class; greater number and variety of classroom materials developed by parents at home; enrichment in areas the teacher could not direct; and improved parental self-image because of successful cooperation with the school. The following comments reflect many of the teachers' remarks about the benefits of parent involvement:

Although my teaching career is near a close, I believe parent involvement is one of the keys to improving education, and it should be encouraged. It will not only promote better pupil performance, but it will improve the self-image of each parent, especially in a school community (Title I) such as ours.

I welcome the parents' help and their expertise that increase my children's understanding in special enrichment areas in which I may not be well-versed. For the most part, any assignment I send home is pursued and completed with parents' help.

I feel a good parent education group or program is needed to help parents enjoy and understand their children's need to try, fail, and try again on their own. Parents can guide and show their love by being there (and giving assistance) when their children need them, but not by doing the work for their children.

Subgroup Differences

Some teachers specified that benefits from parent involvement should be expected only for some children. They described some groups of parents they believed were less able to conduct learning activities successfully at home. However, other teachers pointedly commented that these same groups were successfully involved in parent involvement activities. The important question is whether benefits from parent involvement can be expected from parents of older students, parents with little education, working parents, and single parents.

For example, some teachers believed the benefits will depend on the family structure and the other activities of the parents. The following comments illustrate the debatable issue of involvement of working mothers:

I feel my experience as a working mother and as a single parent has helped tremendously in gearing my relationships and assignments involving parents.

More and more of my "parents" are single parents and sole support. Their time and energy are limited. They do want to cooperate for the most part but are too tired and overworked. I don't even help my own children very much because I am too tired when I get home.

Mother's employment—this factor has nothing to do with parental involvement. You did not ask if parents were alcoholic, drug addicts, child abusers, etc.—You did not ask if parents I work with (and for) are interested in school, impressed with my credentials, comfortable with the administrators and me. These are important facts— mother's employment activities are not.

Working parents have more demands on their time. Helping kids at home becomes a more frustrating task when a parent is tired or has many jobs to do. Other parents get carried away and ask the kids to do too much at home.

Several teachers commented on differences between parents with more or less formal education:

I don't feel the educational level of the parents plays too great a part because in my experience I've had tremendous parent involvement with those whose educational level did not go beyond the eighth grade.

Parent involvement became extremely poor as the years progressed. When the emphasis of education went back to basics, the parents withdrew. This could be attributed to their own poor educational backgrounds and preparedness to help their children.

In general, teachers did not specify the benefits of parent involvement. Most teachers said, "It depends on the students and their parents," as this teacher commented:

I have had excellent cooperation from parents this year. In many instances it has been up to 95 percent. Other years have not produced the same results. Last year, I had the cooperation of approximately 10 out of 32 parents—and it was the same school. It depends on the group of children—if I had completed this questionnaire last year my responses would have been totally different.

Many teachers thought that the school climate and the principal's support were important, as this teacher noted:

Most of my teaching career, my principals have been very much against the teacher working with parents other than when discipline was involved, and have been unwilling for the teacher to have contact with parents outside of regular classroom hours. My breakthrough in working with parents has been due to working with an outstanding teacher who is excellent in home and school relations.

Use of Parent Involvement Coordinators

Many comments were offered by teachers on the Title I programs. These programs often include parent coordinators, whose job it is to get more parents involved in more aspects of school life. The Title I programs are the largest federally funded programs for parent involvement. Several teachers remarked on the benefits from excellent Title I parent programs, but just as many said the programs were poor and wasteful. The contrasting opinions suggest that some organizational strategies are necessary if the programs are to succeed from the teachers' point of view.

I teach in a Title I school where we have an organized Parent Involvement Program headed by two Parent Involvement Aides. They lead many programs and activities once conducted by the teacher, such as home visits, telephone calls, trips with children to dentist or doctor, assistance with clothing needs, recruitment of parent volunteers to operate the Reading Club, and organization of workshops for parents to learn games that can be used at home. So many of these opportunities are out of the hands of the classroom teacher. Twenty-five or 30 years ago when I taught in a rural Appalachian consolidated school, I had much more parent involvement than I do now. From my teaching point of view, I definitely had more support from parents on things I attempted to do. Although our Title I aides have very good rapport with our parents, there seems to be more of a trend to let the aides do things for the parents and less emphasis on helping parents to help themselves. We do have "star" examples of parent volunteers of more than 10 years who now are "super" paid Title I aides. That is progress, as they help not only their own families but others.

Under the Title I program, we have a home visitation aide who takes learning games into homes of our Title I students. Parents are to play these with the students. Of my eight Title I students, only two parents agreed to accept the games and neither of the two children involved ever played any of the games. I consider this a total waste of our federal money.

Many Title I programs mandate parental involvement. I've been active in helping develop and conduct parent-involvement workshops. I often have classroom workshops to bring parents up-to-date on curriculum and let them know that they are their child's primary and most important teachers.

I have found that since the school I have worked in became Title I there is less parent involvement. The conclusion that I have come to is that since there are paid assistants, parents feel that their services are not needed.

Parent volunteers require constant professional supervision and coordination. This is not done by a Title I Parent Coordinator with a high school education. Our Title I parent coordinator has been my greatest influence in working with parents.

The reactions partly reflect the teachers' personal attitudes and partly the fact that some Title I programs are better organized, are staffed by more qualified coordinators, and communicate better with teachers. How do the successful Title I programs operate to strengthen family and school ties? What strategies from successful Title I programs can be incorporated into any school to improve home-school alliances? The teachers' opinions on Title I programs raise important questions for further study.

Problems with Parental Assistance

Many teachers who have had experience working with parents have important concerns about the likely success of parent involvement practices. Some teachers described problems often associated with volunteers: undependability, shortened schedules, low commitment, and different goals and values of volunteers and the schools. Others were concerned about the parents' lack of training in methods and approaches for teaching children who have learning problems. These concerns are related to the teachers' lack of time to provide parents with adequate training in how to teach or how to deal with learning problems. These are especially important concerns for parent volunteers in the classroom, but parents at home are also "volunteers." They are not accountable to the teacher. Some teachers commented on how parents fail to follow through in learning activities at home.

Other teachers were concerned that students might not develop responsibility if parents assume too much of the responsibility for students' assignments:

[T]he more opportunities we give our parents to be in the school and the more information given out by teachers, the more parents tend to take any work that is given to the child as their work rather than developing responsibility in their children.

Other teachers expressed concern that parents have many problems other than academic ones that interfere with teachers' requests for assistance with learning activities at home:

Some parents do not know how to, or will not, control their children. They expect teachers to work miracles and get their children to learn and to behave when the parents cannot make their own children behave. When contacting parents, especially for behavior problems, I hear more and more frequently, "I don't know what to do with them." No teacher can teach if time must be spent on simple discipline and manners that should be learned at home. I believe that it would help many parents to see their children work with others in the classroom.

I have found as a teacher in this transient community that the parents are too busy to bother about how their children are doing. If everything is going smoothly, the parents stay at home. Only if trouble arises does one hear from a parent. Even if you are doing a fantastic, outstanding job you do not hear from parents. Only in time of trouble.

Parent involvement *is* the problem. I have accomplished the impossible when I manage to just get some parents into the school for a conference.

The effectiveness of using these techniques depends on the community(ies) the school is serving. I have taught in a school where the parents were so involved that one did not need to use techniques. I have taught in a school where very few parents were capable of using any technique no matter how simple. I have also had a parent who could have helped her son tell me that that is my job.

Some admitted that teachers fear parents, and this fear inhibits the kinds of programs that teachers attempt:

Most teachers fear parents and I, too, only use parents when I feel I have complete control.

My experience indicates that teachers are even more fearful than the parents of our interaction.

Successful Efforts

Despite the possible problems, some teachers with parents of all educational levels and students at all achievement levels have been able to establish programs that emphasize the link between school and home.

Reading with Children. Many teachers described how they organize a formal program in which parents or students read on a regular basis. For example:

About 4 years ago in a school with a large minority population, most parents were contacted and agreed to see to it that their children read—either to the parent or by themselves for 10 minutes every evening. Many parents cooperated and I believe it helped the children's reading skills. Of course, the children could read longer than 10 minutes if they wished. They brought in slips signed by their parents each morning and were rewarded occasionally by small items donated by local businesses. Very few parents objected.

Signing Papers and Folders. Many teachers have devised different systems to keep parents aware of the children's schoolwork. When teachers ask parents to sign daily work or weekly folders, they are fulfilling an obligation to keep parents informed of children's progress before or between report cards. Some teachers also send home skill-building assignments or games based on the students' problems identified in schoolwork or on tests:

By having parents sign children's graded math tests and units, I cover several problem spots. Parents always have a good idea of grade average; parents can see the child's progress or lack of it; signing math units enables parents to see all of their children's daily assignments before they are disposed of without the hassle of seeing them every night. Units get signed when the test is taken. If a child receives a poor grade, I attach a sheet telling the parents to review and study the needed skills with their child. The signing insures that the parents see the note.

I send a letter to parents each time we start a new phase of work, explaining what we will be doing and how they can help. This is signed and returned. I also send all returnable work home on blue or green paper or attached to a blue or green computer card. Parents and kids know blue papers are to be returned. I have about 95 percent respond.

Some use a system that permits the parents to communicate with the teacher with more than a signature:

A buddy-book: Each day I write a comment concerning the child's work and general behavior in a book devoted just to homework and teacher-parent comments. The parent signs and responds.

Others have devised phone conference systems to talk with working parents, evening and Saturday conferences and workshops, and other means for two-way communication with parents.

Preparation of Materials. Teachers described two ways in which parent-made materials are used for learning activities. Materials made in school are used at home:

I give parents materials to make flashcards just like mine in math or reading for use at home. Also, parents have watched "mini" lessons on skills that they could teach at home.

I like the mini-clinic: Parents of four Kindergarten and seven first-grade children were encouraged to participate. Parents alternated monthly for individual or small group meetings to discuss activities and games they could use to reinforce skills being taught by the teacher. We sent home materials to be used for a month and returned at the next meeting. Children having the most difficulty learning were selected. Of the 11 parents invited, nine participated. One grandmother and two fathers also attended. Personal contact has made a difference. The success of our parent-involvement programs appears to be closely related to teacher commitment.

Materials made at home are also used at school:

In my "read along with the family" program I send home books and a tape recorder for grandparents or parents to tape the child's favorite story or book. They can listen to it in class. I prepare an activity sheet to go with the tape.

Home Visits. Some teachers use home visits to lay the groundwork for communication with parents that will occur throughout the year. Home visits are arranged voluntarily on weekends or before the beginning of the school year by the teacher and parents or are formally organized by the school administration. Some schools give teachers release time while substitute teachers cover their classes; other schools establish half-days for children so that the teachers' visits occur on the afternoons when no school is scheduled; other schools allocate two full days for teachers' visits when there is no school scheduled.

Our most effective technique is used in the first week of school when the first-grade children attend half days only. We make a 20-minute visit to each home, explain the program and needed supplies, hear concerns, etc. I feel I gain 6 weeks of knowledge about the child during that visit. Also, I feel good in being able to greet each parent by name (usually!) the next time we meet.

I visited each child's home before school opened in the fall. I took each child's photograph, chatted about the things he or she liked to do, pets, etc. On the first day of school the photos and the stories of each child were on the bulletin board. The visit also gave me an opportunity to talk with the mother (and often with both parents) about the curriculum, plans for homework, etc. I expect to resume these visits next summer because they are so useful. There are no tearful children the first week. I know the children by name before they come into the classroom. It is very easy to recruit parent volunteers. It forms the basis for continuing parent contact throughout the year—because we know each other. Telephone conversations when a child is absent or seems troubled strengthen my relationships with the parents. It seems to me that education must be a partnership between parent and teacher.

Summer Learning at Home. Summer activities that enable parents to help their children maintain skills from the school year may be an especially important area for home-school programs. One teacher commented on the work she arranged for parents to supervise during the summer:

> At the end of the year I sent home a calendar of summer activities that would involve parent-child participation and would help the child improve or retain basic skills.

Dilemmas of Parent Involvement

The teachers were aware of the dilemmas of home-school relationships:

> Parents are so involved with staying alive and being able to keep up economically, there is little or no energy left to devote to children—much less spend time teaching, disciplining, etc. The time they have is spent being loving, lenient, and feeling guilty for not having time or energy to help their children. The children have no motivation to study. Many of the children I teach are too busy raising the little children in the family, cleaning house, and doing adult work at home because their parents are out trying to make ends meet. It amazes me that the children can run houses, raise siblings, and still find time to learn at all.

> Many homes have no literature in them—everything comes from TV—yet the schools neglect the media. Parents want to be supportive and help, but they can't—yet without their support, schools cannot make any real difference.

> If parents became actively involved and worked with the teachers, our students would be more successful. Our students need lots of motivation that teachers alone cannot provide.

SUMMARY AND DISCUSSION

In some ways, all of the teachers' comments are correct. There is no denying the different reactions of teachers to the parents with whom they have worked. The honest differences in teachers' opinions reflect three perspectives on parent-school relations:

1. Parents care but cannot do much to help the school or their children in actual learning
2. Parents care but should not help with school learning
3. Parents care and can be of great help if they are shown how to help.

There was no disagreement, however, about the fact that successful parent involvement programs require the teachers' and the parents' commitment. There are usually no formal rewards for teachers or parents for the time and effort required to plan and conduct learning activities at home. However, both may have feelings of satisfaction when children make progress in learning.

Many comments stressed the parents' and students' needs for time at home that is free of academic demands; however, an equal number of teachers emphasized that many students who have trouble in school would be assisted with some structured daily work at home. Parental assistance that provides extra time for learning may be one of the few techniques that can bring a slow student up to grade level. Many teachers believe it is worth a try to develop programs for parents to conduct at home that will supplement the teachers' efforts.

Because of an absence of research on the effects of parent involvement, it is impossible to assure teachers that certain practices will lead to improved student skills, improved parent-child exchanges, or improved parent-teacher relations. It is equally impossible to assure teachers that they can be more successful if they ignore parent involvement. The differences in teachers' opinions and the lack of objective evidence on the debated topics suggest how research can contribute to this important aspect of education. From the statistical results of our survey (Reading 3.1) and from the written comments of the teachers, we have identified eight issues that may prompt new research.

1. Of all types of parent involvement, supervision of learning activities at home may be the most educationally significant. In contrast to PTA councils and classroom volunteers that involve relatively few parents, parent activities at home can involve many or all children's parents. We need to know whether and how teachers at different grade levels can successfully implement parent involvement programs to include all families.

2. Some parents work with their children at home, with or without teachers' suggestions. Most parent involvement efforts by teachers focus on parents who normally would not know what to do to assist their children with learning activities at home. We need information on the kinds of tutoring or supervisory skills all parents can learn quickly. We need to know how effective parents can be during the relatively short, added "learning time at home" in improving their children's skills.

3. The attitudes, training, and experiences of individual teachers have a lot to do with whether they choose to develop parent involvement programs. However, the attitudes of parents and principals, the needs of the students, and the assistance the teachers receive from their colleagues at school may also contribute to the development and success of parent involvement programs.

4. The role of the parent in learning activities at home is not well defined, and the benefits or disadvantages from different kinds of parental activities and approaches are not known. For example, the parent may act as a tutor, teacher's monitor, listener, task initiator, reactor, or co-learner in activities conducted at home. Which parent roles are most effective for what kinds of situations, skills, and students?

5. Differences in teachers' opinions about parent involvement techniques may depend on the skills needed by students of different abilities in the classroom. Skill building and drill for remediation or for enrichment

require different kinds of learning materials and make different demands on the teachers' and parents' time and energies. Skill building requires different designs and techniques for students two years behind grade level and for students on or above grade level. How can parent involvement programs take into account the special needs of each student, so that time at home can assist each student's learning?

6. The teacher's role is changed when the teacher acts as a manager of parent involvement. The teacher shares a portion of the teaching authority when parents are given materials and instructions for supervising learning activities at home. New behaviors are required of teachers to coordinate activities for parents, and different reactions to students are required from teachers in response to activities conducted at home. What are the changes in the teacher's role that occur under different parent involvement techniques?

7. Teachers "intrude" on families' schedules and activities whenever homework is given. The older the student, the more homework and the greater the intrusion on family time. However, if homework is accepted as an important mechanism for reinforcing classroom instruction, then homework assignments that involve parents may maximize learning that can occur during the homework period. Carefully constructed assignments will not necessarily be seen negatively by parents. These assignments can be as simple as a weekly spelling drill or as complex as daily lessons in language or math. We need to know how parent involvement can be organized so that the responsibilities and goals of teachers, parents, and students are clear and attainable.

   From a different perspective, we need information on how the experiences and expertise of each parent can productively be included in teachers' schedules and curricula. Parents' skills and ideas may be taught to their own children at home or introduced to whole classes in school. In either case, parent-designed lessons and activities might be used systematically by teachers to extend and enrich the schools' programs.

8. One of the reasons so many teachers and principals conduct and support visit-school nights and parents' conferences is that these activities have become formal, accepted strategies for parent-teacher exchanges. They are school-level activities that recur in similar, predictable form in most schools. In contrast, the techniques of parent involvement in learning activities at home are classroom-level projects that are developed by individual teachers. The patterns of exchange for these activities have not been standardized and so there are no clear expectations.

It is questionable whether the familiar rituals of visit-school night and parent conferences accomplish more than a polite exchange between parents and teachers. Techniques for parent involvement in home-learning activities have greater potential for actively involving parents in important exchanges with the teacher that may assist their own children's progress in school. We need to know how teachers can organize parent involvement so the activities will become as familiar as the traditional parent-teacher events.

New research on parent involvement should take into account the natural variation in characteristics of teachers, students, families, schools, and classrooms. Important questions on the implementation and effects of parent involvement have been raised by this exploratory survey of teachers and by the variety of opinions they expressed. If the problems and possibilities of parent involvement are systematically studied, research can lead quickly and directly to useful information for teachers.

School Programs and Teacher Practices of Parent Involvement in Inner-City Elementary and Middle Schools*

ABSTRACT

This study uses data from 171 teachers in eight inner-city elementary and middle schools to examine the connections between school programs of parent involvement, teachers' attitudes, and the practices that teachers use to involve parents of their own students. Patterns are examined at two levels of schooling (elementary and middle), in different academic subjects, under various classroom organizations (self-contained, semi-departmentalized, departmentalized), and under different levels of shared support for parent involvement by the teachers and significant other groups. Each of these variables has important implications for the types and strengths of school programs and teachers' practices of parent involvement. The results add to the validation of Epstein's five types of school and family connections. The data used in this study were collected in a three-year action research process with the sampled schools. The process is outlined in terms that any school can follow to improve programs and practices of parent involvement.

INTRODUCTION

An extensive and growing literature documents the importance of school and family connections for increasing student success in school and for strengthening school programs. The theory of overlapping spheres of influence of families and schools on students' learning and development and on family and school effectiveness (Epstein, 1987a [Reading 2.1]) is supported by a growing number of studies. For example, when teachers make parent involvement part of their regular teaching practice, parents increase their interactions with their children at home, feel more positive about their abilities to help their children in the elementary grades, and rate the teachers as better teachers overall, and students improve their attitudes and achievement (Becker and Epstein, 1982 [Reading 3.1]; Epstein, 1986 [Reading 3.4], 1991 [Reading 3.7]).

---

* By Joyce L. Epstein and Susan L. Dauber. This research was supported by a grant from the U.S. Department of Education, Office of Educational Research and Improvement (OERI), and by a National Science Foundation Graduate Fellowship awarded to the second author. The opinions expressed do not necessarily reflect the position or policy of the OERI or the NSF, and no official endorsement should be inferred. We are very grateful to the teachers who participated in the survey and to the principals who supported the survey as the first step in a school improvement process. An earlier version of this reading was presented at the 1988 annual meeting of the American Sociological Association and in a technical report at the Center for Research on Elementary and Middle Schools, Johns Hopkins University. Reprinted with permission from *Elementary School Journal* 91 (1991): 289–303.

Despite increased attention to the topic of parent involvement, few studies have focused on teachers' practices of involving parents in "difficult" or "disadvantaged" inner-city schools. Indeed, a recurring theme in many studies and commentaries is that less-educated parents cannot or do not want to become involved in their children's education (Baker and Stevenson, 1986; Lareau, 1987). Other research challenges this generalization by showing that there is wide variation in the nature and quality of the involvement of parents with less formal education (Clark, 1983; Scott-Jones, 1987) and that, when teachers help them, parents of all backgrounds can be involved productively (Dauber and Epstein, 1989; see Reading 3.6; Epstein, 1986).

Even studies that report average differences in involvement based on parent education or social class, however, recognize that family practices vary within any group of parents (Hoover-Dempsey, Bassler, and Brissie, 1987; Lareau, 1989; Stevenson and Baker, 1987; Useem, 1990). Part of the variation among families is due to the fact that schools vary in how much and how well they inform and involve families.

An earlier large-scale study of elementary teachers, parents, and students showed, for example, that teachers who were "leaders" in the frequent use of parent involvement did not prejudge less-educated, poor, or single parents. They rated all groups of parents higher on helpfulness and follow-through on learning activities with their children at home (Becker and Epstein, 1982; Epstein, 1986, 1990 [Reading 3.5]). In contrast, teachers who did not frequently involve parents in their children's education made more stereotypical judgments about the involvement and abilities of less-educated parents, socioeconomically disadvantaged parents, and single parents. Thus, the attitudes and practices of the teachers, not only the educational, socioeconomic status (SES), or marital status of parents, are important variables for fully understanding whether and how parents become knowledgeable and successful partners with schools in their children's education.

Studies will continue to show that better-educated families are more involved, on average, in their children's education until researchers include measures of teacher practices to involve all parents. Most parents need help to know how to be productively involved in their children's education at each grade level. School programs and teacher practices to organize family and school connections are "equalizers" to help families who would not become involved on their own.

FIVE TYPES OF INVOLVEMENT

Earlier studies and reviews suggest that five major types of involvement are part of schools' comprehensive programs to share responsibilities with families for the education of their children (Epstein, 1987b).

1. *Basic obligations of families* include providing for children's health and safety, developing parenting skills and child-rearing approaches that prepare children for school and that maintain healthy child development across the grades, and building positive home conditions that support school learning and behavior all across the school years. Schools assist families to develop

the knowledge and skills needed to understand their children at each grade level through workshops at the school or in other locations, home visitors, family support programs, and other forms of education, training, and information giving.

2. *Basic obligations of schools* include communications with families about school programs and children's progress. This includes the memos, notices, phone calls, report cards, and conferences that most schools conduct and other innovative communications with parents that some schools create. Schools vary the forms and frequency of communications and greatly affect whether the information sent home can be understood by all families.

3. *Involvement at school* includes parent and other volunteers who assist teachers, administrators, and children in classrooms or in other areas of the school. It also refers to family members who come to school to support student performances, sports, or other events. Schools can improve and vary schedules so that more families are able to participate as volunteers and as audiences. Schools can improve recruitment and training so that volunteers are more helpful to teachers, students, and school improvement efforts.

4. *Involvement in learning activities at home* includes requests and guidance from teachers for parents to assist their own children at home on learning activities that are coordinated with the children's classwork. Schools assist families in helping their children at home by providing information on skills required of students to pass each grade. Schools provide information to families on how to monitor, discuss, and help with homework and when and how to make decisions about school programs, activities, and opportunities at each grade level so that all students can be more successful in school.

5. *Involvement in decision making, governance, and advocacy* includes parents and others in the community in participatory roles in the parent-teacher association/organization (PTA/PTO), advisory councils, Title I programs, or other committees or groups at the school, district, or state level. It also refers to parents as activists in independent advocacy groups in the community. Schools assist by training parent leaders and representatives in decision-making skills and in ways to communicate with all of the parents they represent and by providing information needed by community groups for school improvement activities.

    A sixth type of involvement has been suggested as an important component in schools' comprehensive programs for involving families and communities in their children's education (California State Board of Education, 1988).

6. *Collaboration and exchanges with community organizations* include connections with agencies, businesses, and other groups that share responsibility for children's education and future successes. This includes school programs that provide children and families with access to

community and support services, including after-school care, health services, and other resources that coordinate these arrangements and activities to support children's learning. Schools vary in how much they know and share about their communities and how much they draw on community resources to enhance and enrich the curriculum and other experiences of students.

This type of involvement was not part of the earlier research that helped to identify the five major types of involvement, nor is it included in the present study. Future research will determine whether and how this is a separate type of involvement or whether these collaborations offer strategies for strengthening the five types of school and family connections by calling on and coordinating community resources for workshops, communications, volunteers, learning activities at home, and decision making (Epstein and Scott-Jones, 1988). Other types of involvement and different typologies will be suggested by other researchers and practitioners and will require study. The typology offered in this reading is designed to be helpful to educators who are analyzing their schools' practices and developing new programs. Although the five types are not "pure" and involve some aspects that overlap, most practices that schools use to involve families in their children's education fall under one of the five types.

Schools with programs including the five types of involvement help parents build home conditions for learning, understand communications from the schools, become productive volunteers at school, share responsibilities in their children's education in learning activities related to the curriculum at home, and include parents' voices in decisions that affect the school and their children. There are, literally, hundreds of practices that can be selected to implement each type of involvement. Most practices have not yet been formally evaluated, but the available evidence indicates that the different types of involvement lead to different outcomes for parents, teachers, and students (Brandt, 1989; Epstein, 1986). (See Reading 5.1 to study sample practices, challenges, and results for all six types of involvement.)

Research on the typology provides evidence of its validity, and a study of a large sample of parents using measures of the five types of involvement found moderate to high internal reliabilities ranging from .58 to .81 (Dauber and Epstein, 1989). Data from teachers in earlier studies were used to study the design and effects of types of involvement but did not provide information on whether the five types were separable. This study uses reports from teachers about the five types of involvement in school programs to further examine the typology.

Earlier studies of parent involvement have focused on one level of schooling, either elementary (Becker and Epstein, 1982; Epstein, 1986, 1990, 1991; Hoover-Dempsey et al., 1987), the middle grades (Baker and Stevenson, 1986; Leitch and Tangri, 1988; Useem, 1990), or the high school level (Bauch, 1988; Clark, 1983; Dornbusch and Ritter, 1988; Dornbusch, Ritter, Liederman, Roberts, and Fraleigh, 1987), but studies have not included comparisons across levels of schooling. This study compares school programs and teachers' practices of parent involvement in elementary and middle schools. Dauber and Epstein (1989) present a related study on the attitudes and practices of the parents in these elementary and middle schools.

METHOD

Data were collected from 171 teachers in five elementary and three middle schools in Baltimore on the teachers' attitudes and practices of parent involvement. The eight schools were selected at random from a set of comparable Title I schools in economically and educationally disadvantaged neighborhoods to begin a three-year initiative to improve parent involvement programs and practices.

Teacher representatives for parent involvement from the eight schools were invited to attend a summer workshop. They were paid for their time, were provided with a background on the topic, helped write questionnaires, received a planning grant to administer the survey to teachers and to parents, and planned an initial activity based on the survey results. The teachers were awarded three years of support in a series of small grants to design, conduct, help to evaluate, and expand practices of parent involvement in their schools to increase the achievement and success of students.

The teacher questionnaire on which this study is based is organized into 10 questions with many subquestions that obtained 100 pieces of information on teachers' general attitudes toward parent involvement; teachers' practices of communicating with students' families; use of school and classroom volunteers (including the numbers, frequency, tasks, and training of volunteers); strength of school programs on the five types of parent involvement; importance of specific practices of five types of parent involvement to the teacher for his or her grade level and subjects taught; teachers' expectations of parents; the involvement of hard-to-reach subgroups of parents; the level of support for parent involvement of the teacher, other school staff, parents, and community; the characteristics of the student population; classroom organization; subjects taught; grade level(s); numbers of different students taught; and years of teaching experience. Open-ended comments about parent involvement practices and problems were also solicited from the teachers.

Two stages of analyses were conducted. First, descriptive statistics were provided to the teachers, principals, and parents in each school. Each school was given two profiles, or "Clinical Summaries," based on the data collected from teachers and parents. These profiles summarized the strengths and weaknesses of the school on the five types of parent involvement as perceived by the two groups of respondents and reported summary statistics for all survey questions (Epstein, 1988; Epstein and Salinas, 1988). Schools used these data to develop their initial projects to improve parent involvement programs and practices.

Second, in this study, the data from teachers in the eight schools were combined for more formal analyses of patterns and connections of teacher attitudes about parent involvement, school programs, and the actual practices that teachers use at two levels of schooling (elementary/middle); in different academic subjects; under three classroom organizations (self-contained, semi-departmentalized, departmentalized); and under high or low support by significant other groups for parent involvement. In the next sections we present correlates of strong school programs of the five types of involvement, add information to validate the typology of five major types of involvement, discuss the practices of teachers of specific academic subjects, and demonstrate the importance of a school climate that encourages parent involvement. These analyses provide new information on programs of parent involvement in inner-city elementary and middle schools. Finally, we outline the process that these schools are using and that any school could use to improve its connections with families to benefit students.

RESULTS

Teachers' General Attitudes about Parent Involvement

Overall, teachers in the inner-city elementary and middle schools in this sample have strong, positive attitudes about parent involvement. A 10-item scale, scored 1–4 for negative to positive attitudes on each item, has an average mean score of 3.07 (with a standard deviation of .32), indicating strong agreement overall and little variation in teachers' attitudes. Compared to other teachers, attitudes are more positive for teachers who teach in self-contained classrooms (correlation coefficient, $r = .234$) and for those who perceive high support for parent involvement from their colleagues and students' parents ($r = .336$). Teachers with more positive attitudes toward parent involvement place more importance than other teachers on such practices as holding conferences with all students' parents, communicating with parents about school programs, and providing parents with both good and bad reports about students' progress. More positive attitudes also are positively correlated with more success in involving hard-to-reach parents ($r = .383$), including employed parents, parents with less formal education, single parents, parents of older students, young parents, parents new to the school, and other adults with whom children live.

Separate Contributions of the Five Types of Parent Involvement

The items in the questionnaire were designed to measure the five types of involvement described previously. The five types are significantly interrelated, with correlations ranging from $r = .303$ to $r = .569$, as shown in Table 3.3. The modest correlations indicate, however, that the five types also make separate contributions to comprehensive programs of parent involvement.

The range of coefficients suggests a Guttman scale–like pattern: a cumulative property such that schools with more difficult components of parent involvement have the easier ones in place. For example, a strong school program in communications from school to home (type 2) is least predictive of the other types (range of $r = .303$ to .449; range of $r^2 = 9\%$ to 20%). Because most schools communicate with families through notices, phone calls, conferences, and similar means, the power of this type of involvement to predict other types is relatively low. Knowing a school had a strong program of communication would not help much in predict-

TABLE 3.3   Intercorrelations of Measures of Five Types of Parent Involvement*

Type of Involvement	1	2	3	4	5
1. Parenting skills, child development, and home environment for learning		.378	.482	.569	.467
2. Communications from school to home			.341	.449	.303
3. Volunteers at school				.561	.519
4. Involvement in learning activities at home					.567
5. Decision making, leadership, and governance					

* All correlations are significant beyond the .001 level. N = 171.

ing whether other types of parent involvement were also in place. By contrast, a strong school program in learning activities at home (type 4)—perhaps the most difficult type of parent involvement—is more predictive of the other types (range of r = .449 to .569; range of r^2 = 20% to 32%). That is, if schools are conducting programs to involve parents in learning activities at home, we could predict with up to 32 percent accuracy that one or more of the other types of involvement also were in place. The other three types of involvement—in workshops, volunteers, and decision making—are less distinct in their intercorrelations and their predictive powers. It appears that they are usually added to school programs after communications practices and before involvement in learning activities at home.

The values show that there is considerable flexibility and unpredictability in which types of involvement are strongly implemented in schools. We found in this project, for example, that, with guidance and with small grants to enable teachers to obtain and use data from teachers and parents, schools proceed in different ways to build or strengthen parent involvement programs. For example, if schools learn that parents want this information, they initiate type 4 activities to involve parents in their children's learning at home earlier than is typical in the sequence. The data help us see typical patterns, but the actions taken by individual schools help us understand that these patterns are not fixed. Schools can take different directions in program development if they learn about the needs and interests of their families, students, and teachers.

Other cluster analyses not reported here indicate clear connections between specific school programs and teachers' practices of the same type. For example, teachers' own communication practices correlate significantly with the strength of the school communication program (r = .154) but not with the strength of the school volunteer program (r = .058). Teachers' own volunteer practices correlate significantly with the strength of the school volunteer program (r = .390) but not as strongly with the school communication program (r = .155). Teachers place more importance on their own practices in the type or types of involvement that are strong in their school as a whole.

Correlates of Strong School Programs to Involve Parents

Table 3.4 reports the zero-order correlations of the strength of the five types of parent involvement with school level: elementary versus middle schools. Teachers in elementary schools report significantly stronger programs of parent involvement than teachers in middle schools on four of the five types of involvement ($r = -.212$ to $r = -.4$): parenting and child development, volunteers, learning activities at home, and decision making. The exception is that elementary and middle school teachers do not report much difference in their schools' programs to communicate with parents ($r = -.121$, not significant). Specific communications practices, however (including informal notes, telephone calls, the actual number of children's families involved in parent-teacher conferences), are used significantly more often by elementary grade teachers than by their middle-grade counterparts ($r = -.232$).

Other analyses not reported here show similar, slightly weaker correlations of the types of involvement in Table 3.4 with classroom organization (Epstein and Dauber, 1989). Teachers in self-contained classrooms use significantly more parent involvement than teachers in departmentalized classes ($r = -.155$ to $r = -.321$ for the different types). School level is, however, the stronger correlate. More elementary classes are self-contained, and more middle grade classes are departmentalized ($r = .631$), with some overlap in semi-departmentalized arrangements. Elementary teachers in self-contained or semi-departmentalized classrooms are more likely than middle school teachers to have some school programs and some individual practices that include parents in their children's education. Still other analyses show that within elementary schools, the lower the grade level, the more likely the teacher is to use parent involvement, especially volunteers in the classroom. With considerably different measures, Stevenson and Baker (1987) show that parents of younger children (compared to older students through adolescence) are reported by teachers to be more involved in meetings and conferences at their children's schools.

TABLE 3.4 Zero-Order Correlations of Five Types of Parent Involvement with School Level*

How Strong Is This Type of Involvement in Your School or in Teacher's Own Practice?	School Level, Elementary (0) vs. Middle (1)
1. Workshops (school)	−.403
2. Communications:	
School	−.121
Teacher	−.232
3. Volunteers (school)	−.484
4. Learning activities at home:	
School	−.343
Teacher	−.212
5. Decision making, leadership (school)	−.273

* Correlations of .14 are significant at the .05 level; .19 at the .01 level. N = 171.

There were no significant correlations of the types of involvement and the percentage of students below average in ability in the teachers' classrooms. All of the schools in this sample have high proportions of low-ability students: Approximately 70 percent of the teachers report that more than half of their students are below average in ability. Teachers with fewer years of experience in these schools have slightly more communications with their students' parents ($r = -.178$) and are in schools that use more volunteers ($r = -.169$). Years of teaching experience do not correlate significantly with teachers' reports of the strength of their schools' programs to involve parents in workshops, home-learning activities, or decision-making opportunities.

Effects of School Level, Student and Teacher Characteristics, and Teacher Practices on Parent Involvement Programs

Table 3.5 extends the previous discussion by showing the results of multiple regression analyses that identify the influence of four variables on the strength of three types of school programs of parent involvement. The four variables are school level (coded as elementary = 0 or middle = 1), years of teaching experience, percentage of students below average in ability, and the importance to the teachers of specific practices for their own grade levels and students. Data on teachers' practices were available for three types of parent involvement: communications from school to home, volunteers at school, and learning activities at home. Standardized regression coefficients report the independent effects of each variable, after statistically controlling the other variables in each equation.

The first column of Table 3.5 shows that strong programs of communications from school to home are not strongly influenced by school level, years of teaching experience, or percentage of students below average in ability. The strength or weakness of school programs of communications with families is explained mainly by the teachers' attitudes and practices of communicating with their own students' families (standardized regression coefficient ß = .232).

The second column shows that, with other variables statistically taken into account, strong programs of volunteers at school are explained by school level—more volunteers are used in the elementary grades (ß = −.360); years of teaching experience—newer teachers are more likely to report that their schools have strong volunteer programs (ß = −.176); and individual teachers' practices concerning volunteers—teachers who use volunteers themselves say that their school volunteer program is strong (ß = .237).

The third column shows that strong school programs to involve parents in children's learning activities at home are most influenced by school level—elementary schools are more likely than middle schools to have strong programs of this type of involvement (ß = −.310). Regardless of level, however, reports of strong school programs to involve parents in learning activities at home are also explained by teachers' own emphases on practices that help their students' parents know how to help their children with schoolwork at home (ß = .163).

TABLE 3.5   Summary of the Strengths of Three Types of Parent Involvement

| Characteristics and Practices | How Strong Is This Type of Involvement at Your School?[a] (Standardized Regression Coefficients) | | |
	Communications from School to Home[b]	Volunteers at School	Learning Activities at Home
School level (elementary/middle)	−.104	−.360***	−.310***
Years of teaching experience	.003	−.176*	.016
Percentage of students below average ability	−.056	−.022	−.124
Importance to teacher of this type of practice[c]	.232**	.237**	.163*
R2	.07	.30	.16

N = 171.

a Responses range from 1 = not important, 2 = need to develop, 3 = need to strengthen, to 4 = already strong.

b *Strength of school program of communications* includes three items, *volunteers* includes two items, and *learning activities* at home includes two items.

c Teachers reported how important school and family connections were at their own grade level: *communication practices* includes five items on conducting formal conferences with all parents at least once a year, attending evening meetings, and contacts about students' report cards and progress; *use of volunteers* by the teacher includes the frequency of volunteers in teachers' classrooms in an average week; *learning activities at home* includes nine items on giving information on required skills, providing parents with ideas on how to talk with and help students on schoolwork; listen to students read and practice reading, spelling, writing, and social studies skills; and discuss television shows.

   * $p < .05/.06$.

   ** $p < .01$.

   *** $p < .001$.

The four variables explain little of the variance in the strength of communication programs ($r^2 = .07$), a moderate amount of the variance in the strength of programs for increasing involvement in learning activities at home ($r^2 = .16$), and a considerable amount of the variance in the strength of programs to involve volunteers ($r^2 = .30$).

We know, of course, that level of schooling and associated features affect programs and practices of family involvement because the influence process cannot go the other way. However, because these data are cross-sectional—taken at one point in time—the direction of influence of school programs and teacher practices cannot be determined. It may be that the importance teachers place on specific practices of parent involvement at their own grade levels influences their perceptions of the strength of the programs at their schools. That is, the teachers' personal attitudes and practices color their reports of the school as a whole. Or the strength of particular school programs in communication, use of volunteers, or learning activities at home may influence teachers to involve students' parents in these ways. That is, the schools' programs affect the practices individual teachers use.

There is evidence from other schools that, when some teachers succeed with new activities (such as the use of volunteers), other teachers are influenced to use the same practices, thereby strengthening the school program overall (Vargas, 1990). Indeed, among the schools in this study, all of these influence processes have been observed, suggesting that over time school programs and teacher practices change and improve in concert. Longitudinal data would help document and define this continuous process in which school programs and teachers' individual practices influence each other.

Parent Involvement Practices of Teachers of Different Subjects

Teachers were asked to check all of the subjects that they taught in an average week. Analyses of these data show that teachers of the major academic subjects—English/language arts, reading, math, science, and social studies—tend to stress different parent involvement practices (Epstein and Dauber, 1989). Teachers of reading (compared to teachers who did not teach reading) place more importance on involving parents in listening to their children read aloud ($r = .141$) and on involving parents as volunteers in their classrooms ($r = .138$).

Teachers of English/language arts (compared to teachers who did not teach the subject) emphasize the importance of helping parents become involved in several types of learning activities at home, including listening to the child read ($r = .160$), discussing television shows ($r = .164$), practicing skills for spelling and other tests ($r = .133$), listening to the child's writing assignments ($r = .168$), and assigning homework that requires parent-child interaction and discussion ($r = .143$). These teachers also stress the importance of conferences with all parents ($r = .164$). The specific practices of the reading and English teachers encourage parent involvement in language and reading skills and help promote students' success in these subjects. Teachers of reading and English also report stronger and more positive involvement of parents who are typically "hard to reach," including less-educated parents, single parents, young parents, and other adults (not parents) with whom some children live. In effect, they are more likely than other teachers to use practices to involve children and all families in subject-specific activities as part of their regular teaching practice.

Teachers of math, science, or social studies (compared to teachers who did not teach these subjects) do not place great importance on these parent involvement practices. Compared to other teachers, math teachers are significantly less supportive of attending evening meetings or activities ($r = -.135$); science teachers are significantly less supportive of informing parents of the skills required to pass their subject at each grade level ($r = -.117$); and social studies teachers are significantly less supportive of participating in student-parent-teacher clubs and activities ($r = -.148$).

Earlier research found that elementary school teachers who frequently involve parents in learning activities at home are most likely to request involvement in reading or reading-related activities (Becker and Epstein, 1982 [Reading 3.1]) and that these practices have some positive influence on students' growth in reading scores (Epstein, 1991 [Reading 3.7]). In the present data from elementary and middle grade teachers, we see some subject-specific connections between the academic subjects taught and the teachers' use or lack of use of particular practices. Teachers of math, science, and social studies may need even more assistance than other teachers in preservice and inservice education to understand how to involve parents in their children's learning activities in those subjects.

School Climate for Parent Involvement and Program Strength

Teachers were asked about their own and others' support for parent involvement to indicate the climate at their school for supporting school and family connections. They rated their own level of support (i.e., on a four point scale of none, weak, some, or strong) and estimated the level of support for parent involvement of their principal, other administrators, their teacher colleagues, the parents of students in the school, and others in the community. "Discrepancy scores" were derived to represent the differences between the teachers' own support and their perceptions of the support of other individuals or groups around them. We hypothesized that greater discrepancies between teachers and others in the school would be linked to weaker programs of parent involvement.

Overall, the teachers report that they are similar to their principals in their strong support for parent involvement. However, they believe that they, as individuals, are stronger supporters of parent involvement than their teacher-colleagues and much stronger supporters than the parents or others in the community.

Table 3.6 shows that greater discrepancies between teachers' beliefs about their own and parents' support for involvement occur in schools that have more students below average in ability and more departmentalized programs. Teachers in these schools believe that they are more supportive of involvement than are the parents. When teachers differ culturally and educationally from their students (as in schools with many below-average students), or when they teach greater numbers of students (as in departmentalized programs), they are less likely to know the students' parents and, therefore, more likely to believe that parents are uninterested or uninvolved.

The next section of the table shows that greater discrepancies between teachers and parents are linked to weaker programs of the five major types of parent involvement, with the exception of communications. As noted earlier, just about all schools conduct some communications with families, regardless of teachers' personal attitudes or beliefs. If the teachers believe parents are less supportive of parent involvement than they are, however, the teachers report that their schools have fewer workshops ($r = -.152$), fewer volunteers ($r = -.140$), fewer methods to involve parents in learning activities at home ($r = -.230$), and fewer opportunities for decision making ($r = -.132$).

TABLE 3.6   Discrepancy Scores: Correlates of Teachers' Reports of Differences between Their Own and Parents' Support for Parent Involvement*

	Correlation Coefficient[a]
Classroom conditions:	
Percentage of students below average	+.142[b]
Number of different students	+.172
Self-contained vs. departmentalized	+.180
Strength of school program:	
Parenting skills, home conditions	−.152
Communications from school to home	N.S.[c]
Volunteers at school	−.140
Learning activities at home	−.230
Participation in decision making	−.132
Involvement of hard-to-reach parents:	
Working parents	−.175
Less-educated parents	−.209
Single parents	N.S.
Parents of older students	−.222
Parents new to the school	−.192[b]
Other adults with whom children live	−.200[b]

* Correlations of .14 are significant at the .05 level; .19 at the .01 level; N.S. = not significant. N = 171.

a A (+) correlation suggests that a positive discrepancy score (i.e., teachers' views of own support for parent involvement are higher than their views of parents' support) is associated with a higher level of the measured variable; a (−) correlation suggests a positive discrepancy is associated with a lower level of the measured variable.

b Indicates significance when discrepancy is high between self and principal.

c Indicates significance when discrepancy is high between self and colleagues.

The bottom of the table shows that greater discrepancies between teachers' reports about themselves and parents are linked to less successful connections with several groups of hard-to-reach parents. If teachers believe that parents are not interested in becoming involved in their children's schooling, teachers make fewer efforts to contact, inform, and work with them, especially with those parents who are hard to reach and especially on more difficult types of involvement such as involving parents in learning activities at home.

Other analyses indicate that discrepancies with principals and colleagues also reduce practices of parent involvement, as noted in the table. For example, greater discrepancy between self (teacher) and principals occurs in schools with more disadvantaged students. Also, teachers who think that they and their principal differ in supporting parent involvement make fewer contacts with hard-to-reach parents. Greater discrepancy between self and colleagues is linked to weaker school programs and fewer individual practices of traditional communication with families.

Highly discrepant environments (where teachers believe that they differ in attitudes from others at the school) are less likely to support strong, comprehensive programs of parent involvement. Less discrepant environments (where teachers see themselves as more similar to their own school administrators, colleagues, and parents) are more likely to support strong school programs and encourage strong teacher attitudes and practices.

DISCUSSION

This survey of teachers in inner-city elementary and middle schools offers new information about the strengths and weaknesses of programs and practices of parent involvement. We draw the following conclusions from the data.

School Level

Elementary school programs of parent involvement are stronger, more positive, and more comprehensive than those in the middle grades. This is especially evident for workshops for parents on parenting skills, child development, and school programs; volunteers at school; learning activities at home; and involvement in school decisions. One partial exception concerns school programs of communication. Although teachers in elementary and middle schools report their schools have about equally strong communication programs or policies, middle grade teachers use fewer specific communication practices and communicate less often than elementary teachers with fewer individual families. Parents of middle grade students receive less information or guidance at the very time they need more information and more guidance on how to be involved in larger and more complex schools and on new and more complex class schedules and subjects (Useem, 1990). This pattern is changing and will change more as middle grade schools and teachers increase their understanding of school and family connections in early adolescence and begin to develop stronger and more comprehensive programs.

Classroom Organization

Programs of parent involvement are stronger in self-contained classrooms. The organization of classrooms (e.g., self-contained, semi-departmentalized or teamed, and departmentalized programs) determines the number of students that are the teachers' responsibility and affects the frequency of and reasons for teacher contacts with students' parents. Teachers in self-contained classes (mainly in elementary schools) have fewer students to teach and are more apt to make frequent and diverse contacts with parents. They may feel more familiar with a small number of parents or more fully responsible for the students' school programs, including home-learning activities.

Students with many teachers for different subjects could benefit greatly if their parents knew how to monitor and discuss schoolwork and school decisions with their children. To adjust for the difficulties of working with large numbers of students and families, teachers in middle schools and some elementary schools will need extra information, staff development, and guidance in efficient and effective practices that can be used to involve parents of students in departmentalized or semi-departmentalized programs.

Academic Subjects

Teachers of certain academic subjects—particularly English and reading—use more practices than teachers of other subjects to involve parents in their children's education. Many of the same techniques used by English and reading teachers could be used by teachers of any subject (e.g., teachers can ask parents to listen to a child read something the child wrote or practice skills before quizzes or tests). Teachers of any subject can design and assign homework in a way that requires students to interact with a parent about something interesting that they are learning in school.

Support for Parent Involvement

Discrepancy scores show that greater differences between self (teacher) and principal, self and teacher-colleagues, and, particularly, self and parents are associated with weaker parent involvement programs and practices and less involvement with families who are typically hard to reach. Conversely, greater similarities between self and others are reported by teachers in schools with stronger parent involvement programs and practices. Teachers who believe that they share similar beliefs with parents about involvement make more contacts with parents whom other teachers find hard to reach, conduct more types of activities to involve families, and are less affected by disadvantaged characteristics of the student population and by different classroom organizations. The analyses of discrepancy scores suggest that it is important to build common understanding about shared goals and common support among teachers, parents, and principals so that teachers' feelings of isolation or separateness from others will decrease and school and family partnerships will increase.

Five Types of Involvement

The five major types of parent involvement are related but separable.[*] In these schools, type 2 activities (communications from the school to the home) are more prevalent and, therefore, less predictive of other types of parent involvement programs

---

[*] This also applies to the framework of six types of involvement. See Chapter 5.

or practices. In contrast, type 4 activities (involvement in learning activities at home) are difficult for many teachers to organize and so are implemented in fewer places and by fewer teachers, usually after other, more standard practices are in place. Information from parents at the schools in this study showed that parents wanted more information on how to help their own children (Dauber and Epstein, 1989). Some schools used that information to develop type 4 activities even before strengthening other types of involvement. The results support earlier studies that suggest that schools can invest in different types of involvement to address various needs and to attain different benefits.

Families in Inner-City Schools

Educators and researchers often view minority families and families of educationally disadvantaged students in terms of their deficiencies. Often, however, the deficiencies lie in the schools' programs. In this sample of eight inner-city, Title I elementary and middle schools, some schools and, within schools, some teachers have figured out how to mobilize the support of educationally and economically disadvantaged families. In the three-year action research program, all of the inner-city schools discovered that, regardless of where they started from, they could systematically improve their practices to involve the families they serve.

Linking School Programs and Teacher Practices

The study demonstrates important linkages between school programs and teachers' individual practices to involve parents. Although the direction and process of causality remain to be determined in longitudinal studies, this study provides evidence that strong school programs in particular types of involvement go hand in hand with the importance teachers place on the same types of involvement.

Other variables may also influence school programs and teacher practices. In a study of elementary schools, Hoover-Dempsey et al. (1987) found that teacher efficacy (feeling that one is an effective and capable teacher) is related to the strength of school programs of parent involvement, including conferences with more parents, more volunteers, and more interactive homework activities. Although their measure of teacher efficacy raises some questions because it includes estimates of students' ability to learn, the conclusion that schools with more confident teachers use more involvement strategies is provocative. The authors also found that schools with more confident teachers, on average, report more support from parents.

Another study of parent involvement in elementary schools found that parents and principals rated teachers higher in overall teaching ability and interpersonal skills if the teachers frequently used practices of parent involvement (Epstein, 1985 [Reading 4.3], 1986). Teachers' confidence may be boosted by high ratings and appreciation from parents and administrators that result from the use of more involvement practices and encourage continued and expanded use of these practices.

Studies are needed that press these questions further to increase an understanding of the links between school programs and individual teachers' practices across the grades, in different subjects, and in a variety of school communities. This study is based on a small sample of schools and teachers selected because of their initially low and infrequent family and school connections. Despite the somewhat restricted conditions in these schools, the analyses yield robust and credible results about the connections of parent involvement with the level of school, subjects, types of involvement, and climate of support. Other studies of these patterns in more varied sets of schools will help clarify the reported results.

IMPLICATIONS FOR IMPROVING SCHOOL AND FAMILY CONNECTIONS

The schools in this study were participants in the Baltimore School and Family Connections Project—a long-term process to improve school and family connections to improve students' success in school. The process is one that may be followed or adapted by any school that is not satisfied with its present types or strengths of parent involvement. In this case, educators work with researchers and a community foundation that makes small grants to teachers to develop more responsive programs and practices of parent involvement. Small grants can come from other sources, however, such as district and school funds for school improvement and various federal, state, and local programs. Small grants that support and recognize teachers' practices of parent involvement also have been successful in other projects (Davies, 1990; Krasnow, 1990). We have learned of several steps that may maximize success.

1. **Assess present strengths and weaknesses.** Each school needs to identify its own "starting point" on practices of parent involvement to move ahead with more comprehensive and improved programs.

2. **Identify hopes, dreams, and goals.** How would parents, teachers, students, and administrators like the school to involve parents three to five years from the starting point? Rather than looking back at errors or failures in their practices and relationships, we ask the partners in education to look ahead to their goals for the future. What new goals for parents and administrator practice could be attained?

3. **Identify who will have responsibilities for reaching the goals.** Over a three-year period, progress can be made in clear steps, but some individual, team, group, or committee must be put in charge and supported in its responsibilities to conduct and supervise specific activities, revise practices, evaluate progress each year, and expand programs. Comer's (1988) process of school site management to include parents emphasizes formal committee structures; our work acknowledges and develops committees and other flexible arrangements such as large and small teams and groups to design and improve practices. In either case, responsibilities must be clear, and efforts must be supported.

4. Evaluate implementations and results. It is important for teachers, administrators, parents, and students who invest time and energy in a new process and activities to know how well the program is implemented (e.g., are they reaching those they want to reach?). If programs are successfully implemented, one must evaluate whether and how well they promote student success or other goals. Based on each year's evaluations and reviews, programs may be revised, maintained, or extended to move toward ever more effective connections with more families.

5. Continue to support program development activities. Parent involvement is a process that requires teachers, administrators, parents, students, and others in the school community to plan, implement, and reflect on their efforts and goals. This takes time. We found that three years of small grants to teachers provides a minimum period in which to make a good start to improve some practices, particularly if principals exert their leadership to reinforce the concept of partnership with families and to recognize and extend specific activities. As with any aspect of school effectiveness, however, school and family connections are ongoing investments that require continuous attention and support.

WHAT QUESTIONS MUST BE ASKED?

The schools in this sample started with surveys of teachers and parents that the teachers helped design. These questionnaires are available for others' use or adaptation. There are, however, other ways in which schools can assess where they are starting from. These include gathering information from panels of teachers, parents, and students at PTA meetings, grade-level meetings, or other special convocations. Or, principals may conduct focus groups or breakfast meetings with specially invited teachers and parents to outline goals and plans for parent involvement. Questions for panels, focus groups, or discussion groups about their own schools include:

1. Which practices of each of the five types of parent involvement are presently strong at each grade level? Which are weak? What practices are particularly important at each grade level? Which practices should change from grade to grade, and which should be continued?
2. Are our parent involvement practices coherent and coordinated, or are different groups fragmented and following their own agendas? How are all families, Title I families, limited English-proficient families, special education families, and other families who seem hard to reach provided with information and included in their children's schools and education at home?
3. Which families are we reaching, and which are we not yet reaching? Why are we having problems reaching some families, and what can we do to help solve problems of communication and relationships?
4. What do we expect of each other? What do teachers expect of families? What do families expect of teachers and others in the school? What do

students expect their families to be able to do to help them in appropriate ways at each grade level?

5. How do we want this school to look three years from now in its practices of the five types of parent involvement? How would we like parent involvement to work here? What would teachers do? What would parents do? What would administrators do? What would students do? What are specific goals that we want to reach at the end of one year, two years, and three years?

6. How are our students succeeding on important measures of achievement, attitudes, and other indicators of success? How could parent involvement help more students reach higher standards and higher levels of success? Which types of involvement will help students boost their achievements, accomplishments, attitudes, and behaviors?

7. What steps can we take to reach the three-year goals? Who will be responsible for developing, implementing, and evaluating each type of involvement?

8. What costs are associated with the desired improvements? Will staff development, district resources, and/or school leadership and resources be needed? Will small grants or other special funds be needed to implement the programs? How will teachers, parents, and others who design and conduct activities be supported, rewarded, and recognized?

9. How will we evaluate the implementation and results of our efforts to improve practices? What results do we think will actually be attained in one year, two years, and three years, and what indicators, measures, and observations will we use to learn how we are progressing?

10. Other questions about starting points, plans, goals, responsibilities, implementations, and evaluations.

Whether questionnaires, telephone surveys, focus groups, or other group discussions are used, each school must gather information to create a profile of present practices and a coherent plan of action to improve practices in the future.

SUMMARY

Although teachers individually express strong positive attitudes toward parent involvement, most school programs and classroom practices do not support teachers' beliefs in the importance of school and family partnerships. In this survey most teachers wanted all parents to fulfill 12 parent involvement responsibilities, ranging from teaching their children to behave, to knowing what their children are expected to learn each year, to helping them on those skills. Most schools and teachers have not yet implemented practices to help families fulfill these responsibilities at each grade level. Most teachers believe they are stronger supporters of parent involvement than are the other teachers in the school. This is, of course, logically inconsistent and indicates that the teachers do not know their colleagues' attitudes. Teachers say that parents and others in the community are not strong supporters of parent involvement, but surveys of parents in the same schools contradict the teachers' beliefs about parents (Dauber and Epstein, 1989 [Reading 3.6]). Thus, educators may create false or exaggerated discrepancies between themselves and others about parent involvement.

As schools in this study found when they assessed the attitudes and aims of their teachers and parents, more similarities exist than many realize. There is, then, an important (though often hidden) base of shared goals, interests, and investments in children's success on which to build more effective programs of school and family connections.

REFERENCES

Baker, D. P., and D. L. Stevenson. (1986). Mothers' strategies for children's school achievement: Managing the transition to high school. *Sociology of Education* 59: 156–166.

Bauch, P. A. (1988). Is parent involvement different in private schools? *Educational Horizons* 66: 78–82.

Becker, H. J., and J. L. Epstein. (1982). Parent involvement: A study of teacher practices. *Elementary School Journal* 83: 85–102. (Reading 3.1).

Brandt, R. (1989). On parents and schools: A conversation with Joyce Epstein. *Educational Leadership* 47: 24–27.

California State Board of Education. (1988). *Parent involvement initiative: A policy and plan for action*. Sacramento: Author.

Clark, R. (1983). *Family life and school achievement: Why poor black children succeed and fail*. Chicago: University of Chicago Press.

Comer, J. (1988). Educating poor minority children. *Scientific American* 259(5): 42–48.

Dauber, S. L., and J. L. Epstein. (1989). *Parents' attitudes and practices of involvement in inner-city elementary and middle schools*. CREMS Report 33. Baltimore: Center for Research on Elementary and Middle Schools, Johns Hopkins University. (Reading 3.6).

Davies, D. (1990). Shall we wait for the revolution? A few lessons from the Schools Reaching Out project. *Equity and Choice* 6(3): 68–73.

Dornbusch, S. M., and P. L. Ritter. (1988). Parents of high school students: A neglected resource. *Educational Horizons* 66: 75–77.

Dornbusch, S. M., P. L. Ritter, P. Liederman, D. Roberts, and M. Fraleigh. (1987). The relation of parenting style to adolescent school performance. *Child Development* 58: 1244–1257.

Epstein, J. L. (1985). A question of merit: Principals' and parents' evaluations of teachers. *Educational Researcher* 14(7): 3–10. (Reading 4.3).

———. (1986). Parents' reactions to teacher practices of parent involvement. *Elementary School Journal* 86: 277–294. (Reading 3.4).

———. (1987a). Toward a theory of family-school connections: Teacher practices and parent involvement across the school years. In K. Hurrelmann, F. Kaufmann, and F. Losel (Eds.), *Social intervention: Potential and constraints*, Prevention and intervention in childhood and adolescence 1 (pp. 121–136). New York: de Gruyter. (Reading 2.1).

———. (1987b). What principals should know about parent involvement. *Principal* 66(3): 6–9.

———. (1988). Sample clinical summaries: Using surveys of teachers and parents to plan projects to improve parent involvement. Baltimore: Center for Research on Elementary and Middle Schools, Johns Hopkins University.

———. (1990). Single parents and the schools: The effects of marital status on parent and teacher evaluations. In M. T. Hallinan, D. M. Klein, and J. Glass (Eds.), *Change in societal institutions*, The language of science (pp. 91–121). New York: Plenum. (Reading 3.5).

————. (1991). Effects on student achievement of teachers' practices of parent involvement. In S. Silvern (Ed.), *Advances in reading/language research, Vol. 5: Literacy through family, community, and school interaction* (pp. 261–276). Greenwich, CT: JAI. (Reading 3.7).

Epstein, J. L., and S. L. Dauber. (1989). *Teacher attitudes and practices of parent involvement in inner-city elementary and middle schools.* CREMS Report No. 32. Baltimore: Center for Research on Elementary and Middle Schools, Johns Hopkins University.

Epstein, J. L., and K. Salinas. (1988). *Evaluation report forms: Summaries of school-level data from surveys of teachers and surveys of parents.* Baltimore: Center for Research on Elementary and Middle Schools, Johns Hopkins University.

Epstein, J. L., and D. Scott-Jones. (1988). *School-family-community connections for accelerating education for students at risk.* Proceedings from the Stanford University Invitational Centennial Conference, Stanford, CA.

Hoover-Dempsey, K. V., O. C. Bassler, and J. S. Brissie. (1987). Parent involvement: Contributions of teacher efficacy, school socioeconomic status, and other school characteristics. *American Educational Research Journal* 24: 417–435.

Krasnow, J. (1990). Building new parent-teacher partnerships: Teacher-researcher teams stimulate reflection. *Equity and Choice* 6: 25–31.

Lareau, A. (1987). Social class differences in family-school relationships: The importance of cultural capital. *Sociology of Education* 60: 73–85.

————. (1989). *Home advantage: Social class and parental intervention in elementary education.* Education policy perspectives: Social analysis series. New York: Falmer.

Leitch, M. L., and S. S. Tangri. (1988). Barriers to home-school collaboration. *Educational Horizons* 66: 70–74.

Scott-Jones, D. (1987). Mother-as-teacher in the families of high- and low-achieving low-income black first graders. *Journal of Negro Education* 56: 21–34.

Stevenson, D. L., and D. P. Baker. (1987). The family-school relations and the child's school performance. *Child Development* 58: 1348–1357.

Useem, E. (1990, April). *Social class and ability group placement in mathematics in the transition to seventh grade: The role of parent involvement.* Paper presented at the annual meeting of the American Educational Research Association, Boston.

Vargas, D. (1990). Personal communication on P.S. 111 in the League of Schools Reaching Out project in New York City.

Parents' Reactions to Teacher Practices of Parent Involvement[*]

Teachers have strong opinions about parent involvement. Some believe that they can be effective only if they obtain parental assistance on learning activities at home. Others believe that their professional status is in jeopardy if parents are involved in activities that are typically the teachers' responsibilities. The different philosophies and beliefs of teachers reflect the two main, opposing theories of school and family relations.

One perspective emphasizes the inherent incompatibility, competition, and conflict between families and schools and supports the separation of the two institutions (Parsons, 1959; Waller, 1932; Weber, 1947). It assumes that school bureaucracies and family organizations are directed, respectively, by educators and parents, who can best fulfill their different goals, roles, and responsibilities independently. Thus, these distinct goals are achieved most efficiently and effectively when teachers maintain their professional, general standards and judgments about the children in their classrooms and when parents maintain their personal, particularistic standards and judgments about their children at home.

The opposing perspective emphasizes the coordination, cooperation, and complementarity of schools and families and encourages communication and collaboration between the two institutions. It assumes that schools and families share responsibilities for the socialization and education of the child. Teachers and parents are believed to share common goals for children that are achieved most effectively when teachers and parents work together. These assumptions are based on models of inter-institutional interactions and ecological designs that emphasize the natural, nested, necessary connections among individuals, groups, and organizations (Bronfenbrenner, 1979; Leichter, 1974; Litwak and Meyer, 1974).

Although teachers may combine these perspectives, they tend to emphasize the precepts of one theory or the other in organizing their teaching practice. In an earlier survey of teachers, we found that in some classrooms inter-institutional cooperation was low. These teachers made few overtures to parents, rarely requesting their help on learning activities at home. In other classrooms cooperation was high. These teachers made frequent requests for parental assistance in reinforcing or improving students' skills (Becker and Epstein, 1982 [Reading 3.1]; Epstein and Becker, 1982 [Reading 3.2]).

* By Joyce L. Epstein. Many thanks go to the teachers, principals, and families who participated in this survey. I am indebted to my colleague Henry Jay Becker, who shared responsibility for the design and data collection of the study and offered suggestions on earlier drafts of this reading. Thanks, too, go to John H. Hollifield and two anonymous reviewers for helpful suggestions. This research was supported by a grant from the National Institute of Education. The results and opinions of the author do not necessarily reflect the position or policy of the NIE, and no endorsement by the NIE should be inferred. Reprinted with permission from *Elementary School Journal* 86 (1986): 277–294.

Teachers' reports tell only one part of the story. Parents' reports are needed to verify and clarify their experiences with teachers' different practices of parent involvement. Among the most frequently mentioned expected benefits of parent involvement are the increased or sustained interest and support of parents in the school programs and in their child's progress (Gordon, 1979; Keesling and Melaragno, 1983; Mager, 1980; Morrison, 1978; Rich and Jones, 1977; Robinson, 1979; Sowers, Lang, and Gowett, 1980). Little research has been done, however, to link specific teachers' practices with the parents who experience them or to measure differences in attitudes and reactions of parents whose children are in classrooms of teachers with different philosophies and practices of parent involvement. The data collected for this study connect the teachers with the parents of their students. I examine parents' awareness of teachers' efforts, knowledge about the school program, and evaluations of teachers. The results should provide an understanding of parents' perspectives on teachers' practices that emphasize the cooperation or separation of schools and families.

METHOD

Parents of 1,269 students in 82 first-, third-, and fifth-grade classrooms in Maryland completed and returned by mail questionnaires on the parent involvement practices of their children's teachers, a response rate of 59 percent. The questionnaire, administered in the spring of 1981, contained items assessing parents' attitudes toward the schools and teachers, their experiences with different kinds of involvement and communications with the schools, and their reactions to the teachers' programs and practices. The teachers of these parents' children included 36 "case" teachers who were identified in an earlier survey as strong supporters and users of parent involvement in learning activities at home and 46 "control" teachers who, by their own report, did not emphasize parent involvement but who matched the "case" teachers in their teaching assignment by grade level, school district, years of teaching experience, estimated achievement level of the students in their classes, and average education of their students' parents. Among the "case" teachers, 17 were recognized by their principals as especially strong leaders in the use of parent involvement. In this report, "parent involvement" refers to the frequency of participation by parents in 12 types of learning activities that teachers request parents to conduct or monitor at home that support the child's instructional program at school. Overall, the 82 teachers ranged along a continuum from low to high use of parent involvement. This continuum is one measure of teachers' emphasis on the separation or cooperation of schools and families on learning activities.

Table 3.7 describes the characteristics of parents who returned questionnaires. Families were instructed that the parent most familiar with the child's school and teacher should complete the survey. Over 90 percent of the "most knowledgeable" parents were female. Other background and family characteristics showed a representative mix of the families served by Maryland's schools. Approximately one-fourth of the parents had some high school education but no diploma, almost one-third had graduated from high school, about one-fifth had attended some college, and approximately one-fourth graduated from college or attended graduate school. About one-fourth of the sample comprised single parents. Two-fifths of the respondents did not work outside the home, one-fifth worked part-time, and two-fifths had full-time jobs outside the home. Approximately one-third of the respondents were black.

There were some differences between the parents who responded to the survey and those who did not. More parents whose children were above average in math and reading skills in school returned the survey than did parents of children doing average or below average work in these subjects. Regardless of how children fared academically, the response was greater from parents whose children were in the classrooms of teachers who were leaders in parent involvement. Mailing back the questionnaire may be an indicator of parental cooperation on important requests from the teacher (Becker, 1982).

The differences in return rates from parents had offsetting effects. Parents whose children were in classrooms of teachers who emphasized parent involvement tended to be more positive about school than other parents, but parents of high-achieving students tended to be more critical of school and teachers than other parents. The small differences in return rates from some parents did not seriously affect the usefulness of data from the sizable, diverse sample of parents.

TABLE 3.7   Characteristics of Parents*

Characteristics	%
Grade level of children:	
K, 1, 2	45
3, 4	27
5, 6	28
Sex:	
Female	92
Male	8
Race	
White	62
Black	36
Other	2
Highest education completed:	
Some high school (or less)	25
High school diploma	28
Some college	20
Bachelor's degree	10
Some graduate school (or advanced degree)	17
Family structure:	
Two-parent home	76
One-parent home	24
Employment:	
Not working	39
Part-time work	18
Full-time work	43

* N = 1,269.

Statistical methods were used to take into account the multiple characteristics of parents, teachers, and students to isolate effects on parents of teacher practices of parent involvement. The cross-sectional nature of these data prevents us from drawing conclusions about causal relationships between teacher practices and parents' reactions and evaluations. Regression techniques, however, yield information that permits informed guesses about potentially important, independent effects that should prompt new longitudinal studies.

In this article, I briefly examine parents' attitudes toward public elementary schools and their experiences with some common forms of parent involvement and then focus on parents' reactions to teacher practices of parent involvement in learning activities at home. I examine the responses of parents who have different educational backgrounds and whose children are in classrooms of teachers who differ in their leadership in the use of parent involvement practices.

RESULTS

Parents' Attitudes Toward Public Elementary Schools and Teachers

Parents' attitudes toward the public elementary schools and teachers were remarkably positive. About 90 percent of the parents agreed that their elementary schools were well run. Almost as many felt comfortable at their child's school and believed that they and the teachers had the same goals for the child.

The parents' clearly positive attitudes seem to contradict recent national reports that have criticized the curricula, teachers, and standards in the public schools (National Commission on Excellence in Education, 1983; National Task Force on Education for Economic Growth, 1983). The reactions of parents in Maryland are more like the findings of a recent Gallup poll (1983), in which only 9 percent of respondents with children in public schools said that getting good teachers was a problem, only 9 percent cited parents' lack of interest, and only 1 percent reported problems with administrators. Although there are some problems in all schools, most parents were not concerned about the basic administration of the schools or with the quality of teachers. They found fewer problems with elementary than with secondary schools, and they were more positive about the public schools if they sent their children there (Gallup, 1982, 1983; Goodlad, 1983). Other studies also report generally positive attitudes of parents of public school children toward the curriculum (Klein, Tye, and Wright, 1979), parent involvement, and homework (Olmsted, Wetherby, Leler, and Rubin, 1982; Williams, 1983; Zill and Peterson, 1982).

Despite positive attitudes about schools and teachers in general, parents reported that teachers could do more to involve parents in learning activities at home. Approximately 58 percent of the parents rarely or never received requests from the teacher to become involved in learning activities at home. Fewer than 30 percent of the parents reported that teachers gave them many ideas on how to help their child in reading and math. They overwhelmingly agreed that teachers should involve parents in learning activities at home and that homework was useful for their children. More than 80 percent of the parents said they could spend more time helping their children at home if they were shown how to do specific learning activities.

Experiences with Parent Involvement

We look now at several types of parent involvement that the parents experienced. These include involvement in basic obligations at home, communication from the school to the home, assistance at the school, and assistance in learning activities at home.

Involvement in Basic Obligations. The most pervasive form of parent involvement is the parents' provision of school supplies needed by their children and general support and supervision at home. More than 97 percent of the parents in this Maryland survey said that their children had the supplies needed for school, and over 90 percent reported that their children had a regular place to do homework. These management chores are expected by the schools and are accepted as basic responsibilities by almost all parents.

Involvement in School-to-Home Communications. Communication from the school to the home is sometimes considered "parent involvement" but is usually "parent information." All schools send information home to the family about schedules, report card grades, special events, and emergency procedures. Most of these activities flow one way, from the school to the home, often with no encouragement for communication from parents. Some schools organize and require teacher-parent conferences with all parents; others hold conferences with some parents, only on request. A few schools support home visits by teachers or by aides who serve as liaisons between teachers and parents to inform parents about school procedures.

Despite the typical profusion of notices from school to home, some parents receive few communications from teachers. In the Maryland sample, approximately 16 percent of the parents said they received no memos from their child's teacher, more than 35 percent had no parent-teacher conference, and approximately 60 percent never spoke to the teacher on the phone, as shown in Table 3.8. It is not surprising that the more time required for an exchange, the less often that type of communication occurs, but it is revealing that large numbers of parents are excluded from many of the traditional forms of communication that link the school to the home.

Involvement at School. One prevalent form of involvement is parental assistance at the school: in the classroom as an aide to teachers; in other school locations such as the cafeteria, library, or playground; or at special events, such as class parties, trips, or fund-raisers. Although some parents participate, most parents are not active at school:

TABLE 3.8   Parents Who Never Received Personal Communication from Child's Teacher over One Year

Type of Communication	%
Memo from teacher	16.4
Talk to teacher before or after school	20.7
Conference with teacher	36.4
Handwritten note from teacher	36.5
Workshop at school	59.0
Called on phone by teacher	59.5
Visited at home by teacher	96.3

- Approximately 70 percent never helped the teacher in the classroom or on class trips.
- Approximately 70 percent never participated in fund-raising activities for the school.
- Approximately 88 percent never assisted in the library, cafeteria, or other school areas.

Even those parents who did become active were involved infrequently. The average number of days at school per year was:

- 4.1 days helping the teacher and class;
- 7.0 days helping with fund-raising activities; and
- 3.5 days helping in the school cafeteria, offices, or library.

Only about 4 percent of the respondents (51 parents distributed across 82 classrooms) were very active, spending over 25 days per year at the school. Many (42 percent) of the parents who were not active at school worked outside the home during school hours. Others had small children, family problems, or other activities that demanded their time. Others (about 12 percent) simply had not been asked to assist at school. Despite these facts, parent assistance at the school is the type of parent involvement that most teachers and administrators support (Ogbu, 1974).

Involvement with Learning Activities at Home. A less frequently used form of parent involvement, but one that reflects the theory of cooperation between schools and families, is teacher practices that involve all or most parents in learning activities with their children at home. In this study, teachers ranged from low to high in their use of this type of parent involvement. Parents were asked about their experiences with 12 techniques that teachers use to involve parents in learning activities at home. These were grouped under five categories: (1) techniques that involve reading and books; (2) techniques that encourage discussions between parents and children; (3) techniques based on informal activities and games that use common materials at home; (4) techniques based on formal contracts and supervision among parents, teachers, and children; and (5) techniques that involve tutoring and teaching the child in skills and drills. In an earlier survey, teachers rated these techniques as their most satisfying and successful parent involvement practices (Becker and Epstein, 1982 [Reading 3.1]).

Most Frequent Requests to Parents by Teacher-Leaders. Parents whose children's teachers were recognized by their principal as leaders in parent involvement reported significantly more frequent use of 9 of the 12 parent involvement practices, as shown in Table 3.9. These included reading aloud or listening to the child read, talking with the child about the events of the school day, giving spelling or math drills, giving help on worksheets or workbooks, signing the child's homework, taking the child to the library, playing learning games, using things at home to teach, and visiting the classroom to observe teaching techniques. Despite the frequent use of some activities by some teachers, from one-fourth to two-fifths of the parents never were asked to conduct the five most frequently used parent involvement activities. On the three least used practices—borrowing books, entering contracts, and using TV for learning—there were no significant differences in reports from parents of teachers who were leaders compared with other teachers.

TABLE 3.9   Parents Reporting Frequent Requests for Parent Involvement Techniques by Teacher-Leaders and Other Teachers (percent)

| Activity | Parents Reporting Requests By: | | χ^2 Test[a] |
	Teacher-Leaders	Other Teachers	
1. Read aloud to child or listen to child read	68	51	***
2. Sign child's homework	66	52	***
3. Give spelling or math drills	61	54	*
4. Help with worksheet or work book lessons	57	47	**
5. Ask child about school day	49	42	*
6. Use things at home to teach child	44	34	**
7. Play games that help child learn	35	28	**
8. Visit classroom to watch how child is taught	34	25	**
9. Take child to library	26	17	**
10. Borrow books from teacher to give extra help	21	16	
11. Make a formal contract with teacher to supervise homework or projects	21	19	
12. Watch and discuss TV shows with child	15	15	

a χ^2 tests indicate whether parents report more frequent use of parent involvement activities by teacher-leaders than by other teachers, with frequency categorized as several times or often versus never, once, or twice.
    * $p < .05$; ** $p < .01$; *** $p < .001$.

There were basic similarities between the teachers' reports in an earlier survey and the parents' accounts of their experiences with learning activities at home. The most popular involvement techniques that teachers used (i.e., asking parents to read aloud with a child, conduct discussions, sign homework) were the ones parents most frequently experienced. The least popular techniques for teachers (i.e., discuss TV shows, use formal contracts) were least frequently experienced by parents. Both teachers' and parents' responses suggested that, although infrequently used now, activities that the teacher designed to use the TV at home may be useful for structuring parent-child discussions and for building children's listening and speaking skills. The similarities in parent experiences and teacher practices lend credibility to the reports of both groups. Parents' experiences with teacher practices confirm that some parents are guided by teachers who follow the precepts of theories emphasizing the separation of school and family responsibilities, whereas others are directed toward cooperative efforts on behalf of the children.

Experiences of Parents with Different Educational Backgrounds. Teacher-leaders whose practices supported cooperation between schools and families reported that they involved parents with many, average, or few years of formal schooling. Teachers who were not leaders in parent involvement, whose practices emphasized the separation of school and home, reported that parents with little education could not or would not help their children with learning activities at home (Becker and Epstein, 1982 [Reading 3.1]). We wanted to check the teachers' reports against the experiences of parents who had different educational backgrounds.

Parents' reports of their involvement in learning activities at home are shown in Table 3.10. The top half of the table presents the responses of parents with little schooling, average schooling, and advanced schooling. The bottom half groups parents by the teachers' leadership in the use of parent involvement. We see, in the top panel, that, in general, parents with less formal education reported significantly more frequent requests from teachers than did parents with average or advanced education. The bottom panel shows that the differences in reports from parents with different levels of education were significant only for parents with children in classrooms of teachers who were not leaders in the use of parent involvement. In classrooms of teachers who were leaders, parents at all educational levels reported about equally frequent requests by teachers to conduct learning activities at home.

The same pattern was found in separate analyses of each type of parent involvement activity, including reading, discussions, contracts, informal games, worksheets, and signing homework. The differences in the reports from low- and high-educated parents were significant only in classrooms of teachers who were not leaders in using parent involvement practices.

The reports from parents clarify and extend the earlier information from teachers on their use of parent involvement with differently educated parents. According to parents, teachers who were leaders in the use of parent involvement practices established more equitable programs, involving parents regardless of their educational backgrounds. Teachers who were not leaders in parent involvement did not try to reach all parents. They may have seen little need to approach parents whose

TABLE 3.10   Parents Reporting Frequent Use by Teachers of 12 Parent
Involvement Techniques, by Parents' Education and Teachers' Leadership

	% of Parents Reporting Zero, Some or Many Techniques Used Frequently		
	Zero	Some (1–4)	Many (5+)
Parent education[a]			
High	23	40	37
Average	15	39	46
Low	16	30	54
	$\chi^2 = 25.98$; p < .34 (N.S.)[b]		
Parent education/teacher leadership[a]			
High/leader	6	42	52
High/not leader	25	40	35
Average/leader	9	35	56
Average/not leader	17	40	43
Low/leader	18	26	56
Low/not leader	17	31	52
	χ^2 (teacher leader) = 4.55; p < .34 (N.S.)[b]		
	χ^2 (teacher not leader) = 18.45; p < .001[b]		

a Low education includes parents with some high school education (N = 240); average education includes parents with a high school diploma (N = 462); high education includes parents with at least some college education and beyond (N = 543).

b χ^2 tests were conducted to determine the independence or association of parents' education with reports of teacher requests for frequent parent involvement for all parents, parents with children in classrooms of teacher-leaders, and parents with children in classrooms of teachers who were not leaders. Parents' reports were independent of their education only in teacher-leaders' classrooms.

children were doing well in school or parents who helped their children at home without directions from the teacher. Children of parents with less formal education often do less well in school than other children, need more help at home, and have parents who do not know how to help without guidance from the teacher. Teachers may ask these parents to assist their children at home, even when the teachers believe that these parents will not be fully successful in their efforts (Valentine and Stark, 1979).

It could be that parents with less formal education agree more often with survey questions and that the patterns of parents' reports about the frequency of requests reflect response bias associated with educational level. This explanation would be plausible if we looked only at the general reports from parents by educational level. However, in the classrooms of teacher-leaders, parents of all educational levels reported about equal frequency of teachers' requests for involvement, an unbiased pattern of responses.

Effects of Involvement on Parents

Does it matter to parents whether teachers' practices emphasize separation or cooperation with families? There is little research on whether teachers' efforts have any measurable effects on the parents who are involved. It has been left up to the teacher to decide—often in the absence of information—whether to invest time in parent involvement practices.

Regression analyses were conducted to determine whether teacher leadership affected parents' reactions to teachers' efforts and parents' evaluations of teachers' merits. The analyses included other variables that have been found to influence teacher practices of parent involvement: three measures of the teaching situation: grade level, teacher quality as rated by the principal, and teacher education (highest degree); two measures of student characteristics: classroom performance in reading and math and racial composition of the class; and two characteristics of parents: educational level and extent of parent involvement at the school. Because more active parents, those with more formal education, and parents of more advanced students may pressure teachers to use more parent involvement, these variables are taken into account in the statistical analyses, and their effects on parent reactions are examined. Although these cross-sectional data do not show causality, this model is used to identify potentially important independent effects of teacher practices on parent reactions that can be reexamined in longitudinal studies.

Table 3.11 summarizes how teacher practices of parent involvement affected parents' awareness of teachers' policies, knowledge of the child's program, and evaluations of teachers' merits. We compare the effects on parents of three measures of teacher leadership: (1) teachers' reputations as leaders in parent involvement (from principals' ratings); (2) parents' consensus (at the classroom level) that the teacher is a frequent user of the 12 techniques of parent involvement; and (3) parents' consensus (at the classroom level) that the teacher frequently communicates with parents by note, phone, memo, conference, or conversation at school. On each of these measures, teacher practices fall along a continuum from low to high interaction and cooperation with families. Table 3.12 should be read in conjunction with Table 3.11 and contains corresponding statistics of the contribution of each of the three measures of teacher leadership to the explained variance of each measure of parent reactions.

Parents' Awareness of Teacher Practices

Three items measured parents' awareness of teachers' practices. Parents were asked whether the teacher worked hard at getting parents excited about helping their child at home, whether they received most ideas for home learning from the teacher, and whether the teacher made it clear that they should help their child with homework.

Efforts of Teachers. All three measures of teacher leadership had independent effects on parents' estimates of teachers' efforts, as shown in column 1 of Table 3.11. Of the three measures, teachers' frequent use of learning activities at home had the most dramatic impact (ß = .695) on parents' reports that teachers work hard to interest and excite them in helping their children at home.

In Table 3.12, rows 1–3 inform us about how the measures of teacher leadership and the other variables in the regression model explain—uniquely and in combination—parents' reports that the teacher works hard to involve parents. The figures in the far right-hand column show that routine communications from the teacher to the family explained 9 percent of the variance after all other variables in the model were accounted for. The other variables—especially grade level, racial composition, and parents' education—contributed more than 40 percent of the explained variance after routine communications were accounted for.

The figures in the middle column of rows 1–3 indicate that parents' actual experiences with learning activities at home explained 18 percent of the variance in reports that the teacher works hard, after all other variables were accounted for. Other variables in the model added little information (4 percent of the explained variance) after teacher practices were taken into account.

The facts from Tables 3.11 and 3.12 reveal a strong link between parents' actual experiences with teacher practices of parent involvement and parents' awareness that the teacher works hard to interest and excite parents in their children's education.

Ideas from Teachers. Parents received most ideas for home-learning activities from teachers who were rated by principals or by parents as leaders in parent involvement practices, as shown in column 2 of Table 3.11. Teachers' use of home learning activities (ß = .787) was a more important mechanism for obtaining ideas from teachers than was the teacher's reputation for leadership in parent involvement (ß = .268) or the teacher's use of other, general types of school-to-home communications (ß = .216).

The corresponding rows 4–6 of Table 3.12 show how the three measures of teacher leadership explain parents' receipt of ideas for home learning activities. The variance that teacher practices of parent involvement explained (23 percent) was from four to eight times the variance explained by the other measures of teacher leadership, after all other variables were taken into account.

Encouragement from Teachers. Parents believed they should help when teachers frequently asked them to help (ß = .603). Neither the teachers' reputations as leaders (ß = .081) nor routine communications (ß = .150) significantly affected parents' beliefs that they should help their child on school activities at home.

In Table 3.12, rows 7–9 display the dramatic differences in the contributions of the three measures of teacher leadership to the explained variance in parents' beliefs that they should help at home. Teachers' practices explained 14 percent of the variance after all other variables were accounted for. The other variables added only 9 percent to parents' beliefs that they should help after teacher practices of parent involvement in learning activities were accounted for. In contrast, the other variables contributed 42–54 percent to the explained variance of beliefs that parents should help after routine communications or teacher reputation were accounted for.

TABLE 3.11 Effects on Parents' Reactions and Evaluations of Three Measures of Teacher Leadership in Parent Involvement at Classroom Level (Standardized Regression Coefficients)*

	Parents' Reactions				Parents' Evaluations	
Measure of Teacher Leadership	Teacher Works Hard to Interest Parents	Teacher Gives Many Ideas to Parents	Parents Think They Should Help	Parents Know More about School Program	Positive Interpersonal Skills	Excellence of Teaching Skills
Reputation as a leader[a]	.243**	.268*	.081	.065	.251*	.274*
Parents' (classroom) reports of teacher's use of parent involvement	.695**	.787**	.603**	.406**	.712**	.728**
Parents' (classroom) reports of teacher's use of other communication	.356**	.216	.150	.231*	.373**	.581**
Other consistently significant variables	Grade, Race[b], Parent education	Grade[b], Parent education[b]	Grade, Race, Parent education[b]	Grade, Race[b], Parent education		

*N = 82. Standardized regression coefficients are reported so that comparisons of effects across measures can be made. Effects model included these independent variables all at the classroom level: grade level, principal rating of teacher overall quality; teacher's highest degree (measures of the teaching situation); performance level of students, racial composition of students (measures of student population); parents' education composition, degree of parent activity at school (measures of parent factors).

a Reputation is the confirmation by principals of the teachers' leadership in the frequent use of parent involvement practices.

b Not a significant variable when parents' agreement with teachers is the measure of teacher's leadership.

* Significant at the .05 level.

** Significant at or beyond the .01 level.

TABLE 3.12 Contribution of Three Measures of Teacher Leadership to Explained Variance in Parents' Reactions and Evaluations*

Parents' Reactions and Evaluations	Row	R^2 a	Teacher's Reputation as Leader in Parent Involvement	Parents' (Classroom) Reports of Teacher Use of Parent Involvement	Parents' (Classroom) Reports of Teacher Use of Other Communication
Teacher works hard to interest and excite parents	1	$R^2(a)$	11	69	20
	2	$R^2(b)$	5	18	9
	3	$R^2(c)$	49	4	43
Teacher gives many ideas to parents	4	$R^2(a)$	8	30	10
	5	$R^2(b)$	6	23	3
	6	$R^2(c)$	18	13	13
Parents think they should help	7	$R^2(a)$	2	60	15
	8	$R^2(b)$	1	14	2
	9	$R^2(c)$	54	9	42
Parents know more about child's program	10	$R^2(a)$	2	43	17
	11	$R^2(b)$	0	6	3
	12	$R^2(c)$	42	7	30
Parents' ratings of teacher's interpersonal skills	13	$R^2(a)$	6	9	12
	14	$R^2(b)$	6	19	10
	15	$R^2(c)$	9	20	7
Parents' ratings of excellence of teaching skills	16	$R^2(a)$	10	22	28
	17	$R^2(b)$	7	20	24
	18	$R^2(c)$	14	16	13

% of Variance Explained by:

* Equations included the following independent variables, all at the classroom level: measure of teacher leadership in parent involvement; grade level, teacher overall quality, teacher's highest degree (measures of the teaching situation); performance level of students, racial composition of students (measures of student population); parents' education composition, degree of parent activity at school (measures of parent factors).

a $R^2(a)$ refers to the explained variance of the measure of teacher leadership before any other independent variables are entered in the equation. $R^2(b)$ refers to the explained variance of the measure of teacher leadership after all other independent variables are entered in the equation. $R^2(c)$ refers to the explained variance of all other independent variables after the measure of teacher leadership in parent involvement is entered in the equation. $R^2(a) + (c)$ equals the total variance explained.

Effects on Parents' Knowledge about School

Parents feel competent when they know what the school is doing, can help their children through the program, or can request changes to improve activities. But many parents do not understand the instructional program and cannot act in the child's interest as an advocate or mediator between the school and the family.

In this survey, parents reported whether they "understood more this year than [they] did last year about what [their] child is being taught in school." Parents increased their understanding about school most when the teacher frequently used parent involvement practices (ß = .406) and when the teacher frequently communicated with the family (ß = .231), as reported in Table 3.11, column 4. Principals' estimates of teacher leadership did not affect parents' knowledge about the instructional program (ß = .065).

Rows 10–12 in Table 3.12 show that 6 percent of the variance in improved parent understanding about school instruction was explained uniquely by parents' experiences with teacher practices of parent involvement, after all other measures were accounted for. In contrast, little was uniquely explained by other types of school-to-home communications (3 percent) or the reputation of the teacher (0 percent).

Parents of children in lower grades, in predominantly black classes, and in classes with predominantly less-formally-educated parents also reported that they understood more about the school program than they had in prior years. It is reasonable that parents with younger children or with less formal education themselves need more information than do other parents about instructional programs. The findings also reflect teachers' efforts to reach and teach parents of young students, educationally disadvantaged students, or other high-risk students. Rubin, Olmsted, Szegda, Wetherby, and Williams (1983) found that mothers in urban areas who were involved in activities at school or with a home visitor changed most in their behavior toward their children and in their opinions about themselves. Intervention programs often make special efforts to reach low-achieving children and less-formally-educated parents to involve them in learning activities at home (Safran and Moles, 1980). What is important in our findings is that teachers' frequent use of parent involvement practices improved parents' knowledge about their child's instructional program, after the grade level, racial composition, and parent education composition of the classroom were taken into account. Also, teachers' use of these practices mitigated the disadvantages typically associated with race, social class, and grade level.

The Importance of Grade Level

The most consistently important variable in these analyses of parents' reactions to teacher practices was the grade level of the student. Parents with children in lower elementary grades reported significantly more frequent teacher use of parent involvement, more frequent communications from school to family, and more frequent participation at the school. Certain practices occurred more frequently at the lower grade levels: reading aloud or listening to the child read, giving spelling or math drills, and playing learning games. Other techniques were used more with older children:

entering contracts and signing homework. Still others were used about equally with children at all grade levels: discussing school with children at home.

Parents with children in grades 1, 3, and 5 felt differently about their participation in parent involvement activities. Parents of older elementary children more frequently said that they did not have enough training to help their children in reading and math activities at home. They reported that they helped their children but that they felt less confident about their help. This expressed inadequacy was significant even after parent education was taken into account. There was, then, less use by teachers and less self-confidence of parents in helping children in the upper grades.

Compared with parents of first or third graders, fewer parents of fifth grade students said that the teacher worked hard to involve parents or gave them many ideas for home-learning activities. It may be more difficult for teachers to involve parents of older students in learning activities because the abilities and needs of children in the upper grades are more diversified and the academic content is more complex. The data show, however, that when teachers of any grade level involve parents frequently in home-learning activities, they can positively affect the parents' awareness of the teachers' efforts and knowledge about the school program.

Effects on Parents' Evaluations of Teachers' Merits

Parents evaluated teachers on two dimensions, interpersonal skills and professional merit. Parents were asked to judge the quality of their interpersonal contacts with the teacher by rating five positive characteristics (cooperation, friendliness, respect, trust, and warmth) and five negative characteristics (conflict, misunderstanding, distance, lack of concern, and tenseness). An index was constructed of the number of positive minus the number of negative ratings. Parents were also asked to rate the teacher on overall teaching quality on a six-point scale from poor to outstanding. The last two columns of Table 3.11 indicate that all three measures of teacher leadership—teachers' reputations, parents' experiences with frequent use of teacher practices of parent involvement, and parents' reports of other school-to-home communications—had significant positive effects on parental ratings of teachers' interpersonal skills and professional merit. Most dramatically, parents gave high marks to teachers for interpersonal skills ($ß = .712$) and overall teaching quality ($ß = .728$) if the teachers frequently used parent involvement practices.

In Table 3.12, rows 13–15 report that teacher practices of parent involvement added 19 percent to the explained variance in parents' ratings of interpersonal skills after all other variables in the model were taken into account, more than three times the unique contribution of teachers' reputational leadership and about twice the contribution of routine school-to-home communications with parents. The figures in rows 16–18 indicate that teachers' practices and other kinds of communications are about equally important, explaining 20–24 percent of the variance in parents' ratings of overall teaching quality.

These findings suggest that, in general, teacher practices of parent involvement maximize cooperation and minimize antagonism between teachers and parents and enhance the teachers' professional standing from the parents' perspective. Most parents (94 percent) disagreed with the statement that "it is not the teacher's business" to show parents how to help their child learn at home. When teachers frequently used home-learning activities, parents rated them as more skillful teachers. Because these analyses are based on classroom-level averages from reports of the parents of all children in the classroom, the results do not reflect personal favoritism in the relationships of a few parents and teachers.

The analyses reported in Tables 3.11 and 3.12 treated each of the three measures of teacher leadership in separate equations. In other analyses, the measures were considered simultaneously to determine whether teacher practices of parent involvement continued to affect parents' reactions and evaluations, after other school-to-home communications were taken into account. For each measure of awareness of teachers' efforts, improved parental knowledge, and ratings of teachers' merits, the positive effects of parent involvement practices continued after school-to-home communications were accounted for. In contrast, except for the ratings of overall merit, the positive effects of school-to-home communications disappeared after the teachers' actual classroom practices of parent involvement were taken into account. Although communications from school to home are important, they do not have as consistently strong links to parent reactions as practices of parent involvement in learning activities at home.

In other analyses, we found that parent activity at the school did not significantly affect parents' reactions to the school program or evaluations of the teachers' merits (Epstein, 1984). Involvement of some parents at the school requires a different investment from teachers from involvement of all parents in learning activities at home. Involvement of parents at school may help teachers or administrators fulfill their teaching and other duties, but it does not affect most parents' attitudes toward and reactions to the school or teacher.

SUMMARY AND DISCUSSION

This survey of parents revealed some important facts about parents' attitudes toward public elementary schools and reactions to teachers' practices of parent involvement.

Facts

Parents of children in Maryland's elementary schools had, in general, positive attitudes about their public elementary schools and teachers. They believed the schools were generally well-run, comfortable places for parents to visit and assist and that the goals of the teachers were similar to the goals that the parents had for their children.

Despite generally positive attitudes, parents believed the schools could do more to involve them in learning activities to help their children at home.

Surprisingly large numbers of parents were excluded from some of the most basic, traditional communications from the school, such as specific memos, conversations, phone calls, or conferences with teachers about their child's progress, problems, or programs in school.

Few parents were involved at school. A few parents in a classroom sometimes assisted the teacher, but the number of active parents at school did not affect the attitudes or knowledge of all of the parents who were not—and often could not be—active at the school.

Parents' education did not explain their experiences with parent involvement unless teacher practices were taken into account. In the classrooms of teachers who were leaders in the use of parent involvement, parents at all educational levels said they were frequently involved in learning activities at home. In other teachers' classrooms, parents with less formal schooling reported more frequent requests than did other parents to help their child at home. Teacher-leaders conducted more equitable programs, reaching all or most parents as part of their teaching philosophy and instructional strategy. Other teachers did not as often involve parents with more formal education. Their selective use of parent involvement, however, was more often built on negative expectations of a parent's and, possibly, a child's ability to succeed.

Fewer and fewer teachers helped parents become involved as the students advanced through the elementary grades. Thus, parents' repertoires of helping skills are not developed and improved over the school years, and they tend to taper off or disappear as the child progresses through school.

Parents were aware of and responded positively to teachers' efforts to involve them in learning activities at home. Parents with children in the classrooms of teachers who built parent involvement into their regular teaching practice were more aware of teachers' efforts, received more ideas from teachers, knew more about their child's instructional program, and rated the teachers higher in interpersonal skills and overall teaching quality. Teachers' practices had consistently strong and positive effects on parent reactions to the school program and on parent evaluations of teachers' merits for parents at all educational levels, net of all other variables. Teacher practices of parent involvement had more dramatic positive links to parents' reactions than general school-to-home communications or parent assistance at the school.

Implications for Parents and Teachers

What do these research findings mean to teachers' policies and practices of parent involvement? We found interesting differences in whether parents thought the teacher wanted them to help their children (i.e., that they should help), whether they thought they had enough training to help their children in reading and math (i.e., that they could help), whether they actually spent time assisting and supervising homework and learning activities at home (i.e., that they do help), and whether they said they could spend more time helping their children at home (i.e., that they could help if given directions by the teacher).

Parents think they should help if the teachers give them learning activities to do at home. Other kinds of communications, from teachers' and principals' ratings of teachers' reputations, did not make parents think that they should help with home-learning activities.

Parents' feelings that they can help (i.e., that they have adequate training to help their children with reading and math) are based primarily on their own education and their children's grade level. More parents said they could help if they had more education or if their children were in the lower elementary grades where parents needed less specialized knowledge to help the children.

Despite differences in parents' feelings about their ability to help, most parents do help. Only 8 percent of the parents reported they never helped their child with reading and math skills during the school year, whether or not they were asked to do so by the teacher. Over 85 percent of the parents spent 15 minutes or more helping their children on homework activities when asked to do so by the teacher. Most parents reported, also, that they could help more (up to 44 minutes, on the average) if the teacher showed them what to do.

The differences in whether parents believe they should help, can help, do help, and could help suggest strategies for organizing programs of parent involvement. For example, if teachers want parents to think that they should help, then they must demonstrate this with an active program of parent involvement in learning activities at home. Teachers may design or select daily or weekly activities for parents to do with their children at home. These may be skills individualized for each student's needs, general skills for review and practice, or special activities that extend learning.

If teachers want parents to feel confident that they can help, they (and the school administrators) must organize and conduct workshops for parents on how to help in reading, math, and other subjects. With or without workshops, teachers need materials that are clear and easy to follow to prove quickly to parents that they can help. As Ogbu (1974) points out, parents' lack of knowledge does not mean lack of interest. Workshops or special instruction may be less necessary with well-educated parents who feel confident about helping their children with reading and math and who readily ask teachers questions about how to help (Litwak and Meyer, 1974). Parents of younger children tend to feel that they can help, but the parents of older students (including many well-educated parents) may need clear and sequential guidance from teachers. Special assistance to build and maintain confidence of parents with children in the upper elementary grades is especially important.

Because many parents do help whether or not they are asked, teachers who are not already using parent involvement techniques should consider how to mobilize this available resource more effectively. Because parents say they could help more if shown how, teachers need to consider ways to organize home-learning activities to help more parents make productive use of the time they could spend helping their children.

Teachers can work as individuals, with colleagues on grade-level teams, or in other groups to develop trial programs to increase parents' involvement in learning activities at home, improve parents' understanding of the school program, and encourage home-learning activities that build on the common goals parents and teachers hold. Basic features of these programs should include clear objectives of short- or long-term activities, clear instructions for parents, and information that tells parents how the activity fits into the teacher's instructional program. Procedures should be devised that permit parents to call or contact the teacher or some other knowledgeable representative to ask questions about how to help or to comment on the child's progress or problems with the activity. Systematic follow-up of parents' efforts must occur to determine whether the activities were completed and how successfully. There should be opportunities for parents to suggest activities or changes in the parent involvement techniques.

When teachers use parent involvement activities, are they fulfilling or shirking responsibility? Grasping at brass rings or grasping at straws? Displaying strengths or displaying weakness? These findings suggest that from the parents' perspective, teachers' use of parent involvement in learning activities at home is a teaching strength. Frequent use of parent involvement results in larger collections of ideas for parents to use at home, increased understanding by parents of school programs, and higher ratings of teacher quality.

Ideas about the opposing theories of school and family relations have most often been discussed from the school's or teacher's point of view. This study contributes an interpretation of school and family relations from the parents' perspective. Parents' reports did not reflect deep conflict and incompatibility between the schools and families. On the contrary, they responded favorably to programs that stressed the cooperation of schools and families to help their children succeed in school. Teachers who included the family in the children's education were recognized by parents for their efforts and were rated higher than other teachers on interpersonal and teaching skills. Parents' reports suggest that teachers control the flow of information to parents. By limiting communications and collaborative activities, teachers reinforce the boundaries that separate the two institutions.

The message from parents is that almost all parents can be involved in learning activities at home. The message for teachers is that many parents help their children, with or without the teacher's instruction or assistance, and many would benefit from directions and ideas from the teacher that could be useful for the child's progress in school. These results from this study raise many questions for new research at the elementary and secondary levels on the benefits and disadvantages for parents, teachers, and students of cooperation or separation of families and schools.

REFERENCES

Becker, H. J. (1982). *Parents' responses to teachers' parent involvement practices*. Paper presented at the annual meeting of the American Educational Research Association in New York.

Becker, H. J., and J. L. Epstein. (1982). Parent involvement: A study of teacher practices. *Elementary School Journal* 83: 85–102. (Reading 3.1).

Bronfenbrenner, U. (1979). *The ecology of human development*. Cambridge, MA: Harvard University Press.

Epstein, J. L. (1984). School policy and parent involvement: Research results. *Educational Horizons* 62: 70–72.

Epstein, J. L., and H. J. Becker. (1982). Teacher practices of parent involvement: Problems and possibilities. *Elementary School Journal* 83: 103–113. (Reading 3.2).

Gallup, G. H. (1982). Gallup poll of the public's attitudes toward the public schools. *Phi Delta Kappan* 63: 37–50.

———. (1983). Gallup poll of the public's attitudes toward the public schools. *Phi Delta Kappan* 64: 33–47.

Goodlad, J. I. (1983). A study of schooling: Some findings and hypotheses. *Phi Delta Kappan* 64: 465–470.

Gordon, I. (1979). The effects of parent involvement in schooling. In R. S. Brandt (Ed.), *Partners: Parents and schools* (pp. 4–25). Alexandria, VA: Association for Supervision and Curriculum Development.

Keesling, J. W., and R. Melaragno. (1983). Parent participation in federal education programs: Findings from the federal programs surveys phase of the study of parent involvement. In R. Haskins (Ed.), *Parent education and public policy* (pp. 230–256). Norwood, NJ: Ablex.

Klein, M. F., K. A. Tye, and J. E. Wright. (1979). A study of schools: Curriculum. *Phi Delta Kappan* 60: 244–248.

Leichter, H. J. (1974). *The family as educator*. New York: Teachers College Press.

Litwak, E., and H. J. Meyer. (1974). *School, family and neighborhood: The theory and practice of school-community relations*. New York: Columbia University Press.

Mager, G. (1980). Parent relationships and home and community conditions. In D. R. Cruickshank, *Teaching is tough* (pp. 153–198). Englewood Cliffs, NJ: Prentice-Hall.

Morrison, G. S. (1978). *Parent involvement in the home school and community*. Columbus, OH: Merrill.

National Commission on Excellence in Education. (1983). *A nation at risk*. Washington, DC: Government Printing Office.

National Task Force on Education for Economic Growth. (1983). *Action for excellence*. Denver: Education Commission of the States.

Ogbu, J. V. (1974). *The next generation: An ethnography of education in an urban neighborhood*. New York: Academic Press.

Olmsted, P. P., M. J. Wetherby, H. Leler, and R. I. Rubin. (1982). *Parent perspectives on home-school relationships in a compensatory education program*. Paper presented at the annual meeting of the American Educational Research Association in New York.

Parsons, T. (1959). The school class as a social system: Some of its functions in American society. *Harvard Educational Review* 29: 297–318.

Rich, D., and C. Jones. (1977). *A family affair: Education*. Washington, DC: Home and School Institute.

Robinson, J. L. (1979). Another perspective on program evaluation: The parents speak. In E. Zigler and J. Valentine (Eds.), *Project Head Start: A legacy of the war on poverty* (pp. 467–476). New York: Free Press.

Rubin, R. I., P. P. Olmsted, M. J. Szegda, M. J. Wetherby, and D. S. Williams. (1983). *Long-term effects of parent education follow-through program participation*. Paper presented at the annual meeting of the American Educational Research Association in Montreal.

Safran, D., and O. Moles. (1980). *Home-school alliances: Approaches to increasing parent involvement in children's learning in upper elementary and junior high schools*. Washington, DC: National Institute of Education. Mimeographed.

Sowers, J., C. Lang, and J. Gowett. (1980). *Parent involvement in the schools: A state of the art report*. Newton, MA: Education Development Center.

Valentine, J., and E. Stark. (1979). The social context of parent involvement in Head Start. In E. Zigler and J. Valentine (Eds.), *Project Head Start: A legacy of the war on poverty* (pp. 291–313). New York: Free Press.

Waller, W. (1932). *The sociology of teaching*. New York: Russell & Russell.

Weber, M. (1947). *The theory of social and economic organization*. New York: Oxford University Press.

Williams, D. L., Jr. (1983). *Parent perspectives regarding parent involvement at the elementary school level*. Paper presented at the annual meeting of the American Educational Research Association in Montreal.

Zill, N., and J. L. Peterson. (1982). Learning to do things without help. In L. M. Laosa and I. E. Sigel (Eds.), *Families as learning environments for children* (pp. 343–374). New York: Plenum.

Single Parents and the Schools:
Effects of Marital Status on Parent
*and Teacher Interactions**

INTRODUCTION

The one-parent home is one of the major family arrangements of schoolchildren today. Over 15 million children live in one-parent homes, most in mother-only homes and most as a result of separation or divorce. From a total of about 62 million children overall, the number in one-parent homes is an important and growing subgroup of children in the country. Each year over 1 million children under the age of 18 have parents who divorce. In the United States in 1986, 25 percent of the households with children under 18—about one in four—were single-parent homes (U.S. House of Representatives, 1986).** Membership in one-parent homes is greater for black children, with approximately half of all black children under 18 years old in one-parent homes (U.S. Bureau of the Census, 1982). It is estimated that more than 50 percent of all children born after 1980 will live with only one parent for at least three school years before reaching the age of 18. Most will live in poor, female-headed households (Furstenburg, Nord, Peterson, and Zill, 1983; Garbarino, 1982; Glick, 1979; Masnick and Bane, 1980).

In earlier times, single-parent homes were atypical; now they are common. This contrast raises many questions about the effects of single-parent homes on the members of the family. Much has been written about single parents, their children, their numbers, and their problems, but little research has focused on how single parents and their children fit into other social institutions that were designed to serve "traditional" families. When children are in school, the family and school are inexorably linked. Because of this linkage, changes that occur in families must be accommodated by responsive changes in schools.

* By Joyce L. Epstein. This research was supported by Grant NIE-G-83-0002 from the National Institute of Education (now the Office of Educational Research and Improvement) of the U.S. Department of Education. The opinions expressed by the author do not necessarily reflect the position or policy of the OERI, and no official endorsement by the agency should be inferred. An earlier version of the paper was presented at the annual meeting of the American Sociological Association in 1984. The author is grateful to Henry Jay Becker, John Hollifield, Linda Gottfredson, and Gary Natriello for their helpful comments on earlier drafts. Originally published in M. T. Hallinan, D. M. Klein, and J. Glass, eds., *Change in Societal Institutions* (New York: Plenum, 1990), 91–121. Reprinted with permission.

** In 2009, the statistics were similar, with 25 percent of children in single-parent homes (U.S. Census Bureau, 2009).

THEORETICAL PERSPECTIVES

Schools and families are overlapping spheres of influence on student learning and development (Epstein, 1987 [Reading 2.1]). The model of overlapping spheres of influence recognizes that there are some practices that schools and families conduct separately but there are other practices that can best be conducted as partners. This view is in contrast to a long-standing alternative perspective that emphasizes the separateness of these institutions.

An Emphasis on Separateness

One perspective on institutions and their relationships emphasizes the importance of their separate contributions to society. This view assumes, for example, that school bureaucracies and family organizations are most efficient and effective when their leaders maintain independent goals, standards, and activities (Parsons, 1959; Waller, 1932; Weber, 1947). Institutions that are separate and nonoverlapping give little consideration to the ideas or histories of the other groups, or to their common or interlocking aims or goals, until there are problems or trouble. This is, in effect, a "conflict resolution" model, requiring interventions and interactions only when necessary to solve serious problems.

An Emphasis on Overlapping Spheres of Influence

A social-organizational perspective is offered as the basis for research on schools and families (Epstein, 1987) and other inter-institutional connections that influence the education of children (Epstein, 1989). In this model, the key, proximate environments that educate and socialize children are shown as spheres of influence that can, by design, overlap more or less in their goals, practices, messages, and resources for students. Major "forces" are considered in the model, including (1) time, to account for changes in the ages and grade levels of students and the influence of the historic period, and (2) the philosophies, policies, and practices of each institution. These forces affect the nature and extent of "overlap" of families and schools. The model integrates and extends the ecological approach developed by Bronfenbrenner (1979); the educational insights of Leichter (1974); the sociological studies of schools and communities of Litwak and Meyer (1974); the theory of institutions and individuals of Coleman (1974); and a long tradition of sociological research on school and family environments (Coleman et al., 1966; Epstein and McPartland, 1979; McDill and Rigsby, 1973; and others).

The model of overlapping spheres of influence recognizes the interlocking histories of institutions that educate and socialize children and the changing and accumulating skills of the individuals in them as the basis for studying connections that can benefit children's learning and development. This, in effect, is a "conflict prevention" model in which institutions invest resources in shared goals (such as student success) to prevent or reduce tensions and problems that could require later, more costly treatment.

These two theoretical perspectives are reflected in the practices of two types of teachers and may influence their interactions with single and married parents. Some teachers believe that families and schools have different responsibilities that can best be accomplished separately and independently. These teachers may make greater distinctions in their opinions about the effectiveness of single and married parents if they view single parents as lacking the resources needed to carry out family responsibilities. Other teachers believe families and schools overlap in their interests and share responsibilities for the education and socialization of their children. They may make fewer distinctions between single and married parents if they view all parents as important contributors to their children's education.

Opinions differ about whether schools and teachers should be informed about parents' marital status or changes in family structure. Some argue that teachers are biased against children from one-parent homes. They suggest that teachers negatively label children of divorced or separated parents, explain children's school problems in terms of the family living arrangement rather than in terms of their own teaching practices or the children's individual needs, or assume parental inadequacies before the facts about parents' skills are known (Hetherington, Camara, and Featherman, 1981; Laosa, 1983; Lightfoot, 1978; Ogbu, 1974; Santrock and Tracy, 1978; Zill, 1983). This view sets schools and families apart as separate spheres of influence, with families expected to cope on their own with changes and problems.

Others argue that schools should be informed about parental separation or divorce because teachers provide stability and support to children during the initial period of family disruption, can be more sensitive to children's situations when discussing families, and can organize special services such as after-school care for children that may be needed by single parents and working mothers (Bernard, 1984). This view brings schools and families together, as overlapping spheres of influence with both institutions working together to help children cope and succeed even during times of family changes and stress.

The discrepant opinions of how much families should inform schools about family circumstances are each supported by parents' accounts of experiences with teacher bias or with teacher understanding and assistance (Carew and Lightfoot, 1979; Clay, 1981; Keniston et al., 1977; National Public Radio, 1980; Snow, 1982). There are few facts from research, however, about whether and how teachers respond to students in differently structured families or about how single parents perceive, react to, and become involved with their children's schools and teachers.

Many early studies of single parents and some recent ones are based on a "deficit theory" of family functioning. One major underlying assumption of this work is that the number of parents at home is the key variable for understanding effective parenting and children's success. That is, two parents are always better than one. For example, research based on the "confluence" model argues that crucial intellectual resources are lacking when the father is absent from the home (Zajonc, 1976). This theory asserts that the father is the family member with the highest intelligence and is the educational leader of the family. This is a mechanical theory that has not been well supported in research. It establishes an unequivocal bias against one-parent homes, putting mothers in a fixed and forced subordinate position, discounting the roles most mothers play in encouraging their children's education, and ignoring the roles of schools in guiding family activities that concern school skills.

Other research on single parents based on their deficiencies assumes that one-parent homes are unstable, uncaring, and lacking in emotional and academic support or strong role models for students' school success. The number of parents at home is the measure used as a proxy for numerous alleged weaknesses of the one-parent home. Studies that include the number of parents as the only explanatory variable establish a theoretical bias against one-parent homes, without allowing for alternative explanations.

An alternative view focuses more on the strengths and potentials of families, with attention to the activities and practices of families of any size or structure. The underlying assumption of these studies is that the quality of family practices and processes explains more about parental effectiveness than marital status or the number of parents at home (Barton, 1981; Blanchard and Biller, 1971; Dokecki and Maroney, 1983; Hetherington and Camara, 1984; Marotz-Bader, Adams, Bueche, Munro, and Munro, 1979; Shinn, 1978).

The change from a "deficit model" to a "strengths model" has led to more thoughtful studies of children and parents in one- and two-parent homes. Models improved in small steps, from the simple, mechanistic theories of the impact of the number of parents in the home on student achievement or behavior to only slightly more complex theories that added family socioeconomic status (SES) as another explanatory variable. Researchers recognized that because low education and low income often accompany single-parent status, it is necessary to measure these family conditions as well as marital status so that negative effects due to SES or education are not attributed falsely to single-parent status (Barton, 1981; Kelly, North, and Zingle, 1965; Milne, Myers, Rosenthal, and Ginsburg, 1986; Svanum, Bringle, and McLaughlin, 1982). For example, children from well-educated, middle-class, one-parent homes often perform as well as similar children from two-parent homes.

The improvements in knowledge gained from added measures of social class were not enough, however, to clarify the inconsistent results across studies of the effects of marital status on parent behavior and student achievement. Two relatively stable status variables—marital status and socioeconomic status—do not adequately represent the dynamics of family life that contribute to student achievement or success in school (Hanson and Ginsburg, 1986). Even studies of family contacts with the schools (Baker and Stevenson, 1986; Garfinkle and McLanahan, 1986; Kurdek and Blisk, 1983; Milne et al., 1986; Zill, 1983) have ignored the roles of teachers in increasing or reducing differences in parent and student behavior in differently structured families. A comprehensive review by Newberger, Melnicoe, and Newberger (1986) calls for studies of the many factors that may ameliorate and explain the negative conditions of one-parent homes.

The present study looks at some potentially important variables that allow schools to change to meet the changing needs and conditions of families. We use data from teachers and parents to examine family and school connections in one-

and two-parent homes. We focus on the children's living arrangements that affect the day-to-day communications and interactions between schools and families and compare single and married parents' reports of the frequency of teacher requests for parent involvement. We look next at teachers' reports of the quality of involvement of the single and married parents of their students and the teachers' reports of the quality of the homework completed by children from one- and two-parent homes. We also examine other similarities and differences among single and married parents concerning their children's education.

This study asks the following questions: Do single and married parents differ in their perceptions of teacher practices of parent involvement? Are teachers' perceptions of parents and children influenced by family living arrangements? How does marital status relate to other family and school connections? How do teachers' practices reflect the two theoretical perspectives that emphasize separateness or overlap of families and schools? To address these questions, we introduce, first, a simple model that improves upon earlier research on single parents by accounting for marital status, parent education, and teacher leadership to study parent-teacher exchanges and evaluations. We then test a more complete model that places marital status, parent education, and teachers' practices of parent involvement in a fuller social context with other characteristics of the school and family.

This exploration includes many measures of family structure and processes, student characteristics, and school and classroom structures and processes. The independent variables, introduced as they are needed in different analyses, include family size, race, and parent education; student grade level, classroom ability, and behavior in class; teacher leadership in parent involvement, teaching experience, and overall teaching quality; and specific teacher-parent interactions about the child as a student.

Unlike earlier research that often used "special problem" samples to study single-parent families (Shinn, 1978), this is a purposely stratified sample of a normal population of teachers in grades 1, 3, and 5 in public schools in the state of Maryland and the parents and students in their classes (Becker and Epstein, 1982b [Reading 3.1]). Importantly, the data from teachers, parents, and students are linked so that particular teachers' practices can be connected with the parents and students in those teachers' classrooms (Epstein, 1986 [Reading 3.4], 1991 [Reading 3.7]). Few previous studies measured the behavior and attitudes of single parents about the schools their children attend (Clay, 1981), and none linked the teachers' and parents' practices and evaluations of each other.

SAMPLE, VARIABLES, AND APPROACHES

Surveys of teachers, principals, parents, and students in sixteen Maryland school districts were conducted in 1980 and 1981. Approximately 3,700 first-, third-, and fifth-grade teachers and their principals in 600 schools were surveyed (Becker and Epstein, 1982b; Epstein and Becker, 1982 [Reading 3.2]). From the original sample, 82 teachers were selected who varied in their use of parent involvement in learning activities at home. They were matched by school district, grade level, years of teaching experience, and characteristics of their student populations. Among the teachers, 17 were confirmed by their principals as strong leaders in the use of parent involvement activities. In all, the 82 teachers ranged along a useful continuum from high to low use of parent involvement, with the "confirmed leaders" making the most concerted use of parent involvement in learning activities at home.

Data were obtained on the achievements and behaviors of the students in the 82 classrooms. The parents of the children in the 82 teachers' classrooms were surveyed about their attitudes toward and experiences with parent involvement. In all, 1,269 parents responded to a questionnaire by mail, a response rate of 59 percent. Of these, 24 percent were single parents, close to the national average of 22 percent at that time (U.S. Bureau of the Census, 1982).

We requested that the parent complete the survey who was most familiar with the child's school and teacher. More than 90 percent of the respondents were female, and virtually all of the single-parent respondents were female. Thus, the research provided a sizable, useful sample of single and married mothers whose children were in the classrooms of teachers who differed in their use of practices to involve parents in their children's education.

The categories of one-parent home and single parent come from the parents' reports that only one parent lives at home with the child. We prefer the terms *single-parent home*, *one-parent home*, or *mother-only/father-only home* to describe the living arrangements of schoolchildren, rather than the pejorative terms *broken home*, *broken family*, or even *single-parent family*. A single-parent home or a two-parent home may or may not be "broken" by marital, economic, or emotional conditions (Engan-Barker, 1986; Kamerman and Hayes, 1982). To determine if a family is "broken" requires clear and sensitive measures in addition to the structure of living arrangements.

A child in a single-parent home may have contact with two parents, although only one parent lives at home when the child leaves for and returns from school. The data do not include information on the cause, choice, or duration of single-parent status, nor can we identify calm or troubled relations in two-parent homes. Our sample does not permit us to study one-parent homes where the father is the custodial parent or the parent most knowledgeable about the child's schooling. These are important characteristics of families that should be included in new studies of family and school effects (Bane, 1976; Eiduson, 1982; Furstenburg and Seltzer, 1983; Shinn, 1978; Zill, 1983).

Parent involvement refers to 12 techniques that teachers used to organize parental assistance at home, including reading, discussions, informal learning games, formal contracts, drill and practice of basic skills, and other monitoring or tutoring activities. For example, the most popular teachers' practices included asking parents to read to their child or listen to the child read, using books or workbooks borrowed from the school to help children learn or practice needed skills, discussing schoolwork at home, and using materials found at home to teach needed skills. Eight other activities were also used by teachers to establish parents at home as partners with the teacher to help students do better in school. The activities, patterns of teacher use, effects on parents, and effects on student achievements are discussed fully in Readings 3.1, 3.2, 3.4, and 3.7 and in other publications (Becker and Epstein,

1982a, b; Epstein and Becker, 1982; Epstein, 1986; Epstein, 1991). Parent involvement in learning activities at home is a complex, difficult type of teacher-parent partnership (Leler, 1983), but these practices include more parents and have greater positive impact than other forms of parent involvement that occur at the school building (see Epstein, 1986). Involvement in learning activities at home is the type of involvement that most parents would like the schools to increase and improve across the grades (Dauber and Epstein, 1989 [Reading 3.6]; Epstein, 1990).

Characteristics of Parents

Table 3.13 shows the characteristics of the single and married parents in the sample. There are several important differences. Significantly more single parents are black, reside in the city, have fewer years of formal schooling, work full-time, or have one child. The single and married parents are about equally represented by children in the three elementary school grades (1, 3, and 5) in the study and in the classroom of teachers who were confirmed by their principals as leaders in the use of parent involvement. These characteristics of the Maryland sample are similar to those expected from a national sample of single parents.

We use mothers' education rather than both parents' education, or either parent's occupation, to minimize missing or incomparable data for one- and two-parent homes. Mothers' education has traditionally been used as an indicator of family SES (Sewell and Hauser, 1975). As others have noted, mother's education may be more pertinent than other measures for studying family influences on children's school behaviors or as an indicator of a parent's familiarity with school organizations and procedures (Baker and Stevenson, 1986; Milne et al., 1986). In one-parent homes especially, mother's education may be a more important and accurate indicator of school-like activities at home than other occupational or economic indicators.

RESULTS: PARENTS' REPORTS OF TEACHERS' PRACTICES OF PARENT INVOLVEMENT

Parents were asked to report how often their child's teacher requested their involvement in the 12 home-learning activities described previously. Parents' reports of teachers' requests ranged from 0 to 12 frequently used activities, with a mean score of 4.1 and a standard deviation of 3.4. Table 3.14 shows how single and married parents' reports differed by the formal educational level of the parents and by the teachers' leadership in parent involvement. The mean scores and tests of comparisons in the first column of the table show that, compared to married parents, single parents reported significantly more requests from teachers to assist with learning activities at home (4.80 vs. 3.76). The figures in the second column indicate that among single parents, high- and low-educated single parents reported about equally frequent requests from teachers for parent involvement. Among married parents, however, less-educated married parents reported more frequent requests from teachers for parent involvement than did more-educated married parents (4.16 vs. 3.30).

TABLE 3.13   Characteristics of Single and Married Parents

	Single Parents (N = 273) Percentage Respondents	Married Parents (N = 862) Percentage Respondents
Race[a]		
White	35.9	73.2
Black	64.1	26.8
Residence[a]		
City	57.1	27.7
County/suburb	42.9	72.3
Parent education[a]		
Some high school (or less)	27.1	15.2
High school diploma	32.2	38.4
Some college	28.1	22.6
Bachelor's degree	4.8	10.5
Some graduate school (or more)	7.8	13.3
Employment[a]		
No work outside home	33.1	40.4
Part-time work	11.3	21.4
Full-time work	55.6	38.2
Family size[a]		
0 siblings	24.9	11.7
1–2 siblings	58.3	71.9
3–4 siblings	15.0	14.2
Over 4 siblings	1.8	2.2
Extended family (other adults)	23.8	10.2
Grade level of child		
Grade 1	41.8	38.3
Grade 3	27.8	26.9
Grade 5	30.4	34.8
Teacher leadership in parent involvement		
Confirmed leader	27.5	20.4
Not confirmed leader	72.5	79.6

a Chi-square tests yield significant differences in proportions for single and married parents beyond the .001 level.

In the third column, the measure of teacher leadership adds important information about the experiences of parents. Single and married parents with children in the classrooms of teachers who were confirmed by their principals as leaders in parent involvement reported more requests than parents whose children's teachers were not leaders in parent involvement. The differences were especially great between married parents in teacher-leader and nonleader classrooms.

Other comparisons noted in column 4 of Table 3.14 reveal differences in single and married parents' reports about teachers who were not leaders in parent involvement. Highly educated single parents of students in these teachers' classrooms reported significantly more requests than did highly educated married parents (4.47 vs. 3.04). Less formally educated single parents reported significantly more requests than less formally educated married parents (4.73 vs. 3.97).

If we looked only at the differences in involvement by marital status and educational levels in columns 1 and 2 of Table 3.14, we would miss the important link between families and schools due to teachers' practices, reported in column 3. There are two important patterns of results in Table 3.14:

1. Single parents, regardless of their educational level, report more requests from teachers than do married parents to be involved in learning activities at home.
2. According to parents, teachers who are confirmed leaders in parent involvement make more equal requests of all parents, regardless of education and marital status, whereas other, nonleader teachers ask more of single and low-educated parents.

It is not enough, then, to measure only marital status or parent education to explain parents' behavior concerning their children. Research on single parents and the schools must also take into account teachers' practices concerning parents.

Table 3.15 extends the inquiry by introducing other variables that may explain the simple patterns in Table 3.14. The first line of Table 3.15 reports the independent effects of the three variables—marital status, mothers' education, and teachers' practices of parent involvement—that were introduced previously. With the other two variables statistically controlled, single parents, less-educated parents, and parents whose children are in the classrooms of teachers who were leaders report receiving more requests from teachers for their involvement with their children in learning activities at home.

The second line of the table introduces other characteristics of the family, student, and teacher that previous research suggests may also affect parents', teachers', and students' interactions and evaluations of each other. Race clearly helps to explain the effect of single-parent status on parents' reports of teachers' practices. More black parents head one-parent homes in this sample (as in the nation), and black parents report receiving more requests for parent involvement than do white parents, regardless of marital status. These results reflect the practices of the urban district in which most of the black parents in this sample reside. Teachers in the urban district reported that they used more parent involvement practices (Becker and Epstein, 1982a), and the parents' responses verify the teachers' reports. Teachers tend to reach out to parents when children need extra help. The results also may indicate a continuing trend for black parents to let teachers know that they want to be involved in their children's education (Lightfoot, 1978).

The regression coefficients in line 2 of Table 3.15 show that six variables in addition to race have significant independent effects on parents' reports of their

TABLE 3.14 Parents' Reports of Frequency of Teachers' Use of Parent Involvement (12 Techniques) (Means, Standard Deviations, and Test Statistics from Multiple Comparisons of Mean Scores of Single vs. Married, Low- vs. High-Educated Parents, and Parents of Children in Classrooms of Confirmed Leader vs. Nonleader Teacher in Parent Involvement)

	Family Structure			Parent Education[a]			Teacher Leadership in Parent Involvement			Other Significant Mean Score Comparisons
Parents' reports of teachers' use of 12 parent involvement techniques	Single parent	x̄ s.d N	4.80* 3.53 (246)	Low	x̄ s.d. N	4.87 3.42 (144)	Confirmed leader	x̄ s.d. N	5.22 3.50 (41)	Single vs. married, low education in nonleader classroom (x̄ = 4.73* vs. 3.97)
							Nonleader	x̄ s.d. N	4.73 3.39 (103)	
				High	x̄ s.d. N	4.70 3.70 (102)	Confirmed leader	x̄ s.d. N	5.28 3.52 (29)	Single vs. married, high education in nonleader classroom (x̄ = 4.47* vs. 3.04)
							Nonleader	x̄ s.d. N	4.47 3.77 (73)	
	Married parent	x̄ s.d. N	3.76 3.23 (801)	Low	x̄ s.d. N	4.16* 3.30 (433)	Confirmed leader	x̄ s.d. N	4.76* 3.24 (103)	Low vs. high education, married parents, in nonleader classroom (x̄ = 3.97* vs. 3.04)
							Nonleader	x̄ s.d. N	3.97 3.30 (330)	
				High	x̄ s.d. N	3.30 3.08 (368)	Confirmed leader	x̄ s.d. N	4.63* 3.04 (60)	
							Nonleader	x̄ s.d. N	3.04 3.03 (308)	

a Parent education is high if the respondent attended or graduated from post-secondary school; low if parent attended or graduated from high school only.

* T-test significant at or beyond the .05 level.

experiences with teachers' practices of parent involvement. Parents report significantly more frequent requests for involvement from teachers if they have less formal education (PARED), have younger children (GRADE), have children whose teachers are leaders in parent involvement (TCHLDR), or whose teachers use specific strategies to build close family-school relationships. These interpersonal practices are: Parent feels comfortable and welcomed at school (PARCOMF); parent reports that teacher knows child's individual learning needs (TKNOCH); and teacher talks to parent about how to help the child at home (TALKHLP). Separate analyses show that these variables are about equally important for black and white parents.

The percentage of variance explained in parents' reports of teachers' requests for their involvement improved markedly—from 5 to 30 percent—when we added detailed information on the actual practices that bring schools and families together. It is important, too, that even with teacher-parent interpersonal practices accounted for, teacher leadership in the use of specific practices continues to significantly affect parents' reports of their experiences with learning activities at home.

In previous research, the limited focus on marital status veiled the importance of other variables that influence parents' interactions with their children and their children's schools. Single and married parents' reports about their experiences with parent involvement are influenced by many family and school factors, not simply by the categorical label of marital status.

Single and married parents' reports about what teachers ask them to do at home are one indicator of their treatment by the schools. The next two sections explore teachers' evaluations of single and married parents' abilities to conduct the requested activities and the quality of the homework that their children do.

TEACHERS' REPORTS OF SINGLE AND MARRIED PARENTS' HELPFULNESS AND FOLLOW-THROUGH

Parents' marital status is believed to influence teachers' opinions of parents and their children. Teachers were asked to rate the helpfulness and follow-through on home-learning activities of the parents of each student and the quality of homework completed by each student. In contrast to the laboratory study of Santrock and Tracy (1978), which asked teachers to rate hypothetical children from one- and two-parent homes, our questions were designed not to call teachers' attention to the students' living arrangements when the teachers rated parents and students. We were interested in whether, in a natural environment, teachers' evaluations were affected by parent marital status (identified by the parent) or other family characteristics and practices. It is likely that elementary school teachers are aware of family living arrangements from information provided by parents on emergency cards each year, from informal exchanges with parents or children about their families, or from discussions with other teachers. However, our method for collecting information did not ask teachers to base their evaluations on the explicit criteria of the children's living arrangements.

TABLE 3.15 Effects of Measures of Family, Student, and Teacher Characteristics on Parents' Reports about Teacher Practices of Parent Involvement

	FAMSTR[a]	PARED	TCHLDR	PARWORK	RACE	SEX	ACH	DISC	GRADE	YEARST	TQUAL	PARCOMF	TKNOCH	TALKHLP	R^2
Initial model	−.116*[b]	−.108*	.126*												.048
Full model	−.006	−.102*	.071*	.046	−.238*	−.029	−.055	.003	−.114*	.053	.072*	.071*	.238*	.211*	.286
	(−.138)[c]	(−.133)	(.141)	(.047)	(−.306)	(−.039)	(−.134)	(.020)	(−.195)	(−.029)	(.130)	(.114)	(.328)	(.296)	

a Variables are FAMSTR = one- or two-parent homes; PARED = schooling from less than high school (0) to graduate school (5); TCHLDR = teacher's leadership or lack of parent involvement confirmed by principal (0–4); PARWORK = no work (0) or work (1) outside home by parent; RACE = black (0) or white (1); SEX = male (0) or female (1); ACH = reading and math skills ranked by teacher (0–6); DISC = low (−1) or high (+1) discipline problems; GRADE = student's grade in school management (0–4); YEARST = years of teaching experience; TQUAL = principal rating of teacher overall quality; PARCOMF = parent feeling comfortable and welcome at school (1–4); TKNOCH = parent report that teacher knows child's individual learning needs (1–4); TALKHLP = teacher talked to parent about how to help child at home (0/1). The outcome "parents' reports" refers to the number and frequency of teacher requests for up to 12 techniques to involve parents in learning activities at home.

b Standardized regression coefficients are reported. N = 1,135.

c Zero-order correlations are in parentheses.

* Indicates coefficient is significant at or beyond the .01 level.

Table 3.16 presents teachers' evaluations of the quality of involvement of single and married parents. The ratings of parent helpfulness and follow-through on learning activities at home ranged from +1 to –1, with a mean of .18 and a standard deviation of .70, indicating that, on average, parents were perceived as neither particularly helpful nor inept, but more were helpful (35 percent) than not (17 percent). The comparisons in the first column of Table 3.16 show that teachers rated married parents significantly higher than single parents on helpfulness and follow-through on home-learning activities. The second column shows that single and married parents with more formal education received higher ratings from teachers on helpfulness. The difference in ratings was significant between low- versus high-educated married parents (.267 vs. .437) and single versus married high-educated parents (.302 vs. .437).

The third column offers important information about how teachers' practices affected their evaluations of parents' helpfulness. Teachers who were leaders in the use of parent involvement practices rated single parents with less formal education significantly higher in helpfulness and follow-through at home than did teachers who were not leaders in parent involvement (.366 vs. .102). The same pattern appeared for teachers' ratings of single, highly educated parents (.483 vs. .234). Married parents with less formal education were considered less responsible assistants than more-educated married parents, regardless of the teachers' leadership in the use of parent involvement.

If we had not included teachers' practices in our comparisons, we would conclude that, regardless of education, teachers rate single parents as less cooperative and less reliable than married parents in assisting their children at home. What we see instead is that teachers' own practices of parent involvement influence their ratings of the quality of parental assistance. Teachers' frequent use of parent involvement practices reduces or eliminates the teachers' differential evaluations of single and married parents.

Table 3.17 presents the results of the initial and the better specified models. The regression analyses summarized in the table show, as did the previous tables of simple mean scores, that there are significant independent effects of marital status, parents' education, and teacher leadership in parent involvement on teachers' ratings of their students' parents on helpfulness and follow-through at home. Although each variable has significant, independent effects, the three-variable model explains only 4 percent of the variance in teachers' reports of parent helpfulness.

On the second line of the table, other measures of family, student, and teacher characteristics that have been found important in other research on family-school connections are added to the basic model. These variables increase the explained variance to 23 percent. Most dramatically, student achievement levels and behavior in school affect how teachers evaluate the students' parents. Teachers rate parents more positively if their children are high achievers or well behaved in school. Children may be successful in school because their parents help them at home, parents may give more help to children who are good students and easy to assist, or good students may be assumed by teachers to have good parents as part of a school/home "halo" effect.

Teachers of younger children and more experienced teachers tend to rate parents higher in helpfulness and follow-through than do other teachers. Teachers of the lower elementary grades tend to use more parent involvement techniques, and more experienced teachers may be more aware and appreciative of how the efforts of parents supplement the efforts of teachers (Becker and Epstein, 1982a, b). Although race was not an important variable overall for explaining teachers' ratings of parent helpfulness, separate analyses of black and white parents revealed that marital status remained a modest but significant influence on the teachers' ratings of white parents but not of black parents. White, single parents were rated lower in helpfulness and follow-through than white, married parents, with all other variables in the model statistically controlled. White, single parents may be the most distinct group in terms of their marital status because proportionately more white than black parents are married.

These analyses show that it is mainly the characteristics and needs of students—not the simple category of parental marital status—that best explain teachers' evaluations of parents. However, teachers' leadership remained an important influence on their ratings of parents, even after all other variables were statistically taken into account. Teachers who frequently use parent involvement techniques in their regular teaching practice acknowledge the help they receive and view single and married parents in a more positive light than do other teachers. When teachers involve parents in their children's schoolwork on a regular basis, creating more family and school "overlap," they tend to report that the amount and quality of help from single parents is comparable to that of married parents. When teachers use frequent activities as part of their teaching practice, they help parents build better skills to assist their children at home. At the same time, these activities may help teachers develop more positive expectations and appreciation of parents. Teachers who keep schools and families more separate and do not make parents part of their regular teaching practice tend to promote the stereotype of single parents. They rate single parents' assistance and follow-through on learning activities at home lower in quality and quantity than that provided by married parents.

TEACHERS' REPORTS OF THE QUALITY OF HOMEWORK BY CHILDREN FROM ONE- AND TWO-PARENT HOMES

Teachers were asked to rate the quality of homework completed by each of their students. Researchers identified the children from one- and two-parent homes from data provided by parents. Teachers identified the students who were homework "stars" and homework "problems." Scores on the quality of homework ranged from +1 to −1, with a mean of −.01 and a standard deviation of .64, indicating that, on average, students were neither particularly outstanding nor inferior, with about equal numbers of homework stars (20 percent) and homework problems (21 percent). Teachers' ratings of children's homework are shown in Table 3.18 according to children's living arrangements in one- or two-parent homes, parents' education, and their teachers' leadership in the use of parent involvement.

TABLE 3.16 Teachers' Estimates of the Quality of Parents' Responses to Requests for Involvement (Means, Standard Deviations, and Test Statistics from Multiple Comparisons of Mean Scores of Single vs. Married, Low- vs. High-Educated Parents, and Parents of Children in Classrooms of Confirmed Leader vs. Nonleader Teacher in Parent Involvement)

Teachers' estimates of parents' helpfulness	Family Structure	Parent Education[a]	Teacher Leadership in Parent Involvement		$\bar{x}$	s.d.	N	Other Significant Comparison of Means
	Single parent — $\bar{x}$ .227, s.d. .712, N (255)	Low — $\bar{x}$ .174, s.d. .733, N (149)	Confirmed leader		.366*	.733	(41)	Single vs. married, low education ($\bar{x}$ = .302 vs. .437*)
			Nonleader		.102	.723	(108)	
		High — $\bar{x}$ .302, s.d. .679, N (106)	Confirmed leader		.483*	.738	(29)	Single vs. married, low education in nonleader classroom ($\bar{x}$ = .102 vs. .260*)
			Nonleader		.234	.647	(77)	Single vs. married, high education in nonleader classroom ($\bar{x}$ = .234 vs. .436*)
	Married parent — $\bar{x}$ .346*, s.d. .660, N (813)	Low — $\bar{x}$ .267*, s.d. .693, N (438)	Confirmed leader		.291	.736	(103)	Low vs. high education, married, in nonleader classroom ($\bar{x}$ = .260 vs. .436*)
			Nonleader		.260	.680	(335)	
		High — $\bar{x}$ .437*, s.d. .608, N (375)	Confirmed leader		.444	.690	(63)	
			Nonleader		.436	.591	(312)	

a Parent education is high if the respondent attended or graduated from post-secondary school; low if parent attended or graduated from high school only.

* T-test significant at or beyond the .05 level.

185

TABLE 3.17 Effects of Measures of Family, Student, and Teacher Characteristics on Teachers' Reports about Parent Helpfulness and Follow-Through on Learning Activities at Home

	FAMSTR[a]	PARED	TCHLDR	PARWORK	RACE	SEX	ACH	DISC	GRADE	YEARST	TQUAL	PARCOMF	TKNOCH	TALKHLP	R^2
Initial model	.072*[b]	.131*	.135*												.039
Full model	.042	.049*	.136*	.014	-.034*	-.044	-.343	.205	-.099*	.104	-.009*	.041*	.029*	.056*	.226
	(.081)[c]	(.131)	(.121)	(.027)	(.039)	(-.025)	(.365)	(-.256)	(-.079)	(.079)	(.051)	(.092)	(.069)	(.050)	

a Variables are FAMSTR = one- or two-parent homes; PARED = schooling from less than high school (0) to graduate school (5); TCHLDR = teacher's leadership or lack of parent involvement confirmed by principal (0–4); PARWORK = no work (0) or work (1) outside home by parent; RACE = black (0) or white (1); SEX = male (0) or female (1); ACH = reading and math skills ranked by teacher (0–6); DISC = low (−1) or high (+1) discipline problems; GRADE = student's grade in school management (0–4); YEARST = years of teaching experience; TQUAL = principal rating of teacher overall quality; PARCOMF = parent feeling comfortable and welcome at school (1–4); TKNOCH = parent report that teacher knows child's individual learning needs (1–4); TALKHLP = teacher talked to parent about how to help child at home (0/1). The outcome "parents' reports" refers to the number and frequency of teacher requests for up to 12 techniques to involve parents in learning activities at home. N = 1,135.

 b Standardized regression coefficients are reported.

 c Zero-order correlations are in parentheses.

 * Indicates coefficient is significant at or beyond the .01 level.

The first column of Table 3.18 shows that students from two-parent homes were more often rated as "homework stars" and were less often viewed as "homework problems" than were students from one-parent homes. The measures in the second column show that these ratings were linked to parent education. Children whose mothers had little formal education were rated lower in the quality of their homework than other children in one-parent homes (.057 vs. −.101 for more- vs. less-educated mothers) and in two-parent homes (.157 vs. .050). Family socioeconomic status in column 2 of Table 3.18 helps to explain teachers' evaluations of children in one- and two-parent homes, as has been reported before (Barton, 1981; Laosa and Sigel, 1982; Scott-Jones, 1983).

Teachers' practices of parent involvement are taken into account in column 3 of the table. Teachers who were not leaders in parent involvement held significantly lower opinions of the quality of homework of children from single-parent homes than of those from married-parent homes, at both levels of parent education. The results suggest that children from less-educated, single-parent families face disadvantages in school that may be exacerbated by teachers' lack of leadership in organizing parent involvement in learning activities at home.

If estimates of homework quality reflect student achievement in general, children from one- and two-parent homes in teacher-leader classrooms should have more similar grades and achievement test scores, after other important characteristics are taken into account. In classrooms of teachers who are not leaders in parent involvement, children from one-parent homes may do less well than children from two-parent homes in their report card grades and other school achievements.

The regression analyses in Table 3.19 show how teachers' ratings of the quality of students' homework are influenced by other parent, teacher, and student characteristics. On the first line of the table, the familiar three-variable model shows that marital status and parent education have significant independent effects on teacher ratings of student homework. Students from one-parent homes or whose parents have less formal education are given lower ratings on homework quality. Teacher leadership in parent involvement is not a significant independent influence on teachers' ratings of students, after the other variables are accounted for. The basic model, however, explains only 2 percent of the variance in teacher ratings of student homework.

The second line of Table 3.19 shows that 24 percent of the variance in teacher ratings of student homework is explained by other measures. The most important variables are the work students do in class and their classroom behavior. Brighter students—whatever their behavior or other characteristics—were rated higher on the quality of their homework, and well-behaved students—whatever their ability or other characteristics—were given higher ratings on homework quality. Black students were rated significantly higher in homework quality, after achievement level and behavior were taken into account. Even with these highly influential variables taken into account, the quality of homework of students from two-parent homes was still rated slightly higher by some teachers than that of students from one-parent homes.

Several researchers have questioned whether teachers base children's grades and other ratings on criteria other than performance and whether their ratings reflect bias against children from single-parent homes (Barton, 1981; Boyd and Parish,

TABLE 3.18 Teachers' Estimates of the Quality of Children's Homework Completion (Means, Standard Deviations, and Test Statistics from Multiple Comparisons of Mean Scores by Family Structure, Family Education, and Teacher Leadership in Parent Involvement)

	Family Structure	Parent Education[a]		Teacher Leadership in Parent Involvement		Other Significant Comparison of Means
Teachers' estimates of students' homework completion	Single parent	x̄ -.035 s.d. .604 N (255)	Low	x̄ -.101 s.d. .601 N(149)	Confirmed leader	x̄ .073* s.d. .648 N (41)	Single vs. married, low education (x̄ = .101 vs. .050*)
					Nonleader	x̄ -.167 s.d. .572 N (108)	Single vs. married, low education in nonleader classroom (x̄ = -.167 vs. .045*)
			High	x̄ .057* s.d. .599 N (106)	Confirmed leader	x̄ .207* s.d. .620 N (29)	
					Nonleader	x̄ .001 s.d. .585 N (77)	
	Married parent	x̄ .346* s.d. .660 N (813)	Low	x̄ .050* s.d. .640 N(438)	Confirmed leader	x̄ .068 s.d. .630 N (103)	
					Nonleader	x̄ .045 s.d. .644 N (335)	
			High	x̄ .157* s.d. .589 N(375)	Confirmed leader	x̄ .254 s.d. .595 N (63)	
					Nonleader	x̄ .138 s.d. .587 N (312)	

a Parent education is high if the respondent attended or graduated from post-secondary school; low if parent attended or graduated from high school only.

* T-test significant at or beyond the .05 level.

TABLE 3.19 Effects of Family, Student, and Teacher Characteristics on Teacher's Ratings of Children on Their Homework Completion

	FAMSTR[a]	PARED	TCHLDR	PARWORK	RACE	SEX	ACH	DISC	GRADE	YEARST	TQUAL	PARCOMF	TKNOCH	TALKHLP	R^2
Initial model	.085*[b]	.106*	.039												.021
Full model	.068*	.022	.042	−.024	−.107*	.058	.392*	.183*	−.007*	.050*	−.038	−.024	.058*	.055*	.236
	(.097)[c]	(.114)	(.026)	(−.005)	(.007)	(.132)	(.412)	(−.259)	(.001)	(.035)	(.021)	(−.005)	(.105)	(.018)	

a Variables are FAMSTR = one- or two-parent homes; PARED = schooling from less than high school (0) to graduate school (5); TCHLDR = teacher's leadership or lack of parent involvement confirmed by principal (0–4); PARWORK = no work (0) or work (1) outside home by parent; RACE = black (0) or white (1); SEX = male (0) or female (1); ACH = reading and math skills ranked by teacher (0–6); DISC = low (−1) or high (+1) discipline problems; GRADE = student's grade in school management (0–4); YEARST = years of teaching experience; TQUAL = principal rating of teacher overall quality; PARCOMF = parent feeling comfortable and welcome at school (1–4); TKNOCH = parent report that teacher knows child's individual learning needs (1–4); TALKHLP = teacher talked to parent about how to help child at home (0/1). The outcome "parents' reports" refers to the number and frequency of teacher requests for up to 12 techniques to involve parents in learning activities at home.

b Standardized regression coefficients are reported. N = 1,135.

c Zero-order correlations are in parentheses.

* Indicates coefficient is significant at or beyond the .01 level.

1985; Hammond, 1979; Lightfoot, 1978). Our data show that teachers base their judgments about the quality of children's homework mainly on the performance of the children, rather than on other unrelated criteria. There is little bias evident against children in one-parent homes. When they do occur, biased reports are more likely by teachers who have less contact with parents. If teachers do not ask for and guide parent involvement, single parents and their children are assumed to be less qualified than married parents and their children.

The simple lines of inquiry in Tables 3.14, 3.16, and 3.18 suggest that there may be important statistical interactions of marital status, parent education, and teachers' leadership in parent involvement in their effects on school and family communications. For example, when we graph the mean scores in these tables (not shown here), we see that teacher leadership matters more in determining teachers' ratings of single parents' helpfulness and follow-through on learning activities with their children at home and on their ratings of the homework quality of children in one-parent homes. Parent education matters more for married parents on how teachers rate parents' helpfulness and children's homework. New research is needed on the consequences for student learning of these potentially important interactions.

The full models in Tables 3.15, 3.17, and 3.19 reveal other important patterns. Parents' reports of teachers' practices of parent involvement are influenced by several characteristics of students, teachers, parents, and family-school communications. Teachers' reports of parents are influenced especially by the teachers' interactions with the child in school. It often is said that children are reflections of their parents, but it also seems to work the other way. Parents are evaluated, in part, on the basis of their children's success and behavior in school. Teachers' reports of children are mainly determined by the children's schoolwork. However, even after achievement level is taken into account, some teachers report that children from one-parent homes have more trouble completing homework than do children from two-parent homes. The analyses show clearly that the ratings that parents and teachers give each other are significantly affected by teachers' philosophies and practices of parent involvement.

On a related theme, in the full model we also found that whether or not mothers worked outside the home had no important effect on parents' reports about teachers, teachers' reports about parents, or teachers' reports about the quality of children's homework.

PARENTS' AWARENESS, KNOWLEDGE, AND EVALUATIONS OF TEACHERS

Are single and married parents equally aware of their children's instructional program? Is marital status an important variable for explaining parental receptivity to teachers' requests to help their children? Epstein (1986) shows that teachers' practices influenced parental reactions to their children's teachers and schools. In this reading, we examine whether single and married parents react differently to teachers' efforts to involve and inform parents.

The exploration of previous analyses shows that marital status had no significant effect on whether parents think the child's teacher works hard to get parents "interested and excited about helping at home." Rather, frequent experience with teachers' requests to become involved in learning activities at home had a strong effect on parent awareness of the teacher's efforts. Other variables—less formal education of parents, parents' belief that teachers know the individual needs of their children, and teachers' direct conversations with parents about helping their own child at home—also had significant, independent effects on parents' awareness of teachers' efforts to involve parents.

Similarly, teachers' frequent requests for parent involvement in learning activities at home—not marital status—had strong effects on single and married parents' reports that they get many ideas from teachers about how to help at home; the teacher thinks parents should help at home; they know more about the child's instructional program than they did in previous years; and the teacher has positive interpersonal skills and high teaching quality.

OTHER REPORTS ABOUT SCHOOL FROM SINGLE AND MARRIED PARENTS

Other data collected from parents also help explain some of the results reported in the previous tables.

Single parents reported significantly more often than married parents that they spent more time assisting their children with homework but still did not have the "time and energy" to do what they believed the teacher expected. Single parents felt more pressure from teachers to become involved in their children's learning activities. It may be that their children required or demanded more attention or needed more help to stay on grade level. Or it may be that parents who were separated, divorced, or never married felt keenly their responsibility for their children and the demands on their time. Single parents divide their time among many responsibilities for family, work, and leisure that are shared in many two-parent homes (Glasser and Navarre, 1965; Shinn, 1978).

Requests from teachers for parents to help with home-learning activities may make more of an impression on and may be more stressful for single parents (McAdoo, 1981). Our data show, however, that single parents respond successfully to teachers who involve all parents as part of their regular teaching practice. Like other parents, single parents who were frequently involved by the teacher felt that they increased their knowledge about the child's instructional program. Indeed, teachers who organize and guide home-learning activities may especially help single parents make efficient and effective use of often limited time. When teachers convey uniform expectations and guidance for involvement by all parents, single parents receive an important message about their continuing responsibility in their children's education.

Married parents spent significantly more days in the school as volunteers, as classroom helpers, and at PTA meetings than did single parents. Teachers may be more positive toward parents whom they meet and work with in the school building and classroom. These positive feelings may influence some teachers' ratings of the quality of parental assistance at home. An important fact, however, is that the teacher-leaders—whose philosophy and practices emphasized parent involvement at home—did not give significantly lower ratings to single parents or less-educated parents on their helpfulness or follow-through on home-learning activities, despite those parents' lower involvement at the school building. Because many single parents work full- or part-time during the school day or have other demands on their time that keep them away from school, it is important for teachers to emphasize practices that involve all parents with their children's education at home. If all involvement occurs during school hours, single parents and working parents are excluded from school activities.

There were several measures on which there were no significant differences in the reports of single and married parents. Some common beliefs about single and married parents were not supported statistically. For example, single and married parents gave similar evaluations of the overall quality of their children's teachers, the extent to which the teacher shares the parents' goals for their child, their child's eagerness to talk about school, their child's level of tenseness about homework activities, the appropriateness of the amount and kinds of homework that their children's teachers assigned, and the frequency of most communications (e.g., notes, phone calls, and memos) from the school to the home. These findings support Snow's (1982) conclusion that single and married parents had similar contacts with teachers and similar evaluations of teachers, and that socioeconomic status was more predictive than marital status of parents' contacts with teachers. We show, however, that the SES is not the most important variable. Rather, school and family communications of several types reduce or eliminate the importance of marital status and SES.

Marital status is not significantly related to the severity of discipline problems in class. The belief that children from one-parent homes tend to be disruptive in school may be one of the "myths" that has been perpetuated from earlier studies based on "special problem" populations and from studies that did not include measures of student, family, and teacher characteristics and practices—all of which are more important influences than marital status on children's classroom behavior. In our study, children's disciplinary problems in the classroom are significantly correlated negatively with gender ($r = -.262$), academic achievement ($r = -.147$), and whether the child likes to talk about school at home ($r = -.124$), as might be expected. Male students, low-achieving students, and those who do not like to talk about school or homework with their parents are more likely than other students to be disciplinary problems in class. But parents' marital status is not significantly associated with behavior problems in class ($r = -.056$).

Marital status is not correlated with parents' willingness to help at home, feeling welcome at the school, or reports that someone at home reads regularly with the child. Indeed, single and married parents are remarkably positive about the general quality of their children's elementary schools and teachers (see Epstein, 1986). As in earlier reports by Eiduson (1982), Keniston et al. (1977), and Sanick and Maudlin

(1986), our survey shows that, like married parents, single parents are concerned about their children's education, work with their children, and are generally positive about their children's elementary schools and teachers.

SUMMARY AND DISCUSSION

Researchers have contributed three types of information on single parents. First, descriptive reports offer statistics about single parents and their children. Many reports have focused on the dramatic increase over the years in the prevalence of single parents; the number of children in single-parent homes; racial differences in marital patterns; and the economic disparities of single- versus two-parent homes, especially single-mother homes versus other family arrangements (Bane, 1976; Cherlin, 1981; Newberger et al., 1986; Weitzman, 1985). It is important to continue to document and monitor the trends in separation and divorce, the numbers of children affected, and the emergence and increase of special cases such as teenage single parents (Mott Foundation, 1981) and never-married parents (U.S. Bureau of the Census, 1982).

Second, analytic studies of the effects of family structure on children or parents go beyond descriptive statistics to consider family conditions and processes that affect family members. Research of this type has measured a range of family-life variables, such as socioeconomic status, family history, family practices, and attitudes such as parental commitment to their children (Adams, 1982; Bane, 1976; Epstein, 1983; Furstenburg et al., 1983; Marjoribanks, 1979; Svanum et al., 1982; Zill, 1983). These studies increase our understanding of the dynamics of family life under different social and economic conditions.

Third, integrative, ecological studies of the effects of family structure on children and parents go beyond the boundaries of family conditions to include other institutions that affect family members (Bronfenbrenner, 1979; Epstein, 1987; Leichter, 1974; Litwak and Meyer, 1974; Santrock and Tracy, 1978). These studies show that effects of family structure are, in large part, explained by other variables, including teachers' practices of parent involvement and other measures of family and school interaction.

The present study contributes new knowledge based on data from parents and teachers about single parents and their children's schools.

1. Single parents are not a single group. Single parents are highly diverse in their education, family size, family resources, occupational status, confidence in their ability to help their children, and other family practices that concern their children. The diversity in single-parent homes means that we cannot fully understand families by measuring only the simple category of marital status.

2. There is diversity in teachers' practices that concern families. Some teachers' philosophies and practices lead them toward more positive attitudes about single parents and about how all parents can assist the teacher as knowledgeable partners in their children's education. Some teachers' practices exemplify the theory that families and schools are overlapping spheres of influence for children, whereas other teachers' practices exemplify the belief that families and schools are better off when teachers and parents conduct separate and different activities.

Some teachers involve all or most parents successfully. Other teachers demand more but expect less of single parents and their children. Single parents' abilities to help their children may be affected by the teachers' abilities to inform and direct parents about productive activities for parent involvement at home.

Santrock and Tracy (1978) found that teachers rated hypothetical children from two-parent homes higher on positive traits and lower on negative traits than children from one-parent homes. Levine (1982) reported that teachers had lower expectations for children from one-parent homes. In actual school settings, we found that teachers differed in their evaluations of children from one- and two-parent homes. Teachers tend to rate children from one-parent homes lower on the quality of their homework, and teachers who were not leaders made even greater distinctions between children from one- and two-parent homes.

3. Teacher leadership, not parent marital status, influenced parents' knowledge about the school program and the teachers' efforts. Single and married parents whose children were in the classrooms of teachers who were leaders in parent involvement were more aware of teachers' efforts in parent involvement, improved their understanding of their children's school programs, and rated teachers' interpersonal and teaching skills higher than did parents of children in other teachers' classrooms. Evidence has been accumulating in many studies that daily practices are more important than static measures of family structure for understanding children's experiences. This has often been interpreted to refer to practices that parents might conduct on their own. However, parent involvement in school is not the parents' responsibility alone. Contexts influence practice. Kriesberg (1967) found a neighborhood effect on parents' practices. He noted that disadvantaged single mothers in middle-class neighborhoods gave more educational support to their children than similar mothers in poor neighborhoods. Our study reports a school effect on parents' practices. Teachers' practices that support and guide parents boost the involvement of all parents, including single parents—the same parents that other teachers believe cannot or will not help their children.

4. Research on single parents and their children must include measures of family and school structure and processes that affect the interactions of parents, teachers, and students. Marital status will look more important than it is unless studies include measures of teachers' practices. In this study, teachers' approaches to parent involvement; other teacher, parent, and student characteristics; and specific family-school communications were more important and more manipulable variables than marital status or mother's education for explaining parents' and teachers' evaluations of each other. Studies of school and family connections must go beyond simple structural labels such as marital status and education and include measures of the practices and attitudes of parents, teachers, and students. During the school years, it is necessary to measure the characteristics of all overlapping institutions that influence student behavior and particularly the family and the school. This is especially true for particular outcomes such as student learning and development or parental understanding and practices concerning their children as students.

5. Schools' interactions with families need to change because families are changing. Teachers must consider how they perceive and interact with single parents to minimize bias and maximize the support that all parents give their children. Family members may recover relatively rapidly from the disruption caused by divorce or separation (Bane, 1976; Hetherington, Cox, and Cox, 1978; Zill, 1983). But teachers who favor traditional families may have difficulty dealing with families who differ from their "ideal." Some administrators and teachers still consider the primary, two-parent family as the model by which other families should be judged (Bernard, 1984). The primary family—two natural parents and their children—may be an ideal type, but it is no longer the "typical" family for all school-aged children. In 1980, 63 percent of white children and 27 percent of black children lived in primary families; 14 percent of all white children and 43 percent of all black children lived in one-parent homes with their mothers.* Most of the others lived in "blended" families in which at least one parent had remarried (Hernandez and Meyers, 1986). Demographic trends indicate that the one-parent home will be "the new norm" because over half of all children will live in a one-parent home for some of their school years. During that time, teachers' practices to assist and involve all parents can help reduce single parents' stress about their children's well-being and help children's learning and attitudes about school and homework.

Schools need to change their understanding of single parents to better meet the parents' concerns and children's needs. Most suggestions about how the school should assist single parents and their children focus on providing psychological services, family therapy, discussion groups, or individual counseling for children who experience divorce in their families (Brown, 1980). Although discussion or therapy sessions may help children adjust to family disruptions, this study suggests that a more important general direction is to assist all parents in how to help their children at home in ways that will improve their children's success in school. This includes helping parents make productive use of small amounts of time at home for school-related skills, activities, and decisions.

School policies and practices can minimize or exaggerate the importance of family structure. Although school practices cannot solve the serious social and economic problems that single parents often face, our data show that teachers play a pivotal role in the lives of children from one-parent homes and in their parents' lives as well.

---

* In 2009, about 80 percent of white children, 45 percent of black children, and 65 percent of Hispanic children lived in two-parent homes (U.S. Census Bureau, 2009).

REFERENCES

Adams, B. (1982). *Conceptual and policy issues in the study of family socialization in the United States*. Paper presented at the annual meeting of the American Educational Research Association, New York.

Baker, D. P., and D. L. Stevenson. (1986). Mothers' strategies for children's school achievement: Managing the transition to high school. *Sociology of Education* 59: 156–166.

Bane, M. J. (1976). *Here to stay: American families in the twentieth century*. New York: Basic Books.

Barton, W. A. (1981). *The effects of one-parentness on student achievement*. Unpublished doctoral dissertation, Pennsylvania State University.

Becker, H. J., and J. L. Epstein. (1982a). *Influences on teachers' use of parent involvement*. Report 324. Baltimore: Johns Hopkins University Center for Social Organization of Schools.

———. (1982b). Parent involvement: A study of teacher practices. *Elementary School Journal* 83: 85–102. (Reading 3.1).

Bernard, J. M. (1984). Divorced families and the schools. In J. H. Cansen (Ed.), *Family therapy with school related problems* (pp. 91–101). Rockville, MD: Aspen Systems Corporation.

Blanchard, R. W., and H. B. Biller. (1971). Father availability and academic performance among third-grade boys. *Developmental Psychology* 4: 301–305.

Boyd, D. A., and T. S. Parish. (1985). *An examination of academic achievement in light of familial configuration*. Paper presented at the annual meeting of the American Educational Research Association, Chicago.

Bronfenbrenner, U. (1979). *The ecology of human development*. Cambridge, MA: Harvard University Press.

Brown, B. F. (1980). A study of the school needs of children from one-parent families. *Phi Delta Kappan* 61: 537–540.

Carew, J., and S. L. Lightfoot. (1979). *Beyond bias: Perspectives on classrooms*. Cambridge, MA: Harvard University Press.

Cherlin, A. J. (1981). *Marriage, divorce, remarriage*. Cambridge, MA: Harvard University Press.

Clay, P. L. (1981). *Single parents and the public schools: How does the partnership work?* Columbia, MD: National Committee for Citizens in Education.

Coleman, J. S. (1974). *Power and structure in society*. New York: W. W. Norton.

Coleman, J. S., E. Q. Campbell, C. J. Hobson, J. M. McPartland, A. Mood, F. D. Weinfield, and R. L. York. (1966). *Equal educational opportunity*. Washington, DC: U.S. Government Printing Office.

Dauber, S. L., and J. L. Epstein. (1989). *Parents' attitudes and practices of involvement in inner-city elementary and middle schools*. CREMS Report 33. Baltimore: Johns Hopkins University Center for Research on Elementary and Middle Schools. (Reading 3.6).

Dokecki, P. R., and R. M. Maroney. (1983). To strengthen all families: A human development and community value framework. In R. Haskins and D. Adams (Eds.), *Parent education and public policy* (pp. 40–64). Norwood, NJ: Ablex.

Eiduson, B. T. (1982). Contemporary single mothers. In L. G. Katz (Ed.), *Current topics in early childhood education* (pp. 65–76). Norwood, NJ: Ablex.

Engan-Barker, D. (1986). *Family and education: The concepts of family failure and the role it plays in national educational and family policy—A review of the literature*. Unpublished master's thesis, University of Minnesota.

Epstein, J. L. (1983). Longitudinal effects of person-family-school interactions on student outcomes. In A. Kerckhoff (Ed.), *Research in sociology of education and socialization, Vol. 4* (pp. 101–128). Greenwich, CT: JAI.

———. (1986, January). Reactions of parents to teacher practices of parent involvement. *Elementary School Journal* 87: 277–294. (Reading 3.4).

———. (1987). Toward a theory of family-school connections: Teacher practices and parent involvement across the school years. In K. Hurrelmann, E. Kaufmann, and F. Losel (Eds.), *Social intervention: Potential and constraints* (pp. 121–136). New York: De-Gruyter. (Reading 2.1).

———. (1989). *Schools in the center: School, family, peer, and community connections for more effective middle grade schools and students.* Paper prepared for the Carnegie Task Force for the Education of Young Adolescents. Baltimore: Center for Research on Elementary and Middle Schools, Johns Hopkins University.

———. (1990). School and family connections: Theory, research and implications for integrating sociologies of education and family. *Marriage and Family Review* 15(1/2): 96–126.

———. (1991). Effects on student achievement in reading and math of teachers' practices of parent involvement. In S. Silvern (Ed.), *Advances in reading/language research, Vol. 5: Literacy through family, community, and school interaction* (pp. 261–276). Greenwich, CT: JAI. (Reading 3.7).

Epstein, J. L., and H. J. Becker. (1982, November). Teacher reported practices of parent involvement: Problems and possibilities. *Elementary School Journal* 83: 103–113. (Reading 3.2).

Epstein, J. L., and J. M. McPartland. (1979). Authority structures. In H. Walberg (Ed.), *Educational environments and effects* (pp. 293–312). Berkeley: McCutcheon.

Furstenburg, F. F., Jr., and J. A. Seltzer. (1983). *Encountering divorce: Children's responses to family dissolution and reconstitution.* Paper presented at the annual meeting of the American Sociological Association in Detroit.

Furstenburg, F. F., C. W. Nord, J. L. Peterson, and N. Zill. (1983). The life course of children of divorce: Marital disruption and parental contact. *American Sociological Review* 48: 656–668.

Garbarino, J. (1982). *Children and families in the social environment.* New York: Aldine.

Garfinkle, I., and S. S. McLanahan. (1986). *Single mothers and their children: A new American dilemma.* Washington, DC: Urban Institute Press.

Glasser, P., and E. Navarre. (1965). Structural problems of the one parent family. *Journal of Social Issues* 21: 98–109.

Glick, P. C. (1979). Children of divorced parents in demographic perspectives. *Journal of Social Issues* 35: 170–182.

Hammond, J. M. (1979, November). A comparison of elementary children from divorced and intact families. *Phi Delta Kappan* 61: 219.

Hanson, S. L., and A. Ginsburg. (1986). *Gaining ground: Values and high school success.* Washington, DC: Decision Resources Corporation.

Hernandez, D. J., and D. E. Myers. (1986). *Children and their extended families since World War II.* Paper presented at the annual meeting of the Population Association of America in San Francisco.

Hetherington, E. M., and K. A. Camara. (1984). Families in transition: The process of dissolution and reconstitution. In R. D. Parke (Ed.), *Review of child development research: Vol. 7* (pp. 398–440). Chicago: University of Chicago Press.

Hetherington, E. M., K. A. Camara, and D. L. Featherman. (1981). *Cognitive performance, school learning, and achievement of children for one parent households.* Washington, DC: National Institute of Education.

Hetherington, E. M., M. Cox, and R. Cox. (1978). The aftermath of divorce. In J. H. Stevens Jr. and M. Matthews (Eds.), *Mother-child, father-child relations* (pp. 149–176). Washington, DC: National Association for the Education of Young Children.

Kamerman, S. B., and C. D. Hayes. (1982). *Families that work: Children in a changing world.* Washington, DC: National Academy Press.

Kelly, F. J., J. North, and H. Zingle. (1965). The relation of the broken home to subsequent school behaviors. *Alberta Journal of Educational Research* 11: 215–219.

Keniston, K., and the Carnegie Council on Children. (1977). *All our children: The American family under pressure.* New York: Harcourt Brace Jovanovich.

Kriesberg, L. (1967). Rearing children for educational achievement in fatherless families. *Journal of Marriage and the Family* 29: 288–301.

Kurdek, L. A., and D. Blisk. (1983). Dimensions and correlates of mothers' divorce experiences. *Journal of Divorce* 6: 1–24.

Laosa, L. M. (1983). Parent education, cultural pluralism, and public policy. In R. Haskins and D. Adams (Eds.), *Parent education and public policy* (pp. 331–345). Norwood, NJ: Ablex.

Laosa, L. M., and I. E. Sigel. (1982). *Families as learning environments for children*. New York: Plenum Press.

Leichter, Hope Jensen. (Ed.). (1974). *The family as educator*. New York: Teachers College Press.

Leler, H. (1983). Parent education and involvement in relation to the schools and to parents of school-aged children. In R. Haskins and D. Adams (Eds.), *Parent education and public policy* (pp. 114–180). Norwood, NJ: Ablex.

Levine, E. R. (1982). *What teachers expect of children from single parent families*. Paper presented at the annual meeting of the American Educational Research Association, April, in New York.

Lightfoot, S. L. (1978). *Worlds apart: Relationships between families and schools*. New York: Basic Books.

Litwak, E., and H. J. Meyer. (1974). *School, family, and neighborhood: The theory and practice of school-community relations*. New York: Columbia University Press.

Marjoribanks, K. (1979). *Families and their learning environments: An empirical analysis*. London: Routledge & Kegan Paul.

Marotz-Bader, R., G. R. Adams, N. Bueche, B. Munro, and G. Munro. (1979). Family form or family process? Reconsidering the deficit family model approach. *Family Coordinator* 28: 5–14.

Masnick, G., and M. J. Bane. (1980). *The nation's families: 1960–1990*. Cambridge, MA: Joint Center for Urban Studies of MIT and Harvard University.

McAdoo, H. (1981). *Levels of stress in single black employed mothers of school-aged children*. Washington, DC: Howard University. Mimeographed.

McDill, E. L., and L. Rigsby. (1973). *Structure and process in secondary schools: The academic impact of educational climates*. Baltimore: Johns Hopkins University Press.

Milne, A., D. Myers, A. Rosenthal, and A. Ginsburg. (1986). Working mothers and the educational achievement of school children. *Sociology of Education* 59: 125–139.

Mott Foundation. (1981). *Teenage pregnancy: A critical family issue*. Flint, MI: The Charles Stewart Mott Foundation.

National Public Radio (NPR). (1980, November). *Single parent families*, Parts 1–4, programs 272–275. Washington, DC: National Public Radio.

Newberger, C. M., L. H. Melnicoe, and E. H. Newberger. (1986). *The American family in crisis: Implications for children*. Current Problems in Pediatrics, Volume 16, Number 12. Chicago: Yearbook Medical Publishers.

Ogbu, J. V. (1974). *The next generation: An ethnology of education in an urban neighborhood*. New York: Academic Press.

Parsons, T. (1959). The school class as a social system: Some of its functions in American society. *Harvard Educational Review* 29: 297–318.

Sanick, M. M., and T. Maudlin. (1986). Single vs. 2-parent families: A comparison of mothers' time. *Family Relations* 35: 53.

Santrock, J. W., and R. L. Tracy. (1978). Effects of children's family structure on the development of stereotypes by teachers. *Journal of Educational Psychology* 20: 754–757.

Scott-Jones, D. (1983). *One-parent families and their children's achievement*. Pittsburgh: University of Pittsburgh. Mimeographed.

Sewell, W. H., and R. M. Hauser. (1975). *Occupation and earnings: Achievement in the early career*. New York: Academic Press.

Shinn, M. (1978). Father absence and children's cognitive development. *Psychological Bulletin* 85: 295–324.

Snow, M. B. (1982). *Characteristics of families with special needs in relation to school.* AEL Report Series. Charleston, WV: Appalachian Educational Laboratory.

Svanum, S., R. G. Bringle, and J. E. McLaughlin. (1982). Father absence and cognitive performance on a large sample of six-to-eleven-year old children. *Child Development* 53: 136–143.

U.S. Bureau of the Census. (1982). *Marital status and living arrangements: March 1982.* Current Population Report Series. Washington, DC: U.S. Government Printing Office.

U. S. Census Bureau. (2009). *America's Families and Living Arrangements: 2007.* Washington, DC: U.S. Department of Commerce (P20–56). (Updated reference.)

U.S. House of Representatives. (1986, June 17). *Divorce: A fact sheet.* Washington, DC: Select Committee on Children, Youth, and Families.

Waller, W. (1932). *The sociology of teaching.* New York: Russell and Russell.

Weber, M. (1947). *The theory of social and economic organization.* New York: Oxford University Press.

Weitzman, L. (1985). *The divorce revolution: The unexpected social and economic consequences for women and children in America.* New York: Free Press.

Zajonc, R. (1976). Family configuration and intelligence. *Science* 192: 227–236.

Zill, N. (1983, March). *Perspectives: Mental health of school children from single-parent families.* Paper presented at the National Conference of Single Parents and the Schools, Washington, DC.

Parents' Attitudes and Practices of Involvement in Inner-City Elementary and Middle Schools*

Parent involvement—or school and family connections—is a component of effective schools that deserves special consideration because it contributes to successful family environments and more successful students. Research conducted for nearly 25 years has shown convincingly that parent involvement is important for children's learning, attitudes about school, and aspirations. Children are more successful students at all grade levels if their parents participate at school and encourage education and learning at home, whatever the educational background or social class of their parents.

Most research on parent involvement has focused on parents who become involved on their own, without connecting parents' actions to the practices of their children's teachers. Some research on parent involvement conducted in the late 1980s asks more crucial questions by focusing on the actions of the schools: Can schools successfully involve all parents in their children's education, especially those parents who would not become involved on their own? How can schools involve parents whose children are at risk of failing in school? If schools involve all parents in important ways, are there measurable benefits to students, parents, and teaching practice?

From research we have learned that schools' programs and teachers' practices to involve parents have important positive effects on parents' abilities to help their children across the grades; on parents' ratings of teachers' skills and teaching quality; on teachers' opinions about parents' abilities to help their children with schoolwork at home; on students' attitudes about school, homework, and the similarity of their school and family; and on students' reading achievement (Becker and Epstein, 1982 [Reading 3.1]; Epstein, 1982 [Reading 3.9], 1986 [Reading 3.4], 1991 [Reading 3.7]; Epstein and Dauber, 1991 [Reading 3.3]).

However, few studies focused on schools with large populations of educationally disadvantaged students or hard-to-reach parents (Epstein, 1988a). A recurring theme in some studies is that less-educated parents do not want to or cannot become involved in their children's education (Baker and Stevenson, 1986; Lareau, 1987). However, other research challenges this assumption by showing that some teachers successfully involve parents of the most disadvantaged students in important ways (Clark, 1983; Comer, 1980; Epstein, 1990 [Reading 3.5]; Epstein and Dauber, 1991;

* By Susan L. Dauber and Joyce L. Epstein. The research was supported by grants from the U.S. Department of Education, Office of Educational Research and Improvement (OERI), and by a National Science Foundation Graduate Fellowship awarded to the first author. The opinions expressed do not necessarily reflect the position or policy of the OERI or the NSF, and no official endorsements should be inferred. The authors, listed alphabetically, shared responsibility for this chapter. We are grateful to the parents who participated in the survey and to the teachers and principals who conducted the survey as the first step in a school improvement process. Reprinted with permission. From N. Chavkin, ed., *Families and Schools in a Pluralistic Society* (Albany: State University of New York Press, 1993), 53–71.

Rich, Van Dien, and Mattox, 1979; Rubin, Olmsted, Szegda, Wetherby, and Williams, 1983; Scott-Jones, 1987).

Earlier studies of teachers and parents focused on one level of schooling, either elementary schools (see Becker and Epstein, 1982; Epstein, 1986, 1990, 1991); middle or junior high schools (Baker and Stevenson, 1986; Leitch and Tangri, 1988); or high schools (Bauch, 1988; Clark, 1983; Dornbusch and Ritter, 1988). This study used comparable data from two levels of schooling: elementary and middle grades. The study asked inner-city parents in economically disadvantaged communities how they are involved or want to be involved and how family involvement differs in the elementary and middle grades.

STUDY DESIGN

Eight Title I schools in the Baltimore area were involved in an "action research" program in cooperation with a local foundation. The Fund for Educational Excellence in Baltimore made small grants directly to schools to help teachers increase and improve parent involvement. Teacher representatives for parent involvement from the eight schools attended a two-day summer workshop on school and family connections. They helped design questionnaires for teaches and parents (Epstein and Becker, 1990) for use in each school to identify where schools are starting from on five major types of parent involvement (Epstein, 1987). The teachers were provided with small planning grants to help them distribute and collect the surveys.

Each school was given nontechnical "clinical summaries" of the data from teachers and from parents to help them understand their strengths and weaknesses in parent involvement (Epstein, 1988b; Epstein and Salinas, 1988). The schools used the data to develop action plans for improving parent involvement programs and practices. The teachers who are directing the projects are supported by small grants ($1,000) each year to cover expenses to implement and evaluate the activities they designed.

Data from 171 teachers in these schools on their attitudes and practices of parent involvement were reported in a separate paper (see Epstein and Dauber, 1991 [Reading 3.3]). The data from teachers showed that:

- Teachers generally agreed that parent involvement is important for student success and teacher effectiveness.
- Teachers were more sure about what they wanted from parents than about what they wanted to do for parents. Almost all teachers reported that they expected all parents to fulfill 12 responsibilities, ranging from teaching their children to behave, to knowing what children are expected to learn each year, to helping their children with homework. Few teachers, however, had comprehensive programs to help parents attain these skills.
- Elementary school practices were stronger, more positive, and more comprehensive than those in the middle grades.

- The individual teacher was a key, but not the only, factor in building strong school programs. Analyses of "discrepancy scores" showed that perceived similarities between self and principal, self and teacher-colleagues, and self and parents were significantly associated with the strength of schools' parent involvement programs. Programs and practices were stronger in schools where teachers perceived that they, their colleagues, and parents all felt strongly about the importance of parent involvement.

The reports about parent involvement from teachers in inner-city elementary and middle schools are important but tell only half the story about what is happening in any school. Data from parents are needed to understand fully where schools are starting from and their potential for improving parent involvement practices. This reading combines the data from the parents in all eight schools to study the present practices and patterns of parent involvement in inner-city elementary and middle grades. We examine parents' reports of their attitudes about their children's schools, their practices at home, their perceptions of how the schools presently involve parents, and their wishes or preferences for actions and programs by the schools.

The questionnaires included more than 75 items of information on parent attitudes toward their children's school; the school subjects that parents want to know more about; how frequently the parents are involved in different ways in their children's education; how well school programs and teacher practices inform and involve them in their children's education; what workshop topics they would select; the times of day that parents prefer meetings or conferences at school to take place; how much time their children spend on homework and whether the parents help; and background information about parents' education, work, and family size.

Parents responded in large numbers to the opportunity to give their opinions about their involvement and school practices. More than 50 percent of the parents in each school returned the questionnaires (N = 2,317), a respectable rate of return given that no follow-ups were possible because of school schedules and budget constraints.

The eight Title I inner-city schools, five elementary and three middle schools, were selected at random from sets of similar Title I schools that serve children and families who live in public housing projects, rental homes and apartments, and privately owned homes in economically disadvantaged neighborhoods. Table 3.20 outlines the characteristics of the parent population. Although parents of both elementary- and middle-grade students are well represented, the sample includes almost twice as many single parents as the national average, more parents without high school diplomas, and larger family sizes than in the general population.

It is possible, of course, that the 50 percent who did not respond are among the least involved or lowest in literacy. They include parents whose children did not bring the questionnaires home or did not return them, parents who chose not to answer questionnaires, or parents who cannot read well enough to answer the questions. The surveys were written, rewritten, and tested for use in Title I schools. More than 30 percent of the parents who returned the surveys did not complete high school; more than 40 percent are single parents. Thus, despite some under-representation

TABLE 3.20   Characteristics of the Sample of Parents*

	Percent
Elementary school parents (N = 1,135)	49.0
Middle school parents (N = 1,182)	51.0
Single parents	43.4
Working outside home (full- or part-time)	63.7
Did not complete high school	31.0
Completed high school	40.6
Beyond high school	28.3
Average family size (adults and children)	4.4
Parent rating of student ability:	
Top student	7.6
Good student	32.4
Average/OK student	35.2
Fair student	21.8
Poor student	3.0

* N = 2,317.

of the most educationally disadvantaged families in these schools, the sample is highly diverse and highly representative of the schools.

Despite some limitations of the sample, this study offers unique comparable data from parents with children in elementary and middle schools. Indeed, because of the educational and economic disadvantages of the sample, we can put questions of parent involvement to a stringent test.

MEASURES

Parents' Reports of Their Involvement

Parents rated the frequency of their involvement in conducting 18 different practices included under five major types of parent involvement: parenting and supervising at home, communicating with the school, volunteering at the school, conducting learning activities at home, and participating in PTA or parent leadership activities. The main measures of parents' practices are:

> *Parent Involvement at the School* (PINVSCH)—a five-item measure of the frequency of helping (never, not yet, one to two times, many times) at the school building.
> *Parent Involvement with Homework* (PINVHW)—a five-item measure of the frequency of assisting and monitoring homework.
> *Parent Involvement in Reading Activities at Home* (PINVREAD)—a four-item measure of the frequency of parent help to students in reading.

Total Parent Involvement (PINVIOT)—an 18-item measure of the frequency of parents' use of all types of parent involvement at home and school, including the 14 items in the three scales listed previously and four other items on games, chores, and trips that involve parents and children in communication and learning activities at home.

Parents' Reports of Schools' Practices to Involve Parents

Parents rated their children's schools on whether and how well the schools conduct nine parent involvement practices. The activities include the five types of parent involvement, ranging from the school telling parents how the child is doing in school to giving parents ideas of how to help at home. The main measures of school practices as reported by parents are:

School Practices to Communicate with Parents and Involve Them at School (SCHCOMMPI)—a five-item measure of how well the school communicates with parents to provide information about school programs and activities.

School Practices to Involve Parents at Home (SCHHOMEPI)—a four-item measure of how well the school contacts and guides parents to help their own children at home.

Total School Program to Involve Parents (SCHTOTPI)—a nine-item measure of the extent to which the school contacts and guides parents to involve them in their children's education at home and at school.

TABLE 3.21   Measures of Parent Involvement and Attitudes

		Mean	Reliability
Parent Involvement at the School (PINVSCH)	5 items	2.36	.69
Parent Involvement with Homework (PIVHW)	5 items	3.54	.63
Parent Involvement in Reading Activities at Home (PINVREAD)	4 items	3.00	.58
Total Parent Involvement (PINVTOT)	18 items	3.07	.81
Parent Attitudes about the School (PATT)	6 items	3.29	.75
School Practices to Communicate with Parents and Involve Them at School (SCHCOMMPI)	5 items	2.35	.71
School Practices to Involve Parents at Home (SCHHOMPI)	4 items	2.04	.81
Total School Program to Involve Parents (SCHTOTPI)	9 items	2.21	.81

Other measures are:

Parent Attitudes about the School (PATT)—a six-item measure of the quality of the child's school.
Family Background Measures—Parent Education, Marital Status, Family Size, Parent Work outside the Home, and Parent Ratings of Student Ability.

The several scales of parents' reports of their practices, the schools' practices to involve them, and their attitudes toward their children's school have modest to high reliabilities. These are reported in Table 3.21.

EFFECTS ON PARENT INVOLVEMENT

Table 3.22 summarizes analyses of the effects of parent and student characteristics, school level, and school practices to involve families on parents' reported involvement at school and at home. The four columns of the table report the variables that significantly explain parent involvement at school (column 1); at home on homework (column 2); at home on reading in particular (column 3); and on total parent involvement at school, with homework, with reading, and in all activities (column 4).

Level of Schooling (Elementary or Middle School)

School level has strong independent effects on all measures of involvement reported by parents. Parents of children in the elementary grades are more involved than parents of children in the middle grades. According to the parents' reports, elementary school teachers do more and do better to involve parents in their children's education at school ($ß = -.13$), at home with homework ($ß = -.14$), with reading activities at home ($ß = -.08$), and with all types of involvement ($ß = -.16$).

Within middle schools, parents of sixth and seventh graders are more likely to be involved in their children's education at home. Parents of eighth graders are more involved at the school building. Because these data were collected early in the school year, parents of sixth graders were still relatively new to the school and may not have been included in the small core of parent volunteers in middle schools. Sixth-grade students may be more apt to ask for help at home if they are still unsure of themselves in a new school setting. Older students (eighth graders) may feel that they are more knowledgeable than their parents about schoolwork and school decisions.

Family Characteristics

In all cases, parents who are better educated are more involved at school and at home than parents who are less educated. Other family characteristics affect different types of involvement. Parents with fewer children are more involved with their

TABLE 3.22   Effects on Extent of Parents' Involvement of School Level, Family Characteristics, and Reported Teacher Practices to Involve Parents

	Extent of Involvement Reported by Parents:			
	At School	At Home on Homework	At Home on Reading Skills	Total Parent Involvement
	(β = standardized beta coefficient)[a, b]			
	(β)	(β)	(β)	(β)
School level (elementary/middle)	−.13	−.14	−.08	−.16
Parents' education	.11	.08	.13	.13
Family size	NS	−.07	−.06	−.07
Parent works outside home	−.06	NS	NS	NS
Rating of student ability	.06	.10	.15	.13
Teacher practices to involve parents[c] at school	.27			
at home		.18	.16	
Overall				.30
N	1,447	1,489	1,512	1,248
R^2	.14	.09	.08	.18

a Listwise regression analyses are reported to eliminate all cases with missing data. This procedure was checked with pairwise procedures that add about 300 cases to analyses. The results were all but identical.

b All reported coefficients are significant at or beyond the .05 level; coefficients of .10 or more are particularly important.

c Each equation includes the parents' reports of teachers' practices that most directly link to the type of involvement of the parents. That is, school practices that include asking the parent to come to school are used in the equation to explain parents' involvement at school; school practices that guide parents in how to help at home are used in the equation to explain parents' involvement at home on homework and reading skills; and the sum of all school practices is used in the equation to explain parents' total involvement.

children at home (β = −.07), but family size is not a significant factor for explaining parent involvement at school. Parents who work are significantly less likely to participate at the school building (β = −.06), but working outside the home is not a significant predictor of involvement at home. Marital status had no significant effects on the extent of involvement either at school or at home. These results confirm other reports at the elementary level (see Epstein, 1986) and at the middle level (Muller, 1991).

Student Characteristics

In all analyses, parents were more involved in their children's education if the children were better students. These cross-sectional data cannot be interpreted to mean that students whose parents are involved become better students. However, the results of earlier studies that used fall-to-spring test scores over one school year suggest that teachers' practices to involve parents in reading resulted in greater reading gains for children in those teachers' classrooms (Epstein, 1991). Parents whose children are doing well or are doing better in school are more likely to do more to ensure their children's continued success.

School Programs and Teachers' Practices

The strongest and most consistent predictors of parent involvement at school and at home are the specific school programs and teacher practices that encourage and guide parent involvement. Regardless of parent education, family size, student ability, or school level (elementary or middle school), parents are more likely to become partners in their children's education if they perceive that the schools have strong practices to involve parents at school (ß = .27), at home with homework (ß = .18), and at home with reading activities (ß = .16). The sum of all nine school practices has the strongest effect on parents' total involvement (ß = .30) after all other factors have been statistically controlled.

When parents believe the schools are doing little to involve them, they report doing little at home. When parents perceive that the school is doing many things to involve them, they are more involved in their children's education at school and at home. The schools' practices, not just family characteristics, make a difference in whether parents become involved in and feel informed about their children's education.

CLASSROOM-LEVEL REPORTS OF SCHOOL PRACTICES

Individual parents in one teacher's class may view the teacher's practices from a personal perspective. For example, one parent may receive special advice from a teacher about how to help a child at home or become involved at school. Or all parents of students in a classroom may report the teacher's practices similarly if they recognize that the teacher's regular practice is to involve all parents. We checked to see how individual parent reports compared to the reports of other parents in the same classroom. We can begin to understand whether parent involvement is a phenomenological process or a general classroom process by examining how parents of entire classrooms of students report the teacher's requests for involvement.

In this sample, only parents of children in the elementary grades could be identified by classroom for aggregated reports. The 1,135 parents of children in 86 classrooms provided assessments of school practices to inform and involve parents. An average or "consensus" score was calculated for each classroom and merged with the individual parent records.

Individual reports were significantly and positively correlated with the reports of other parents in the classroom (between $r = .28$ and $r = .44$). The highest agreement among parents came on the parents' reports about the amount of time that their children spend on homework ($r = .44$). Individual and aggregate scores were

TABLE 3.23   Comparison of Effects of Individual-Level and Classroom-Level Reports of Teacher Practices to Involve Parents (Elementary School Level Only)

	Extent of Involvement Reported by Parents:			
	At School	At Home on Homework	At Home on Reading Skills	Total Parent Involvement
	(β = standardized beta coefficient)[a, b]			
	(β)	(β)	(β)	(β)
Individual parent's report of teacher practices[b]	.28	.20	.16	.33
Classroom parents' consensus about teacher practices, individual parent's background with variables controlled[b, c]	.07	NS	NS	.13
Classroom parents' consensus about teacher practices, aggregate parent background with variables controlled[b, d]	.22	.24	.14	.27

a Listwise regression for these analyses include from 603 to 782 cases for elementary school parents, depending on the type of involvement measured. The same background variables are statistically controlled as shown in Table 3.15.

b Linked measures of teachers' practices (as shown in Table 3.15) are used in these analyses.

c Aggregate reports from all parents in a classroom about teachers' practices of parent involvement are used instead of an individual's report.

d Aggregate reports about teacher practices of parent involvement from all parents in a classroom, including aggregate family background variables.

correlated slightly lower on whether the teacher guides parents on how to help with homework ($r = .32$).

Parents also were in high agreement about the overall quality of their children's school. The correlation was +.38 between an average parent's report that a school was good or poor and the reports of all the parents in the same classroom. The modest but significant correlations suggest that there is agreement about school and teacher practices to involve parents. The figures also show considerable variation in the interpretations of teacher practices by individual parents in the same classroom.

Classroom averages of parents' reports may be more objective measures than one parent's report of a teacher's practices. We compare the effects of the classroom-level and individual-level measures on parents' practices in Table 3.23. The first line shows the individual effects; the second line shows the effects on parent involvement of the classroom aggregate measures of teachers' practices. On all types of involvement, the individual reports have stronger effects than the aggregated reports on parents' practices at school and at home. Line 2 substitutes the average of the parents' reports for that classroom, but retains the parents' individual background variables. This analysis uses the aggregate report as an alternative "truth" about the teacher's practices as if all parents received and interpreted the same information about involvement from the teacher. The results in lines 1 and 2 can be viewed as providing a "range of effects," with the "truth" somewhere between the two coefficients. Line 3 is a classroom analysis. It uses the average reports of all parents in a classroom about teacher practices and the average family background variables. These effects are highly consistent with the individual analyses. Importantly, they show that when classroom agreement about specific teachers' practices is high, individual parents tend to respond with those practices at home.

The differences raise two questions for future studies: How accurately does any one parent report a teacher's practices? Do teachers treat all parents in a classroom similarly to involve them at school and at home? The coefficients in Table 3.23 suggest that despite some consensus about teachers' practices among parents in a class, there is considerable evidence of individual interpretation of teacher practices and the translation of those practices into parent practices. All parents of children in a classroom may not be treated the same by a teacher, and they may not interpret messages, requests, and opportunities in the same way. The strongest effects on parent involvement at school and at home are demonstrated by parents who personally understand and act on the teacher's practices that encourage their involvement.

We believe that in strong or "improving" schools, the correspondence between one parent's report and those of all other parents in the class should increase over time. This would indicate that parents were becoming increasingly similar in how they perceived and understood the teacher's practices. There would, of course, always be some differences in individual responses to requests for involvement.

STUDENT TIME ON HOMEWORK AND PARENT INVOLVEMENT

Helping with homework is one common and important means by which parents become involved in what their children are learning in school. We asked parents several questions about their children's homework practices and their own involvement in homework activities. Table 3.24 shows comparisons of homework activities of elementary and middle school students and the help they receive from parents. According to parents:

- Middle school students spend more time doing homework on an average night than do elementary students.
- Parents of elementary school children help their children for more minutes and feel more able to help with reading and math than do parents of middle school students.
- Parents of children at both levels of school say they could help more (up to 45–50 minutes, on average) if the teacher guided them in how to help at home.

- Parents of children at both levels of school say they have time to help on weekends. Often, students are not assigned homework on weekends, when many parents have more time to interact with their children.
- More parents of elementary school students than parents of middle school students report that their children's schools and teachers have good programs that guide them in how to help at home to check their child's homework. Even at the elementary level, only 35 percent of the parents think their school "does well" on this. At the middle level, only 25 percent believe their school does well to help them know what to do.
- More parents of elementary school students than parents of middle school students report that their child likes to talk about school at home. But even at the elementary level, many parents, close to 40 percent, do not think that their children really enjoy such discussions.

Other data (not reported in Table 3.24) indicate that parents with more formal education say that their children spend more time on homework. These parents may be more aware of the homework that their children have to do, the parents may make sure the children do all of their homework, or the children may be in classrooms where the teachers give more homework. Parents with less formal education say they could help more if the teachers told them how to help. Those with more education may believe they are already helping enough or that they are already receiving good information from the teacher on how to help.

Table 3.25 reports the results of multiple-regression analyses conducted to determine the factors that affect how much time parents spend monitoring, assisting, or otherwise helping their children with homework. As noted, level of schooling affects the amount of time parents spend helping at home. With all other variables statistically controlled, parents of elementary students spend more time helping on homework ($ß = -.18$). Regardless of school level, parents help for more minutes if their children spend more time on homework. Alternative explanations are that when parents help, it takes students more time to do their homework, or parents help when their children have a lot of homework assigned by the teacher.

Parents' education, family size, and marital status—all indicators of family social class and social structure—are not significantly associated with the amount of time parents help with homework. Parents who work outside the home spend fewer minutes helping their children than do other parents. Parents whose children need the most help in schoolwork (rated by parents as "fair" or "poor" students) spend more minutes helping with homework ($ß = -.08$). Other analyses show that this is especially true in the elementary grades. Parents of struggling students may believe that if they give their children extra help on homework, the students have a chance to succeed in school. By the middle grades, parents who rate their children as "poor" students do not help their children as much as parents of "average" students. In the middle grades, parents may feel they are not able to help their academically weak children without special guidance from teachers about how to help. Parents of top students do not help for as many minutes in the middle grades, in part because the

TABLE 3.24 Parents' Reports about Homework

	School Level	
	Elementary (N = 1,135)	Middle (N = 1,182)
Average time on homework	30–35 min.	35–40 min.
Average time parent helps	30–35	25–30
% Strongly agree they are able to help with reading	75.9	67.1
% Strongly agree they are able to help with math	71.8	55.4
Average time parent could help if teacher gave information	45–50 min.	45–50 min.
% Have time to help on weekends	95.3	91.9
% Report school explains how to check child's homework	35.7	25.0
% Strongly agree child should get more homework	40.0	35.6
% Strongly agree child likes to talk about school at home	62.4	45.3

TABLE 3.25 Effects on Minutes Parents Help with Homework of School Level, Family Characteristics, Students' Homework Time, and Teachers' Practices to Involve Parents in Homework

	β[a,b]
School level (elementary or middle)	−.18
Students' homework time	.51
Parent education	NS
Family size	NS
Single parent	NS
Parent works outside home	−.08
Rating of student ability	−.08
Teachers' practices to guide parent help on homework	.10
N	1,560
R^2	.28

a Standardized beta coefficients for listwise regression analyses are reported.

b All reported coefficients are significant at or beyond the .05 level; coefficients of .10 are particularly important.

students do not need or ask for assistance and in part because teachers do not guide parents' involvement.

Other analyses show that in the middle grades, struggling students spend the least amount of time on homework. Thus, there is less investment in homework time by middle-grade students who are academically weak, less investment in helping behavior by parents of these students, and less investment by middle-grade teachers in informing parents about how to help their children at this level.

Even after all family and student characteristics are statistically accounted for, there is a significant, positive, and important effect of teachers' reported practices to guide parents in how to help their children with homework ($ß = .10$). Teachers who more often conduct practices that involve families influence parents to spend more time with their children on homework. The variables in these analyses explain about 28 percent of the variance in the amount of time parents spend helping on homework.

There is an interesting contrast between Tables 3.22 and 3.25 concerning parent involvement at home with homework. Table 3.22 shows that parents with more formal education and parents of more successful students report that they are involved in more and different ways of helping at home with homework. Table 3.25 reports that parents of weaker or academically struggling students spend more minutes helping their children on an average night. Types of help and time spent helping are different indicators of involvement. It may be that, over time, many different ways of helping and more minutes spent helping lead to more success for students on schoolwork.

The different patterns suggest that students' different needs are being addressed by parents. Students who need more help take more minutes of their parents' time. Students who are better students may require different kinds of assistance. The important similarity between the two tables is that the specific practices of teachers to guide parents in how to help at home increase the types of help parents say they give and the time they give to help their children.

DISCUSSION

Several other findings from the data regarding inner-city parents increase our understanding of parent involvement in children's education in the elementary and middle grades:

- Most parents believe that their children attend a good school and that the teachers care about their children, and the parents feel welcome at the school. However, there is considerable variation in these attitudes, with many parents unhappy or unsure about the quality of schools and teachers. Interestingly, parents' attitudes about the quality of their children's school are more highly correlated with the school's practices to involve parents (.346) than with the parents' practices of involvement (.157). Parents who become involved at home and at school say that the school has a positive climate. Even more so, parents who believe that the school is actively working to involve them say that the school is a good one. This connection supports earlier findings that parents give teachers higher ratings when teachers frequently involve parents in their children's education (Epstein, 1985 [Reading 4.3], 1986).
- Parents report little involvement at the school building. Many parents work full-time or part-time and cannot come to the school during the school day. Others report that they have not been asked by the school to become volunteers, but would like to be.

- Parents in all the schools in this sample are emphatic about wanting the school and teachers to advise them about how to help their children at home at each grade level. Parents believe that the schools need to strengthen practices such as giving parents specific information on their children's major academic subjects and what their children are expected to learn each year.
- Parents of young children and parents with more formal education conduct more activities at home that support their children's schooling.
- Parents who were guided by teachers on how to help at home spent more minutes helping with homework than other parents.
- In many schools, parents are asked to come to the building for workshops. An interesting sidelight in these data is that in all eight schools, elementary and middle, parents' top request for workshop topics was "How to Help My Child Develop His/Her Special Talents." Across the schools, from 57 to 68 percent of parents checked that topic (average 61 percent). By contrast, an average of 54 percent were interested in workshops on helping children take tests, and an average of 45 percent checked interest in discipline and control of children.
- Inner-city parents need information and assistance to help develop the special qualities they see in their children. Time and resources to develop talent may be as important as time for homework for helping children's self-esteem and commitment to learning. The parents' requests for help from the schools on the topic of developing children's special talents are important calls for action, along with their requests for schools to increase information on how to help on homework.

Most important for policy and practice, parents' level of involvement is directly linked to the specific practices of the school that encourage involvement at school and guide parents in how to help at home. The data are clear that the schools' practices to inform and involve parents are more important than parent education, family size, marital status, and even grade level in determining whether inner-city parents stay involved with their children's education through the middle grades.

Although teachers in these urban Title I schools reported that most parents are not involved and do not want to be (see Epstein and Dauber, 1991), parents of students in the same schools tell a different story. They say that they are involved with their children but that they need more and better information from teachers about how to help at home. Parents and teachers have different perspectives that must be recognized and taken into account in developing activities to improve parent involvement.

Earlier research showed that some of the strongest immediate effects of teachers' practices of parent involvement are on parents' attitudes and behaviors (see Epstein, 1986). This study suggests that the same is true for inner-city parents. Parents are more involved at school and at home when they perceive that the schools have strong programs that encourage parent involvement. The implication is that all schools, including inner-city schools, can develop more comprehensive programs of parent involvement to help more families become knowledgeable partners in their children's education.

In these schools the survey data were used to help the schools plan three-year programs to improve their parent involvement practices to meet the needs and requests of the parents and the hopes of the teachers for stronger partnerships. The data served as Time 1, the starting point, for a longitudinal study of the impact of three years of work to improve practices. In this and in other research, the next questions must deal with the results of efforts to improve school and family partnerships.

REFERENCES

Baker, D. P., and D. L. Stevenson. (1986). Mothers' strategies for children's school achievement: Managing the transition to high school. *Sociology of Education* 59: 156–166.

Bauch, P. A. (1988). Is parent involvement different in private schools? *Educational Horizons* 66: 78–82.

Becker, H. J., and J. L. Epstein. (1982). Parent involvement: A study of teacher practices. *Elementary School Journal* 83: 85–102. (Reading 3.1).

Clark, R. (1983). *Family life and school achievement: Why poor black children succeed and fail.* Chicago: University of Chicago Press.

Comer, J. P. (1980). *School power.* New York: Free Press.

Dornbusch, S. M., and P. L. Ritter. (1988). Parents of high school students: A neglected resource. *Educational Horizons* 66: 75–77.

Epstein, J. L. (1982). *Student reactions to teacher practices of parent involvement. Parent Involvement Report Series P-21.* Paper presented at the annual meeting of the American Education Research Association. Baltimore: Johns Hopkins University Center for Research on Elementary and Middle Schools. (Reading 3.9).

———. (1985). A question of merit: Principals' and parents' evaluations of teachers. *Educational Researcher* 14(7): 3–10. (Reading 4.3).

———. (1986). Parents' reactions to teacher practices of parent involvement. *Elementary School Journal* 86: 277–294. (Reading 3.4).

———. (1987). What principals should know about parent involvement. *Principal* 66(3): 6–9.

———. (1988a). How do we improve programs in parent involvement? *Educational Horizons* (special issue on parents and schools) 66(2): 58–59.

———. (1988b). *Sample clinical summaries: Using surveys of teachers and parents to plan projects to improve parent involvement.* Parent Involvement Series, Report P-83. Baltimore: Johns Hopkins University Center for Research on Elementary and Middle Schools.

———. (1990). Single parents and the schools: Effects of marital status on parent and teacher interactions. In M. T. Hallinan, D. M. Klein, and J. Glass (Eds.), *Change in societal institutions* (pp. 91–121). New York: Plenum. (Reading 3.5).

———. (1991). Effects of teacher practices of parent involvement on student achievement in reading and math. In S. Silvern (Ed.), *Advances in reading/language research, Vol. 5: Literacy through family, community, and school interaction* (pp. 261–276). Greenwich, CT: JAI. (Reading 3.7).

Epstein, J. L., and H. J. Becker. (1990). Hopkins Surveys of School and Family Connections: Questionnaires for teachers, parents, and students. In J. Touliatos, B. Perlmutter, and M. Straus (Eds.), *Handbook of family measurement techniques* (pp. 345–346). Parent Involvement Series, Report P-81. Newbury Park, CA: Sage.

Epstein, J. L., and S. Dauber. (1991). School programs and teacher practices of parent involvement in inner-city elementary and middle schools. *Elementary School Journal* 91: 289–303. (Reading 3.3).

Epstein, J. L., and K. Salinas. (1988). *Evaluation report forms: Summaries of school-level data from surveys of teachers and surveys of parents*. Parent Involvement Report Series P-82. Baltimore: Center for Research on Elementary and Middle Schools, Johns Hopkins University.

Lareau, A. (1987). Social class differences in family-school relationships: The importance of cultural capital. *Sociology of Education* 60: 73–85.

Leitch, M. L., and S. S. Tangri. (1988). Barriers to home-school collaboration. *Educational Horizons* 66: 70–74.

Muller, C. (1991). *Maternal employment, parental involvement, and academic achievement: An analysis of family resources available to the child*. Paper presented at the annual meeting of the American Sociological Association in Cincinnati.

Rich, D., J. Van Dien, and B. Mattox. (1979). Families as educators for their own children. In R. Brandt (Ed.), *Partners: Parents and schools* (pp. 26–40). Alexandria, VA: Association for Supervision and Curriculum Development.

Rubin, R. I., P. P. Olmsted, M. J. Szegda, M. J. Wetherby, and D. S. Williams. (1983). *Long-term effects of parent education on follow-through program participation*. Paper presented at the annual meeting of the American Education Research Association in Montreal.

Scott-Jones, D. (1987). Mother-as-teacher in families of high- and low-achieving low-income black first graders. *Journal of Negro Education* 56: 21–34.

READING 3.7

Effects on Student Achievement of Teachers' Practices of Parent Involvement*

ABSTRACT

This study uses longitudinal data from 293 third- and fifth-grade students in Baltimore City who took the California Achievement Test (CAT) in the fall and spring of the 1980–1981 school year. The students were in the classrooms of 14 teachers who varied in their use of techniques to involve parents in learning activities at home. With data from parents, students, and teachers, we examine the effects over time of teachers' practices of parent involvement on student achievement test scores.

INTRODUCTION

Social science research on school and family environments has documented the importance for student development and achievement of family conditions and practices of parent involvement in school (Clausen, 1966; Coleman et al., 1966; Epstein, 1983; Heyns, 1978; Leichter, 1974; Marjoribanks, 1979; Mayeske, 1973; McDill and Rigsby, 1973; Gordon, 1979; Henderson, 1987; Sinclair, 1980). There is consistent evidence that parents' encouragement, activities, interest at home, and participation at school affect their children's achievement, even after the students' ability and family socioeconomic status are taken into account. Students gain in personal and academic development if their families emphasize schooling, let their children know they do, and do so continually over the school years.

The earlier research considers family practices that vary naturally in the study samples. It recognizes that in any population some parents become involved in their children's education, based on their own knowledge about school and their ability to guide and encourage their children. This study examines parent involvement that results from teachers' efforts to involve more parents in their children's education, not just those who would become involved on their own. We want to know what

---

* By Joyce L. Epstein. An earlier version of this paper was presented at the 1984 annual meeting of the American Educational Research Association. The author is grateful to Henry Jay Becker and Doris Entwisle for their helpful comments and suggestions and to others who reviewed or reacted to earlier drafts. Many thanks to the teachers, principals, families, and students who contributed to this study. This research was supported by grants from the Department of Education Office of Educational Research and Improvement. The results and improvements do not necessarily reflect the position or policy of the OERI. Originally published in S. Silvern, ed., *Advances in Reading/Language Research*, vol. 5: *Literacy Through Family, Community, and School Interaction* (Greenwich, CT: JAI, 1991), 261–276. Reprinted with permission.

happens if we change the expected variation among families to increase the number of parents who can knowledgeably assist their children to improve or maintain their academic skills. We need to know: Are there ways to increase the number of parents who become involved in their children's learning activities at home? If teachers and administrators take the responsibility to involve all parents, are there measurable effects on student achievement test scores and other important school outcomes?

Over the years there have been many programs and practices designed to increase home-school cooperation to improve students' academic skills and attitudes or parents' attitudes (Collins, Moles, and Cross, 1982). Few programs or practices, however, have been systematically evaluated for their effects on students. Tidwell (1980) describes positive effects on parents, although the data to evaluate Los Angeles's "Project AHEAD" were admittedly poor. Gotts (1980) reports small effects on "adaptability to school" for children in family-school preschool programs. Cochran (1986) describes a preschool program designed to "empower" parents, but the linkages in the model to the children's schools and teachers' practices are weak. Rich and Jones (1977) present important early evidence suggesting that extra learning time at home produces gains in early elementary students' reading scores equivalent to those made by students under more expensive "pull-out" programs in schools. The data, statistical controls, and methods of analysis in these studies, however, were seriously limited. Gordon (1979) reviews several studies and unpublished dissertations suggesting that there are generally positive effects of the programs on parents and on young children, but the measures of parent involvement in these studies are incomplete and the connections to schools and instructional programs are unmeasured.

Several Follow-Through models emphasized parent involvement at school and at home (Rivlin and Timpane, 1975), but in all cases the effects of the parent involvement components were poorly measured. The most reliable data and consistent results from the Follow-Through studies seem to be effects on parents' attitudes and parent-teacher relations. (See the exchange in the *Harvard Educational Review* by Anderson, St. Pierre, Proper, and Stebbins, 1978; Hodges, 1978; Wisler, Burnes, and Iwamoto, 1978.) Other studies and commentaries suggest that direct contact of parents with their own children on learning activities at home (as opposed to the contact of a few parents in the school building) should have important consequences for student achievement and other outcomes such as school attendance and classroom behavior (Comer, 1980; Gillum, Schooley, and Novak, 1977; Rich, Van Dien, and Mattox, 1979).

Previous studies did not link specific teachers' practices with their own students and parents, and there was little information on characteristics of the teachers, parents, or students for even cursory controls on other influences on achievement. Few studies focused on upper elementary school or older students. Overall, there is little "hard" data that address the question of whether teachers' practices of parent involvement directly influence student achievement (Olmsted, Wetherby, Leler, and Rubin, 1982). This study begins to fill some of the gaps in the earlier work by focusing on the effect of teacher practices of parent involvement on gains in reading and math achievement test scores over one school year.

DATA AND APPROACH

We use longitudinal data from 293 third- and fifth-grade students in Baltimore City who took the California Achievement Test (CAT) in the fall and spring of the 1980–1981 school year. The full study involved many districts in the state of Maryland, but only one district administered fall and spring achievement test scores to permit analyses of change in math and reading scores over one school year.

The students were in the classrooms of 14 teachers who varied in their emphases on parent involvement. The continuum ranged from "confirmed leaders"—teachers who reported frequent use of parent involvement in learning activities at home and who were confirmed by their principals as leaders in these practices—to infrequent users, to confirmed nonusers of parent involvement in learning activities at home— teachers who reported, and whose principals confirmed, their lack of emphasis on parent involvement (see Becker and Epstein, 1982 [Reading 3.1]). The parents of students in these teachers' classrooms were surveyed about their reactions to and experiences with teacher practices of parent involvement (see Epstein, 1986 [Reading 3.4]). The data link teacher practices to the families' responses and to the achievement of students, and enable us to analyze the consequences of teachers' uses of instructional strategies that emphasize parent involvement at home.

Several types of variables that theoretically could influence change in achievement scores are included in the analyses: student and family background (sex, race, and grade level of students, parent education, and students' fall achievement test scores), teachers' characteristics and practices (overall teaching quality as rated by the principal, years of experience, and teachers' and principals' reports of the teachers' leadership in parent involvement), parent reactions (parents' reports of teacher requests for involvement and parents' rating of the quality of homework assigned by the teacher), and student effort (teachers' rating of the quality of homework completed by the students). The variables are described in detail in Becker and Epstein (1982) and Epstein (1985 [Reading 4.3], 1986, 1990 [Reading 3.5]). Multiple regression analysis is used to identify the important independent effects of these variables on gains in reading and math achievement. We are especially interested in whether teacher practices of parent involvement affect reading and math achievement, after the other potentially influential variables are taken into account.

We use students' residual gain scores as our measure of growth or change over the school year. Because earlier family and school factors influenced prior student achievement, we must statistically control the students' initial, fall achievement test scores that reflect the earlier influences. Then we examine the effects of the ongoing teachers' practices on change in reading and math skills over the school year in our study. As Richards (1975, 1976) showed, changes in scores over a reasonable interval, such as a school year, measure school impact and individual growth as accurately as other methods (Cronbach and Furby, 1970). Changes in scores also have the conceptual advantage of giving a clear picture of growth from pretest to posttest.

Ideally, we would like to have more measures of teachers' classroom practices. It may be, for example, that teachers who frequently use parent involvement strategies also differ from infrequent users or nonusers in their other classroom activities and instructional methods. In this study we control for differences in teachers' quality and approaches by taking into account principals' ratings of the teachers' skills, including their preparation of lessons, knowledge of subject, classroom discipline, and creativity. We focus, then, on the effects of teacher practices of parent involvement, net of overall teacher quality. Although new studies of parent involvement and achievement may add other measures of specific teacher practices, our statistical controls on teacher quality and early student achievement greatly strengthen the models, measures, and methods used in previous studies.

RESULTS

Effects on Change in Reading Achievement

Table 3.26 shows the significant correlates of gains in reading achievement and the results of the regression analysis to identify the significant, independent effects of these variables on achievement gains. The variables were entered in four steps to illustrate the type, magnitude, and persistence of influence. Line 1 of the table shows the effects on change in reading scores of initial or starting characteristics of students and teachers: the students' initial, fall reading scores and the overall quality of the teacher as rated by the principal. Students with lower reading scores in the fall make greater gains by the spring than do other students ($\beta = -.259$). This effect is partly a "regression to the mean" but is also partly a consequence of the room to change and the need to change. Students who are initially low may be able to move their scores more easily than those who are at or near the "ceiling" in a range of scores, and, we assume, they and their teachers are working to improve the students' basic skills. The positive effect of teacher quality ($\beta = +.157$) shows that, independent of students' starting scores, teachers whose principals give them high ratings in classroom management, control, instructional effectiveness, and creativity help students make greater gains in reading than do teachers who receive lower ratings for teaching quality. These two variables explain 10 percent of the variance in change in reading scores.

Line 2 of the table reports that teacher leadership in parent involvement in learning activities at home positively and significantly influences change in reading achievement, adding about 4 percent to the variance explained by the initial characteristics of students and teachers.

Line 3 of the table takes into account two measures of parental resources and responses. Parents with more formal education and parents who report that they have learned more this year than they knew previously about their child's instructional program positively influence change in the reading achievement of their children.

Thus, we see that student gains in reading achievement are influenced by parents who usually help their children (i.e., those with more formal education) and, importantly, parents who are helped to help their children (i.e., those whose children's teachers involve parents in learning activities at home to increase their knowledge

TABLE 3.26   Influence on Change in Reading Achievement Test Scores from Fall to Spring*

Variables Added	Initial Reading Score (Fall)	Overall Quality of Teacher	Leadership in Parent Involvement	Parent Education	Parent Knows More This Year Than Before	Student Homework Quality	R^2
1. Student and Teacher (Starting) Characteristics	-.259	.157					.105
2. Teacher Leadership in Parent Involvement at Home	-.243	.201	.193				.141
3. Parent Resources and Response to Involvement	-.275	.164	.171	.185	.153		.185
4. Homework Completion Quality	-.330	.138	.128	.162	.122	.193	.216
5. (Zero-order Correlation with Reading Achievement)	(-.285)	(.200)	(.162)	(.092)	(.191)	(.186)	

* Achievement test scores are fall and spring scores (percentiles) on the Reading Subtest of the California Achievement Tests for 293 third- and fifth-grade students. Standardized regression coefficients are reported. In this table, all unstandardized coefficients are twice their standard errors.

about the school program). An additional 4 percent of the variance is explained by these parental characteristics.

Teachers rated their students as homework stars, homework problems, or as neither stars nor problems. We see in line 4 of the table that students who complete their homework well gain more in reading achievement than do other students. When homework quality is added to the equation in Table 3.26, its effects on achievement are clearly important, and the effects of teachers' practices and parents' responses decrease slightly but remain significant. This indicates not only the generally robust importance of these variables but also the crucial contribution of students' investments in schoolwork for improving their own achievement.

Although many factors influence learning, we were especially interested in whether teachers' practices of involving parents have persistent, independent effects on student achievement. We see that teachers' leadership in parent involvement in learning activities at home contributes independently to positive change in reading achievement from fall to spring, even after teacher quality, students' initial achievement, parents' education, parents' improved understanding of the school program, and the quality of students' homework are taken into account. Indeed, the influence of teachers' practices of parent involvement may be even more important than the coefficient suggests, because improved parents' understanding and better homework quality are also influenced by these practices (Epstein, 1982 [Reading 3.9], 1986).

Effects on Change in Math Achievement

Table 3.27 tells a different story about change in math achievement scores. Again, all variables are included in this analysis that are significantly correlated with change in math achievement. We also include teachers' leadership in parent involvement, despite its low correlation, to compare its effects on math with those reported for reading.

Line 1 of Table 3.27 shows that students who start with lower math scores in the fall change more in math skills over the school year. In part this reflects regression to the mean, but also, as in reading, slower students with more room to change and greater need to change make greater gains by spring than do students who score well. Students also gain more if they have relatively new, recently trained teachers, or if they are in the younger grades (i.e., here, grade 3 rather than grade 5). It may be that making progress in math is easier for students in the lower grades, where teachers tend to help students master basic skills and do not stress the swift coverage and competitive knowledge of more advanced math topics. Younger students and their teachers may be able to improve needed math skills more easily than can older students who have, with each passing year, more skills to cover and more ground to make up if they have fallen behind. The overall quality of the teacher, as rated by the principal, is a significant correlate of students' growth in math but does not have an independent influence on change in math achievement after other measures of student and teacher characteristics are accounted for. The four characteristics of students and teachers shown in line 1 of the table explain approximately 25 percent of the variance in math gains.

TABLE 3.27 Influence on Change in Math Achievement Test Scores from Fall to Spring[1]

Variables Added	Initial Math Score (Fall)	Overall Quality of Teachers	Years of Teaching Experience	Grade Level	Leadership in Parent Involvement	Homework Not Busy Work	R^2
1. Student and Teacher (Starting) Characteristics	−.349*	−.038	−.152*	−.266*			.253
2. Teacher Leadership in Parent Involvement at Home	−.348*	−.047	−.148*	−.277*	−.028		.254
3. Assigned Homework Quality	−.334*	−.047	−.146*	−.258*	−.025	.104‡	.264
4. (Zero-order Correlation with Math Achievement)	(−.428)	(.131)	(−.151)	(.326)	(.040)	(.216)	

[1] Achievement test scores are fall and spring scores (percentiles) on mathematics subtest of the California Achievement Tests for 293 third- and fifth-grade students. Standardized regression coefficients are reported.

* Indicates unstandardized coefficient is at least twice its standard error.

‡ Indicates coefficient is approaching twice its standard error.

Line 2 of the table shows that teachers' leadership in the use of parent involvement is not an important variable for understanding change in math scores. In contrast to its influence on reading achievement gains in Table 3.26, teachers' parent involvement practices are neither correlated with math gains nor significantly affected by other variables in this model.

Line 3 of the table suggests that parents' reports that teachers assign purposeful homework (not busy work) have a small, positive effect on change in math achievement, but explains only an additional 1 percent of the variance in math gains. This measure may reflect a combination of parents' awareness of their children's math work, the parents' general acceptance of their children's school programs, better quality of the teachers' decisions about homework assignments, and the students' interest and investment of time at home on their homework. New research should look into these components of homework assignments by teachers, as well as aspects of homework completion by students discussed in Table 3.26.

Comparing Effects on Change in Reading and Math Scores

Table 3.28 shows a common model consisting of variables from Tables 3.26 and 3.27 used to compare effects on changes in reading and math achievement. Two variables—student sex and race—have been added to Table 3.28 even though they lack a significant zero-order correlation with the dependent measure. We include them here to show that although sex and race are usually of interest in studies of reading and math achievement, they are not important explanatory variables for students' growth over the school year. The table presents the standardized regression coefficients and identifies the independent influences of the variables on change in reading and math over one school year. We have arranged the variables to focus on student and family background factors, teacher characteristics, and home-learning activities.

The top section of the table focuses attention on student and family background variables. As in the earlier tables, we see that initial (fall) scores influence change in both reading and math scores: Students who initially have low scores change more from fall to spring. Neither sex nor race of students influences changes in scores in either subject. Parent education and grade level are important independent influences, but for different subjects. Parents with more formal education independently influence positive change in reading scores, but parents' education is not an important influence on students' math gains. Younger students (in grade 3) make greater gains in math than do students in grade 5, but grade level is not an important independent influence on change in reading achievement.

The middle section of the table presents the variables in the model that concern the teachers' background and skills. The two variables have important independent effects, but on different subjects. Overall teacher quality—the reputational index based on principals' ratings of four instruction and management skills—influences change in students' reading scores but not math. More recent teacher training (reflected in fewer years of teaching) promotes greater gains in math but does not influence change in reading.

TABLE 3.28 Comparing a Common Model of Effects on Change in Reading and Math Scores

Variables	Measures	Change in Reading Achievement		Change in Math Achievement	
		ß	(r)	ß	(r)
Student and Family Background	Sex	.048	(.022)	.009	(.050)
	Grade Level	−.053	(−.222)	−.247*	(−.326)
	Parent Education	.170*	(.092)	.067	(−.024)
	Race	.068	(−.004)	.088	(.022)
	Fall Score‡	−.294*	(−.285)	−.357*	(−.427)
Teacher Skills and Experience	Overall Quality of Teacher	.175*	(.200)	−.033	(.131)
	Years of Teaching Experience	−.004	(−.026)	−.152*	(−.151)
Home-Learning Activities	Teacher Leadership Involving Parents in Learning Activities at Home	.144*	(.162)	−.037	(.040)
	Homework Not Busy Work	.028	(.072)	.109*	(.216)
	R^2	.173		.274	

NOTES: ß = Standardized regression coefficients.

(r) = Zero-order correlations.

N = 293.

* Indicates unstandardized coefficient is at least twice its standard error.

‡ Fall score is the initial reading score in the analysis of change in reading achievement, and the initial math score in the analysis of change in math achievement.

The bottom section of the table focuses attention on two types of home-learning activities. Teacher leadership in the use of parent involvement in learning activities at home has a positive influence on change in reading scores, but not in math scores. Parents' reports of pertinent homework assignments influence positive change in students' math scores, but not reading scores.

The common model explains 17 percent of the change in students' reading scores compared to 27 percent of the variance in the change in math scores. The different explanatory power of the model is due mainly to the impact of low initial scores and younger grade level on growth in math skills. Table 3.26 shows more variance explained (about 22 percent) in change in reading achievement because the equation included parents' increased understanding of their children's instructional program and the quality of students' completed homework, two measures that are, in part, explained by teachers' practices of parent involvement and that, in part, boost reading achievement.

DISCUSSION

Why do teachers' practices of parent involvement influence change in reading but not math scores? Why should changes in reading and math achievement test scores be influenced by different variables? And what do these patterns mean for understanding parent involvement and student achievement?

We have some clues about these questions from other data collected from the teachers and parents in the study. For example, teachers report that reading activities are their most frequently used and most satisfying parent involvement practices, and principals report that they encourage teachers to involve parents in reading activities more than in other subjects (see Becker and Epstein, 1982). Parents report that they receive most requests for assistance on reading-related activities at home (see Epstein, 1986). It appears that these emphases on parent involvement in reading have real consequences for improving students' reading achievement. There is little reason to expect that these practices would have direct and immediate effects on students' math skills. This would require teachers' sequential and coordinated practices to involve parents in math activities.

More parents of fifth-grade students feel that they do not have enough training to help their children with reading and math skills at home (Epstein, 1984). Their feelings of inadequacy may be more serious about math. Teachers of older students have fewer parent volunteers in their classes and give less guidance to parents in how to help their children at home. Teachers may need to give more help to parents of older children so that they understand what to discuss about school and how to assist, guide, and monitor their children in reading, math, and other subjects at home.

Table 3.29 shows that there was dramatic improvement in reading and math scores for third- and fifth-grade city students in this sample from fall to spring. But our analyses suggest that the dramatic changes in reading and math scores are attributable to different factors. Gains in reading achievement are influenced sharply by several sources, including the teachers' leadership in parent involvement, the

TABLE 3.29 Third- and Fifth-Grade City Students' Reading and Math Scores

	Fall 1980	Spring 1981
Reading achievement scores		
Mean	38.60	50.69
Standard deviation	(25.51)	(25.20)
Math achievement scores		
Mean	43.75	57.46
Standard deviation	(25.70)	(24.74)

teachers' overall quality of instruction, the students' need to improve, the quality of the students' homework, the parents' education, and the parents' improved knowledge about the school program.

Gains in math achievement may have more to do with the grade level, methods of teaching math, and traditional homework assignments. Recently trained teachers may be more responsive to current pressures to increase attention to math and to ensure mastery of basic skills in the early grades. In present practice, few teachers ask parents to become involved in math activities at home, but most teachers assign math homework. When parents see that homework is pertinent and purposeful, the students make important math gains.

Previous research shows consistently that school effects are stronger for math achievement than for reading or language arts achievement. Here, we see one explanation for that finding. Some teachers help families help their children practice reading: listening to the child read, reading aloud to the child, borrowing books to use at home, and other reading-related practices (see Becker and Epstein, 1982). More formally educated parents independently influence their children's growth in reading skills. These would be the parents who usually are involved in their children's education. More important, after parent education is taken into account, teacher practices of parent involvement help families become informed and involved, and they influence students' reading skills.

There are many important questions raised by the findings of this study that need to be answered in new research. For example, how do teachers implement their parent involvement programs to get all or most parents involved? What happens to students' achievements and attitudes if their parents will not or cannot help their children even when the teacher requests and guides parent involvement? There are many real and difficult problems that must be solved for teachers to successfully use parent involvement in learning activities at home. These questions will be best answered by studies of the implementation and evaluation of well-designed and well-planned procedures, including the teachers' goals for parent involvement, the orientation of parents, and the management and follow-up of learning activities at home.

Teachers can take new directions to make stronger connections with the family. The Teachers Involve Parents in Schoolwork (TIPS) process helps teachers improve their own approaches to parent involvement and to improve the parents' skills with their children at all grade levels (Epstein, 1987; Epstein, Salinas, and Jackson, 1995 [see Chapter 6]). The TIPS process includes math and science models and prototypic activities for the elementary grades and language arts and science/health models, and prototype activities for the middle grades that may enable teachers to assist parents and students in becoming involved as knowledgeable partners in learning activities at home in other subjects, as well as in reading.

For some teachers, the "bottom line" for their decisions about whether to use parent involvement practices rests with the documentation of effects on students. This study finds significant effects on changes in reading achievement from fall to spring for children in the classrooms of teachers who are leaders in the use of parent involvement practices. Additional studies with longitudinal achievement test scores in specific subjects, with more specific measures of teacher practices of parent involvement and with data from parents on their responses to teachers' requests, are needed to verify and support these results.

Although this study adds to an understanding of linkages between practices of parent involvement and student achievement in specific subjects, there are some serious limitations that should be addressed in new research. For example, the sample includes only urban schools and large numbers of African American families. Future studies will want to focus on other populations and various communities to check the generalizability of the findings.

Another issue is the lack of specificity of the practices of involving parents. In this study, we can identify only the overall effects of multiple practices that almost exclusively involve parents in reading activities at home. Because educators need to choose among many practices, we need a more clearly defined menu of specific reading involvement practices and their associated effects on reading achievement, as well as information on specific practices to involve parents in other subjects and their effects on student achievement in those subjects.

These data do not account for prior differences in the involvement of the families in the study and the practices of earlier teachers to involve families that may cumulatively affect student achievement. A full complement would include longitudinal measures of parents' involvement, teachers' practices, and student outcomes over more than one school year.

Also, teachers who use frequent practices of parent involvement may differ from other teachers in the ways in which they influence student achievement. Although this study statistically controls teacher "quality" using principals' ratings of teachers' classroom organization, management, and pedagogical approaches, this measure does not necessarily capture all of the important differences in teacher attitudes, classroom activities, teacher-student relations, and other factors that also may affect student achievement gains. More comprehensive measures of teacher practices would strengthen analyses and clarify the contribution to achievement gains of teachers' practices to involve all families.

Despite its limitations, this study contributes new information on the subject-specific connections of teacher-guided parent involvement, parent responses and interaction with their children, students' investments in the quality of their own work, and achievement gains. It supports and extends the studies of Rich and Jones (1977);

Walberg, Bole, and Waxman (1980); Tizard, Schofield, and Hewison (1982); and others reviewed by Henderson (1987) that suggest that teachers' strong implementation of parent involvement and parents' responsive involvement with their children at home on schoolwork should increase student achievement, even in families with little formal education. The results of this study reveal the need for even more comprehensive and longitudinal inquiries on specific linkages of practices to involve parents and their effects on students. The study also emphasizes the importance of including school and family environments and their connections on the agenda of new research in reading and language arts.

Lightfoot (1978) and Scott-Jones (1987) caution against too great expectations of the effects of parent involvement on academic or social outcomes. Their concerns are important. It is not the parents' responsibility to teach their children new skills in the school curriculum or to take over the teachers' job. However, teachers and parents share a responsibility to their children to monitor and understand their progress in school. This includes assisting students to master the skills needed to pass each grade and to feel good about themselves as learners. Our evidence on reading achievement gains suggests that teachers can help more parents understand how to help their children when questions arise at home about schoolwork. Most parents report that they want teachers to tell them that it is all right to help their children and to explain how to use time at home productively to work toward school goals (see Epstein, 1986). Parents are one available but untapped and undirected resource that teachers can mobilize to help more children master and maintain needed skills for school, but this requires teachers' leadership in organizing, evaluating, and continually building their parent involvement practices.

REFERENCES

Anderson, R. B., R. G. St. Pierre, E. C. Proper, and L. B. Stebbins. (1978). Pardon us but what was the question again? A response to the critique of the Follow-Through evaluation. *Harvard Educational Review* 48: 161–170.

Becker, H. J., and J. L. Epstein. (1982). Parent involvement: A study of teacher practices. *Elementary School Journal* 83: 85–102. (Reading 3.1).

Clausen, J. A. (1966). Family structure, socialization and personality. In L. W. Hoffman and M. L. Hoffman (Eds.), *Review of child development research, Vol. 2* (pp. 1–53). New York: Russell Sage.

Cochran, M. (1986). *Empowering families: An alternative to the deficit model.* Paper presented at the First Bielefeld Conference on Social Prevention and Intervention in Bielefeld, West Germany.

Coleman, J. S., E. Q. Campbell, C. J. Hobson, J. M. McPartland, A. Mood, F. D. Weinfeld, and R. L. York. (1966). *Equality of educational opportunity.* Washington, DC: U.S. Government Printing Office.

Collins, C., O. Moles, and M. Cross. (1982). *The home-school connection: Selected partnership programs in large cities.* Boston: Institute for Responsive Education.

Comer, J. P. (1980). *School power.* New York: Free Press.

Cronbach, L. J., and L. Furby. (1970). How should we measure change—or should we? *Psychological Bulletin* 74: 68–80.

Epstein, J. L. (1982). *Student reactions to teachers' practices of parent involvement.* Paper presented at the annual meeting of the American Educational Research Association in New York. (Reading 3.9).

———. (1983). Longitudinal effects of person-family-school interactions on student outcomes. In A. Kerchkoff (Ed.), *Research in sociology of education and socialization, Vol. 4* (pp. 101–128). Greenwich, CT: JAI.

———. (1984). School policy and parent involvement: Research results. *Educational Horizons* 62: 70–72.

———. (1985). A question of merit: Principals' and parents' evaluations of teachers. *Educational Researcher* 14(7): 3–10. (Reading 4.3).

———. (1986). Reactions of parents to teacher practices of parent involvement. *Elementary School Journal* 86: 277–294. (Reading 3.4).

———. (1987). *Teachers' manual: Teachers involve parents in schoolwork [TIPS].* Baltimore: Johns Hopkins University Center for Research on Elementary and Middle Schools.

———. (1990). Single parents and the schools: Effects of marital status on parent and teacher interactions. In M. T. Hallinan, D. M. Klein, and J. Glass (Eds.), *Change in societal institutions* (pp. 91–121). New York: Plenum. (Reading 3.5).

Epstein, J. L., K. C. Salinas, and V. E. Jackson. (1995). *Manuals for teachers and prototype activities: Teachers Involve Parents in Schoolwork (TIPS) for the elementary and middle grades.* Baltimore: Center on School, Family, and Community Partnerships, Johns Hopkins University.

Gillum, R. M., D. E. Schooley, and P. D. Novak. (1977). *The effects of parental involvement on student achievement in three Michigan performance contracting programs.* Paper presented at the annual meeting of the American Educational Research Association in New York.

Gordon, I. (1979). The effects of parent involvement in schooling. In R. S. Brandt (Ed.), *Partners: Parents and schools* (pp. 4–25). Alexandria, VA: Association for Supervision and Curriculum Development.

Gotts, E. (1980). Long-term effects of a home-oriented preschool program. *Childhood Education* 56: 228–234.

Henderson, A. (1987). *The evidence continues to grow: Parent involvement improves achievement.* Columbia, MD: National Committee for Citizens in Education.

Heyns, B. (1978). *Summer learning and the effects of schooling.* New York: Academic Press.

Hodges, W. L. (1978). The worth of the Follow-Through experience. *Harvard Educational Review* 48: 186–192.

Leichter, H. J. (1974). *The family as educator.* New York: Teachers College Press.

Lightfoot, S. L. (1978). *Worlds apart: Relationships between families and schools.* New York: Basic Books.

Marjoribanks, K. (1979). *Families and their learning environments: An empirical analysis.* London: Routledge and Kegan Paul.

Mayeske, G. W. (1973). *A study of the achievement of our nation's students.* Washington, DC: U.S. Government Printing Office.

McDill, E. L., and L. Rigsby. (1973). *Structure and process in secondary schools: The academic impact of educational climates.* Baltimore: Johns Hopkins University Press.

Olmsted, P. P., M. J. Wetherby, H. Leler, and R. I. Rubin. (1982). *Parent perspectives on home-school relationships in a compensatory education program.* Paper presented at the annual meeting of the American Educational Research Association in New York.

Rich, D., and C. Jones. (1977). *A family affair: Education.* Washington, DC: Home and School Institute.

Rich, D., J. Van Dien, and B. Mattox. (1979). Families as educators of their own children. In R. Brandt (Ed.), *Partners: Parents and schools* (pp. 26–40). Alexandria, VA: Association for Supervisors and Curriculum Development.

Richards, J. M., Jr. (1975). A simulation study of the use of change measures to compare educational programs. *American Educational Research Journal* 12: 299–311.

————. (1976). A simulation study comparing procedures for assessing individual educational growth. *Journal of Educational Psychology* 68: 603–612.

Rivlin, A. M., and P. M. Timpane. (1975). *Planned variation in education: Should we give up or try harder?* Washington, DC: The Brookings Institution.

Scott-Jones, D. (1987). Mother-as-teacher in the families of high- and low-achieving black first graders. *Journal of Negro Education* 56: 21–34.

Sinclair, R. L., ed. (1980). *A two-way street: Home-school cooperation in curriculum decision making.* Boston: Institute for Responsive Education.

Tidwell, R. (1980). *Evaluation of the accelerating home education and development (AHEAD) program, 1979–1980.* Los Angeles: University of California at Los Angeles. Mimeographed.

Tizard, J., W. N. Schofield, and J. Hewison. (1982). Collaboration between teachers and parents in assisting children's reading. *British Journal of Educational Psychology* 52: 1–15.

Walberg, H. J., R. E. Bole, and H. C. Waxman. (1980). School-based family socialization and reading achievement in the inner city. *Psychology in the Schools* 17: 509–514.

Wisler, C. E., B. P. Burnes, and D. Iwamoto. (1978). Follow-Through redux: A response to the critique by House, Glass, McLean, and Walker. *Harvard Educational Review* 48: 171–185.

Homework Practices, Achievements, and Behaviors of Elementary School Students[*]

ABSTRACT

Data from 82 teachers and 1,021 students and their parents are used to explore the correlates of homework activities and elementary school students' achievements and behaviors in school. Six groups of variables that concern homework are examined: homework time, homework appropriateness, student attitudes, teacher practices of parent involvement in learning activities at home, parent abilities and resources, and other student and family background variables.

Results suggest that at the elementary school level, students with low achievement in reading and math spend more time doing homework, have more minutes of parent help, and have parents who receive more frequent requests from teachers to help at home. Questions are raised about the design of homework, the involvement of families, and the need for research that builds on the reported correlates.

INTRODUCTION

Homework is considered one of the most important practices for establishing a successful academic environment in high school. Coleman, Hoffer, and Kilgore (1982) concluded that homework and discipline were two features of private schools that made them more successful learning environments than public schools. The implication is that if public schools assigned more homework, their students would learn more, and the schools would be more effective.

This prescription may be too simple. The notion that more is better may not be true for all students, in all subjects, at all skill levels, and at all grade levels. Indeed, if more homework is assigned than can be completed, or if inappropriate homework is assigned, then home assignments may be counterproductive for student achievement.

Most research on the effects of homework has been conducted at the secondary school level. Rutter, Maughan, Mortimore, and Ouston (1979) included three items about homework in their report on secondary school effects. They reported that the assignment of homework by teachers and the completion of homework by students were positively associated with student academic performance and school behavior.

* By Joyce L. Epstein. This work was supported by grants from the U.S. Department of Education, Office of Educational Research and Improvement. The opinions are the author's and do not necessarily reflect the policies or positions of OERI. Earlier versions of this paper were included in *ERS Information Folio: Homework* (Arlington, VA: Educational Research Service, 1987, 1990) and in the first edition of this volume, 2001.

They found that schools in which teachers gave frequent, substantial homework assignments had better student outcomes than did schools in which teachers assigned little homework. It is important to note, however, that their cross-sectional data were reported only as zero-order correlations, and could mean that schools with good, hardworking students had diligent teachers who assigned more homework more often.

Similarly, a National Assessment of Educational Progress (NAEP) study of students' mathematics skills showed that among 10,000 17-year-olds, good students did about 10 hours of homework and watched about 5 hours of TV per week. Poor students often received no homework and varied in the amount of TV they watched (Yeary, 1978).

Keith (1982) conducted an important study of the effects of homework on the achievement of secondary school students. Using data collected in the High School and Beyond (HSB) survey, he found a significant, positive effect of homework on high school grades (path coefficient = .192). Race, family background, ability, and school program (i.e., track) were statistically controlled, providing a rigorous analysis of cross-sectional data. He also showed an interesting linear relationship between hours of homework per week and school grades for students at three ability levels. The grades of low-ability students who did 10 hours of homework or more per week were as good as the grades of high-ability students who did no homework. Keith's findings suggest that students' personal commitments to school and homework may have positive consequences for students at all levels of ability.

The extant studies of homework, based on limited data, leave many questions unanswered. They yield mixed results, with some showing positive results from homework and others showing no results or negative correlations (Austin, 1978; Gray and Allison, 1971). Little is known about why or how homework is associated with student achievement, behavior, attendance, or attitudes. We need to understand why homework is assigned, whether it is appropriate in quantity and quality, and how it is structured to fit into teaching and reteaching skills in the classroom. It is important to determine if there are measurable effects on students of homework time, habits, completion, and assistance or support from parents and peers.

We also need to examine homework policies and practices at the elementary school level, because the achievements of young students largely determine the ability group or curriculum track they enter in middle and high schools. Homework could be important if it were shown to help more elementary students attain skills that are needed for success in the middle grades. Also, we need to understand parental involvement as a feature of homework, including whether parental assistance helps students who need the most help and whether and how these interactions affect parent-child relationships.

PURPOSES OF HOMEWORK

From the literature, I have identified 10 reasons that homework is assigned to students. Some are more defensible than others. The 10 Ps, or purposes, of homework are:

Practice: Increase speed, mastery, and maintenance of skills.

Preparation: Ensure readiness for the next class; complete activities and assignments started in class.

Participation: Increase the involvement of each student with learning tasks to increase the immediacy and enjoyment of learning.

Personal Development: Build student responsibility, perseverance, time management, self-confidence, and feelings of accomplishment; also develop and recognize students' talents in skills that may not be taught in class; extension and enrichment activities.

Parent-Child Relations: Establish communications between parent and child on the importance of schoolwork, homework, and learning; demonstrate applications of schoolwork to real-life situations and experiences; promote parental awareness of and support for students' work and progress.

Parent-Teacher Communication: Enable teachers to inform and involve families in children's curricular activities and enable parents to know what topics are being taught and how their children are progressing.

Peer Interactions: Encourage students to work together on assignments or projects, to motivate and learn from each other.

Policy: Fulfill directives from administrators at the district or school level for prescribed amounts of homework per day or week.

Public Relations: Demonstrate to the public that the school has rigorous standards for serious work, including homework. Also, productive interactions with the public may be designed as student-community homework assignments.

Punishment: Correct problems in conduct or productivity (not a defensible purpose).

All but the last purpose for homework are valid and important, although most teachers say that the main reason they assign homework is to give students time to practice skills learned in class (see Becker and Epstein, 1982 [Reading 3.1], and see Chapter 6 for more on the purposes and on improving the homework process).

Homework for Practice and Preparation

Homework enables students to practice skills, increase the ease with which skills can be used, and increase understanding of how and when to use the skills. Garner (1978) studied 400 fifth-, eighth-, and tenth-grade students. He measured both class time and homework time for specific subjects to establish exposure or total time in and out of school allocated to specific subjects. He found greater variation in homework than in class time for math and language arts. For example, almost one-third of the fifth-grade students in his sample had approximately eight hours' more total exposure to language arts skills and activities than the rest of the students, or more than one extra day per week for learning and using language arts. Older students received more homework than did younger students. At the tenth-grade level, one-half hour of homework in math extended class time by 75 percent for more math learning. Even at the fifth-grade level, 25 minutes of math homework added half again the time of a typical math class period for learning, reviewing, or practicing math. In Garner's study, high-ability students were given more homework and class time, especially at the high school level. Garner's findings point to the potential value of well-planned use of homework time to extend learning time and to give time to practice skills.

Homework for Participation

Homework increases individual participation in lessons. In many classrooms, only a few children participate frequently and "carry the class," while other children passively absorb information or not. By contrast, homework requires each student to participate actively and continually by reading, thinking, and recording ideas and answers on paper and by making decisions about how to complete the work. Homework is a structured opportunity for students to take control of their learning and thinking. At home, students control the amount of time they need to learn something and the number of consultations with others (including parents and peers) to make discoveries or to receive support for academic work. Students make self-assessments on the quality of their work and may compare their self-assessments with their teachers' marks or grades on homework completed.

Homework for Personal Development

Some teachers assign homework to help students take responsibility for schoolwork. Students must record the assignment, create a schedule to do the work, finish it, store it in their notebooks, and bring it to school when it is due. Homework may be designed to help students build "study skills"; follow directions; and increase perseverance, neatness, and completeness as they take responsibility for their own work.

Homework for Parent-Child Relations and Parent-Teacher Communications

Sometimes homework is the only form of serious communication about school and learning between parents and school-age children. Children may need help in following directions, remembering and interpreting what was learned in school, relearning information that was misunderstood or incompletely learned, and deciding whether their approach and presentation will be acceptable to the teacher.

Homework provides a reason for parents and children to exchange information, facts, and attitudes about school. Maertens and Johnston (1972) found that students who had homework assignments and who received immediate or delayed feedback from parents had better mastery of math skills than did students who received no homework.

Homework provides a reasonable, feasible way for teachers to communicate regularly with all families about what their children are learning in school and how their children's skills are progressing. Parents see, via homework assignments, how their children write, think, and execute an assignment. Teachers sometimes assign homework so that parents will not be surprised by their children's report card grades that reflect the quality of classwork.

There are important questions for new studies to ask about parent involvement in learning activities at home. For example: How can teachers advise all parents on how to monitor, check, and interact with children on homework? What practices help teachers guide parents to help when students have specific learning weaknesses and needs? If parents are guided in how to help at home, how can teachers and researchers measure if students improve in homework quality and achievement?

Homework for Peer Interactions

Homework may be designed to encourage students to work with each other on assignments and projects. Students may check each other's math, listen to and edit stories, explore their community, and engage in other exchanges and activities to learn from and with one another. Assignments may enable pairs or small groups of students to combine their talents in art, music, writing, drama, and other skills.

Homework as School Policy

Homework may be assigned to comply with district or school directives that a certain amount of homework must be given to all students on a certain number of days each week. Surveys of parents indicate that they have time to interact with and help their children on weekends (see Epstein, 1986 [Reading 3.4]), but schools often assign homework only on weekdays. Homework policies should be reviewed from year to year, with input from teachers, parents, and students to ensure that homework is designed to meet various positive purposes, including family-friendly schedules for parent-child interactions.

Homework as Public Relations

Homework is sometimes assigned to fulfill public expectations for rigorous demands for high student achievement. If parents and the public believe that a "good school" is one that gives homework, then educators may assign homework to meet this standard for school organization.

Homework as Punishment

Some teachers have assigned homework to punish students for lack of attention or for poor behavior in school. This includes the infamous assignments to write "I must not chew gum in school," or 500 words on appropriate behavior, or other reminders of school standards for behavior. These assignments focus on improving behavior more than on building academic skills, and produce embarrassment more than mastery. It is generally believed that punishment is an inappropriate purpose for homework. There are no known studies of the effects of punishing assignments on students.

The 10 purposes of homework require different homework designs. It is clear that not all desired outcomes for students will result from just any assignment. That is, assigning minutes or more minutes of homework will not necessarily produce greater achievement, better study habits, more positive attitudes about school, better connections of teachers and parents, more positive interactions of parent and child, or any other single desired outcome.

Thus, in research on homework, the outcome or result measured should be directly related to the *purpose* and *design* of homework. For example, if the stated purpose of homework is public relations, then the outcome measured should concern the understanding and attitudes of parents or the public. If the purpose is improved basic skills, then the homework should focus on specific skills, and studies should measure how those skills are affected by doing or not doing homework. If teachers, administrators, and parents define several purposes simultaneously, then multiple measures of results will be needed to determine whether any or all purposes are met.

For some purposes, the design of homework—how it is structured, introduced, and followed up—may be as important as its topic or content. Keshock (1976) reported that when college science homework was graded and counted as part of the course grade, homework performance improved, but test scores did not. Also, in a Los Angeles PUSH-EXCEL program, students were asked to work uninterrupted from 7:00 to 9:00 P.M. on home-learning activities. This requirement improved homework behaviors, but reports were not available on whether achievement improved (Yeary, 1978).

Using data from the International Association for the Evaluation of Educational Achievement (IEA), Wolf (1979) reported that homework time was important for specific academic subjects. He reported significant correlations between homework in science and literature and achievement in those subjects at the school and individual student levels. However, in regression analyses that accounted for family background and instructional program (or curriculum track), variables were entered in blocks, making it impossible to pinpoint the independent effects on achievement of homework compared to other instructional variables. The results show only that good students do more homework than do poor students in science and literature. The important point from this research, however, is that homework in one subject may affect outcomes in that subject only and may not have a general effect on achievement test scores or on other student attitudes and behaviors.

DATA AND APPROACH

In this study, the following information about homework was collected from each source involved in the homework process.

Data from Teachers

Teacher data included homework policies of the school and district, the amount of homework assigned, subjects of homework, the purpose of homework, attitudes and policies about parental help with or corrections of homework, the policy of requiring parents to sign homework, estimates of students who complete homework, nominations of students who have problems with homework or who are homework "stars," and use of class time to check or correct homework.

Data from Principals

Principal data included district and school policies, procedures to check teachers' homework assignments, and attitudes about whether parents should help with homework.

Data from Parents

Parent information included reports of the amount of time the child spends on homework, parents' understanding of teachers' policies on parental help on homework, evaluation of appropriate level of difficulty of the child's homework, the child's understanding and completion of homework, and communications with the teacher about homework.

Data from Students

Student information included the amount of homework assigned and completed, weekend homework, habits of doing homework, help at home on homework, parents' knowledge of homework assignments, problems and completion of homework, the appropriate level of challenge in homework, attitudes about homework, and written comments.

Surveys of teachers, principals, parents, and students in 16 Maryland school districts were conducted in 1980 and 1981. Approximately 3,700 first-, third-, and fifth-grade teachers and their principals in 600 schools were surveyed (see Becker and Epstein, 1982 [Reading 3.2]; Epstein and Becker, 1982 [Reading 3.2]). From the original sample, 36 teachers were identified who strongly emphasized parent involvement in learning activities at home. These "case" teachers were selected at random from a stratified sample of leaders in parent involvement to represent the three grade levels; urban, suburban, and rural districts; socioeconomic conditions of the communities in the state; and teachers' education, experience, and teaching conditions. Forty-six "comparison" teachers were then matched to the case teachers on the same selection criteria, but these teachers were not leaders in their use of parent involvement in learning activities at home.

The case and comparison teachers and their principals were interviewed at length about instructional practices in general and parent involvement practices and leadership. The parents of the children in the 82 teachers' classrooms were surveyed about their attitudes toward and experiences with parent involvement. In all, 1,269 parents responded by mail to the survey, a response rate of 59 percent. Approximately 600 fifth-grade students were surveyed about their homework activities. This report uses data from parents and teachers to explore the correlates of homework activities and student achievements and behaviors in school.

EXPLORATORY ANALYSES

In this study, selected data from teachers, principals, students, and parents were explored to learn more about how homework assignments and home-school interactions were linked to student achievements and behaviors. Table 3.30 presents six sets of variables on homework and their zero-order correlations with reading and math achievements, homework performance, and classroom behavior. The six sets of selected variables and their scoring are described below.

Homework Time. Minutes spent per day is a 5-point score from no homework to one hour or more; minutes parent helps or could help per day is an 8-point score from no minutes to one hour or more.

Homework Quality. Appropriate amount and difficulty are 3-point scores from too easy to too difficult, and too little to too much; appropriate purpose is a 4-point score of parent disagreement that homework is just busy work (scored negatively).

Student Attitudes. Parent assessment of whether the child likes to talk about school and homework and whether the child is tense about homework (scored negatively) are 4-point scores from strongly agree to strongly disagree.

Teacher Practices. Parents reported the frequency of use of 12 practices of parent involvement, including reading, discussion, informal activities, formal contracts, signing homework, tutoring, and drill and practice. Parents' reports that the teacher thinks parents should help, and reports that they receive many ideas from the teacher, are 4-point scores from strongly agree to strongly disagree. Parents agreed or disagreed that the teacher talked to them directly about their child's homework, need for parental help at home, or classroom behavior. Ratings by parents or principals on the overall quality of the teacher are 6-point scores from poor to outstanding.

TABLE 3.30   Homework Variables as Correlates of Student Achievements and Behaviors[a, b]

	Achievements		Student Measures			Mean/S.D.
				Behaviors		
	Reading	Math	Homework Star	Homework Problem	Discipline Problem	
1. Homework Time						
Minutes spent	−.108	−.052	.081	.000	−.011	3.00/1.25
Minutes parent helps	−.180	−.195	−.010	.070	.134	26.32/15.40
Minutes parent could help	−.042	−.077	.090	−.137	.045	43.84/17.34
2. Homework Quality						
Appropriate amount	.019	−.033	−.075	.030	.041	2.16/0.53
Appropriate difficulty	.032	.025	−.021	.012	.053	2.07/0.40
Appropriate purpose	.047	.025	.045	.009	.012	3.61/0.72
3. Student Attitudes						
Likes to talk about school and homework	.131	.117	.140	−.132	−.124	3.35/0.93
Not tense about homework	.179	.141	.074	−.119	−.032	2.90/1.16
4. Teacher Practices						
Frequent requests for parent involvement	−.137	−.123	.054	.043	.020	3.98/3.36
Teacher thinks parents should help	−.187	−.172	−.025	.013	−.007	2.20/0.82
Parent receives ideas from teacher	−.061	−.077	.063	.019	−.042	2.44/1.17
Teacher talked to parent about:						
(a) Homework	−.087	−.137	−.070	.118	.012	0.18/0.38
(b) Parent help at home	−.132	−.110	.018	−.008	−.032	0.22/0.42
(c) Behavior	−.055	−.072	−.012	.061	.275	0.46/0.50
Parent rating of teacher quality	.060	.093	.105	−.026	−.077	3.76/1.19
Principal rating of teacher quality	.113	.093	−.044	−.085	.003	2.52/1.04
5. Parent Abilities and Resources						
Parent education	.196	.238	.027	−.100	−.057	2.60/1.23
Confidence in ability to help	.140	.166	.085	−.073	−.034	3.12/1.11
Educational items at home	.238	.262	.071	−.105	−.136	4.67/2.53
Number of books at home	.161	.192	.060	−.095	−.078	3.97/1.20
Regular place for homework	−.043	−.056	−.053	.080	.019	1.09/0.29

(continues)   239

TABLE 3.30 *(continued)*

	Achievements			Student Measures Behaviors		Mean/S.D.
	Reading	Math	Homework Star	Homework Problem	Discipline Problem	
6. Other Student and and Family Factors						
Sex (Female)	.093	.033	.129	–.075	–.201	1.50/0.50
Race (White)	.083	.155	–.015	–.005	–.064	0.64/0.48
Residence (City)	–.043	–.146	.008	–.018	.034	0.35/0.48
Two-parent home	.057	.142	.085	–.066	–.056	1.76/0.43
Mother works	–.018	.021	.015	.027	–.019	0.61/0.49
Hours TV	–.053	–.082	.009	.003	.057	2.36/1.17
Parent expectations for education	.316	.308	.090	–.137	–.082	2.39/1.13
Grade level	–.002	.045	.033	.036	–.015	2.89/1.70

a N = 1,021 students whose parents participated in the survey for whom information on classroom achievements and behavior was provided by the teacher.

b Correlations of .08 or higher are significant at or beyond the .01 level.

Parent Abilities and Resources. Parent education is a 6-point score from less than high school to graduate school; confidence in ability is a 4-point score from strongly agree to strongly disagree that they have enough training to help the child in reading and math. Educational items is a checklist of 10 items that students may use at home for homework, including a ruler, dictionary, globe, and others. Number of books at home is a 5-point score ranging from fewer than 10 to more than 100 books. Regular place for homework is a single item of agreement or disagreement.

Other Student and Family Factors. Sex of student is scored female = 1, male = 0; race is scored white = 1, black = 0; residence is scored 1 = city, 0 = suburb/rural; family structure is scored 1 or 2 for one or two parents home, 1 or 0 for mother works or does not work outside the home, hours of TV per day ranging from none to 5 or more hours; parent expectations for child's education is a 4-point score from finish high school to finish graduate school; and grade level refers to the student's grade, 1, 3, or 5.

RESULTS: HOMEWORK PRACTICES AND STUDENT SKILLS AND BEHAVIOR

Homework Time

Section 1 of Table 3.30 shows how three measures of homework time correlate with student achievements and behaviors. The three measures are the average number of minutes spent by the child on homework per day; the average number of minutes the parent helps the child in response to teacher requests; and the number of minutes the parent could help if shown how to do so.

Time spent doing homework ranged from none (13 percent) to 15 minutes (21 percent), 30 minutes (36 percent), 45 minutes (13 percent), or one hour or more (17 percent). Parents helped on the average of 25 minutes per night when asked to do so by teachers but said they could help about 45 minutes per night if the teacher showed them how to help.

The relationships between homework time and parent help on student achievements in reading and math are negative. That is, students with lower achievement in reading and math spend more time on homework and get more help from parents. The negative relationships may indicate that teachers are reaching out to parents to obtain extra help for children who need additional learning time and/or that parents who recognize their children's weaknesses are trying to help on their own. This probability is supported by the fact that parents of children who are deemed homework and discipline "problems" spend more time helping their children than do other parents. Children who are doing well in school spend less time and need less help from parents than do weaker students.

The right side of the table in section 1 shows the associations of homework time and school-related behaviors. Teachers consider children who do more homework as homework "stars." Parents of homework stars say they could spend more time assisting their children. The parents of students who are homework and discipline "problems" already spend more time than do other parents assisting their children.

These data should not be interpreted to mean that if more time is spent on homework and more help is given, student achievement will decline. This is a good example of the inadequacy, indeed inappropriateness, of correlations to address questions of effects on students. These cross-sectional data simply tell what associations of variables exist, not whether one variable leads to or causes the other.

The patterns reported here are, however, indicative of some well-known facts about elementary school students and their homework. First, at the elementary school level, all students are likely to be assigned the same homework. The same assignment—such as learning 20 spelling words or completing 10 math problems—may take some students longer than others to complete. Students who have problems learning in school need to spend more time on an assignment to understand what other children master in class and complete quickly at home. Also, teachers may ask parents to see that their elementary school children finish their work, even if they do not ask the parents to help the child with needed skills. Thus, slower students may spend more time on homework, and parents will spend more time monitoring or helping students who need more time to learn or complete their work.

Homework Quality

Section 2 of Table 3.30 features three measures of parents' estimates of the appropriateness and value of the homework their children receive. There are no significant correlations of these measures with achievements or behaviors. One reason for this is the lack of variation in the parents' ratings. Approximately 92 percent of the parents agreed that homework was not busy work, 90 percent said that the child's homework was the appropriate level of difficulty, and 78 percent thought the child received the right amount of homework. Because parents of successful and unsuccessful students generally agreed about the value and appropriateness of homework, these variables do not explain differences in student skills, homework completion, or classroom behavior.

Student Attitudes

Section 3 explores relationships of student attitudes toward homework with student achievement and behaviors. Children who like to talk about school and homework with a parent have higher reading and math skills and are more often considered homework stars. Children who do not like to talk about school and homework are more apt to be homework and discipline problems. Also, children who are not tense about homework are higher achievers and less likely to be identified as having homework problems.

In this sample, close to 20 percent of the elementary school students do not like to talk about school with their parents, and 35 percent say they are tense when working with their parents on homework. These attitudes and behaviors may be early warning signs of more serious problems of commitment to schoolwork. Teachers may be able to help parents learn how to help their children build confidence and positive attitudes about school and homework. Positive attitudes toward school are good indicators of day-to-day success in school, commitment to school goals, and the likelihood of staying in school, even if they do not directly relate to high achievement (see Reading 3.9). Here we see, however, that a very specific behavior—talking about school and homework at home—is correlated with reading and math achievement and with successful actions and behaviors.

Teacher Practices

Section 4 includes measures of teacher practices of parent involvement concerning homework. The correlations indicate that teachers make more requests of parents whose children achieve at lower levels. These results support the information reported in section 1 that parents spend more time with children who need more help, and suggest that parent time is given in response to requests from teachers.

The data indicate that homework and discipline problems are addressed through specific communications with parents. Teachers talk directly with parents about homework activities if the students are identified as having homework problems ($r = .118$), and teachers talk directly with parents about school behavior if students are identified as having discipline problems ($r = .275$). Teacher practices of parent involvement are more highly and consistently correlated with student achievement, showing clearly that teachers reach out especially when they need parents' help with students whose math and reading skills are low.

Parents say they receive more frequent requests, more messages that they should help, and more direct communications from teachers about how to help at home when their children are low in reading and math skills. Principals and parents, however, rate teachers higher in overall teaching quality when students are high in achievement, and parents give higher ratings to teachers if their children are homework stars.

Parent Abilities and Resources

Section 5 of the table examines five family resources that may aid student achievement and behavior. Four measures are significantly and positively correlated with reading and math skills: parent education, parental confidence about ability to help in reading and math, educational items in the home, and books in the home. When these resources are lacking at home, children are more likely to have homework problems.

Having a regular place for homework is not highly associated with achievement or behavior. Others have also reported that a regular place for homework is not as important as a regular habit of completion, regardless of where homework is done (McCutcheon, 1983). In these data, however, the lack of importance of the variable is probably due to the lack of variation in the responses, with about 91 percent of the families reporting that the children have a regular place for doing homework.

Other Student and Family Factors

Section 6 shows the association of other student and family factors that are believed to affect homework activities, achievements, and behaviors. There are strong correlations of race (white), location (non-city residence), and two parents at home with higher math skills, but not with reading skills. Female students tend to have higher reading scores and are more often viewed as homework stars, whereas males are more often labeled discipline problems.

Parental educational expectations for children are strongly associated with higher reading and math achievement, more homework stars, and fewer homework and discipline problems. Even more than socioeconomic status variables, parents' expectations are positively associated with student achievement. Parents' expectations are, in part, based on students' history of high achievement, good work, and good behavior. Thus, parents' expectations reported at one point in time reflect their children's prior tests, report card grades, homework assignments, and other parent-child and parent-teacher interactions. Parents have higher expectations for students who are achieving and behaving well in school.

Some family variables are less important than might be expected from popular opinion. Hours of TV watched per day are not highly correlated with reading or math skills and not at all correlated with being a homework star or having school-linked problems. There is no significant association of the mother working outside the home with reading or math achievements, homework completion, or classroom behavior. Student achievement and behavior are not significantly affected by grade level. There are high- and low-achieving students, and well- and poorly behaved students, at all grade levels.

SUMMARY AND DISCUSSION

Several intriguing patterns emerge from the six groups of variables reviewed in Table 3.30 to guide future studies.

Reading and Math Skills

Low achievement is associated with more time spent doing homework, more minutes of parent help, and more frequent requests from teachers for parent involvement in learning activities at home. The significant negative associations indicate that in the elementary school parents are asked to assist children who need more help. At this level of schooling, not much homework is assigned per night, and students who have trouble with the work can work a little longer to complete the assignment.

By the time students are in high school, much more homework is given, and more is given to brighter students. Poor students in high school tend not to work very long on what they do not understand and typically do not expect and may not want their parents' help. Most middle and high school teachers do not ask parents to help with or even monitor students' homework. These patterns are particularly interesting for what they might mean for improving homework designs, assignment, and connections with families.

Homework and Classroom Behavior

Parents report spending more time helping children who teachers say are discipline and homework problems. The parents of other children say they could spend more time helping their children at home, if they were shown how to do so. There is a supply of untapped parental assistance available to teachers that may be especially useful in improving the skills of average and below-average students who could do better with additional time and well-guided attention.

One important correlate of homework and discipline problems is the lack of educational trappings at home (e.g., books, rulers, globes, dictionaries, art supplies). Teachers who seek parental help in solving student homework and discipline problems may need to find ways (perhaps including connections to business partners) to make educational resources available for use at home.

Importance of Positive Attitudes and Exchanges about Schoolwork and Homework

Children who like to talk about school and homework with their parents and are less tense about their work tend to be good students, homework stars, and well behaved in class. Children who are tense when working with their parents on homework activities are more often homework problems. Yet children with achievement and discipline problems are those whose parents are spending more minutes helping at home. It is pretty clear that parents of children who have problems in school require guidance on how to help their children at home, or ineffective teaching at home could redouble the school problems.

Homework is a manipulable variable. Teachers and administrators control whether to assign homework and how much homework to assign. They design activities that encourage or prevent parental involvement in learning activities that students bring home.

Need for Full Analyses and Longitudinal Data

This study provides a base on which to build. It also shows that a simple association of homework time (assigned or spent) and student achievement is not enough to understand if or when homework is important for effective teaching and learning. The array of correlates makes it clear that future research must include multivariate analyses that take into account the variables from sections 5 and 6 of Table 3.30 of family resources and family and student factors that affect achievements and behaviors. The correlates are an important start for understanding the independent effects of homework time, quality, attitudes, and parent involvement on achievement and behavior.

The bottom line concerning homework is whether time spent pays off for improving and maintaining school achievement, homework completion, and other school attitudes and behaviors. This question is particularly important for students who need extra time and extra help to learn basic and advanced skills. Future studies will need longitudinal data to learn whether achievement and behavior improve when students put in time on homework and when they are monitored and assisted by their families. More broadly, new measurement models will be needed to study the complexities underlying homework design, assignment, completion, follow-up, and interactions with families.

The relationships of homework time, achievements, and behaviors at the elementary school level are important because they differ markedly from relationships reported for secondary school students. Younger students and their families are more responsive to school demands for mastering basic skills, and the children and their parents spend more time working on needed skills.

Somewhere between the elementary and middle grades, the philosophies and practices of teachers, students, and parents change. In the upper grades, brighter students tend to spend more time on homework, and many slower students stop doing homework altogether. In many cases, teachers in middle and high schools assign more homework to brighter students because they expect it will be done. Many parents in middle and high schools stop monitoring homework, especially if they are not given information about homework policies or how to work with their adolescents. There are many interesting questions for future research on the differences in the amount of time slower and brighter students spend on homework in the elementary and secondary grades, and why these patterns occur.

REFERENCES

Austin, J. D. (1978). Homework research in mathematics. *School Science and Mathematics* 78: 115–121.

Becker, H. J., and J. L. Epstein. (1982, November). Parent involvement: A study of teacher practices. *Elementary School Journal* 83: 85–102. (Reading 3.1).

Coleman, J. S., T. Hoffer, and S. Kilgore. (1982). *High school achievement.* New York: Basic Books.

Epstein, J. L. (1986). Parents' reactions to teacher practices of parent involvement. *Elementary School Journal* 86: 277–294. (Reading 3.4).

Epstein, J. L., and H. J. Becker. (1982, November). Teacher reported practices of parent involvement: Problems and possibilities. *Elementary School Journal* 83: 103–113. (Reading 3.2).

Garner, W. T. (1978). Linking school resources to educational outcomes: The role of homework. *Teachers College Research Bulletin* 19: 1–10.

Gray, R. F., and D. E. Allison. (1971). An experimental study of the relationship of homework to pupil success in computation with fractions. *School Science and Mathematics* 71: 339–346.

Keith, T. Z. (1982). Time spent on homework and high school grades: A large-sample path analysis. *Journal of Educational Psychology* 74: 248–253.

Keshock, E. G. (1976). The relative value of optional and mandatory homework. *Teaching Method News* 8: 3–32.

Maertens, N., and J. Johnston. (1972). Effects of arithmetic homework on the attitudes and achievements of fourth, fifth, and sixth grade pupils. *School Science and Mathematics* 72: 117–126.

McCutcheon, G. (1983). *How does homework influence the curriculum?* Paper presented at the annual meeting of the American Educational Research Association in Montreal.

Rutter, M., B. Maughan, P. Mortimer, and J. Ouston. (1979). *Fifteen thousand hours: Secondary schools and their effects on children.* Cambridge, MA: Harvard University Press.

Wolf, R. M. (1979). Achievement in the United States. In H. J. Walberg (Ed.), *Educational environments and effects* (pp. 313–330). Berkeley: McCutchan.

Yeary, E. E. (1978). What about homework? *Today's Education* (September–October): 80–82.

Student Reactions to Teachers' Practices of Parent Involvement*

Decades of studies indicate that home environments and family involvement in education are important for student success in school (Coleman et al., 1966; Epstein, 1984; Leichter, 1974; Marjoribanks, 1979; Mayeske, 1973; McDill and Rigsby, 1973). The evidence is clear that parental encouragement and involvement at school and at home boost children's achievement, even after student ability and family socioeconomic status are taken into account.

However, not all families get involved in school-related activities or show interest in their children's work (Lightfoot, 1978). It is important to learn what would happen if schools took steps to engage all parents, not just those who become involved on their own. Another crucial question is: What do students think about parent involvement? Ironically, although students are ultimately responsible for their own education, they are rarely consulted for ideas about how to improve their schools, or about how they, their teachers, and their families might best work together to enhance student success in school (Epstein, 1981). This study explores (1) what students know and say about home-school connections and (2) the results of students' experiences with family involvement on their school attitudes and behaviors.

STUDY BACKGROUND

Research shows that teachers vary in the extent to which they use different practices and strategies to involve parents in learning activities at home (see Becker and Epstein, 1982 [Reading 3.1]; Epstein and Becker, 1982 [Reading 3.2]). In a survey of 3,700 first-, third-, and fifth-grade teachers, some reported a high emphasis on parent involvement ("case" teachers), and some reported average or low emphasis on parent involvement ("comparison" teachers).

A sample of 30 case and 30 comparison teachers was matched on characteristics of their teaching situation, including grade level, city or county, district, socioeconomic status of the children taught, and type of teaching assignment. Additional data were collected in extended interviews with the case and comparison teachers and with their principals, surveys were administered to parents of these teachers' students, and surveys were obtained from fifth-grade students in case and comparison teachers' classes. The case and comparison teachers also provided data on their students' achievements, school behaviors, and homework completion patterns. School records were culled for third- and fifth-grade students' achievement test scores. This study focuses on 390 fifth-grade students in the matched classrooms of nine case and nine comparison teachers.

* By Joyce L. Epstein. (2001). This research was supported by grants from the U.S. Department of Education/OERI. The results and opinions do not necessarily reflect the position or policy of OERI.

Few previous studies of family involvement focus on upper elementary school-age children. Several researchers and program developers report evidence from several completed studies and unpublished dissertations suggesting generally positive effects of the programs on parents and students (Comer, 1980; Gordon, 1979; Henderson, 1981; Rich, Van Dien, and Mattox, 1979). However, most studies are uneven and their measures of parent involvement are incomplete.

One study of 764 sixth-grade students by Benson, Medrich, and Buckley (1980) is interesting, even though it does not focus on teachers' practices of parent involvement on school-related activities. The researchers examined the natural variation in how parents spend time with their children at home in everyday interactions such as eating dinner together, in cultural enrichment activities, in participation at school, and in setting rules for their children. They looked at the relationship of parents' time and student achievement for students from low, middle, and high SES families. They found that family time in cultural and other activities positively influenced the achievement of students from all socioeconomic levels, but especially students from high and middle SES families. The results illustrate, again, how the self-initiated activities of some families are advantageous to their children.

In the present study, data from fifth-grade students are explored to determine if teachers' practices of parent involvement and reports of parents' assistance differ among students in case and comparison teachers' classes. The next sections give an overview of the data collected from students, principals, and teachers, and the results of analyses of the effects of multiple measures of parent involvement and support on student attitudes and school behaviors.

DATA

Surveys were collected from 390 fifth-grade students in case and comparison teachers' classrooms. The surveys asked students about their homework assignments, homework completion, parents' help at home, attitudes about school and homework, success in school, behavior, college plans, and open-ended comments about homework activities. In most classes the teachers administered the short, anonymous surveys and collected them in mailing envelopes that were returned directly to the researchers.

In one district, local regulations required students to obtain individual, signed parental permission slips to take surveys in class. The timing of the study in the spring of 1981 made it risky to wait for signed permission slips. Teachers did not have time to distribute and collect permission slips, then administer the surveys, when they were concluding tests and other end-of-year activities. In this set of classrooms, student surveys were included with the parents' surveys and were completed by the students at home and mailed back to the researchers.

In the school-administered settings, the response rate of students was from 90 to 100 percent, depending on number of children present the day of the survey. In the home-administered settings, the response rate averaged about 50 percent. The lower response rate of home-administered surveys reflects the parents' responses to the survey, parents' decisions to give the student survey to their children, and children's willingness to complete the survey at home. These obstacles highlight the benefits of conducting no-risk surveys of students as part of standard school and district evaluations of their own programs.

Independent Variables

Multiple Measures of Parent Involvement. Multiple measures of teachers' practices of parental involvement were collected from teachers, principals, and students. These included teachers' reports of their parental involvement practices; teachers' ratings of parents who are "helpful" to their children on school activities at home; principals' ratings of teachers' leadership in involving parents; students' estimates of the frequency of assignments from teachers that request parent involvement at home; and students' estimates of the extent of parental awareness and support of homework activities.

Because no single measure is perfect, multiple indicators of the construct of parent involvement were used to try to correct for measurement problems and check for consistent patterns of effects of parent involvement on students' achievements and behaviors. For example, teachers' reports of their parental involvement practices were collected one year before the survey of students was conducted. Principals may not be fully aware of how much and how well their teachers involved parents with students at home. Students' estimates of teachers' practices and parental support were obtained from a limited number of questions in a short survey. Teachers' estimates of parents who were helpful at home were based on different degrees of contact with the parents of the students in their classes.

Each of these measures, used alone, would raise doubts about the effects of parent involvement. By contrast, patterns of results from more than one measure should provide more credible and convincing information about positive, negative, or no effects of involvement on student achievements and behaviors.

Other Explanatory Variables. Student gender, race, location of school in city or suburb, student ability (i.e., ratings of low, average, and high ability provided by teachers), and the general quality of teachers' skills (i.e., quality of lessons, knowledge, creativity, and discipline) are used as statistical controls in regression analysis. These variables have been found to affect student outcomes and teaching effectiveness, and, therefore, must be taken into account in estimates of effects on students of teachers' practices of parent involvement.

Dependent Variables

Just as multiple measures of parent involvement were used to identify patterns of effects, this study incorporates a variety of dependent variables from the student surveys and teachers' reports to identify patterns of effects of involvement on indicators of student success or problems in school. The dependent variables include:

- Two measures of student attitudes: Two items on attitudes toward homework (i.e., Homework is a waste of time; I learn a lot from homework) and five items of student satisfaction with school (Epstein, 1981).
- One measure of home-school similarity: Three items (i.e., My parent is a teacher; I learn important things at home; School teaches what my family wants me to learn).
- One measure of extra schoolwork done at home: Two items (i.e., I do weekend projects assigned by my teacher; I complete work on weekends on my own).
- One measure of teacher-family exchanges: Two items (i.e., My teacher knows my family; If I am in trouble, my teacher lets my family know).
- One measure of student homework habits: Two items (i.e., I do my homework at the same time; I do my homework in the same place).
- One measure of parent support: Four items (i.e., My parent reminds me to do my homework; My parent knows when I need help with homework; My parent knows when my homework is finished; My parent knows when I have done a good job with homework).
- Teacher estimates of student behavior, including the identification of students who are homework stars, homework problems, and discipline problems.

RESULTS

Table 3.31 shows the background characteristics of students in the case and comparison teachers' classrooms, along with teachers' ratings of student and parent qualities and principals' ratings of teachers. In case teachers' classrooms, there were fewer males and more females, fewer white and more black students, and more students with average reading and math abilities. These characteristics are statistically controlled in all analyses of effects of teacher practices of parent involvement on the dependent variables.

Teachers were asked to nominate as many of their children as fit a set of descriptors: "homework star," "homework problem," and "discipline problem." The teachers also nominated families who were "helpful" or who typically provided "no follow-through" on homework and home-learning activities. More students in case teachers' classrooms were nominated as homework stars, and fewer were considered discipline problems, than in comparison teachers' classrooms. About equal numbers were homework problems. More students in case teachers' classrooms had parents whom teachers considered "helpful," and fewer parents showed "no follow-through," than in comparison teachers' classrooms. Overall, the raw data suggest that case teachers had more positive estimates of more of their students and families on homework and home-school connections than did the comparison teachers, reflecting and confirming the case teachers' emphasis on family involvement.

TABLE 3.31   Summary of Student Characteristics, Teacher Characteristics, and Student Opinions in Nine Case and Nine Control (Matched) Fifth-Grade Teachers' Classrooms

Student Background Characteristics	% Students in Case Teachers' Classrooms N = 199	% Students in Comparison Teachers' Classrooms N = 191
Male	41	56
Female	59	44
White	46	55
Black	54	45
Urban	53	52
Other	47	48
Reading ability		
Low	11	9
Middle	54	49
High	35	40
Math ability		
Low	14	26
Middle	48	34
High	35	40
Teachers' evaluations of student behaviors and family support for parent involvement		
Homework star	30	20
Homework problem	19	19
Discipline problem	11	18
Helpful parents	56	20
No follow-through by parent	12	17
Principals' estimates of teachers' qualities and excellent teaching skills (i.e., quality of lessons, knowledge, creativity, discipline)	51	45

Student Attitudes and Behaviors

Table 3.32 summarizes the effects of the indicators of parent involvement and support on students' attitudes about school, homework, and home-school connections. Five measures of parent involvement and support derived from data from teachers, principals, and students are featured. The columns are labeled Case/Comparison Teachers (an indicator based on teachers' reports of the extent of practices of parental involvement); Helpful Parents (from a checklist from teachers of parents' helpfulness and follow-through); Teacher Practices to Involve Parents at Home (from principals' ratings); Homework That Involves Parents; and Parent Awareness and Support (two reports from students on the kinds of homework they receive and their interactions with parents on homework).

Each dependent variable is regressed, separately, on each of the parent involvement measures along with student background characteristics (gender, race, reading and math abilities), school location (urban/suburban), and teacher quality. With these potentially important influences statistically controlled, we can look at the effects of parent involvement practices on student outcomes. Table 3.32 reports the standardized regression coefficient (ß) and, for significant associations, the test statistic (F). The last column of the table lists other explanatory variables that significantly affect students' attitudes and behaviors.

Student Attitudes. The first row shows that student attitudes toward school are positively and significantly influenced by four of the five parent involvement measures provided by teachers, principals, and students. Students have more positive attitudes about school if they report that their parents are aware of and are involved in helping with homework, if their teachers rate the parents as helpful, and if principals report that the teacher works to involve families at home. Student attitudes toward homework, in the second row of the table, also are significantly more positive when students say their teachers assign interactive homework and their parents are aware of and involved with them on homework.

Gender and race also influence attitudes toward school and homework. Female students and African American students have more positive attitudes than do other students, with all other background and ability measures statistically controlled. Interestingly, student reading and math abilities do not significantly influence student attitudes, echoing earlier evidence that achievement and attitudes about school are not necessarily highly related measures (Epstein, 1981).

Student Reports of Home-School Connections. The middle three rows of Table 3.32 indicate that student interactions with parents at home about homework affect their beliefs that their home and school are similar and that their teacher knows their family. Student beliefs about strong home-school connections are explained by all five indicators of parent involvement from teachers, principals, and the students themselves.

Student ability and teacher quality also affect beliefs about home-school connections. Students with high reading and math abilities, and those with excellent teachers as rated by principals, also are more likely to see their home and school as more similar and their teachers and parents in closer communication.

Parent involvement indicators are less powerfully linked to student reports that their teacher would inform their family if they were in trouble in school, in part because there is less variation on this measure. Most students believe that their teachers would, indeed, contact their parents about trouble in school.

Homework Habits. The last four rows of Table 3.32 reveal that students' knowledge and reports about their own experiences at home are the best predictors of their homework habits. Students are more likely to do their homework at the same time and in the same place if they frequently interact with parents and if parents are aware

TABLE 3.32 Summary of Analyses of Effects of Multiple Measures of Parent Involvement on Multiple Measures of Student Attitudes and Behavior*

Parent Involvement Measure:		Case/Comparison Teachers Surveys (Teachers) ß	(F)	Helpful Parents Checklist (Teachers) ß	(F)	Teacher Practices to Involve Parents Rating Scale (Principals) ß	(F)	Homework That Involves Parents at Home Survey (Students) ß	(F)	Parent Awareness and Support Survey (Students) ß	(F)	Which Other Variables Are Significant
Attitudes toward school		.028		.083	(4.19)	.151	(11.40)	.235	(33.31)	.139	(12.94)	Female, Black
	R^2	.293		.301		.318		.364		.323		
Attitudes toward homework		.047		-.013		-.032		.218	(27.71)	.149	(14.58)	Female, Black
	R^2	.266		.253		.255		.233		.293		
Home-school similarities		.040		-.044		.153	(11.01)	.198	(21.86)	.142	(12.68)	Not City, High Ability
	R^2	.167		.177		.216		.251		.222		
Teacher knows Ability, family		.073	(3.21)	.219	(28.59)	.153	(11.05)	.158	(13.89)	.099	(6.10)	Not City, High
	R^2	.198		.280		.229		.238		.211		Teacher Quality
Teacher informs family if trouble		.055		.092	(4.85)	.040		-.029		.079	(3.85)	Female, Black
	R^2	.177		.180		.161		.159		.175		
Do homework at the same time		-.043		.024		.091	(3.82)	.142	(10.94)	.108	(7.22)	None
	R^2	.110		.118		.140		.176		.158		
Do homework in the same place		.058		.015		.027		.139	(10.45)	.136	(11.40)	None
	R^2	.110		.087		.091		.156		.161		
Assigned weekend homework		.143	(12.55)	.057		.018		.110	(6.74)	.033		White, City, High Ability
	R^2	.251		.229		.223		.245		.225		
Do homework on weekend		.068		.059		.071		.157	(14.08)	.165	(18.03)	Female, Black, Not Urban
	R^2	.263		.255		.256		.289		.298		

*Data from teachers, principals, and students, with gender, race, ability, location, and teacher quality controlled. N = 390.

253

of their work. These homework habits are not explained by any of the other variables used in the equations, such as student gender, race, ability, and teacher quality.

Teachers' practices of parent involvement are, however, significantly linked to student reports that they are assigned homework on weekends. Teachers who frequently involve parents in learning activities at home are more likely to take advantage of available weekend time to encourage these interactions. Students say they do more homework on the weekend when their parents support their work.

Suburban students and those with high reading and math abilities are more likely than other students to see similarities between home and school, think the teacher knows their family, and have teachers who assign weekend homework, net of all other student and school characteristics. These analyses indicate, however, that if parent involvement is activated by teachers and experienced at home, students in any neighborhood and with low or high academic skills report strong family and school connections and do their homework whenever assigned, including weekends.

SUMMARY AND DISCUSSION

Overall, more than half (25) of the 45 tests of effects of the five measures of parental involvement on nine student behaviors and attitudes were significant. Many were not only significant, but also were strong and educationally important, even after other highly influential student ability, family background, and school and teacher characteristics were taken into account. Although gender, race, location, teacher quality, and student ability were sometimes important, these explanatory variables did not extinguish the positive effects of teachers' efforts to involve families and parent support at home on student attitudes and behaviors.

Two cross-cutting patterns in Table 3.32 are worthy of note. First, the most consistent positive effects on all nine measures of student attitudes and behaviors are linked to students' reports of having assignments that encourage interactions at home, and their recognition of parental awareness, support, and involvement. Second, the most consistent effect across the five measures of parent involvement from students, teachers, and principals is on student reports that the "teacher knows my family." Students are significantly more likely to say their teacher knows the family when their teachers report that they frequently involve parents; the teachers see parents as helpful; the principals recognize that teachers are working to involve families; and the students themselves say that their parents are aware of and engaged in homework activities.

The use of multiple measures of involvement, multiple reporters, and multiple measures of student attitudes and behaviors strengthens any single result reported in Table 3.32. Principals' views of teachers' skills in involving parents, teachers' reports of their practices of involvement, and their views of parents are important indicators of home-school connections. In this study, students' reports add significantly to an understanding of parent involvement. The data suggest that when their families are involved with them on school matters, students are significantly more likely to develop attitudes and conduct activities that will keep them in the students' role and on a successful path through school. At the same time, had only student reports been included, the self-reports might be considered distorted or inflated by self-interests. By including confirmatory reports from teachers and principals, the effects of parent involvement on student attitudes and homework habits are more clear and more credible than in the past.

Where do these results lead? Positive attitudes about school and homework and good homework habits are likely to help students stay in school, even if they are not the top or most academically successful students. Students are more likely to be successful in school if they see their parents as teachers, hear that their families want them to learn what their teachers teach at school, and say that the things they learn at home are important.

There is a growing consensus among educators that parents must play a more active role in their children's education. It is believed that parent involvement assists educators' efforts to help individual students attain basic skills and reach high academic standards. It is expected that if schools systematically and equitably informed and involved all parents, many more students would see that their families and teachers have similar goals for high achievement and good behavior in school and expectations for completing homework at home. This study suggests that parents' influence may be most powerful when they communicate directly with their children, so that students experience interactions, conversations, and activities at home that clearly translate parental interest in their work into students' positive attitudes and commitment to their work.

Studies of students at all grade levels are needed to check and confirm the results reported here. In particular, studies should explore the long-term results of family involvement and positive student attitudes, behaviors, and investments on student achievement and graduation from high school. Data on direct links among teacher practices, parent responses, student experiences, and ultimately, student grades and achievement test scores are needed to extend understanding of the benefits for students of well-organized and equitable home-school connections.

REFERENCES

Becker, H. J., and J. L. Epstein. (1982). Parent involvement: A study of teacher practices. *Elementary School Journal* 83: 85–102. (Reading 3.1).

Benson, C., E. Medrich, and S. Buckley. (1980). A new view of school efficiency: Household time contributions to school achievement. In J. Guthrie (Ed.), *School finance policies and practices—the 1980s: A decade of conflict* (pp. 169–204). Cambridge, MA: Ballinger.

Coleman, J. S., et al. (1966). *Equality of educational opportunity*. Washington, DC: U.S. Government Printing Office.

Comer, J. P. (1980). *School power*. New York: Free Press.

Epstein, J. L. (Ed.). (1981). *The quality of school life*. Lexington, MA.: Lexington Books.

———. (1984). A longitudinal study of school and family effects on student development. In S. A. Mednick, M. Harway, and K. Finello (Eds.), *Handbook of longitudinal research, Vol. 1* (pp. 381–397). New York: Praeger.

Epstein, J. L., and H. J. Becker. (1982). Teacher practices of parent involvement: Problem and possibilities. *Elementary School Journal* 83: 103–113. (Reading 3.2).

Gordon, I. (1979). The effects of parent involvement in schooling. In R. S. Brandt (Ed.), *Partners: Parents and schools* (pp. 4–25). Alexandria, VA: Association for Supervision and Curriculum Development.

Henderson, A. (Ed.). (1981). *Parent participation—student achievement: The evidence grows.* Columbia, MD: National Committee for Citizens in Education.

Leichter, H. J. (1974). *The family as educator.* New York: Teachers College Press.

Lightfoot, S. L. (1978). *Worlds apart: Relationships between families and schools.* New York: Basic Books.

Marjoribanks, K. (1979). *Families and their learning environments: An empirical analysis.* London: Routledge and Kegan Paul.

Mayeske, G. W. (1973). *A study of the achievement of our nation's students.* Washington, DC: U.S. Government Printing Office.

McDill, E. L., and L. Rigsby. (1973). *Structure and process in secondary schools: The academic impact of educational climates.* Baltimore: Johns Hopkins University Press.

Rich, D., J. Van Dien, and B. Mattox. (1979). Families as educators of their own children. In R. Brandt (Ed.), *Partners: Parents and schools* (pp. 26–40). Alexandria, VA: Association for Supervisors and Curriculum Development.

DISCUSSION AND ACTIVITIES

The comments in this section extend and update the content of the readings in this chapter. Main concepts and results are summarized and used to promote discussions and debates. Questions and activities are provided for class discussion and homework assignments. They may suggest other exercises, field activities, or research projects.

MAIN CONCEPTS

Key Results

The results and issues reported in the readings in this chapter provide a base on which to build new research on school, family, and community partnerships and useful approaches in practice. Three important results, introduced in Chapter 2 and featured in this chapter, deserve particular attention because they changed the way we study and develop programs of partnership.

1. School and teacher programs and practices of partnership influence whether and which families become involved in their children's education and schools.
2. School programs and practices of partnership increase teachers' awareness and appreciation of family assistance and reduce teachers' stereotypes of nontraditional families as uncaring and uninvolved.
3. Subject-specific activities that involve families with their children in learning activities at home help to increase student achievement in specific subjects.

COMMENT

School Practices Influence Family Involvement (Featured Result Number 1)

In an early study, Baker and Stevenson (1986) reported interesting results about the connections of parents' knowledge or beliefs about involvement and their actions. Their data indicated that almost all parents (including those with more and less formal education) have similar knowledge about the importance of involvement in their children's education and about ways they might become involved. However, parents with more formal education were more likely to translate their knowledge into actions for and with their children.

This result looks, at first, like a simple story of social class differences. Parents with more formal education are better able to translate knowledge into action. However, the readings in this chapter cast Baker and Stevenson's results and other studies in a different light. Data from parents, teachers, and students show that schools' programs and practices help parents with less formal education to more successfully put their knowledge to work. Good information and guidance from school principals, teachers, counselors, and other parents help all parents translate their knowledge about the importance of involvement into actions in working with the schools and with their children.

Although family background variables are important, they are not the only explanation for which parents influence their children's learning and development. The nature and quality of teachers' and administrators' practices to involve families are as important as or more important than family background variables such as race or ethnicity, social class, marital status, parental education, and mother's work status for determining whether and how parents become involved in their children's education. Family practices of involvement are also as important as or more important than family background variables for determining whether and how students progress and succeed in school.

Surveys of parents reveal that their activities and conversations about school with children at home are directly influenced by the types of practices that schools conduct to involve parents. That is, if schools invest in practices to involve families, most or all parents respond by taking part in those practices, including parents who might not have otherwise become involved on their own.

Surveys of teachers reveal a related result. Teachers' classroom practices to involve their students' families are strengthened when their schools' programs for involving families are strong. When teachers know that other teachers and administrators in their schools and districts place high importance on involving families, they conduct more activities to involve their own students' families. Thus:

- Families do more when schools guide their involvement.
- Teachers do more when others in their schools and districts share a commitment to practices of involvement.
- Family behavior (what families do) is as powerful as or more powerful than family characteristics (what families are) in influencing their children's schoolwork and success.

These results should encourage educators to develop comprehensive, schoolwide programs to reach out to inform and involve all families, including those who might not otherwise become involved on their own.

ACTIVITY

Classroom Debate and Discussion

A. Create a panel to debate the following resolution: *Resolved: What families do is more important than what families are.*

1. Explain the distinction between family characteristics and family behaviors.
2. Take one side of this debate. Prepare your main argument in a paragraph or two.
3. Imagine your adversary in the debate. Prepare a paragraph or two taking that position.
4. Discuss or debate this issue in class.

B. Why is it important for schools to develop programs and implement practices to involve families in different ways, rather than simply to expect or demand that families get more involved? Give at least one idea of why such programs and practices are important:
1. for the school as a whole
2. for an individual teacher, student, family, and for the community

C. Why is it important for all families to know every year that their schools and all teachers will:
1. provide useful information about school programs and children's progress?
2. ask for and use information from them about their children?
3. create a climate of partnership as children progress through the grades?

D. Give one idea why C1, C2, and C3 are particularly important to one of the following:
1. a family with an excellent student
2. a family with a failing student
3. a family of a student with special needs

COMMENT

Teachers Who Involve Parents Rate Them More Positively and Are Less Likely to Stereotype Nontraditional Families (Featured Result Number 2)

Practices of partnership assist teachers as well as parents. For example, when they work to involve all parents, teachers gain a greater understanding of parents' interests in and potential for assisting their children. Teachers who frequently involve families in their children's education rate single and married parents, low-income and middle-income parents, and more and less formally educated parents more positively and more equally in helpfulness and follow-through with their children at home. By contrast, teachers who do not frequently involve families give more stereotypic ratings to single parents, poor parents, and those with less formal education, marking them lower in helpfulness and follow-through than other parents.

QUESTIONS TO DISCUSS

1. a. Why do you think teachers who involve families more frequently give more positive ratings to all families?
   b. Why do you think teachers who do not involve families frequently are more likely to stereotype single parents, poor parents, or those with less formal education?
2. What other group(s) of families or students might these two types of teachers treat or rate differently? Explain your ideas.
3. Labels create stereotypes because they ignore important variations in family practices. That is, not all families in any category behave the same way. As stated in Reading 3.5, "Single parents are not a single group."
   a. How do labels such as *single parent, working mom, welfare family,* and *less-educated parents* affect school, family, and community partnerships?
   b. How do labels such as *illegitimate child, latchkey child,* and *poor student* affect students in school and the roles the students play in school, family, and community partnerships?
   c. How would you revise the labels listed in (A) and (B) to improve the wording of the descriptors and correct any distortions that they create?
4. a. How are the following phrases defined statistically and colloquially?
      (1) *nontraditional family*
      (2) *traditionally uninvolved family*
      (3) *traditionally underserved family*
   b. Justify or refute each of the above three terms as they relate to employed mothers, single parents, and parents with less formal education. Should these families be included in one or more of the categories listed above?
   c. How do you think the three phrases affect school, family, and community partnerships?
5. Reading 3.6 reports data from a sample of parents who, some educators and researchers believe, are not involved in their children's education. Reexamine the data reported in Reading 3.6.
   a. Select and identify two results that indicate whether parents in inner-city schools are involved or wish to be involved in their children's education.
   b. Explain why each of the two results you selected is important for understanding parents of elementary- and middle-grade students in inner-city schools.

There Are Subject-Specific Links between Family Involvement and Student Achievement (Featured Result Number 3)

Practices to involve families at home in interactions with their children about a specific subject are likely to affect student achievement in that subject. In the study reported in Reading 3.7, data connected teacher practices, parent responses, and student achievement over one year. We learned that:

- Teachers' practices to involve parents in learning activities at home were mainly limited to reading, English, or related activities. Also, principals encouraged teachers to involve parents in reading and related skills.
- Parents reported more involvement in reading activities.
- Students improved reading scores more from fall to spring if their teachers frequently involved parents in reading-related learning activities at home, but the students' math scores were not affected.

The data indicate that when parents are involved in reading, students respond by focusing on and completing more reading activities at home. This may lead to greater attention, motivation, and success in reading in school.

The data from this study suggest that practices of partnership may be purposely designed to help boost student achievement in specific subjects. There also were some important related findings. Family involvement in one subject will not necessarily benefit the child in another subject. Family involvement in activities at home may not benefit students at all unless the activities are well designed, well implemented, and accompanied by excellent teaching every day in school.

Updated Resource: Surveys of Teachers, Parents, and Students

The early surveys of teachers, parents, and students about patterns of parental involvement and schools' partnership programs have been updated. The questionnaires and information on the internal reliability of scales used in various studies are available for researchers, graduate students, and others conducting studies on related topics. Options include:

Epstein, J. L., L. Connors-Tadros, and K. C. Salinas. (1993). *High School and Family Partnerships: Surveys for Teachers, Parents, and Students in High School.* Baltimore: Center on School, Family, and Community Partnerships, Johns Hopkins University.

Epstein, J. L., and K. C. Salinas. (1993). *Surveys and Summaries: Questionnaires for Teachers and Parents in the Elementary and Middle Grades.* Baltimore: Center on School, Family, and Community Partnerships, Johns Hopkins University.

Sheldon, S. B., and J. L. Epstein. (2007). *Parent Survey on Family and Community Involvement in the Elementary and Middle Grades.* Baltimore: Center on School, Family, and Community Partnerships, Johns Hopkins University.

———. (2007). *Student Survey on Family and Community Involvement in the Elementary and Middle Grades.* Baltimore: Center on School, Family, and Community Partnerships, Johns Hopkins University.

The measures and materials are described on the website http://www.partnershipschools.org in the section "Publications and Products."

FIELD EXPERIENCE

Interview a Parent/Quick Survey

When the study in Reading 3.7 was conducted, most teachers in the elementary grades asked parents to become involved in reading more than other subjects. Find out whether this is still true.

A. Interview one parent of an elementary school student. Identify whether you are interviewing a mother, father, or other family member and the grade level of the child. Note any other factors about the family or community that you think may influence responses. Ask:
1. Does your child's teacher ask you to become involved with your child on homework?
2. If YES, ask:
   a. In which subjects?
   b. If more than one subject is mentioned, check: In which subject are you most often asked to be involved?
3. If NO, ask:
   a. Do you and your child work together on any subject or skills at home?
   b. If so, in which subject most of all?
B. Document your questions and the responses. Write a paragraph summarizing what you learned from the parent you interviewed.
C. *Optional class activity:* Discuss the responses to these interviews in class. Do the results of your classmates' interviews suggest that there is more parent involvement in reading/English, as we found in the original study, or is there evidence of other patterns of subject-specific involvement?

What Is and What Might Be

Research helps identify "what is" and "what might be" in school practices to involve families. An average score on a scale or measure tells what usually is, whereas the variance of a scale or measure helps point to what might be. Of course, variations in scores are higher and lower, better and worse than the average score. For example, studies indicate that some teachers go far beyond average in conducting many activities to involve all students' families. Other teachers conduct far fewer involvement activities than the average.

The variation in practices of partnership is often more interesting than the average. Within a state, a district, and even a school, teachers' and administrators' approaches to families vary. Some educators conduct many activities to inform and involve all families; others have not yet thought about how to integrate partnerships into their work as professional educators. The teachers and administrators who have already developed effective partnerships help researchers and other educators identify and study what might be possible in all schools. Those who avoid communicating with families help inform the field about problems that must be solved. Reading 3.2 presents ideas from both groups of teachers.

QUESTIONS TO DISCUSS

Select two challenges that teachers in Reading 3.2 described as "barriers" to parent involvement.

Example: One challenge discussed in Reading 3.2 is that telephoning parents takes time. To meet this challenge, you might think about organizing a schedule to guide teachers about whom to call, how often to call, how to mix positive messages with calls about problems, how to get help from volunteers in making certain kinds of calls, how to supplement phone calls with other communications, and other solutions. You may use this challenge as one of your answers, or select two different challenges from Reading 3.2.

1. State the two challenges that you selected.
2. Outline at least two important issues that need to be resolved to meet each challenge.
3. List at least one activity that might be implemented to address the issues you outlined to meet each challenge.
4. Share the challenges, issues, and solutions in class. Examine the activities suggested for their feasibility, sensitivity to families' situations, and likely success.
5. *Optional class activity*: Collect the most promising ideas for a resource notebook or an electronic idea file on school, family, and community partnerships for use in schools or for researchable topics.

Discrepancy Scores

Data in Reading 3.3 indicate that, on average, teachers are more likely to support the involvement of families if they think that other teachers and administrators in their schools have similar beliefs and goals about the importance of parent and community involvement. They also are more likely to conduct activities to involve their students' families if their school has a well-organized program of school, family, and community partnerships. By contrast, if they think that their colleagues do not support parent involvement, teachers are less likely to implement many practices themselves. In some schools, however, you will find outliers: teachers who are leaders in involving families, even if no other teachers do so.

Interview on Patterns of Collegial Support

A. Interview one school-based educator about his or her practices and school experiences to involve families and communities to see which model—the *group-support process* or the *individual-leader phenomenon*—seems to be working in the school. The educator may be a teacher, principal, counselor, or other specialist at a preschool or elementary, middle, or high school. Identify the school level and position of the person you interview. Ask:
   1. At your school, does the power of the group influence practices to involve or avoid parents, or does each individual teacher decide whether and how to involve parents? Explain.
   2. Do most teachers conduct the same kinds of activities, or do individual leaders do more and better activities with parents than most other teachers? Explain.
   3. What is one example of a practice that all teachers in the school conduct with all or most families?
   4. What is one example of a particularly good practice that only one or two teachers conduct with the families of their students?
   5. Are formal plans written each year outlining all of the activities to involve parents and communities in the school at each grade level? If so, who writes these plans? If not, how are activities scheduled?
B. Add at least one question of your own about group or individual approaches to involve parents or communities.
C. Document your questions and the responses.
D. Write a paragraph summarizing what you learned or questions raised in this interview.

Diverse and Changing Families

For the past several decades, families have been changing structures and diversifying functions. There are more single parents, blended families, gay and lesbian parents, and other family forms than in the past. There are more families with two parents employed and single parents working outside the home. Some fathers are at home while mothers work outside the home. Some parents are unemployed. Some families are homeless or in temporary shelters. Some families are highly mobile, moving frequently to new homes, schools, and communities.

Families will continue to vary in structure, composition, and situation. Nevertheless, just about all families send their children to school with high hopes for their success and happiness.

The results of the studies in Readings 3.4, 3.5, and 3.6 suggest that some parents (e.g., single parents and parents with less formal education) are less involved in their children's education unless they receive good information and guidance from the schools.

QUESTIONS TO DISCUSS

Many parents—single and married—work full-time or part-time during the day, evening, or night. Employed mothers and fathers have limited time for meetings and events at the school building. These realities should affect the variety and schedule of activities to involve families at school or at home across the grades.

1. Describe two activities that would permit parents who are employed during the school day to participate at the school building.
2. Describe two activities that would permit parents who are employed at night to participate at the school building.

Parent Interviews about Work and Family

A. Interview two single mothers (i.e., separated, divorced, widowed, or never married) or two married mothers who are employed full-time outside the home about the ways in which they are involved in the education of their school-aged children.
B. Before your interviews, write three questions that you will ask both interviewees about involvement in their children's education at home and at school and whether or how their children's schools welcome and guide their involvement.

C. Identify whether you are interviewing single or married mothers. Note the school and grade level of one child in the family and other factors that you think may influence responses to questions about parent involvement (e.g., parents' education; occupation; race/ethnicity; total number of children at home; urban, suburban, or rural community; or other factors).

D. List the questions you ask and the responses of each interviewee.

E. Summarize the results of the two interviews. Respond to the following questions:

1. How are the two individuals you interviewed alike and different in their patterns of involvement at home and at school?

2. What do you think are some reasons for the similar or different patterns of involvement?

F. Is the information that you obtained representative or not representative of the views that would be obtained from a random sample of 100 single mothers or married and employed mothers? Explain.

G. *Optional class activity*: See how increasing the sample affects the results and conclusions of individual interviews. In class, combine and summarize the data from all interviews with single mothers. Then, combine and summarize the data from all interviews with married mothers. Discuss the full set of results:

1. In what ways are the combined data more useful than the individual reports? Which results might be important in school practice?

2. Which results raise questions that should be studied further?

COMMENT

Partnerships with Diverse and Changing Families

Families not only differ in form and function (see Reading 3.5), but they change from one year to the next. Single parents marry, married parents divorce, employed parents become unemployed, unemployed mothers start to work outside the home, and so forth. However they change, families still are responsible for their children and share responsibilities with schools for their children's education and development. Families that face stressful changes are more likely to remain partners with schools if administrators and teachers understand how to involve families who are in transition.

QUESTIONS TO DISCUSS

1. List two school, family, and community partnership activities that you believe are appropriate and important for all families to conduct, regardless of how families differ or how they change.

a. Explain why these activities are important for all families to conduct.
b. Explain one way in which schools could help families with each of the activities that you listed.

2. List one school, family, and community partnership activity that needs to be tailored for (a) single parents, (b) employed parents, and (c) parents who separate, divorce, or remarry to feel comfortable about participating. Describe how and why you would tailor or adapt the activity you listed for these three groups.

COMMENT

One-Parent Homes but Two-Parent Families

Some students live with one parent, and the other parent lives nearby. Many non-resident parents (usually fathers) would like to be more active in their children's education. Some nonresident parents have joint custody of their children and expect to be fully involved in their education, but the school may officially record the address of only one parent. Many nonresident parents would appreciate information and invitations from the school to become more involved. Studies suggest that children whose nonresident fathers are involved in their schooling are more likely to like school, do well in school, and participate in extracurricular activities than are children in one-parent homes whose nonresident fathers are uninvolved.

Some children have no contact with their nonresident parent. These students may be particularly sensitive to questions or school activities that refer to "your parents."

Depending on their situations, students may appreciate options to communicate with one or both parents or other relatives to involve important adults in their lives and in their school activities and experiences. These complex topics of how schools understand and interact with families that are differently structured require systematic study and innovative school and classroom practices.

ACTIVITY

Review or Interview

A. Identify a level of schooling that interests you. Use your experience or interview a teacher or school administrator to address these questions:
1. What is your school's policy about providing information or invitations to nonresident parents?
2. What is your school's policy about vocabulary referring to a parent or parents:

- in memos or other communications to the home?
- in activities in class?

B. Write a short critique of the policies that are described. Is each one a good policy? Why or why not? If no policy exists, draft a short, workable policy statement on whether and how to provide information and invitations to nonresident parents.

C. *Optional follow-up activity*: Interview one nonresident parent of a school-age child to learn if and how he or she is presently involved in a child's school and education. Identify whether this parent has joint custody of the youngster.

1. Write at least five questions for your interview. Include one on the changes in school policies or practices concerning nonresident parents this individual would recommend.
2. Record your questions and document the responses you obtain.

COMMENT

Students Who Live with One Parent

In Reading 3.5, teachers' practices made a difference in whether single and married parents were productive partners with the schools in their children's education. This result reinforces the importance of measuring school and family practices simultaneously to understand what parents do and whether they are assisted to become involved by the programs and practices at their children's schools. Without attention to the schools' efforts, many studies distort the desires and abilities of all families to be productively involved in their children's education.

A study of Midwestern youth in one- and two-parent homes concluded that, on average, kids do better in two-parent homes, but some students in single-parent families thrive, and some in two-parent homes do not. Family structure does not fully determine or explain children's and adolescents' well-being.

What matters most, regardless of family structure, is what happens within the family (Benson, 1993). For example, adolescents in single-parent homes are much less at risk of failing or getting in trouble in school if they report that their families are involved in their schooling, provide social support, and monitor other aspects of their lives. Examine the chart on the next page (Benson, 1993).

What Percent of Successful and Unsuccessful Students in One-Parent Homes Are Supported by Their Families in Different Ways?

As shown in the chart, higher percentages of adolescents in single-parent homes who "thrive" in school (i.e., achieve well, have high aspirations, do homework, stay

| | Percent of Students Who Report | | | |
Students in one-parent homes	Family support for education	Parent involvement in schooling	Parental standards	Discipline at home
Of students who thrive:	64	29	85	60
Of students who do *not* thrive:	34	18	47	41

out of trouble) report that they receive support and guidance from an involved parent at home, compared with students who do not thrive in school (i.e., have academic or behavior problems). Another way to say this is that more students from single-parent families who are successful in school report having strong parental support, standards, discipline, and involvement.

Saying that some single parents are involved in their children's education while others are not is important, but not surprising. Many studies conducted in the United States and other nations show that in all kinds of families, some parents are involved, and others are not. Regardless of family structure, children of involved parents are more likely to succeed in school in many different ways. Reading 3.5 adds evidence that when teachers implement activities to involve all families, more single parents become involved in their children's education across the grades. Then, their children have a better chance of succeeding in school.

QUESTIONS TO DISCUSS

1. In the chart, which variable—family support, involvement, standards, or discipline—do you think presents the most important contrasting percentages for students in one-parent homes who thrive compared with those who do not thrive?
   a. Identify the variable and percentages you will discuss.
   b. Explain why you think the percentages reported for that variable are important.
2. Write two questions that you would like to ask the students who were in Benson's study to better understand the family and school circumstances that contributed to the results in the chart. State your two questions, and explain why each is important for understanding the variables in the chart.
3. Use at least two examples from Reading 3.5 to discuss this statement: *Family involvement and support in one-parent and two-parent homes is partly determined by school practices.*

Who Is Hard to Reach?

Who are the hard-to-reach parents? In some ways, some of the time, every family is hard to reach. Parents who work outside the home may be hard to reach. Parents who are at a distance from the school may be hard to reach. Fathers may be hard to reach. Young parents, teen parents, older parents, parents of older children, parents with less formal education, those who do not speak English, single parents, stepparents, noncustodial parents, and foster parents may be hard to reach. In some cases parents with advanced education or great wealth also may be hard to reach. Some families fit more than one of these descriptors and may be particularly hard to reach.

Not all schools have the same hard-to-reach families. Some schools have figured out how to contact and involve families who seem unreachable at other schools.

FIELD EXPERIENCE

Reaching Hard-to-Reach Parents

   A. Interview one teacher or administrator from two different schools. Identify the positions of your interviewees, their school or grade levels, and important characteristics of their students, families, or communities. Ask:
     1. Who are the hard-to-reach parents in your school?
     2. Why are they hard to reach?
     3. What strategies have been used at your school to try to reach one or more of the groups of families that you listed?
   B. Add at least one question of your own.
   C. List the questions you ask and the responses.
   D. Write a paragraph on the similarities or differences in the responses of educators from the two schools—and possible reasons.
   E. *Optional class activity*: Share and compare ideas with others in the class. Identify useful strategies for reaching hard-to-reach parents.

COMMENT

Paired Data from Teachers and Parents

Readings 3.1 and 3.4 are "paired" with data from teachers and parents from the same schools, respectively, in a statewide sample of urban, suburban, and rural schools. Data in Readings 3.3 and 3.6 also are "paired" with data from teachers and parents from the same schools in a sample of urban elementary and middle schools. The data from these studies reveal common themes and important contrasts among teachers and parents. For example, most teachers think parents are not involved in their children's education, whereas most parents report they are involved—or try to be—often without guidance or assistance from the school or from their children's teachers.

As another example, almost all teachers (more than 90 percent) say they held conferences with parents, but 36 percent of the parents say they never had a conference with their child's teacher. These discrepancies must be discussed, explained, and addressed for parents and teachers to understand each other's work and their common interests in children.

QUESTIONS TO DISCUSS

1. How can the reports from 90 percent of teachers and 36 percent of parents about parent-teacher conferences both be true?
2. What are the implications of these contrasting results for improving the way in which parent-teacher conferences are organized, scheduled, and counted?
3. Read one pair of readings (3.1 and 3.4 or 3.3 and 3.6).
    a. Identify one set of results (not those discussed above) that indicate that parents and teachers, on average, view things similarly or differently.
    b. Explain how the similar or different results that you identified might affect school, family, and community partnerships.

COMMENT

Teachers as Parents

Despite the fact that most teachers are parents, data from many surveys show that teachers misunderstand what most parents try to do at home. Many teachers blame parents for their lack of involvement, despite the teachers' knowledge of how hard it is to stay informed and involved in their own children's education from year to year. It may be that teachers characterize all parents according to their worst experiences with families, rather than according to their best experiences. Determine if this is true through the following field experience.

Interview Teachers Who Are and Are Not Parents

A. Interview one teacher who is a parent of a school-age child and one teacher who is not a parent. Write their responses to the following questions:
  1. As a teacher, what is your best experience with a parent?
  2. As a teacher, what is your worst experience with a parent?
  3. How would you describe the involvement of most parents of the students you teach?
B. Add a question of your own for these teachers.
C. Ask the teacher who *is* a parent:
  1. In what grade level is your oldest school-age child?
  2. How easy or difficult is it for you to be involved at this child's school?
  3. How easy or difficult is it for you to be involved with this child at home?
  4. How much information or guidance do you get from this child's school and teacher to help you be productively involved?
D. Add a question of your own for this teacher.
E. Summarize what you learned from the two teachers you interviewed. Include the following reflections as well as other ideas:
  1. From the first set of questions, how were the teachers' assessments of most parents influenced by their best and worst experiences?
  2. From the second set of questions, how did the teacher's role as an educator affect interactions with his or her own child's teacher(s)? How did the teacher's role as an educator affect interactions with the child at home?

Student Achievement and Family Involvement

Reading 3.7 uses gain scores to measure achievement (i.e., how much a student grows over one year), after accounting for initial skills. There are some typical or expected patterns in these data. For example, students who start with lower scores make greater gains over one year.

There are statistical reasons for this result. One technical explanation is a general "regression to the mean," which suggests that, by chance and human nature, poor students will, on occasion, score higher than they did before. Similarly, good students will, on occasion, score lower than they did before. It may be more than chance or naturally occurring corrections, however, when measures are made after one year's time. For example, students who start out lower in skills have more "room to grow," whereas students who start with high scores near the ceiling or top of a range of scores will not be able to show as much positive growth or change. They may be working hard simply to maintain their high scores.

There also are substantive reasons why students with low scores may gain more in one year than students with high scores. For example, schoolwork may be easier at the lower levels, making it possible for students to jump ahead more quickly from low starting points, once they are motivated to work. Or schools may promote student learning with innovative and responsive curricula and instructional methods that enable slower students to make progress and brighter students to maintain their skills. These alternative, complex, statistical, and substantive issues need to be sorted out in research on the effects of family involvement on student achievement.

The data in Reading 3.7 suggest that gains in reading and math by students in urban elementary schools are influenced by different characteristics of parents, students, and teachers. Examine the following summary chart of results from that study.

SUMMARY CHART

Factors Influencing Gains in Reading and Math in the Elementary Grades

QUESTIONS TO DISCUSS

1. Select one result in the summary chart that surprised you, and explain why.
2. Explain how the result you selected might affect school, family, and community partnerships.
3. If you were studying student progress in reading or math, what is one additional variable that you would measure to clarify the results in the summary chart? Explain why you think the variable you selected might be important.

Factors that affect gains in *reading*	Factors that affect gains in *math*
• Initial reading scores—low scoring reading students gain more	• Initial math scores—low scoring math students gain more
• Parent education	—
—	• Younger grade levels
• High quality rating of teacher	—
—	• Recency of teacher training
• Teacher use of learning activities at home (in reading)	(Family involvement in reading does not affect gains in math test scores)
—	• Parent reports of high quality homework

Giving Credit Where Credit Is Due

One intriguing result of the analyses of data from the study reported in Reading 3.8 is that teachers tend to evaluate parents based on their children's achievement. Parents of students who were homework "stars" were viewed more positively by teachers than were parents of students who had homework or discipline problems. Parents of homework stars were rated significantly more helpful than other parents. By contrast, parents of children who had trouble with homework or who behaved badly in school were rated significantly lower in helpfulness and follow-through than were other parents.

Student Ability/Behavior	Teachers' Ratings of Parents' Helpfulness and Follow-Through	
	ß	(F)
Homework Star	.225	(35.76)
R²	.47	
Homework Problem	− .146	(14.02)
R²	.38	
Discipline Problem	− .110	(7.54)
R²	.33	

NOTE: This figure uses the same control variables as Table 3.32.

FIGURE 3.5   Teachers' Ratings of Parents' Helpfulness and Follow-Through

Parents make similar assessments of teachers. Table 3.30 shows that parents rate teachers higher in quality if their children are homework stars and if their children are doing well in math. Use these results and your experiences to answer the following questions.

1. Are students high achievers *because* their parents help them, or are parents helpful *because* their students are high achievers? Give one example of how each of these causal patterns could be true.
2. Do students have trouble in school *because* their parents are not involved, or do parents disengage *because* their children have trouble in school? Give one example of how each of these causal patterns could be true.
3. Are teachers more effective *because* their students are high achievers, or are children high achievers *because* they have better teachers? Give one example of how each of these causal patterns could be true.
4. *Optional*: Discuss these issues in class. What are the implications of the examples for research on the effects of family involvement on student achievement?

COMMENT

Studying and Improving Homework

Homework is a strategy that can be designed to motivate students, increase learning, involve families, and improve teaching (Cooper and Valentine, 2001; see also Reading 6.1). For too long, however, homework has been studied as an either/or, more/less variable. Many studies still focus only on the number of minutes or hours of homework that are assigned or spent. The debates about minutes of homework miss important distinctions between assigning more homework and designing better homework. There is a difference between focusing on time spent on homework and the complex issues of the purpose, content, and form of homework.

After reviewing more than two dozen U.S. and international studies of homework and its effects on students, I developed a model for studying, understanding, discussing, and improving homework. This model (see Figure 3.6) shows an extensive set of variables that could be measured to more fully study and understand the design and effects of homework on student learning, teacher effectiveness, and family understanding and involvement in children's education.

Variables in the Model

The chart on pp. 277–280 shows examples of variables for each section of the conceptual model. Some or all of these or related variables may be included in a measurement model to study the background, design, and effects of homework on students, teaching practice, and family practice. Of course, no single study of homework can include all of these variables, but studies may select variables that make sense in well-specified theoretical and measurement models.

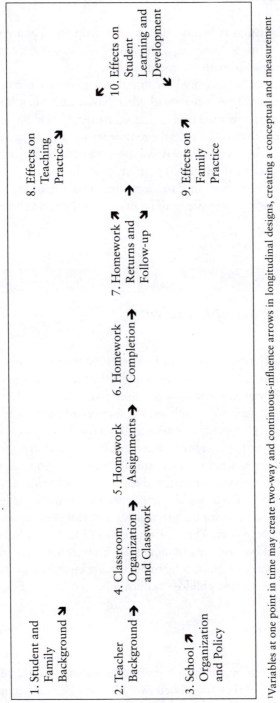

1. Student and Family Background

2. Teacher Background

3. School Organization and Policy

4. Classroom Organization and Classwork

5. Homework Assignments

6. Homework Completion

7. Homework Returns and Follow-up

8. Effects on Teaching Practice

9. Effects on Family Practice

10. Effects on Student Learning and Development

[1]Variables at one point in time may create two-way and continuous-influence arrows in longitudinal designs, creating a conceptual and measurement "loop" for studying the effects of homework over time.

FIGURE 3.6   Research Model for Studying Effects of Homework[1]

Examples of Variables that May Be Addressed in Studies of the Nature and Effects of Homework

1. **Student and Family Background**
   Gender
   Race/ethnicity
   Parent education
   Other family socioeconomic status (SES) indicators, e.g.:
   - Occupation
   - Income
   - Family size

   Student program/curriculum track/ability group
   Student personality variables affecting homework completion, e.g.:
   - Self-concept of ability
   - Locus of control
   - Diligence, persistence
   - Neatness
   - Creativity

   Student prior or starting achievement
   Student prior or starting attitudes about school, homework
   Peer/friendship group homework patterns
   Student part-time work hours/schedule
   Home conditions supporting learning, e.g.:
   - Place for homework
   - Time for homework
   - Supplies for homework
   - Resources for learning (e.g., books, newspapers, art materials)

   Climate and support for homework, e.g.:
   - Interruptions
   - Competing responsibilities
   - Interactions
   - Final check

   Parental knowledge about school and classroom
   Parental connections with school and teachers
   Community resources/library/museums

2. **Teacher Background and Practice**
   Education
   Teaching experience
   Quality of teaching
   Subject specialization
   Attitudes toward students
   Philosophy and attitudes about homework
   Practices of family and community involvement

3. **School Organization and Policy**
   Grade span
   Program definition, e.g.:
   - Magnet
   - Charter
   - Other special school program

   Community characteristics
   Aggregate student/family population characteristics
   District, school, and classroom homework policies
   Standards for homework
   Supervision of teachers' lessons and homework
   Articulation of feeder and receiver schools

(continues)

(continued)

4. **Classroom Organization and Classwork**
   Grade level
   Subject
   Teacher planning time
   Interdisciplinary connections across subjects
Classroom organization, e.g., TARGET structures of:
   - Task
   - Authority
   - Reward
   - Grouping
   - Evaluation
   - Time to organize classwork
   Plan for homework in instruction
   Classroom behavior, discipline
   External interruptions

5. **Assigning Homework (by Teacher)**
   Amount and time expected
   Frequency
   Design/form/novelty/diversity/level of interest
   Clarity
   Coordination with curriculum
   Coordination with student ability, e.g.:
   - Group/individual ability
   - Common/individualized assignments
   Content:
   - Review
   - Remediation
   - Critical thinking
   - Creative thinking
   - Enrichment, extension of skills
   - Completion of classwork
   Purpose:
   - Practice and mastery of knowledge/skills
   - Preparation for new lesson
   - Participation, enjoyment of learning
   - Parent involvement:
     - Parent-child communication, interaction
     - Parent-teacher communications
   - Peer interactions
   - Public relations
   - Policy
   Alternative assignments, extra credit assignments
   Makeup assignments due to absence
   After-school activities
   Parents' roles in identifying issues for homework assignments
   Students' roles in identifying issues for homework assignments

6. **Completing Homework (by Student)**
   Time spent:
   - On assigned homework
   - On unassigned homework
   Location:
   - In-school time for homework
   - After-school place for homework

Level of interest in subject, topic
Use of special skills or talents
Parent support, monitoring, assistance
Parent pressure, conflict, avoidance
Parent communications with teachers, e.g.:
- Daily homework log
- Computerized messages
- Required signature

Competing activities for time at home, e.g.:
- Chores
- TV
- Internet
- Part-time work
- Sports or talents
- Other lessons
- Responsibilities

Availability of peers for interactions, and extent of interactions of friends/class-mates/siblings by telephone, in the neighborhood, and other ways

7. **Returning and Following up on Homework (by Teacher)**
Timing of return
Frequency of collection, checking
Feedback, e.g.:
- Correction
- Evaluation
- Tally
- Grade
- Comment

Follow-up to redo/resubmit assignment
Role of parent after return
Rewards/penalties/consequences for student
Class time, other school time, after-school time to make up work
Homework part of report card grade
Extra homework assignments
Notification of parents

8. **Effects on Student Learning and Development**
Completion rate, quantity
Completion quality, accuracy, creativity
Improved learning:
- Readiness for next lesson
- Classroom subject tests
- Report card grades
- Achievement test scores

Improved behavior and attitudes toward:
- School
- Subjects
- Homework
- Learning
- Teachers

Attendance:
- Motivation to learn and to work as a student
- Willingness to work to improve
- Continued enrollment in school
- Selection of advanced courses

(continued)

(continued)

- Self-control/discipline
- Positive self-concept of ability

9. **Effects on Teaching Practice**
   Organization of instructional time:
   - Pace of lessons
   - Homework as segment of instructional time
   Introduction of homework, questions from students
   Follow-up of homework, extension, enrichment
   Design of homework and remedial instruction or assignments for individuals
   Communications with parents and students
   Attention to community and family conditions, interests, talents, and resources

10. **Effects on Family Practice**
    Organization of home environment to support student homework
    Frequency of interactions with child on homework
    Content of interactions with child on homework
    Quality of interactions with child on homework
    Parent attitudes:
    - About quality of school, teacher(s)
    - About responsiveness of school and teacher(s) to child
    - Importance of instructional program for preparing child for future
    - Understanding of what child is learning in school
    Quality of communications with teachers
    Support for school program

Variables that Affect Homework and Learning

Photocopy and complete the chart in Figure 3.7, or create it on your computer.

A. Select a grade level and a school subject that interest you.
B. In the chart on the next page, list *one* variable that interests you from *each section* of the model given above. For each variable, describe *one problem* that the variable may cause in the design, conduct, or results of homework and *one solution* for correcting the problem to improve the homework process. An example for a School Organization and Policy variable is shown at the top of the chart.

Grade level selected: _____

Subject selected: _____

VARIABLE from homework model	ONE PROBLEM caused by the design, conduct, or results of homework	ONE POSSIBLE SOLUTION to the problem that would improve the design, conduct, or results of homework
EXAMPLE VARIABLE School Organization and Policy—District, school, and classroom homework policies	EXAMPLE PROBLEM Teacher's homework policy is not clear to all students and parents.	EXAMPLE SOLUTION Homework policy should be provided in written and other forms and discussed with all students and parents.
1. Student and family background		
2. Teacher background, practice		
3. School organization and policy		
4. Classroom organization and classwork		
5. Assigning homework		
6. Completing homework		
7. Returning and following up homework		
8. Effects on teaching practice		
9. Effects on family practice		
10. Effects on student learning and development		

FIGURE 3.7 Variables that Affect Homework Design and Completion

QUESTIONS TO DISCUSS

Homework is not cost free. There are investments that students, teachers, and parents make for students to complete homework. For example, it "costs" teachers planning time to design homework that will be assigned to students. The investments in homework should yield benefits for students, teachers, and parents. Identify one cost and one benefit of homework for each group listed in the chart on the next page. Include one reason why you think each of your listings is a cost or a benefit.

	Homework Cost	Why is this a cost?	Homework Benefit	Why is this a benefit?
Teachers				
Students				
Parents/ Families				

Interview Students about Homework

Reading 3.8 uses data from teachers, principals, parents, and students to better understand homework and its links with student achievement and behavior.

A. Interview two students who are in different grade levels.
B. Audio-record or take notes on the students' responses to the following. Ask:
  1. What is the best homework assignment that you remember?
  2. What is the worst homework assignment that you remember?
C. For the best and worst examples, ask:
  1. Describe the homework assignment you remember.
  2. Do you remember the purpose of this homework?
  3. About how long did this homework take you to complete?
  4. Did a lesson in class lead to the homework, or did the homework lead to a lesson later on? Or was this just a separate activity?
  5. Did you show this homework to a parent, friend, or someone else?
  6. What made the assignment especially good/especially bad?
D. Also check each student's age, gender, and grade level, and ask each student:
  1. General attitude about school: Do you like school a lot, a little, not much, or not at all?
  2. Average grades: Do you get mostly As, Bs, Cs, Ds, or Fs in school?
E. Summarize the students' responses. Write a reflective paragraph on whether the students' reactions to homework were thoughtful or uninformed. Did the students' reactions have any implications for teachers' designs of good homework? Do you see any connections between the students' experiences or ideas about homework with the students' age, grade level, gender, attitude about school, or report card grades?

F. *Optional class activity*: Combine the data collected by all students in the class. Analyze one or more connection between the interviewed students' attitudes about homework with their grade level (or report card grades or attitudes about school).

QUESTIONS TO DISCUSS

Most studies of homework indicate that, regardless of their starting skills, *if* students do their homework, they are more likely to improve their skills and do better in school than similar students who do not do their homework. One interesting result discussed in Reading 3.8 is that in the elementary grades struggling students spend more time than do advanced students completing their homework. By the middle and high school grades, data indicate that advanced students spend more time on homework than do slower students.

1. Do you think it is possible to design homework that will encourage middle and high school students at all ability levels to spend the time they need to complete their homework? Explain.
2. *Optional class activity*: Discuss these ideas in class. Identify the most interesting ideas for improving the design and assignment of homework in middle and high schools to encourage all students to complete their assignments regardless of their ability levels.

ACTIVITY

Reading to Understand Homework

A. Early and recent research on homework adds information to the data presented in Readings 3.8 and 3.9. Select an article, chapter, or book from the following list, or select another recent research report on homework, and answer the questions on the next page.

Balli, S. J. (1998). When mom and dad help: Student reflections on parent involvement with homework. *Journal of Research and Development in Education* 31: 142–146.
Cooper, H. (1989). *Homework*. White Plains, NY: Longman.
Cooper, H., and J. C. Valentine. (2001). Using research to answer practical questions about homework. *Educational Psychologist* 36: 143–154.
Corno, L., and J. Xu. (2004). Homework as the job of childhood. *Theory into Practice* 43: 227–233.
Hoover-Dempsey, K. V., A. C. Battiato, J. M. Walker, R. P. Reed, J. M. Dejong, and K. P. Jones. (2001). Parental involvement in homework. *Educational Psychologist* 36: 195–209.
Hoover-Dempsey, K. V., O. C. Bassler, and R. Burow. (1995). Parents' reported involvement in students' homework: Strategies and practices. *Elementary School Journal* 95: 435–450.

Hyde, J. S., N. M., Else-Quest, M. W. Alibali, E. Knuth, and T. Romberg. (2006). Mathematics in the home: Homework practices and mother-child interactions doing mathematics. *Journal of Mathematical Behavior* 25: 136–152.

Keith, T. Z., and V. A. Cool. (1992). Testing models of school learning: Effects of quality of instruction, motivation, academic coursework, and homework on academic achievement. *School Psychology Quarterly* 7: 207–226.

MetLife. (2007). *The MetLife survey of the American teacher: The homework experience*. New York: MetLife, Inc.

Patall, E. A., H. Cooper, and J. C. Robinson. (2008). Parent involvement in homework: A research synthesis. *Review of Educational Research* 78: 1039–1104.

Van Voorhis, F. L. (In press). Adding families to the homework equation: A longitudinal study of mathematics achievement. *Education and Urban Society*.

———. (2003). Interactive homework in middle school: Effects on family involvement and students' science achievement. *Journal of Educational Research* 96: 323–339.

Villas Boas, A. (1998). The effects of parental involvement in homework on student achievement in Portugal and Luxembourg. *Childhood Education* 74: 367–371.

Xu, J. (2004). Family help and homework management in urban and rural secondary schools. *Teachers College Record* 106: 1786–1803.

B. Answer the following questions about the article, chapter, or book that you selected:

1. List the title, author(s), date, and place of publication.

2. Identify three important variables that are discussed or analyzed in the publication you selected. Tell where you would place each of these variables in the 10 sections of Figure 3.6.

3. Identify one main result of the study you selected. Explain whether and how this result increases an understanding of the design and effects of homework.

COMMENT

Paired Data from Parents and Students on Homework

Reports from parents and students in Readings 3.8 and 3.9 suggest that weekends are underused as time for interactive homework. Parents overwhelmingly report that they have time on weekends to talk with their children about school and to help with homework. Students complete more homework and extra work on weekends if their teachers frequently involve their families in learning activities at home. Some schools give no homework on weekends as a matter of policy. Yet weekends may provide family-friendly time for students to talk with someone at home about something interesting they are learning in class and about important decisions they must make about schoolwork and activities.

QUESTIONS TO DISCUSS

1. Identify a grade level that interests you.
2. Make a chart summarizing one pro and one con argument from the perspective of a teacher, parent, and student in the grade level you selected on the following:
   a. Assigning homework to students on weekends.
   b. Assigning homework on weekends that requires students to talk with a parent or other family member about something interesting they are learning in class or about a school-linked decision.
3. Write a paragraph from your point of view about assigning homework on weekends in the grade level you selected.
4. An important result described in Reading 3.8 is that children who like to talk about school at home complete more homework and have higher academic skills than students who do not talk about school at home. This finding raises two "chicken or egg" questions:
   • Which came first, doing well in school *or* talking about school at home?
   • Which came first, doing poorly in school *or* not talking about school at home?

These questions require longitudinal studies to monitor changes in skills over time, but you can begin to explore these issues by discussing the following questions:

A. For the grade level you selected, describe two ways in which children show their distress or anxiety about homework.
B. For the grade level you selected, give one idea of how a teacher might:
   1. Design homework assignments that minimize distress and anxiety.
   2. Encourage children and parents to talk about schoolwork at home.
C. Which do you think comes first, doing well in school *or* talking about school at home? Discuss or write a paragraph about one activity that links home and school that might lead students on the positive path you selected.
D. Which do you think comes first, doing poorly in school *or* not talking about school at home? Discuss or write a paragraph about one activity that links home and school that might lead students on the negative path you selected.

CROSSCUTTING THEMES

Three quite different themes cut across the readings in this chapter:

1. Partnerships change across school levels as students mature and as school programs increase in complexity.

2. Partnerships are affected by the school authority and decision-making structures.
3. Researchers must use multiple measures to study the nature and effects of school, family, and community partnerships.

The following comments and questions will help you explore these crosscutting themes.

COMMENT

Grade Level and Academic Subject Differences

The theory of overlapping spheres of influence assumes that school, family, and community responsibilities and activities will change over time across grade levels and from teacher to teacher. The readings in this chapter document that on average, elementary schools involve families more than do middle schools. In most middle schools, teachers give less information to parents, and parents report less involvement in their children's education than in the younger grades. Reading 3.6 reports, however, that parents of middle-grade students want to be as informed and involved as parents of younger children, although they require different information and must conduct different interactions with their early adolescent children.

The data also reveal differences in practices among teachers of different subjects. Reading 3.1 shows that teachers were most comfortable in the early grades involving parents in reading and reading-related activities at home. Data in Reading 3.3 show that reading and English teachers involved families more than other teachers, even in the middle grades.

The data about what is typical or normative in the elementary and middle grades raise many questions about the age-appropriate family and community involvement activities that could or should be conducted across the grades and by teachers of different subjects.

QUESTIONS TO DISCUSS

1. Give examples from the readings and your experiences to address the following questions. (*Optional*: Interview a teacher, parent, or student about these questions. Identify your source, the grade level, and the responses.)
   a. How do school, family, and community partnerships presently change from one grade level to the next? Provide two examples.
   b. How do school, family, and community partnerships presently vary in different school subjects? Provide two examples.
   c. How do partnership activities presently change from the beginning to the end of the same school year? Provide two examples.

d. How are communications from home to school affected when children move to a new school (e.g., in the middle of the year, at the start of a new school year, or when they graduate to the next level of schooling)? Provide two examples.

2. Use the results reported in the readings in this chapter and your own ideas to discuss:

a. Should the nature (design of practices, activities, subject matter) of involvement change as children move from the elementary to the middle grades? Provide two examples that support your view.

b. Should the extent (time, number of activities) of involvement change in the elementary and middle grades? Provide two examples that support your views.

COMMENT

Transitions to New Schools and New Grade Levels

Parents, teachers, and students must create new partnerships every year. Parents often are unsure about what is expected by their children's new teachers or how to help their children in new grade levels or new schools. Teachers are unfamiliar with most new students and families who enter their classes each year. Among many unknowns, students are unaware of whether and how their new teachers will keep families informed and involved about school programs and students' progress. For these and other reasons, commitments to school, family, and community partnerships must be renewed every year.

Data show dramatic declines in involvement after each transition to new levels of schooling (i.e., from preschool to elementary school, from elementary to middle school, and from middle to high school). Also, if students transfer to new schools during the school year, families are often uninformed about the school and how to become involved. Educators must have ways to welcome and connect with entering students and their families whenever they arrive at school.

Transitions are risky but important and exciting points of change and promise in students' lives. Appropriate and important school, family, and community partnerships should minimize problems and maximize success for students at points of transition.

QUESTIONS TO DISCUSS

1. Select a school transition that interests you (e.g., preschool to elementary school, elementary to middle school, middle to high school, or high school to postsecondary education/training). Think about students and their families entering a new school at the transition point that you selected.

a. Identify or design and describe one activity that would help students and parents make a successful transition to the new level of schooling that you selected.

b. Identify or design and describe one activity that would give the teachers and administrators the information they need about the children and families who are making a transition to the new level of schooling that you selected.

2. Select a grade level that interests you. Think about students and their families entering a new grade level within their present school (not a transition to a new school).

a. Identify or design and describe one activity that could be implemented at the start of a new school year to give parents the information they need to help their children make a successful transition to the grade level that you selected.

b. Identify or design and describe one activity that could be implemented at the start of a new school year to give the teachers and administrators the information they need to make a good start with students and their families in the grade level you selected.

3. *Optional class activity*: Share and critique examples of activities to involve families at points of transition from school to school and from grade to grade. Add the most promising examples to a resource notebook or electronic idea file for use in practice or for research and development.

COMMENT

Student Mobility

A study of the effects of family mobility indicates that elementary school students in two-parent homes who move up to seven times experience no more academic or behavioral problems than students who do not move. However, even one move increases the academic and behavioral problems of elementary school students in other family arrangements, such as mother-only, step-, or blended families, and other family forms (Tucker, Marx, and Long, 1998). The researchers statistically accounted for many family characteristics (such as parent education, income, and recency and distance of moves) to explore the effects of diverse family arrangements and the number of family moves on students' success in school.

Two variables missing from the study should be included in new research. First, it is important to know whether the children had academic or behavior problems before they moved, to determine whether mobility and family arrangements are responsible for academic and behavioral problems. Second, it is important to know what schools do to welcome and orient new students and their families with useful information on school policies and parent involvement. Some school practices may reduce the stress of moving to a new community by integrating new students and families into the school community.

Research is needed on whether and how schools with comprehensive programs of school, family, and community partnerships intervene to reduce the risks of mobility to student success in school, especially in single-parent homes, stepparent families, or blended families. A related study indicates that students in military families are not particularly affected when a parent is deployed as part of military duty (TDY—temporary duty assignments) (Thompson, 1998). In this study, one influential variable was parental satisfaction with the school's efforts to help students cope with the TDY. Some students are relatively resilient when their families move or when parents are temporarily absent, particularly if the school and community offer helpful information and support during turbulent times.

If schools are aware of stressful family situations and take action to assist students and their families, student achievement and behavior may not be as negatively affected as when families and students are left on their own to adjust to new schools and changes in family life.

QUESTIONS TO DISCUSS

1. In studies of effects of mobility on student success in school, why is it important to know whether schools conduct practices to welcome, inform, and involve families at school and at home?
2. Why might these partnership practices be particularly important to single parents in new neighborhoods and schools?
3. In studies of effects of mobility on student success in school, why is it important for researchers to measure whether youngsters were good or poor students, well or poorly behaved prior to the move from one school to another?

COMMENT

The Authority Structure

School, family, and community partnerships are part of the authority structure of schools (see comment on authority and control in Chapter 2). The authority structure is defined, in part, by who participates in school decisions; how families are informed and involved in their children's education; and how often and why students, families, educators, and others in the community interact.

The distribution and definition of power are altered by the way teachers, administrators, parents, and others in communities think about, talk about, and act to share responsibilities for education. Decisions about schools may be shared on any or all topics, including school organization; management; staffing; curriculum; student motivation; instructional methods; annual evaluations and recognition of teachers, administrators, and students; school climate; and specific policies and programs.

QUESTIONS TO DISCUSS

Use the articles and comments in this chapter to support your responses to the following questions:

1. *Teacher authority.* Is teacher and administrator authority more like a pie or an empire?
   a. How do you view a teacher's authority? Is it like a pie: If some authority is shared with families, there is less of the authority pie left, and, therefore, the teacher loses power? Or is it like an empire: If some authority is shared and alliances are made with families, the teacher gains power, influence, and effectiveness? Or do you view the effects of partnerships on a teacher's authority in some other way?
   b. Explain your ideas.
   c. Discuss the above questions, substituting "principal" for "teacher." Does the substitution affect your response? Why or why not?
2. *Family influence.* Is family influence on children weakened or enhanced when children go to school?
   a. How do you view the effects of school, family, and community partnerships on the influence families have to socialize, educate, motivate, and encourage their children? Do partnerships weaken and diffuse family authority and influence because teachers and others educate and socialize children? Or do partnerships strengthen and enhance family influence by providing parents with information and opportunities to interact with their children and educators about school decisions and school life? Or do you view the effects of partnerships on families' authority and influence in some other way?
   b. Explain your ideas.
3. *Student independence.* Is student independence boosted or delayed by school, family, and community partnerships?
   a. How do you view the effects of school, family, and community partnerships on student self-direction and independence? Do partnerships act as a catalyst through which parents, teachers, and others guide students toward greater independence? Or do partnerships act as an inhibitor, with collaborative activities delaying independence and keeping students dependent for too long on teachers, parents, or others? Or do you view the effects of partnerships on student independence in some other way?
   b. Explain your ideas.

Using Multiple Measures, Reporters, and Methods to Understand Family Involvement and Student Outcomes

Several readings in this chapter report multiple measures to study school, family, and community partnerships. The studies include (1) two or more measures from the same reporter, (2) two or more reporters on similar or related measures, or (3) multiple measures and multiple reporters. These techniques may produce consistent or inconsistent patterns of results that instantly confirm or dispute conclusions.

For example, in one study we identified teacher-leaders by using two measures, one from teachers' self-reports about their partnership practices and one from principals' ratings of the same teachers' practices. The principals' ratings confirmed or refuted teachers' self-reports on the extent to which they involved families of their students. The measures were cross-checked to identify concordant cases of teachers who were confirmed leaders who were particularly effective in their connections with families. The multiple measures created a better, more reliable independent variable of "teacher-leaders" than either measure could do alone.

As another example, in Reading 3.9, multiple measures were used to determine if reports about the level of family involvement from students, teachers, and principals produced consistent effects on students' attitudes, behaviors, and experiences. In this study, perspectives of different reporters at home and at school supported the conclusion that family involvement was linked to positive attitudes and higher student productivity.

QUESTIONS TO DISCUSS

1. Why might a researcher want to use two, three, or more measures of the *same* concept from the *same* reporter? Describe one problem that is solved and one problem that is created by this method of inquiry.

2. Why might a researcher want to obtain information from *two or more reporters* on the same concept? Describe one problem that is solved and one problem that is created by this method of inquiry.

3. Research on family and community involvement may be conducted using many different methods of data collection and analyses. There is no one right way to study partnerships. Various methods contribute different kinds of information to increase understanding and to raise new questions for future studies. For example, Readings 3.1 and 3.2 present quantitative analyses of survey data and qualitative analyses of teachers' comments, respectively.

   a. What do quantitative analyses of survey research (Reading 3.1) contribute that cannot be learned only by observations or "testimonies" about programs?

   b. What do the personal comments of teachers (Reading 3.2) contribute that cannot be learned from quantitative analyses of survey data?

Effects of Partnerships on Students

Studies of effects on students of school, family, and community partnerships have increased and improved over time (Jeynes, 2005). Most early research did not control for students' prior skills when studying whether family involvement increased student achievement. When prior skills are omitted from such analyses, the results mainly indicate that high-achieving students have families who are involved or that families are involved when students are high achieving.

Also, most early research did not account for what schools do to involve families in various ways. When school programs and teacher practices are omitted from such analyses, results mainly indicate that some families become involved on their own and that their children benefit from self-initiated family involvement.

Thus, information on students' prior skills and on the nature and quality of school programs and teacher practices of partnership is needed to fully answer questions about whether family involvement increases the achievement of students with initially different skill levels.

Analyses in Reading 3.7 statistically control for students' prior skills, teacher quality, and other variables that affect learning to identify the independent effects on students' standardized achievement test scores of teacher practices of involving families. The data link teachers' practices, parents' responses, and children's achievements.

If you see studies—early or new—that do not account for students' starting skills or behaviors, or for schools' practices to involve all families, you should be wary of claims that family involvement increases student achievement or other positive results. Such studies may be showing only that good students usually have parents who are more involved at school and at home.

Similarly, you should be wary of correlational results from cross-sectional or anecdotal data that show that family involvement links to poor achievement or problem behavior. This pattern—reported in Reading 3.8—may simply indicate that slower students require extra help at a particular point in time. The help they receive will vary in quality and may or may not have a positive impact on the problem at hand.

Researchers need well-specified measurement models and data that include students' starting skills to identify whether and how family involvement affects students' skills, achievement test scores, or behavior. Quantitative and qualitative studies must account for these complexities to address such questions as the following: Do school, family, and community partnerships lead to better achievement or other positive results for all students? If students need and receive help from school, home, and the community, do they improve their skills or attitudes?

Hypothetical Study

Choose question A or B, according to your interests.

A. Students in Lincoln Elementary School start the fifth grade with very different reading and math skills and with different histories of family involvement. The fifth graders are placed in three classrooms with teachers who differ in how much and how well they involve parents in reading and math. Suppose Lincoln Elementary School has set goals that all fifth graders will move on to middle school with at least sixth-grade reading and math skills. Two of many possible research questions linked to school, family, and community partnerships are:
   • Do students have higher math and/or reading skills if their parents are involved in their education at school and at home?
   • Do more students graduate with at least sixth-grade math and/or reading skills if their teachers conduct activities to involve all families with their children in these subjects?

   How might you study these topics to help Lincoln Elementary School learn whether and how well it is reaching its reading and math goals?

   1. Select one of the bulleted questions above that interests you.
   2. There are many methods to use to address these questions. Outline the steps for studying the question that you selected. How many teachers, students, and families will be involved in your hypothetical study and in what ways? How many months or years will your study take?
   3. List three major variables that you would include in your study and explain why each variable is important.

B. Students enter Roosevelt High School in the ninth grade with very different reading, math, and other skills and with different histories of family involvement. Each ninth grader has several teachers who have not done much in the past to involve students' parents at school or in students' learning activities and school decisions at home. Suppose Roosevelt High School has set a goal that at least 90 percent of all students who enter ninth grade will graduate from high school on time (in four years). Two of many possible research questions linked to school, family, and community partnerships are:
   • Do entering students with similar backgrounds complete grade 12 and graduate from high school on time if their families are involved in their education at school and at home?
   • If students fail one or more courses in grade 9, how are they helped by their school, family, and community to get back on the path to high school graduation? How successful are these students?

How might you study these topics to help Roosevelt High School learn whether or how well it is reaching its graduation goal?

1. Select one of the bulleted questions above that interests you.
2. There are many methods to use to address these questions. Outline how you might go about studying the question that you selected. How many teachers and students will be involved in your hypothetical study of Roosevelt High School? How many families will be included, and in what ways? How many months or years will your study take?
3. List three major variables that you would include in your study and explain why each variable is important.

C. *Optional class activity*:

1. Share and discuss the designs of the hypothetical studies of Lincoln Elementary School and Roosevelt High School and the variables that students selected for their studies. Consider: Are the study procedures clear? Are the variables essential? If the proposed study were conducted, would the selected question be clearly addressed?
2. Discuss: Are the questions about fifth graders in Lincoln and high school students in Roosevelt equally easy to study? Explain your ideas.

COMMENT

Importance of Reading Original Research

Although literature reviews, syntheses, meta-analyses, annotated bibliographies, and other summaries (such as Reading 2.2) provide useful overviews of a field or topic, they do not replace original research. Syntheses of research ask you to accept the reviewers' interpretations of large numbers of studies. They provide an efficient way to scan a field, but you also need to read original research to learn how an individual researcher conducts and reports a study. By reading original research (e.g., the readings in this chapter), you can consider:

- Are the sample and data adequate?
- Are the methods credible?
- Do the results add new knowledge to the field?
- What debatable issues are raised?
- What new questions should be studied to extend, confirm, or contest the reported results?

By reading original research, you should be able to frame your own studies more successfully or judge and select the most promising approaches for educational practice.

Reading Original Research

A. Select and read one original research article or book chapter—not a review or synthesis—on the effects of school, family, and community partnerships on students, teachers, administrators, or parents. The work may be a quantitative or qualitative study.

You may choose one reading in this chapter, a reference reported in this chapter, an article or chapter of original research in a book listed below, or one of the listed articles or chapters. Or you may select a recent article or chapter on your own.

Choose one chapter reporting an original research study in one of these books:

Booth, A., and J. Dunn (Eds.). (1996). *Family-school links: How do they affect educational outcomes.* Hillside, NJ: Lawrence Erlbaum Associates.

Bryk, A. S. and B. Schneider. (2002). *Trust in schools: A core resource for improvement.* New York: Russell Sage Foundation.

Chavkin, N., (Eds.). (1993). *Families and schools in a pluralistic society.* Albany: State University of New York Press.

Deslandes, R., (Eds.). (2009). *International perspectives on contexts, communities and evaluated innovative practices: Family-school-community partnerships.* New York: Routledge.

Lareau, A. (2003). *Unequal childhoods: Class, race, and family life.* Berkeley: University of California Press.

Or choose one of the following articles:

Catsambis, S., and A. A. Beveridge. (2001). Does neighborhood matter? Family, neighborhood, and school influences on eighth grade math achievement. *Sociological Focus* 34: 435–457.

Grolnick, W. S., C. Benjet, C. O. Kurowski, and N. H. Apostoleris. (1997). Predicators of parent involvement in children's schooling. *Journal of Educational Psychology* 89: 538–548.

Heymann, S. J., and A. Earle. (2000). Low-income parents: How do working conditions affect their opportunity to help school-age children at risk? *American Educational Research Journal* 37: 833–848.

Hill, N. E. (2004). Parent academic involvement as related to school behavior, achievement, and aspirations: Demographic variations across adolescence. *Child Development* 75: 1491–1509.

Ho, E. S., and J. D. Willms. (1996). Effects of parental involvement on eighth-grade achievement. *Sociology of Education* 69: 126–141.

Lee, V. E., and R. G. Croninger. (1994). The relative importance of home and school in development of literacy skills for middle-grade students. *American Journal of Education* 102: 286–329.

Lonigan, C. J., and G. J. Whitehurst. (1998). Relative efficacy of parent and teacher involvement in a shared-reading intervention for preschool children from low-income backgrounds. *Early Childhood Research Quarterly* 13: 263–290.

Lopez, G. R., J. D. Scribner, and K. Mahitivanichcha. (2001). Redefining parent involvement: Lessons from high-performing migrant-impacted schools. *American Educational Research Journal* 38: 253–288.

McBride, B. A., S. H. Schoppe-Sullivan, and H. Moon-Ho. (2005). The mediating role of fathers' school involvement on student achievement. *Journal of Applied Developmental Psychology* 26: 201–216.

Reynolds, A. J. and M. Clements. (2005). Parental involvement and children's school success. In E. Patrikakou et al. (Eds.), *School-family partnerships for student success* (pp. 109–127). New York: Teachers College Press.

Sheldon, S. B. (2003). Linking school-family-community partnerships in urban elementary schools to student achievement on state tests. *Urban Review* 35: 149–165.

B. Answer the following questions about the article, chapter, or book that you selected.

1. List the full bibliographic information of the publication you selected.

2. In one or two paragraphs, summarize the main questions and main results of the study.

3. Describe in a sentence or two:
    a. Were the sample and data adequate?
    b. Were the variables clear and measures reliable?
    c. In studies measuring student outcomes (e.g., achievement, behavior, attendance), were the measures of parental involvement theoretically linked to the outcome of interest?
    d. Were the analyses and results convincing?
    e. How did this study contribute to the knowledge base on school, family, and community partnerships?

C. Write two questions that you think should be studied to follow up on the results of the publication that you reviewed.

REFERENCES

Baker, D. P., and D. L. Stevenson. (1986). Mothers' strategies for children's school achievement: Managing the transition to high school. *Sociology of Education* 59: 156–166.

Benson, P. (1993, June). The troubled journey, and youth in single parent families. *Source* (Search Institute) 9(2): 1–3.

Cooper, H., and J. C. Valentine. (2001). *Educational Psychologist: Special Issue on Homework* 36(2).

Jeynes, W. (2005). A meta-analysis of the relation of parental involvement to urban elementary school student academic achievement. *Urban Education* 40: 237–269.

Thompson, E. K. (1998). *The effects of military deployment on children's adjustment at school*. Unpublished doctoral dissertation, University of Arizona, Tucson.

Tucker, C. J., J. Marx, and L. Long. (1998). Moving on: Residential mobility and children's school lives. *Sociology of Education* 71: 111–129.

PART TWO

Applying Research on School, Family, and Community Partnerships

4

Policy Implications

POLICIES AT THE FEDERAL, STATE, DISTRICT, AND SCHOOL levels increasingly include goals for school, family, and community partnerships. Importantly, legislation and guidelines are beginning to go beyond broad objectives for "parental involvement" by including explicit requirements and commitments for states, districts, and schools to develop effective partnership *programs*.

The trend—too slow, but encouraging—is to provide leadership and finances at state, district, and school levels to enable every school to create stronger connections with families, businesses, community agencies, and other groups in ways that benefit students. The trend is too slow because most state and district leaders have not established strong leadership and sustainable programs of family and community involvement. Most have not assigned the staff and budgets needed to conduct state and district leadership activities that guide and support all preschools and elementary, middle, and high schools in planning and implementing comprehensive, goal-linked partnership programs that engage all families and help all students succeed in school.

At the state level, there have been too few incentives for action and too few consequences for inaction from state boards and state leaders to encourage all districts and their schools to develop policies and enact programs that engage families in productive ways at all grade levels. Similarly, in most districts, neither incentives nor consequences from superintendents and school boards are pressing and guiding all school principals to establish official committees of educators and parents who share responsibilities for organizing and maintaining comprehensive, goal-linked, site-based partnership programs.

These deficiencies in leadership and organization reflect a general lack of will to translate strong rhetoric and broad policy statements on the importance of family and community involvement into viable programs and practices of partnership. The absence of incentives and consequences allows too many superintendents and principals to put partnership programs on the back burner, instead of placing school, family, and community connections front and center as an essential ingredient of school improvement. Too many leaders still view parental involvement as their personal agenda, rather than as a topic for shared leadership with a committee structure that could make a seemingly overwhelming topic into one that is manageable and successful.

The trend is encouraging, however, because over the past few years increasing numbers of states, districts, and schools have written policies and guidelines, identified leaders for partnerships, mobilized leadership teams, planned their work to improve over time, and started to implement partnership programs that mobilize family and community involvement in ways that support student learning and development. The knowledge gained from these efforts should help other states, districts, and schools take similar actions to involve all families and communities in their children's education.

STATES

Some states are actively developing and improving their leadership and programs that support districts and schools in their work on partnerships. A few have established permanent bureaus, offices, or departments of school, family, and community partnerships with directors, coordinators, and facilitators as experts on involvement. At this writing, over 20 state departments of education have joined the National Network of Partnership Schools (NNPS) at Johns Hopkins University to work on this agenda. These states have a designated leader whose responsibility is to inform, encourage, and assist districts and schools throughout the state to develop plans, programs, and practices of family and community involvement for increasing student success in school.

The investments and efforts of state leaders for partnerships vary, however, in quality, intensity, and duration. State departments of education are complex organizations with leaders who change frequently, with offices that overlap in responsibilities and operate at a distance from their districts and schools.

Some state leaders are guiding districts and schools to improve their partnership programs. State leadership activities include writing state goals and policies, providing federal and state funding and targeted grants for partnerships, providing professional development and ongoing training on partnership program development, conducting conferences, sharing best practices, evaluating work and progress, and recognizing and rewarding excellent practices. Examples of state leadership are discussed in the readings, comments, and activities in this chapter.

Nevertheless, too few of the 50 states have designated offices and leaders charged with increasing partnership program development in the districts and their schools in the state. Too few state leaders have long-term plans for partnerships or line-item budgets to support state experts who actively guide districts and schools to involve all families in their children's education. Too few state leaders have organized their work in ways that integrate family and community involvement agendas across departments. Efforts remain fragmented in most states, with many different offices conducting aspects of family and community involvement. Without clear leadership for partnerships, state departments of education cannot guide all districts and all schools to plan and implement programs that involve more families in more productive ways.

DISTRICTS

Some districts in all states are implementing policies to help schools improve connections with students' families and communities. With or without state guidance and financial support, most districts are responding to federal requirements for Title I funds that mandate policies, plans, and programs of family and community involvement. Some districts not only write policies on partnerships, but also have expert leaders who guide and support all preschools and elementary, middle, and high schools to improve the quality of their programs of family and community involvement for student success.

At this writing, over 150 districts are members of the National Network of Partnership Schools (NNPS) at Johns Hopkins University. They have identified a leader for partnerships and use research-based approaches to build capacities in all schools to conduct goal-linked partnership programs so that families and communities support student success in school. Some districts are moving swiftly and surely on this agenda; others lag. The work in leading districts will help other districts learn how to develop and maintain effective district-level leadership and school-based partnership programs.

Still, too few of about 14,000 public school districts in the United States are engaged in systematic efforts to develop, implement, evaluate, and continually improve their programs of school, family, and community partnerships. Most districts still need to identify professional staff to serve as leaders for partnerships, allocate adequate budgets, establish clear structures, and follow feasible processes to help all preschools and elementary, middle, and high schools to organize and improve their school-based partnership programs.

Noteworthy efforts by district leaders include allocating federal, state, and local funds for site-based partnership program development; providing ongoing staff development for school teams focused on family and community involvement and other educators to keep improving their programs; enabling schools to share best practices; and evaluating school-based programs. Even in very small districts, superintendents, school boards, principals, and lead teachers can support the development of partnership programs in their schools. Ultimately, every school must have the capacity to plan, implement, and continually improve its own partnership program.

SCHOOLS

Just about all schools conduct some activities to inform and involve parents in their children's education. Indeed, all schools that receive Title I funds are required to engage parents in productive ways. Not all schools—Title I or otherwise—plan their programs systematically, link the involvement activities to school goals for student success, or evaluate the quality and progress of their efforts.

At this writing, over 1,200 schools located in more than 30 states are members of the National Network of Partnership Schools (NNPS) at Johns Hopkins University. They aim to use research-based approaches to establish programs of family and community involvement that create a positive school climate and that help students improve skills and attitudes in reading, math, and other subjects; attendance; behavior; postsecondary planning; and other outcomes. Not all schools in NNPS, however, proceed at the same pace. The work of leading schools is helping to identify essential and effective components of partnership programs and should help other schools understand the new directions needed to improve their programs of family and community involvement.

There are, however, over 98,000 public and 35,000 private elementary and secondary schools in the country. Too few of these schools have an organized committee of educators and parents dedicated to guiding the school to plan, implement, evaluate, and continually improve its program and practices of family and community involvement in ways that support all students' learning, development, and success in school.

FEDERAL PROGRAMS

In the 1990s, the U.S. Department of Education and Secretary of Education Richard Riley shined a spotlight on school, family, and community partnerships. The department framed a vision, supported research and development, published reports, conducted traditional and satellite conferences, and contributed to a national conversation about improving the connections of home, school, and community.

Attention waned to some extent after 2002, when federal programs focused narrowly on test scores and emphasized parents' options to change schools that did not meet test-score targets. Some officials lost sight of the importance of family and community involvement as a mechanism for organizing successful schools and increasing student learning. Even when partnership programs were not emphasized, federal requirements for research-based parent involvement programs were written into the No Child Left Behind Act (NCLB) in Section 1118 and in other sections of the law. These regulations—many based on results of research and improved in each reauthorization of the Elementary and Secondary Education Act (ESEA)—influenced the development of partnership programs in some states, districts, and schools, as described above.

For more than 50 years, federal policies have guided educators, families, businesses, and other community groups to improve parental involvement in education. These include Head Start policies in the 1960s, family leave policies, Title I regulations in one form or another since the mid-1960s, Even Start legislation, Goals 2000 targets, Individuals with Disabilities Education Act (IDEA), Improving America's Schools Act (IASA)—which preceded NCLB as the renewed version of ESEA—and other laws and guidelines from the departments of Education, Labor, Health and Human Services, Commerce, and Justice.

Although federal policies and related funds to improve schools and to increase parental involvement have been continuous, the emphases at any point in time reflected the politics of education. As a result, there is little coherence across federal laws from different departments and no clear way to evaluate progress or problems in federally funded programs of family and community involvement. At this writing, for example, NCLB's Section 1118 requires states, districts, and schools to meet important requirements that *could* result in well-planned partnership programs in every school. All kinds of "monitoring" are conducted to see if programs meet the federal guidelines, but checklists cannot gauge the quality of partnership programs, the equity of outreach to all families, whether and how programs and results improve from year to year, or how local leaders should strengthen weak programs.

Federal laws are too distant from districts, schools, and families to serve as the main guide for developing permanent partnership programs. Rather, federal guidelines must be interpreted by state, district, and school leaders. Their policies and practices must integrate multiple funding streams for family involvement for general education programs, special education, homeless education, drug abuse prevention, health improvement, and other programs to produce a unified partnership program in every district and in every school that is open to evaluation and improvement.

SUMMARY

Leadership and research-based actions at all levels—federal, state, district, and school—are needed to enable all schools to improve their partnership programs. The main work of school, family, and community partnerships occurs at the school level where principals, teachers, parents, and students meet daily. Federal, state, and district policies, funds, and professional development will be most valuable if they guide educators, parents, students, and community members to work together to implement effective school-based programs that welcome, respect, inform, and involve all families in ways that support student learning and success in school.

Federal, state, and district policies and actions should be reviewed and revised periodically to ensure that they encompass the latest, proven approaches. Leadership goes beyond checking for compliance with federal or state rules. Leadership includes ongoing assistance to evaluate progress and to continually improve plans, involve more families, and increase students' success in school. School policies must be judged on whether they enable teachers, families, and others in the community to work effectively together—as an action team—on behalf of the children they share (see Chapters 5, 6, and 7).

This chapter includes a short reading outlining useful state policies and several examples of state and district policies that are consistent with the theory, research, and framework for school, family, and community partnerships presented in this volume. The examples show how education leaders are beginning to (1) correct vague goals for parental involvement by using the vocabulary of *school, family, and community partnerships*; (2) identify the six major types of involvement to link practices of partnership to school improvement goals; (3) provide staff development to school action teams of principals, teachers, parents, and others; and (4) offer incentives and recognition for innovative and effective programs and practices.

This chapter also includes one reading that reports the results of research on whether and how well districts are addressing requirements for parental involvement in federal policy—NCLB. Taken together, the readings and activities in this chapter introduce you to viable policies for school, family, and community partnerships and to research on challenging policy questions.

Parent Involvement:
State Education Agencies Should Lead the Way[*]

Words about the importance of parent involvement are meaningless without financial and technical support.

ABSTRACT

Parent involvement is on everyone's list of practices to make schools more effective, to help families create more positive learning environments, to reduce the risk of student failure, and to increase student success. Although most state education agencies have policies on parental involvement, there still is little financial support for leadership, programs, and actions needed to improve school programs, teachers' practices, and parents' understanding of ways to become involved in their children's education. This reading draws from research on school and family partnerships to outline actions needed at the state level to improve programs to involve families in every school.

OVERVIEW

One major finding from the research reported in Chapter 3 is that teacher leadership, outreach, and involvement activities—not parent education, marital status, or other background variables—made a difference in whether parents improved their knowledge about the school and actions to help their children, and whether children improved their reading scores. Because teachers and administrators play key roles in including or excluding parents from their children's education, state policies and actions should aim to improve district-level and school-level leaders' capabilities to conduct parent involvement programs and practices that make a difference for student success in class.

STATE SUPPORT OF PARENT INVOLVEMENT

State policies, bylaws, guidelines, and funds for educational programs strongly influence district and school leadership, teaching practice, and community support. These policies can either recognize or ignore the connections between educational and socializing institutions in a child's life—the family, the school, and the community.

---

[*] By Joyce L. Epstein. Article updated 2010. An earlier version of this article was published in *Community Education Journal* 14, no. 4 (1987): 4–10.

State programs that address the needs of all families for useful information and involvement in their children's education give something back to families and citizens for their education tax dollars. Parent involvement in a sequential, continuing program from preschool through high school is one important factor for reducing students' school failure and dropping out, and increasing the probability of students' graduating from high school. The quality of family and school connections all through school can dramatically affect the students' futures and determine whether they become dependent on or contribute to the state. Programs through high school that support family and community involvement and parent-child interactions about school may be the most beneficial investments that can be made at the state, district, and school levels to prevent more costly social and educational problems.

PARENT INVOLVEMENT AND CHOICE

In the mid-1980s, the National Governors' Association Task Force on Parent Involvement and Choice focused a great deal of attention on the pros and cons of increasing parents' choices of the schools their children attend, especially choices among public schools with different programs. However, after the choice of schools is made—even if children attend their neighborhood schools—parents and educators must choose whether or not to emphasize parental involvement. Important family and school connections start with the choice of or assignment to schools and continue when teachers, parents, and students interact on a daily basis.

Students make many decisions each year. Their choices of programs, courses, activities, opportunities, and special services affect their futures. Parents need to be involved as knowledgeable partners in these decisions. They must understand how the school system works; the goals and programs of the schools their children attend; the options and consequences of decisions that concern their children each school year; the course objectives and requirements for a passing grade; how teachers define success and grade progress; the programs that are available to their children before and after school, on weekends, and on Saturdays; and how their children may participate in those programs.

Some parents have the information and experience they need to guide their children through the elementary and secondary grades and into postsecondary schooling or work. Other parents—most parents—need and want information from teachers and administrators about how to help their children make key decisions and how to guide students' in learning activities. This is true in all schools—public, charter, or private; religious or secular; chosen or assigned—at all levels of schooling.

Even today, there is much discussion about parent involvement in the choice of schools for their children, but too little attention paid to the importance of parent involvement after the choice of schools is made. The strongest influences on partnership programs will come from districts and schools, but state departments of education, governor's offices, and other state programs can and should establish policies and take action to encourage and support district and school leaders to improve their programs and practices of family and community involvement.

STATE LEADERSHIP FOR PARENT INVOLVEMENT

Research suggests that the following policies and actions at the state level will help districts and schools improve programs and practices of school, family, and community partnerships and help to produce better academic and behavioral results for more students.

1. Write a policy that outlines the state's commitment to research-based and goal-oriented programs of school, family, and community partnerships. An official policy should recognize the importance of family and community involvement and the need for well-planned partnership programs in districts and schools. The policy should make explicit the state's perspectives, expectations, and services that will support research-based programs in districts and schools. A strong state policy will recognize leadership at the district level and action-oriented teams of teachers, parents, administrators, and others at the school level to plan, implement, evaluate, and sustain partnership programs linked to school improvement goals. The policy should call educators' attention to the six types of involvement that can be activated to inform and engage all families in more ways to support student learning and development.

It is not enough to mandate only parent advisory councils, or only parent-teacher organizations, or only parent volunteers at the school building. These activities typically involve only a small number of parents and have little impact on helping all parents monitor and guide their children's education at all grade levels. Other types of involvement must be implemented, including effective parent-teacher and parent-teacher-student conferences with all parents, parent involvement in learning activities at home, and connections with the community. All children benefit if their parents are knowledgeable about school programs and students' options, and if their parents are knowledgeable partners with teachers in their education.

A state policy must be clear and comprehensive, but also flexible and responsive. Good policies recognize that districts and schools in the state have different starting points in their practices of partnerships and serve diverse populations of parents and students. An official policy on school, family, and community partnerships should be accompanied by "enactments" that specify the services that the state will provide to help every district and every school implement the policy. The following are some activities that states may select to support the implementation of a policy on school, family, and community partnerships.

2. Establish an office or department with an expert leader and adequate staff to facilitate the development and continuous improvement of programs of school, family, and community partnerships. Every state should have a director of school, family, and community partnerships who is an expert on partnership program development and who is known as the "go to" leader on partnership program development for the state. This leader not only will continue to increase his or her knowledge and skills for state-level leadership on partnerships, but also will increase awareness, develop knowledge, and encourage the actions of colleagues in the state department of education and in districts and schools in the state. Interdepartmental connections with colleagues will help state leaders for partnerships strengthen their programs and improve outreach to districts and schools in the state.

3. Write an annual Leadership Action Plan for Partnerships. To be effective, state leaders for partnerships must write a Leadership Action Plan that outlines and schedules the activities they will conduct each year to promote and support school, family, and community partnerships at the state level and with districts and schools. Research and field work reveal six leadership strategies for state and district leaders that will be represented in activities selected to match the state's policy context and education goals. A strong state plan for partnerships will include activities to *create awareness, align program and policy, guide learning and program development, share knowledge, celebrate milestones, document progress,* and *evaluate outcomes* of partnership programs (Epstein et al., 2009). The actions discussed in this section will help state leaders fulfill these six leadership strategies.

4. Identify funds for state-level leadership on school, family, and community partnerships to cover staff and program costs. State leaders must have a budget for partnership program development that covers staff salaries, training programs, small grants for partnership projects, conferences to share best practices, evaluation studies, and/or other selected activities in the Leadership Action Plan for Partnerships. A line item in the state education budget stabilizes support for leadership on partnerships, for state-level activities, and for the work state leaders do with districts and schools.

The most effective parent involvement programs and practices are conducted at the school level—where the students and families are located. State grants to districts that are, then, channeled to schools can help to increase the number and quality of school-based programs to involve all families—including those typically hard to reach—in their children's education. State funds also might be used to provide sabbaticals or summer salaries for district and school leaders to develop and adapt materials to improve outreach to all families and effective practices.

There are potentially important connections between state funds and the quality of partnership programs and practices in districts and schools. In most districts and schools, funds are needed to translate materials for parents who do not speak or read English, support interpreters at parent-teacher meetings, and develop effective practices to involve special populations of single parents, young parents, parents of children with special needs, and other groups that need specialized support. State funds can be used to develop, test, and disseminate approaches and materials that districts and schools can use or adapt to reach targeted populations of parents and community groups. (Also see discussions and activities on funding for programs of family and community involvement on pp. 362–368).

5. Conduct ongoing inservice education on partnerships. State leaders for partnerships should provide or support others to provide inservice education on beginning and advanced topics for developing programs of school, family, and community partnerships. Well-organized inservice education will outline scheduled dates for professional development for district leaders to prepare them for their work on partnerships and advance their skills over time. Other inservice activities help state, district, and school professionals continually improve their knowledge and their programs of partnerships.

6. Collect, assess, and help leaders improve district policies on partnerships *and* the organization of district leadership for partnership program development. Some federal policies (e.g., Title I in ESEA) and some state policies ask state leaders to collect and monitor districts' policies on parental involvement and related practices to gauge compliance with requirements for funding. It is not enough, however, to collect and rate policies or plans as "in" or "out" of compliance. State leaders must also guide district leaders to continually improve their leadership and programs that fulfill state policy requirements. This means that state leaders themselves must be up-to-date on research and resources that will help district and school leaders implement effective programs of family and community involvement that support student success in school.

7. Evaluate teachers and administrators for their work on partnerships. State boards of education should provide guidelines for districts to evaluate the quality of efforts to conduct and improve family and community involvement in educators' annual or periodic evaluations. This component of professional work should be included in the evaluations of district superintendents, district-level leaders for partnerships, school principals, teachers, counselors, and instructional aides. Although these professional evaluations are conducted at the district and school levels, state leaders may assist with information, templates, and examples of rigorous yet reasonable evaluations of educators' competencies on leadership for partnerships and on partnership program development and improvement.

8. Support a master teacher, lead teacher, or other career ladder program to build a cadre of district and school-based specialists in organizing, evaluating, and improving programs of family and community involvement. In a national survey, teachers reported strong interest in developing leadership skills that enable them to be more active participants in school improvement activities in their schools and in their districts (MetLife, 2010). States may support innovative plans to improve the status of teachers in this "hybrid" role of teacher and leader of an area for school reform.

Some professional development programs prepare teachers to become subject matter specialists or "coaches" to assist other teachers in a school or within a district. It also is possible to prepare and promote teachers who are specialists in school, family, and community partnerships. For example, teachers who are chairs or co-chairs of schools' Action Teams for Partnerships tend to become expert in organizing effective partnership programs. They not only lead their own schools' work on partnerships but also may climb a career ladder to become district-level leaders for partnerships who guide other school-based teams to develop their programs of family and community involvement. State support of career ladder programs may provide financial support, planning time, or other recognition for teacher leaders.

9. Develop partnership tools or products. State leaders for partnerships not only use available tools and guidelines to develop their partnership programs but also develop and customize tools to meet the needs and goals of schools, families, and students in their locations. Leaders create brochures, calendars, newsletters, periodic communiqués, translations of information and materials for families with limited English skills, websites, summaries of research results, and other publications and products. Districts and schools must solve various challenges (e.g., in involving fathers, in engaging families who do not speak or read English, in welcoming new families to the community, in explaining state assessments, and many other topics) as they improve their partnership programs. State leaders for partnership can help by developing "tailor-able tools" that district leaders and school teams can use or adapt to engage all families in ways that support their children's success in school.

10. Encourage business, industry, and other community connections to strengthen school, family, and community partnerships. Some businesses have policies that permit and encourage employees who are parents to become involved in their children's education and attend parent-teacher conferences. Some businesses have policies that enable all employees, with or without school-age children, to volunteer time to assist local schools. State leaders may work with legislators, business leaders, and community groups to draft legislation or develop other incentives (e.g., tax incentives, tax credits, preferred status, or other types of recognition for businesses) that encourage businesses to support family and community involvement in schools. State leaders also may encourage business, industry, university, and community leaders to establish day care programs for young children, summer and vacation programs for school-age students, and information centers on child and adolescent development for employees who are parents, and they may recognize organizations that conduct these family-friendly and student-support activities. See the discussion and activities on support by business and industry for family and community involvement of employees on pp. 376–378.

11. Establish an advisory committee so that state education leaders hear from parents and the community about partnerships and other educational issues. Each state should have an advisory committee with representatives of key stakeholders that meets on a regular schedule with the state superintendent of schools and/or the office on partnerships. The members of the advisory committee should represent the diverse population of students and families served in the state. They will represent varied perspectives on how state leaders can strengthen family and community involvement in all districts and schools.

12. Establish a website, library, clearinghouse, and/or dissemination center for research on partnerships, promising practices of family and community involvement, and useful materials and resources. State offices for family and community involvement may collect and disseminate information on partnerships and share best practices on a website, in family resource centers, and in other convenient locations. State leaders can use new technologies to collect and share summaries of research results on partnerships; effective approaches for organizing partnership programs; teachers' practices for involving parents in conferences, homework, and extracurricular and other activities; tools to evaluate the quality and progress of partnership programs; forms and technologies for communicating with parents; information on child and adolescent development and parenting strategies; and other information and materials. The materials developed at the state level may be tailored and disseminated by district leaders in forms useful to educators, parents, and the public in their areas.

13. Support requirements for preservice and advanced education to prepare new teachers and administrators to conduct excellent partnership programs. State leaders should support legislation for state certification that requires future teachers and administrators to take at least one course on how to conduct an effective program of school, family, and community partnerships. State grants and other awards should support state colleges and universities in developing preservice and advanced courses on family and community involvement for future teachers and administrators. The content must go beyond coverage of traditional communications with families (e.g., parent-teacher conferences) to include education for future educators on how to plan, implement, evaluate, and improve outreach to parents and results for students.

Currently, in most states, future teachers, principals, counselors, and other administrators are not required to obtain and demonstrate knowledge and skills on developing effective and sustainable programs of family and community involvement linked to school improvement goals for student success in school (see Chapter 1 for an overview). Yet every educator entering a school or classroom must work every day with children and their families. Future teachers' abilities to implement home and school connections are as critical to their success as their abilities to teach reading or manage classrooms. Future principals, too, need to know how to guide teams of educators, parents, and community partners to work together to develop an effective school-based program of family and community involvement.

14. Support research and evaluation on the quality and effects of programs and practices of school, family, and community partnerships. State leaders should collect and analyze data to learn whether and how well state level partnership programs are working and how districts and schools improve the quality, outreach, and results of partnership programs over time. Or state leaders should arrange for periodic external evaluations of these activities.

Educators know that what gets measured gets done. Many educators will continue to consider parental involvement "extra stuff" or "fluff" until there is clear accountability for partnership programs. This includes clarity on what data to collect to learn if district leaders are effectively guiding schools to develop goal-linked partnership programs and whether and how school teams are organizing effective programs to involve all families in ways that support student learning and development.

Measures must be made of current involvement activities, quality of implementation, extent of outreach to families and community partners, responses from families and community partners, and, ultimately, results for students. Some documentation is relatively simple, such as gathering district policies and providing feedback on these documents. Other evaluations are complex, such as collecting longitudinal data to study whether the quality of school partnership programs affects student attendance, achievement, and behavior over time (Epstein et al., 2009).

DISCUSSION

The policies and actions outlined in this chapter require leadership, time, funds, and commitments for the long term. State departments of education that establish these four requirements will have more successful and sustainable programs of school, family, and community partnerships.

Funding is particularly important, not only to support the state leaders for partnerships, but also for the investments in teacher training, evaluation studies, and the other activities discussed above. Funds for state leaders should be ensured for an extended period of time (just as funds support curricular improvements) to develop state leaders' expertise on partnerships and to help district and school leaders improve and sustain their programs of family and community involvement that contribute to student success in school. Funds to increase the number and quality of partnership programs in districts and schools in the state are likely to be returned to the state in the form of better-informed parents, more successful students, more effective teachers, fewer student failures, higher graduation rates, and fewer demands on other state and local resources for expensive social services when the students are adolescents and young adults.

Parent involvement is not the parents' responsibility alone. Nor is it the state's, district's, or school's responsibility alone. Parent involvement is everybody's job but nobody's job until a structure is put in place to support it. Without financial and technical support from state education agencies, words about the importance of parent involvement are meaningless. State policies—the words—are necessary but not sufficient for enabling all districts and schools to develop strong programs of family and community involvement. Policies that are unfunded and unsupported will be unwelcome and ineffective.

In sum, state leaders have important responsibilities for developing and continually improving their knowledge, skills, and activities of school, family, and community partnerships. They also must take steps to facilitate the knowledge and skills of district leaders and school-based Action Teams for Partnerships so that every elementary, middle, and high school is able to develop its own program of partnership.

REFERENCES

Epstein, J. L. (2009). District and State Leadership for School, Family, and Community Partnerships. In J. L. Epstein et al., *School, family, and community partnerships: Your handbook for action* (3rd ed.; pp. 235–273). Thousand Oaks, CA: Corwin.

MetLife. (2010). *Survey of American teachers: Collaborating for student success, part 3, teaching as a career*. New York: Author.

READING 4.2

Sample State and District Policies on School, Family, and Community Partnerships[*]

Three state policies from California, Connecticut, and Wisconsin and three district policies from Buffalo, New York, Middletown, Connecticut, and Saint Paul, Minnesota, are included in this chapter. The policies were selected because they are thoughtfully written, research-based, and comprehensive and because they include administrative commitments to help schools enact the policies. The policies call for well-planned programs that reach out to involve all parents, [*3] with district leaders and school-based teams to organize and plan programs that use the framework of six types of involvement and recognize work done well. The words and emphases of these policies may help other states and districts to develop simple yet responsive policies and enactments on school, family, and community partnerships.

Having a good policy is the first step on the path to partnerships. The featured policies should not be interpreted to mean that these states and districts have completed their work or fulfilled their policies. Indeed, all of the states and districts noted here still have a great deal of work to do to help all schools develop and sustain comprehensive programs of school, family, and community partnerships.

STATE POLICIES: CALIFORNIA, CONNECTICUT, AND WISCONSIN
California State Board of Education Policy
Subject: Parent Involvement in the Education of Their Children

---

Introduction

A critical dimension of effective schooling is parent involvement: Research has shown conclusively, that parent involvement at home in their children's education improves student achievement. Furthermore, when parents are involved at school, their children go farther in school and they go to better schools.

From research studies to date, we have learned the following important facts:

1. Families provide the primary educational environment.
2. Parent involvement in their children's education improves student achievement.

---

[*] The term *parent* refers to any caregiver who assumes responsibility for nurturing and caring for children, including parents, grandparents, aunts, uncles, foster parents, stepparents, guardians, etc. Some educators and researchers use the terms *parent involvement, family involvement, family engagement,* and related terms. In my view, these terms focused on parents' behaviors are embedded in the overarching goal of developing excellent programs of school, family, and community partnerships that increase student learning and success in school.

3. Parent involvement is most effective when it is comprehensive, supportive, long-lasting and well-planned.
4. The benefits of parent involvement are not limited to early childhood or the elementary level; there are continuing positive effects through high school.
5. Involving parents in supporting their children's education at home is not enough. To ensure the quality of schools as institutions serving the community, parents must be involved at all levels in the schools.
6. Children from low-income and culturally and racially diverse families have the most to gain when schools involve parents. The extent of parent involvement in a child's education is more important to student success than family income or education.
7. We cannot look at the school and the home in isolation from one another; families and schools need to collaborate to help children adjust to the world of school. This is particularly critical for children from families with different cultural and language backgrounds.

Schools that undertake and support strong comprehensive parent involvement efforts are more likely to produce students who perform better than identical schools that do not involve parents. Schools that have strong linkages with and respond to the needs of the communities they serve, have students that perform better than schools that don't. Children who have parents who help them at home and stay in touch with the school, do better academically than children of similar aptitude and family background whose parents are not involved. The inescapable fact is that consistently high levels of student success are more likely to occur with long-term comprehensive parent involvement in schools.

The California State Board of Education recognizes that a child's education is a responsibility shared by school and family during the entire period the child spends in school. Although parents come to the schools with diverse cultural backgrounds, primary languages, and needs, they overwhelmingly want their children to be successful in school. School districts and schools, in collaboration with parents, teachers, students and administrators, must establish and develop efforts that enhance parent involvement and reflect the needs of students and families in the communities which they serve.

To support the mission of California schools to educate all students effectively, schools and parents must work together as knowledgeable partners. All of the grade level reforms, Here they come: Ready or Not!, It's Elementary, Caught in the Middle, Second to None, and other major initiatives such as Healthy Start (SB 620) and School Restructuring (SB 1274), emphasize parent and community involvement in school restructuring. The reform efforts support school-based shared decision-making at the school site that includes all stakeholders, including teachers, administrators, students, parents and other community members.

The State Board of Education will continue to support, through the California Department of Education, assistance to school districts and schools in developing strong comprehensive parent involvement. Comprehensive means that parents are involved at all grade levels in a variety of roles. The efforts should be designed to:

1. Help parents develop parenting skills to meet the basic obligations of family life and foster conditions at home, which emphasize the importance of education and learning.
2. Promote two-way (school-to-home and home-to-school) communication about school programs and students' progress.
3. Involve parents, with appropriate training, in instructional and support roles at the school and in other locations that help the school and students reach stated goals, objectives and standards.
4. Provide parents with strategies and techniques for assisting their children with learning activities at home that support and extend the school's instructional program.
5. Prepare parents to actively participate in school decision making and develop their leadership skills in governance and advocacy.
6. Provide parents with skills to access community and support services that strengthen school programs, family practices, and student learning and development.

These six types of parent involvement roles require a coordinated school-wide effort that has the support of parents, teachers, students and administrators at each school site. Furthermore, research indicates that home-school collaboration is most likely to happen if schools take the initiative to encourage, guide and genuinely welcome parents into the partnership. Professional development for teachers and administrators on how to build such a partnership is essential.

The issue of parent involvement in the education of their children is much larger than improving student achievement. It is central to our democracy that parents and citizens participate in the governing of public institutions. Parent involvement is fundamental to a healthy system of public education.

ADOPTED JANUARY 14, 1989; UPDATED SEPTEMBER 9, 1994

Connecticut State Board of Education
Adopts a Definition of School-Family-Community

Public Act 97-290, Section 14, requires each local and regional board of education to "develop, adopt, and implement written policies and procedures to encourage parent-teacher communication. These policies and procedures may include monthly newsletters, required regular contact with all parents, flexible parent-teacher conference, drop in hours for parents, home visits, and the use of technology such as homework hot lines to allow parents to check on their children's assignments and students to get assistance if needed." The state law went into effect September 1, 1998.

In 1997 and again in 2009, the Connecticut State Board of Education issued a *Position Statement on School-Family-Community Partnerships for Student Success* to guide state, district, and school leaders, parents, and the public to understand and implement the short policy statement. Following is the most recent version of the statement:

The Connecticut State Board of Education believes education is a shared responsibility throughout a student's life from birth to adulthood. Families, school staff and community members make important contributions to student success and the best results come when all three work together as equal partners. The purpose of these three-way partnerships is to support students' success in school and through life.

A Definition of School-Family-Community Partnerships

The State Board of Education endorses a research-based definition of school-family-community partnerships that can be applied to policies and practices across the state that result in student success.

School-family-community partnerships are:

- A shared responsibility with schools and other community organizations committed to engaging families in meaningful, culturally respectful ways as well as families actively supporting their children's learning and development;
- Continuous across a student's life, beginning in infancy and extending through college and career preparation programs; and
- Carried out everywhere that children learn including homes, early childhood education programs, schools, after-school programs, faith-based institutions, playgrounds, and community settings.

Taken together, this definition supports the creation of pathways to partnerships that honor the dynamic, multiple and complementary ways that children learn and grow. Family engagement is everything family members do to support their children's learning, guide them through a complex school system, advocate for them when problems arise, and collaborate with educators and community groups to achieve more equitable and effective learning opportunities. The terms parent or family are intended to mean a natural, adoptive or foster parent, or other adult serving as a parent, such as a close relative, legal or educational guardian and/or a community or agency advocate.

As students become older and more mature, they should and will take increasing responsibility for their learning. Nevertheless, they will need support from the adults in their lives throughout their educational careers.

A Comprehensive Approach

In order to encourage a comprehensive approach to school-family-community partnerships, the Board recommends that school districts develop programs addressing each of the following six standards:

1. Parent education. Identify and prioritize as needed, secondary school completion options and English language learning services for parents of school age children. Support the family's essential role in encouraging children's learning at every age and in developing positive parent-child relationships.

2. Communicating and creating a welcoming climate. Promote ongoing, clear, meaningful, and two-way communication about school programs and student learning, and develop personal relationships among school staff, families, students and community members.

3. Volunteering. Involve families in instruction and support, both in and out of school, and in creating a family-friendly atmosphere at school.

4. Supporting learning at home. Involve families in learning and enrichment activities at home and in the community that are linked to academic standards.

5. Decision-making and advocacy. Provide opportunities for families to develop and strengthen their leadership roles in school decisions, especially those related to student performance and school improvement.

6. Collaborating with community. Provide coordinated access to community resources, serve as a resource to the community and offer opportunities for community service.

To be effective, these standards of engagement should be connected to the goals of the school district's improvement planning, and designed to engage students and families in strengthening specific knowledge and skills identified as needing work by assessment data. Parent and community engagement that is linked to student learning has a greater effect on achievement than more general involvement.

Characteristics of Successful School-Family-Community Partnerships

The State Board of Education recognizes that school-family-community partnerships must focus on activities that are linked to children's learning. They also must reflect the many ways in which families, community organizations, and school staff engage with and support one another, from promoting family literacy, to improving schools and advocating for greater educational quality and opportunity.

Successful partnerships are as varied as their local communities, yet they share certain common characteristics. Effective partnerships are:

1. Respectful. All partners develop relationships that recognize, respect and build on the diverse strengths, talents, needs, and interests of families and students.

2. Inclusive. Staff reach out to all families, especially those who are culturally diverse or have low levels of income. They examine their assumptions and come to know and learn from families as individuals. All families are honored and valued as partners in their children's education.

3. Flexible. Partnerships are tailored to all stages of a student's educational career, and offer a variety of times, locations and opportunities for participation.

4. Democratic. Families and young people are equal partners with staff, together constructing programs, policies and information. Leadership is open to families, students and other partners.

5. Systematic. Partnerships focus on student achievement and help families and community members understand what students are learning and what the district's standards for successful performance mean for different ages and grade levels.

Benefits of High-Quality School-Family-Community Partnership Programs

Research shows that well-planned partnerships among families, school and community members can make a powerful contribution to greater student success. No matter what their income or background, students with involved families tend to have higher grades and test scores, better attendance, and higher rates of homework completion. They enroll in more challenging classes, have better social skills and behavior, and are more likely to graduate and go on to college.

Families and schools also benefit. Families engaged in partnerships have a greater sense of efficacy, stronger social ties and are more likely to continue their own education. Teachers report greater job satisfaction when they work with families, and families who are more involved hold more positive views of teachers and schools. Increased involvement develops feelings of ownership, resulting in greater family and community support for public education.

The State Board of Education understands that it takes more than engaged families and communities to sustain high student achievement. High-performing schools have many characteristics, including high standards and expectations for student learning, effective school leadership as well as high quality curriculum and instruction. Research also shows, however, that successful schools also have strong ties with families and their community. An effective program of school-family-community partnerships is a critical support students require to realize their potential, and one essential step toward eliminating our state's achievement gaps.

ADOPTED: NOVEMBER 4, 2009

SUPPLEMENT TO POSITION STATEMENT, NOVEMBER 2009

The Connecticut State Board of Education in its 2009 *Position Statement on School-Family-Community Partnerships for Student Success* calls for a shared responsibility among three equal partners to support students' success in school and through life. This document is intended to offer additional guidance to the *Position Statement*.

To develop effective school-family-community partnership programs, state, district and school leaders, along with parents, community leaders and students, must identify goals for their collaboration. Each member of the team has an important role to play and unique contributions to make to the partnership.

State Department of Education Responsibilities

Develop and promote school-family-community partnership programs that contribute to success for all students.

- Provide resources and technical assistance to school districts to help them implement programs of partnership, in accordance with this policy statement. This leadership includes promoting the six standards of family engagement and the full involvement of all major partners.
- Expand the message from a focus on parenting to emphasize the shared responsibility of families, schools and communities to create pathways for family engagement to support student achievement.
- Hold public forums, summits and other meetings to solicit ideas from parents, educators and others about how families, schools and communities can work together to support student learning.

Coordinate and strengthen the family and community engagement components of all major state and federal programs.

- Identify all state and federal programs that have family and community engagement requirements and assess their implementation and effectiveness.
- Collect and disseminate information about current research, best practice and model policies and programs.

School Districts' Responsibilities

Create a culture of partnership.

- The district must make family engagement a priority, set clear goals for school-family-community partnerships that all schools are expected to meet and monitor progress on those goals.

- The school board should establish policies that support partnerships, such as making school facilities available to the community and families and creating roles for businesses and community organizations.
- Connect school-family-community partnerships directly to the district's improvement initiative.
- The district should designate a senior level administrator responsible for school-family-community partnerships to provide leadership for program implementation, coordination and accountability.
- The district should guide all schools to develop and implement a systematic and effective plan for engaging families in improving student achievement that aligns with school and district improvement plans.

Organize district resources to create a structure of support so that all schools can and will establish and sustain strong partnerships.

- The district should develop structures to implement fully the six standards of family engagement and monitor progress to determine which practices produce the best results.
- The district should provide training and support for teachers, administrators, other staff members and families in developing partnership skills, especially understanding and appreciating diversity, developing skills to work with people from different backgrounds and linking programs and activities to student learning.
- The district should provide learning and development opportunities for families such as parent leadership and advocacy training, adult education, literacy and English language instruction so that parents may be full partners in their children's education.
- The district should prioritize engagement of parents of school age children who may need English as a Second Language program and high school completion programs such as GED test preparation.

Schools' Responsibilities

Welcome all family and community members to the school.

- The principal should consistently demonstrate commitment to families and expect and support all staff to create a respectful, inclusive and family-friendly environment.
- School staff should make every effort to build trusting, relevant relationships among families, staff and community members.

Engage families and community members in a systematic way to help the school meet its student achievement goals.

- All family engagement programs and activities should be linked to student learning so that families can understand what their children are learning in class and gain skills to help them at home.
- Teachers should learn and practice effective, research-based strategies linking family engagement to student success.

Communicate regularly with families about student learning.

- The school should use many two-way pathways for communication, in everyday language that is translated into families' home languages.
- Schools should make it easy for any family to communicate with teachers, the principal and other administrators.

Encourage families to be advocates for their own and others' children, to ensure that students are treated fairly and have access to meaningful learning opportunities.

- Give families information about how the school system works and how to raise questions or concerns.
- Give families information and support to monitor their children's progress and guide them toward their goals, including college.
- Promote opportunities for families to take part in learning and development programs related to leadership, advocacy and adult education including literacy and English language instruction.

Make families and school staff equal partners in decisions that affect children and families.

- A school council or other decision-making group should include families and give them a voice in major decisions, including principal selection.
- Every school should have a strong, broad-based parent organization that can advocate on behalf of families and children.

Collaborate with community organizations to connect students, families and staff to expand learning opportunities, community services and civic participation.

- School staff should work closely with community organizations, businesses and institutes of higher education to make resources available and turn the school into a hub of community life.

Families' Responsibilities

Create a home environment that promotes learning and holds children to high expectations.

- Engage in family reading activities and support homework. Emphasize the value of education and hard work. Talk to children about school and help them think about and plan for their future.

Build a relationship with children's teachers.

- Let teachers know families want to work with them as a partner to ensure children's success. Ask teachers to keep families informed about children's progress.

Take advantage of the opportunities the school and district provide.

- Join the parent organization and seek out ways to contribute at home or at school. Attend meetings and get to know school staff.
- Engage in parent leadership and family literacy programs that build parents' own skills and knowledge.

Make sure children go to school every day and closely monitor how they are doing in school.

- If a child is struggling or falling behind, contact the teacher or a counselor and insist on getting help.
- Make sure children are taking challenging classes or programs. Ask teachers or counselors for help if children need it to succeed. Learn about what students must do to graduate on time and be ready for college.

Community Leaders' Responsibilities

Work with the district to create community schools that provide integrated family support services.

- Survey families and staff at each school to find out their interests and needs. Respond by mapping the assets in the community, building upon existing resources and co-locating social and health services in schools.

Form a network of organizations that can partner with schools to strengthen families and support student success.

- Community members and employees can: serve as volunteers, role models and mentors; give students individual attention; and demonstrate the value the community places on education. Businesses can sponsor partnership activities and encourage employees to play an active role. Libraries, museums, colleges and cultural agencies can reduce fees and make special programs available for families.

Students' Responsibilities
(as developmentally appropriate)

Take responsibility for learning.

- Students are entitled to a free public education and should take full advantage, asking for help when needed.
- Take initiative to find and explore new areas of learning that are of personal interest.

Form a student organization at school.

- Let the teachers and principal know what is working well in the school and how it could be better.

Join the school improvement team.

- Ask the principal and teachers for student-led conferences where students can display work, explain what has been learned and discuss what students want and will need to learn.

Plan for your future and think carefully about goals in life.

- Discuss ideas with family, teachers, counselors and other adults. Find out how to reach those goals.

ADOPTED: NOVEMBER 4, 2009

Wisconsin Department of Public Instruction
Policy on Family-School-Community Partnerships

The Wisconsin Department of Public Instruction (DPI) recognizes that parents and families are a child's first and most important teachers. When children enter school, the responsibility for their learning is shared by the schools, families, communities, and the children themselves.

Further, the DPI believes that:

- All children deserve to grow up in nurturing, healthy, and safe learning environments in which families are supported in their roles and responsibilities;
- Families of all cultures, languages, and incomes care deeply about their children's success; and
- Family-school-community collaboration and partnerships benefit all children.

Successful family-school-community partnerships include the following goals:

- Communication between home and school is regular, two-way, and meaningful.
- Responsible parenting, quality teaching, and caring communities are promoted and supported.
- Families and the community play a key role in helping students learn.
- School staff provide a welcoming environment for parents and other community members and seek their support.
- Parents participate in advocacy and decisions, including budget and curriculum, that affect children and families at the local, district, and state levels.
- Community resources are made available to strengthen school programs, family practices, and student learning, and community partners participate in helping schools meet their learning goals.

To meet its mission that all school-age children have access to quality educational programs that meet high standards of excellence, the DPI provides leadership and resources to enable communities, schools, and families, including students, to work as knowledgeable partners. Therefore, the DPI:

- Educates and expects its staff to promote family-school-community partnerships and community collaborations;
- Is responsive to parents and other citizens who contact the DPI for help or to offer suggestions;
- Encourages school leaders to create a respectful, safe, and caring school climate welcoming family and community participation;
- Promotes and supports education and training for educators, families, and other citizens to develop and maintain partnerships and collaborations for life-long learning; and
- Promotes schools and communities that work together to improve student learning and citizenship development.

APPROVED: APRIL 28, 2004

School District Policies:
Buffalo (NY), Middletown (CT), and Saint Paul (MN)
Buffalo Public Schools
Parent Involvement Policy 3170
2008
Subject: Parent Involvement Policy

Parent Involvement Beliefs

The Buffalo Public Schools believes that education is a partnership among the student, parent/guardian, school, and community. The academic achievement and success of our students depend on the actions, relationships, and strengths of these partnerships.

Students, who are at the center of the partnerships, have unique skills, talents, and learning styles and are ultimately accountable for their own academic achievement. Parents and families provide their children with the foundation of their values, including educational values, responsibilities, expectations, rules for home/school environment, and aspirations. Parents are the primary providers in preparing their children for school readiness and academic success. Parents' knowledge of their children's unique histories, traditions, life experiences, and learning experiences are important to their success. Parents also share knowledge about community resources and challenges, both of which are valuable and critical to their child's progress. The educational responsibility for our students is shared by the parents, district, schools, and community.

Parent Involvement Framework

In 1999, the Buffalo Public Schools adopted the framework of the National Network of Partnership Schools, a research-based model of parent involvement designed by Dr. Joyce Epstein of Johns Hopkins University. The Buffalo Chapter of this Partnership assists our schools in developing comprehensive programs of school, family, and community partnerships as part of their efforts to increase parent involvement. This model is based on the following six types of parental involvement:

1. **Parenting.** Assist families with parenting and child-rearing skills, understanding child and adolescent development, and setting home conditions that support children as students at each grade level.

2. **Communicating.** Communicate with families about programs and student's progress through effective school-to-home and home-to-school communication.

3. **Volunteering.** Improve recruitment, training work, and schedules to involve families as volunteers and audiences at the school or in other locations to support students and school programs.

4. Student Learning at Home. Involve families with their children in learning activities at home, including homework and other curriculum-related activities and decisions.

5. Decision Making. Include families as participants in school decisions, governance, and advocacy through PTO/PTA, school councils, committees, and other parent organizations.

6. Collaborating With the Community. Coordinate resources and services for families, students, and the school with businesses, agencies, and other groups, and provide services to the community.

District Responsibilities/Expectations

To successfully implement the District's beliefs in parent involvement, support will be comprised of, but not limited to the following:

1. Continuing to foster a network of sharing among schools through the Buffalo Chapter of the National Network of Partnership Schools framework.
2. Providing a budget allocation to support district and school parental involvement initiatives.
3. Establishing a parent organization in every school.
4. Hiring a parent facilitator in every school.
5. Disseminating information relevant to student achievement and parents' rights through community meetings, telephone contact, and individual schools.
6. Providing for parent participation on all district decision-making teams.
7. Supporting a District Parent Center that provides academic assistance to parents, students, and community.
8. Ensuring compliance with Section 1118 (parent involvement) of the No Child Left Behind legislation.
9. Providing an effective mechanism to ensure mutual respect and accountability between school/parent partnerships.

The District Parent Coordinating Council

The purpose of the District Parent Coordinating Council is to ensure that a partnership with the District is created and to monitor the implementation of the Board of Education's Parent Involvement Policy. The Council is the venue for disseminating relevant and important information from the Superintendent, as well as serving as a conduit for parental feedback to the District. The Council receives support from Erie I BOCES Regional School Support Center, including having a member working in conjunction with the Council's Executive Board. The general Council meetings are held monthly. All district parents are welcome, including all organizations that represent parents, such as the Special Education Parent Advisory Committee and the Title I District Advisory Council.

Building Responsibilities and Expectations

Principals, in collaboration with parents and the support of the District Parent Co-ordinating Council, Buffalo Chapter of the National Network of Partnership Schools, and the Erie I BOCES Regional School Support Center, will:

1. Establish a parent/family organization in each school and shall:
   - Call at least one business meeting of the parent organization each year in order to encourage the inclusion of new parents into the organization.
   - Elect officers and have regular meetings, scheduled in consultation with parents and announced publicly, inviting all to attend.
   - Be maintained as a viable entity to ensure that parents, who are full partners in their child's education, have an opportunity to be included in meetings and decision-making.
   - Elect/appoint members to represent all parents from the school community to the District Parent Coordinating Council, School Based Management Team, and Action Teams related to student achievement.
2. Establish a parent room in each school.

Parent Responsibilities and Expectations

Parent involvement is the action parents take to participate in regular, two way, and meaningful communication with their children's schools to provide an education that graduates productive citizens. All parent involvement is aimed at increasing student achievement through various levels of involvement.

Parents can be defined as any parent, guardian, and/or person in parental relation to a child or children. Parents are expected to:

1. Ensure that children come to school prepared and ready to learn.
2. Provide high-quality nutrition, adequate sleep, and exercise for their children.
3. Provide a learning environment for children to do homework and actively monitor their children's homework and level of completion.
4. Review and support the District Attendance Policy.
5. Review and support the District Code of Conduct.
6. Attend parent/family organization meetings, parent/teacher conferences, and workshops designed to increase student achievement.

7. Communicate with teachers and principals as partners in their children's academic success.

The Buffalo Board of Education and the Superintendent of Buffalo Public Schools endorse and support this plan to help ensure the BPS mission of "Putting children and families first to ensure high academic achievement for all."

NOTE: Refer also to Policies #7660—Parent Involvement—Children with Disabilities and #8260—Programs and Projects Funded By Title I.

ADOPTED: APRIL 24, 2002

REVISED: FEBRUARY 13, 2008

Middletown (CT) Board of Education Parent Involvement Policy 6172.4(a)

The Middletown Board of Education actively supports and encourages parent involvement in all of its schools and programs. This policy also meets the applicable No Child Left Behind guidelines in the district's Title I schools. The Board recognizes that cooperative efforts among the parents,* school and community are essential to building strong educational programs for all children.

Toward this end and pursuant to federal law, the Middletown School District has developed and will distribute this written parent involvement policy based on discussion and consultation with parents of children participating in the Title I program along with parents of non-participating children. In turn, each Middletown school, both Title I and non-Title I, will develop and distribute its own parent involvement policy/compact, consistent with district policy but specific to that school's interests and needs.

As recommended by Connecticut's State Board of Education, the Middletown Board recognizes and supports these six standards for building and maintaining effective school-family-community partnerships. The illustrations noted are some, not all, of the programs and activities that help Middletown meet these standards.

1. Parenting: Promote and support effective parenting skills and the family's primary role in encouraging children's learning at each age and grade level.
   - Middletown meets this standard through its family math and language arts nights, Parent Leadership Training Institutes (PLTI), pre-school workshops for parents, parenting workshops, and Even Start (adult ed.), and Family Resource Centers initiatives.
2. Communicating: ongoing, two-way, and meaningful communication between schools, families, and the community.
   - Middletown meets this standard through its PTAs and PTOs, principals' coffees, parent-teacher conferences, curriculum nights,

---

* "Parents" or "Parent" also includes guardians and other family members involved in supervising children's schooling.

Comcast programs, newsletters, and district, school, and classroom web pages. The new parent involvement committees will strengthen this communication.

3. Volunteering: provide training to parents and community members to support learning both in and out of school.
   - Middletown meets this standard through its extensive student mentor program, family outreach worker efforts, PLTIs, read-ins, student tutor collaborations with Middlesex Community College and Wesleyan University, parent volunteer program, and several student volunteer/service activities.

4. Learning at home: encourage family involvement in school and curriculum related enrichment activities.
   - Middletown meets this standard through its parent math and language arts nights, numerous school-related and educational websites, newsletters (weekly to monthly), and curricular activities that focus on and engage families. Again, the new parent involvement committees will help us better meet this standard.

5. Decision making: help all families strengthen their leadership in school decisions.
   - Middletown will better meet this standard through the formation of parent involvement committees at all of its eleven schools, continued support of PLTIs, inviting greater parent participation on curriculum development efforts, and giving greater attention to student performance and curriculum initiatives at its PTA, PTO, and MSA (Middletown Schools Association—the umbrella organization for Middletown's PTAs and PTOs) meetings.

6. Collaborating with the community: enable schools and families to access—and serve as—community resources.
   - Middletown meets this standard through its work with the NAACP, United Way, Ascend, Excel, Upward Bound, park and recreation department, local colleges and universities, school-business partnerships, and neighborhood outreach through community centers and religious organizations.

Annually, parents of both Title I and non-Title I students will help evaluate, revise, and implement their school's policies for the following year. Every effort will be made to engage these parents and to comply with the new federal and state regulations. Both at the district and school levels, the parent committees will convene annually to assess the district's success in meeting the six standards and improving overall academic quality. The district parent involvement advisory committee will comprise representatives from all eleven schools and will include Title I parents. Building principals and the assistant superintendent will be responsible for organizing and maintaining both district and building level parent involvement committees. The school-based committees will each compile a brief report, submitting this to the district parent involvement advisory committee. The advisory committee will review the reports and compile a summary report to be shared with the Board of

Education and community. Specifically, the committees will consider data from the district's many assessments (i.e., DRAs, CMTs, CAPTs, SATs, in-house grades and assessments, GPAs, drop-out and behavioral information), success at fulfilling the objectives and recommendations in the annual district/school/department improvement and diversity enhancement plans. The committee will also review Reading First, Literacy Collaborative, and Early Reading Success progress as revealed through these and other measures.

Beyond the annual review and planning meetings, schools receiving Title I funds will conduct three additional meetings—again, scheduled to accommodate as many Title I parents as possible—to provide parents with:

- Information about Title I funded programs;
- Clear and coherent descriptions of curricula, including the kinds of assessments and levels of expected proficiency;
- Opportunities to make suggestions and participate in decisions affecting their children's educational experiences;
- Opportunities to bring to the district level any concerns that are not satisfactorily addressed at the building level.

The district and schools will ensure that parents of children identified to participate in Title I programs shall receive from the school principal and Title I staff an explanation of the reasons supporting each child's selection for the program, a set of objectives to be addressed, and a description of the services to be provided. Opportunities will be provided for the parents to meet with the classroom and Title I teachers to discuss their child's progress. Parents will also receive guidance about how they can assist in educating their children at home.

As part of its school's parent involvement policy, each Title I school in Middletown shall jointly develop with parents of children served a "School-Parent Compact" outlining the roles and responsibilities of parents, staff, and students for improved student academic achievement in meeting state and federal standards. Each school's "School-Parent Compact" shall:

1. Describe the school's responsibility to provide high-quality curriculum and instruction in a supportive and effective learning environment enabling children in the Title I program to meet the State's academic achievement standards;
2. Indicate the ways in which parents will be responsible for supporting their children's learning (e.g., monitoring attendance, completing homework, monitoring TV and video viewing, attending school activities, and participating, as appropriate, in decisions related to their children's education and extra-curricular time); and
3. Address the importance of parent-teacher communication on an ongoing basis, with at a minimum, parent-teacher conferences, frequent reports to parents, and reasonable access to staff.
4. Address the six standards for building and maintaining school-family-community partnerships.

POLICY ADOPTED: FEBRUARY 10, 2004
POLICY READOPTED: JUNE 20, 2006, MIDDLETOWN, CONNECTICUT

Saint Paul Public Schools
Family Involvement Policy 615.00

Purpose (2002)

The Board believes that the involvement of families in the children's education every year, preK–12, has positive impact on the student's success in school. Research indicates that planned, comprehensive family involvement can contribute to the achievement of key school goals. The Board also believes that children are more likely to be successful when parents or families and school staff work as a team to support each student.

General Statement of Policy (Revised, 2008)

1. Each school site shall collaborate with its community of families to ensure family involvement in the education of their children. Each school shall implement a strategy that takes a research-based, comprehensive approach to parent involvement and expectations that includes the following elements:
    *   Parenting
    *   Communicating
    *   Volunteering
    *   Learning at Home
    *   Decision Making
    *   Collaborating with the Community
    *   Shares responsibility for high expectations and student performance.
    *   Builds the involvement capacity of school, program staff and families.
    *   Increases access and engagement of *all* families with children.
2. The end result will be to insure integration of family-school involvement throughout district activities, including development and evaluation of district and school improvement plans.

ADOPTED: MAY 14, 2002, SAINT PAUL PUBLIC SCHOOL POLICY 615.00
REVISED: JUNE 17, 2008
LEGAL REFERENCES:
20 U.S.C. § 6318 (PARENTAL INVOLVEMENT)
MINN. STAT. § 124D.8955 (PARENT AND FAMILY INVOLVEMENT POLICY)

Research Meets Policy and Practice:
How Are School Districts Addressing NCLB
Requirements for Parental Involvement?*

The No Child Left Behind Act (NCLB, Public Law 107-110), signed into law in 2002, reauthorized the Elementary and Secondary Education Act (ESEA), thereby updating the legislation, first passed in 1965, that provides federal funds to improve schools serving children from economically disadvantaged families and communities. In addition to well-publicized requirements for high-quality teachers, achievement tests, and accountability for the progress of major subgroups of students, NCLB includes important requirements for district leaders to develop district-level and school-based policies and programs for more effective parental involvement.

The regulations in Section 1118 have improved with each reauthorization of ESEA, reflecting advances in sociological and educational theories about district leadership for school improvement. The requirements also call for the application of research-based approaches for program development (Borman, Cookson, Sadovnik, and Spade, 1996; Epstein, 2001). For example, early Title I legislation on parental involvement mandated minor, often symbolic, participation of a few parent representatives on district and school advisory committees. Most other parents were left on their own to figure out whether and how to become involved in their children's education across the grades. Now the law outlines a "nested" system of actions at the state, district, and school levels for developing programs to involve all families in ways that support student achievement and success in school.

Historically, there have been notable pendulum swings in assessments of the contributions of district leaders to school improvement. Some have labeled district leaders irrelevant and inadequate managers of school reform; others have called them essential guides for improving schools (Coburn, 2003; Datnow, Hubbard, and Mehan, 2002; Fullan, 2001; Learning First Alliance, 2003; Mac Iver and Farley, 2003) and for strengthening programs of school, family, and community partnerships (Chrispeels, 1996; Epstein, 2001; Sanders, 2005). The consensus across studies is that district leaders are responsible for creating a culture of reform with all schools and that they must not allow one school to improve while others decline (Burch and Spillane, 2004).

The new understanding of effective district leadership emphasizes shared, distributed, or democratic leadership and teamwork for school reform (Fullan, 2001; Pounder, Reitzug, and Young, 2002). In practice, shared leadership typically refers to collaborative work conducted by administrators and teachers. Although educators

* By Joyce Epstein. (2010). This work was supported by a grant from the National Institute of Child Health and Human Development, Grant R01 HD0471. A shorter version of this chapter was published in A. R. Sadovnik, J. O'Day, G. Bohrnstedt, and K. Borman, eds., *No Child Left Behind and the Reduction of the Achievement Gap: Sociological Perspectives on Federal Educational Policy* (New York: Routledge, 2008), pp. 267–279.

know that family and community involvement is important, educators often are reluctant to share leadership with parents and community members. Most teachers and administrators have not been prepared in college courses to conduct collaborative work (Darling-Hammond and Bransford, 2005; Epstein and Sanders, 2006; Leithwood and Prestine, 2002). Most districts do not offer effective inservice education on new strategies for organizing school, family, and community partnerships (Epstein et al., 2009).

Despite these gaps in the education of educators, NCLB requires district leaders to organize effective partnership programs and to share leadership for children's education with parents. Specifically, Section 1118 specifies that districts *shall* (which in legislative language means *must*) provide professional development and ongoing technical assistance to help schools implement programs that inform families about state standards and tests, guide parents to support student achievement at home, communicate messages in languages parents can understand, resolve other "barriers" or challenges that limit the involvement of economically disadvantaged and linguistically diverse parents, and build the capacity of both schools and parents to conduct and improve programs. The law states that districts *must*:

- Provide the coordination, technical assistance and other support necessary to assist participating schools in planning and implementing effective parent involvement activities to improve student academic achievement and school performance.
- Build the schools' and parents' capacity for strong parent involvement.

The law also outlines several optional activities that districts *may* conduct, including establishing district-level advisory councils; providing parents with literacy classes, leadership training, and transportation and child care to attend school meetings and workshops; scheduling meetings at varied times to increase parental participation, working with businesses and community partners; and adopting model approaches to help organize partnership programs.

The specifications in NCLB redirect district leaders from simply monitoring schools' compliance with the law to actively guiding schools to improve the quality and results of their partnership programs (Cowan, 2003; U.S. Department of Education, 2004).

FRAMEWORK OF POLICY INSTRUMENTS

The required and optional actions in NCLB for district leadership on partnerships can be understood with a theoretical framework that outlines a range of policy instruments for school reform. McDonnell and Elmore (1991) identified important differences of mandates that require and regulate actions, inducements that reward or sanction actions, capacity building that increases knowledge and skills for action, and system changing that reassigns decision-making activities to new groups or individuals. NCLB includes all four policy instruments to guide district leaders on varied ways to improve programs of family and community involvement.

NCLB's Section 1118 includes the mandates for actions districts must take, outlined above. Title I, Part A, includes inducements for action through funding that districts must allocate to schools to implement effective school-based parental involvement programs. The funding is tied to sanctions, which federal monitors may impose if districts fail to meet the requirements. Overall, the law states its goal to build capacities of district leaders, school leaders, and parents to plan, implement, and evaluate productive family involvement through the required professional development activities. District leaders who implement the required actions could help all schools develop more equitable programs of involvement by involving families who are typically labeled "hard to reach." Such actions would produce system-changing behaviors at the district level and in all schools (Epstein, 2005; Epstein and Sheldon, 2006).

Additional system-changing requirements are legislated in other sections of NCLB that require district leaders to offer parents of eligible students options to change schools and select supplemental services if their child's school fails to meet state standards for achievement or safety for two years or more (Lauen, 2008; Mickelson and Southworth, 2008). These options change the way decisions about student placement are made in school districts.

NATIONAL NETWORK OF PARTNERSHIP SCHOOLS

Although NCLB specifies that research-based programs should be implemented, the law does not indicate how the actions can be accomplished. Most district leaders need help in enacting NCLB Section 1118 and other requirements for family and community involvement. Studies and field tests are required in order to understand the structures and processes that enable districts and schools to develop and sustain effective partnership programs. In this study, we draw from data collected by the National Network of Partnership Schools (NNPS) at Johns Hopkins University, which includes a large number of school districts that share an interest in improving school, family, and community partnerships.

NNPS guides districts to use research-based approaches to understand family and community involvement and to help schools develop goal-linked programs that will help more students succeed in school (Epstein et al., 2009). Of course, not all leaders apply new knowledge or use handbooks, tools, or professional development training with the same speed or effectiveness. The variations in district leadership permit NNPS to study whether and how particular practices contribute to the quality of district partnership programs over time. We asked two main research questions:

- How are school districts addressing NCLB's requirements for family involvement? Are the requirements in Section 1118 for districts reasonable and attainable?
- How do district leaders' efforts on partnerships affect their reports of the quality of their schools' programs of family and community involvement?

DATA

Data were collected in 2004 on end-of-year *Update* surveys from 69 U.S. school districts in NNPS. Of these, 51 districts also provided data in 2003, permitting longitudinal analyses of progress in districts' partnership program development. The districts, ranging in size from 1 school to over 200 schools, were located in urban, suburban, and rural communities in 24 states.* They had been members of NNPS for from one year (20.8 percent) to eight years (11.1 percent). *Update* surveys are required by NNPS to renew membership and services for the next school year.

Therefore, all districts that returned the surveys were, in effect, restating their interest in improving their partnership programs.

MEASURES

In NNPS, district leaders for partnerships are guided to assume two major responsibilities, which also are required by NCLB. They are expected to establish district-level leadership and directly assist individual schools with their partnership programs, as measured by the following scales.

Dependent Variables

Leadership. This measure of 13 items ($\alpha = .79$) assessed the extent to which district leaders organized their work by setting up an office, identifying a budget, writing a leadership plan, writing or reviewing policy on parent involvement, and conducting other district-level activities.

Facilitation. This scale of 16 items ($\alpha = .92$) gauged the extent to which district leaders directly assisted individual schools to form an Action Team for Partnerships, write annual plans, evaluate progress, share ideas, and conduct other school-based activities.

Solve challenges to increase involvement. Six items ($\alpha = .71$) identified whether district leaders actively helped schools address basic challenges to reach more diverse families or left the schools on their own to solve problems. Challenges included involving parents who do not speak or read English, getting information to families who cannot attend school meetings, providing opportunities to volunteer at school and other locations, preparing teachers to guide families on helping children with homework, ensuring that diverse families are represented on school committees, and identifying community resources for school improvement.

---

* The U.S. districts providing data were in Alabama, Arkansas, California, Florida, Georgia, Kentucky, Louisiana, Massachusetts, Maryland, Michigan, Minnesota, Missouri, North Carolina, New Jersey, New York, Ohio, Oklahoma, Pennsylvania, South Carolina, Tennessee, Texas, Utah, Washington, and Wisconsin.

Report of schools' progress. A single item asked district leaders for the number of schools making "good progress" on partnerships. This number was transformed into the percentage of all schools that were assisted with work on partnerships.

Independent Variables

The explanatory variables in this study included measures that were of interest in prior studies of district leadership on partnerships.

Demographic characteristics. The size of the district (number of schools) and poverty level (the percentage of students receiving free- or reduced-price meals in the district) were statistically controlled.

Collegial support for partnerships. This 13-item scale (α = .93) reported the average level of cooperation (from none = 1 to a lot = 4) that district leaders for partnerships reported receiving from colleagues at the district level, in schools, from parent organizations, and from others in the community.

Program development tools and guidelines. This 7-item scale (α = .87) reported district leaders' average ratings of helpfulness (from not helpful = 1 to very helpful = 4) of major tools and materials for program development, including a comprehensive handbook, newsletters, books on best practices, website information, monthly communications, and other connections with NNPS.

Evaluation tools. A 6-item scale (α = .53) identified whether district leaders used tools designed to help them evaluate district and school partnership programs, including reflective documentations, on-site inventories, and survey instruments.

Other NCLB requirements. A 10-item scale (α = .79) assessed leaders' reports of whether the district, as a whole, was addressing specific NCLB requirements. One item in this scale—*communicate in languages that parents can understand*—had the greatest variation across districts. It is used as an explanatory variable in selected analyses of district leaders' work on partnerships.

RESULTS

Districts varied on the nature and extent of their leadership and facilitation activities for developing district-level and school-based programs of family and community involvement. They implemented an average of 7.37 activities to organize their offices and their work on partnerships. Some (16.9 percent) conducted 11 to 13 district-level leadership activities, whereas others (19.7 percent) conducted only 1 to 4 of the actions listed. District leaders also reported conducting an average of 7.25 facilitation activities to directly assist schools in developing their partnership programs.

TABLE 4.1 Variables Affecting District-Level Leadership and Facilitation from 2003 to 2004

| | NCLB Requirements for Districts | | | |
| | Leadership Structure | | Facilitation of Schools | |
	β	(t)	β	(t)
District Characteristics				
Size of district (# schools)	−.085	ns	−.050	ns
Percent free of reduced-price lunch	.156	ns	−.025	ns
Program Components				
Prior Year's Leadership Structure	.539	(4.24)***	—	
Prior Year's Facilitation of Schools			.629	(5.78)***
Collegial Support (District, School, Families)	.176	ns	.208	(1.89)*
NNPS Program Tools and Guidelines	.325	(2.66)**	.347	(3.17)***
Adjusted R^2	.501		.597	

N = 51 U.S. school districts in NNPS.
Standardized regression coefficients are shown.
Levels of significance: * $p < .05$; ** $p < .01$; *** $p < .001$
Source: 2003 and 2004 *Update* surveys.

About 24 percent conducted 13 to 16 activities, whereas 14.1 percent reported that, as yet, they conducted *no* (0) actions to assist individual schools.

A few NCLB requirements were almost universally addressed, such as having a policy on parental involvement (85 percent) and providing information to parents about their child's achievement test scores (98.4 percent). By contrast, only 51 percent of the district leaders said their districts were working well to communicate with families in the languages parents speak at home.

The *Update* survey also measured overall program quality in the form of a "portrait" of the district's partnership program. Districts' programs ranged from *low* (26.7 percent in a planning year or just beginning), to *average* (46.5 percent with a good start or good programs), to *high* quality (26.7 percent with very good or excellent programs). The variation in district leaders' efforts inform the analyses of how partnership programs develop.

District Leaders' Work

OLS regression analyses were conducted to test whether districts in NNPS improved their leadership and facilitation of schools from 2003 to 2004, as shown in Table 4.1. Districts' demographic characteristics of size and poverty level did not signifi-

TABLE 4.2 Influence on District Leaders to Help Schools Meet Challenges to Involve All Families

	β	(t)
District Characteristics		
Size of district (# of schools)	.278	(1.98)[+]
Percent free or reduced-price lunch	−.151	ns
District Program Components		
Prior Year's Attention to Meet Challenges	.379	(2.56)**
District's Emphasis on Communicating with All Parents	.264	(1.82)[+]
Use NNPS Evaluation Tools	.296	(2.05)*
Adjusted R^2	.407	

N = 51 U.S. school districts in NNPS for at least two years.
Standardized regression coefficients are shown.
Levels of significance: + $p < .10$; * $p < .05$; ** $p < .01$
Source: 2003 and 2004 *Update* surveys.

cantly affect the number of leadership or facilitation actions conducted by district leaders for partnerships. Some leaders in large and small, affluent and poor districts successfully set up their offices and worked with schools on partnerships, whereas other leaders lagged on these actions.

Table 4.1 also shows the importance of sustaining work on program development. District leaders who conducted more leadership actions in 2003 continued to do so in 2004 (β = .539, $p < .001$), and those who previously assisted their schools also did so in 2004 (β = .629, $p < .001$).

After accounting for prior work in 2003, district leaders who reported strong collegial support for partnerships (β = .208, $p < .10$) and who used and found helpful more NNPS tools for program development (β = .347, $p < .001$) significantly increased the number of facilitative activities they conducted to assist schools. Useful tools and guidelines also helped leaders organize their own work on partnerships (β = .325, $p < .01$). About 50 percent of the variance in leadership and nearly 60 percent of the variance in facilitation were explained by prior work on partnerships, collegial support, and the use of helpful tools and materials. These basic factors helped explain district leaders' attention to the requirements listed in NCLB Section 1118 to improve programs of parental involvement.

Solving Challenges to Involve All Families

Table 4.2 explores the influences on district leaders' efforts to help schools address challenges to reach more diverse families, as required by NCLB. The results indicate that district leaders who worked with schools to address challenges in 2003 continued to provide schools with ideas to involve all families in the next school year (β = .379, p < .01).

Over and above the work of the prior year, district leaders were more likely to give schools ideas for addressing key challenges to involve parents from all racial, educational, and socioeconomic groups if the district as a whole was addressing the NCLB requirement to communicate in understandable languages with all families (β = .264, p < .10) and if the leaders for partnerships used more NNPS evaluation tools (β = .296, p < .05).

District leaders in larger districts assisted schools more than in smaller districts (β = .278, p < .05), perhaps because the challenges were more common in large districts. Poverty level of students did not strongly influence whether leaders for partnerships worked with schools to solve challenges to involve all families or left it up to the schools. The district's history of attention to challenges, priority for communicating in languages families understand, and the use of evaluation tools explained 40 percent of the variance in whether district leaders directly assisted schools to work on challenges to reach all families.

The quantitative results in Table 4.2 were reflected in comments the district leaders wrote about their schools' progress, as in these typical responses:

> More schools . . . included parents on teams, representing the demographic makeup of the school.

> (The district developed) a new school improvement format (that) requires . . . family and community partnerships . . . for each major initiative.

Schools' Progress on Partnerships

District leaders reported whether their schools were making *little, some,* or *good progress* on partnerships. Table 4.3 shows that neither the size nor the poverty level of the district significantly affected leaders' reports of their schools' progress. By contrast, leaders' actions of *leadership* and *facilitation* had strong but varying effects on their reports of schools' progress on partnership program development.

Column 1 of Table 4.3 shows that the extent of district leadership to organize an office, budget, and plans for partnerships was important for how leaders reported schools' progress (β = .343, p < .01). Those who conducted more leadership actions reported that more of their schools were making good progress on partnerships. Column 2 shows even more dramatic effects of leaders' direct assistance to schools on reports of schools' progress (β = .575, p < .001) and of the level of collegial support on schools' progress (β = .283, p < .05). District facilitation and collegial support—two measures that indicate whether district leaders made contact with schools and witnessed the work on school-based partnership programs—explained more than twice the variance as the more distal measure of leadership structure (43 percent compared to 20 percent) in reports of schools' progress on partnerships.

TABLE 4.3 Influence of District Leadership and Facilitation on Reports of Schools' Progress in Family and Community Involvement

	Model 1		Model 2	
	β	(t)	β	(t)
District Characteristics				
Size of district (# schools)	.052	ns	−.060	ns
Percent free of reduced-price lunch	−.098	ns	−.048	ns
Program Components				
Prior Year's Leadership Structure	.343	(2.31)*	—	
Prior Year's Facilitation of Schools			.575	(4.88)***
Collegial Support (District, School, Families)	.278	(1.87)+	.283	(2.23)*
Adjusted R^2	.203		.433	

N = 69 U.S. school districts in NNPS.
Standardized regression coefficients are shown.
Levels of significance: + $p < .10$; * $p < .05$; ** $p < .001$
Source: 2004 *Update* surveys.

In open-ended comments about their work, district leaders for partnerships reported improvements in helping schools increase the involvement of parents with children around achievement, as in the following representative statements:

Programs are directed more at academics. New sites have become more into it. They seem to get it.

[We had a] 60% increase in school memberships [to work on partnerships], and more parent engagement activities are connected to student achievement goals at school sites.

In separate analyses, not reported here, we found that district leaders for partnerships who evaluated their district and school programs did more than other districts to help teachers involve parents with children to increase achievement in school subjects ($β = .425$, $p < .01$). Prior studies also found that when districts evaluated their programs, they showed a seriousness of purpose in increasing improving their leadership and facilitative activities (Epstein and Williams, 2003; Epstein, Williams, and Jansorn, 2004; Sanders, 2008). Over 30 percent of the variance in districts' efforts to involve families with students on achievement was explained by districts' commitment to communicate with all families and actions to evaluate partnership programs.

Asked how they evaluate their work on partnerships, district leaders explained that they asked *schools* to document the activities they conducted and parents' participation. Most schools gathered parents' reactions after each involvement activity. Some districts organized evaluations in systematic ways, as noted in these comments:

[We conduct] phone surveys, surveys in newsletters, focus groups.

[A] comprehensive survey is administered annually and carefully analyzed.

[Our program of] partnership is part of the strategic plan and is evaluated by staff, parents and administration.

Contrasting Correlates of District Leadership

Not every leadership action is equally important for the quality of district-level partnership programs. Analyses were conducted to "unpack" the above results. NCLB requires districts to have a parental involvement policy. In addition, NNPS asks district leaders to write a leadership plan each year that schedules their actions at the district level and in assisting schools on partnerships.

Table 4.4 shows that leaders with written plans were significantly more likely to fulfill other requirements in NCLB's Section 1118 for district leadership on parental involvement. Those with a plan and schedule for actions were more likely to identify a budget for partnerships ($r = .543, p < .001$), conduct professional development ($r = .317, p < .01$), actively facilitate their schools ($r = .552, p < .001$), disseminate best practices ($r = .440, p < .001$), and conduct other activities to increase district-level and school-level capacities for productive parental involvement. Having a policy was not significantly correlated with any of the other actions by district leaders.

These patterns are due, in part, to the greater variation among districts in writing detailed plans than in having a policy. Although most districts (85 percent) had a policy, just over half (58 percent) wrote a detailed work plan in 2004. The results reinforce the importance for district leaders to go beyond the minimum of having a policy to increase the quality of their leadership and facilitation on partnerships.

DISCUSSION

This study presents the first quantitative analyses of whether and how well districts are addressing NCLB requirements for improving programs of family involvement. The data collected in 2004, as NCLB completed its second full school year, showed that most districts in NNPS had started to address NCLB's requirements for district leadership on parental involvement. The results point to four policy-related conclusions that could help other districts organize more effective leadership for partnerships.

1. Writing a policy is important but not sufficient for districts to conduct viable partnership programs. Most districts in NNPS had formal policies on parental involvement and were trying to disseminate information to parents on their children's

TABLE 4.4   Contrasting Correlates of District Policies and Written Plans with NCLB Requirements

Leadership actions on partnerships linked to NCLB requirements (Sec. 1118)	Have a district policy		Have a written plan	
	Mean .85 (s.d. .35)		Mean .58 (s.d. .50)	
	r	sig.	r	sig.
Have a district budget	.222	ns	.543	***
Conduct professional development for schools	.042	ns	.317	**
Offer grants to schools for partnerships	.058	ns	.405	***
Recognize excellent programs	.118	ns	.417	***
Disseminate best practices	.088	ns	.440	***
Make connections with colleagues to coordinate family involvement	.084	ns	.472	***
Facilitate schools' Action Teams for Partnerships (scale)	.176	ns	.552	***
Help schools address challenges to reach all families (scale)	.035	ns	.251	+
Evaluate district and school partnership programs (scale)	.008	ns	.263	*
Use NNPS evaluation tools (scale)	.101	ns	.378	**

N = 69 school districts.
+ $p < .10$; * $p < .05$; ** $p < .01$; *** $p < .001$
Source: 2004 *Update* surveys.

achievement and on schools' status in making adequate yearly progress (AYP), as required by NCLB. Fewer were addressing more difficult challenges of helping schools communicate with families who did not speak English and helping families become involved in ways that could increase students' achievement in school subjects. Some others (14 percent) had taken no steps to directly assist schools in developing educators' and parents' capacities to create comprehensive school-based partnership programs.

The results suggested that having a district policy on parental involvement was just one step on a much longer path to partnerships. Another document—a detailed plan for leadership and facilitation—was associated with the enactment of more NCLB requirements for district leadership on partnerships. In open-ended comments, district leaders listed the following typical goals for the next school year:

[We need to] assist buildings in fully implementing their action plans and to monitor the progress of implementations.

[We need to] get principals on board and help them recognize the value of family and community partnerships.

Even as they worked to communicate with families, districts in NNPS met new challenges. Some found that their communications about students' test scores were not clear and understandable for large numbers of parents. For example, a clinical review with district leaders revealed that annual "school report cards" often were issued in print that was too small to read, placed in hidden locations on district and state websites, or distributed without needed explanations of educational terms and statistics. It was clear that having a policy on parental involvement was a first step on a long path toward excellent and equitable partnership programs.

2. A district leader for partnerships must be assigned to enact a district-wide partnership program. Each district in this study had a leader for partnerships who served as a "key contact" to researchers at Johns Hopkins University for guidance on their work on partnerships. By contrast, other districts may have policies for parental involvement but have *no one* assigned to lead this component of school organization and school improvement. This kind of "unstaffed mandate" would not be tolerated in schools working to improve their reading or math curricula, where curriculum coaches or consultants are expected. By contrast, many districts have lagged in assigning leaders for partnerships to guide schools in this work.

Assigning a leader for partnerships still was not enough to ensure high-quality partnership programs. District leaders must take action to improve their partnership programs. In this study, leaders varied widely in the number and quality of activities they conducted. Leaders did more to organize work and facilitate schools if they had strong collegial support, used research-based program development and evaluation tools and materials, and sustained their efforts over time. Further, leaders who directly assisted their schools were more likely to report that the schools were making good progress in their programs of family and community involvement.

There was wide variation and considerable room for improvement in the quality of all of these activities. Many district leaders seemed to be moving slowly in providing school teams with professional development on partnerships and encouraging and motivating schools to improve their programs from year to year. One leader explained why progress was slow:

> Over the past 2–3 years, due to retirements and resignations, the person designated to lead this program (for the district) has changed (3 times). In addition the district has just rewritten its strategic plan. Consequently, not much progress has been made.

3. District leaders for partnerships need support from others to conduct district-wide partnership programs. Neither a district policy on partnerships nor an assigned leader was enough to ensure a high-quality partnership program. This study showed that collegial support from other district leaders, school principals, educators, families, and tools and guidelines offered by NNPS helped some district leaders for partnerships do more to assist schools and to report progress on partnerships. The results suggest that collegial contacts and using research-based tools for program development and evaluation may increase the seriousness of purpose of leaders' work on partnerships.

Many district leaders for partnerships noted that they needed to keep improving their assistance to their schools. The comments reinforce this study's findings that district leaders' direct assistance to schools is linked to the progress that is observed in schools and to schools' detailed plans for involving all parents in productive ways. The district leaders said that in the next school year they needed to:

> ... [have] more school contact to work with team development and planning

> ... [provide] staff development to all staff-administration, teachers, teacher assistants

The nested nature of support for involvement relies heavily on the district superintendent's messages, as noted in this representative comment:

> [Our superintendent should identify] partnership as a district priority by sending clear messages to administrators, participating in [partnership] activities at the school and district levels, and include the quality of partnership programs as part of administrators' evaluations.

The district leaders recommended other actions that their superintendents should take to legitimate the district's work on partnerships:

- Make public statements about the importance of partnerships.
- Give greetings at professional development sessions on partnerships for schools' Action Teams for Partnerships.
- Mandate a detailed action plan for partnerships as one part of the annual school improvement plan.
- Expect other district administrators to understand and support partnerships.
- Make partnerships part of the annual evaluation of principals and teachers.
- Provide targeted funding at the district level and for each school for programs of partnership.
- Include the quality of partnership programs in the data collected to assess school improvement.
- Develop ties with community partners to support the schools.

In one district leader's words, such activities would make partnerships an "unshakable expectation" for all schools in the district.

4. The four policy instruments embedded in NCLB Section 1118 are influencing leadership for parental involvement. This study suggests that NCLB's mandates for partnerships are beginning to affect district leaders' awareness and actions. The scales and measures showed that leaders were able to distinguish between mandates that they were and were not addressing. In written comments, respondents recognized the legitimacy of NCLB's mandates by noting that they wanted to improve their programs in the next school year by providing more staff development on partnerships, getting more principals on board, and helping all schools fully implement their action plans for partnerships.

NCLB inducements in the form of Title I targeted funds are beginning to influence district leaders' actions on family and community involvement. District leaders rated whether there were not enough funds for partnerships or whether their programs were adequately or well funded. More adequate funding was correlated with more district-level leadership activities ($r = .433$, $p < .001$) and with more actions to facilitate schools on partnerships ($r = .363$, $p < .01$).

NCLB requirements for capacity building were enacted by district leaders who conducted professional development on partnerships for school teams, including teachers, administrators, parents, and community partners and other workshops and presentations on family involvement for district colleagues. District leaders who provided team training for schools' Action Teams for Partnerships reported higher quality partnership programs overall ($r = .365$, $p < .004$).

Finally, system-changing actions were emerging. Many district leaders were using tools and materials to improve their work on partnerships and to help schools organize their programs and practices. Some were addressing challenges to help schools involve families who would otherwise be excluded from exchanges and decisions about their children's education. Many were guiding schools to write annual goal-oriented action plans with activities that involved families with their children to improve achievement in reading, math, attendance, and other indicators of success in school, as directed by NCLB (see Hutchins et al., 2009, for district and school programs that apply research in practice and in award-winning programs at www.partnershipschools.org in the section "Success Stories").

LIMITATIONS AND FUTURE STUDIES

Although this study provides new knowledge about district leaders' work on partnerships in response to NCLB, it is limited by the lack of comparable data from districts that were not members of NNPS. We cannot say if or how well other districts are addressing NCLB requirements for parental involvement. The data provided some useful clues, however, because districts in this study varied widely in their leadership activities. Those that used fewer program development and evaluation tools, for example, conducted fewer leadership and facilitation activities and had weaker partnership programs. These districts may be more like many other districts that are struggling to enact NCLB requirements. Still, studies are needed of matched samples of NNPS and non-NNPS districts to clearly show whether targeted tools, guidelines, and networking on partnerships increase districts' responses to NCLB requirements.

A second limitation is that this study examined only data from district leaders, not reports from the schools in these districts. Separate studies have shown that schools' Action Teams for Partnerships that reported receiving support from their district leaders conducted more family involvement activities, reached more diverse families, and implemented more NCLB requirements for family involvement (see Sheldon 2005, 2008; Sheldon and Van Voorhis, 2004). New studies are needed that examine the "nested" systems of districts and their schools to learn whether and which district leadership actions contribute significantly to the quality of schools' partnership programs, over and above what schools do on their own. With appropriate samples of schools nested within districts, researchers could use Hierarchical Linear Modeling (HLM) analyses to separate the independent effects of district policies and actions from the effects of leadership and support that occurs at the school level.

CONCLUSION

NLCB Section 1118 appears to be raising district leaders' awareness of partnerships and encouraging leaders to take action. The regulations for parental involvement require attention to the structure of district leadership and to processes for planning, implementing, and evaluating programs and practices of partnerships at the district level and in all schools. In this study, data from districts showed that with time, collegial support, and helpful guidelines and tools, district leaders addressed more NCLB requirements for family and community involvement. By their actions, these leaders are showing that districts can meet the spirit and the letter of the law.

REFERENCES

Borman, K. M., P. W. Cookson Jr., A. R. Sadovnik, and J. Z. Spade. (Eds.). (1996). *Implementing educational reform: Sociological perspectives on educational policy.* Norwood, NJ: Ablex.

Burch, P., and J. Spillane. (2004). *Leading from the middle: Midlevel district staff and instructional improvement.* Chicago: Cross City Campaign for Urban School Reform.

Chrispeels, J. H. (1996). Evaluating teachers' relationships with families: A case study of one district. *Elementary School Journal* 97: 179–200.

Coburn, C. (2003). Rethinking scale: Moving beyond numbers to deep and lasting change. *Educational Researcher* 32: 3–12.

Cowan, K. T. (2003). Parental involvement. In K. T. Cowan and C. J. Edwards (Eds.), *The new Title I: The changing landscape of accountability* (pp. 139–149). Washington, DC: Thompson.

Darling-Hammond, L., and J. Bransford. (2005). *Preparing teachers for a changing world: What teachers should learn and be able to do.* San Francisco: Jossey-Bass.

Datnow, A., L. Hubbard, and H. Mehan. (2002). *Extending educational reform: From one school to many.* New York: Routledge Falmer.

Epstein, J. L. (2001). *School, family, and community partnerships: Preparing educators and improving schools.* Boulder: Westview.

———. (2005). Attainable goals? The spirit and letter of the *No Child Left Behind Act* on parental involvement. *Sociology of Education* 78(2): 179–82.

Epstein, J. L., and M. G. Sanders. (2006). Prospects for change: Preparing educators for school, family, and community partnerships. *Peabody Journal of Education* 81: 81–120.

Epstein, J. L., and S. B. Sheldon. (2006). Moving forward: Ideas for research on school, family, and community partnerships. In C. F. Conrad and R. Serlin (Eds.), *SAGE Handbook for research in education: Engaging ideas and enriching inquiry* (pp. 117–137). Thousand Oaks, CA: Sage. (Reading 2.2).

Epstein, J. L., and K. J. Williams. (2003, April). *Does professional development for state and district leaders affect how they assist schools to implement programs of partnership?* Paper presented at the annual meeting of the American Educational Research Association, Chicago.

Epstein, J. L., et al. (2009). *School, family, and community partnerships: Your handbook for action, third edition.* Thousand Oaks, CA: Corwin.

Epstein, J. L., K. J. Williams, and N. R. Jansorn. (2004, April). *Does policy prompt partnerships? Effects of NCLB on district leadership for family involvement.* Paper presented at the annual meeting of the American Educational Research Association, San Diego.

Fullan, M. (2001). *Leading in a culture of change.* San Francisco: Jossey-Bass.

Hutchins, D. J., et al. (Eds.). (2009). *Promising partnership practices 2009.* Baltimore: National Network of Partnership Schools, Johns Hopkins University. (See annual collections of practices at www.partnershipschools.org in the section "Success Stories.")

Lauen, D. L. (2008). False promises: The school choice provisions in NCLB. In A. R. Sadovnik, J. O'Day, G. Bohrnstedt, and K. Borman (Eds.), *No Child Left Behind and the reduction of the achievement gap: Sociological perspectives on federal educational policy* (pp. 203–226). New York: Routledge.

Learning First Alliance. (2003). *Beyond islands of excellence: What districts can do to improve instruction and achievement in all schools.* Baltimore: ASCD. www.learnignfirst .org/lfaweb/rp?pa=docanddocId=62.

Leithwood, K., and N. Prestine. (2002). Unpacking the challenges of leadership at the school and district level. In J. Murphy (Ed.), *The educational leadership challenge: Redefining leadership for the 21st century* (pp. 42–64). Chicago: University of Chicago Press.

Mac Iver, M., and E. Farley. (2003). *Bringing the district back in: The role of the central office in improving instruction and student achievement.* CRESPAR Report #65. Baltimore: Center for Research on the Education of Students Placed at Risk.

McDonnell, L. M., and R. F. Elmore. (1991). Getting the job done: Alternative policy instruments. In A. R. Odden (Ed.), *Education policy implementation* (pp. 157–184). Albany: State University of New York Press.

Mickelson, R., and S. Southworth. (2008). When school choice leaves many children behind: Implications for NCLB for the Charlotte-Mechlenberg schools. In A. R. Sadovnik, J. O'Day, G. Bohrnstedt, and K. Borman (Eds.), *No Child Left Behind and the reduction of the achievement gap: Sociological perspectives on federal educational policy* (pp. 227–241). New York: Routledge.

Pounder, D., U. Reitzug, and M. D. Young. (2002). Preparing school leaders for school improvement, social justice, and community. In J. Murphy (Ed.), *The educational leadership challenge: Redefining leadership for the 21st century* (pp. 261–288). Chicago: University of Chicago Press.

Public Law 107-110. (2002, January 8). *No Child Left Behind Act of 2001.* Congressional Record, 115 STAT. 1501–1505.

Sanders, M. G. (2005). *Building school-community partnerships: Collaboration for student success.* Thousand Oaks, CA: Corwin.

———. (2008). Using diverse data to develop and sustain school, family, and community partnerships: A district case study. *Education Management, Administration, and Leadership* 36: 530–545.

Sheldon, S. B. (2005). Testing a structural equations model of partnership program implementation and family involvement. *Elementary School Journal* 106: 171–87.

———. (2008). Getting families involved with NCLB: Factors affecting schools' enactment of federal policy. In A. R. Sadovnik, J. O'Day, G. Bohrnstedt, and K. Borman (Eds.), *No Child Left Behind and the reduction of the achievement gap: Sociological perspectives on federal educational policy* (pp. 281–294). New York: Routledge.

Sheldon, S. B., and F. L. Van Voorhis. (2004). Partnership programs in U.S. schools: Their development and relationship to family involvement outcomes. *School Effectiveness and School Improvement* 15: 125–48.

U.S. Department of Education. (2004). *Parental involvement, Title I, Part A: Non-regulatory guidance.* Washington, DC: Author.

DISCUSSION AND ACTIVITIES

The comments in this section extend and update the content of the readings in this chapter. Key concepts and results are summarized. Questions and activities are provided for class discussions, debates, and homework assignments. They may suggest other exercises, field activities, and research projects.

KEY CONCEPTS

1. State, district, and school policies on school, family, and community partnerships must be clear, comprehensive, flexible, and responsive to be implemented in ways that meet the goals and needs of students, families, and schools.

2. State, district, and school policies on school, family, and community partnerships require enactments or other official commitments to ensure adequate staff, funding, training, dissemination, and other support needed to implement the policies.

COMMENT

Policies and Enactments

Policies concerning school, family, and community partnerships must be clear and comprehensive, but also flexible. Good policies encourage state, district, and school programs to account for their starting points on partnerships and focus partnership practices on specific school and family goals for student success. Policies also should set high standards for excellent, ongoing programs of school, family, and community partnerships; they should specify ways to measure how well programs are implemented and progressing and whether and how well goals are met.

At the state and district levels, policies on partnerships should include explicit enactments for leadership, funding, professional development, and other assistance that will enable schools to implement the policies with family and community involvement plans and practices to engage all parents in their children's education. As noted in Reading 4.1, policies without enactments are unfunded and unsupported, and will be unwelcome and ineffective.

State and district policies on partnerships must clearly outline how schools will be assisted to develop and evaluate partnership programs with training, funds, and other assistance, encouragement, and recognition from the state and district. The emphasis on assistance to schools is in contrast to top-down policies with rigid directives or prescribed activities that leave educators, parents, and students no flexibility to design programs or practices of partnership that they can call their own.

The seemingly simple guidelines for clear, comprehensive, flexible, funded, and facilitated policies are not as simple to implement as you might think. The readings, discussions, and activities in this chapter should help you to explore, critique, and consider policies for improving school, family, and community partnerships in states, districts, and schools.

Review State and District Policies

The sample policies (see Reading 4.2 in this chapter) show how state and district boards of education are working to promote the development of effective programs and practices of school, family, and community partnerships. Some of the sample policies include enactments outlining the actions taken to help districts and/or schools implement programs that fulfill the policies. It is useful to compare, contrast, and critique the samples to identify words and actions that you think are particularly important for producing good programs of school, family, and community partnerships at the state, district, and school levels.

    A. Select and identify *one* state and *one* district sample policy in Reading 4.2 that interest you.

    B. For each one, write your ideas on these questions.
1. Does the policy include reference to all six types of involvement (parenting, communicating, volunteering, learning at home, decision making, and collaborating with the community) in any order? Explain.
2. Does the policy refer to the involvement of parents at all grade levels?
3. Does the policy focus family and/or community involvement on student learning and success in school?
4. Does the policy commit to helping districts and/or schools improve their partnership programs?
5. Discuss one other feature of each policy that you think is particularly important.
6. Give each policy an overall rating: E for Excellent, S for Satisfactory, or N for Needs Improvement. Explain why you rated the policy as you did.

    C. Give your ideas of two ways to improve the policy you selected.

Changes in Technology

When Reading 4.1 was first published, there were no state or district websites on partnerships. A library or clearinghouse was a physical, not a virtual, place. Now, state departments of education and districts across the country use their websites to provide educators, parents, and the public with easy access to policies, publications, and other information on school, family, and community partnerships.

Some state and district websites are informative and understandable. Some are confusing to the extreme. It helps to see the difference. You may be in a position to assist district and state leaders to develop clear and useful websites for educators, parents, students, and the public.

ACTIVITY

Explore and Rate Websites

State Departments of Education Websites

A. Explore *one* of the following state department of education websites, and answer the questions on the next page. Search to find the state's policy on parental involvement or school, family, and community partnerships and evidence that the policy is being supported. Some of these states' policies are provided in Reading 4.2.

- **California**: www.cde.ca.gov

   Click on "Specialized Programs." Then use the search box to find "School, Family, and Community Partnerships."

- **Connecticut**: www.sde.ct.gov

   Follow the path from "Parents and Community" to "Family & Community Involvement and Youth Development Programs" to "School-Family-Community Partnerships." See newsletters called *Schools and Families* and related documents. Or use the search box to find "School-Family-Community Partnerships."

- **Ohio**: www.ode.state.oh.us

   Use the search box to find "Family and Community Engagement." See the state's collection of promising practices on the website.

- **West Virginia**: wvde.state.wv.us

   Follow the sidebar link to "State Board" and then "Policies," and scroll down to the links for "Policy 2200: Parent, Family, and Community Involvement in Education."

- **Wisconsin:** dpi.wi.gov

In the left-hand navigation bar click on "Divisions & Teams" under "DPI Menu." Under the heading "Division for Libraries, Technology, & Community Learning," click on "Community Learning and Partnerships." Then in the sidebar click on "Family-School-Community Partnerships."

Or select a state that interests you that has a section of its website on family and community involvement to address the questions below.

1. Use the chart below. Give the name of the state's Department of Education and the website URL.
2. Explore the website that you selected, and rate the features outlined in the chart.
3. Rate the website overall from A (Excellent/Informative) to F (Failing/Headache-Producing).
4. Explain, in writing, two things that are clear and good about the website's section or information on partnerships.
5. Write two recommendations that would improve this website, and explain why each improvement is needed.

State Department of Education and Website URL:

_____

_____

Feature	Rating (A–F)
Ease of locating the policy on parental involvement or partnerships	
Ease of locating information on parental involvement or partnerships	
Clarity of information provided	
Usefulness of information to educators, parents, or the public	
Attractiveness/ease of reading	
Multiple languages provided	
Add another factor you consider important: _____	
Overall Rating	
List two features that are clear and good: 1. 2.	
Recommendation 1:	
Recommendation 2:	

District Websites

B. Explore *one* of the following district websites, and answer the questions below. Search to find the district's policy on parental involvement or school, family, and community partnerships and evidence that the policy is being supported. Some of these districts' policies are provided in Reading 4.2.

- Anoka-Hennepin School District, MN: www.anoka.k12.mn.us

    Hover over "Parents" in the menu at the top of the page, and then click on "Parent Involvement."

- Buffalo Public Schools, NY: www.buffaloschools.org

    At the top of the page, hover over "Parents," and then click on "Family, Schools & Community." In the sidebar click on "Parent Involvement."

- Howard County Public Schools, MD: www.hcpss.org

    Use the search box to find "Parent, Family and Community Involvement."

- Middletown Public Schools, CT: www.middletownschools.org

    Click on "Board of Education," and follow links to "Policies & By-laws." Click on the link "Community Relations," and then click on the link for policy #1110.1 (a PDF), and see the section "Parent Resources."

- Naperville Community School District 203, IL: www.naperville203.org

    Hover over "Parents and Students," and then click on "School Family Community Partnership."

- Pasco School District, WA: www.psd1.org

    Hover over "Families," and click on "School & Family Partnerships."

- Saint Paul Public Schools, MN: www.spps.org

    Hover over "Community" and then "Office of Community Relations," and click on "Family and Community Involvement."
    Or select a school district that interests you that has a section of its website devoted to family and community involvement to address the questions below.

1. Use the chart on the next page. Give the name of the district and the website's full URL.

2. Explore the website that you selected, and rate the features outlined in the chart.
3. Rate the website overall from A (Excellent/Informative) to F (Failing/Headache-Producing).
4. Explain, in writing, two things that are clear and good about the website's section or information on partnerships.
5. Write two recommendations that would improve the website and explain why each improvement is needed.

NOTE: State and district websites change over time. Some connections may no longer be correct. If one URL is no longer functioning, find another state or district website for this activity.

District: _____
Website URL: _____

Feature	Rating (A–F)
Ease of locating a policy on parental involvement or partnerships	
Ease of locating information on parental involvement or partnerships	
Clarity of information provided	
Usefulness of information to educators, parents, or the public	
Attractiveness/ease of reading	
Multiple languages provided	
Ease of connecting to a particular school	
Add another factor you consider important: _____	
Overall Rating	
List two features that are clear and good: 1. 2.	
Recommendation 1:	
Recommendation 2:	

Compare State and District Leadership on Partnership Program Development

The state policy initiatives recommended in Reading 4.1 also may be important leadership actions in school districts. State policies are written and programs organized to guide districts and schools in different geographic locations and political contexts within a state. District policies are written and actions taken to guide preschools and elementary, middle, and high schools serving diverse student and family populations to develop their partnership programs. Some state-level leadership strategies also may enable district leaders to help all schools develop effective partnership programs.

A. Photocopy Figure 4.1 on pages 354–355.
B. Write "yes" or "no" to indicate whether you think each entry (drawn from the outline for states in Reading 4.1) is appropriate for state and/or district leaders to enact their policies that support family and community involvement.
  1. If *yes* for districts, explain one way in which the action might differ in a district compared to a state.
  2. If *no* for districts, explain one reason why the action is not important or appropriate for district leaders for partnerships to conduct.

The Power of Linked Policies and Practices

States may take actions that encourage partnership programs whether or not they are guided by federal mandates or supported by federal funds. Districts may take actions that enable all schools to develop partnership programs whether or not they are actively supported by their state departments of education. Schools may develop programs of school, family, and community partnerships whether or not they are directly supported by their districts or states. Individual teachers may establish good partnerships with students' families and communities whether or not they are guided or aided by their schools or by other policy levels and leaders.

Although each policy level may work on partnerships independently, research and exemplary practice suggest that programs are stronger and of higher quality when federal, state, district, and school policies; funding; and technical assistance are linked or "nested." That is, programs are more effective in design and in results when federal policies support states, districts, and schools; when state policies support districts and schools; and when district policies enable schools to strengthen and sustain excellent partnership programs. The best connections will lead ultimately to improving programs at the school level, where educators, families, and students interact on a daily basis to help students learn and grow.

| | Is this an appropriate policy initiative for: | | If YES for districts, tell *one* way the policy or resulting activities might differ in a district compared to a state. |
POLICIES AND ACTIVITIES	STATES? DISTRICTS? (Write YES or NO for each.)		If NO for districts, give *one* reason why the policy is not appropriate.
a. **Write a policy** that supports comprehensive programs of school, family, and community partnerships.	——	——	—————— —————— ——————
b. **Establish an office or department** with an expert leader and adequate staff to facilitate the development and continuous improvement of programs of partnership.	——	——	—————— —————— ——————
c. Write an **annual Leadership Action Plan for Partnerships.**	——	——	—————— —————— ——————
d. **Identify funds** for school, family, and community partnerships to cover staff and program costs.	——	——	—————— —————— ——————
e. **Conduct ongoing inservice** education on partnerships.	——	——	—————— —————— ——————
f. Collect, assess, and **improve policies** on partnerships, and improve the organization of leadership for partnership program development.	——	——	—————— —————— ——————
g. **Evaluate teachers** and administrators for their work on partnerships.	——	——	—————— —————— ——————
h. **Support a master teacher, lead teacher, or other career ladder program** to increase expertise on partnerships.	——	——	—————— —————— ——————

(continues)

FIGURE 4.1   Policies and Activities Comparing State and District Policies

i. **Develop partnership tools or products** (e.g., brochures, lunch menus, templates for calendars, newsletters, publications for all schools and families, guidelines for communicating with non–English-speaking families). —— —— _____

j. **Encourage business, industry, and other community connections** to strengthen school, family, and community partnerships. —— —— _____

k. **Establish an advisory committee** for school, family, and community partnerships including educators, parents, and community members. —— —— _____

l. **Establish a website,** library, clearinghouse, or dissemination center for research on partnerships, best practices, other materials. —— —— _____

m. **Support and conduct evaluations** of the quality of partnership programs and practices. —— —— _____

n. **Conduct an annual conference** for schools to share best practices with each other and to continueannual plans for improving partnership programs. —— —— _____

FIGURE 4.1   *(continued)*

QUESTIONS TO DISCUSS

1. On the one hand: Give two examples from readings in this chapter or from your experience that indicate why policies that are linked (or "nested") across federal, state, district, and/or school levels are likely to create stronger and more effective programs to involve families and communities than do policies that are not linked or that are issued at just one level.

2. On the other hand: Give two examples of how a single school might establish a policy and effective partnership program even if its state and district are not actively supporting such actions.

3. What advice would you give to a district leader who is considering whether to (a) develop a district policy, guidelines, and assistance to help all schools in the district develop programs of school, family, and community partnerships, or (b) leave it up to each school to do this without district support? Draw from Reading 4.3 to list two recommendations you would give a district leader and the reasons for your advice.

COMMENT

Federal Leadership and Federal Guidelines

At the federal level, some policies of the departments of Education, Labor, and Health and Human Services, as well as other departments, concern connections among students, families, schools, and communities. Several programs have long histories of including family involvement among their required components.

Head Start, initiated in 1965, recognized that all families, including those with low incomes, are important in their children's education. Head Start legislated roles and opportunities for parents in economically distressed communities to become involved in preschools, encouraged parents to volunteer or work as paid aides, and required parents to serve on advisory committees to be involved in policy decisions that affected their own and other children. Head Start programs included home visits to help families learn age-appropriate parenting skills and activities to support their preschool child's learning and healthy development at home and to find health and other services in the community.

Follow-Through, initiated in 1967, attempted to continue Head Start's emphasis on parental involvement and activities for children and families through the primary grades.

The Education of All Handicapped Children Act (Public Law 94-142), initiated in 1975, required teachers and parents to cooperate in setting annual educational and developmental goals for children with special needs.

Title I of the Elementary and Secondary Education Act (ESEA) of 1965 (also called Chapter 1 for a while and then Title I again) included guidelines and mandates for school and family partnerships that are congruent with the theory and framework in this volume. In its present form, Title I recognizes the importance of family involvement in the education of children who, because of educational and economic difficulties, are not doing well or are at risk of failing in school. This ongoing federal policy requires large districts to spend some Title I funds to develop positive partnership programs to include families in their children's education in productive ways.

Along with Title I, other sections of ESEA (e.g., Even Start; Titles III, IV, V, and VI; the Individuals with Disabilities Education Act [IDEA]) include requirements or guidelines for home-school-community connections to improve students' chances of success.

There have been two main problems in implementing federal guidelines and programs for home-school connections. First, educators in states, districts, and schools have not always understood the intent of the legislative language to establish coherent and important programs of partnership, and they faced no serious consequences for inaction. Second, in the past, the legislative guidelines led educators to separate Title I parents from other parents. The first problem stalled action and progress on partnerships in many locations. The second problem caused the separation and segregation of parents within schools, limiting the sense of community and contradicting the concept of partnerships. Although schoolwide Title I programs aim to create more cohesive school communities, the two historic problems still plague many Title I programs.

ACTIVITY

Find and Critique Federal Policies on Partnerships

Use the Internet to learn more about federal policies that include attention to parental involvement, community connections, or other aspects of school, family, and community partnerships.

A. Explore federal legislation, regulations, and other policy guidelines on www.ed.gov, the website of the U.S. Department of Education. Or explore the website of the departments of Labor, Commerce, or Health and Human Services for policies concerning connections among home, school, and community. Look for information on Titles I, III, IV, V, or VII; Head Start; Even Start; free- or reduced-price meals; or another policy that concerns the families of economically and educationally distressed children, children with special needs, or gifted and talented children.

B. Identify *one* federal policy that interests you.

C. Summarize and critique the policy (or section) you selected.
   1. What does the policy require or request of a state, district, school, family, or community concerning school, family, and community partnerships?
   2. Explain: Is the policy you selected clear? Is it flexible for diverse districts? Does it increase educators' capacities to organize effective programs at the selected policy level?
   3. In your view, what is one positive or negative feature of the policy for improving programs of school, family, and community partnerships in schools, districts, or state departments of education?
   4. Describe one way that you would improve the federal policy that you selected.

Federally Funded Programs and Policies

Interview one educator who is associated with a Head Start, Even Start, Title I, or other federally funded program for children and families in a school, district, or community location. This may be an individual interview or one conducted in class for and with all students.

A. Identify the program and the position of the person you are interviewing. Briefly summarize the goals of the selected program.
B. Ask the interviewee:
   1. Does your program have a written policy and plan for school, family, and community partnerships?
      a. If yes, briefly summarize the policy.
      b. If no, briefly summarize the program's approach to school, family, and community partnerships.
   2. Are only federal funds used in this program, or are other funds also used to support the program and activities of school, family, and community partnerships?
   3. Describe one of the program's most effective and one of its least effective activities for family and community involvement.
   4. Overall, how effective is this program in informing and involving all of the families that are eligible for its services?
   5. What transitional activities help children and families move from this program to their next school?
   6. What is one way that you would like to improve the way this program works with families and communities in the future?
C. Add one question of your own about the federally funded program you selected.
D. Document your questions and responses.
E. Write a reflective paragraph on the information you obtained on the nature and quality of the program and the contributions of federal funds to its work.

Identify Policy Instruments in ESEA

Reading 4.3 discusses four policy instruments (McDonnell and Elmore, 1991) that, at this writing, are embedded in the federal Elementary and Secondary Education Act (ESEA) in sections on parental involvement. The reading examines whether and how these different guidelines and requirements affect district leadership on partnerships and school-based programs of family and community involvement.

The four policy instruments are *mandates*, *inducements*, *capacity-building opportunities*, and *system-changing actions*.

A. Use the search function at www.ed.gov to find the current Elementary and Secondary Education Act.
B. Examine *all* sections of ESEA that refer to parental involvement.
C. Document one example of the legislative language in *one* section of the law (give the identifying section code, and cite the content, or note "none") that specifies or reflects:
   1. A mandate (a requirement or regulation that must be fulfilled to comply with the law)
   2. An inducement (a reward that encourages or a sanction that punishes particular actions)
   3. Capacity building (a way to build new skills and knowledge for action on the topic)
   4. System change (actions that permanently alter typical decision-making or leadership patterns on the topic)
D. Write a paragraph or two to tell which section and policy instrument in ESEA you think would have the strongest effects on district leaders' actions to improve district-level and/or school-based programs of parental involvement and why.

COMMENT

Top-Down, Bottom-Up, or Side-by-Side Policy

There are recurrent controversies about the differences, benefits, and disadvantages of "top-down" versus "bottom-up" policies and directives. In several readings throughout this book, I suggest that the most important policies for school, family, and community partnership find expression in programs and practices at the school level. The readings and activities also suggest, however, that some federal, state, and district policies, leadership, activities, and support enable schools to develop skills and programs of school, family, and community partnerships.

QUESTIONS TO DISCUSS

Use the information in this chapter and your experience to answer the following questions.

1. Do you think that a federal, state, district, or school policy can change educators' and families' attitudes and behaviors about school, family, and community partnerships? Explain your yes or no answer.

2. Give one example of "side-by-side" federal, state, district, and/or school policies that shows how leadership, investments, and practices of partnership across policy levels might affect the involvement of families and communities in their children's education at the school level.

COMMENT

The Flow and Ebb of Policy and Practice

In the real world of education, the ebb and flow (or flow and ebb) of policies and practices may encourage or prevent the development of permanent partnership programs. It is common for policies and actions to be passed, revised, and then halted before the original goals are achieved.

In some states and districts, policies, leadership, goals, and activities for school, family, and community partnerships are started and stopped, delayed, limited in scope, or redirected because of leadership and staff changes, changes in "missions," or budget cuts. In other states and districts, partnerships are maintained and expanded despite changes in personnel.

State Example

For example, at the state level, California's Department of Education's policy on parental involvement (included in Reading 4.2) was passed in 1989 and, with revisions, is still on the books. California was one of the first states to use research as the basis for a short, clear policy that named the six types of involvement (parenting, communicating, volunteering, learning at home, decision making, and collaborating with the community) as components of school-based partnership programs (Solomon, 1991).

The original policy included detailed plans for state-sponsored staff development and assistance for district leaders and school teams to maximize the chances that the state policy would be enacted. After a good start, progress was slowed by politics and by serious budget cuts that affected the state's options for fulfilling its plans for widespread, cost-free professional development. Later, the state reestablished and strengthened its policy and initiatives on partnerships.

California is a large state with over 1,000 school districts. It is not possible for a state office to order or control the work that occurs in all of these districts, large and small. However, it is important for this state and all states to have a policy that is meaningful to and can be customized and implemented in all districts and schools.

District Example

At the district level, Indianapolis provides an example of "flow and ebb" in leadership, policies, and practices of family and community involvement. In the 1980s, the Indianapolis Public Schools (IPS) Parents in Touch office led the nation in district-level leadership on partnerships (Warner, 1991). Progress was seriously affected when key staff retired and the superintendent and other leaders changed more than once. These are common occurrences in school districts. Although some schools in IPS still refer to Parents In Touch as one of their school-based approaches, and although the district states its intention to develop effective partnership programs in all schools, IPS remains in a period of reconstructing district-level leadership, policies, and actions on partnerships.

No Need for Progress to Ebb

It should be noted that progress on partnerships is not always halted by changes in personnel and budget cuts. Several states and many districts working on partnerships experience changes in leaders and budgetary crises but continue to increase the quality of their partnership programs. Several factors support continuous program improvement, including clearly written policies; documented plans and activities; evaluations of progress; broad participation and expertise, so that new leaders may be drawn from those already working in the state or district; and attention to transitions, so that new leaders are informed about past successes and are able to build on the work of those who left.

For example, when its superintendent changed once in the early 1990s and then again, and when its leader for partnerships left and a new leader was appointed, St. Paul Public Schools in Minnesota maintained a clear vision about family involvement and *increased* efforts to improve home, school, and community connections in all schools. Similarly, despite leadership changes and budget woes, Buffalo Public Schools continued to assign leaders to guide schools to strengthen their school-based partnership programs. The new superintendents and leaders in these and other locations were able to learn about and expand the goals of their predecessors.

Personnel changes are guaranteed to occur in schools, districts, and state departments of education. Individuals move, are promoted, retire, or transfer to new assignments. Budgets are challenged as departments compete for limited funds. Even with these inevitable changes and challenges, state, district, and school investments in school, family, and community partnership programs can be protected and improved—just as reading, math, science, testing, and other programs continue despite the ups and downs of budgets and the comings and goings of leaders and staff.

Think of the permanence and predictability of a reading, math, or testing program in schools, districts, or states. What might be done to organize ongoing programs of school, family, and community partnerships that will not disappear with staff or budget changes?

1. Select and identify a policy level—state, district, or school—that interests you.
2. Using the readings in this chapter and your experience, describe two structures, processes, or activities that you think would help prevent setbacks in the progress of partnership programs from staff or budgetary changes.
3. Explain why you think each idea might help stabilize or "institutionalize" a program of partnerships at the policy level that you selected.

COMMENT

What Are School, Family, and Community Partnerships Worth?

Programs of school, family, and community partnerships may be funded using a formula allocating a *per-pupil expenditure* or a *lump-sum investment* to support staff and program costs. Several years ago, I suggested a minimum per-pupil expenditure of $5, $10, and $25 at the state, district, and school levels, respectively, or minimum lump-sum investments of $100,000 per state, $50,000 per large district, and $15,000 per school to fund the leadership, development, training, implementation, evaluation, and continuous improvement of programs of partnership in states, districts, and schools (Epstein, 1991).

Since that initial modest proposal, my colleagues and I have collected data from states, districts, and schools on the levels and sources of their investments in staff and activities to develop comprehensive partnership programs (Epstein et al., 2009). The following comments and activities draw from those data to address the question: What are school, family, and community partnerships worth?

Exploring Funding Options: Per-Pupil Allocations

Imagine the following allocations for school, family, and community partnership programs at the state, district, and school levels:

- $0.15–$1 per student of state funds to be used at that level to fund salaries and benefits of a state director of partnerships and staff, state programs, and services for activities that assist districts and schools in their work on partnerships. State funds may support staff salaries and benefits, grants to districts and schools, training and other inservice education, and other state leadership functions.

- $5–$10 per student of district funds to be used at that level to fund salaries and benefits of district coordinator(s) and facilitator(s), district programs, and services to assist all schools in the district to develop expertise and programs of school, family, and community partnerships. District funds may support training and other inservice education, grants to schools, the dissemination of effective practices, and other district leadership functions. The district's work should be coordinated with state policies and activities, when appropriate.

- $12–$20 per student of funds at the school level to support a program of activities planned each year by the school's Action Team for Partnerships. This includes activities conducted on the six types of involvement designed to inform and involve all students' families in their children's education at school and at home. Each school's program includes activities that are selected and tailored to meet important goals for student success and to meet the needs and interests of students and families. This may include a part-time, site-based coordinator, printed materials, refreshments, incentives, workshop presenters, website development, and other specific involvement activities. The school policies, programs, and practices should be coordinated with state and district policies and activities, when appropriate.

Any state, district, or school could justify investing *more* than the modest amounts suggested above, but few presently make even these minimal investments. Different formulas could be used, for example, if a district offers large grants to all schools to support activities in a written plan for partnerships, if districts fund full-time facilitators for partnerships in each school, or if districts include in their allocations for partnerships full-service program components such as school-site health, recreation, after-school, and other educational programs and services for children and families.

Another way to determine a reasonable per-pupil investment is to assign 1 percent of the total per-pupil costs to educate youngsters to fund all state and district leadership, training, and support activities and all school-based programs of school, family, and community partnerships. For example, if it costs $6,000 per student per year for a full educational program, then $60 per student would be divided to fund the state, district, and school programs of partnership. This would exceed the minimum allocations suggested above for the state, district, and school levels, but still would be a reasonable allocation for organizing, sustaining, and continually improving family and community involvement that supports student learning and success in school.

Exploring Funding Options: Lump-Sum Allocations

Another funding alternative is based on the allocation of a lump sum for partnerships. States, districts, and schools may allocate new funds or reallocate existing funds to support staff salaries and benefits, grants, training, and other activities to ensure that there are leadership and funds for the development of district-level and school-based partnership programs. Table 4.5 summarizes the range of investments reported by schools, districts, and states in the National Network of Partnership Schools in 2007. The reported average investments indicate that:

- state leadership and support for programs of partnership averages about $211,000 (median of $175,000);
- district leadership and support for programs of partnership average about $214,000 for districts with more than 30 schools, and proportionately more or less for larger and smaller districts (median of $65,000);
- school leadership and support for programs of partnership averages about $6,000 for schools with 400–800 students and proportionately more or less in larger or smaller schools (median of $2,000).

Combining the per-pupil expenditures for parental involvement programs in Table 4.5 across all three policy levels indicates that all states, districts, and schools could begin to build comprehensive programs of school, family, and community partnerships for a total of about $30 per student per year. This remarkably reasonable level of funding may be drawn from funds that are available in federal, state, and local programs that already are targeted to school, family, and community partnerships for student success. The estimates suggest that all states, districts, and schools can afford to identify leaders and support the development of programs that fulfill basic goals for improving school, family, and community partnerships.

Table 4.5 also shows that, at this writing, states, districts, and schools are using many sources of funds to cover their programs of school, family, and community partnerships to increase student success in school. Some funds come from federal, state, and local programs that include requirements and recommendations for family and community involvement (e.g., Title I; Title III; Title IV, including Safe and Drug Free Schools; Title V on choice and innovative programs; Title VI on flexible approaches for increasing student achievement and effective rural schools; and others). For example, Title IV funds for Safe and Drug Free Schools may be used for prevention activities, including home, school, and community connections to improve and maintain good student attendance, behavior, and learning. Title VI funds may be applied creatively to improve curricular connections in school, family, and community partnerships, such as improving designs of homework, enriching the curriculum through volunteers, creating community-based career development and job shadowing programs, and other attention to school subjects. Title VII funds may be applied to programs that help students with limited English to increase school skills, including connections with families to motivate student learning.

TABLE 4.5   Levels and Sources of Funds for Programs of Family and Community Involvement in Schools, Districts, and States

	Schools (N = 356)[1]	Districts (N = 83)[1]	States (N = 12)[1]
Levels of Funding	**Range: $100 to $88,000** Median: $2,000 Average: $5,722 Suggested per-pupil expenditure range: $12 to $20	**Range: $800 to $2.78 million** Median: $65,000 Average: $213,958 Suggested per-pupil expenditure range: $5 to $10	**Range: $2,000 to $600,000** Median: $175,000 Average: $211,088 Suggested per-pupil expenditure range: $0.15 to $1.00
Sources of Funds for Family and Community Involvement Programs	Bilingual education Community partners District budget Drug prevention General funds Principals' discretionary funds PTA School fund-raisers Special education funds State funds Title I Titles III, IV 21st Century Schools grants Other federal, state, district, and local funds	Bilingual education Community partners District budget Drug prevention District fund-raisers General funds Local foundations PIRC support PTA Special education State funds Title I Titles II, III, IV United Way 21st Century Schools grants Other federal, state, and district funds	IDEA–special education funding PIRC support State professional development funds State department of education general funds Title I 21st Century Schools grants Other federal and state funds

[1] Source: *Update* surveys of schools, districts, and states in the National Network of Partnership Schools (NNPS) at Johns Hopkins University. School data are from 1998 and are corrected for inflation to reflect 2007 dollars. District and state data are from 2007 *Update* surveys.

States, districts, and schools also use general funds, donations from parent associations, and grants and donations from businesses, foundations, community groups, and other sources. Funds from all sources are combined or blended to support state coordinators, district facilitators, activities planned by school Action Teams for School, Family, and Community Partnerships, and other personnel and program costs.

Funding Options: Other Factors

The number of districts in a state, the number of schools in a district, and the number of students and families in a school all may affect funding formulas. For example, a state with over 400 school districts with an average of 7 schools in each will need a different plan and funding formula than a state with 50 districts with an average of 60 schools in each. Consider the following hypothetical states.

State A has about 400 districts that average 10 schools per district (ranging from 1 to 50 schools per district across the state).	State B has about 50 districts that average 60 schools per district (ranging from 10 to 100 schools per district across the state).
This state will need more staff and leadership activities at the state level or by region to assist all districts and schools to organize and develop their expertise and programs of partnership. In small districts, with fewer than 15 schools, part-time leaders for partnerships may assist the schools. In very small districts (e.g., fewer than 5 schools) school leaders may work relatively independently, with state, regional, or other organizational support (e.g., service providers), as needed.	This state will need only one or two full-time professional staff at the state level, adequate support staff, and a budget to assist districts and schools with their leadership and work on school, family, and community partnerships. Large districts in this state will need a full-time-equivalent facilitator to assist every 15–30 schools to develop and maintain their partnership programs.
In State A, state leadership (with assistance from various organizations) may be more complex than in State B.	In State B, district leadership may be more complex than in State A.

Both hypothetical states need to identify a state leader for partnerships who will write a plan to organize state leadership activities, including some of the actions outlined in Readings 4.1 and 4.2. Each state will need to develop within-state, interdepartmental connections among programs that include attention to families and communities. Other state and regional organizations, intermediate staff development units, and universities also may take leadership roles at the state and/or district levels to help districts and schools develop their knowledge, skills, and programs of partnership.

Districts in each hypothetical state must identify a leader on partnerships and related program costs, and all schools will need adequate funding each year to support activities planned by their Action Teams for Partnerships. The level of support needed will depend on the size of the district or school, goals for students, student and family needs, the community context, and other factors.

Summary of Funding Options

There are many possible formulas for per-pupil or lump-sum allocations at the state, district, and school levels to support the real costs of developing and maintaining programs of school, family, and community partnerships at all three policy levels. Decisions will vary based on the conditions and needs in large and small states, districts, and schools. However derived, a reasonable plan for adequate funding is needed in every state, district, and school to ensure that all students' families are welcome in their children's schools and are informed about and active partners in their children's education at all grade levels. The examples of alternative funding plans force attention to such questions as:

- How much is it worth to develop and maintain productive school, family, and community partnerships so that all families are involved in their children's education across the grades?
- Where will the money come from, and how will it be spent?
- Who will decide?
- How will results of the investments be evaluated?
- How will investments and programs be sustained?

ACTIVITY

Design a Feasible Plan for Funding Partnerships

A. Select and identify one state, district, or school that interests you.
B. List its name, location, and size (e.g., number of districts, schools, and/or number of students served). This information may be obtained on the Internet (e.g., nces.ed.gov), by phone, or in federal, state, or local directories, or through other sources. Or use the following hypothetical information:

New State has 100 school districts and approximately 1,600 schools. Every district, including New District, has 10 elementary schools (grades K–5) with 300 students in each school; 4 middle schools (grades 6–8) with 750 students in each school; and 2 high schools (grades 9–12) with 1,500 students in each.

C. Working with the information in this chapter, create a realistic funding plan for school, family, and community partnerships for the state, district, or school that you selected.

1. Begin with a paragraph summarizing the philosophy or policy on which you will base your funding plan. Consider these requirements:
   a. The program you outline must enable educators, parents, and community members to work together in ways that support student success in school.
   b. The program and budget you describe must enable each school to build its capacity to plan, conduct, and maintain partnerships with all families, not just a few.
2. a. Outline the funding approach you will use (i.e., per-pupil expenditure or lump-sum allocation); at least five sample activities that you will fund at the state, district, or school level that you selected; and the level of funding you recommend for one year to support the activities you outlined.
   b. Give details on the allocations you recommend for staff salaries and benefits, training workshops, grants, and other activities in your comprehensive program of partnerships.
D. *Optional class activity*: In class, present and critique classmates' funding plans. Discuss:
   1. Are the funding estimates realistic?
   2. What would the plan permit and exclude in a full program of partnerships?
   3. Do you think that the plan could be implemented in the school, district, or state you selected? Why or why not?

COMMENT

Partnerships Start at Birth

Parents As Teachers (P.A.T.) is a long-standing early education intervention program that grew from a 1981 pilot program in Missouri to a nationally replicated model. The program was designed to serve all families of infants and very young children, not just those with high-risk characteristics. P.A.T. prepares parent educators who make a series of home visits each year to help participating families understand child development from birth to age three so that their children are ready to learn in school. Services include home visits, screening to monitor children's development and to identify and reduce risks to healthy development, parent education, group meetings for parents, and play experiences for children in a community center. In Missouri, one early estimate of the cost of the pilot P.A.T. program was $210 per family, with $170 coming from the state and $40 from local funds. Since the early 1980s, costs have increased to cover the salaries of parent educators and program costs, though the program is rarely fully funded to serve all families, as originally intended. P.A.T. remains a popular program that is part of early childhood education policies in many states and districts.

Early evaluations of P.A.T. suggested positive effects on parents' attitudes and confidence and on children's readiness skills and social development, fewer undetected hearing problems, and reduced effects of risk conditions on children's language development (Pfannenstiel, Seitz, and Zigler, 2002; Pfannenstiel and Seltzer, 1989). Research is needed on how children in P.A.T. proceed through their educational careers and whether and which families continue to be involved in their children's education after their children start elementary school.

P.A.T. is one of many successful early education programs that assist families and their infants and toddlers. A logical next step for all such programs is to ensure that information for families about child and adolescent development and parental involvement in education continues as children progress through the elementary and secondary grades. This would require the kinds of policies and practices featured in Readings 4.1 and 4.2 that outline how state and district leaders can help all schools develop and maintain effective partnership programs that aim to increase student success in school.

QUESTIONS TO DISCUSS

1. Give two reasons why it is important for a state to focus on families of children from birth to age three, as in P.A.T. and similar programs.
2. Give two reasons why it is *not enough* to focus on families of children from birth to age three in organizing home, school, and community partnerships.

COMMENT

Chart a District's Progress in Developing Partnership Programs

Reading 4.3 and other studies indicate that district policies are necessary but not sufficient for schools to build capacity to organize their own partnership programs. Rather, district leaders who are expert on partnership program development have two responsibilities: to conduct activities at the district level that benefit all schools and to conduct activities that guide each school to develop effective programs of family and community involvement. School-based partnership programs increase the options for all students' families to be involved in their children's education at every grade level in ways that support student success in school.

To fulfill both responsibilities, district leaders must take the following steps on the path to partnerships:

Step 1. Write a policy.
Step 2. Build knowledge at the district level. Identify a leader for partnerships.

Step 3.　　Implement district-level activities, such as conducting workshops for parents or compiling a handbook of ideas.

Step 4.　　Assist schools on request.

Step 5.　　Take initiative to help every school create an Action Team for Partnerships.

Step 6.　　Provide all school teams with needed professional development and support to help them organize, implement, evaluate, and sustain their partnership programs.

Step 7.　　Assist schools on a regular schedule, organize ways for schools to share their best activities, and conduct midyear or end-of-year activities to address challenges and discuss solutions.

Step 8.　　Evaluate the quality of district and school programs and effects of partnerships in order to improve programs from year to year.

Most districts start this work with steps 1, 2, and 3 but never get to steps 5 through 8.

Discuss a District's Progress on Partnerships

Select and identify a school district with at least 10 schools that is of interest to you. Arrange to interview one district leader (a district leader for partnerships or other administrator) and one principal from the district. Or invite a district leader and a principal from a local district to class for a group interview.

A. Ask the district leader:
1. Does your district have a policy on parental involvement or school, family, or community partnerships?
   a. If yes, what is one feature of this policy?
   b. If no, why is there no policy on partnerships?
2. Is there a district leader who is expert on partnerships to oversee work at the district level and in the schools?
   a. If yes, what are this leader's responsibilities at the district level and in aiding schools to develop their own site-based partnership programs?
   b. If there is no leader, who in the district is responsible for advancing family and community involvement?
3. What is one strong district leadership activity for family and community involvement conducted this year?
4. How should your district's partnership program improve in the next year or two?
5. Add at least one question of your own.

B. Ask the school principal:
  1. Does your school implement the district's policy on partnerships, or does the school have a separate and different policy? Or both? Or none?
     a. If it has *any* policy, please explain how this policy is shared with teachers, parents, and student.
     b. If it has none, please explain whether a written policy would help your school strengthen its partnership program.
  2. Does the school have an Action Team for Partnership or an equivalent committee that organizes a plan, implements activities, and evaluates its outreach to engage all parents in useful ways each year?
  3. How do district leaders assist your school to improve its partnership program?
  4. What is one strong activity for family and community involvement in your school?
  5. How does your school's partnership program need to improve in the next year or two?
  6. Add at least one question of your own.
C. Document the questions and responses. Indicate which step (see steps 1–8) the district is working on to build its leadership on partnerships.
D. Reflecting on the responses from the two interviewees, write a reflective paragraph telling whether this district is at an early or advanced stage in developing district-level and school-based partnership programs.

COMMENT

District Policies: Focus on Choice

Some states and districts have policies about school choice and about school, family, and community partnerships. As discussed in Reading 4.1, school choice and partnerships are simultaneously *linked* and *separate* policies. They are linked because choice involves families in major decisions about where their children will attend school or which program within a school a child will elect. They are separate because choice is a discrete event that may or may not be followed by other opportunities for ongoing involvement.

Many states and districts have policies that permit, encourage, or require families to choose their public schools within or across school districts. In various places, parents may choose magnet schools, charter schools, career academies, and other special schools or programs at the elementary, middle, and high school levels. At the time of this writing, districts were required to allow parents to choose new schools for their children if, over two years, the current school failed to make adequate progress on state achievement tests. Policies that enable parents to choose their child's school are designed to build students' talents and interests, increase competition among schools and improve the quality of school programs, respond to court orders for racially integrated schools, or meet other policy goals.

Some policies on school choice are clear and equitable. Others are murky and do not inform or involve all families about the choices they may make. In some cases, parents do not receive timely information about their choices. Sometimes, information is not written in languages that parents and students can understand.

Parents need information on the consequences of different choices for their children's learning, transportation, and special programs. Changing schools entails changing friends and locations. The new schools may not have programs that meet the needs of particular children and could be a poorer match than the current school. The choice process is, in fact, complicated. Information and processes on choice must be clear, equitable, and timely.

After the choice of a school is made, every school must inform and engage all families to support their children's learning and development. This requires each school to have a comprehensive program of school, family, and community partnerships that involves all parents every year as students proceed through school.

QUESTIONS TO DISCUSS

1. a. How might choosing a school *increase* the involvement of families?
   b. How might choosing a school *decrease* the involvement of families?
2. Select and identify the level of schooling (elementary, middle, or high school) that interests you. Suppose a family moved into a new community with a child entering the level of schooling you selected.
   a. Write three questions you think a parent should ask in the new community if public school choice were an option. Note to whom each question should be addressed. Explain why each question is important to a parent.
   b. Write three questions you think a parent should ask in the new community if all students were assigned to their schools and there were no options for school choice. Note to whom each question should be addressed. Explain why each question is important to a parent.
   c. *Optional class activity*: Discuss the concerns parents may have about the choice or assignment of schools. Whose responsibility (e.g., district administrators, school leaders, others) is it to address these issues?

Organizations' Policies for Preparing Educators

States and districts are not the only leadership units that write policies and guidelines on school, family, and community partnerships. Professional organizations, including the American Association of Colleges for Teacher Education (2009), the National Association of State Boards of Education (2009), and the National School Boards Association (2003), recognize the importance of programs of partnership to increase student success in school and to reduce school dropout rates.

Accrediting and professional organizations also have policies and recommendations on partnerships that influence education and practice. Following are two examples.

New Teachers: NCATE Standards for Teacher Credentials

The National Council for Accreditation of Teacher Education (NCATE, 2008) includes a standard for parental involvement for candidates for teaching and for teacher preparation institutions. The standards aim to ensure that new teachers understand and are prepared to involve families in their children's education. For example, NCATE's standards for preparing elementary teachers include the following goals for teachers' professionalism:

Professional Growth, Reflection, and Evaluation. Elementary teachers are aware of and reflect on their practice in light of research on teaching, professional ethics, and resources available for professional learning; they continually evaluate the effects of their professional decisions and actions on students, families, and other professionals in the learning community and actively seek out opportunities to grow professionally.

Collaboration with Families, Colleagues, and Community Agencies. They know the importance of establishing and maintaining a positive collaborative relationship with families, school colleagues, and agencies in the larger community to promote the intellectual, social, emotional, physical growth, and well-being of children. (Standard 5.2)

Explanation. Candidates understand different family beliefs, traditions, values, and practices across cultures and within society and use their knowledge effectively. They involve families as partners in supporting the school both inside and outside the classrooms. They involve families in assessing and planning for individual children, including children with disabilities, developmental delays, or special abilities. Candidates understand schools as organizations within the larger community context and the operations of relevant aspects of the systems in which they work. They also understand how factors in the elementary students' environments outside of school may influence the students' cognitive, emotional, social, and physical well-being and, consequently, their lives and learning. Candidates participate in collegial activities designed to make the entire school a productive learning environment and develop effective collaborations with specialists.

Similarly, in outlining what middle school teachers should know and be able to do, NCATE (2008) states: "Middle school teachers understand how prior learning experiences and family backgrounds influence young adolescent learning. They form relationships with the students' families and community to create a collaborative learning experience."

Experienced Teachers: National Board for Professional Teaching Standards (NBPTS)

The National Board for Professional Teaching Standards (NBPTS) defines what an experienced, exemplary teacher should know and be able to do. One standard specifies that excellent teachers establish family partnerships. For example, in the outline for the Early Adolescence/Generalist Certificate (NBPTS, 2001), the following standard describes how experienced teachers in the middle grades should work with families and communities to help students succeed:

> Standard XI: Family Partnerships
> Accomplished generalists work with families to achieve common goals for the education of their children.

Explanation. In explaining how teachers "clearly signal through word and deed the importance of families as partners with the school in their children's education," NBPTS explains how exemplary teachers cultivate family support for their children's education:

> Accomplished generalists understand that active, involved, and informed families create a network that supports vital, effective instructional programs. They see collaboration with parents as an essential tool in providing students with the support, motivation, and understanding they desire and need. Teachers effectively communicate with families about their children's accomplishments, successes, and needs for improvement, including means for attaining higher goals. They ensure that this communication extends to families whose primary language is not English. Teachers search for ways to share the school's objectives and expectations for its students, as well as the rationales for assignments. Teachers interpret and discuss students' work as well as report cards and test scores in a manner that gives parents an accurate portrait of their children's progress. They can discuss course selection and consequences, including the importance of planning for high school and future education. They work constructively with parents to help their children develop good learning habits and study skills, complete homework, set goals, and improve performance. As necessary, they assist families in finding additional resources and services outside the school, such as health care, counseling, and child care.

Teachers who apply for NBPTS certification must submit a portfolio with four entries that demonstrate their best practices, one of which shows their accomplishments outside of the classroom—with families, the community, or colleagues—and how that entry affects student learning. Every NBPTS certificate includes one standard for family and community involvement, making clear that exemplary teachers conduct productive partnerships to increase students' success.

QUESTIONS TO DISCUSS

Compare and contrast the NCATE guidelines for new teachers and the NBPTS guidelines for experienced teachers on practices to involve families and communities in children's education.

1. How might the NCATE and NBPTS guidelines encourage new and experienced teachers to develop and conduct activities to involve the families and communities of the students they teach? Give two ideas of how each of the guidelines might influence an individual teacher's practice.
2. How might the NCATE and NBPTS guidelines encourage teachers to contribute to their schools' partnership programs, beyond the work they do with the families of their own students? Give two ideas of how each of the guidelines might influence teachers to work collaboratively with others at their schools.
3. How might the NCATE and NBPTS guidelines encourage teacher education programs to provide undergraduate courses for new teachers and advanced graduate courses for experienced teachers to develop knowledge and skills to involve families in their children's education? Give one idea of how each of the guidelines might affect teacher education.

ACTIVITY

Explore State Requirements for Teaching Credentials

A. Locate on the Internet or otherwise obtain a copy of the requirements for teacher, administrator, or counselor credentials from a state that interests you. Identify the state and credential that you selected.
   1. Do the requirements *explicitly* specify competencies in involving families and communities in children's education?
      If yes:
      a. List the requirements for competencies in partnerships.
      b. Do you think these requirements are adequate for preparing the educator to work productively with families? Explain why or why not.
      c. Suggest one change that you believe would improve the requirements.
      If no:
      a. Do the requirements *implicitly* refer to family and community involvement (e.g., refer to teaching culturally diverse children, which implies also working with students' families)?
      b. Create a state requirement concerning school, family, and community partnerships that you believe would be important for the professional credential you selected.

    c. Explain why you think your recommendation is important and attainable.

B. Obtain a current catalog for your college or university.

   1. List the required and elective courses offered in education that would prepare future teachers, administrators, or counselors to understand students' families and have skills to work with family and community partners in students' education.

   2. Do you think the available courses are adequate for preparing teachers, administrators, counselors, or other professionals to conduct effective programs of family and community involvement?

      a. If yes, give two reasons why you think so.

      b. If no, suggest two additions, revisions (e.g., changes in course titles), or other changes that you think would improve the courses and content on partnerships.

Other Policy Issues

Many other important and provocative policy-related questions have emerged as the field of school, family, and community partnerships has grown. This section discusses a few policies and proposals that could affect state, district, and school policies on school, family, and community partnerships.

COMMENT

Laws that Enable Parents Who Work Outside the Home to Attend Parent-Teacher Conferences and School Meetings

In 2007, 12 states and the District of Columbia passed laws that require employers to allow employees who are parents to take leave time to attend their children's school meetings and events. The laws differed in how "leave time" was defined and regulated, including which employers must comply by size of business, which employees are eligible, the number of hours covered, which school meetings qualify, how employers are notified for approval, whether parents use paid or unpaid time, and other factors.

One report identified the states as California, Hawaii, Illinois, Louisiana, Massachusetts, Minnesota, Nevada, North Carolina, Rhodes Island, Tennessee, Texas, and Vermont (A Better Balance, 2007). At least 13 other states (Colorado, Delaware, Georgia, Iowa, Maryland, Mississippi, New Jersey, New York, Ohio, Pennsylvania, South Carolina, West Virginia, and Wisconsin) have designed, are reviewing, or may reconsider similar legislation.

For example, among the early laws on this topic:

- A 1990 law passed by the state legislature in Minnesota permitted workers who are parents to use up to 16 hours of accrued vacation time, sick leave, or other arranged time to attend parent-teacher conferences or other meetings related to their own children's education or to attend to their children's illnesses.
- A similar bill in California (AB 2590, Chapter 1290 in the Statutes of 1994, expanded in 1997) specified that employers with 25 or more employees should allow each employee (parents, grandparents, or guardians) up to 40 hours of time to participate in their children's schools using vacation time, personal or sick leave, compensatory time, or leave without pay.
- By contrast, a 1992 policy in Virginia pertained only to parents who were employees of the Commonwealth of Virginia. The law provided paid leave of up to eight hours per year, credited to full-time employees each year, with proportional awards of leave time to part-time employees to meet with teachers, attend functions, or volunteer at school. This policy was designed to serve as a model for large businesses in the state to duplicate to demonstrate their commitment to families, children, and schools. Similarly, Tennessee's first law pertained to state employees.

Reports from Minnesota and other states suggest that flexible leave policies promoted greater involvement of parents in their children's education, including more communication with their children's teachers and more involvement of fathers. Research suggests why and how this happens.

An early study by Espinoza (1988) found that employers' typical short-term leave policies affected the involvement of employees who were parents. He studied a phone company where women in clerical jobs were not permitted to take less than a full day of unpaid leave when they wanted to attend parent-teacher conferences. In addition, nonmedical, unexcused absences worked against them when they were considered for transfers and promotions. Thus, the women were doubly disciplined by a loss of pay for more time off than they needed to attend conferences at their children's schools and by penalties for taking time off. They had to balance these factors with the personal and family benefits of attending the conferences to demonstrate good parenting and to learn more about their children's progress and success in school.

Most parents in blue-collar jobs still face difficulties and penalties at work if they take time from work to attend parent-teacher conferences or to volunteer at their children's schools. Most white-collar workers have greater flexibility with compensatory time, flexible leave time, or other arrangements to attend conferences or other meetings and to volunteer, with no loss in pay and no penalties for their actions. Although mothers attend most of these activities, more fathers in white-collar jobs with flexible work conditions participate in school conferences and activities than do fathers in blue-collar jobs that impose more rigid work rules and penalties for absences (Espinoza, 1988).

QUESTIONS TO DISCUSS

1. What changes in behavior, actions, or attitudes might result from state laws that require employers to permit employees who are parents to attend parent-teacher conferences or other required school meetings?
   a. Describe one result that you would expect (regardless of state).
   b. Explain why you would expect the results you described.

ACTIVITY

Examine an Employer's Support for Family Involvement in Education

Does your state, place of employment, or a local company with over 100 employees have laws or guidelines that permit workers to take time to attend parent-teacher conferences or other meetings at their children's schools? Use the Internet and other reference materials, or interview a local employer about this issue.

   A. Identify the employer you selected (e.g., state or business) and your method of inquiry. Address section B-1 (below) if the employer has a parental leave policy and B-2 if not.
   B-1. If the employer you selected *permits* parental leave for meetings at children's schools, report the following:
   1. Describe the formal or informal guidelines and requirements for parental leave.
   2. Are the guidelines used by employees? In what ways or why not?
   3. Do you think the current guidelines are adequate and clear?
      a. If so, how do the guidelines benefit the participating families, students, schools, communities, and the employer?
      b. If not, how would you improve the guidelines or their applications?
                                    OR
   B-2. If the state or business you selected *does not permit* parental leave:
   1. Write a hypothetical guideline that you think is clear, fair, and workable for the state or business you selected.
   2. Explain why the components you included are important for families, students, schools, communities, and the employer.
   C. Whether or not guidelines about parental leave exist:
   1. Give one example of an activity that a school might conduct to adjust the schedule of conferences, meetings, and events to accommodate parents who work full-time or part-time during the day or evening.
   2. Give one example of an activity that a community organization or group (e.g., faith-based organization, neighborhood group) might conduct to assist working parents or single parents to maintain involvement in their children's schools.

Communicate in Languages that Parents Understand

Most federal, state, and district policies call attention to the need to create positive partnerships with all families, including those who do not speak or read English well. In some cases, information from school to home needs to be written more clearly in *English*. In other cases, information needs to be in the languages that parents speak and read at home.

For example, policies to improve the education of children who are limited in English proficiency could be applied to the families of these children. Policies also are needed to communicate with parents who are limited in their proficiency with English, even if their children speak English well. In a modest proposal, I suggested (Hidalgo, Siu, and Epstein, 2004) that the *Lau v. Nichols* (414 U.S. 563, 1974) decision, which required schools to provide non–English-speaking students with equal opportunities to learn in a language they could understand, should be reworded to reflect the results of research on school, family, and community partnerships, as follows (added text is in italics):

> Where the inability of *parents of* school children to speak and understand the English language excludes the children from effective participation in the education program, the school district must take affirmative steps to open its instructional program to these *parents and their* children.

The proposed revision recognizes that language barriers between parents and teachers—like barriers between children and teachers—impede the equal participation of children in educational programs. If parents cannot understand their children's teachers, classroom programs, and communications from the school, then parents cannot effectively guide their children, monitor their work and progress, raise questions or concerns with teachers, or act as advocates for their children. Without clear and understandable communication, parents cannot effectively evaluate the quality of the schools or the education of their children.

The suggestion to extend *Lau v. Nichols* to apply to communications with parents as well as to instruction for children raises questions about schools' responsibilities to ensure that appropriate communications are conducted with *all* parents, whether or not their children are limited in English proficiency. Indeed, the 2002 NCLB's Section 1118 supported this call for more equitable, understandable communications with all parents. The law required states, districts, and schools to communicate policies and involvement practices with all parents "in a language the parents can understand," but added "to the extent practicable." This is a reasonable qualification, but even in schools that serve families who speak many different languages at home, educators, parents, students, and community members are developing innovative ways to inform and involve all families with neighborhood translators, high school student bilingual interpreters, foreign language media, and other connectors (Hutchins et al., 2009). See examples in the section "Success Stories" at www.partnershipschools.org.

1. Do you think it is necessary to ensure two-way communications with non–English-speaking parents and those whose English is limited? Give two reasons why or why not.

2. As states, districts, and schools work to comply with federal and state legislation to communicate with all parents, educators and their family and community partners will have to develop and implement creative practices with parents who do not speak or read English well or speak other languages at home. Give two examples of practical activities that could inform and involve families who do not speak or read English well.

COMMENT

Equity in Out-of-School Activities

Students gain knowledge and build cultural capital when they engage in and enjoy activities, events, and services in school and in their communities. In recent years, after-school programs have become more common, but they do not serve all students at any age or grade level.

Some families cannot afford the transportation, admission fees, lessons, and dues that more affluent families easily invest in their children's education outside of school. Federal, state, and local "vouchers" or certificates could be created for educational and cultural activities that support and enhance children's school learning and development. An "enrichment voucher"—a kind of "food-for-thought stamp"—could be distributed to families who cannot presently provide their children with supplementary learning and talent development activities after school. The subsidies could be funded by governmental or community agencies and distributed to families whose children are eligible for free or reduced-price meals in school. These enrichment vouchers would help families support their children's participation in educational experiences and activities in their communities.

Enrichment or talent development vouchers could cover payments for children's and parents' transportation and admissions to museums, zoos, science centers, and aquariums; dance, music, theater, and other performances; sports activities; and other community cultural activities, classes, and events. The mix of after-school, summer, weekend, vacation, and evening activities would supplement the school curriculum, promote students' success in school, and help develop students' special talents and skills. In addition to traditional after-school programs (which are not available in all communities or for all students), innovative, well-designed enrichment programs could provide care and learning opportunities for children while their parents are at work. In addition, unlike traditional after-school programs, the enrichment vouchers would enable parents and children to attend some activities, events, and programs together as a family on evenings and weekends and during holidays and vacation periods.

Why Vouchers for Community
Enrichment Activities Are Needed

Recognized Need by Parents. In several surveys of families of elementary, middle, and high school students, the workshop topic of most interest to parents was: "How do I help my child develop his or her talents?" This was of particular interest to parents with low incomes who know that their children have special, sometimes hidden, talents that must be discovered and nourished. Many families need to know where or how to gain access to community enrichment programs and services, but may not be able to afford to do so.

Evidence of Long-Term Positive Effects. Studies of middle and high school students and families indicate that student and family visits to museums during the middle grades have long-term effects on student success in high school, even after prior achievement scores are taken into account (Bodilly and Beckett, 2005; Catsambis, 2001; Griffin, 2004). The results suggest that cultural and educational activities may have lasting value for student success in school, but only some students have opportunities to benefit from these experiences.

Unresponsive Community Schedules. Some communities and schools create opportunities for families and children to participate in enriching educational and cultural community activities. These include free days at zoos and museums, community fairs, "first nights" for family New Year's Eve celebrations, and other special events and festivals on holidays and weekends throughout the year. Unfortunately, many families with low incomes and limited English skills do not hear about these offers, do not have transportation to get to them, or do not feel welcome and comfortable at the events. The opportunities are often inaccessible to families and students who need them most. For example, free days at art, science, or history museums may be scheduled when children are in school or when parents are at work, making it difficult or impossible for children and families to attend.

In sum, there are major inequities in opportunities for student learning outside of school and for developing skills and talents that help define who students are as individuals and as members of their communities. How might more equal access to enriching and educational events and opportunities in communities be provided? Enrichment or talent development vouchers is one idea. Expansion of effective after-school programs is another.

Schools, families, and communities must think together in new ways to enrich and extend students' experiences after school, on weekends, and during summer and other vacations, including family cultural activities in their communities. In the absence of direct federal, state, or local subsidies to families for the educational and cultural enrichment of their children, federal, state, or local tax credits or other incentives might be offered to community organizations, agencies, cultural groups, businesses, and others who organize such programs for children and their families.

QUESTIONS TO DISCUSS

1. Do you think communities should offer free admission and transportation to enrichment activities to:
   a. Students who cannot afford these fees? Explain your views.
   b. Families who cannot afford these fees? Explain your views.
2. In your *home community*, which community groups, cultural organizations, businesses, and others might be able to support "enrichment vouchers" for children and for families? Describe one strategy that one of the groups you listed might conduct to enact this modest proposal for all or some students and families.

ACTIVITY

How Do Policies Link to Programs, Practices, and Results of Partnerships?

The readings, comments, questions, and activities in this chapter suggest that federal, state, district, and school policies are needed to sustain strong school-based programs of family and community involvement that engage all parents in their children's education. Policies may affect the results discussed in Part 1 (Chapters 1, 2, and 3) of this volume. Among other results, four major findings of the research studies were:

- More parents become involved when welcoming schools have well-planned goal-linked partnership programs that involve families and the community in ways that support student success in school.
- Teachers are more positive about their work and about family and community involvement in schools that have effective partnership programs.
- All communities have resources that could support students' social, emotional, physical, and talent development and academic achievement in school.
- Students are more successful in school, and more students graduate from high school on time, if their families and communities support their learning and development at every grade level.

A. Write a sentence or two to explain how a good policy at any *one* level—federal, state, district, or school—could affect each of four results listed above.
B. Write a sentence or two to explain how good and linked policies at all four levels—federal, state, district, and school—could strengthen each of the four results listed above.

Read and Report More about State and District Policies on Partnerships

To increase your understanding of policies on partnerships, read at least one article, chapter, or book listed below, or choose a recent, important publication on federal, state, district, or school policies on school, family, and community partnerships.

A. Identify the article, chapter, or book that you selected, the policy level it addresses (federal, state, district, or school), and its full bibliographic reference.

B. Write a one-page summary of the publication. Include a brief overview of the main topic(s) or question(s) that are raised in the publications, data (if any), and main results or conclusions.

C. Write a one-page critique of whether and how the selected publication is useful to educators or policy leaders for improving programs of school, family, and community partnerships.

D. Write two questions that you think should be asked to extend the work that you read. Explain why you think each question is important for improving policies of partnerships.

READING LIST FOR THIS ACTIVITY

Federal Policies

Appleseed. (2006). *It takes a parent: Transforming education in the wake of the No Child Left Behind Act.* Washington, DC: Author.

Moles, O. C. (2005). School-family relations and student learning: Federal education initiatives. In E. N. Patrikakou et al. (Eds.), *School-family partnership for children's success* (pp. 131–147). New York: Teachers College Press.

Sadovnik, A. R., J. O'Day, G. Bohrnstedt, and K. Borman. (Eds.). (2008). *No Child Left Behind and the reduction of the achievement gap: Sociological perspectives on federal educational policy.* New York: Routledge. (See Section IV, "School Choice and Parental Involvement," chapters 10–14.)

Schneider, B. (1996). School, parent, and community involvement: The federal government invests in social capital. In K. Borman, P. Cookson, and A. Sadovnik (Eds.), *Implementing federal education legislation* (pp. 193–213). Norwood, NJ: Ablex.

State Policies

M-Pac. (2005). *A shared responsibility: Recommendations for increasing family and community involvement in schools.* Baltimore: Maryland State Department of Education. www.marylandpublicschools.org/MSDE/programs/familylit/mpac/.

National PTA. (2009). *State laws on family engagement in education*. Chicago: Author.

Redding, S., and P. Sheley. (2005). Grass roots from the top down: The state's role in family-school relationships. In E. N. Patrikakou et al. (Eds.), *School-family partnership for children's success* (pp. 148–163). New York: Teachers College Press.

Epstein, J. L. (2009). Develop district and state leadership for partnerships. In J. L. Epstein et al. (Eds.), *School, family and community partnerships: Your handbook for action* (3rd ed.; pp. 235–273). Thousand Oaks, CA: Corwin.

District Policies

Chavkin, N. F. (1995). Comprehensive districtwide reforms in parent and community involvement programs. In B. Rutherford (Ed.), *Creating family/school partnerships* (pp. 77–106). Columbus: National Middle School Association.

Henderson, A. T., K. L. Mapp, V. R. Johnson, and D. Davies. (2007). Scaling up: Why can't all schools in a district create strong partnerships with families? In A. T. Henderson, K. L. Mapp, V. R. Johnson, and D. Davies, *Beyond the bake sale: The essential guide to family-school partnerships* (pp. 219–250). New York: the New Press.

Sanders, M. G. (2008). Using diverse data to develop and sustain school, family, and community partnerships: A district case study. *Education Management, Administration, and Leadership* 36: 530–545.

Westmoreland, H., H. M. Rosenberg, E. Lopez, and H. Weiss. (2009). *Seeing is believing: Promising practices for how school districts promote family engagement*. Chicago: National PTA and Harvard Family Research Project.

School Policies

Chrispeels, J. H., and K. J. Martin. (2002). Four school leadership teams define their roles within organizational and political structures to improve student learning. *School Effectiveness and School Improvement* 13: 327–365.

Edwards, P. A. (2004). *Children's literacy development: Making it happen through school, family, and community involvement*. Boston: Pearson.

McKenna, M., and D. J. Willms. (1998). The challenge facing parent councils in Canada. *Childhood Education* 74: 378–382.

Sanders, M. G., and S. B. Sheldon. (2009). *Principals matter: A guide to school, family, and community partnerships*. Thousand Oaks, CA: Corwin.

REFERENCES

A Better Balance. (2007). *Fact sheet: Educational leave*. New York: The Work and Family Legal Center.

American Association of Colleges for Teacher Education. (2009). Resolutions. www.aacte.org.

Bodilly, S., and M. K. Beckett. (2005). *Making out-of school time matter: Evidence for an action agenda*. Santa Monica, CA: Rand Corporation.

Catsambis, S. (2001). Expanding knowledge of parental involvement in children's secondary education: Connections with high school seniors' academic success. *Social Psychology of Education* 5: 149–177.

Epstein, J. L. (1991). Paths to partnership: What we can learn from federal, state, district, and school initiatives. *Phi Delta Kappan* 72: 344–349.

Epstein, J. L., et al. (2009). *School, family and community partnerships: Your handbook for action* (3rd ed.). Thousand Oaks, CA: Corwin.

Espinoza, R. (1988). Working parents, employers, and schools. *Educational Horizons* 66: 62–65.

Griffin, J. (2004). Research on students and museums: Looking more closely at the students in school groups. *Science Education* 88: 59–70.

Hidalgo, N., S-F. Siu, and J. L. Epstein. (2004). Research on families, schools, and communities: A multicultural perspective. In J. Banks (Ed.), *Handbook of research on multicultural education* (2nd ed.; pp. 631–655). San Francisco: Jossey Bass.

Hutchins, D. J., et al. (Eds.). (2009). Promising partnership practices 2009. Baltimore: National Network of Partnership Schools at Johns Hopkins University.

McDonnell, L. M., and R. F. Elmore. (1991). Getting the job done: Alternative policy instruments. In A. R. Odden (Ed.), *Education policy implementation* (pp. 157–184). Albany: State University of New York Press.

National Association of State Boards of Education. (2009). *Partners in prevention: The role of school-community partnerships in dropout prevention.* Arlington, VA: NASBE.

National Board for Professional Teaching Standards (NBPTS). (2001). *Early adolescence generalist standards, second edition.* Arlington, VA: Author. (See www.nbpts.org for certificate requirements for all subjects and grade levels.)

National Council for Accreditation of Teacher Education (NCATE). (2008). *Professional standards for the accreditation of teacher preparation institutions.* Washington, D.C.: Author. (See www.ncate.org, and click on "Standards" and then "Program Standards.")

National School Boards Association. (2003). *Guiding principles for business and school partnerships.* Arlington, VA: The Council for Corporate and School Partnerships.

Pfannenstiel, J. C., V. Seitz, and E. Zigler. (2002). Promoting school readiness: The role of the Parents as Teachers Program. *NHSA Dialog: A Research-to-Practice Journal for the Early Intervention Field* 6: 71–86.

Pfannenstiel, J., and D. Seltzer. (1989). New parents as teachers: Evaluation of an early parent education program. *Early Childhood Research Quarterly* 4: 1–18.

Solomon, Z. P. (1991). California's policy on parent involvement: State leadership for local initiatives. *Phi Delta Kappan* 72: 335–362.

Warner, I. (1991). Parents in touch: District leadership for parent involvement. *Phi Delta Kappan* 72: 372–375.

A Practical Framework for Developing Comprehensive Partnership Programs

THIS CHAPTER TURNS FROM THEORY, research, and policy to practice. If theoretical concepts, research results, and policies are clear, then good practices of school, family, and community partnerships should follow. Reading 5.1 serves as a touchstone for Chapters 5, 6, and 7. You will hear "echoes" of themes from the early chapters. Here we focus on the research-based framework of six types of involvement. You will find examples of practices for each type of involvement, discuss challenges that must be met to conduct excellent activities, and learn about the results of well-designed and well-implemented activities. Reading 5.1 also outlines the steps for organizing and maintaining goal-oriented, school-based partnership programs.

The comments, discussions, and activities in this chapter delve deeply into the six types of involvement. There are hundreds of activities that may be selected for each type of involvement. Here we explore ways to understand how each type of involvement contributes to the quality of partnership programs in preschools, elementary, middle, and high schools. The information in this chapter provides the background and understanding needed to resolve difficult challenges that arise for some types of involvement (also see Chapter 6) and for organizing comprehensive programs of school, family, and community partnerships (also see Chapter 7).

Based on research, development, and innovative practice, there are new ways to think about the six types of involvement, including new definitions and designs for workshops for parents, new structures for parent-teacher-student conferences and other communications, new locations for volunteers, new approaches to interactive homework, new responsibilities of parent organizations and leadership, and new goals for community-school collaborations. The basic and advanced activities explored in this chapter should help every teacher and principal connect with more families and community groups. The activities should help every district leader for partnerships understand how to help their schools improve the quality of their partnership programs. By reviewing, discussing, and designing ideas for the six types of involvement, you will begin to see how activities for each type meet the needs of today's families and contribute to the attainment of school improvement goals for student success.

If you are in education, you will be able to use the practical framework of six types of involvement to guide discussions and to customize plans and actions for programs of school, family, and community partnerships in the schools, districts, or states in which you work. If you are in research and evaluation, you will be able to use Reading 5.1 as a base on which to build new studies of the organization and results of specific types of involvement. Such studies will contribute to the field by extending, elaborating, confirming, or contradicting information on the challenges and results of different family and community involvement activities.

School, Family, and Community Partnerships— Caring for the Children We Share*

The way schools care about children is reflected in the way schools care about the children's families. If educators view children simply as *students*, they are likely to see the family as separate from the school. That is, the family is expected to do its job and leave the education of children to the schools. If educators view students as *children*, they are likely to see both the family and the community as partners with the school in children's education and development. Partners recognize their shared interests in and responsibilities for children, and they work together to create better programs and opportunities for students.

There are many reasons for developing school, family, and community partnerships. Partnerships can improve school programs and school climate, provide family services and support, increase parents' skills and leadership, connect families with others in the school and in the community, and help teachers with their work. However, the main reason to create such partnerships is to help all youngsters succeed in school and in later life. When parents, teachers, students, and others view one another as partners in education, a caring community forms around students and begins its work.

What do successful partnership programs look like? How can practices be effectively designed and implemented? What are the results of better communications, interactions, and exchanges across these three important contexts? These questions have challenged research and practice, creating an interdisciplinary field of inquiry into school, family, and community partnerships with "caring" as a core concept.

The field has been strengthened by supporting federal, state, and local policies. Since the late 1980s, Title I of the Elementary and Secondary Education Act has included increasingly specific, research-based mandates and guidelines for programs and practices of family and community involvement. Most recently, the No Child Left Behind Act (NCLB) outlines a "nested" system of school, district, and state requirements for developing research-based programs that involve parents in ways that contribute to student achievement and success in school. These guidelines must be met to qualify for and maintain federal funding.

As important, many states and districts have developed or are preparing their own policies to guide schools in creating more systematic connections with families and with community partners. The policies reflect research results and exemplary practices that show that goals for more effective programs of family and community involvement are attainable (Epstein, 2005a).

---

* By Joyce L. Epstein. Originally published in *Phi Delta Kappan* 76 (1995): 701–712. Updated as Chapter 1.1 in J. L. Epstein et al., *School, Family, and Community Partnerships: Your Handbook for Action*, 3rd ed. (Thousand Oaks, CA: Corwin, 2009).

Underlying all of the policies and programs is a theory of how social organizations connect with each other; a framework of the basic components of school, family, and community partnerships for children's learning; a growing literature on positive and negative results of these connections for students, families, and schools; and an understanding of how to organize excellent programs. In this chapter, I summarize the theory, framework, and guidelines from our research that should help elementary, middle, and high schools and education leaders take steps toward successful partnerships.

OVERLAPPING SPHERES OF INFLUENCE: UNDERSTANDING THE THEORY

Schools make choices. They may conduct only a few communications and interactions with families and communities, keeping the three spheres of influence that directly affect student learning and development relatively separate. Or they may conduct many high-quality communications and interactions designed to bring all three spheres of influence closer together. With frequent interactions among schools, families, and communities, more students will receive common messages from various people about the importance of school, of working hard, of thinking creatively, of helping one another, and of staying in school.

The *external* model of overlapping spheres of influence recognizes that the three major contexts in which students learn and grow—the family, the school, and the community—may be drawn together or pushed apart. In this model, there are some practices that schools, families, and communities conduct separately and some that they conduct jointly to influence children's learning and development.

The *internal* model of the interaction of the three spheres of influence shows where and how complex and essential interpersonal relations and patterns of influence occur between individuals at home, at school, and in the community. These social relationships may be enacted and studied at an *institutional* level (e.g., when a school invites all families to an event or sends the same communications to all families) and at an *individual* level (e.g., when a parent and a teacher meet in conference or talk by phone). Connections between educators or parents and community groups, agencies, and services also can be represented and studied within the model (Epstein, 1987, 1992, 1994).

The model of school, family, and community partnerships locates the student at the center. The inarguable fact is that students are the main actors in their education, development, and success in school. School, family, and community partnerships cannot simply "produce" successful students. Rather, partnership activities may be designed to engage, guide, energize, and motivate students to produce their own successes. The assumption is that if children feel cared for and if they are encouraged to work hard in the role of student, they are more likely to do their best to learn to read, write, calculate, and learn other skills and talents, and to remain in school.

Interestingly, studies indicate that students are crucial for the success of school, family, and community partnerships. Students are often their parents' main source of information about school. In strong partnership programs, teachers help students understand and conduct both traditional communications with families (e.g., delivering memos or report cards) and new communications (e.g., interacting with family members about homework, using e-mail to communicate with teachers, or participating in or leading parent-teacher-student conferences). As we gain more information about the role of students in partnerships, we are developing a more complete understanding of how schools, families, and communities must work with students to increase their chances for success.

HOW THE THEORY WORKS IN PRACTICE

In some schools there still are educators who say, "If the family would just do its job, we could do our job." And there still are families who say, "I raised this child; now it is your job to educate her." These words embody a view of *separate* spheres of influence. Other educators say, "I cannot do my job without the help of my students' families and the support of this community." And some parents say, "I really need to know what is happening in school in order to help my child." These phrases embody the theory of *overlapping spheres of influence*.

In a partnership, teachers and administrators create more *family-like* schools. A family-like school recognizes each child's individuality and makes each child feel special and included. Family-like schools welcome all families, not just those that are easy to reach. In a partnership, parents create more *school-like* families. A school-like family recognizes that each child is also a student. Families reinforce the importance of school, homework, and activities that build student skills and feelings of success.

Communities, too, including groups of parents working together, create *school-like* opportunities, events, and programs that reinforce, recognize, and reward students for good progress, creativity, contributions, and excellence. Communities also create *family-like* settings, services, and events to enable families to better support their children. *Community-minded* families and students help their neighborhoods and other families. The concept of a community school or full-service school is gaining acceptance (Dryfoos and Maguire, 2002). This refers to a place where programs and services for students, parents, and others are offered before, during, and after the regular school day.

Schools and communities talk about programs and services that are family-friendly—meaning that they take into account the needs and realities of family life, are feasible to conduct, and are equitable toward all families. When all these concepts combine, children experience *learning communities* or *caring communities* (Epstein, 1995; Henderson, Mapp, Johnson, and Davies, 2007; Lewis, Schaps, and Watson, 1995).

All of these terms are consistent with the theory of overlapping spheres of influence, but they are not abstract concepts. You will find them daily in conversations, news stories, and celebrations of many kinds. In a family-like school, a teacher might say, "I know when a student is having a bad day and how to help him along."

A student might slip and call a teacher "Mom" or "Dad" and then laugh with a mixture of embarrassment and glee. In a school-like family, a parent might say, "I make sure my daughter knows that homework comes first." A child might raise his hand to speak at the dinner table and then joke about acting as if he were still in school. When communities reach out to students and their families, youngsters might say, "This program really made my schoolwork make sense!" Parents or educators might comment, "This community really supports its schools."

Once people hear about the concepts of family-like schools and school-like families, they remember positive examples of schools, teachers, and places in the community that were "like a family" to them. They may remember how a teacher paid individual attention to them, recognized their uniqueness, or praised them for real progress, just as a parent would. They might recall things at home that were "just like school" and that supported their work as a student, or they might remember community activities that made them feel smart or good about themselves and their families. They will recall that parents, siblings, and other family members engaged in and enjoyed educational activities and took pride in the good schoolwork or homework that they did, just as a teacher would.

HOW PARTNERSHIPS WORK IN PRACTICE

These terms and examples are evidence of the *potential* for schools, families, and communities to create caring educational environments. It is possible to have a school that is excellent academically but ignores families. However, that school will build barriers between teachers, parents, and children that affect school life and learning. It is possible to have a school that is ineffective academically but involves families in many good ways. With its weak academic program, that school will shortchange students' learning. Neither of these schools exemplifies a caring, educational environment that requires academic excellence, good communication, and productive interactions involving the school, all families, and the community.

Some children succeed in school without much family involvement or despite family neglect or distress, particularly if the school has excellent academic and support programs. Teachers, relatives outside the immediate family, other families, and members of the community may provide important guidance and encouragement for these students. As support from school, home, *and* community accumulates, more students feel secure and cared for, understand and adopt the goals of education, work to achieve their full potential, build positive attitudes and school behaviors, and stay in school. The shared interests and investments of schools, families, and communities create the conditions of caring that work to "over-determine" the likelihood of student success (Boykin, 1994).

Any practice can be designed and implemented well or poorly. Even well-implemented partnership practices may not be useful to all families. In a caring school community, participants work continually to improve the nature and effects of partnerships. Although the interactions of educators, parents, students, and community members will not always be smooth and successful, partnership programs establish a base of respect and trust on which to build. Good partnerships encourage questions and debates, and withstand disagreements; provide structures and processes to solve problems; and are maintained—even strengthened—after conflicts and differences have been resolved. Without a firm base of partnerships, the problems and concerns about schools and students that are sure to arise will be harder to solve.

WHAT RESEARCH SAYS

In surveys, experimental interventions, and other field studies involving teachers, parents, and students at the elementary, middle, and high school levels, some important patterns relating to partnerships have emerged.

- Partnerships tend to decline across the grades, *unless* schools and teachers work to develop and implement appropriate practices of partnership at each grade level.
- Affluent communities tend to have more positive family involvement, on average, *unless* schools and teachers in economically distressed communities work to build positive partnerships with their students' families.
- Schools in more economically depressed communities make more contacts with families about the problems and difficulties their children are having, *unless* they work at developing balanced partnership programs that also include contacts about the positive accomplishments of students.
- Single parents, parents who are employed outside the home, parents who live far from the school, and fathers are less involved, on average, at the school building, *unless* the school organizes opportunities for families to become involved and to volunteer at various times and in various places to support the school and their children. These parents may be as involved as other parents with their children at home.

Researchers from the U.S. and other nations have drawn the following conclusions from their studies of family and community involvement:

- Just about all families care about their children, want them to succeed, and are eager to obtain better information from schools and communities in order to remain good partners in their children's education.
- Just about all teachers and administrators would like to involve families, but many do not know how to efficiently and effectively build positive and productive programs, and, consequently, are fearful about trying. This creates a "rhetoric rut," in which educators are stuck expressing support for partnerships without taking necessary actions.

- Just about all students at all levels—elementary, middle, and high school—want their families to be more knowledgeable partners about schooling and are willing to take active roles in assisting communications between home and school. However, students need much better information about how their schools view partnerships and more guidance about how they can conduct important exchanges with their families about school activities, homework, and school decisions.

The summary of results reflect findings in articles and chapters by Baker and Stevenson (1986), Bauch (1988), Becker and Epstein (1982), Booth and Dunn (1996), Burch and Palanki (1994), Clark (1983), Connors and Epstein (1994), Dauber and Epstein (1993), Davies (1991, 1993), Dornbusch and Ritter (1988), Eccles and Harold (1996), Epstein (1986, 1990, 2001, 2005c), Epstein and Connors (1994), Epstein and Dauber (1991), Epstein, Herrick, and Coates, (1996), Epstein and Lee (1995), Epstein and Sanders (2000), Lareau (1989), Lee (1994), Sanders (2005), Scott-Jones (1995), Sheldon (2005, 2007a, b), Sheldon and Van Voorhis (2004), Simon (2004), Van Voorhis (2003), Van Voorhis and Sheldon (2004), and others.

The research results are important because they indicate that caring communities can be built intentionally; that they include families that might not become involved on their own; and that, by their own reports, just about all families, students, and teachers believe that partnerships are important for helping students succeed across the grades.

Good programs of family and community involvement will look different at each site, as individual schools tailor their practices to meet the needs and interests, time and talents, and ages and grade levels of the student. However, our studies have identified some commonalities across successful partnership programs at all grade levels. These include attention to the overlapping spheres of influence on student development; attention to various types of involvement that promote many different opportunities for schools, families, and communities to work together; and an Action Team for Partnerships (ATP) to coordinate each school's work and progress on family and community involvement. The best school-based programs are supported by district leaders for partnerships, whose expertise grows and who help all elementary, middle, and high schools in the district to plan, implement, and evaluate their programs and share best practices (Epstein, 2007).

SIX TYPES OF INVOLVEMENT—SIX TYPES OF CARING

A framework of six major types of involvement is based on the results of many studies and from many years of work by educators and families in elementary, middle, and high schools. The framework (summarized in the accompanying tables) helps educators develop more comprehensive programs of school and family partnerships. The framework also helps researchers locate their questions and results in ways that can inform and improve practice (Epstein, 1992, 1995).

TABLE 5.1 Epstein's Framework of Six Types of Involvement for Comprehensive Programs of Partnership, with Sample Practices

Type 1—Parenting	Type 2—Communicating	Type 3—Volunteering	Type 4—Learning at Home	Type 5—Decision Making	Type 6—Collaborating with the Community
Help all families establish home environment to support children as students.	Design effective forms of school-to-home and home-to-school communications about school programs and their children's progress.	Recruit and organize parent help and support.	Provide information and ideas to families about how to help students at home with homework and other curriculum-related activities, decisions, and planning.	Include parents in school decisions, developing parent leaders and representatives.	Identify and integrate resources and services from the community to strengthen school programs, family practices, and student learning and development.
Sample Practices	**Sample Practices**	**Sample Practices**	**Sample Practices**	**Sample Practices**	**Sample Practices**
Suggestions for home conditions that support learning at each grade level.	Conferences with every parent at least once a year, with follow-ups as needed.	School and classroom volunteer program to help teachers, administrators, students, and other parents.	Information for families on skills required for students in all subjects at each grade.	Active PTA/ PTO or other parent organizations, advisory councils, or committees (e.g., curriculum, safety, personnel) for parent leadership and participation.	Information for students and families on community health, cultural, recreational, social support, and other programs or services.
Workshops, videotapes, and computerized phone messages on parenting and child rearing for each age and grade level.	Language translators assist families, as needed.	Parent room or family center for volunteer work, meetings, and resources for families.	Information on homework policies and how to monitor and discuss schoolwork at home.	Independent advocacy groups to lobby and work for school reform and improvements.	Information on community activities that link to learning skills and talents, including summer programs for students.
Parent education and other courses or training for parents (e.g., GED, college credit, family literacy).	Weekly or monthly folders of student work sent home for review and comments. Parent-student pickup of report cards, with conferences on improving grades.	Annual postcard survey to identify all available talents, times, and locations of volunteers.	Information on how to assist students to improve skills on various class and school assessments. Regular schedule of homework that requires	District-level councils and committees for family and	Service integration through partnerships involving school; civic, counseling, cultural, health,

(continues)

TABLE 5.1   *(continued)*

Sample Practices	Sample Practices	Sample Practices	Sample Practices	Sample Practices	Sample Practices
Family support programs to assist families with health, nutrition, and other services. Home visits at transition points to preschool, elementary, middle, and high school. Neighborhood meetings to help families understand schools and to help schools understand families.	Regular schedule of useful notices, memos, phone calls, newsletters, and other communications. Clear information on choosing schools or courses, programs, and activities within schools. Clear information on all school policies, programs, reforms, and transitions.	Class parent, telephone tree, or other structures to provide all families with needed information. Parent patrols or other activities to aid safety and operation of school programs.	students to discuss and interact with families on what they are learning in class. Calendars with activities for parents and students to do at home or in the community. Family math, science, and reading activities at school. Summer learning packets or activities. Family participation in setting student goals each year and in planning for college or work.	community involvement. Information on school or local elections for school representatives. Networks to link all families with parent representatives.	recreation, and other agencies and organizations; and businesses. Service to the community by students, families, and schools (e.g., recycling, art, music, drama, and other activities for seniors). Participation of alumni in school programs for students.

The six types of involvement are *parenting, communicating, volunteering, learning at home, decision making,* and *collaborating with the community*. Each type of involvement includes many different *practices* of partnership (see Table 5.1). Each type presents particular *challenges* that must be met to involve all families and needed *redefinitions* of some basic principles of involvement (see Table 5.2). Finally, each type is likely to lead to different *results* for students, parents, teaching practices, and school climates (see Table 5.3). Thus, schools must select which practices will help achieve the goals they set for student success and for creating a climate of partnerships. The tables provide examples of practices for each type of involvement, challenges for successful implementation, redefinitions for up-to-date understanding, and results that have been documented and observed in diverse school settings.

CHARTING THE COURSE

The entries in the tables are illustrative. The sample practices displayed in Table 5.1 are a few of hundreds of activities that may be selected or designed for each type of involvement. Although all schools may use the framework of six types as a guide, each school must chart its own course in choosing practices to meet the needs of its families and students.

The challenges in Table 5.2 are a few of many that relate to the sample practices for each type of involvement. There are challenges—that is, problems—for every activity that must be resolved in order to reach and engage all families in the best ways. Often, when one challenge has been met, a new one will emerge.

The redefinitions, also in Table 5.2, redirect old notions so that involvement is not viewed solely as or measured only by "bodies in the building." For example, the table calls for changes in how we define, organize, and conduct workshops, communications, volunteers, homework, decision making, and connections with community. By redefining these familiar terms, it is possible for partnership programs to reach out in new ways to many more families.

The selected results in Table 5.3 should help correct the widespread misperception that any practice that involves families will raise children's achievement test scores. Instead, it can be seen that certain practices are more likely than others to influence students' attitudes, attendance, and behavior in school, whereas other practices will influence skills, test scores, and other achievements over time.

Although students are the main focus of partnerships, the various types of involvement also promote various results for parents and teachers. For example, expected results for parents include not only leadership in decision making, but also confidence about parenting, productive curriculum-related interactions with children, and many interactions with other parents and the school. The expected results for teachers include not only improved parent-teacher conferences and clearer school-home communications, but also helping teachers understand students' families, take new approaches to homework, and make productive connections with families and the community.

The results listed in Table 5.3 have been measured in at least one research study and/or observed as many schools conducted their work on partnerships. The entries are listed in positive terms to indicate the results of well-designed and well-implemented practices. It should be fully understood, however, that results may be negative if poorly designed practices exclude families or create barriers to communication and exchange. More research is needed on the results of specific practices of partnership in various schools, at various grade levels, and for diverse populations of students, families, and teachers. It will be important to confirm, extend, or correct the information on results listed in Table 5.3 to help schools make purposeful choices among practices that foster various types of involvement.

The tables cannot show the connections that occur when one activity promotes several types of involvement simultaneously. For example, volunteers may organize and conduct a clothing swap-shop (Type 3) that allows parents to obtain school uniforms or children's clothes at no cost (Type 1), and community businesses may

TABLE 5.2   Challenges and Redefinitions for the Successful Design and Implementation of the Six Types of Involvement

Type 1—Parenting	Type 2—Communicating	Type 3—Volunteering	Type 4—Learning at Home	Type 5—Decision Making	Type 6—Collaborating with the Community
Challenges	Challenges	Challenges	Challenges	Challenges	Challenges
Provide information to all families who want it or who need it, not just to the few who can attend workshops or meetings at the school building. Enable families to share information about culture, background, and children's talents and needs. Make sure that all information for families is clear, usable, and linked to children's success in school.	Review the readability, clarity, form, and frequency of all memos, notices, and other print and nonprint communications. Consider parents who do not speak English well, do not read well, or need large type. Review the quality of major communications (e.g., the schedule, content, and structure of conferences; newsletters; report cards). Establish clear two-way channels for communications from home to school and from school to home.	Recruit volunteers widely so that *all* families know that their time and talents are welcome. Make flexible schedules for volunteers, assemblies, and events to enable employed parents to participate. Organize volunteer work; provide training; match time and talent with school, teacher, and student needs; and recognize efforts so that participants are productive.	Design and organize a regular schedule of interactive homework (e.g., weekly or bimonthly) that gives students responsibility for discussing important things they are learning and helps families stay aware of the content of their children's classwork. Coordinate family-linked homework activities, if students have several teachers. Involve families with their children in all important curriculum-related decisions.	Include parent leaders from all racial, ethnic, socioeconomic, and other groups in the school. Offer training to enable leaders to serve as representatives of other families, with input from and return of information to all parents. Include students (along with parents) in decision-making groups.	Solve turf problems of responsibilities, funds, staff, and locations for collaborative activities. Inform families of community programs for students, such as mentoring, tutoring, and business partnerships. Ensure equity of opportunities for students and families to participate in community programs or to obtain services. Match community contributions with school goals; integrate child and family services with education.

(continues)

TABLE 5.2   *(continued)*

Type 1— Parenting	Type 2— Communicating	Type 3— Volunteering	Type 4— Learning at Home	Type 5— Decision Making	Type 6— Collaborating with the Community
Redefinitions	Redefinitions	Redefinitions	Redefinitions	Redefinitions	Redefinitions
Workshop to mean more than a meeting about a topic held at the school building at a particular time.	*Communications about school programs and student progress* to mean two-way, three-way, and many-way channels of communication that connect schools, families, students, and the community.	*Volunteer* to mean anyone who supports school goals and children's learning or development in any way, at any place, and at any time, not just during the school day and at the school building.	*Homework* to mean not only work done alone but also interactive activities shared with others at home or in the community, linking schoolwork to real life.	*Decision making* to mean a process of partnership, of shared views and actions toward shared goals, not just a power struggle between conflicting ideas.	*Community* to mean not only the neighborhoods where students' homes and schools are located but also any neighborhoods that influence their learning and development.
Workshop also may mean making information about a topic available in a variety of forms that can be viewed, heard, or read anywhere, anytime.			*Help* at home to mean encouraging, listening, reacting, praising, guiding, monitoring, and discussing, not "teaching" school subjects.	*Parent leader* to mean a real representative, with opportunities and support to hear from and communicate with other families.	*Community* rated not only by low or high social or economic qualities but also by strengths and talents to support students, families, and schools.
					Community means all who are interested in and affected by the quality of education, not just those with children in the schools.

offer discounts on uniforms purchased at the swap-shop (Type 6). The participating parents may serve as volunteers to keep the swap-shop operating, thereby perpetuating activities and results for Types 1, 3, and 6.

As another example, an after-school program may be conducted by parent and community volunteers and the community's Parks and Recreation Department, combining Types 3 and 6. The after-school program also serves as a Type 1 activity because it assists families in supervising their children in a safe and purposeful place. The program also may alter the way homework is completed and how interactions about homework are conducted at home between students and parents (Type 4). Research is needed to understand the combination of types of involvement in complex activities. Practitioners should realize that various practices may activate several types of involvement.

The tables also simplify the influences that produce results over time. For example, the involvement of families with children in reading at home may make students more strongly motivated to read and to give more attention to reading instruction

TABLE 5.3   Expected Results for Students, Parents, and Teachers of the Six Types of Involvement

Type 1—Parenting	Type 2—Communicating	Type 3—Volunteering	Type 4—Learning at Home	Type 5—Decision Making	Type 6—Collaborating with the Community
Results for Students	Results for Students	Results for Students	Results for Students	Results for Students	Results for Students
Awareness of family supervision; respect for parents. Positive personal qualities, habits, beliefs, and values, as taught by family. Balance between time spent on chores, on other activities, and on homework. Good or improved attendance. Awareness of importance of school.	Awareness of own progress and of actions needed to maintain or improve grades. Understanding of school policies on behavior, attendance, and other areas of student conduct. Informed decisions about courses and programs. Awareness of own role in partnerships, serving as courier and communicator.	Skill in communicating with adults. Increased learning of skills that receive tutoring or targeted attention from volunteers. Awareness of many skills, talents, occupations, and contributions of parents and other volunteers.	Gains in skills, abilities, and test scores linked to homework and classwork. Homework completion. Positive attitude toward schoolwork. View of parent as more similar to teacher and home as more similar to school. Self-concept of ability as learner.	Awareness of representation of families in school decisions. Understanding that student rights are protected. Specific benefits linked to policies enacted by parent organizations and experienced by students.	Increased skills and talents through enriched curricular and extracurricular experiences. Awareness of careers and options for future education and work. Specific benefits linked to programs, services, resources, and opportunities that connect students with community.

(continues)

in school. This, in turn, may help students maintain or improve their daily reading skills in class and their reading report card grades. Over time, good classroom reading instruction and ongoing home support should increase students' skills and confidence in reading and significantly improve their reading achievement test scores. The time between a Family Reading Night or other family involvement activities in reading and the time that students' increase their reading achievement test scores will vary, depending on the quality and quantity of the reading-related activities in school and out.

Consider one more example. Studies using longitudinal data and rigorous statistical controls on student background and prior influences found important benefits

TABLE 5.3   *(continued)*

Type 1— Parenting	Type 2— Communicating	Type 3— Volunteering	Type 4— Learning at Home	Type 5— Decision Making	Type 6— Collaborating with the Community
Results for Parents	Results for Parents	Results for Parents	Results for Parents	Results for Parents	Results for Parents
Understanding of and confidence about parenting, child and adolescent development, and changes in home conditions for learning as children proceed through school. Awareness of own and others' challenges in parenting. Feeling of support from school and other parents.	Understanding school programs and policies. Monitoring and awareness of child's progress. Responding effectively to students' problems. Interactions with teachers and ease of communications with school and teachers.	Understanding teacher's job, increased comfort in school, and carryover of school activities at home. Self-confidence about ability to work in school and with children or to take steps to improve own education. Awareness that families are welcome and valued at school. Gains in specific skills of volunteer work.	Knowledge of how to support, encourage, and help student at home each year. Discussions of school, classwork, and homework. Understanding of instructional program each year and of what child is learning in each subject. Appreciation of teaching skills. Awareness of child as a learner.	Input into policies that affect child's education. Feeling of ownership of school. Awareness of parents' voices in school decisions. Shared experiences and connections with other families. Awareness of school, district, and state policies.	Knowledge and use of local resources by family and child to increase skills and talents or to obtain needed services. Interactions with other families in community activities. Awareness of school's role in the community and of the community's contributions to the school.

(continues)

TABLE 5.3   (continued)

Type 1—Parenting	Type 2—Communicating	Type 3—Volunteering	Type 4—Learning at Home	Type 5—Decision Making	Type 6—Collaborating with the Community
Results for Teachers	Results for Teachers	Results for Teachers	Results for Teachers	Results for Teachers	Results for Teachers
Understanding families' backgrounds, cultures, concerns, goals, needs, and views of their children	Increased diversity and use of communications with families and awareness of own ability to communicate clearly	Readiness to involve families in new ways, including those who do not volunteer at school	Better design of homework assignments	Awareness of parent perspectives as a factor in policy development and decisions	Awareness of community resources to enrich curriculum and instruction
Respect for families' strengths and efforts	Appreciation and use of parent network for communications	Awareness of parent talents and interests in school and children	Respect of family time	View of equal status of family representatives on committees and in leadership roles	Openness to and skill in using mentors, business partners, community volunteers, and others to assist students and augment teaching practice
Understanding of student diversity	Increased ability to elicit and understand family views on children's programs and progress	Greater individual attention to students, with help from volunteers	Recognition of equal helpfulness of single parent, dual income, and less formally educated families in motivating and reinforcing student learning		
Awareness of own skills to share information on child development			Satisfaction with family involvement and support		Knowledgeable, helpful referrals of children and families to needed services

for high school students' attitudes, behaviors, and report card grades as a result of continuing several types of family involvement from middle school through high school (Lee, 1994; Simon, 2004). However, achievement test scores, stable by 12th grade, were not greatly affected by partnerships at the high school level. By contrast, elementary school students' math achievement test scores increased significantly when their teachers assigned interactive math homework (Epstein, 2005b; Van Voorhis, in press). Even with prior math test scores accounted for, elementary students' standardized achievement can be influenced by effective homework designs and interactions with parents. In the future, longitudinal studies of practical interventions at different grade levels will increase an understanding of the complex patterns of results that can develop from various partnership activities (Epstein, 1991; Epstein and Dauber, 1995; Epstein and Sanders, 2000; Henderson and Mapp, 2002; Sheldon, 2009).

The six types of involvement guide the development of a balanced, comprehensive program of partnerships, including opportunities for family involvement at school, at home, and in the community, with potentially important results for students, parents, and teachers. The results will depend on the particular activities that are implemented and the quality of the design, implementation, and outreach.

ACTION TEAMS FOR PARTNERSHIPS

Who will work to create caring school communities that are based on concepts of partnership? How will the necessary work on all six types of involvement get done? Although a principal or a teacher may be a leader in working with some families and with some community groups, one person cannot create a lasting, comprehensive program that involves all families as their children progress through the grades.

From the hard work of many educators and families in hundreds of schools and districts, we have learned that, along with clear policies and strong support from district and state leaders and from school principals, an Action Team for Partnerships (ATP) in each school is an essential structure. The ATP—a committee of the school council or school improvement team—is dedicated to improving plans and practices of family and community involvement. The ATP guides the development of a comprehensive partnership program linked to school improvement goals for student success. Using the framework of six types of involvement, the ATP integrates all family and community connections that occur in the school in a single, unified plan and program.

The trials and errors and the efforts and insights of hundreds of schools across the country have helped identify five important steps that any school can take to develop more positive school, family, and community connections.

Step 1: Create an Action Team for Partnerships

A team approach is an appropriate and effective way to build school, family, and community partnerships. The Action Team for Partnerships (ATP) is an "action arm" of a School Council or School Improvement Team, if one exists in the school. The ATP takes responsibility for assessing present family and community involvement practices, organizing options for new partnerships, implementing selected activities, delegating leadership for other activities, evaluating next steps, and continuing to improve and coordinate practices for all six types of involvement. Although the members of the ATP lead some of the activities, they are assisted by other teachers, parents, students, administrators, and community members who take leadership or support roles for planned partnerships.

The ATP team should include at least two or three teachers from different grade levels, departments, or specialties; at least two or three parents from different neighborhoods or cultural groups with children in different grade levels; and at least one administrator. Teams may also include at least one member from the community at large and, at the high school level, at least two students from different grade levels. Others who are central to the school's work with families also may be included as team members, such as a school counselor, social worker, nurse, school psychologist, cafeteria worker, secretary, or custodian. Such diverse membership ensures that the team will plan activities that take into account the various needs, interests, and talents of teachers, parents, the school, and students.

The chair (or, better, co-chairs) of the action team should be members who have the respect of the other members, as well as good communication skills and an understanding of the partnership approach. At least one member of the action team should also serve on the school council, school improvement team, or other advisory body.

Members of the ATP may serve as chair or co-chairs of subcommittees organized to implement family and community involvement activities on specific school improvement goals (e.g., family and community involvement to help improve students' reading, math, and behavior, and to improve the school's climate of partnerships) or on the six types of involvement. A team with at least 6 members (or as many as 12 or more) ensures that responsibilities for leadership can be shared and delegated so that one person is not overburdened with all family and community involvement activities. The work of the action team also ensures that plans for partnership will continue even if members move or change schools or positions. Members may serve renewable terms of two to three years, with the replacement of members who leave in the interim. Other thoughtful variations in assignments and activities may be created by small or large schools using this process. See Chapter 7 for details on organizing effective Action Teams for Partnerships.

In the first phase of our field work in 1987, projects were led by "project directors" (usually teachers) and were focused on one type of involvement at a time. Some schools succeeded in developing good partnerships over several years, but others were thwarted if the project director moved, if the principal changed, or if the project grew larger than one person could handle. Other schools were guided to try a team approach to work on many types of involvement simultaneously, and to focus on activities that create a climate of partnerships and that help students reach important results in learning and behavior. These schools showed that the team approach was the best structure for strong and sustainable program. Now, a team approach guides all of our research and development projects in elementary, middle, and high schools.

Step 2: Obtain Funds and Other Support

A modest budget is needed to guide and support the activities planned by each school's Action Team for Partnerships. Funds also are needed for district leaders for partnerships who will help each school with its plans and programs of family and community involvement. Investments are needed at the state level for leadership on partnerships as well.

Funds for schools, districts, and states may come from a number of sources. These include federal, state, and local programs that mandate, request, or support family involvement, including Title I and other "titled" funding streams. At the district level, funds are needed to support the salaries of a director and facilitators who help all schools develop their partnership programs, and for program costs (e.g., staff development and training workshops on school, family, and community partnerships; parent coordinators or liaisons to serve as ATP chairs or co-chairs; activities in schools' One-Year Action Plans for Partnerships). In addition, local school-business partnerships, school discretionary funds, and fundraising targeted to the schools' partnership programs can support the plans and activities of school-based ATPs. Recent data indicate that schools' ATPs need at least $2,500 per year to support activities in a typical, start-up Action Plan for Partnerships. See details on levels and sources of funds for partnership programs at the school, district, and state levels in Chapter 4.

The ATP also must have sufficient time and social support to do its work. This requires explicit support from the principal and from district leaders for team training, meetings to plan and evaluate activities, and time to conduct the activities in the annual plan for partnerships. Time during the summer also may be used to plan new approaches and projects for the start of the new school year.

Step 3: Identify Starting Points

Most schools have some teachers and administrators who conduct some practices of partnership with some families some of the time. How can good practices be organized and extended so that all teachers at all grade levels inform and involve all families in ways that support student learning and success in school? How can some schoolwide involvement activities build a sense of community with all students and families?

The Action Team for Partnerships (ATP) works to systematize and improve typically haphazard patterns of involvement. The ATP starts by gathering information about the school's current practices of partnership, along with the views, experiences, and wishes of teachers, parents, administrators, and students (see "Starting Points" and "Measure of School, Family, and Community Partnerships" in Epstein et al. [2009] for two ways of assessing the nature and extent of present practices).

Starting points also may be identified in other ways, depending on available resources, time, and talents. For example, the ATP might use formal questionnaires (Epstein, Connors, and Salinas, 1993; Epstein and Salinas, 1993; Sheldon and Epstein, 2007) or telephone interviews to survey teachers, administrators, parents, and students, if funds and experts are available to process, analyze, and report survey data. Or the ATP might organize a panel of teachers, parents, and students to speak at a PTA or PTO meeting to discuss the goals and desired activities for improving family and community involvement. Structured discussions may be conducted at a series of principal's breakfasts for representative groups of teachers, parents, students, and others; random-sample phone calls may also be used to collect suggestions and reactions; and formal focus groups may be convened to gather ideas about school, family, and community partnerships at the school.

What questions should be addressed to take stock of present practices and to plan next steps? Regardless of how information is gathered, the following areas should be part of any information gathering:

Present strengths. Which practices of school, family, and community partnerships are, presently, working well for the school as a whole? For individual teachers and specific grade levels? For which types of involvement? On what school goals for student success?

Needed changes. Ideally, how do we want school, family, and community partnerships to work at this school three years from now? Which present practices should continue, and which should change?

Expectations. What do teachers expect of families? What do families expect of teachers and other school personnel? What do students expect of their families and teachers?

Sense of community. Which families are presently involved, and which are not yet engaged with the school and with their children's education? Who are the "hard-to-reach" families? What might be done to communicate with and engage these families?

Links to goals. How are students doing on measures of academic achievement, including test scores and report card grades? On measures of attitudes and attendance? On other indicators of success? How might family and community connections assist the school in helping more students reach higher goals and achieve greater success?

Step 4: Develop a One-Year Action Plan

With the information on a school's starting points and with understanding of the goals and ideas for partnerships collected from teachers, administrators, parents, and students, the Action Team for Partnerships (ATP) will develop a detailed One-Year Action Plan for Partnerships. The annual action plan includes a set of selected goals or objectives, desired results, measures to assess results, specific involvement activities that will be implemented, improved, or maintained each year; dates scheduled; types of involvement; actions needed to prepare the activity; people responsible for implementing the activities and those assisting; funds or resources required; and other important details.

The One-Year Action Plan for Partnerships should be shared with the school council or school improvement team, parent organization, all teachers, and, in various ways, all parents and students. Corrections and additions from the various groups contribute to a final plan for partnerships for the school year.

If the ATP takes one step forward each year to improve family and community involvement for each of the specific academic and behavioral goals in the One-Year Action Plan, it will continually improve the quality of partnerships and student success. If the ATP makes one step forward each year on each of the six types of involvement, it will take 18 steps forward over three years to improve the school climate for partnerships. Good plans and actions lead to a more comprehensive, coordinated, and goal-oriented program of school, family, and community partnerships.

In short, the ATP, with input from others, will complete an annual, detailed action plan for partnerships that addresses these issues:

Details. What will be done each year to implement activities that involve families in ways linked to specific goals for student success? What activities for the six types of involvement will be activated? How will these activities also create a welcoming school climate for all students and their families? What, specifically, will be accomplished over the next school year to improve family and community involvement?

Responsibilities. Who will be responsible for developing and implementing the practices of partnership that are in the One-Year Action Plan for Partnerships? Will staff development or other guidance be needed to plan and implement activities? How will teachers, administrators, parents, and students be supported and recognized for their work? What role will district leaders for partnership or others play in assisting schools' ATPs with activities?

Costs. What costs are associated with implementing the planned activities? What sources will provide the needed funds? Will small grants or other special budgets be needed? What funds and in-kind contributions are needed to maintain and improve the activities from year to year?

Evaluation. How well are activities implemented? What are the effects of each activity on the school climate and/or on students, teachers, and families? What indicators will be used to measure the quality of implementation and the results?

Step 5: Continue Planning, Evaluating, and Improving Programs

The ATP should schedule an annual presentation and celebration of progress at the school so that all teachers, families, and students know about the work that was done each year to build partnerships. Or a district coordinator for school, family, and community partnerships may arrange an annual midyear or end-of-year conference for all schools in the district. At a district-wide annual meeting, ATPs from all schools can display and share their accomplishments and best practices for involving families and the community in ways that improve students' attitudes, behaviors, and achievements in specific subjects. Panels of ATP members may discuss serious challenges and solutions for reaching all families, share ideas for the six types of involvement, and gather ideas for improving programs in the next school year.

In short, the ATP considers the following questions: How will the ATP increase the number of families who are partners with the school in their children's education over the next school year? What opportunities will be arranged for teachers, parents, and students to come together as individual teachers, grade levels, or a whole school to support student learning and development? How will the ATP evaluate, strengthen, and sustain the school's partnership program to continue to improve results for students?

Each year, the Action Team for Partnerships develops a new and improved One-Year Action Plan for Partnerships for the next school year. The ATP shares its plans and gathers input so that educators, families, students, and the community are aware of progress, new plans, and how they can help.

CHARACTERISTICS OF SUCCESSFUL PROGRAMS

Hundreds of schools have taken these five steps over the years. Their experiences helped identify some important properties of successful partnership programs.

Incremental Progress

Progress on partnerships is incremental, including more families each year in ways that benefit more students. Like reading or math programs, assessment programs, sports programs, or other school investments, partnership programs take time to develop, and must be periodically reviewed, evaluated, and continuously improved. Schools and districts in our projects have shown that some progress can be made immediately, but it tends to take at least three years to demonstrate that a partnership program is a "permanent" component of school and district organization.

The development of an excellent partnership program is a process, not a single event. All teachers, families, students, and community groups are unlikely to participate all at once. Not all activities that are implemented the first time will succeed in engaging all families. But with good planning, thoughtful implementation, well-designed activities, thoughtful evaluations, and pointed improvements, more and more families and teachers can learn to work with one another on behalf of the children they share.

Similarly, not all students instantly improve their attitudes or achievements when their families become involved in their education. After all, student learning depends mainly on good curricula, engaging and appropriate instruction, the students' interests and commitment, and the work the students' complete. However, with a well-implemented program of partnerships, more students receive support from their families, and more will be motivated to work harder in school.

Connections to Curricular and Instructional Reform

A program of school, family, and community partnerships that focuses on children's learning and development is an important component of curricular and instructional reform. For example, helping families understand, monitor, and interact with students on homework is an extension of classroom instruction. Volunteers who bolster and broaden student skills, talents, and interests extend classroom learning. Improving the content and conduct of parent-teacher-student conferences and goal-setting activities are important aspects of curricular reform; family support and family understanding of child and adolescent development and school curricula are necessary to assist students as learners. All of these activities—homework-help interventions, volunteers and tutors linked to student learning, the redesign of parent-teacher-student conferences, and similar activities—are part of curricular and instructional reform and should be supported with the appropriate federal, state, and local funds for school improvement.

One important new direction for partnership programs connects family and community involvement directly to the school improvement plan. This is done by focusing family and community involvement on specific curricular and instructional goals for student learning and by appending the One-Year Action Plan for Partnerships to the annual school improvement plan. These organizational changes move partnerships from being peripheral and unplanned activities for parents to being official components of a school's program for student learning and development.

Redefining Professional Development and Shared Leadership

The action team approach to partnerships changes the definition of "professional development" because teachers, administrators, parents, and other partners are trained together, as a team, to develop, implement, evaluate, and continue to improve practices of partnership. The development of a well-functioning Action Team for Partnerships is not the result of a "dose" of inservice education, but is a long-term process of developing and extending educators' and parents' talents and capacities for organizing and conducting effective partnerships. Teachers, administrators, parents, and others on the Action Team for Partnerships must be helped to become the experts on this topic for their school. With this definition, program development can be supported by various federal, state, and local funds for professional development for school improvement.

An effective program of family and community involvement also stretches the definition of *shared leadership*—an important concept in educational administration. Usually, the term means that teachers will share leadership with principals and specialists in improving school organization, curriculum, and instruction. In effective partnership programs, shared leadership means that all members on the team of teachers, administrators, parents, and community partners will take responsibility for developing, implementing, evaluating, and continually improving plans and practices of family and community involvement.

Developing excellent partnership programs in all districts and schools would be easier if educators came to their positions prepared to work productively with families and communities. Courses or classes are needed in preservice teacher education, continuing studies, and advanced degree programs that define professional work in terms of partnerships. Today, most teachers, principals, counselors, and district leaders enter their professions without an understanding of family backgrounds, concepts of caring, the framework of six types of involvement, or partnership program development. Thus, most principals and district leaders are not prepared to guide school teams in developing, evaluating, and sustaining effective partnership programs.

Schools, colleges, and departments of education that prepare future teachers, administrators, and others who work with children and families should identify where in the curriculum students are asked to study and learn the theory, research, policy, and practical ideas of partnerships, or where these topics should be added to better prepare their graduates for their professional work (Chavkin and Williams, 1988; Christenson and Conoley, 1992; Epstein, 2001; Epstein and Sheldon, 2006; Hinz, Clark, and Nathan, 1992; Swap, 1993).

Even with improved preservice and advanced coursework, however, each school's Action Team for Partnerships and other practicing educators will need inservice education and targeted team training to tailor plans for partnerships to the needs and goals of the teachers, families, and students in the school. The framework and guidelines in this chapter can be used by thoughtful educators to organize high-quality, ongoing professional development on partnerships, school by school.

THE CORE OF CARING

Years ago, a school in Baltimore named its partnership program the I Care Program. It developed an I Care Parent Club that fostered fellowship and leadership of families, an I Care newsletter, and many other events and activities. Other schools also gave catchy, positive names to their programs to indicate that families, students, teachers, and community partners were developing relationships and conducting actions to assist all students toward success.

Interestingly, synonyms for *caring* match the six types of involvement:

Type 1—Parenting: *Supporting, nurturing, loving,* and *child raising*
Type 2—Communicating: *Relating, reviewing,* and *overseeing*
Type 3—Volunteering: *Supervising* and *fostering*
Type 4—Learning at Home: *Managing, recognizing,* and *rewarding*
Type 5—Decision Making: *Contributing, considering,* and *judging*
Type 6—Collaborating with the Community: *Sharing* and *giving*

Underlying all six types of involvement are two defining synonyms of *caring*: *trusting* and *respecting*. Of course, the varied meanings are interconnected, but it is striking that various elements of caring are associated with activities for the six types of involvement. If all six types of involvement are operating well in a school's program of partnerships, then all of these caring behaviors could be activated to assist children's learning and development.

SUMMARY: BATTLEGROUND OR HOMELAND?

Despite real progress in many states, districts, and schools over the past few years, there still are too many schools where educators do not understand the families of their students. There still are too many families who do not understand their children's schools, and too many communities that do not understand or assist their schools, families, or students. There still are too many districts and states without the policies, departments, leadership, staff, and fiscal support needed to help all schools develop excellent and permanent programs of partnership.

Relatively small financial investments are needed to support district leaders for partnerships and the work of school-based Action Teams for Partnerships. Yet, those investments yield significant returns for all schools, teachers, families, and students. Educators who have led the way in constructing research-based programs with the necessary components provide evidence that any state, district, or school can create similar programs.

Schools have choices. There are two opposing approaches to involving families in schools and in their children's education. One approach emphasizes conflict and views the school as a battleground. The conditions and relationships in this kind of environment guarantee power struggles and disharmony. The other approach emphasizes partnership and views the school as a homeland. The conditions and relationships in this kind of environment invite mutual respect, shared leadership on partnerships, and direct energies to activities that foster student learning and development. Even when conflicts flare, however, peace must be restored, and the partners in children's education must work together.

NEXT STEPS: STRENGTHENING PARTNERSHIPS

Collaborative work and thoughtful give-and-take among researchers, policy leaders, educators, parents, and community partners are responsible for the progress that has been made over the past two decades in understanding and developing school, family, and community partnerships. Similar collaborations will be important for future progress in this and other areas of school reform.

To promote these approaches, I established the National Network of Partnership Schools (NNPS) at Johns Hopkins University in 1996. NNPS provides school, district, state, and other education leaders with research-based tools and guidelines to help elementary, middle, and high schools plan, implement, and maintain comprehensive and goal-oriented programs of school, family, and community partnerships. With the efforts of many colleagues, NNPS has been able to encourage and guide educators, parents, and other community leaders to organize stronger program of family and community involvement.

Partnership schools, districts, and states have worked hard to put the recommendations of this chapter into practice in ways that are appropriate for their locations. Implementation includes applying the theory of overlapping spheres of influence, the framework of six types of involvement, and the action team approach. Systemic advances include district leaders who assist all schools to use teamwork and develop and sustain partnership programs. The researchers and staff of NNPS at Johns Hopkins University disseminate information, guidelines, and newsletters; offer e-mail and website assistance; hold annual conferences; and conduct workshops to help state and district coordinators and school leaders learn new strategies and share successful ideas. The members of NNPS share best practices at all policy levels in annual collections of *Promising Partnership Practices* (Hutchins et al., 2009). With a strong research base, NNPS guides state and district leaders, educators, and parents to recognize their common interests in the children they share, and to work together, with care, to strengthen programs of family and community involvement that contribute to student success.

REFERENCES

Baker, D. P., and D. L. Stevenson. (1986). Mothers' strategies for children's school achievement: Managing the transition to high school. *Sociology of Education* 59: 156–166.

Bauch, P. A. (1988). Is parent involvement different in private schools? *Educational Horizons* 66: 78–82.

Becker, H. J., and J. L. Epstein. (1982). Parent involvement: A study of teacher practices. *Elementary School Journal,* 83: 85–102.

Booth, A., and J. F. Dunn, J. F. (Eds.). (1996). *Family-school links: How do they affect educational outcomes?* Mahwah, NJ: Lawrence Erlbaum.

Boykin, A. W. (1994). Harvesting culture and talent: African American children and educational reform. In R. Rossi (Ed.), *Schools and students at risk* (pp. 116–139). New York: Teachers College Press.

Burch, P., and A. Palanki. (1994). Action research on family-school-community partnerships. *Journal of Emotional and Behavioral Problems* 1: 16–19.

Chavkin, N., and D. Williams. (1988). Critical issues in teacher training for parent involvement. *Educational Horizons* 66: 87–89.

Christenson, S. L., and J. C. Conoley. (Eds.). (1992). *Home-school collaboration: Enhancing children's academic competence.* Silver Spring, MD: National Association of School Psychologists.

Clark, R. M. (1983). *Family life and school achievement: Why poor Black children succeed or fail.* Chicago: University of Chicago Press.

Connors, L. J., and J. L. Epstein. (1994). *Taking stock: The views of teachers, parents, and students on school, family, and community partnerships in high schools* (Center Report 25). Baltimore: Center on Families, Communities, Schools and Children's Learning, Johns Hopkins University.

Dauber, S. L., and J. L. Epstein. (1993). Parents' attitudes and practices of involvement in inner-city elementary and middle schools. In N. Chavkin (Ed.), *Families and schools in a pluralistic society* (pp. 53–71). Albany: State University of New York Press.

Davies, D. (1991). Schools reaching out: Family, school and community partnerships for student success. *Phi Delta Kappan* 72: 376–382.

———. (1993). A more distant mirror: Progress report on a cross-national project to study family-school-community partnerships. *Equity and Choice* 19: 41–46.

Dornbusch, S. M., and P. L. Ritter. (1988). Parents of high school students: A neglected resource. *Educational Horizons* 66: 75–77.

Dryfoos, J., and S. Maguire. (2002). *Inside full-service community schools.* Thousand Oaks, CA: Corwin.

Eccles, J. S., and R. D. Harold. (1996). Family involvement in children's and adolescents' schooling. In A. Booth and J. F. Dunn (Eds.), *Family-school links: How do they affect educational outcomes?* (pp. 3–34). Mahwah, NJ: Lawrence Erlbaum.

Epstein, J. L. (1986). Parents' reactions to teacher practices of parent involvement. *Elementary School Journal,* 86: 277–294.

———. (1987). Toward a theory of family-school connections: Teacher practices and parent involvement. In K. Hurrelmann, F. Kaufmann, and F. Losel (Eds.), *Social intervention: Potential and constraints* (pp. 121–136). New York: DeGruyter.

———. (1990). Single parents and the schools: Effects of marital status on parent and teacher interactions. In M. Hallinan, *Change in societal institutions* (pp. 91–121). New York: Plenum.

———. (1991). Effects on student achievement of teacher practices of parent involvement. In S. Silvern, *Literacy through family, community, and school interaction* (pp. 261–276). Greenwich CT: JAI.

———. (1992). School and family partnerships. In M. Alkin (Ed.), *Encyclopedia of educational research* (6th ed.; pp. 1139–1151). New York: Macmillan.

———. (1994). Theory to practice: School and family partnerships lead to school improvement and student success. In C. L. Fagnano and B. Z. Werber (Eds.), *School, family and community interaction: A view from the firing lines* (pp. 39–52). Boulder: Westview Press.

———. (1995). School/family/community partnerships: Caring for the children we share. *Phi Delta Kappan* 76: 701–712.

———. (1996). Perspectives and previews on research and policy for school, family, and community partnerships. In A. Booth and J. F. Dunn (Eds.), *Family-school links: How do they affect educational outcomes?* (pp. 209–246). Mahwah, NJ: Lawrence Erlbaum.

———. (2001). *School, family, and community partnerships: Preparing educators and improving schools, first edition.* Boulder: Westview.

———. (2005a). Attainable goals? The spirit and letter of the No Child Left Behind Act on parental involvement. *Sociology of Education* 78: 179–182.

———. (2005b). Results of the Partnership Schools-CSR model for student achievement over three years. *Elementary School Journal* 106: 151–170.

———. (2005c). School, family, and community partnerships in the middle grades. In T. O. Erb (Ed.), *This We Believe in action: Implementing successful middle level schools* (pp. 77–96). Westerville, OH: National Middle School Association.

———. (2007). Research meets policy and practice: How are school districts addressing NCLB requirements for parental involvement? In A. R. Sadovnik, J. O'Day, G. Bohrnstedt, and K. Borman (Eds.), *No Child Left Behind and the reduction of the achievement gap: Sociological perspectives on federal educational policy* (pp. 267–279). New York: Routledge.

Epstein, J. L., and L. J. Connors. (1994). *Trust fund: School, family, and community partnerships in high schools* (Center Report 24). Baltimore: Center on Families, Communities, Schools and Children's Learning, Johns Hopkins University.

Epstein, J. L., L. J. Connors, and K. C. Salinas. (1993). *High school and family partnerships: Surveys and summaries (Questionnaires for teachers, parents, and students).* Baltimore: Center on School, Family, and Community Partnerships, Johns Hopkins University.

Epstein, J. L., and S. L. Dauber. (1991). School programs and teacher practices of parent involvement in inner-city elementary and middle schools. *Elementary School Journal* 91: 289–303.

———. (1995). Effects on students of an interdisciplinary program linking social studies, art, and family volunteers in the middle grades. *Journal of Early Adolescence* 15: 237–266.

Epstein, J. L., S. C. Herrick, and L. Coates. (1996). Effects of summer home learning packets on student achievement in language arts in the middle grades. *School Effectiveness and School Improvement* 7: 93–120.

Epstein, J. L., and S. Lee. (1995). National patterns of school and family connections in the middle grades. In B. A. Ryan, G. R. Adams, T. P. Gullotta, R. P. Weissberg, and R. L. Hampton (Eds.), *The family-school connection: Theory, research and practice* (pp. 108–154). Thousand Oaks, CA: Sage.

Epstein, J. L., and K. C. Salinas. (1993). *School and family partnerships: Surveys and summaries.* Baltimore: Center on School, Family, and Community Partnerships, Johns Hopkins University.

Epstein, J. L., and M. G. Sanders. (2000). School, family, and community connections: New directions for social research. In M. Hallinan (Ed.), *Handbook of sociology of education* (pp. 285–306). New York: Plenum Press.

———. (2002). Family, school, and community partnerships. In M. Bornstein (Ed.), *Handbook of parenting* (2nd ed.; pp. 407–437). Mahwah, NJ: Lawrence Erlbaum.

Epstein J. L., and S. B. Sheldon. (2006). Moving forward: Ideas for research on school, family, and community partnerships. In C. F. Conrad and R. Serlin (Eds.), *SAGE handbook for research in education: Engaging ideas and enriching inquiry* (pp. 117–137). Thousand Oaks, CA: Sage.

Henderson, A., and K. L. Mapp. (2002). *A new wave of evidence: The impact of school, family, and community connections on student achievement.* Austin, TX: Southwest Educational Development Laboratory.

Henderson, A. T., K. L. Mapp, V. R. Johnson, and D. Davies. (2007). *Beyond the bake sale.* New York: New Press.

Hinz, L., J. Clarke, and J. Nathan. (1992). *A survey of parent involvement course offerings in Minnesota's undergraduate preparation programs.* Minneapolis: Center for School Change, Humphrey Institute of Public Affairs, University of Minnesota.

Hutchins, D. J., et al. (Eds.). (2009). *Promising partnership practices 2009.* Baltimore: School, Family, and Community Partnerships, Johns Hopkins University Center. (See annual collections of practices at www.partnershipschools.org in the section "Success Stories.")

Lareau, A. (1989). *Home advantage: Social class and parental intervention in elementary education.* Philadelphia: Falmer.

Lee, S. (1994). *Family-school connections and students' education: Continuity and change of family involvement from the middle grades to high school.* Unpublished doctoral dissertation, Johns Hopkins University.

Lewis, C. C., E. Schaps, and M. Watson. (1995). Beyond the pendulum: Creating challenging and caring schools. *Phi Delta Kappan* 76: 547–554.

Lloyd, G. (1996). Research and practical application for school, family, and community partnerships. In A. Booth and J. F. Dunn (Eds.), *Family-school links: How do they affect educational outcomes?* (pp. 255–264). Mahwah, NJ: Lawrence Erlbaum.

Sanders, M. G. (2005). *Building school-community partnerships: Collaborating for student success.* Thousand Oaks, CA: Corwin.

Scott-Jones, D. (1995). Activities in the home that support school learning in the middle grades. In B. Rutherford (Ed.), *Creating family/school partnerships* (pp. 161–181). Columbus, OH: National Middle School Association.

Sheldon, S. B. (2005). Testing a structural equation model of partnership program implementation and parent involvement. *Elementary School Journal* 106: 171–187.

———. (2007a). Getting families involved with NCLB: Factors affecting schools' enactment of federal policy. In A. R. Sadovnik, J. O'Day, G. Bohrnstedt, and K. Borman (Eds.), *No Child Left Behind and reducing the achievement gap: Sociological perspectives on federal educational policy* (pp. 281–294). New York: Routledge.

———. (2007b). Improving student attendance with school, family, and community partnerships. *Journal of Educational Research* 100: 267–275.

———. (2009). Improving student outcomes with school, family, and community partnerships: A research review. In J. L. Epstein et al., *School, family, and community partnerships: Your handbook for action* (3rd ed.; pp. 40–56). Thousand Oaks, CA: Corwin Press.

Sheldon, S. B., and J. L. Epstein. (2007). *Parent and Student Surveys on Family and Community Involvement in the Elementary and Middle Grades.* Baltimore: Center on School, Family, and Community Partnerships, Johns Hopkins University.

Sheldon, S. B., and V. L. Van Voorhis. (2004). Partnership programs in U.S. schools: Their development and relationship to family involvement outcomes. *School Effectiveness and School Improvement* 15: 125–148.

Simon, Beth S. (2004). High school outreach and family involvement. *Social Psychology of Education* 7: 185–209.

Swap, S. M. (1993). *Developing home-school partnerships: From concepts to practice.* New York: Teachers College Press.

Van Voorhis, F. L. (2003). Interactive homework in middle school: Effects on family involvement and science achievement. *Journal of Educational Research* 96: 323–338.

———. (In press). Longitudinal effects of family involvement with students on math homework. *Education and Urban Society.*

Van Voorhis, F. L., and S. B. Sheldon. (2004). Principals' roles in the development of U.S. programs of school, family, and community partnerships. *International Journal of Educational Research* 41: 55–70.

DISCUSSION AND ACTIVITIES

This section extends and updates the content of Reading 5.1. It summarizes key concepts and results and provides questions and activities for class discussions, debates, and homework assignments, which may suggest other exercises, field activities, and research projects.

KEY CONCEPTS

1. Six types of involvement. A framework of six types of involvement (parenting, communicating, volunteering, learning at home, decision making, and collaborating with the community) grew from analyses of data collected from educators, parents, and students at the elementary, middle, and high school levels. The six types of involvement are demonstrably separable; include different practices; set different challenges for excellence; and lead to different results for students, families, schools, and communities.

2. Practices or activities. These terms are used interchangeably to describe specific implementations in schools. For district and state policies, practices, and activities, see Chapter 4.

3. Challenges. Challenges are problems that must be solved to improve the outreach or quality of school, family, and community partnerships. Some researchers, educators, and parents talk of "barriers" that prevent the involvement of some parents or community groups in children's education. However, every challenge that we identify has been solved by some educators, families, students, and community partners working together. Therefore, although every school will face challenges in designing and implementing activities for all types of involvement, the challenges can be solved to sustain excellent partnership programs.

4. Results. The results of school, family, and community partnerships are complex because not every activity leads to all good things. Indeed, any activity may be designed and conducted well or poorly, and, thereby, may lead to positive or negative results. Moreover, there are two main patterns of effects. First, each type of involvement produces some unique results. For example, Type 5—Decision Making activities, done well, will increase parents' support for their children's schools, whereas Type 4—Learning at Home activities, done well, will help students complete homework and gain skills in particular subject areas.

Second, all types of involvement can be designed to produce the *same* targeted results. For example, activities for all six types of involvement may focus on engaging families and the community to help students improve reading skills, math skills, or other desired results for student success.

Educators, parents, and others must understand the potential and patterns of results of involvement to knowledgeably and purposely design or select activities that will help meet school improvement goals.

5. Resource/idea file. The discussions and activities in Chapters 5, 6, and 7 focus on how to design and implement practical programs of school, family, and community partnerships. Future teachers, administrators, and other education professionals should compile a resource notebook or electronic file of ideas to use in practice teaching and in their work in schools, districts, and other education settings. Students who are preparing to conduct research may compile ideas and questions that they might address and clarify in future studies.

COMMENT

Website Resource: Promising Partnership Practices

Many activities in this chapter ask you to think of examples of practices for the six types of involvement that meet particular challenges or that produce specific results. You can use Tables 5.1, 5.2, or 5.3 for ideas. Or, you can draw from hundreds of exemplary practices that are featured in annual books of *Promising Partnership Practices* by schools, districts, states, and organizations in the National Network of Partnership Schools (NNPS). These collections are on the NNPS website at www.partnershipschools.org in the section "Success Stories." Use the search feature to sort the activities in each book by type of involvement.

COMMENT

Why Six Types?

Over the years, a framework of six types of involvement grew from research, field studies with practicing educators and families, and emerging policies. The types of involvement—parenting, communicating, volunteering, learning at home, decision making, and collaborating with the community—were first identified in the elementary grades and became clearer with data from middle and high schools.

The types of involvement comprise activities conducted at school, at home, and in the community. Activities may be conducted by students, teachers, parents, administrators, and others to improve schools, strengthen families, and increase student success. This large and varied agenda could get lost if categories were too simple.

For example, if all involvement activities were labeled "at home" or "at school," it would not be possible to make important distinctions between and among activities that occur in both locations. For example, volunteers may become involved at school or at home—assisting teachers, administrators, and/or students in either location. If categories are confounded, other distinctions are lost. For example, some programs define parents as "supporters" or "learners," but these labels are confusing because families and educators are supporters *and* learners in all six types of involvement—often in the same involvement activity.

The framework of six types of involvement corrects too-simple and confounded labels. With this framework, it is possible to categorize all activities that involve families and community members; identify challenges; and link activities to short-term and long-term goals for students, parents, and the schools. There is general agreement about the usefulness of the framework. It was adopted and applied by the National PTA (1998, 2009) to the work of that organization, and it was incorporated into publications and training of the National Education Association (Dianda and McLaren, 1996) and American Federation of Teachers (1999, 2009). Many states, districts, and schools use the framework as the basis for their policies of parental involvement (see Chapter 4). The framework has made it possible to move away from the task of "defining" involvement to the harder work of implementing comprehensive programs of school, family, and community partnerships.

The following comments and exercises will increase your understanding of the six types of involvement. I hope that familiarity will breed attempt! If you understand the framework and many ways to activate it in practice, you should be more likely to create and conduct comprehensive programs of school, family, and community partnerships. You may develop these programs with colleagues in the schools, districts, and state departments of education where you work as a professional educator, as an active parent, and as an involved member of the community.

Researchers, too, should be able to use the framework to improve their studies of the effects of different types of involvement on student achievement and other outcomes for students, families, teachers, and school climate. Details are needed on who benefits from specific partnership activities, how much, and at which grade levels. The summary charts in Reading 5.1 are extensive, but each entry is based on relatively few studies. Many studies—using different methods, in diverse communities, and with students and families at all grade levels—are needed to extend knowledge and strengthen all six types of involvement.

SUMMARY: TYPE 1—PARENTING

Basic Responsibilities of Families

Type 1—Parenting activities help families fulfill their basic responsibilities of providing for children's nutrition, health, safety and protection, clothing, supervision, discipline, development of independence, and other attributes. Activities may include family support programs, parent education, workshops, and parent-to-parent connections that strengthen parents' understanding of child and adolescent development, parenting skills, and home conditions that support learning at each age and grade level. Type 1 activities also assist schools in understanding families' backgrounds, cultures, parenting styles, and goals for children.

Many schools address topics of parenting by conducting workshops for parents. One of the many Type 1 challenges is to get information from workshops to parents who cannot come to the school but want and need the information. Schools are meeting this challenge with old and new technologies to share information in written summaries, by e-mail, on websites, on CDs, through parent-to-parent networks, and in other ways using high-tech and low-tech communications.

If Type 1—Parenting activities are well designed and well implemented, specific results can be expected. For example, student attendance and promptness should improve if parents are helped to understand the school's attendance policies, their responsibility to get their children to school every day and on time, and the health and community services available to support student attendance.

Focus of Type 1 Activities

- Housing, health, nutrition, clothing, safety
- Parenting skills for all age levels
- Home conditions that support children as students at all grade levels
- Information and activities to help schools understand children and families

Challenges

- Provide information to all families who want it or who need it, not only to the few who attend workshops/meetings at the school building.
- Enable families to share information with schools about background, culture, talents, goals, and needs.

Redefinitions

- *Workshop* is not only a meeting on a topic held at the school building but also the content of that topic, which may be viewed, heard, or read at convenient times and varied locations.

Measurable Results for Students

- Balance of time spent on chores, other activities, and homework
- Regular attendance
- Awareness of family belief in the importance of school

Measurable Results for Parents

- Self-confidence about parenting as children proceed through school
- Knowledge of child and adolescent development

Measurable Results for Teachers and Schools

- Understanding of families' goals and concerns for children
- Respect for families' strengths and efforts

See Tables 5.1, 5.2, and 5.3 in Reading 5.1 for more on Type 1.

COMMENT

Understanding Type 1—Parenting

Parents have a continuous responsibility for raising their children, whereas most teachers have students for only one year, and most schools work with children for just a few years. To meet their children's needs, families say they want clear, understandable, ongoing information about child and adolescent development. Many families benefit from contacts with other parents about parenting skills, problems, and solutions at each age level. Others request or require professional, personal services for themselves and their children.

Just about all parents deserve respect and appreciation from educators for their ongoing efforts at home to raise their children and for the support they provide to their children as students. Families want and need up-to-date information, conversations, and guidance to revise and adapt home activities and family discussions every year. With good information, many, most, or all parents would better understand their children and the expectations of teachers.

At the same time, teachers and administrators deserve respect and appreciation from parents for their dedication to educating every child and for the attention they pay to bring out the best in each child. Educators need information from families about their children and about family backgrounds, cultures, talents, goals, and expectations for students. Without such information, schools and teachers may operate on erroneous ideas about students and their families.

Most schools do not gather information from families about their children on a regular schedule. Most do not routinely give clear information to help all families remain knowledgeable partners in their children's education from year to year. It is not surprising, then, that many families feel unassisted and unappreciated by their children's schools and unsure about the development stages their children experience. A good mix of Type 1 activities includes information for parents and from parents about children and families. This creates two main challenges that must be met for programs of partnership to effectively implement Type 1—Parenting.

Challenge Number 1: Provide Information to Families Who Cannot Come to Meetings and Workshops at School

Many families cannot come to meetings and workshops on parenting, child and adolescent development, or other topics designed to help families understand their children. Most workshops, parent-to-parent meetings, and social activities with educators are attended only by a small number of the families served at a school. Even when a workshop is well attended, some families will not be there. An important challenge raised by Type 1 activities is: *How shall schools get information to those who cannot come to the school building at a particular time?*

The absentees are not bad parents. They may be busy with other children, work outside the home, live far from school, feel unwelcome or frightened by the school, speak languages other than English, or have other reasons for not attending a meeting at school on a particular day. The absentees may be just as caring, loving, and interested in their children as the parents who attend. Ironically, some absentees are parents who are teachers, administrators, or child care providers who are working with other people's children during the school day and who cannot leave their schools to attend meetings at their own children's schools.

Challenge Number 2: Gather Information from Families to Help Schools Understand the Students and Their Families

In addition to increasing families' understanding of their children at each age and grade level, some Type 1 activities should increase educators' understanding of the students and their families, including their backgrounds, goals, strengths, and needs. As they become aware of and sensitive to the strengths of families, educators are better able to support all students and involve all families.

QUESTIONS TO DISCUSS

1. What information do you think families want and need every year from schools to understand child and adolescent development? List five items of information that you believe all families need to know every year from their children's schools.

2. What information do you think all schools want and need each year from families to understand the students and their families? List five items of information that you believe teachers, administrators, and/or counselors need to know every year from families.

Linking Type 1 Challenges and Results

What results would you expect from Type 1—Parenting activities designed to meet the two challenges discussed above?

A. Use the chart in Figure 5.1.
B. Select and identify a grade level that interests you.
C. Describe one Type 1—Parenting activity that you think would meet each of the listed challenges. You can use the list of ideas that you developed in the questions above, the website for *Promising Partnership Practices*, or other ideas that you may have.
D. For each activity that you describe, give one short-term result that you would expect if the activity were well implemented.
E. Make clear whether the expected result will benefit students, parents, teachers, or others.

Name: _____ Grade level selected:_____ Date _____

Sample Challenges for Success with Type 1—Parenting	One activity to meet this challenge	One short-term result of the activity	Who will benefit?
Provide information for parents who cannot attend a workshop or meeting			
Obtain information from parents to help teachers understand their children and families			

FIGURE 5.1 Type 1 Challenges

Parent Education Programs

Type 1 activities may be provided by a school or by family support, parent education, or other programs that serve families. If these programs are well designed, responsive to families' needs, and well implemented, they should increase parents' confidence and the quality of their parenting.

A. Interview (or invite for a class interview) the director and a participant of a family support, family literacy, parent education, or other parenting program. Identify the interviewees and the program.
B. Discuss the goals of the program and how the results of the program are measured. Prior to the interview, prepare at least five questions about the program on these topics:
1. One question about the goals of the program and participants.
2. One question about eligibility requirements or fees for services.
3. One question about how the quality of the implementation of the program is measured.
4. One question about the results of the program for participants and their families and how results are monitored and measured.
5. At least one more question that interests you about the program.
C. Document your questions. Listen to the director's and participant's views, and document their responses.
D. Summarize the similarities and/or differences in views of the director and the participant.
E. Write two commendations on the program's successes and/or two recommendations for improving the program based on your interpretations of the interviewees' comments.

COMMENT

Looking Deeper into "Workshops"

Under the new definition of workshop stated above, the location, presenter, time, and technology of a workshop may vary. The content of a workshop may be presented in various ways to reach more parents.

Location: Workshops may be offered at the school building or at a location in the community. Some businesses or organizations host lunchtime or weekend workshops on school-related topics for their employees.

Presenter: Workshops may be offered by teachers, administrators, counselors, parents, other professionals, or members of the community. Some workshops for parents and teachers may be presented by students. Expertise is available in all communities on topics that are important to all families and students.

Time: Workshop information may be made available at various times, not just at one scheduled time, at the school or in the community. Some workshops are presented twice—once during the school day and once in the evening to reach more families. Some are available "on demand" and may use new technologies (e.g., video, website, summaries in a parent center, etc.).

Technology: Workshops may be offered in traditional meetings and in other forms. Videotapes, CDs, audiotapes, and printed summaries of homegrown or commercial workshops may be viewed and heard in the media center or parent room at school; borrowed to view at home; or distributed to neighborhood libraries, businesses, family resource centers, health centers, or other locations. Workshop topics and main results can be summarized in computerized phone messages, in school or local newspapers, on local cable TV or radio, on school or district websites, or in other forms. Follow-up discussions might include parent, educator, and student reactions, experiences, and suggestions. Different workshops may be scheduled each year to develop a "library" of important information for families on child development and other topics concerning education. The workshop products could then be shared among schools or districts.

Workshop topics should be thoughtfully selected with input from parents to meet their needs and interests in child and adolescent development. Each year and across time, workshop topics should "add up" to something that helps parents understand their children and that helps schools understand families.

ACTIVITY

Workshop Topics

A. Select and identify a grade level that interests you.
B. List one workshop topic about which educators have important information about children and schools that you think should be shared with parents at the grade level you selected.
C. Describe two ways in which the information could be shared with parents who were unable to attend the workshop.
D. Discuss one result that you would expect for:
   - parents who attended the workshop
   - parents who received information in the ways you described in item C
E. List one topic about which parents have important information about their children or families that you think should be shared with educators at the school.
F. Describe two ways to share the information you listed in item E. If the activity is conducted at school, include at least one idea of how families who cannot come to school might participate.
G. Discuss one result that you would expect from the activities you described in item F.

Organize a Type 1—Parenting Activity

A. Select item 1 *or* item 2 to organize a Type 1—Parenting activity.
1. Workshop for parents.
   a. Select and identify a grade level that interests you.
   b. List one topic that you believe parents want to know more about concerning their children's development at that grade level. You may use your ideas from the activity above or other ideas.
   c. Organize a workshop of about one hour on the topic you selected. Use the new definition of *workshop* to ensure that all parents obtain good information on the topic you selected. Consider various locations, times, and technologies that would help convey information to all families. Write a complete plan outlining the content, facility, targeted audience, schedule, responsibilities for publicity, other organizational issues, and follow-up plans, if any.
2. Family exchange and information for schools. Remember, in addition to workshops *for* parents, Type 1—Parenting activities help schools learn more about their students' families. For example, an annual Family Fair might help families share histories, talents, stories, customs, foods, crafts, and other specialties. Such activities could be photographed, collected in school albums, videotaped, and edited over time to establish a "family history" of the school that may be shared with each new class that enrolls.
   a. Select and identify a grade level that interests you.
   b. Describe one strategy that would encourage families to exchange important information with each other and with educators at the school.
   c. Write a complete plan for organizing, conducting, and following up the activity you selected.
B. *Optional activity*: In class, critique the plans for the workshops and family exchange activities. Consider the importance of the topics, timing, technologies, strategies for providing information to nonattendees, and likely results. Save good ideas in your resource notebook or electronic idea file.

SUMMARY: TYPE 2—COMMUNICATING

Basic Responsibilities of Schools

Type 2—Communicating activities help educators and families share information about school programs and student progress in varied, clear, and productive ways.

Schools send information home in notes, newsletters, report cards, folders, and e-mail, and they share information in conferences, phone calls, and other ways. Increasingly schools are using voice mail, e-mail, and websites to communicate with families. Type 2 activities create *two-way communication channels* from school to home and from home to school so that families can easily communicate with teachers, administrators, counselors, and other families.

Most schools communicate in many ways with at least some parents about school programs and children's progress, but not all of the communications are understood by all families. One of the many Type 2 challenges is to use clear and understandable language in written and verbal exchanges to reach all families. Schools are meeting this challenge by writing more clearly in English, translating written documents into major languages spoken by students' families, and providing interpreters for parents who speak different languages at meetings and conferences.

Many schools are working to make their report cards and the criteria for students' grades clear to all students and parents. If Type 2 communications are well designed and well implemented, specific results can be expected. For example, if more families feel welcome and comfortable at parent-teacher-student conferences (Minke and Anderson, 2003), they will be better able to follow up the conference with help for their children or with more questions for the teacher. If more parents understand criteria for report card grades, they may be better able to recognize and celebrate good work and progress at home and help their children maintain or improve their grades.

FOCUS OF TYPE 2 ACTIVITIES

School-to-Home Communications

- Memos, notices, report cards, conferences, newsletters, phone calls, e-mail and other computerized messages, websites
- Information on school programs, tests, and children's progress
- Information needed to choose or change schools, courses, programs, and activities

Home-to-School Communications

- Two-way channels of communication for questions, comments, and other interactions

Challenges

- Make all memos, notices, and other print and nonprint communications clear and understandable for all families.

- Obtain ideas from families to improve the design and content of communications such as newsletters, report cards, and conference schedules.

Redefinitions

- *Communications about school programs and student progress* are not only from school to home but also from home to school and with the community.

Measurable Results for Students

- Awareness of their own progress in subjects and skills
- Knowledge of actions needed to maintain or improve grades
- Awareness of their roles as courier and communicator in partnerships

Measurable Results for Parents

- Support for child's progress and responses to correct problems
- Ease of interactions and communications with school and teachers
- High rating of quality of the school

Measurable Results for Teachers and Schools

- Ability to communicate clearly with parents
- Use of a network of parents to communicate with all families

See Tables 5.1, 5.2, and 5.3 in Reading 5.1 for more on Type 2.

COMMENT

Two-Way Communications between Home and School

One Type 2 challenge is to establish easy-to-use, two-way communications between home and school about school programs and student progress. Teachers need to know when parents can be reached at home or at work and what numbers to call. Parents need to know when teachers, counselors, and principals can be reached at school or home and what numbers to call. Families may want to know how to connect with other helpful people such as the school counselor, nurse, social worker, officers of the parent organization, class parents, family center coordinator, parent representatives on the school council and Action Team for Partnerships, and others. Some schools develop "telephone trees" or family directories each year for each grade level so that all parents have information on school contacts and so that parents can easily contact each other.

Parents also need to be encouraged to ask questions and offer ideas that will help their children proceed successfully through the grades. Although this is a simple idea, many schools have not opened two-way communication channels so that information, questions, and conversations may flow easily from school to home and from home to school. This is a particular challenge when families speak many languages, have diverse reading skills, work different shifts and schedules, and have other circumstances that require thoughtful and responsive actions. Parents' requests for more and better information are indicators of family strengths, not weaknesses.

FIELD EXPERIENCE

Interview about Type 2 Communications

A. Select a parent or educator (teacher, principal, or counselor) to discuss the two-way communications that he or she presently conducts and about needed improvements. Also identify the grade level of one school-age child who links home and school for the interviewee. Ask:
   1. What are two productive forms of school-to-home or home-to-school communications that you presently use?
   2. In your view, what are two ways that improve your present practices or experiences to encourage two-way communications between parents and teachers or between parents and school administrators?
   3. Some teachers give parents their home phone numbers. Others prefer not to do so. What are your feelings about this exchange of information?
B. Document the questions and responses.
C. What do you think is the most difficult challenge to effective two-way communications that was identified in your interview? Explain why you think this challenge is formidable.
D. Share information in class to compare responses of educators and parents and how some have solved the challenges that others have not yet addressed.

The Role of Students in Type 2 Communications

Students are important for the success of all six types of involvement, including Type 2—Communicating. Communications from school to home and from home to school almost always involve students as couriers, commentators, observers, and targets of attention in both settings. From preschool through high school, students need guidance and recognition from teachers and administrators to effectively serve as home-school communicators and connectors. In a study we conducted at the high school level, a parent joked, "If teachers could pin notices to students' sweaters the way they did in kindergarten, more of their communications would reach me." Of course, that is not an age-appropriate solution for high school teachers, students, or parents.

Students and families need good information about the curriculum, tests and assessments, standards for success, report card marking systems, and other features and changes in school programs. Students and families should be involved in creating, reviewing, and improving all aspects of schooling that determine student success.

With good information and participation, families can assist educators in helping students adjust to new schools, new curricula, and other changes that affect their success in school. With good information and participation, students themselves can more successfully respond to changes that affect their work and progress.

QUESTIONS TO DISCUSS

1. What do families and students need to know about the following aspects of school programs, and what might families and students contribute to the success of these aspects of schooling?

	Families need to know	Students need to know	Families or students may contribute in this way
A. Curriculum/ school subjects			
B. Tests and assessments			
C. Report cards			
D. Standards for students' work			
E. Add one more Topic: _____			

2. a. Give two examples of how students might help conduct school-to-home or home-to-school communications about school programs and student progress in learning and behavior.
   b. Give two examples of how students might hinder school-to-home or home-to-school communications about school programs and student progress in learning and behavior.
   c. Give two examples of what teachers and/or parents could say or do to help students understand the importance of their roles in school-to-home and home-to-school communications.

COMMENT

Back-to-School Night

At the start of a school year, most preschools and elementary, middle, and high schools hold a Back-to-School Night or open house to help families learn about school programs, meet their children's teachers, and hear about plans and requirements for specific subjects. These initial, annual gatherings are group meetings, not individual parent-teacher conferences. Some principals and teachers use the occasion to talk about their approaches to school, family, and community partnerships and to obtain information from parents about their families' goals for their children and their children's special talents.

FIELD EXPERIENCE

Site Visit

The following activity may be completed alone, with a partner, or in cooperation with a teacher, administrator, or parent.

A. Visit a local school on Back-to-School Night. If that cannot be scheduled, interview a teacher, administrator, or parent who has attended a Back-to-School Night, or use your own experience. Indicate whether you made a visit, conducted an interview, or are relying on reflection.
B. Describe the type of school, location of the community, number of families attending the event, agenda and activities, and other observations or descriptions.
C. Evaluate the event for its strengths and weaknesses in welcoming parents; providing information about school programs and grade-level requirements; gathering information from parents; and establishing a climate for school, family, and community partnerships for the year.

Letter Writing from School to Home

A. Identify a school level or grade level that interests you.
B. Write four letters that a teacher or administrator might send to families of students, including:
   - An introductory letter to greet all families at the start of the year, along with your ideas and plans for school, family, and community partnerships;
   - A letter to set up and schedule an individual conference with each parent at school or by phone at a time that is convenient for both of you;
   - A "good-news" letter to share students' accomplishments with their families; and
   - A letter to all families or to an individual family on another topic of your choice (e.g., a special conference to discuss an academic or behavior problem, a follow-up letter to report progress in solving a problem, or some other topic).
C. *Optional class activity*: In class, share the letters that were drafted. In small groups, pairs, or as a whole class, critique the letters for their form, vocabulary, readability for all families, awareness of family interests and needs, sensitivities to children's ages and grade levels, and other issues. Make changes to improve your letters. Collect examples as prototypes for future reference in your resource notebook or electronic idea file.

Newsletters

A. Collect one example of a school or classroom newsletter. It may be a paper copy or a copy from a school website.
B. Identify the school level (preschool or elementary, middle, or high school) or grade level of the example.
C. Analyze the purpose(s) and content of the newsletter. Critique the format; readability; quality of information; participation of students, teachers, administrators, and parents; two-way communication strategies; and other qualities.
D. Give two suggestions of how you would improve the newsletter you reviewed.
E. Draw a diagram or layout to show what an excellent newsletter might look like for the school or grade level that you critiqued.
F. *Optional activity*: In class, share some of the sample newsletters and critiques.

Contacts and Meetings with Parents—What Is Realistic?

Many educators say, "If we could just get the parents to the school, we would know they were involved." The fact is that most parents cannot come to school very often. Most work full-time or part-time during the school day. Others are too far from the school; have other family, faith, and neighborhood obligations; or have other reasons why it is not easy to come often to the school building.

Realistically, how often each year might a teacher or administrator contact every student's family individually? As a group? How might these contacts occur—in face-to-face meetings, in writing, by phone, or in other ways? What resources or support from the school or from the school district might be needed to encourage parents to come to school at certain times during the school year?

One method is to share information with individual families. The following are some ways to share information with individual families about their own children.

- Parent-teacher conferences
- Parent-teacher-student conferences
- Student-parent interviews, conversations, or conferences at home
- Telephone conversations
- Informal meetings
- Notes, letters about individual students
- E-mail to individual parents or students
- Student report cards
- Weekly folders of students' work
- Interactive homework
- Add another example: _____

Another method is to share information with groups of families. The following are some ways to share information with groups of families:

- Back-to-School Night or open house
- School or class newsletters
- Grade-level meetings
- PTA or other parent organization meetings
- School and district policy statements
- School handbooks
- Websites
- Listservs
- Other social networking method (e.g., blog, Twitter)
- Add another example: _____

Mapping Communications for a Year

A. Select and identify a grade level that interests you. For middle and high school grades, also select and identify a subject area. Estimate the number of students a teacher may teach at that grade level/subject.

B. Think of the time and resources needed for group meetings, individual parent-teacher conferences, home visits, phone calls, e-mail, positive postcards, and the other communications listed above.

C. Create a paper or computerized calendar of the months and weeks of one school year (typically 180 days from September to June, or 36 full weeks; in year-round schools, four 9-week sessions). If you wish, you may add vacation months.

D. Outline a feasible communication schedule that you believe is positive and realistic and encourages two-way communication and problem solving between a teacher and the families of students in the grade (and subject) you selected.

    1. Put an *I* next to the *individual* communications with each student's family.

    2. Put a *G* next to *group* communications that are the same for all families.

    3. Identify whether the communications would be conducted by the teacher(*T*), school administrators (*SA*), counselors (*C*), parents (*P*), students (*S*), or others (*O*).

    4. On your calendar, estimate the hours or minutes needed to plan, conduct, and complete the communications you listed.

E. *Optional activity*: Exchange and critique the calendars of communications in class. Are the activities realistic for teachers and for parents? Which activities ensure two-way channels of communication from school to home and from home to school? Discuss: Do the activities emphasize "bodies in the building," or is there a useful mix of communication strategies so that all parents can participate even if they cannot come to the school building?

Parent-Teacher Conferences

Interview a teacher or parent about a parent-teacher conference in which he or she participated. Identify a few key characteristics of the interviewee and the grade level of the child who was the subject of the conference.

A. Ask the interviewee to think of one recent parent-teacher or parent-teacher-student conference and answer the following questions about that conference:
   1. What was the purpose of the conference? What was the content? How was it organized?
   2. How would you describe the tone of the conference, feelings of the participants, and quality of the exchanges?
   3. Was the student present?
      a. If yes, how did this affect the conference?
      b. If no, how might that have affected the conference?
   4. Give an example of how you:
      a. Exchanged information about the student as a person with interests, strengths, talents, concerns, and needs.
      b. Gained information about the student's progress on work in school in specific subjects, general knowledge, and social skills.
      c. Discussed important goals and strategies for reaching goals for progress in learning and success, including help needed to reach new goals.
      d. Celebrated the uniqueness and potential of the student as a part of the school, class, and community.
B. Add at least one question of your own about a parent-teacher conference and its schedule, content, and follow-up or another important related topic.
C. Document your questions and responses.
D. Write a short critique of whether and why you think this was a good or poor conference.

ACTIVITY

Role Play on Conferences and Meetings with Parents

A. With others in class, take the part of a parent, teacher, administrator, or student in one of the following school meetings:
   1. Conference with a parent about a behavior problem
   2. Conference with a parent about an academic problem
   3. PTA meeting about a dress code or homework policy
   4. Committee on the selection of textbooks
   5. Meeting on special programs or services for children (e.g., library, guidance, summer school, after-school program, free breakfasts, student health issues, or a topic that you add)
B. List the topic, the roles, and the players.
C. The players should meet for at least 15 minutes to discuss the topic and plan a mock interaction to perform for the class.

D. Conduct the interaction for the class. For each presentation, discuss:
1. What were the goals, fears, strengths, and needs of each participant?
2. If this were a real interaction of educators and family members, would all participants have felt that the exchange was positive and productive?
    a. If yes, explain why.
    b. If no, explain what each participant might have done differently to produce a better result.

COMMENT

Students in Conferences

One of the most common comments about parent involvement is that the best way to get parents to attend events at school is to have students involved. Student concerts, plays, sports activities, choruses, award assemblies, and, of course, graduation are just a few activities that parents attend happily. This common pattern alerts us to the need to consider when, why, and how students are included in school, family, and community partnerships. Increasingly, students are being given active roles in parent-teacher-student conferences.

A. Students may help *prepare* parents for parent-teacher conferences by:
- describing and discussing the subjects they study;
- drawing a map of the school to help parents find their teacher(s) and classroom(s);
- providing a schedule of their classes, names of teachers, and room numbers; and
- writing some questions for their parents to discuss with their teacher(s).

B. Students may *participate* in parent-teacher-student conferences by:
- attending parent-teacher-student conferences; and
- leading one part or all of the parent-teacher-student conferences.

C. Students may *follow up* conferences with needed actions by:
- discussing the results and recommendations of conferences they did not attend with their teachers and parents;
- setting goals and creating a work plan, as needed, to fulfill important recommendations; and
- following up at regular intervals to discuss with their teachers and parents how their work is continuing at high levels or improving.

To lead or conduct parent-teacher-student conferences, students need clear explanations and time with their teachers to prepare for the conference. Also, parents need to be prepared for the nontraditional format of a student-led conference. By conducting parent-teacher-student conferences, students demonstrate that they are the main actors in their education and that they can plan and reflect on their work and progress.

QUESTIONS TO DISCUSS

1. a. Add one more example to list A (above) of how a student might prepare a parent for a parent-teacher conference.
   b. What are one benefit and one problem with any entry in list A?
2. a. Add one more example to list B (above) of how a student might actively participate in a parent-teacher-student conference.
   b. What are one benefit and one problem with any entry in list B?
3. a. Add one more example to list C (above) of how a student might follow up the results and recommendations of a parent-teacher conference.
   b. What are one benefit and one problem with any entry in list C?

ACTIVITY

Inviting Parents to a Meeting at School

A. Select and identify a school level and grade level that interest you. Tell whether you will be thinking about this as a teacher or as a principal.
B. Select one of the following events that interests you: Back-to-School Night or parent-teacher-student conference.
C. Suppose you wanted all parents of your students to attend the event you selected.
   1. Describe one way that you would maximize the number of parents who attended the event you selected.
   2. Some families in your class or school are difficult to reach and rarely come to such events. Select and identify one group of the following families who sometimes are hard to reach or reluctant to come to school events:
      - Parents who disliked school when they were children
      - Parents who do not speak English
      - Parents who do not read English well
      - Parents who work at night
      - Parents who live at a distance
      - Fathers or significant males in students' lives
      - Foster parents
      - Noncustodial parents
      - Other (please specify): _____

3. Describe two ways that you might try to reach the special group you selected to encourage them to attend the event.
4. Explain why you think your two communication strategies might work with the group you selected.

QUESTIONS TO DISCUSS

All students move through the grades and change schools at key points, such as from preschool to elementary, elementary to middle, and middle to high school. Even within schools with K–8, K–12, 7–12, or other broad grade spans, there are important within-school transitions from one school level to the next. How might students and their families be helped to make successful transitions from one school level to the next?

1. Select and identify one transition point in schooling that interests you.
2. If you were in the "feeder" school or grade, what is one piece of information about going to a new school that you would share with all students and families? How might you provide that information?
3. If you were the "receiving" school or grade, what is one piece of information about coming to a new school that you would share with all students and all families? How might you provide that information?
4. *Optional activity*: Critique the ideas in class, and collect the most promising ones for a resource notebook or electronic idea file.

FIELD EXPERIENCE

Communicating with Families Who Are New to a School

What information is typically shared with families when they enroll their children in a new school, either because of a move to a new neighborhood or because of a change in school levels? Interview a principal, counselor, or teacher about his or her school's policies and practices of communicating with families who enroll children at or after the start of the school year. (Or invite all three for a class panel interview.)

A. Identify your interviewee's position and level of schooling. Ask:
   1. What *formal connections* are made with all families that are new to the school? What information is routinely provided to these families?
   2. What *informal connections* are made with some families that are new to the school?
   3. What is one improvement that you would make to better inform or assist families that are new to your school?
B. Add a question of your own.

C. Document your questions and responses. Summarize your opinion of how well new families are welcomed and included in this school.

SUMMARY: TYPE 3—VOLUNTEERING

Involvement at and for the School

Type 3—Volunteering activities help educators and families work together to support the school program and children's work and activities. Type 3 activities include recruiting and training volunteers; arranging schedules, locations, and activities for volunteers; and recognizing parents who serve as audiences for students' events and performances as volunteers. Type 3 activities enable educators to work with regular and occasional volunteers who assist and support students in the school and in other locations. Type 3 activities enable parents and other family members to offer their time, talent, and ideas for productive activities for volunteers.

Many schools have at least a few volunteers—often the same group of active parents. One of the many Type 3 challenges to excellent volunteer programs is to recruit widely so that all families know they are valued as volunteers. Schools are meeting these challenges by enabling parents to volunteer their time and talent at convenient times in the evening, on weekends, and on vacation days. These decisions greatly increase the number of parents and others who can assist schools and students. If Type 3—Volunteering is well designed and well implemented, some or all students may gain or improve skills taught by or practiced with volunteer aides, lecturers, tutors, and mentors.

Focus of Type 3 Activities

- Volunteers *in* schools or classrooms—assist administrators, teachers, students, or parents as aides, tutors, coaches, lecturers, chaperones, and other leaders
- Volunteers *for* schools or classrooms—assist school programs and children's progress in any location and at any time
- Volunteers as members of audiences—attend assemblies, performances, sports events, recognition and award ceremonies, celebrations, and other events

Challenges

- Recruit widely, provide training, and create flexible schedules and locations for volunteers so that all families know that their time and talents are welcomed and valued.

Redefinitions

- *Volunteer* not only means a person who comes during the school day but also a person who supports school goals and children's learning in any place and at any time.

Measurable Results for Students

- Skills that are tutored or taught by volunteers
- Skills in communicating with adults

Measurable Results for Parents

- Understanding of the teacher's job
- Self-confidence about ability to work in school and with children
- Enrollment in programs to improve their own education and to prepare for jobs in education

Measurable Results for Teachers and Schools

- Readiness to involve all families in new ways, not only as volunteers
- More individual attention to students because of help from volunteers

See Tables 5.1, 5.2, and 5.3 in Reading 5.1 for more on Type 3.

QUESTIONS TO DISCUSS

1. The number of families who become volunteers at the school building may be increased if parents and other family members can volunteer to assist in classrooms, in parent rooms, on the playground, in the lunchroom, and in other locations. Give one idea for how each of the following old ways of working with volunteers might be expanded or changed to enable more families to participate.

OLD way	NEW way
A. Volunteers must come to the school building.	_____
B. Volunteers must come during school hours.	_____
C. Volunteers must come during the school year.	_____
E. Volunteers must have children in the school.	_____
F. Volunteers must not be involved in curriculum-related activities.	_____
G. Other idea:	_____

2. Suppose you notice, as the research shows, that working parents, single parents, or parents who live far from the school do not volunteer as much as other parents. What is one new approach to increase the number of each of the following groups of parents to volunteer in ways that help student learning and success?

Potential Volunteers	One way to increase participation:
A. Working parents	_____
B. Single parents	_____
C. Parents who live far from the school	_____
D. Fathers	_____

Improving the Effectiveness of Volunteers

Not every task at school should be assigned to a volunteer. And not every volunteer is successful at every task.

A. Use the chart in Figure 5.2. Give one idea of how a principal, teacher, or coordinator of volunteers might identify the problems that are listed.
B. Give one idea of how to solve the problems should they occur.

Potential Type 3 Problem	How to Identify the Problem	Possible Solution
A. Ineffective volunteers who want to help but do not do well		
B. Underachieving volunteers whose talents are not well used		
C. Unsavory characters who should not be in school or working with children		
D. Add one other possible problem with volunteers that might arise: _____ _____		

FIGURE 5.2 Type 3 Problems

QUESTIONS TO DISCUSS

Some parents cannot or do not volunteer at school. Many parents work full-time or part-time during the school day, when most volunteer activities are scheduled. Those who work at night may not be able to volunteer during the school day. What if you redefined *volunteer*, as suggested above, to mean "any one who supports school goals and children's learning in any place and at any time."

1. How would this definition enable more parents to become volunteers?
2. How would this definition assist a school, a teacher's classroom, families, and the community?
3. What is one problem with the new definition? What is one way to resolve that problem?
4. How far would you extend the new definition? Answer the following questions and explain your reasons:
   a. Should we consider parents and family members "volunteers" when they attend sports activities, drama productions, concerts, and other performances and assemblies? Why or why not?
   b. Should we consider parents "volunteers" when they come to school for parent-teacher conferences, for meetings on Individual Education Plans (IEPs) for students with special needs, to readmit children who have been suspended, or for other required meetings? Why or why not?

COMMENT

Matching Volunteers'
Talents and School Needs

One way that some schools begin to think about expanding Type 3—Volunteering, is to ask teachers, administrators, and school staff for a "wish list" of how volunteers' time and talents might be helpful. The activities on a wish list might be conducted by volunteers at school, in classrooms, on the way to and from school, in the community, or at home. The activities may be frequent and periodic, or occasional.

Another way that some schools begin to think about volunteers is to create a "talent pool" by asking parents, other family members, and even members of the community to indicate how they might like to help the school and students; what their talents, time, range of interests, or willingness to help are, and what a good location for their assistance would be.

Wish Lists or Talent Pools for Volunteers

A. Select one of the approaches above—a *school's wish list* or a *parent talent pool*—that interests you.

B. Design a tool that would help a school gather the information you selected. Make the form you design short, clear, and to the point, as well as easy to categorize, tally, and search for/find.

C. *Optional activity*: Invite a cooperating principal or teacher to work with your class.

   1. Ask a teacher, administrator, or counselor to critique one or more forms for collecting information about volunteers and give feedback on whether the forms are clear enough for teachers or parents.

   2. Ask the cooperating educator to share with you any similar approaches that are used to develop a wish list for volunteers or a talent pool of volunteers.

Website Exploration: Organizing Volunteers

Explore the annual collections of *Promising Partnership Practices* at www.partnershipschools.org in the section "Success Stories."

A. Select one year's book, and search on Type 3—Volunteers.

B. Select one activity reported by a school, and critique it.

   1. What were two positive features of the activity that increased the number of volunteers or the activities conducted by volunteers?

   2. What were two weaknesses or limitations to the activity that could be corrected for even greater success? Tell how.

Creating Strong Volunteer Programs

Suppose you were working with a preschool or elementary, middle, or high school that wanted to organize and implement a useful volunteer program.

A. Identify the level of schooling that interests you (e.g., preschool or elementary, middle, or high school).

B. Identify whether you are thinking about the needs of the whole school or the needs of one teacher in a specific grade level or subject.
C. Include the following components in your plan for a successful volunteer program. List one example of how you will address each component.
   •   Recruit volunteers
   •   Match talents of volunteers with needs of teachers, students, others
   •   Train volunteers
   •   Schedule work for volunteers
   •   Evaluate volunteers
   •   Continue the program from year to year
D. Share the plans for organizing volunteers in class. For each idea, discuss:
   1. Is the design feasible?
   2. Would the proposed program reach out to involve parents, other family members, and/or community members who would not typically become volunteers on their own?
   3. Will the recruitment, training, and assignments of volunteers be easy to maintain from year to year?
E. Collect promising ideas for a resource notebook or electronic idea file.

See Chapter 6 for one targeted program to organize Type 3—Volunteering for social studies and art in the middle grades and additional discussion topics and activities on volunteers.

SUMMARY: TYPE 4—LEARNING AT HOME

Involvement in Academic Activities

Type 4—Learning at Home activities involve families with their children in homework, goal setting, and other curriculum-related activities and decisions. Information on homework policies, course choices, prerequisites, goal setting, and other academic decisions can help parents influence students' choices and learning in many different ways. Some schools encourage teachers to design homework that enables students to share and discuss interesting work and ideas with family members. These activities create two-way connections between home and school about the curriculum and academic learning without parents having to come to the school building.

Students in all schools learn many different subjects, but most parents are unaware of all that their children are learning or how to interact with their children on curricular matters. Most parents are uninvolved in important academic decisions that affect their children's and the family's future. One of many Type 4 challenges is for teachers to effectively and realistically assign students homework and guide parents in how to interact with students about schoolwork at home. Some activities draw on the knowledge that all parents have, based on their backgrounds and experiences (Moll, Amanti, Neff, and Gonzalez, 1992). Other activities enable students to conduct conversations, demonstrations, and other interactions with parents to share ideas and examples of what they are learning in class (Van Voorhis and Epstein, 2002).

If Type 4—Learning at Home activities are well designed and well implemented, more students will complete their homework and improve the quality of their work, and more parents will be well informed about what students are learning in class. With family encouragement and input, students will be more actively involved in setting goals for success in school and in planning postsecondary educational pathways.

Focus of Type 4 Activities

- How to help at home with homework
- Skills required to pass each subject
- Curriculum-related decisions
- Students' goal setting for success in school and postsecondary planning
- Development of other skills and talents

Challenges

- Design and implement interactive homework in which students take responsibility to discuss important classwork and ideas with their families.
- Sequence information and activities to help students and families set ambitious goals and strategies for improving or maintaining success in school every year, and for postsecondary education, training, and work.

Redefinitions

- *Homework* means not only work that students do alone but also interactive activities that students share and discuss with others at home.
- Help at home means how families encourage and guide children, not how they teach school subjects.

Measurable Results for Students

- Skills, abilities, and test scores linked to classwork; homework completion
- Self-confidence in ability as learner; positive attitudes about school
- Viewing parent as similar to teacher and home as in sync with school

Measurable Results for Parents

- Discussions with child about school, classwork, homework, future plans
- Understanding curriculum, what child is learning, and how to help at home

Measurable Results for Teachers and Schools

- Respect for family time; satisfaction with family involvement and support
- Recognition that single parents, dual-income families, economically disadvantaged families, and families that do not speak English can encourage and assist student learning

See Tables 5.1, 5.2, and 5.3 in Reading 5.1 for more on Type 4.

COMMENT

Understanding How Families Link to Homework

Many studies show that there are serious problems with the design, assignment, completion, and follow-up of homework in many elementary, middle, and high schools. School policies, teachers' designs of homework, student investments, and family activities all may need to be improved for students to benefit from their homework assignments.

Scott-Jones (1995a and 1995b) discussed four levels of involvement of parents and children in homework: valuing, monitoring, assisting, and doing. Families need good information each year to convey to their children that they value homework as an important task, they will monitor the completion of homework, and they want to assist students as best they can with their work. Everyone agrees that parents should not *do* their children's homework and that homework is the students' responsibility. For example, the Teachers Involve Parents in Schoolwork (TIPS) Interactive Homework process (see Chapter 6) is designed to expedite the first three levels of valuing, monitoring, and assisting homework and to prevent the fourth, with directions for students to conduct the interactions with their families.

QUESTIONS TO DISCUSS

How does family valuing, monitoring, and assisting or interacting on homework change across the grades?

1. Select and identify in ascending order three grade levels that interest you.
2. For each grade level, list one example of what you think parents might say or do to show their children that they (a) value homework, (b) monitor homework, and (c) will assist or interact with them on homework.

Grade Levels:	(a) Value Homework	(b) Monitor Homework	(c) Assist or Interact with Homework
Grade __			
Grade __			
Grade __			

3. How do the messages you listed differ or remain the same across the grade levels you selected? Explain.
4. Select one grade level from your chart. How might a teacher help all parents convey the messages you listed on how they value, monitor, and assist with student homework?

COMMENT

Homework Policies and Procedures

Parents help their children with homework based on their own knowledge about school and school subjects. An early study found that most parents say that they need information every year to help their children do their best on homework. Over 70 percent of parents surveyed in elementary, middle, and high schools wanted to know: What is the school's homework policy? Over 90 percent wanted to know: How do I help my child at home this year? (See Chapter 3 for surveys of parents.)

QUESTIONS TO DISCUSS

1. How are parents affected if teachers do or do not provide the following information on students' homework? List one result for parents that you would expect:

How Are Parents Affected . . . ?

	If teachers *do* provide information on . . .	If teachers *do not* provide information on . . .
A. Homework policies each year		
B. How homework is factored into students' report card grade in each subject		
C. How to monitor students' homework		
D. How to ask good questions so that students talk about their classwork and ideas		
E. How students can show and explain something that they learned in class		
F. How to choose academic courses in math, science, foreign languages, and electives in high school		

2. Select one result from your chart that you believe is particularly compelling. Describe one activity that might help teachers provide the information to all parents and that would produce the result that you expect.
3. Select one result from the chart that you believe is particularly troublesome. Describe one problem that could arise and an activity that would help solve that problem.

COMMENT

Innovative Designs for Interactive Homework

One way to redefine family involvement in homework and in academic decisions is to place the *student* in charge of the interactions. This strategy acknowledges that parents are not and should not be expected to teach school subjects to their children every year. Rather, students are expected to share with families interesting things they are learning in class or important decisions that must be made about academic courses, programs, or other opportunities.

In addition to the special focus on Teachers Involve Parents in Schoolwork (TIPS) in Chapter 6, there are many other ways to help families monitor their children's work and interact with them about ideas and academic decisions. The following comments and activities introduce a few interactive strategies for increasing conversations at home about students' skills in different subjects.

ACTIVITY

Purposes of Homework

You often hear people say that students should do their homework on their own in a quiet place. Indeed, some homework should be completed independently to help students learn how to study on their own. But other homework can be *interactive* to enable students to share their work and to keep families informed about what their children are learning in school. Thus, homework may be either independent or interactive. Also see Chapter 6.

A. Select and identify a grade level that interests you.
B. In the chart below, list three purposes of *independent* homework. If homework were designed for each purpose, what might be accomplished for students and for parents?
C. List three purposes of *interactive* homework. If homework were designed for each purpose, what might be accomplished for students and for parents?

Three Purposes of *Independent* Homework	What might be accomplished for students?	What might be accomplished for parents?
1.		
2.		
3.		
Three Purposes of *Interactive* Homework	What might be accomplished for students?	What might be accomplished for parents?
1.		
2.		
3.		

Student-Parent "Home Conference"

Many years ago, Ross Burkhardt, a talented middle-grade educator, designed home conferences on writing that students conducted at home. Each student made a formal appointment with a parent or family member to discuss the student's writing. The students provided their parents with folders containing selected pieces of their writing or arranged to read the work aloud. Then students conducted a structured interview that the class developed to gather parents' reactions to their work. Finally, students summarized their parents' reactions and wrote their own reactions to their parents' comments. They listed plans for improving or maintaining the quality of their writing.

The interaction enabled each student to share writing samples with a parent; gather reactions, ideas, and suggestions from a parent; and write a reflective response to what he or she learned from the discussion. A student-parent home conference could be scheduled in any subject as an interactive homework assignment once or twice a year to keep families aware of students' work and to encourage curriculum-related conversations.

ACTIVITY AND FIELD EXPERIENCE

Student-Parent "Home Conference"

A. Select a subject other than writing and a grade level that interest you.
B. Design a student-parent home conference for the subject and grade level that you selected. Include guidelines for students to:
   - arrange an appointment with a parent
   - obtain a parent's reactions to the work
   - record the parent's reactions
   - write their own reflections
C. Add one more component that you believe should be part of a home conference in the subject and grade level you selected.
D. *Optional activity*:
   1. Identify a cooperative teacher.
      a. Ask the teacher for feedback on the guidelines that you wrote for a home conference in item B above.
      b. Arrange for one class to conduct the student-parent home conference that you developed, or work with the teacher to design a set of guidelines for a home conference in writing or another subject.

Part b will require the cooperating teacher to

    (1)   use some class time to develop with students or explain the elements of a structured interview that all students will conduct with their parents

    (2)   develop with students or explain a recording form for students to report the parents' and their own reactions

    (3)   have students select a few pieces of their work in the selected subject for the home-conference folder

    (4)   assign the home conference as homework to the students and conduct the follow-up activity.

2.   Collect and summarize the students' reactions to their parents' reviews.

3.   Write a paragraph to explain your views on whether the activity succeeded in increasing student-parent communications, parents' awareness of student work, and students' understanding of their own skills and goals.

COMMENT

"Homemade Homework" Designed by Students and Families

Another way to vary homework assignments is to periodically ask children and parents to design a family-related homework activity for the student to conduct. For example, students or parents may design activities for homework such as writing a story, poem, or speech; creating artwork; taking a photograph; planning a budget and activities for a special trip; making a list to complete an important family project; or other tasks that help students practice and demonstrate real-world applications of writing, speaking, math, science, social studies, and other school skills or develop personal talents. The student and a parent or family member might create or select one assignment each month, such as:

- Write a letter to a grandparent, other relative, or family friend.
- Learn to play or sing a new song, practice it at home, and perform it in class on a traditional or created instrument.
- Write a critical summary or review of a movie, drama production, piece of music, restaurant, neighborhood location, or other family experience.
- Draw or paint a poster of a family holiday or celebration.
- Compose a speech on a topic of importance to the student or family.
- Describe an activity that the student conducted at home or in the community to help someone.
- Write a description or draw a portrait of a favorite relative or interesting person in the neighborhood.

- Write a story of something interesting that happened while conducting an ordinary activity at home (e.g., what happened when babysitting, lawn mowing, fixing a door, washing clothes, making dinner).
- Critique a website on a topic or hobby of interest to the student.
- Build a building, bridge, or box out of toothpicks, spaghetti, Legos, ice cream sticks, or other matter.
- Add one idea of your own of an activity a parent and child might choose or design for the child's homework.

ACTIVITY AND FIELD EXPERIENCE

"Homemade Homework"

Student-designed or student-and-family-designed homework assignments may be linked to different school subjects each month or on some other regular schedule.

A. Select and identify a grade level of your choice.
B. Create a plan from October to May that would guide students and families to design or select a "homemade homework" assignment for the student to conduct. In elementary grades, vary the plan for different subjects or skills each month. In middle or high school grades, vary the plan for different skills or topics for one subject that you select and identify.
C. *Optional activity*:
   1. Identify a cooperative teacher at the grade level you selected. Ask the teacher for feedback on your plan and an opportunity to test one of the activities with a class.
   2. Collect the assignment, and review in writing the results of the homemade assignments.

COMMENT

Schoolwide Interactive Homework

A school may select a key theme or topic once a month or once a marking period and assign the same homework to everyone in a particular grade or to everyone in the school. This kind of assignment directs younger and older students to think about an issue or idea that is important to everyone. For example, all students may address questions such as:

What should a new playground for the school or community look like?
How can we get more books for the library?

How can we help our community or local senior citizens' center?

Alternatively, the assignment may help all students focus on topics that are important for personal and social development, such as:

How can students be kind to each other?
What does it mean to study for a test?
How can we welcome new students to our school?

Or an assignment may focus all students on a matter of history or current events, such as:

What issues are important to you in the next election?
What should this school ask the mayor about education and school
    improvement?
What do we mean by *freedom* and *democracy*?

Schoolwide or grade-level homework assignments also could be purposely interactive with sections for students to interview a friend or a family member about the topic, as in TIPS activities (see Chapter 6).

ACTIVITY AND FIELD EXPERIENCE

Schoolwide Homework

Schoolwide homework assignments may address different issues once a month, once a marking period, twice a year, or on some regular schedule.

A. Select and identify a school level that interests you (i.e., preschool or elementary, middle, or high school).
B. Select a topic that you think is important for students at all grade levels in the school to think and talk about.
C. Create a design for schoolwide interactive homework on the topic you selected. Outline how this work might be assigned to all students, noting
   1. if adaptations are needed for younger and older students
   2. what the students will be asked to do
   3. how they will be guided to conduct interactions with a family member, friend, or member of the community.
D. *Optional activity*: Identify a cooperative school.
   1. Ask the principal, master teacher, or department chair for reactions to your design for schoolwide homework.
   2. If possible, test the idea schoolwide or with more than one collaborating teacher.

3. Collect the assignments, and write a short critique of whether and how a common assignment worked with students in different grades or classes.

Homework Assignments in Practice Teaching

A. Select a subject that you are observing or assisting with as a practice teacher.
B. Identify the subject, grade level(s) of the students, and dates of at least two observations.
C. Summarize the main content of the classroom lessons, skills taught, and homework assigned on the dates of your observations.
D. For each observation, discuss whether you think the homework assigned was well designed or poorly designed for the students in the class. If the homework or some elements were well designed, explain why. If the homework or some elements were poorly designed, explain why, and design and explain one improvement.
E. Discuss your observations with your cooperating teacher and/or your practice teaching supervisor. Discuss the difficulties or ease with which homework is designed, assigned, and completed by students.

Student Goal Setting

Another aspect of Type 4—Learning at Home focuses on parental involvement in discussions with students about their goals and strategies for success in school. Every student should be guided to set goals for each school term or marking period, the school year, and the future. Of course, teachers set goals for students, but it also is important for students—the main actors in learning—to set some of their own goals and to identify strategies and resources to reach their goals. Often, parents are unaware that their children are setting academic and behavioral goals or how to help them reach their goals each year in school.

In our early studies of high schools, one high school devised an interesting way of bringing families into student goal-setting activities. First, during an English class, all students set goals for attendance, report card grades in all subjects, and a personal goal for increasing their skills and self-confidence over the next marking period. Second, at home, students shared their goals with a parent or other family partner, discussed various strategies for reaching their goals, and how the family partner could help. Then, during a social studies period in school, students reflected on their discussions with their families and their own ideas, and wrote their final goals and strategies for the next marking period. The goals and strategies were kept in folders in the students' English classes. At the end of each marking period, students conducted another interactive homework assignment with a family partner to review and discuss whether they attained their goals, made progress, or needed more help. They wrote their new goals and strategies for the next marking period and continued the process throughout the school year.

ACTIVITY

Helping Students Discuss Goals for Success at Home

A. Select and identify a grade level that interests you. At the middle and high school levels, also select and identify a subject that interests you.

B. Using the description of a goal-setting strategy in the Comment above, develop a set of directions and forms that a teacher in the grade level or subject selected might use at the start of the school year to do the following:

- Guide students to set four important goals for success in school. You might choose attendance, achievement (in at least two subjects), homework completion, behavior, or another important goal for students in the grade level you selected.
- Have students identify strategies that they will use to reach their goals.
- Enable students to conduct an interactive homework assignment as a structured interview with a family partner at home to discuss their goals, strategies to reach their goals, and how parents or other family members may help the students with their goals and strategies.
- Guide students to write their final goals and strategies to reach their goals, after reflecting on their discussion with a family partner.

C. Share designs for goal-setting activities with a partner in class. Check whether the directions and processes are clear, well timed for students and families, and appropriate for the grade levels and subjects selected.

See Chapter 6 for one targeted program to organize Type 4—Learning at Home for Teachers Involve Parents in Schoolwork (TIPS) Interactive Homework and additional discussion topics and activities on school, family, and community partnerships for student learning.

Participation and Leadership

Type 5—Decision Making activities include families as participants in school decisions, governance, and advocacy activities on school councils or school improvement teams, Action Teams for Partnerships, other committees, PTA/PTO, and other school-based or independent parent organizations. Type 5 activities prepare some parents for leadership roles and enable parent representatives to obtain information from and give information to the families they represent. Type 5 activities also prime all parents to serve as advocates for their own child so that they have equitable access to programs, services, and opportunities that are offered by a school, district, or community.

Increasingly, schools are recognizing the importance of parent representatives on school councils, site-based management teams, committees that focus on partnerships and other aspects of school improvement, and other advisory groups. One of the many Type 5 challenges is for parent representatives to reflect the diverse populations and neighborhoods served by the school. It also is important for parent representatives to communicate well with other parents to obtain input on school decisions and to report the results of school meetings. Schools are meeting this challenge by creating leadership positions for neighborhood representatives to reach out to traditionally underrepresented groups and ensure that all families have a voice in policy decisions.

If Type 5—Decision Making activities are well designed and well implemented, more families should feel a strong attachment to their school. They may be willing to serve on committees or assist committees with ideas and resources. Some families may be willing to lobby for more effective state and district policies and funding to benefit their school and all students. Also, educators learn that parents' views improve and extend discussions that lead to more inclusive and responsive decisions.

Focus of Type 5 Activities

- PTA/PTO membership, participation, leadership, representation
- Advisory councils, school improvement teams, Action Teams for Partnerships
- Title I councils, school-site management teams, other committees
- Independent advocacy groups

Challenges

- Include parent leaders from all racial, ethnic, socioeconomic, and other groups in the school.
- Offer training for parent representatives to develop leadership skills.
- Include student representatives along with parents in decision making.

Redefinitions

- *Decision making* means a process of partnership to share views and take action toward shared goals, not a power struggle.

Measurable Results for Students

- Awareness that families are represented in school decisions
- Specific benefits linked to policies enacted by parent organizations

Measurable Results for Parents

- Awareness of and input on policies that affect children's education
- Shared experiences and connections with other families

Measurable Results for Teachers and Schools

- Awareness of families' perspectives on policies and school decisions
- Acceptance of family representatives as equals on school committees

See Tables 5.1, 5.2, and 5.3 in Reading 5.1 for more on Type 5.

COMMENT

Type 5—Decision-Making Partnerships, Not Power Plays

Type 5—Decision Making activities recognize and increase parents' abilities to express their opinions and contribute to school plans and policies. In Type 5 activities, parent representatives take leadership roles along with educators. Parent leaders help other parents understand and contribute ideas to issues and policies that affect the design and quality of school programs and opportunities for all children. Because parents and teachers share an interest in and responsibility for children's learning and development, parents' voices and ideas add important dimensions to school decisions about children's education.

To successfully implement Type 5—Decision Making, it is necessary for schools to address several challenges. One is to help parent leaders serve as true representatives of other families. This includes helping leaders obtain ideas from and return information to the families they represent about school decisions, programs, and activities.

In many schools, parents' opinions about school policies are not taken seriously. Some schools have no parent organization (e.g., PTA, PTO, PTSA). Some have no school council, site-management team, or committee structure that includes family representatives. Often, even when such groups include parents, only a few parents participate actively. When they do participate, few parent representatives collect information from other families or share the results of school meetings and decisions with other parents.

Consequently, in most schools, only a few parents know what topics, issues, and decisions are discussed or enacted. Typically, only a few voices arc heard from parent leaders who may or may not represent the views of other parents. These patterns and problems of selective participation are even more evident on district-level councils and committees.

Interestingly, most families do not want to serve on committees or in leadership roles, but most do want parents' voices represented in school decisions. In a study of high schools, for example, we found that about 8 percent of parents wanted to serve on committees, but just about all others wanted parent representatives on councils and committees so that parents' had a say in school decisions.

For parent leaders to represent all parents on major committees, it is necessary to develop Type 5—Decision Making skills and strategies. For example:

- Parent leaders must be numerous and be selected or elected in ways that give the parents of all groups of students (from different neighborhoods, racial and ethnic groups, special interests) representative voices in school decisions.
- Parent leaders must be assisted to effectively represent other parents by gathering their ideas on important issues and by reporting back to the families they represent. Because not every parent attends committee meetings, communication with parent leaders is evidence of all parents' participation.
- Similarly, administrators, teachers, students, or others from the community who serve on decision-making teams also must gather and give information to those they represent.
- New leaders must be continually prepared to serve as representatives and active participants in all schools. Processes must be organized and ongoing for selecting representatives and conducting decision-making activities because parent leaders, at one time, move to other schools and to other neighborhoods as their children progress through the grades.

In comprehensive programs of school, family, and community partnerships, there must be adequate and effective representation of all parents' ideas by parent leaders.

QUESTIONS TO DISCUSS

Should parents' views be represented in all school decisions?

1. Select and identify a level of schooling that interests you.
2. Divide a page in half.
   a. On one side, list arguments that support a response of *yes* to the above question for the level of schooling that you selected. Give at least two reasons why parents' views should be represented in all school decisions.
   b. On the other side, list arguments that support a response of *no* to the question for the level of schooling that you selected. Give at least two reasons why parents' views should not be represented in all school decisions, and give at least two examples of decisions that should be made only by teachers or administrators.
3. Share your ideas in a class discussion or debate.
4. After hearing others' ideas and considering your own arguments, write a policy statement about family representation in school decisions that you believe would work in a school or district. Discuss whether the policy statement would be feasible to implement.

FIELD EXPERIENCE

Parent Participation in School Decisions

A. Interview a state, district, or school administrator or a teacher for ideas about how families should be and could be involved in school decisions and on policy-related committees. (This may be conducted as an individual assignment or by inviting an administrator for a class interview.)
B. Identify the policy level you selected and the job title of your interviewee. Ask:
   1. Approximately how many students are served in your state/district/school?
   2. In your work, which organizations, committees, or other formal policy-making groups presently include parent representatives?
   3. If any, ask:
      a. This year, about how many parents serve on these decision-making or advisory bodies?
      b. What contributions do you think parents make to these groups?
      c. What leadership training is provided to parent leaders and to others on these committees?

4. If none, ask:
   a. What committees, task forces, or other groups or organizations do you think would benefit from parent representatives?
   b. What contributions do you think parents would make to these groups?
   c. What leadership training would be needed to prepare parent leaders and others on these committees?
C. What is one successful example of family participation in school decisions that you have experienced or heard about?
D. What is one problem that you have experienced or heard about concerning family involvement in school decisions? What is one possible solution to this problem?
E. Add at least one question of your own about parent or community representation.
F. Document your questions and the interviewee's responses. From the information in this chapter and the answers from your interview:
   1. Summarize your assessment of the quality of participation of families in Type 5—Decision Making in the state/district/school in your interview.
   2. Include one recommendation to improve the quality of parent participation in Type 5—Decision Making in the location you examined.

QUESTIONS TO DISCUSS

1. Suppose that your school or district served five different neighborhoods of mainly white, African American, Latino, Asian American, and American Indian families, respectively. Your school has a PTA, a school improvement team, and an Action Team for Partnerships (ATP). Your district has a district advisory committee, a community development committee, and a business outreach committee. Right now, just about all of the parent representatives on these six school and district committees are from one of the five neighborhoods served by the school. Is this a problem that needs a solution?
   a. If yes, explain why, and provide one solution to the problem you defined.
   b. If no, explain why this is not a problem.
2. Mr. Jones has been PTA president for nine years. His children have graduated from school, but he is still the PTA president of their prior elementary school. Is this a problem that needs a solution?
   a. If yes, explain why, and provide one solution to the problem you defined.
   b. If no, explain why this is not a problem.

3. The monthly PTA meetings are poorly attended. Only the officers and a few regulars attend these meetings. Minutes are taken, but they are not distributed. Is this a problem that needs a solution?
   a. If yes, explain why, and provide one solution to the problem you defined.
   b. If no, explain why this is not a problem.

SUMMARY: TYPE 6—COLLABORATING WITH THE COMMUNITY

Where Is the School Community?

Type 6—Collaborating with the Community activities bring extra human, fiscal, and physical resources, programs, and services from the community to the school. Connections with small and large businesses; government agencies; cultural, religious, civic, and fraternal organizations; colleges and universities; and other community groups and individuals should benefit students, families, or the school. Type 6 activities also enable students, staff, and families to contribute their services to the community.

All schools are located in communities, but many schools are strangely isolated from the businesses, agencies, senior citizens, cultural centers, and other potentially helpful groups and individuals in their locations. Students often live in one community, travel to the school community, attend religious services in another community, have after-school care somewhere else, and link to businesses in still other locations. Schools rarely tap the full set of resources from all communities that have ties to and interest in students. One Type 6 challenge is to identify the resources in the community that will advance school improvement goals, enrich school programs, and meet the needs of students and families.

If Type 6 activities are well designed and well implemented, students and families will learn about and use the various community services and programs to improve health, increase skills, and develop the talents of all family members. Schools will enrich their curriculum and instruction and improve the school climate by collaborating with the community.

Focus of Type 6 Activities

- Community contributes to schools, students, and families
- Business partners, agencies, cultural groups, health services, recreation, and many other groups strengthen programs and classroom curricula

- Schools, students, and families contribute to community
- Students in service learning programs conduct projects to share talents and to solve community problems

Challenges

- Solve problems of turf, responsibilities, funds, and goals to effectively organize school-community collaborations.
- Inform all families and students about community programs and services.
- Ensure equal access and opportunities for participation.

Redefinitions

- *Community* includes not only families with children in the schools but also all who are interested in and affected by the quality of education.
- Communities are rated not only on economic qualities but also on the strengths and talents available to support students, families, and schools.

Measurable Results for Students

- Knowledge, skills, and talents from enriched curricular and extracurricular experiences and from exploring careers in the community
- Self-confidence, feeling valued by and belonging to the community

Measurable Results for Parents

- Knowledge and use of local resources to improve health, increase skills, develop talents, and obtain needed services for families
- Interactions with other families and contributions to community

Measurable Results for Teachers and Schools

- Knowledge and use of community resources for curriculum and instruction

See Tables 5.1, 5.2, and 5.3 in Reading 5.1 for more on Type 6.

Getting to Know the "Community"

It is not easy for educators to know about all of the resources in their communities. Few teachers or principals live near their schools, as was common in the distant past. There are several reasons, however, why it may benefit students if educators and parents conduct Type 6 activities to learn more about their communities and to draw on available resources to help students succeed in school and in life.

One Type 6 challenge is to identify and mobilize community support of school goals for student learning. In some schools, contributions by business partners of equipment or volunteer time are unconnected to the goals of the school or to student learning. Ties with businesses and industries, organizations, agencies, and other groups and individuals in the community should be designed to support, enrich, and extend the school's agenda to promote success for more students (Mickelson, 1996; Sanders, 2005).

For example, several years ago, one school's business partner (the local office of a national telephone company) placed phones in all teachers' classrooms, making it possible for teachers to communicate more easily with parents. Other business partners have funded small grants to schools to develop better school, family, and community partnerships on all types of involvement. Some community partners organize food banks with low-income families' assistance and participation, clothing for parents to attend school functions, eyeglasses for students, books for students or school libraries, Internet connections to scientists, mentors, job-shadowing programs for high school students, and other goal-oriented activities that are linked to student and family needs or interests and to school improvement plans. In this way, Type 6—Collaborating with the Community comes full circle to link with Type 1—Parenting to help families fulfill basic obligations to feed, clothe, care for, and guide their children.

A second challenge is for schools to view the term *community* broadly to build connections with many members and groups who have an interest in developing successful students and good citizens. These include the businesses, organizations, and other groups and individuals in and around the school, in neighborhoods where students live, in faith communities where students worship, in locations that hire students for part-time employment, in areas where parents work, and in other places that are important to students, families, and the school.

The *school community* includes all family and community members who care what happens to the school and to children, whether or not they have children in the school. Because children are the future adults, workers, and families in communities, it is important to foster positive and productive connections with all who have a stake in good schools and student success.

Community Portraits

Many educators, families, and students are unaware of the resources in their communities. Indeed, many are unclear where their community begins and ends. The boundaries of a school community may be narrowly defined to include only the neighborhood around the school, broadly drawn to include the home communities of all who are served by the school, or even more inclusive of the whole town or city.

Students, teachers, and families can learn about available resources if they create a "community portrait" of the area around the school, home neighborhoods, and other locations where children, families, and teachers spend time and give or receive services (Family Resource Coalition, 1996; Goode, 1990). These include museums, zoos, libraries, shops, places for child care, places of worship, and other locations where students and families visit, work, give or obtain services, learn, or play. This activity asks you to think about your community, then consider how you might address the same questions in a school setting to help students and families think about their communities.

A. Divide a page in half with:

Side A: YOUR OWN community   Side B: OTHER communities

Answer the A questions on one side of the page and the B questions on the other side. Then answer the summary questions.

1a. Where are the boundaries of your community?

1b. How might you guide students, teachers, and families to identify the geographic boundaries of what they consider their community?

2a. Who lives in your community?

2b. How might you guide students, teachers, and families to identify and report information on the various groups of people who live in their communities?

3a. What are the social and economic conditions in your community that identify its strengths and needs?

3b. How might you guide students, teachers, and families to collect information and report on the diverse social and economic conditions, strengths, and needs in their communities?

4a. What organizations, groups, programs, or special resources in your community are interested in schools, students, and families?

4b. How might you guide students, teachers, and families to collect information on groups that are interested in and have resources, services, programs, and opportunities for students and families in their communities?

B. Present the information on your community (from questions 1a, 2a, 3a, and 4a) in a community portrait as a report, chart, picture, or other form that you think might be useful for a particular audience of your choice (e.g., families, students, community group).

C. From your ideas for questions 1b, 2b, 3b, and 4b, summarize an activity that would enable teachers or a team of teachers and parents to create a community portrait that they could use to enrich their school and services for students and families.

COMMENT

Finding Community

We need to define the school community to include all who have a stake in the quality of students' education. This includes families in the community with children in school and people in the community who have no children in school. The latter group is growing in size and is sometimes described as hostile to or uninterested in public schools.

Contrary to some beliefs, however, people with no children in school are connected to schools, families, and to children in many ways. They have grandchildren, nieces, nephews, and other relatives or friends and neighbors in school. They hire students to work for them. They live next door to students and see them in the neighborhood. They follow school sports in the news and are served by students and graduates in restaurants, stores, hospitals, and other locations in the community. Future policies, products, programs, services, and qualities of life in communities depend on the education, skills, and talents of the children they know and the children they do not know who are presently in schools.

FIELD EXPERIENCE

Community Interview

A. Interview one community member who has no children in the public schools. Identify this person's occupation, approximate age, and other characteristics that you think are important. Ask:
1. How do you rate the public schools presently in your community: excellent, good, average, or poor? Explain.
2. Did you attend public or private school in elementary school, middle grades, and high school? What was the quality of your educational program at each school level?
3a. Do you have any children?
3b. If yes, and they are older than school age: Did your children attend public or private school? Was it in this community? How would you rate the quality of the education they received at their schools: excellent, good, average, or poor?

3c. If yes, and they are younger than school age: Will your children attend public or private school in this community?

4a. Do you have any relatives whose children presently attend public schools in this or another community?

4b. About how many in all?

4c. About how many in this community?

5. Do you have any friends whose children presently attend public schools in this or other communities?

5a. About how many in all?

5b. About how many in this community?

6. Do you ever talk with children, adolescents, or graduates of the public schools in this community? If so, what is one example of an interaction you have had?

7. How are you presently affected by the quality of education offered by the local public schools?

8. How do you think you will be affected in the future by the quality of the local public schools?

B. Add at least one question of your own.

C. Document your questions and the responses.

D. Summarize your views of how this person is linked to the public schools. What are the implications of the responses that you obtained? How typical do you think this person is compared to others in the community?

E. Compare notes in class to learn about the variety of connections that community members have with schools and students, whether or not their children are attending public schools.

COMMENT

Meetings with Parents at School and in the Community

Schools are the most common place for meetings with parents, but they are not the only possible sites. Meetings for parents and others in the community may be held in other locations that are open and accessible to all, including libraries, churches, community centers, apartment or community meeting rooms, and business or community auditoriums.

Some small meetings or "coffees" have been organized in volunteers' living rooms, apartment buildings' common rooms, and centrally located community spaces. Individual home visits also may be conducted to meet with parents. One year, a school in the National Network of Partnership Schools (NNPS) reported an innovative *Promising Partnership Practice* held mid-summer on a local beach! The activity brought together teachers, administrators, parents, and students to encourage summer reading.

Notices of school and community meetings may be posted in supermarkets, Laundromats, and other neighborhood locations, and information on school programs, schedules, events, newsletters, and other announcements also may be distributed at these sites.

Although some meetings about school may be conducted in other settings, it is important for teachers and families to communicate easily with each other. Indeed, schools must make all families welcome and comfortable about coming to school for important meetings, conferences, celebrations, student presentations, and other school-linked activities.

QUESTIONS TO DISCUSS

1. Select and identify a grade level that interests you and one of the following activities: Back-to-School Night, parent-teacher conference, meeting about a school policy, or a topic of your choice.
2. What are the pros and cons about conducting the activity you selected at school or in the community? Consider the location; the ease of access for all families; time, travel, and other conditions that are likely to affect attendance and participation of families; and the success of the activity. Create a chart that lists your ideas:
   a. Which activity did you select? _____
   b. Which grade level did you select? _____

	PROS Two reasons this *is* a good location	CONS Two reasons this is *not* a good location
At school?	1. 2.	
In the community In what location? _____	1. 2.	

COMMENT

Community Connections for Student Success

On any given day, students are either in school or out of school. When they are not in school, their families, peers, and communities either reinforce, complement, or counter school goals for student learning and development. Heather Weiss and others call out-of-school activities for students *complementary learning* (Bouffard and Weiss, 2008). Gordon, Bridglall, and Meroe (2005) call out-of-school-activities *supplementary education*. These terms focus on after-school activities and community programs and services that increase students' skills and talents. Dryfoos and others advocate for out-of-school activities to be housed within a *full-service* school, so that students, families, and community members use the school building throughout the day and evening for positive programs and services that support student learning (Dryfoos, 1994; Dryfoos and McGuire, 2002). In *partnership schools*, the goal is for educators, parents, and community partners to work together to provide in-school and out-of-school opportunities, at school, at home, and in the community, that increase student learning, talents, and success in school.

Community partners are valuable participants in partnership programs—in or out of school, with complementary, supplementary, or simply excellent programs and services. When educators, families, and the community reinforce and extend student learning and success, the spheres of influence of home, school, and community overlap in productive ways, and students experience strong support in school and out. Alternatively, when home, school, and community are disconnected, youngsters may reject the student's role and may be more likely to drop out of school.

QUESTIONS TO DISCUSS

Example A. Some community groups recognize and reward students for excellence and improvement. For example, a few communities created a "Gold Card" program to give middle and high school students discounts on purchases for a defined period of time if they attained and maintained high attendance or good grades or improved significantly over a marking period.

  A. Describe one other community recognition or support program for students that you know or have heard about.
  B. How might something like a Gold Card program or the program that you described help a student, a family, a school, and a community?

Example B. Most students are assisted when schools, families, peers, and communities reinforce and enrich school, learning, and service. There are times, however, when this rule does not hold. For example, students who are not succeeding in school may be positively influenced by community programs and services that treat them *better* than they are treated in school. Nonschool contacts may give these students more respect and more rewarding messages than they receive in school. Nonschool contacts, including peers, families, employers, and other community members, may appreciate students' ideas, assistance, special skills, and talents more than their teachers, administrators, and classmates do.

1. Describe one program or activity that you know or have heard about in which a student who is failing or having trouble in school is succeeding in an activity in the community.
2. How would the program or activity you described help a student, a family, a school, and a community?
3. Discuss one way in which a student's success in community activities might be directly linked to schoolwork and might increase a failing students' chances of success in school.

FIELD EXPERIENCE

Interview with a Community Organization Representative

How do community groups link to schools? One district working with the National Network of Partnership Schools worked with its foreign language radio stations and newspapers to place notices about school events in places that would reach families who did not speak English at home. A high school working to improve students' success in school worked with a clothing firm to increase students' experiences in marketing, design, and career exploration.

Select a local community agency, cultural group, citizens' group, religious institution, government office, fraternal or other social organization, college or university public relations office, radio, TV, cable TV, newspaper community relations office, local foundation or philanthropic group, business, or other community location that has an interest in children and their success in school.

A. Identify the place and your contact person. Ask the contact person:
   1. In what way(s) is your organization interested in children, learning, schools, and families?
   2. In what way(s) does your organization presently assist children, schools, or families? What are your programs and their goals? How many participate? How long have the programs operated?
   3. What programs or activities would you like to add or improve in the future to link your organization to children, schools, and families? In your organization, how would decisions be made to implement these changes?
B. Add at least one question of your own.
C. Document your questions and responses.
D. From the information you obtained, write a short summary on the quality and purposes of this organization's connections to students, families, and/or schools. Include one recommendation for improving this organization's partnerships in the future.

E. Share all students' summaries in class to gain a broader view of the many ways that community groups partner with schools to improve school programs and to increase students' learning and development.

COMMENT

Part-Time Jobs in Communities

When they are in middle and high school, adolescents increase their connections with businesses, community groups, agencies, and others in the community. Students join clubs and organizations in their communities, shop, help neighbors with odd jobs, have part-time jobs, join summer programs, take lessons outside of school, volunteer to serve their community, and participate in many other community activities. In some school districts, middle and high school students must earn service-learning credits as a graduation requirement.

Many high school students and some middle school students work part-time during the school year. According to the Bureau of Labor Statistics (2005) from 41 percent of high school freshman to 87 percent of high school seniors (over 70 percent of all high school students) worked during the school year or summer. Often, students' part-time or summer jobs or activities in the community are treated as if they were unrelated to the school program. Yet students gain academic and social skills on the job, meet and solve problems, and contribute to the community in their work and with their earnings.

There are important debates about whether students should work during high school, for how many hours, and in what kinds of jobs. Some early studies that concluded that students should not work too many hours during the school year were emotionally interpreted to mean that part-time work is bad for students. Recent studies based on national samples of students, longitudinal data, and more rigorous analyses found that most students were not adversely affected by their work experiences within the current range of hours worked, from a few hours to about 20 hours per week (Mortimer, Finch, Dennehy, Lee, and Beebe, 1994; Schoenhals, Tienda, and Schneider, 1998). Clearly, students need guidance about balancing school and employment, and some need to be limited in their part-time work if their schoolwork is suffering (The College Board, 2009). An equally important question is whether and how employers should require students to have or maintain excellent school attendance and report card grades to continue employment during the school year.

Linking School and Part-Time Employment

How can students' part-time and summer jobs be more productively linked to their school programs? Interview an employer of a high school student, a parent or teacher of a student who has a part-time job, or a student who is employed part-time. Or invite one or more of these people for a class interview.

    A. Identify the person you are interviewing: an employer, parent, teacher, or student. Ask:

       1. What are two things that an employer might do to help student employees place high priority on school attendance, classwork, homework, studying, course grades, completing high school, and continuing their education?

       2. What are two things that families might do to ensure that their children do not fall behind in school as a result of part-time work?

       3. What are two things schools might do to link students' employment with required courses?

       4. What are two things students might do to demonstrate that they can successfully balance school, work, leisure, and family responsibilities?

       5. Give two ideas of how such school-family-community linkages might benefit students who work while they are in high school.

    B. Add one question of your own.

    C. List your questions and the interviewee's responses.

    D. Write a summary of the most important ideas that were discussed for connecting student jobs and student learning.

Community Forums and Advocates for Education

Some research and development activities focus on the roles of community leaders and members, task forces, advocates, and other groups in improving schools. Often called *community engagement*, this type of involvement may be sponsored by a governor's Office on Children, Youth, and Families; a mayor; community organizers; business roundtables; chambers of commerce; citizens for school improvement; or others. The goal is to encourage participants from all parts of the community to share their views, concerns, and goals for excellent schools, highly competent and responsive teachers and administrators, and new programs for students.

There are two views on community roles in school improvement. On one hand, community-led discussions and initiatives may result in new and innovative ideas. On the other hand, most community gatherings produce a list of good and common goals, often the same goals as teachers and all parents have for their schools and for their children. The list is then filed and often forgotten.

Years ago, community leaders thought they could simply "organize" and tell the leaders of districts and schools what to do. That never worked. Schools are embedded in a complex educational system with regulations and requirements that develop at the federal, state, district, and school levels. Community groups may think they have different and better goals than do district and school leaders, but most forums reveal that educators, parents, business leaders, and citizens have very similar goals for their schools and for their students.

New efforts in community engagement show how important it is for community groups to collaborate with (not fight with) the educators in their districts and schools. This is very clear in a recent study of how community groups in seven cities worked with school leaders to improve programs and promote student success in attendance, achievement, high school graduation, and postsecondary plans (Blank, Melaville, and Shah, 2003; Bodilly and Beckett, 2005; Mediratta, Shah, and McAlister, 2009).

QUESTIONS TO DISCUSS

1. What roles do community members play in improving elementary, middle, and high schools in their area?
2. Why is it important for elected officials or for school district leaders to conduct periodic community forums on education and on school reform?

ACTIVITY

Who Can Improve the Schools?

A. Select one of the following statements to discuss, defend, or dispute.
   1. Resolved: People in business, industry, and other professions and occupations know how to improve schools better than educators do.
   2. Resolved: Educators at the state, district, and/or school levels know how to improve schools better than other citizens in communities do.
   3. Resolved: The best way to improve schools is for educators and community leaders to exchange ideas and work together.
   4. Resolved: If the community is engaged in improving schools, then educators need not organize programs and activities to involve all students' families in their education.
B. Use one of the following references (or a recent article that you select on connections with community) to learn more and to support your views.

Chadwick, K. G. (2004). *Improving schools through community engagement*. Thousand Oaks, CA: Corwin.

Mediratta, K., S. Shah, and S. McAlister. (2009). *Community organizing for stronger schools: Strategies and successes*. Cambridge, MA: Harvard Education Publishing Group.

Nettles, S. M. (1991). Community involvement and disadvantaged students. *Review of Educational Research* 61: 379–406.

Sanders, M. G. (2005). *Building school-community partnerships: Collaborating for student success*. Thousand Oaks, CA: Corwin.

Sanders, M. G., and A. Harvey. (2002). Beyond the school walls: A case study of principal leadership for school-community collaboration. *Teachers College Record* 104(7): 1345–1368.

Waddock, S. A. (1995). *Not by schools alone: Sharing responsibility for America's education reform*. Westport, CT: Praeger.

C. Write a paragraph or two describing your views, and be ready to defend your ideas in class. Identify the reference that you used.

SUMMARY: THE 6 TYPES OF INVOLVEMENT

To summarize, it is important to understand how the six types of involvement can be used to develop comprehensive programs of school, family, and community partnerships in all schools. We have learned that it is necessary to redefine parent involvement with new designs for school, family, and community partnerships. It also is imperative to meet the challenges that have prevented many families from becoming involved in their children's education. In this section, we explore how the six types of involvement are connected. This includes how basic and advanced activities contribute to a balanced program of partnerships, how one type of involvement promotes another, and how several types of involvement may strengthen the chances of reaching important results. The summary comments and activities should increase your understanding of the types of involvement, separately and in combination.

SUMMARY: NEW DEFINITIONS FOR FAMILY AND COMMUNITY INVOLVEMENT IN THE 21ST CENTURY

The framework of six types of involvement helps school-based teams of teachers, administrators, and parents responsible for planning and improving family and community involvement, as well as individual educators, develop comprehensive programs of school, family, and community partnerships. Such programs include activities that are designed and implemented to involve all families in new ways at school, at home, and in the community. Data from many studies contributed to the following "redefinitions" of involvement that must be understood and activated for effective school, family, and community partnerships in the twenty-first century. (See Reading 5.1 and the summaries of the six types in this chapter for examples.)

QUESTIONS TO DISCUSS

1. Give one example of a school, family, and community partnership activity that would fulfill the spirit of each of the following redefinitions for selected activities for the six types of involvement.

Sample Redefinition—Type 1

A *workshop* not only is a meeting on a topic held at the school building but also the content of that meeting, which may be viewed, heard, or read at convenient times and varied locations.

a. One activity that represents this new definition is:

_____

Sample Redefinition—Type 2

Communications about school programs and student progress are not only from school to home but also from home to school and with the community.

b. One activity that represents this new definition is:

_____

Sample Redefinition—Type 3

Volunteers are not only parents or others who come to help during the school day but also those who give their time to support school goals and children's learning in any location.

c. One activity that represents this new definition is:

_____

Sample Redefinition—Type 4

Help at home does not mean that parents must know how to teach school subjects but that families guide, encourage, and interact with their children on homework and school-related decisions.

d. One activity that represents this new definition is:

_____

Sample Redefinition—Type 5

Decision making means exchanging views to plan and implement an effective, co-ordinated partnership program that will help students succeed in school, not an endless, contentious power struggle.

 e. One activity that represents this new definition is:

_____

Sample Redefinition—Type 6

Community includes not only families with children in school but also all community members who are interested in and affected by the quality of education.

 f. One activity that represents this new definition is:

_____

2. Select one of the above redefinitions that interests you. Write a short paragraph on:
  a. One major difference between the "old" and "new" definitions of the term you selected.
  b. One way the new definition might affect how school, family, and community partnerships are conducted.

COMMENT

Meeting Challenges for Excellent Partnerships

Even if the redefinitions of involvement were applied, there still would be many challenges to meet in implementing high-quality partnership programs. By meeting key challenges, more or all parents will be informed and involved in their children's education. The questions in the next section start with a *challenge* for each of the six types of involvement that must be met with well-designed activities for preschools and elementary, middle, and high schools to reach out to all families.

QUESTIONS TO DISCUSS

1. Rewrite each of the following "challenge sentences" to give one idea of how all schools (preschools and elementary, middle, and high schools) might meet that challenge to try to involve more parents or all parents. An example is given for one of the Type 1 challenges.

Sample Type 1 Challenge

Challenge: Not all parents provide information to schools about their goals for their children.

   Rewrite: To meet this challenge, all schools could conduct a short survey of all parents about their goals, dreams, and expectations for their children each year.

Type 1 Challenge

Not all parents can attend workshops at school when they are scheduled.
   a. To meet this challenge, all schools could

_____

Type 2 Challenge

Not all parents feel comfortable asking teachers or principals questions about school programs and their children's progress or giving suggestions for improvements.
   b. To meet this challenge, all schools could

_____

Type 3 Challenge

Not all parents can volunteer to assist at the school building during the school day.
   c. To meet this challenge, all schools could

_____

Type 4 Challenge

Not all parents understand the teacher's homework policies or how to monitor and assist their children with homework.

d. To meet this challenge, all schools could

_____

Type 5 Challenge

Not all parents want to serve on school committees or in other organized leadership roles, but they want parents' voices represented in school decisions.
     e. To meet this challenge, all schools could

_____

Type 6 Challenge

Not all parents have good information about the programs, resources, and services in their communities that could assist and benefit their children and families.
     f. To meet this challenge, all schools could

_____

COMMENT

Basic and Advanced Practices

Basic Activities

A common question about the types of involvement is: Which basic activities should our school conduct to involve families? Are there some things that all schools should do with all families? Should some practices for each of the six types of involvement be implemented before other practices?

There are no right answers to these questions. What is basic or essential in one school may be unnecessary in another. What is essential one year may not be needed the next year if the population of students and families changes or if school goals are changed or attained. These unknowns emphasize the importance of customizing plans and selecting activities for the six types of involvement to meet the needs, interests, goals, and capabilities at each school. For example:

- If many families need help in obtaining food or clothing for their children, then a food bank or a clothing swap-shop may be a basic Type 1—Parenting activity at a school. If these are not major problems, it would be foolish to spend time and effort in organizing and conducting a food bank or a swap-shop.

- If most families do not feel comfortable at school or knowledgeable about the school's programs, then a Family Fun and Learning Night (Type 2) may be basic for increasing parents' feelings of welcome and for initiating positive parent-teacher communications.
- If students are chronically absent, then family and community involvement focused on improving attendance is basic and essential for increasing student success.

Schools with different goals or different challenges to partnerships would select different basic activities to involve families and members of the community in important and useful ways. Thus, it is the framework of six types of involvement that is basic and prescribed for an effective program of school, family, and community partnerships, not any one particular activity. Every school must know its families, students, teachers, and goals to select practices that create a balanced and productive partnership program. Although every program will include some different practices, there are some common home, school, and community connections that are valued by parents and by educators in many or most schools.

For example, one basic Type 2—Communicating activity in all schools is to communicate that all families are welcome and that two-way communications will be a regular feature of every teacher's practice. Some schools need to hang welcome signs in many languages; some need to develop friendly sign-in procedures for parents and visitors who enter the building. Just about all schools need to organize ways to gather families' ideas for improving school programs from year to year.

Conferences also are basic Type 2—Communicating activities. These may be designed as parent-teacher, parent-teacher-student, or student-led parent-teacher-student conferences. Such conferences may be individual, group, or grade-level meetings, using face-to-face, phone, or other communications. Whatever their format, conferences need to be scheduled so that all parents are able to attend.

Similarly, school or class newsletters are basic Type 2—Communicating practices in most schools. All newsletters should be readable in languages parents can understand. Newsletters in California schools are often written on tri-folds in English, Spanish, and Chinese as a matter of state law. Newsletters will differ, however, in whether they are long or short; with or without student work; on paper, on a website, or sent via e-mail to families who request that format. Whatever the content or format, newsletters need to include two-way communication formats for families to respond with ideas, comments, or questions.

Preschools and elementary, middle, and high schools will select different basic activities for all six types of involvement to meet important needs and goals. At all school levels, however, all activities must be designed to meet key challenges to involve all families. That means, for example, that parent-teacher conferences should not be conducted only with parents of students who are having serious problems, nor only with the families of successful students. Newsletters should not be written using vocabulary that only some can read. Although basic communications will vary in design and quality, all excellent partnership programs will include some basic activities that are well planned, well implemented, and continually reviewed and improved.

Advanced Activities

In addition to basic or common activities to involve families and communities, there are advanced, complex, or specially targeted practices that may require more time and resources to design and conduct. For example, it takes considerable time and a large number of participants to plan and implement a multicultural fair, a monthly series of family workshops on curricular topics, a "turn-off-the-TV" series of events, weekly interactive homework assignments in particular subjects, a four-year sequence to help families and students develop postsecondary plans for college or work, community improvement projects, and other large-scale projects.

Specially targeted advanced practices may be designed and implemented to meet the special needs of selected students and families. For example, some schools need to translate all print and nonprint communications with families into Spanish or other languages and to have translators at parent-teacher conferences and other meetings to assist some parents. District resources may be needed for this advanced agenda, or other creative solutions may be developed that require time to organize. By including these targeted activities, families who would not be involved can be included by design.

A comprehensive partnership program should include a reasonable mix of basic and advanced partnership activities that can be conducted by educators, parents, and others working together. The activities should be designed to meet major challenges to excellent involvement and contribute to the attainment of school improvement goals. (See Chapter 7 for an action team approach that supports good planning and continual improvement of partnership programs.)

ACTIVITY

Identifying Basic and Advanced Partnerships

What are some basic and advanced activities for each type of involvement?

A. Identify a level of schooling that interests you (preschool or elementary, middle, or high school).
B. In the chart on the next page, create a hypothetical school at the level you selected. Give the school a name.
C. List a few key features of your hypothetical school, including its size (number of students), locale (urban, suburban, rural), and some features of the students and families served (e.g., racial and ethnic composition, family education background, and levels of student achievement).
D. Which family or community involvement activities will be *basic* at your school? Use Reading 5.1, the summaries in the chapter, and the website for *Promising Partnership Practices* to fill in the chart.

1. List one *basic* activity for each of the six types of involvement that is common in most schools and that should be conducted in your hypothetical school.
2. Give one reason why you think each basic activity is essential for your school.

Name of your hypothetical school: _____

School Features:
Size of school (number of students): _____
Locale (urban, suburban, rural): _____
Racial/ethnic composition of students: _____
Mix of education levels of parents: _____
Mix of levels of student achievement: _____

Type of Involvement	One Basic Activity	Why Is It Important?
Type 1—Parenting: To help parents understand child and adolescent development.		
Type 2—Communicating: To help parents understand school programs and children's progress.		
Type 3—Volunteering: To support the school and students.		
Type 4—Learning at Home: To help students and families interact at home on homework and the curriculum.		
Type 5—Decision Making: To develop parent leadership and to encourage parent input on school matters.		
Type 6—Collaborating with the Community: To connect people and resources in ways that assist students, families, and the school.		

E. Which *advanced* or more complex activities are needed in your hypothetical school? Use Reading 5.1, the summaries in the chapter, and the website resource of *Promising Partnership Practices* to fill in the chart below.

1. List one advanced, complex, or specially targeted activity for each type of involvement that will enrich your school's partnership program or meet some unique needs and interests of students, families, and the community.

2. Give one reason why you think each advanced activity will strengthen, enrich, extend, or enliven your school's program of partnerships.

Type of Involvement	One Advanced Activity	Why Is It Important?
Type 1—Parenting		
Type 2—Communicating		
Type 3—Volunteering		
Type 4—Learning at Home		
Type 5—Decision Making		
Type 6—Collaborating with the Community		

COMMENT

Beyond "Bodies in the Building"

The framework of six types of involvement balances activities that are conducted at school, at home, and in the community so that parents who cannot easily come to the school building still can be productively involved in their children's education. This is important because some parents feel guilty or frustrated if they cannot be at the school building to volunteer or attend meetings. The framework also helps educators understand that parents who are not at school may be very much involved in their children's education.

Activities that require "bodies in the building" limit the involvement of many parents who cannot get to the building at a specific time. Thus, the redefinitions that we discussed are particularly important for helping families become and remain involved in school and in other settings. Face-to-face communications must be supplemented by voice-to-voice, note-to-note, e-mail–to–e-mail, and other responsive technologies.

The fact is that some parents come to school regularly, whereas others come occasionally or rarely. What can you learn about whether, why, and when parents, other family members, or others in a community come to the school building?

What Kinds of Family and Community Involvement Can You See at School?

A. Visit a school for at least one hour to observe and record the family and/or community involvement that you see during a time of day that you select.
   1. Identify the name, location, and level of the school (i.e., preschool or elementary, middle, or high school).
   2. Identify the date and day of your observation.
   3. Identify the time of your observation (select one).

      _____ A. *at the start* of a typical school day, time: _____

      _____ B. *during selected hours* of a school day, time: _____

      _____ C. *at the end* of a school day, time: _____

      _____ D. *at a scheduled evening meeting*, time: _____

      _____ E. *other time* (describe): _____
   4. Identify where in the school you made your observations:

      _____
   5. Describe whether, where, how many, and how parents or others from the community were involved at the school during your observation.
   6. If parents are at the school, briefly interview two parents about:
      • why they are at school at the time you observed
      • how often they come at this time
      • how often they are involved with their children at home
      • at least one other question that you add

      If no parents are at the school, briefly interview two teachers, administrators, or staff about:
      • why they think there are no parents present at the time you observed
      • when most parents come to the school
      • how much they believe parents are involved with their children at home
      • at least one other question that you add

B. Record your questions and responses. Summarize your ideas about the nature and quality of family involvement that you observed. Are your observations sufficient for judging the involvement of parents and others at this school? Explain.

C. Compare observations in class to get a "big picture" from many observers of why and when parents are involved at the school building and in other locations.

SUMMARY: CONNECTING THE SIX TYPES OF INVOLVEMENT

The six types of involvement are labeled according to their main goals or purposes. The labels are designed to help schools classify and identify present practices, plan a results-oriented program of partnerships, monitor progress, and continually improve the quality of family and community involvement. As in all typologies, however, there are no "pure" types. Although some activities represent just one type of involvement, other activities promote more than one type to produce particular results.

For example, school or classroom newsletters aim to inform families about school programs and events (Type 2—Communicating). Depending on their designs, however, newsletters also may promote other types of involvement. A school or classroom newsletter may be formatted electronically by parent volunteers (thereby increasing Type 3—Volunteering). In addition, students' academic work and curricular skills may appear in some newsletters for students to share their work and ideas with their parents (thereby extending Type 4—Learning at Home). Community programs for children and families may be announced in newsletters (thereby strengthening Type 6—Collaborating with the Community). Thus, all school or classroom newsletters have the *goal* of Type 2—Communicating, but some also may promote other types of involvement.

There are many such examples. A food cooperative or clothing swap-shop has the *goal* of assisting parents with basic responsibilities to feed or clothe their children (Type 1—Parenting), but the activity may be organized and conducted by parent volunteers (Type 3—Volunteering) with contributions from the community (Type 6). The goal determines the activity's classification, but the structure, organization, and scope of an activity may promote additional types of involvement that strengthen a school's partnership program.

QUESTIONS TO DISCUSS

How may the six types of involvement be combined to successfully organize and conduct the following?

1. A workshop has the *goal* of helping parents understand their children's development at different grade levels (Type 1—Parenting). List activities for at least two other types of involvement that may contribute to the successful conduct of a Type 1—Parenting workshop.

   Activities contributing to a successful workshop for parents:

   Type _____

   Type _____

2. A read-a-lot program has the *goal* of helping parents interact with their children who read at home for school or for pleasure (Type 4—Learning at Home). List activities for at least two other types of involvement that might contribute to the successful conduct of a Type 4 activity that guides families to read with their children at home.

   Activities contributing to a successful read-a-lot at-home program:

   Type _____

   Type _____

COMMENT

Correlated Types of Involvement

The six types of involvement contribute to a comprehensive program of school, family, and community partnerships. Research reveals a few prominent patterns of how the types of involvement work independently and in combination.

For example, Type 2—Communicating activities are implemented in most schools, even if other types of involvement are not. Just about all schools communicate with families through memos, report cards, conferences, phone calls, and other technologies, even if they need to improve the quality of these connections to reach and involve all families. Not all schools organize parent volunteers to work at the school (Type 3), invite parents to serve on decision-making committees (Type 5), or systematically involve families in other ways.

Because most research on Type 2 simply tallies whether schools ever communicate with *any* families, there is little variation across schools on this type of involvement. Therefore, in many studies, Type 2 activities do not strongly correlate with or predict the use of other types of involvement.

By contrast, Type 4—Learning at Home activities are less prevalent in schools because they require every teacher to involve all families in children's learning activities at home in homework, decisions about courses, and other curricular-related activities. There is, then, considerable variation across schools in the use of Type 4 involvement. Type 4 activities tend to strongly predict the use of all other types of involvement. This suggests that schools may not conduct Type 4 activities until they have successfully implemented other, less complicated, types of involvement.

Other correlations between types of involvement also are informative. Most studies indicate strong, positive correlations of Type 3—Volunteering and Type 5—Decision Making. These connections have been reported at the school level (i.e., when school programs and practices are measured) and at the individual parent level (i.e., when parents report their personal experiences). That is, schools with Type 3—Volunteering activities also tend to conduct Type 5—Decision Making activities with parents on school committees. In some cases, parents who volunteer during the school day are the same parents who participate in and lead the PTA/PTO or other parent association activities. This is due, in part, to the fact that both types of involvement typically require parents who can come to the school building and require parents who feel welcome and confident at the school.

The size and direction of correlations of types of involvement are not fixed. They will change with newly designed activities, research samples, and measures. For example, if schools begin to define volunteers as parents who assist in different ways at home, at school, and in the community, then parent volunteers (Type 3) may no longer be the same parents who are active leaders in the PTA or on decision-making committees (Type 5). By redefining volunteers, the previously strong correlations of Types 3 and 5 may be reduced in future studies.

Even if schools conducted comprehensive partnership programs with all six types of involvement, they would vary in which activities were selected, how well the activities were designed and implemented, and how results were measured. Most prior studies of involvement used relatively simple measures to denote a "type" of involvement. With a better understanding of school, family, and community partnerships and with better measures of the quality and results of partnerships, future studies will be able to contribute new knowledge about the connections of the six types of involvement (Epstein, Connors-Tadros, and Salinas, 1993; Epstein and Salinas, 1993; Sheldon and Epstein, 2007).

QUESTIONS TO DISCUSS

1. What is one reason why volunteers at a school might increase the likelihood that the school also will have an active PTA or PTO?
2. What is one reason why an active PTA at a school might increase the likelihood that the school also will have many volunteers?
3. Another prominent correlation in studies of involvement is reported between Type 5—Decision Making and Type 6—Collaborating with the Community. Give two reasons why schools that include parents on decision-making committees or in an active PTA/PTO might also conduct activities that involve their communities.

Understanding Results of Involvement

Even if all of the challenges to excellent partnerships were solved, there still would be questions about which activities should be implemented to produce the most successful partnership programs and to produce important results for students. To date, research suggests several important patterns that link family and community involvement to results for students, families, and schools (Sheldon, 2009).

1. Each type of involvement includes activities that produce different or unique results for students, families, and schools. Table 5.3 in Reading 5.1 and the summaries in this chapter show that each type of involvement may lead to some unique results for students, parents, and teachers. This is important because too many people still believe that any activity for any type of involvement will increase student achievement test scores. This is not the case. For example, well-implemented Type 1—Parenting activities should help families understand child and adolescent development. It will take many steps for that knowledge to affect student learning. By contrast, well-implemented Type 4—Learning at Home Activities should help families understand their children's school curricula, their children as "learners," and how to assist their children with homework at each grade level. Parents' connections with their children about their daily work may directly affect whether the student completes homework and pays attention in class for immediate learning. In this way, it may take fewer steps for well-implemented Type 4 activities to affect student learning.

2. Each type of involvement includes activities that can be designed to help produce and strengthen the same, specific results for students, families, and teachers. Because there are hundreds of practices that may be selected for each type of involvement, educators and parents can design or select activities to contribute to specific results such as improving or maintaining good student attendance, school safety, and even student achievement. Examine these examples:

> *Example: Focus on Attendance.* National and local surveys and extensive fieldwork confirm that activities for several types of involvement engage families and community partners in ways that help students improve their attendance and on-time arrival at school.
>
> *Type 1:* Workshops and information for parents explain the family's role in getting children to school every day on time.
>
> *Type 2:* Administrators clearly outline the school's attendance policies; all report cards communicate students' attendance and promptness to all families.
>
> *Type 3:* Volunteers call parents of children who are absent to let families know that the school cares about student attendance and to remind parents and students about making up work that is missed.

Type 6: Businesses and community groups provide alarm clocks to families that need them; health services provide needed information to families so that they can get assistance if students are ill.

Example: Focus on Writing. Schools may focus on helping students improve their writing skills by implementing activities for several types of family and community involvement that focus on writing.

Type 2: Student writing is featured in school newsletters.

Type 4: Families are involved with students on weekly interactive homework assignments in writing, as students read aloud their paragraphs, essays, poems, and other forms to obtain parents reactions.

Type 5: PTA/PTO sponsors annual "meet-the-authors" events for students, families, and the community.

Type 6: Community members come to the school on a regular schedule to show and share how writing is used in their various occupations.

There are many examples of how the six types of family and community involvement may be activated to help improve student attendance; behavior; reading, math, and science skills; and other results (Epstein et al., 2009). The mix of activities across types of involvement enables all families to become involved in productive ways even if they cannot come to the school building. The variety of activities makes it more likely that students will reach the stated goals than if only one activity for one type of involvement were conducted.

ACTIVITY

Design Different Types of Involvement to Contribute to Same Results

A. Add one more activity to each of the above lists to show another type of family or community involvement that might help improve student attendance and writing skills.
1. One more family or community involvement activity to improve *student attendance*:
Type _____ Activity: _____
2. One more family or community involvement activity to improve *student writing*:
Type _____ Activity: _____
B. Identify a grade level that interests you.
1. Select a goal for student success in a school subject (other than improving writing) that interests you. You may choose to focus on improving skills in reading, math, science, social studies, foreign languages, or another subject.

2. List activities for at least three of the six types of family and community involvement that you think would help produce the goal you selected.

3. Explain how each activity would help produce the desired results.

COMMENT

Steps from Family Involvement to Student Success

Not all family and community involvement activities will improve student learning, achievement test scores, or report card grades. Some activities produce other, different, and important results. We are beginning to learn which involvement activities produce what results, for whom, in what amount of time, and with what inevitable challenges.

Following are two involvement activities (discussed briefly above) that some people believe will increase student success in school. However, they differ in whether, how, and when they affect parents and students in the short term and in the long term.

Type 1—Parenting

A workshop for parents on child development may first increase parents' confidence about their interactions with their children.

If parents attend the workshop or obtain information from the workshop in other ways, and if the information they receive from the school is understandable and important, then some parents might apply the information at home in their attitudes and actions. If parents implement the activities successfully, then some of their children may process the information and increase, improve, or maintain their motivation to learn in school or other positive school behaviors.

As children proceed through the grades, parents will need additional information to continue this chain of effects. If parents, students, or the school misses any of these or other intermediate steps, then the long and fragile chain of effects from workshops for parents to student learning will be broken.

This chain of potential effects and some common "detours" or failures are shown in Figure 5.3.

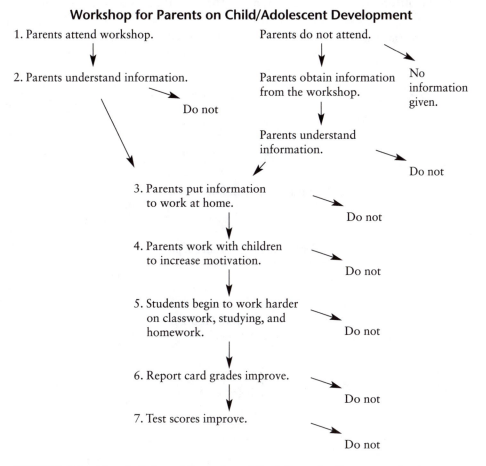

Workshop for Parents on Child/Adolescent Development

1. Parents attend workshop.

2. Parents understand information.

   Do not

Parents do not attend.

Parents obtain information from the workshop.

No information given.

Parents understand information.

   Do not

3. Parents put information to work at home.

   Do not

4. Parents work with children to increase motivation.

   Do not

5. Students begin to work harder on classwork, studying, and homework.

   Do not

6. Report card grades improve.

   Do not

7. Test scores improve.

   Do not

FIGURE 5.3   Map 1: Selected Steps from Workshops for Parents to Student Learning

Type 4—Learning at Home

Homework is a key connector between school and home. Weekly interactive homework and other school-family-student connections about homework should help more students complete their assignments and talk about schoolwork at home. Students who regularly complete their homework not only practice and strengthen their skills but also tend to be better prepared for the next day's classwork. The completion of homework also should help students improve their report card grades and may improve their performance on weekly tests. Over time, all of these improvements may affect achievement test scores. Interactive homework activities also help families remain aware of their children's curriculum, monitor their children's work, show interest in what their children are learning, and motivate their children to work in school.

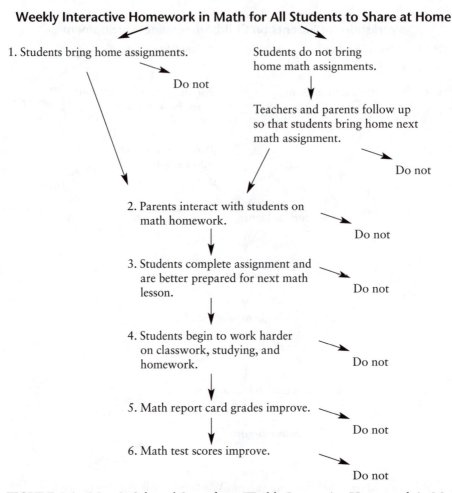

Weekly Interactive Homework in Math for All Students to Share at Home

1. Students bring home assignments.

    Do not

Students do not bring home math assignments.

Teachers and parents follow up so that students bring home next math assignment.

    Do not

2. Parents interact with students on math homework.

    Do not

3. Students complete assignment and are better prepared for next math lesson.

    Do not

4. Students begin to work harder on classwork, studying, and homework.

    Do not

5. Math report card grades improve.

    Do not

6. Math test scores improve.

    Do not

FIGURE 5.4   Map 2: Selected Steps from Weekly Interactive Homework in Math to Student Learning

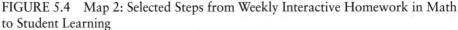

If students attend school regularly, experience excellent teaching, participate in class, complete their homework, and are reinforced by their families, then students should improve their skills and success in school. The interactions at home in reading should contribute to improved reading skills, interactions in writing to improved writing skills, and so forth. It may be that all of these elements are needed for students to benefit from family involvement in learning activities at home.

This chain of potential effects and some common "detours" or failures are shown in Figure 5.4.

School-family-community connections are less likely to increase student learning if the activities focus on developing parents' attitudes and behaviors without clear, immediate, and effective links to the students. Because most parents do not attend workshops at school, only a few parents and students benefit from these activities.

Even if workshop information is disseminated to all parents, many steps are needed for parents to transfer their own new knowledge and new parenting behaviors to the students, who then must incorporate their parents' guidance into their behavior and learning.

QUESTIONS TO DISCUSS

- Figure 5.3 (Map 1) shows major steps that may be needed to transfer information from a workshop for parents on child development (Type 1—Parenting) to increased student learning.
- Figure 5.4 (Map 2) shows typical steps that may be needed to transfer weekly interactive homework in (Type 4—Learning at Home) to student learning and success in school.

1. Compare the two maps.
   a. What are two factors that might make a difference in whether and how a student is affected positively by the involvement of a parent in Map 1 and Map 2?
   b. What are two factors that might make a difference in how many students in a school are assisted by the involvement of parents in Map 1 and Map 2?
2. Each step indicated by an arrow ($\downarrow$) along the path to partnerships takes time to implement and to produce results. Each step may lead to progress (i.e., the next step) or to failure. The timing, risks, and successes will, of course, vary from parent to parent and from student to student.
   a. Create a "time chart" for the successful steps in each of the maps.
   b. Estimate the time it would take a typical family and average student to complete each step ($\downarrow$) from the parent involvement activity to student success.
   c. Show and label your time estimates for the six steps in Map 1 and Map 2.
3. Write a summary of your conclusions from your review of the two maps and time charts about the impact of family involvement on student achievement.

ACTIVITY

Mapping Family Involvement to Student Success

Following are four more family involvement activities that some believe should improve student success in school.

A. Select one of these activities, or write a sequence of your own.
1. **School or Class Newsletters (Type 2—Communicating).** School or classroom newsletters may first increase families' awareness of school and classroom programs and help parents talk with their children about school activities. If parents regularly discuss school activities with their children, then parents may reinforce the school's messages to students about the importance of their participation in school and in class. If students understand and accept that message and increase their participation in class, then students may improve their attitudes about school and, over time, increase their attention in class, work, and achievement.

2. **Parent Volunteers at School (Type 3—Volunteering).** Volunteers at school may lead first to more adult supervision of students, improve the safety in and around the school building, and improve the overall climate of the school. If volunteers are engaged in classrooms, then the closer adult supervision may improve student behavior in class. This may make it more likely that students who are in class will pay attention to their teachers and to their classwork, which, in turn, may boost learning. If volunteers are well trained in assisting students with specific learning skills, then the students who are assisted should improve the skills on which they are assisted and, over time, other skills that build on what they learn.

3. **Parent Leaders (Type 5—Decision Making).** Inviting parents to contribute to school decisions as members of a school council or committee may first increase the parent leaders' support for the school. If the parent leaders communicate well, then other parents, too, may improve their understanding of and support for school programs. Over time, parents' input on school decisions may improve the quality of school programs, teaching conditions, curriculum and instructional advances, and how children succeed in school. Families with strong ties to the school may be more likely to understand and reinforce the school's messages to students about the importance of school and their work in school. Over time, parents' messages about school, vigilant monitoring, and continuous communications with their children may increase students' positive attitudes toward school, their attention in class, the quality of their classwork and homework, and their learning.

4. **Before- and After-School Classes (Type 6—Collaborating with the Community).** Before-school and after-school programs conducted with community support and volunteers may help some students develop special talents and learn new skills. If students participate in these programs, then they should improve or learn skills in sports, music, dance, art, photography, computer use, chess, math, foreign languages, and other topics. Students who do not or cannot attend

before- and after-school coaching and classes should not be expected to benefit in the same way as those who attend. The activities may affect student attendance, behavior, attitudes about school, and other specific skills that are taught and, over time, may increase student learning and achievement test scores.

5. **An Activity You Select.** Write a sequence of steps from an involvement activity to student success.

B. Draw a map of major steps from the implementation of a family and community involvement activity to student achievement or success in school. Show the possible detours or failures of action along the way.

C. Estimate the time it would take for an average family and student to complete each step ($\downarrow$) on your map from the involvement activity to student success.

D. Share and critique the maps and timelines in class. Discuss:

- Are the estimated timelines realistic?
- Is the selected family involvement activity likely to improve student achievement for most students in a school?

REFERENCES

American Federation of Teachers. (1999). *Parent and family involvement course.* Educational Research and Dissemination Program. Washington, DC: Author.

———. (2009, January 16). *AFT Teachers Winter Institute.* Baltimore: Maritime Institute.

Blank, M., A. Melaville, and B. P. Shah. (2003). *Making the difference: Research and practice in community schools.* Washington, DC: Coalition for Community Schools/Institute for Educational Leadership.

Bodilly, S., and M. K. Beckett. (2005). *Making out-of-school time matter: Evidence for an action agenda.* Santa Monica, CA: Rand Corporation.

Bouffard, S., and H. Weiss. (2008). Building the future of family involvement: A complementary learning framework. *Evaluation Exchange* 14: 2–5.

Bureau of Labor Statistics. (2005). *Employment of high school Students rises by grade.* www.bls.gov.

Chadwick, K. G. (2004). *Improving schools through community engagement.* Thousand Oaks, CA: Corwin.

The College Board. (2009). *Students and part-time work.* professionals.collegeboard.com.

Dianda, M., and A. McLaren. (1996). *Building partnerships for student learning.* Washington, DC: National Education Association.

Dryfoos, J. (1994). *Full-service schools: A revolution in health and social services for children, youth, and families.* San Francisco: Jossey-Bass.

Dryfoos, J., and S. Maguire. (2002). *Inside full-service community schools.* Thousand Oaks, CA: Corwin.

Epstein, J. L., L. Connors-Tadros, and K. C. Salinas. (1993). *High school and family partnerships: Surveys for teachers, parents, and students in high school.* Baltimore: Center on School, Family, and Community Partnerships, Johns Hopkins University.

Epstein, J. L., and K. C. Salinas. (1993). *Surveys and summaries: Questionnaires for teachers and parents in the elementary and middle grades.* Baltimore: Center on School, Family, and Community Partnerships, Johns Hopkins University.

Epstein et al. (2009). *School, family, and community partnerships: Your handbook for action* (3rd ed.). Thousand Oaks, CA: Corwin.

Family Resource Coalition. (1996). *Know your community*. Chicago: Author.

Goode, D. A. (1990). The community portrait process: School community collaboration. *Equity and Choice* 6(3): 32–37.

Gordon, E. W., B. L. Bridglall, and A. S. Meroe. (Eds.). (2005). *Supplementary education: The hidden curriculum of high academic achievement*. Lanham, MD: Rowman & Littlefield.

Mediratta, K., S. Shah, and S. McAlister. (2009). *Community organizing for stronger schools: Strategies and successes*. Cambridge, MA: Harvard Education Publishing Group.

Mickelson, R. A. (1996). Opportunity and danger: Understanding the business contribution to public education reform. In K. M. Borman, P. W. Cookson, A. R. Sadovnik, and J. Z. Spade (Eds.), *Implementing educational reform: Sociological perspectives on educational policy* (pp. 245–272). Norwood, NJ: Ablex.

Minke, K. M., and K. J. Anderson. (2003). Restructuring routine parent-teacher conferences: The family-school model. *Elementary School Journal* 194: 49–69.

Moll, L. C., C. Amanti, D. Neff, and N. Gonzalez. (1992). Funds of knowledge for teaching: Using a qualitative approach to connect homes and classrooms. *Theory into Practice* 31(2): 132–141.

Mortimer, J., M. Finch, K. Dennehy, C. Lee, and T. Beebe. (1994). Work experience in adolescence. *Journal of Vocational Education Research* 19: 39–70.

National PTA. (1998). *National standards for parent/family involvement programs*. Chicago: Author.

———. (2009). *Ready, set, lead! PTA national standards for family-school partnerships*. Chicago: Author.

Nettles, S. M. (1991). Community involvement and disadvantaged students. *Review of Educational Research* 61: 379–406.

Sanders, M. G. (2005). *Building school-community partnerships: Collaborating for student success*. Thousand Oaks, CA: Corwin.

Sanders, M. G., and A. Harvey. (2002). Beyond the school walls: A case study of principal leadership for school-community collaboration. *Teachers College Record* 104(7): 1345–1368.

Schoenhals, M., M. Tienda, and B. Schneider. (1998). The educational and personal consequences of adolescent employment. *Social Forces* 77: 723–762.

Scott-Jones, D. (1995a). Activities in the home that support school learning in the middle grades. In B. Rutherford (Ed.), *Creating family/school partnerships* (pp. 161–181). Columbus: National Middle School Association.

———. (1995b). Parent-child interactions and school achievement. In B. A. Ryan, G. R. Adams, T. P. Gullota, R. P. Weissberg, and R. L. Hampton (Eds.), *The family-school connection: Theory, research, and practice* (pp. 75–107). Thousand Oaks, CA: Sage.

Sheldon, S. B. (2009). Improving student outcomes with school, family, and community partnerships: A research review. In J. L. Epstein et al., *School, family, and community partnerships: Your handbook for action* (3rd ed.; pp. 40–56). Thousand Oaks, CA: Corwin.

Sheldon, S. B., and Epstein, J. L. (2007). *Parent surveys and student surveys on family and community involvement in the elementary and middle grades*. Baltimore: Center on School, Family, and Community Partnerships, Johns Hopkins University.

Van Voorhis, F. L., and J. L. Epstein. (2002). *Teachers involve parents in schoolwork: Interactive Homework CD* (for math, K–5; language arts and science, 6–8). Baltimore: Center on School, Family, and Community Partnerships, Johns Hopkins University.

Waddock, S. A. (1995). *Not by schools alone: Sharing responsibility for America's education reform*. Westport, CT: Praeger.

Practical Applications: Linking Family and Community Involvement to Student Learning

TEACHERS INVOLVE PARENTS IN SCHOOLWORK (TIPS): INTERACTIVE HOMEWORK AND PRODUCTIVE VOLUNTEERS

Educators must understand all six major types of involvement (parenting, communicating, volunteering, learning at home, decision making, and collaborating with the community) to implement, evaluate, and sustain comprehensive programs of school, family, and community partnerships. Some types of involvement are implemented with familiar activities, such as workshops for parents in Type 1—Parenting or parent-teacher conferences in Type 2—Communicating. Even common practices, however, pose challenges that must be met to involve all families in their children's education (see Chapter 5).

Some types of involvement are not so familiar or have not been well organized in the past. In this chapter, we examine two research-based approaches to involve families in their children's education in ways that are important to teachers, students, and parents; these approaches have not been well implemented in most schools. The applications were designed, developed, and tested to help educators systematically, equitably, and productively involve families at home and in school to improve student learning.

Reading 6.1 introduces the topic of "interactive homework" with a research summary of early studies that were conducted to focus on rarely discussed issues. First, homework is not only about the time that students spend on homework. Second, homework has different purposes that should affect the design of the assignments.

Third, certain interactive homework designs inform and involve families without requiring parents to think they should know how to teach school subjects.

Reading 6.2 elaborates the research summary with details on the Teachers Involve Parents in Schoolwork (TIPS) Interactive Homework process, which helps educators implement Type 4—Learning at Home Activities. This is a difficult component of a comprehensive partnership program to establish and sustain because it requires every teacher to connect class lessons, students' work, and families as influential partners for children's learning. The TIPS Interactive Homework process helps teachers design and use homework assignments to connect home and school on curriculum-related activities. TIPS activities improve parents' understanding of what their children are learning; guide conversations at home; and, if well implemented, improve students' homework completion, subject-matter skills, and readiness for classwork.

New definitions and ideas about volunteers were discussed in Chapter 5. Just about all schools have some volunteers, but educators have found it difficult to establish and sustain productive roles and activities for parent and community volunteers, particularly in middle schools. Two aspects of organizing volunteers are particularly challenging. First, middle schools wrestle with the common belief that students do not want their parents at school. Our studies in middle schools indicated that this was partly true and partly false. It was true that students did not want parents working in the same way as in elementary schools—meaning parents should not wave to or hug their children or make a "big deal" about their presence. But middle school students actually appreciated parents in helpful roles. Second, many schools struggle with developing volunteers who can help teachers create interdisciplinary experiences—that is, connect one subject with another in ways that extend student learning.

Reading 6.3 describes the Teachers Involve Parents in Schoolwork (TIPS) Volunteers in Social Studies and Art process, which helps educators implement productive and interdisciplinary Type 3—Volunteering in the middle grades. In social studies and art, volunteers are trained to present famous art prints linked to the social studies curriculum for grades six, seven, and eight. The process can be adapted for other subjects and grade levels. If well implemented, TIPS volunteers help teachers enrich and extend the curriculum and increase students' knowledge and appreciation of art.

Both TIPS approaches focus on students. In TIPS Interactive Homework, students conduct conversations and other interactions with family partners, because homework is always the students' responsibility. Students' skills are evaluated to determine whether and how TIPS interactive homework contributes to learning. In TIPS Volunteers, students are the focus of the interdisciplinary lessons in social studies and art. Students' knowledge and attitudes about art are evaluated to determine if the volunteers' presentations are effective.

A common question is, "How does family and community involvement help students to succeed?" The question assumes a direct link between involvement and student learning. Research reveals, however, that not every type of involvement leads to higher student achievement (see related discussions in Chapters 2, 3, 5, and 7). The TIPS approaches illustrate two different ways to link family and community involvement to student learning: by involving all families at home in supporting homework and by involving parents and other volunteers at school in activities that enrich the curriculum and extend students' experiences.

The TIPS research-based processes are not "canned" programs. Teachers cannot simply distribute someone else's homework assignments. Homework—including interactive homework—must be directly linked to a teacher's course objectives and to students' classwork. Similarly, interdisciplinary art and social studies lessons must be linked to specific units of work. Thus, the prototype materials that have been developed for both approaches at Johns Hopkins University (referenced in Readings 6.2 and 6.3) must be reviewed, revised, and supplemented to match each school's curriculum and other school, family, and student characteristics. The TIPS approaches require educators to work with families to organize family-friendly schedules, conduct and improve activities, orient families and students to new approaches, conduct follow-up activities in class, evaluate results, and continue to improve the effectiveness of these programs.

By understanding the research on interactive homework and by looking at two different processes for improving Type 3—Volunteering and Type 4—Learning at Home, you will see what it takes to organize productive partnerships linked to student learning. The descriptions and examples of TIPS materials in this chapter may be particularly helpful in courses on curriculum and instruction, methods of teaching specific subjects, practice teaching seminars, and related instruction for future teachers and administrators. Principals, superintendents, curriculum leaders, and teachers of all subjects should know how to design and implement family and community connections that enhance student learning.

More Than Minutes: Teachers' Roles in Designing Homework*

Homework has long been a topic of social research, but relatively few studies have focused on the teacher's role in the homework process. Most research examines what students do and whether and how the completion of homework or time spent affects student achievement or success in school (Cooper, 1989; Paschal, Weinstein, and Walberg, 1984; and see Cooper and Valentine, 2001). Yet the homework process begins with teachers who choose the topics and content of assignments to help students meet particular learning goals. Thus, teachers not only *assign* homework but also *design* homework. Designing homework requires teachers to consider the purposes, format, and other elements of assignments that will engage students and help them succeed. Assignments reflect not only teachers' knowledge of the curriculum, but also their understanding of the skills, abilities, and needs of their students, and the characteristics and situations of their students' families (Epstein, 2001).

Homework is recognized as one indicator of successful schools and successful students. Coleman, Hoffer, and Kilgore (1982) concluded that more homework and better discipline were two reasons why private schools were more successful learning environments than public schools. Similarly, studies have shown that students in the U.S. do less homework than do students in other countries (Chen and Stevenson, 1989; Stevenson et al., 1990). The implication is that if teachers in U.S. public schools assigned more homework, students would learn more, and the schools would be more effective.

This prescription may be too simple. Just assigning *more* homework is a mechanical response to a set of complex issues. Students who presently do little or no homework are unlikely to work harder and longer just because more homework is assigned (Corno, 1996). The call for more homework is based on a belief that the more time students spend on schoolwork, the more they will learn. However, as the next sections show, the purposes of homework are varied, and the connections of time on homework and student achievement are complex. In addition to time, other aspects of homework design also are important for encouraging more students to do their assignments. For example, parental involvement is one element of homework design that may encourage students to spend more time and complete their assignments with higher quality work (Epstein, 2001; Hoover-Dempsey et al., 2001).

This article begins with a review of the purposes of homework that have been identified by educators in survey research, and in interviews and workshops on homework. We then draw from research to understand how homework completion, time on homework, and parental involvement inform and affect the teacher's role in the homework process. Finally, we review the results of research on one new homework design—interactive homework—that teachers have implemented in lan-

---

* By Joyce L. Epstein and Frances L. Van Voorhis. Reprinted with permission from *Educational Psychologist* 36 (2001): 181–193. References have been updated.

guage arts, math, and science to meet the specific purposes of improving student skills, increasing parent-teacher communication, and improving parent-child relations.

PURPOSES OF HOMEWORK

Early surveys and interviews of teachers (Becker and Epstein, 1982; Epstein and Becker, 1982 [Reading 3.2]; Epstein, 1988), comprehensive reviews of research on homework (Cooper, 1989; Paschal et al., 1984), recent studies (Corno, 2000; Muhlenbruck, Cooper, Nye, and Lindsay, 2000), and periodic workshops with educators (Epstein and Van Voorhis, 2000) indicate that there are many reasons that teachers assign homework. A content analysis of information from these sources revealed ten broad purposes of homework: *practice, preparation, participation, personal development, parent-child relations, parent-teacher communications, peer interactions, policy, public relations,* and *punishment* (Epstein, 1988, 2001). Assignments designed to meet these purposes should help increase student learning and development, develop home-school-community partnerships, and improve teaching and administrative practice. In order to understand the teacher's role in the homework process, we believe it is important to begin with information on why teachers assign homework to students. (Also see Reading 3.8).

Practice

Some homework is designed to give students opportunities to practice skills taught in class, increase speed, demonstrate mastery, retain skills, review work, and study for tests. Teachers reported that the main reason they assigned homework in the elementary grades is to give students time to practice skills from class lessons (Becker and Epstein, 1982). In an early study of fifth, eighth, and tenth grade students, Garner (1978) observed that 25–30 minutes of math homework a day in middle and high school would add more than three and one half years of time for practicing and mastering math.

Preparation

Teachers may assign homework to ensure that each student is ready for the next lesson. This may include homework that asks student to complete unfinished classroom activities and assignments. Homework may be designed to help students study and internalize what they learned in school in preparation for the next lessons that will be taught (Muhlenbruck et al., 2000; Paulu, 1995). For example, students may begin a series of math problems in school, and complete the work for homework. Homework also may be designed to stimulate students' thinking about a topic, as when teachers ask students to outline ideas for an essay that will be written in class.

Participation

Homework may increase each student's involvement in learning, in applying specific skills and knowledge, and in conducting projects. Often in class, some students are hesitant to participate. Homework may be designed to engage all students in active learning, such as conducting and reporting experiments in science, writing essays, critiquing a book, or conducting other projects (Corno, 2000; Epstein, 2001).

Personal Development

Another purpose of homework is to build student responsibility, perseverance, time management, self-confidence, and feelings of accomplishment; also to develop and recognize students' talents in skills that may not be taught in class. Some teachers design homework to help students learn to manage their time, establish work schedules, build study skills, and develop research skills (Featherstone, 1985; McDermott, Goldman, and Varenne, 1984; Muhlenbruck et al., 2000). At home, students may control the amount of time they spend on different skills, the books or resources they use, and the number of consultations with parents, siblings, and friends to complete their work (Leone and Richards, 1989). Students also may need to learn to deal with distractions at home (Cooper, Lindsay, and Nye, 2000; Xu and Corno, 1998). Homework for personal development also may be designed to extend or enrich skills and talents in music, art, drama, mechanics, construction, and other areas of interest to students that are not developed in class (Corno, 2000; Epstein, 2001).

Parent-Child Relations

Homework may be designed to guide and promote positive communications between parent and child. Parent-child conversations may help reinforce the importance of schoolwork, homework, and learning, and promote students' understanding of how schoolwork is used in real-life situations. Homework may spark conversations between parents or other family partners and children about what students are learning in class (Balli, 1995; Epstein, Simon, and Salinas, 1997; Scott-Jones, 1995; Van Voorhis, 2003). Some homework assignments may help bring parents and children closer together to enjoy learning and exchange ideas (Acock and Demo, 1994), and enable parents to show their children that they support their schoolwork (Balli, Demo, and Wedman, 1998; González, Andrade, Civil, and Moll, 2001; Levin et al., 1997; Merttens and Woods, 1994). Decades ago, Maertens and Johnston (1972) found that students who received feedback from their parents on their math homework had better mastery of math skills than did other students. More recently, Van Voorhis (2003) found that when students and their parents were enthusiastic about science homework, the students completed more homework and earned more points for accuracy than did students whose attitudes about science were not positive or did not match their parents' views.

Parent-Teacher Communications

Homework may be purposely designed to enable teachers to inform and involve all families in their children's curricular activities. Teachers may organize procedures and assignments to keep families aware of topics that are taught in class, how their children are progressing, how to support their children's work and progress, and how to connect with the teachers. Some teachers ask parents to sign students' homework agendas or completed assignments (Epstein and Becker, 1982). Some homework may be designed for parents to give extra help to students with specific weaknesses. These assignments require teachers to provide clear guidelines or training so that parents can succeed in the role of "tutor" (Lehrer and Shumow, 1997; Xu and Corno, 1998). Also, teachers may design homework that encourages students to conduct conversations with family partners in order to complete the assignments (Balli et al., 1998; Epstein, Salinas, and Jackson, 1995; Van Voorhis, 2003).

Peer Interactions

Some homework may be designed to encourage students to work together, and motivate and learn from each other. Students may work with friends and peers on short-term or long-term assignments, projects, and studying for tests (Corno, 2000; Paris, Yambor, and Packard, 1998). Peer interactions may be formal, with assigned partners and roles, or informal, with friends at home or on the telephone. Research suggests that when adolescents support one another on homework, students have higher math and English report card grades (Azmitia and Cooper, 2001).

Policy

Teachers may make assignments to fulfill school or district policies for a prescribed amount of homework. Individual teachers, principals, the whole school staff, district superintendents, or educator-parent teams may decide that students should receive a certain amount of homework each day or each week (Hoover-Dempsey, Bassler, and Burow, 1995; Zernike, 2000). Policy directives should be integrated with other homework processes. For example, elementary, middle, and high school parents report that they have time to help their children with homework on weekends (Connors and Epstein, 1994; Dauber and Epstein, 1993; Epstein, 1986), but some schools assign homework only on weekdays, thereby reducing opportunities for parent-child interactions.

Public Relations

Homework may be assigned to demonstrate to parents and to the public that a school has a rigorous academic program and high standards for student work.

Researchers have suggested that good schools give homework (Coleman, Hoffer, and Kilgore, 1982), that good students do homework (Rutter, Maughan, Mortimore, and Ouston, 1979), and that good teachers assign more homework (Corno, 1996). When expectations for schoolwork and homework are met, families, businesses, and other community partners may be more likely to support schools and students in other ways.

Punishment

Historically, some teachers used homework to try to correct problems with student conduct or productivity. Teachers now report that assigning homework to punish students for inattention or poor behavior is not a valid purpose (Epstein and Van Voorhis, 2000). Some researchers have described homework, itself, as a punishing activity, referring particularly to poorly designed or overly burdensome assignments that confuse or frustrate students (Cooper and Valentine, 2001; McDermott, Goldman, and Varenne, 1984; Xu and Corno, 1998).

The different purposes of homework are not mutually exclusive; homework may be designed to fulfill one or several purposes. For example, elementary and secondary teachers reported that they assign homework to help students learn, build study skills, and manage time (Muhlenbruck et al., 2000), thereby recognizing practice, preparation, and personal development as three purposes for homework assignments. Research is needed that examines whether the design and content of homework match the teachers' stated purposes, and how different homework designs affect student outcomes. The next section summarizes how research on homework completion and time informs and affects teachers' roles in the homework process.

HOW RESEARCH ON HOMEWORK INFORMS TEACHERS' ROLES AND ACTIONS

Homework Completion

Early research examined the effects of homework completion on student achievement and other indicators of student success. Most studies concluded that students who complete their homework have better report card grades and higher achievement test scores than do students who do not complete their work (see reviews by Cooper, 1989; Cooper and Valentine, 2001; Paschal et al., 1984). Measures of homework completion accept the fact that students vary in the amount of time they spend on their assignments and focus, instead, on whether students fulfill their responsibility to do their work. For example, Cooper, Lindsay, Nye, and Greathouse (1998) found that in both the upper and the lower grades, the more homework that students completed (i.e., none, some, about half, most, or all of their assignments), the higher their report card grades and achievement test scores. Homework completion still is an important variable to study, but, in our view, measurement models should be improved to study the effects, over time, of contrasting homework designs and content on students' homework completion, accuracy of work, and their achievement, attitudes, and homework habits.

Time on Homework

The results of studies of time spent on homework are complex, with important implications for teachers' actions in designing homework. One early study of elementary school students collected information on homework from students, parents, and teachers (Epstein, 1988). This cross-sectional study found that, on average, students with lower levels of ability spent more time on homework. Also, the elementary school teachers reported that they asked parents of low-ability students to help their children more than they asked other parents to help. Finally, parents of low-ability students reported that they spent more time helping their children with homework. Similar results were reported by Levin and her colleagues (1997).

In cross-sectional studies, the negative correlation of student ability and time on homework must not be interpreted as a causal pattern (Babbie, 1990). Rather, the association suggests that in the elementary grades where assignments are relatively short, students at all levels of ability tend to take the time they need to complete their work (Muhlenbruck et al., 2000). Also, in the elementary grades, teachers and parents are more likely to work together to help all students complete their assignments (Epstein and Dauber, 1991).

Other studies indicate that in the secondary grades, high-ability students tend to spend more time on homework (Campbell, Hombo, and Mazzeo, 2000). Importantly, some studies of secondary students have used longitudinal data or measures of students' prior skills to identify causal patterns between time and achievement. These studies show that *if* students spend time on and complete their homework, *then* their skills improve over time. For example, Keith (1982) reported that, regardless of their initial levels of ability, high school students who did homework regularly received higher report card grades than did other students. With students' race, family background, prior ability, and high school curricular track statistically controlled, low-ability students who did ten hours of homework or more per week had as good report card grades as high-ability students who did no homework. That study identified a persuasive linear relationship between time on homework and report card grades for low-, middle-, and high-ability students in high school.

Because, on average, fewer students do all of their homework in the older grades, there is greater variation in secondary school students' investments in homework and greater variation in their rates of homework completion (Sheldon and Epstein, 2005). The greater variation in these indicators helps produce the stronger associations in secondary than in elementary grades of time on homework and achievement (Cooper and Valentine, 2001). Epstein (1988) speculated about three reasons for the variation in secondary students' homework habits and results.

First, some low-ability students in the upper grades may stop doing homework if it is frustrating, if it does not help them learn, or if they are pressured by peers not to do homework. This explanation is supported by 1999 NAEP data that indicate that 13 percent of high school students do not do any homework that is assigned (i.e., 0 minutes) compared with 5 percent and 4 percent at the middle and elementary levels, respectively (Campbell et al., 2000). Also, a detailed study of middle school students found that many low-ability students do their work hastily and less accurately than average-ability or honors students, or do not do their assignments at all (Van Voorhis, 2003).

Second, some teachers may assign students in low-ability classes less homework or less interesting assignments than students in honors or advanced classes, or convey low expectations that slower students will do the work. The 1999 NAEP data indicate that about one-fourth of high school students are assigned 5 pages or less to read in school or at home per day, whereas another one-fourth are assigned over 20 pages per day. These discrepant assignments are linked to significant differences in students' reading scores, suggesting that brighter students are assigned and do more work (Campbell et al., 2000).

Third, parents of middle and high school students may not monitor adolescents' homework as faithfully as they did when their children were younger, in part because they are not asked to do so by secondary school teachers. For example, analyses of the National Education Longitudinal Survey (NELS) data show that 26 percent of parents in 8th grade, 45 percent of parents in 10th grade, and 51 percent of parents in 12th grade report that they rarely or never help their children with homework (Lee, 1994; Simon, 2004). Low-ability students in middle and high school may not feel the degree of parental pressure to complete their assignments that low-ability students in the elementary grades experience.

The first two reasons may be explained by greater differences in secondary versus elementary students' attitudes about and actions in fulfilling their responsibilities for homework. Students' personal investments also may be influenced by the strength and clarity of teachers' messages and expectations for good work, and by whether the design and content of the homework are well matched to students' increasingly diverse skills and interests. The third reason is related to the persistent finding that fewer parents are involved in secondary schools or feel able to help their teens with increasingly difficult schoolwork at home (Epstein and Lee, 1995; Lee, 1994; Scott-Jones, 1995; and see Hoover-Dempsey et al., 2001). The greater variation in parents' monitoring and assisting with homework may contribute to the degree of students' dedication to and time on homework, which in turn result in fewer secondary than elementary students completing their assignments. It is likely that a combination of these influences—individual attitudes and investments, teachers' homework designs and processes, parent and peer messages and support— not any one alone, affect secondary students' homework habits and the results of their efforts.

Other studies confirm these basic patterns of results. Reported zero-order correlations show that young students with weaker skills tend to take more time to complete their homework (Cooper et al., 1998; Epstein, 1988; Muhlenbruck et al., 2000). In these studies, time on homework leads more students to complete their assignments, which may contribute to improved skills or other indicators of success. Middle and high school students with advanced skills are assigned more homework

and spend more time on homework (Garner, 1978; Keith et al., 1993). In these studies, students' achievement influences teachers to assign more demanding homework
that requires more time, which, in turn, may continue to help increase the achievement of more successful students. Causal models that account for students' prior
abilities and coursework show, however, that time on homework contributes to the
achievement of middle and high school students at all ability levels (Keith and Cool,
1992). Time series studies are needed to clarify whether there is a reinforcing, spi-
raling pattern whereby time on homework leads to completion of assignments and
higher achievement or success in school, which in turn affects the nature and extent
of ongoing homework assignments, and so on.

Implications for Research and Practice

The research on homework time and completion has important implications for
teachers' actions, and alerts researchers to studies that are needed to clarify the discrepant patterns of results. First, the reported zero-order correlations suggest that
secondary school teachers should design homework that more effectively encourages
and enables low-ability students to take the time they need to complete their work.
That should produce the same pattern of negative or null associations of student ability and time on homework as reported in studies at the elementary level. Second, the
causal analyses that account for students' prior skills suggest that all teachers should
strive to design high-quality homework so that students who complete their assignments will, in fact, benefit from their efforts. More longitudinal research is needed,
especially at the elementary level, to determine if completing homework and doing it
well improves student achievement over time, as reported at the secondary level.

As indicated above, parent involvement in children's education is recognized as
a positive force for homework completion, student learning, and success in school.
The next section summarizes research on parental involvement in homework that
may affect how teachers design and use homework (also see Hoover-Dempsey et
al., 2001, for a comprehensive review).

HOW RESEARCH ON PARENT INVOLVEMENT
INFORMS TEACHERS' ROLES AND ACTIONS

Homework is one part of a comprehensive program of school, family, and community partnerships, which includes six major types of involvement: *parenting, communicating, volunteering, learning at home, decision making,* and *collaborating with
the community* (Epstein, 1995; Epstein et al., 2009). As one example of a learning-
at-home activity, homework is an inevitable connector of home and school. Interestingly, of all the types of involvement, parents say they most want to help their
children with homework so that they will do better in school (Epstein, 1986;
Sanders, Epstein, and Connors-Tadros, 1999).

Scott-Jones (1995) identified four ways that parents may be involved with their children on homework by valuing, monitoring, assisting, and doing homework. That is, parents may tell their children that they value homework as an important task for increasing learning; monitor the completion of homework; and show that they will assist their children with their work. It is well understood that parents should not *do* their children's homework (Scott-Jones, 1995), and that homework is the students' responsibility (Epstein, 2001). Research indicates that, presently, involvement is influenced by parents' education, students' grade levels, teachers' attitudes, and schools' programs and practices of partnership.

Parent Involvement and Family Educational Background

Research consistently reports that just about all parents know they should monitor their children's work, and that they view homework as an important part of schooling (Delgado-Gaitan, 1990; Epstein, 1986; Hoover-Dempsey et al., 1995; Simon, 2004). However, those with more formal education are more likely to act on their beliefs (Astone and McLanahan, 1991; Baker and Stevenson, 1986; Lareau, 1989; Xu and Corno, 1998).

Parent Involvement and Students' Grade Levels

Parents of younger children are more frequently involved in their children's education than are parents of students in the upper grades (Eccles and Harold, 1996; Epstein and Lee, 1995; Hoover-Dempsey and Sandler, 1997; Stevenson and Baker, 1987). Parents of older students report feeling increasingly less able to help with homework (Dauber and Epstein, 1993; Grolnick and Slowiaczek, 1994; Simon, 2004). Studies using data from the National Education Longitudinal Surveys (NELS) indicate that students benefit if their parents remain involved in their education through the middle and high school grades (Catsambis, 1998; Fehrmann, Keith, and Reimers, 1987; Ho and Willms, 1996; Keith et al., 1993; Lee, 1994; Simon, 2004).

These studies show that students do better on outcomes such as attendance, credits completed, report card grades, preparedness for school from grade 8 to grades 10 and 12 if they continue to communicate with their parents about schoolwork and school decisions, regardless of family background, parents' education, and students' prior skills.

Parent Involvement and Teacher Attitudes

Research shows that family involvement also benefits teachers. They report more positive feelings about teaching and about their schools when there is more parent involvement in the school (Epstein and Dauber, 1991; Hoover-Dempsey, Bassler, and Brissie, 1987). Moreover, teachers who frequently conduct activities to involve parents in their children's learning activities at home are more likely to report that all parents can help their children, whereas other teachers are more likely to stereotype parents with less formal education, and report that they are not interested in education and cannot help their children at home (Becker and Epstein, 1982; Epstein, 1990). Teachers who communicate with parents tend to increase their expectations and appreciation of all parents, and continue to add activities for family involvement.

School Programs to Increase Parental Involvement

Studies are accumulating that show that *if* schools and teachers implement specific practices, *then* parents respond by becoming more involved on those very practices (Ames, DeStefano, Watkins, and Sheldon, 1995; Balli, 1998; Delgado-Gaitan, 1990; Epstein and Dauber, 1991; Ho and Willms, 1996; Lee, 1994; Sanders et al., 1999; Simon, 2004; Snow, Barnes, Chandler, Goodman, and Hemphill, 1989; Van Voorhis, 2003).

Hoover-Dempsey and Sandler (1997) explored why some parents become involved in their children's schooling. They found that parents were influenced by their beliefs about their roles and responsibilities to become involved, their feelings of efficacy or competence to help their children, and their understanding of teachers' expectations for involvement (see Hoover-Dempsey, 2001). Without new approaches to help parents to understand their roles and build their feelings of competence, it is likely that the prevailing pattern that only some parents are involved will continue.

The challenges are clear. Most teachers and administrators report that they *want* parents to support their children's learning and to monitor homework, but they think that most parents do not do enough (Farkas, Johnson, and Duffett, 1999). Parents want to be involved, but say they need guidance in how to help at home (Corno, 2000; Dauber and Epstein, 1993; Eccles and Harrold, 1996; Hoover-Dempsey and Sandler, 1997; Sanders et al., 1999). Most teachers need new approaches, organized strategies, and specific tools to help parents become productively involved at home (Ames et al., 1995; Epstein, 2001; McDermott et al., 1984; Pratt, Filipovich, and Bountrogianni, 1995).

NEW DESIGNS FOR FAMILY INVOLVEMENT IN HOMEWORK

The results of research on homework completion, time on homework, and parental involvement suggest that teachers have a responsibility to select or design assignments that are purposeful, engaging, and of high quality so that (a) students at all grade levels—including low-ability students—take the time they need to complete their assignments; (b) students benefit from their effort; and (c) parents at all grade levels are appropriately and effectively involved in their children's education. This three-fold challenge was addressed by researchers and teachers working together to improve the design of homework and to study the effects of interactive assignments on homework completion, family involvement, and student learning (Epstein, Salinas, and Jackson, 1995).

New Approaches to Interactive Homework

"Interactive homework" encourages students to share interesting things they are learning in class with family members, friends, peers, or others in the community (Epstein, 2001). The Teachers Involve Parents in Schoolwork (TIPS) process is one design for interactive homework that guides students to conduct conversations and interactions with family partners in math, science, language arts, or other subjects (Epstein et al., 1995).

The TIPS interactive homework process grew from early research that showed when elementary school teachers frequently involved families in reading activities at home, more parents conducted reading activities with their children, *and* more of these students improved their reading test scores from fall to spring of the school year. Interestingly, involvement in reading had no impact on students' math achievement scores. These results suggested a potentially important *subject-specific link* between parent involvement in reading and gains in student reading achievement (Epstein, 1991). The same study revealed that teachers in the younger grades often asked parents to be involved with their children in reading homework, but rarely in other subjects. In the middle grades, few teachers involved parents on curricular matters or homework (Dauber and Epstein, 1993; Eccles and Harrold, 1996; Scott-Jones, 1995).

TIPS Design Elements. As in all homework, TIPS assignments are the students' responsibility. Parents play supportive roles in discussing homework with their children; they are *not* asked to teach school skills. With their family partners, students demonstrate math skills, conduct science experiments, share ideas and obtain reactions to written work, conduct surveys or interviews, gather parents' memories and experiences, apply school skills to real life; or work with parents or other family partners in other ways.

Other features of the TIPS process include: (1) Teachers and principals orient parents and students to the TIPS process; (2) teachers send home TIPS activities on a regular schedule (e.g., once a week or twice a month); (3) teachers allot extra time (e.g., two days or over a weekend) for TIPS homework to accommodate family schedules; (4) TIPS are designed for two sides of one page and include simple instructions that the student can explain to a family partner; (5) all activities use readily available materials at home, and require no expensive purchases; (6) TIPS activities include a home-to-school communication for parents to check or comment whether they enjoyed the activity with their child, and whether they learned something about what students are learning in class; (7) teachers use the same methods for collecting, grading, and discussing TIPS as they use for other homework; (8) teachers use family and student feedback for redesigning activities, or to contact families who may have questions about their students' work or progress. Used on a weekly or bimonthly schedule, TIPS activities aim to keep parents aware of what their children are learning in school.

Research on TIPS proceeded from questions about the feasibility of implementing interactive homework, to studies of the effects of interactive homework works, for whom, and in what subjects.

Research on the TIPS Interactive Homework Process

Three studies have been conducted on the effects of teachers' implementations of TIPS interactive homework on students' skills, parent involvement, and student and parent attitudes about homework (Balli, 1995; Epstein et al., 1997; Van Voorhis, 2003), as summarized in Table 6.1. The three longitudinal studies also report the effects of homework completion on students' skills, report card grades, and other measures of achievement, after accounting for students' prior skills and family background.

TIPS Language Arts

Research was conducted on the influence of TIPS Language Arts on students' homework completion, writing skills, and language arts report card grades (Epstein et al., 1997). This study included 683 students in grades 6 and 8 in two central city middle schools where over 70 percent of the students qualified for free- or reduced-price lunch.

TIPS language arts writing assignments guided students to read aloud the "prompts" that set the stage for their writing, converse with family partners about the topic, read aloud their first drafts of written work, gather reactions to their stories or essays, and conduct "family surveys" to discuss their family partners' experiences that related to their own.

Records were kept of the homework completed, and writing samples were collected and scored by an independent coder in the fall, winter, and spring of the school year. Students and parents were surveyed for their reactions to TIPS. Analyses statistically controlled for parent education, student grade level, attendance, fall report card grades, and fall writing sample scores, to identify the effects of TIPS interactive homework on students' skills in the winter and spring, and on student and family attitudes at the end of the school year.

As would be expected in any longitudinal study of student achievement, students with higher writing scores in the fall also had higher scores in the winter and spring. However, after taking into account their initial skill levels, students who completed more TIPS homework assignments had higher language arts report card grades. When parents participated, students improved their writing scores from fall to winter and from winter to spring, regardless of their initial abilities.

Over 80 percent of the students reported that TIPS gave them a way to show their parents what they were learning in class. Nearly 100 percent of the families surveyed agreed that TIPS gave them information about what their children were learning in class. The more parents participated, the better they liked TIPS interactive homework. This study demonstrated that TIPS interactive homework could be successfully implemented in the middle grades, and that parents with little formal education could become productively involved in ways they had not been before. Results indicate that students at all ability levels benefited, over time, from completing their language arts homework by improving their writing skills. Future

	TIPS Language Arts	TIPS Math	TIPS Science
Author(s)	Epstein, J. L., Simon, B. S., and Salinas, K. C.	Balli, S. J., Balli, S. J., Wedman, J. F., and Demo, D.	Van Voorhis, F. L.
Date of Publication	1997	1995, 1997	2003 (reference updated)
Sample Size	683 students 218 parents 16 classes 8 teachers	74 students 69 family partners 24 parent interviews 3 classes 1 teacher	253 students 180 family partners 10 classes 4 teachers
Research Design	Longitudinal (1 year) and developmental Weekly assignments	Quasi-Experimental 3 groups: no prompts for family involvement, student prompts for family involvement, and student and family prompts for family involvement. Longitudinal (3 months) 20 assignments, about 2 per week	Quasi-Experimental 2 groups with same homework content: one group had detailed guidelines for student and family interaction, and the other group had no family involvement guidelines. Longitudinal (1/2 school year) Developmental 18 assignments, weekly
Student Sample Characteristics	6th and 8th grade students 70% Free/reduced-price lunch 15% Special education services 12–15% Enter during year 20–27% Withdraw during year East Coast middle school Predominantly poor African American families	6th grade students Mean MMAT scores of 3 groups 378.0 Similar ability level in all 3 classes 46% Reported that one or both parents held a college degree Midwestern middle school Predominantly middle class, white families	6th and 8th grade students 36% African American 53% White 25% Free/reduced-price lunch 15% Low-ability classes 39% Average-ability classes 46% Honors classes East Coast middle school Predominantly middle class, but heterogeneous population

TABLE 6.1 Summary of TIPS Interactive Homework Intervention Studies

(continues)

	TIPS Language Arts	TIPS Math	TIPS Science
Main Outcome Measures	Reported level of family involvement Writing samples Language arts report card grades Surveys of parents and students' attitudes toward TIPS	Reported level of family involvement Mathematics posttest administered after 20 homework assignments completed Surveys of students and parents Telephone surveys of 24 selected parents	Reported level of family involvement Accuracy (number of points out of 10 for each assignment) Science report card grades Science homework test questions Student and parent attitudes about homework and TIPS
Results: Effects on Achievement	Parent participation on TIPS added significantly to students' writing scores as the year progressed ($\beta = .180$, $p < .01$ for winter; $\beta = .234$, $p < .001$ for spring), after accounting for prior fall writing scores.	No significant differences in math achievement across the three groups, with prior math achievement as a covariate.	TIPS students (with detailed instructions for family involvement) earned significantly higher science report card grades ($\beta = .15$, $p < .05$) than students without detailed family involvement instructions. The effect held after accounting for prior science achievement and percent of homework returned.
Subject Contrasts	None tested. Focused only on language arts/writing.	TIPS homework design in math prompted family involvement in math more than in non-TIPS subjects.	TIPS homework design in science prompted family involvement in science more than in non-TIPS subjects.
SES Effects	No SES difference in extent of family involvement.	No SES difference in extent of family involvement.	No SES difference in extent of family involvement.
Other Results	Completing more TIPS homework assignments positively influenced student report card grades, with prior grades and attendance controlled. Eighty-two (82%) percent of students agreed "TIPS gives me a way to show my parent what I am learning in class," and nearly 100% of parents also agreed.	Students in the groups with prompts for family involvement more often involved families in math homework than did students whose homework designs excluded prompts.	Students in the group with prompts for family involvement more often involved families in science homework than did students whose homework designs excluded prompts. Eighty-eight (88%) percent of TIPS students agreed, "TIPS gives me a way to show my parent what I am learning in class," and 93% of parents also agreed.

TABLE 6.1 (continued)

studies of TIPS language arts are needed that vary the homework condition (see math and science studies below), and that are conducted in schools with diverse student populations.

TIPS Math

A study of 74 suburban sixth graders explored the effects of TIPS math interactive homework (Balli, 1995; Balli et al., 1998), as outlined in Table 6.1. In this study, students in three classes with the same teacher were assigned math homework that was identical in content, but that varied in guidelines for parental involvement. One class received TIPS math homework with guidelines for students to discuss their work with family partners and for family partners to sign and send comments and observations to the teachers. The second class received modified TIPS math homework with some guidelines for students, but no options for parents' comments or signature. The third class had the same assignments but no references to family involvement for the student or for parents.

TIPS math assignments guide students to show parents how specific math skills are taught by the teacher in class; practice and demonstrate their mastery of math skills; and engage their family partners in conversations about how math skills are used in the real world. Parents are asked to provide reactions, comments, and a signature in the section for home-to-school communications.

Balli's results indicated that family involvement was significantly higher in both TIPS groups that guided students to involve their parents in demonstrations and discussions about math. More parents of these students reported being involved with their children on math homework. Parents felt most involved in the full TIPS process, when they were encouraged to provide their observations, comments, and questions to teachers.

The study of TIPS math revealed that, in the middle grades, parents appreciated the student-guided interactions about math. Students and parents reported more positive conversations about math, and most students believed that the interactions helped them be more prepared and successful in math class (Balli, 1998). This study also advanced knowledge about homework with subject-specific measures and analyses that showed that parents' involvement in math using the TIPS design did not translate to parent involvement in other subjects which did not use TIPS (Balli, 1995).

All three classes advanced similarly in math skills, in part because they had the same effective math teacher and because their homework and tests covered the same content. By holding the teacher-effect constant, this study contributed component analyses that demonstrated the effects on parent involvement of the portions of the TIPS assignments that guide students to share their math work with their family partners, discuss real-world math applications, and that ask parents for their reactions to the interactive experience.

TIPS Science

Van Voorhis (2003) conducted a quasi-experimental study of 253 sixth and eighth grade science students in 10 classrooms of four teachers in a suburban middle school. The racial and socioeconomic characteristics and the ability levels of students were more diverse in this study than in the other two studies, as shown in Table 6.1. Van Voorhis examined the effects of contrasting science homework designs on students' homework completion, science report card grades, science test scores, and student and parent attitudes about homework and science.

Students in six classes received weekly Teachers Involve Parents in Schoolwork (TIPS) science activities with specific guidelines for students to interact with family partners on science experiments and activities. Students in the remaining four classes received the same homework but with no guidelines for family involvement (ATIPS). TIPS science activities were designed by the students' teachers to match the units and topics covered in grades 6 (i.e., science skills and processes, oceanography, machines) and in grade 8 (i.e., ecology, geology, heredity).

TIPS science assignments are designed to help students summarize what they are studying in science, conduct science activities with family partners as their assistants, discuss their conclusions with family partners, and conduct surveys or discussions about how the science topic is part of everyday life. There is a home-to-school communication section for parents to send their comments and reactions to the science teacher (Epstein et al., 1995; Van Voorhis, 2003).

Van Voorhis and her collaborating teachers strengthened the consequences of completing science homework by assigning points to each section of the assignment, and by including questions based on the homework on each unit test. She also extended an understanding of subject-specific effects by showing that family involvement in TIPS science was higher than family involvement in subjects that did not use interactive homework designs.

Students completing TIPS assignments reported significantly higher family involvement in science than did students in the ATIPS classes. TIPS students also had higher science report card grades, even after accounting for other influential variables of students' prior science abilities, parent education, and the amount of homework completed. Thus, over and above the effects of homework, the impact of the TIPS interactive design added significantly and positively to students' report card grades. This study provides strong evidence that the TIPS homework process is effective in increasing family involvement and in boosting science achievement of students who involve family partners in homework.

Summary

The three TIPS studies were conducted in poor, urban and middle-class, suburban communities. Family socioeconomic status did not determine whether parents became involved with their children in math, science, or language arts. Without the

TIPS design that guides all students to conduct conversations with their family partners, one would expect the typical result that parents with more formal education and advantage would be more involved.

Also, the three studies were conducted in middle schools where, traditionally, there is little involvement of parents with students on homework. Yet, in these schools, parents were overwhelmingly appreciative of the TIPS design and the way that their middle school students were able to demonstrate and share their skills and ideas at home.

In all three studies, students agreed that the TIPS interactive homework design enabled them to show their parents what they were learning in class, and parents agreed that the TIPS homework design helped them know what their children were learning in school. These were two major purposes that teachers identified for using interactive homework.

The TIPS studies indicate that teachers can take decisive roles in designing and implementing math, language arts, and science homework to fulfill several purposes of homework. Each TIPS assignment is designed to extend time for students to practice skills and participate actively in learning; increase teacher-parent communications about the curriculum; and improve parent-child connections on learning activities at home, as outlined in Table 6.2. TIPS manuals and prototype materials in math, science, and language arts may be of interest to teachers and researchers who want to develop interactive homework for their curricula and study the effects on students at different grade levels and with diverse abilities and backgrounds (ASCD, 2001; Epstein et al., 1995; Epstein and Van Voorhis, 2000). (See Reading 6.2 for more information.)

The results of the TIPS studies are supported by interventions and research in other countries including Australia, Chile, Great Britain, Portugal, and Scotland (Davies and Johnson, 1996). Generally, the international studies of "shared learning" and interactions in the elementary grades indicate that children can be effective "connectors" between school and home. For example, when spelling homework was designed to involve families in Scotland, more parents participated in discussions with their children and helped students practice and extend spelling skills (MacBeath, 1998). As another example, more families with very little formal education interacted with their children on Portuguese language development skills (Villas-Boas, 1998).

OTHER NEW HOMEWORK DESIGNS

TIPS is not the only innovative homework design that teachers may use or adapt for specific purposes. Moll and his colleagues (Moll, Amanti, Neff, and González, 1992; González and Moll, 1996) have worked with teachers and parents to develop curricular approaches that bring students' cultural backgrounds and families' "funds of knowledge" (Vélez-Ibáñez and Greenberg, 1992) into the classroom. In turn, the class lessons spark homework that requires students to bring school skills home to discuss with family members, and other assignments that enable students to draw

TABLE 6.2   Components of Teachers Involve Parents in Schoolwork (TIPS) Interactive Homework Assignments, by Subject

All TIPS Assignments
Letter to parent, guardian, or family partner briefly explains in one sentence the topic and skill of the assignment. The student writes in the due date and signs the letter.

Math Elements
Look this over shows an example of how a particular math skill was taught in class, and guides the student to explain the skill to a parent or family partner. The answer to this example is given.
Now try this presents another example for the student to show a family partner how the particular skill is done. The answer is given on the back of the page.
Practice and more practice are additional examples for the student to master the skill.
Let's find out or *In the real world* interactions help the student and family partner discover and discuss how the math skill is applied at home or in common situations.

Language Arts Elements
Objectives explain the learning goal(s) of the activity, if this is not clear from the title or letter.
Prewriting gives the student space to plan a letter, essay, story, or poem by outlining, brainstorming, listing, designing nets and webs, or using other planning strategies.
Prewriting gives the student space to plan a letter, essay, story, or poem by outlining, brainstorming, listing, designing nets and webs, or using other planning strategies.
First draft gives the student space to write and edit. A student who needs more space may add paper. Some teachers ask the student to write a final copy on other paper at home or at school.
Interactions guide the student to conduct a family survey or interview, talk with a family partner about ideas or memories, read work aloud for reactions, edit work, practice a speech, or conduct other interactions. Other assignments include exchanges focused on grammar, vocabulary, reading, and other language arts skills.

Science Elements
Objectives explain the learning goal(s) of the activity.
Materials are common, inexpensive, and easily available at home, or the school provides the materials.
Procedure guides the student, step by step, in a hands-on activity that requires the student to think and act like a scientist, and to interact with a family partner.
Lab report or data chart gives space for the student to report findings.
Conclusions guide the student to discuss results and real-world applications of science with a family partner.

End of All TIPS Assignments
Home-to-school communication invites the parent to send an observation, comment, or question to the teacher about the skill the student demonstrated and the homework experience.
Parent signature is requested on each activity.

Sources: Epstein, Salinas, and Jackson, 1995; Epstein and Van Voorhis, 2000.

ideas, information, and experiences from family and community knowledge and expertise. Class lessons and related homework may be based on how mothers use math in sewing (González et al., 2001), how workers in many occupations use reading and math to build a house (Mehan, Lintz, Okamoto, and Wills, 1995), and similar investigations. These school-family-community connections help students see that, regardless of the socioeconomic status of the community, many people in their families and neighborhoods have useful, interesting, and enriching skills that link to and enhance school topics.

Corno (2000) discusses other ways that innovative teachers may design homework assignments to spark students' creative thinking, talent development, and community service and problem solving. For example, teachers may design assignments so that students work with one another after school at home, by telephone, or on the Internet. Assignments and projects done with peers and friends help students connect, draw from each other's talents, and communicate about schoolwork at times that they may otherwise be at home alone. As another example, Corno (2000) describes how the writing process (Calkins, 1994) can be used in homework assignments. Students keep notebooks of ideas drawn from family events, photographs, characters, and other activities as the basis for writing stories, essays, and poems in class. The homework notebooks help students improve their observation skills and focus their writing on what they know. Evaluations of interactive homework show that practice in writing improves the quality of students' work (Epstein et al., 1997), and so it is possible that students' writing notebooks also may help students become better writers.

Epstein (2001) outlines new approaches for *homemade homework*, in which parents and children design a family-related activity for students to conduct based on important activities and responsibilities at home. For example, students and parents may elect to write a letter to a relative; draw or take a photo of something important to the family; plan activities and a budget for a special trip; start a collection of critical reviews of TV shows, movies, or restaurants that they experience; or other family activities that use and advance school skills. Epstein (2001) also describes *home conferences*, originally created by a middle school educator. In these assignments students select a few examples of their writing, read or discuss them with a family partner, and write a reflection on the suggestions they received in order to improve their writing in the future. This strategy could be used once or twice a year in any subject to help students and parents review and discuss student work. (See Chapter 3 for discussions and activities on these.)

In these innovative approaches, students always are responsible for their homework, but all of the interactions with peers, family partners, or members of the community aim to promote conversations and active learning. These and other innovative homework interventions require systematic development and research on their impact on student homework habits and learning.

IMPLICATIONS FOR FUTURE RESEARCH AND PRACTICE

The results of this review prompt three recommendations for improving research on homework and its connections with policy and practice.

The results of the TIPS interventions are promising, but serious homework problems in many, if not most, schools need to be addressed (Campbell et al., 2000). Some students do not do their work, some parents are not informed about or involved in their children's education, and some teachers do not design or use homework effectively. Educators need to assess the homework successes and problems in their schools, and plan specific actions to correct the problems that presently limit many students' learning. Researchers can help educators conduct these assessments, and can work more closely with educators to design and test solutions to the homework problems that are identified.

The topic of homework should be covered more pointedly in preservice, advanced, and inservice education for teachers and administrators. This review suggests that homework not only is something that students do, but also is part of teachers' professional work. When they worked with researchers to develop TIPS activities in language arts and science, the collaborating teachers had never before worked together systematically to design homework for the purposes of informing parents about students' work or for guiding students to talk with their parents about schoolwork (ASCD, 2001). They had to learn how to use research-based design elements to develop effective assignments (Epstein and Van Voorhis, 2003). Prospective and practicing educators need clear information on the purposes of homework, various designs for assignments, research on the effects of homework, and how to link classwork, homework, and assessments. Most teachers are presently guided and monitored on the quality of class lesson plans and classroom teaching, but are not well prepared, supervised, or evaluated on their homework designs and actions (see Epstein, 2001).

More rigorous research is needed to better understand how contrasting homework designs affect specific student outcomes across the grades. Research shows that homework can be an important tool for teachers to help students develop basic and advanced skills, but there still is much to learn about homework. The TIPS studies illustrate one way to broaden research from measures of minutes or completion of homework to focus on the design and content of assignments to meet specific purposes or goals for student learning and development. These studies also raise questions about teachers' roles in using homework as an instructional tool, including whether and how well they introduce assignments and follow up assignments with discussions, marks, and related quiz or test questions. Research on these topics would open the "black box" of homework, and should make research on homework more useful in policy and in practice.

CONCLUSIONS

Homework is a daily activity for most students for at least twelve years of schooling. Every assignment takes the time, energy, and emotions of teachers, students, and families. Given these investments, it is important to ask: How can homework be an effective teaching tool, a useful communication strategy, and a beneficial learning experience? The research reviewed in this article suggests that when teachers design homework to meet specific purposes and goals, more students complete their homework and benefit from the results, and more families remain involved in their children's education through the middle grades.

ACKNOWLEDGMENTS

This research was supported by grants from the U.S. Department of Education, Office of Educational Research and Improvement/OERI, Disney Learning Partnership, and the Wallace–Reader's Digest Funds. The opinions are the authors' and do not necessarily represent the policies or positions of these funding sources. Special thanks to the many teachers who, over the years, assisted in designing and testing the TIPS interactive process, and to students and parents who participated in the research studies. Thanks, too, to the editors and three anonymous reviewers for suggestions on an earlier version of this article.

REFERENCES

Acock, A. C. and D. H. Demo. (1994). *Family diversity and well-being*. Thousand Oaks, CA: Sage.

Ames, C., L. DeStefano, T. Watkins, and S. Sheldon. (1995). *Teachers' school-to-home communications and parent involvement: The role of parent perceptions and beliefs*. Report 28. Baltimore: Center on Families, Communities, Schools, and Children's Learning, Johns Hopkins University.

Association of Supervision and Curriculum Development (ASCD). (2001). *How to make homework more meaningful*. (Video). Alexandria, VA: Author.

Astone, N. M., and S. S. McLanahan. (1991). Family structure, parental practices and high school completion. *American Sociological Review* 56: 309–320.

Azmitia, M., and C. R. Cooper. (2001). Good or bad? Peers and academic pathways of Latino and European American youth in schools and a community college outreach program. *Journal of Education of Students Placed at Risk* 6: 45–71.

Babbie, E. (1990). *Survey research methods* (2nd ed.). Belmont, CA: Wadsworth.

Baker, D., and D. Stevenson. (1986). Mothers' strategies for school achievement: Managing the transition to high school. *Sociology of Education* 59: 156–167.

Balli, S. J. (1995). *The effects of differential prompts on family involvement with middle-grades homework*. Unpublished doctoral dissertation, University of Missouri, Columbia.

———. (1998). When mom and dad help: Student reflections on parent involvement with homework. *Journal of Research and Development in Education* 31: 142–146.

Balli, S. J., D. H. Demo, and J. F. Wedman. (1998). Family involvement with children's homework: An intervention in the middle grades. *Family Relations* 47: 149–157.

Becker, H. J., and J. L. Epstein. (1982). Parent involvement: A survey of teacher practices. *Elementary School Journal* 83: 85–102.

Calkins, L. M. (1994). *The art of teaching writing* (new ed.). Portsmouth, NH: Heinemann.

Campbell, J. R., C. M. Hombo, and J. Mazzeo. (2000). *NAEP 1999 trends in academic progress: Three decades of student performance.* NCES 2000-469. Washington, DC: U.S. Department of Education.

Catsambis, S. (1998). *Expanding knowledge of parental involvement in secondary education: Effects on high school academic success.* Report 27. Baltimore: Center for Research on the Education of Students Placed at Risk (CRESPAR), Johns Hopkins University.

Chen, C., and H. W. Stevenson. (1989). Homework: A cross-cultural examination. *Child Development* 60: 551–561.

Coleman, J. S., T. Hoffer, and S. Kilgore. (1982). *High school achievement: Public, Catholic, and private schools compared.* New York: Basic Books.

Connors, L. J., and J. L. Epstein. (1994). *Taking stock: Views of teachers, parents, and students on school, family, and community partnerships in high schools.* Report 25. Baltimore: Johns Hopkins University, Center on Families, Communities, Schools, and Children's Learning.

Cooper, H. (1989). *Homework.* White Plains, NY: Longman.

Cooper, H., J. J. Lindsay, and B. Nye. (2000). Homework in the home: How students, family and parenting style differences related to the homework process. *Contemporary Educational Psychology* 25: 464–487.

Cooper, H., J. J. Lindsay, B. Nye, and S. Greathouse. (1998). Relationships among attitudes about homework, amount of homework assigned and completed, and student achievement. *Journal of Educational Psychology* 90: 70–83.

Cooper, H., and J. Valentine. (2001). Using research to answer practical questions about homework. *Educational Psychologist* 36: 143–53.

Corno, L. (1996). Homework is a complicated thing. *Educational Researcher* 25: 27–30.

———. (2000). Looking at homework differently. *Elementary School Journal* 100: 529–548.

Dauber, S. L., and J. L. Epstein. (1993). Parents' attitudes and practices of involvement in inner-city elementary and middle schools. In N. Chavkin (Ed.), *Families and schools in a pluralistic society* (pp. 53–71). Albany: State University of New York Press.

Davies, D. and V. R. Johnson. (Eds.). (1996). Crossing boundaries: Family, community, and school partnerships. *International Journal of Educational Research* 25 (Special Issue).

Delgado-Gaitan, C. (1990). *Literacy for empowerment: The role of parents in children's education.* New York: Falmer.

Eccles, J., and R. D. Harold. (1996). Family involvement in children's and adolescents' schooling. In A. Booth and J. F. Dunn (Eds.), *Family-school links: How do they affect educational outcomes?* (pp. 3–34). Mahwah, NJ: Lawrence Erlbaum.

Epstein, J. L. (1986). Parents' reactions to teacher practices of parent involvement. *Elementary School Journal* 86: 277–294.

———. (1988). *Homework practices, achievement, and behaviors of elementary school students.* Report 26. Baltimore: Center on Families, Communities, Schools, and Children's Learning, Johns Hopkins University.

———. (1990). Single parents and the schools: Effects of marital status on parent and teacher interactions. In M. Hallinan (Ed.), *Change in societal institutions* (pp. 91–121). New York: Plenum.

———. (1991). School programs and teacher practices of parent involvement in inner-city elementary and middle schools. *Elementary School Journal* 91: 289–305.

———. (1995, May). School/family/community partnerships: Caring for the children we share. *Phi Delta Kappan* 76: 701–712.

———. (2001). *School, family, and community partnerships: Preparing educators and improving schools.* Boulder: Westview.

Epstein, J. L., and H. J. Becker. (1982, November). Teacher reported practices of parent involvement: Problems and possibilities. *Elementary School Journal* 83: 103–113. (Reading 3.2).

Epstein, J. L., and S. L. Dauber. (1991). School programs and teacher practices of parent involvement in inner-city elementary and middle schools. *Elementary School Journal* 91: 289–305.

Epstein, J. L., and S. Lee. (1995). National patterns of school and family connections in the middle grades. In B. A. Ryan, G. R. Adams, T. P. Gullota, R. P. Weissberg, and R. L. Hampton (Eds.), *The family-school connection: Theory, research, and practice* (pp. 108–154). Thousand Oaks, CA: Sage.

Epstein, J. L., et al. (2009). *School, family, and community partnerships: Your handbook for action* (3rd ed.). Thousand Oaks, CA: Corwin.

Epstein, J. L., K. C. Salinas, and V. E. Jackson. (1995). *Manual for Teachers and Prototype Activities: Teachers Involve Parents in Schoolwork (TIPS) language arts, science/health, and math interactive homework in the middle grades.* Baltimore: Center on School, Family, and Community Partnerships, Johns Hopkins University.

Epstein, J. L., B. S. Simon, and K. C. Salinas. (1997, September). Effects of Teachers Involve Parents in Schoolwork (TIPS) language arts interactive homework in the middle grades. *Research Bulletin* 18.

Epstein, J. L., and F. L. Van Voorhis. (2000). *Teachers Involve Parents in Schoolwork (TIPS) Interactive Homework Training Materials.* Baltimore: Center on School, Family, and Community Partnerships, Johns Hopkins University.

Farkas, S., J. M. Johnson, and A. Duffett. (1999). *Playing their parts: Parents and teachers talk about parental involvement in public schools.* New York: Public Agenda.

Featherstone, H. (1985, February). Homework. *Harvard Education Letter* 1(1).

Fehrmann, P. G., T. Z. Keith, and T. M. Reimers. (1987). Home influences on school learning: Direct and indirect effects of parental involvement on high school grades. *Journal of Educational Research* 80: 330–337.

Garner, W. T. (1978). Linking school resources to educational outcomes: The role of homework. *Teachers College Research Bulletin* 19: 1–10.

González, N., R. Andrade, M. Civil, and L. Moll. (2001). Bridging funds of distributed knowledge: Creating zones of practice in mathematics. *Journal of Education of Students Placed at Risk* 6: 115–132.

González, N., and L. Moll. (1996). Teachers as social scientists: Learning about culture from household research. In P. M. Hall (Ed.), *Race, ethnicity, and multiculturalism* (pp. 89–114). New York: Garland.

Grolnick, W. S., and M. L. Slowiaczek. (1994). Parents' involvement in children's schooling: A multidimensional conceptualization and motivational model. *Child Development* 65: 237–252.

Ho, E. S., and J. D. Willms. (1996). Effects of parental involvement on eighth-grade achievement. *Sociology of Education* 69: 126–141.

Hoover-Dempsey, K. V., O. C. Bassler, and J. S. Brissie. (1987). Parent involvement: Contributions of teacher efficacy, school socioeconomic status, and other school characteristics. *American Educational Research Journal* 24: 417–435.

Hoover-Dempsey, K. V., O. C. Bassler, and R. Burow. (1995). Parents' reported involvement in students' homework: Parameters of reported strategy and practice. *Elementary School Journal* 95: 435–450.

Hoover-Dempsey, K. V., A. B. Battiato, J. M. T. Walker, R. P. Reed, J. M. DeJong, and K. P. Jones. (2001). Parental involvement in homework. *Educational Psychologist* 36: 195–210.

Hoover-Dempsey, K. V., and H. M. Sandler. (1997). Why do parents become involved in their children's education? *Review of Educational Research* 67: 3–42.

Keith, T. Z. (1982). Time spent on homework and high school grades: A large-sample path analysis. *Journal of Educational Psychology* 74: 248–253.

Keith, T. Z., and V. A. Cool. (1992). Testing models of school learning: Effects of quality of instruction, motivation, academic coursework, and homework on academic achievement. *School Psychology Quarterly* 7: 207–226.

Keith, T. Z., P. B. Keith, G. C. Troutman, P. G. Bickley, P. S. Trivette, and K. Singh. (1993). Does parental involvement affect eighth-grade student achievement? Structural analysis of national data. *School Psychology Review* 22: 474–496.

Lareau, A. (1989). *Home advantage: Social class and parental intervention in elementary education.* Philadelphia: Falmer.

Lee, S. (1994). *Family-school connections and students' education: Continuity and change in family involvement from the middle grades to high school.* Unpublished dissertation, Johns Hopkins University.

Lehrer, R., and L. Shumow. (1997). Aligning the construction zones of parents and teachers for mathematics reform. *Cognition and Instruction* 15: 41–83.

Leone, C. M., and M. H. Richards. (1989). Classwork and homework in early adolescence: The ecology of achievement. *Journal of Youth and Adolescence* 18: 531–548.

Levin, I., R. Levy-Schiff, T. Appelbaum-Peled, I. Katz, M. Komar, and N. Meiran. (1997). Antecedents and consequences of maternal involvement in children's homework: A longitudinal analysis. *Journal of Applied Developmental Psychology* 18: 207–222.

MacBeath, J. (1998). The development of student study centres to improve homework and learning in Scotland. *Childhood Education* 74: 383–386.

Maertens, N. W., and J. Johnston. (1972). The effects of arithmetic homework upon the attitudes and achievement of fourth, fifth, and sixth grade pupils. *School Science and Mathematics* 72: 117–126.

McDermott, R. P., S. V. Goldman, and H. Varenne. (1984). When school goes home: Some problems in the organization of homework. *Teachers College Record* 85: 391–409.

Mehan, H., A. Lintz, D. Okamoto, and J. S. Wills. (1995). Ethnographic studies of multicultural education in classrooms and schools. In J. A. Banks and C. A. M. Banks (Eds.), *Handbook of research on multicultural education* (pp. 129–144). New York: Macmillan.

Merttens, R., and P. Woods. (1994, April). *Parents' and children's assessment of maths in the home: Towards a theory of learning congruence.* Paper presented at the Annual Meeting of the American Educational Research Association, New Orleans.

Moll, L. C., C. Amanti, D. Neff, and N. González. (1992). Funds of knowledge for teaching: Using a qualitative approach to connect homes and classrooms. *Theory into Practice* 31: 132–141.

Muhlenbruck, L., H. Cooper, B. Nye, and J. J. Lindsay. (2000). Homework and achievement: Explaining the different strengths of relation at the elementary and secondary school levels. *Social Psychology of Education* 3: 295–317.

Paris, S. G., K. M. Yambor, and B. Packard. (1998). Hands-on biology: A Museum-school-university partnership for enhancing students' interest and learning in science. *Elementary School Journal* 98: 267–289.

Paschal, R. A., T. Weinstein, and H. Walberg. (1984). The effects of homework on learning: A quantitative synthesis. *Journal of Educational Research* 78: 97–104.

Paulu, N. (1995). *Helping your child with homework.* Washington, DC: Office of Educational Research and Improvement, U.S. Department of Education.

Pratt, M. W., T. Filipovich, and M. Bountrogianni. (1995). Teachers' views of parents: Family decision making styles and teacher-parent agreement regarding homework practices and values. *Alberta Journal of Educational Research* 41: 175–187.

Rutter, M., B. Maughan, P. Mortimore, and J. Ouston. (1979). *Fifteen thousand hours: Secondary schools and their effects on children.* Cambridge, MA: Harvard University Press.

Sanders, M. G., J. L. Epstein, and L. Connors-Tadros. (1999). *Family partnerships with high schools: The parents' perspective.* Report 32. Baltimore: Center for Research on the Education of Students Placed At Risk (CRESPAR), Johns Hopkins University.

Scott-Jones, D. (1995). Parent-child interactions and school achievement. In B. A. Ryan, G. R. Adams, T. P. Gullota, R. P. Weissberg, and R. L. Hampton (Eds.), *The family-school connection: Theory, research, and practice* (pp. 75–107). Thousand Oaks, CA: Sage.

Sheldon, S. B., and J. L. Epstein. (2005). Involvement counts: Family and community partnerships and math achievement. *Journal of Educational Research* 98: 196–206.

Simon, B. S. (2004). High school outreach and family involvement. *Social Psychology of Education* 7: 185–209.

Snow, C., W. S. Barnes, J. Chandler, I. Goodman, and L. Hemphill. (1989). *Families and schools: Effects on literacy.* Cambridge, MA: Harvard University Press.

Stevenson, D. L., and D. P. Baker. (1987). The family-school relation and the child's school performance. *Child Development* 58: 1348–1357.

Stevenson, H. W., S. Lee, C. Chen, J. W. Stigler, C. Hsu, and S. Kitamura. (1990). Contexts of achievement: A study of American, Chinese, and Japanese children. *Monographs of the Society for Research in Child Development* 55: Serial No. 221.

Van Voorhis, F. L. (2003). Interactive homework in middle school: Effects on family involvement and science achievement. *Journal of Educational Research* 96(6): 323–338.

Vélez-Ibáñez, C., and J. Greenberg. (1992). Formation and transformation of funds of knowledge among U.S. Mexican households. *Anthropology and Education Quarterly* 23: 313–335.

Villas-Boas, A. (1998). The effects of parental involvement in homework on student achievement in Portugal and Luxembourg. *Childhood Education* 74: 367–371.

Xu, J., and L. Corno. (1998). Case studies of families doing third grade homework. *Teachers College Record* 100: 402–436.

Zernike, K. (2000, October 10). As homework load grows, one district says "enough." *New York Times.*

Teachers Involve Parents in Schoolwork (TIPS): Interactive Homework in Math, Science, and Language Arts

LINKING FAMILY INVOLVEMENT
WITH STUDENT ACHIEVEMENT

Although all six types of involvement discussed in Chapter 5 are important, not every type of family or community involvement will immediately increase student achievement and success in school. Type 4—Learning at Home is one type of involvement that may directly influence students' skills and achievements. Family interactions with children about schoolwork and homework may, if well designed and effectively implemented, increase students' completion of homework, improve students' attitudes toward school, boost students' readiness for the next class lesson, and improve students' performance on tests and report card grades.

Type 4—Learning at Home requires every teacher to activate the important connections between what is taught and learned in school and what is encouraged, practiced, discussed, and celebrated at home. It requires every teacher to inform and involve families about the work that their children do in class.

This could be a daunting, even impossible, task if it meant that teachers had to show every parent how to teach every skill in every subject. It would be equally unfair, even absurd, to expect all parents to know how to teach their children all school subjects every year. It is possible, however, to implement useful Type 4 activities to help students gain and strengthen skills, interact with parents or other family members about schoolwork at home, and keep parents informed about the skills their children are learning from week to week or month to month.

Most teachers and administrators report that they want parents to support their children's learning, help students practice important skills, and monitor homework. Most, however, have not organized ways to guide all parents in productive interactions with their children about homework or curriculum-related decisions. Some teachers and administrators worry that involving families with children in learning activities at home will diminish teachers' professional status. Studies indicate, however, that when teachers implement frequent, family-friendly practices of partnership, parents increase their respect for teachers and for the work that teachers do (Epstein and Van Voorhis, 2001 [Reading 6.1]; Xu, 2003; Xu and Corno, 2003; and see Reading 4.3).

Most parents do not want to teach school subjects to their children. Rather, parents want to know: "*How can I help my child do well in school?*" Many studies and interviews with thousands of parents about what they mean by "help" indicate that parents want to support, encourage, and motivate their children, monitor their work, celebrate progress, and conduct interactions that will help their children complete their homework and do well in school (Hoover-Dempsey and Sandler, 1995; and see Readings 3.4, 3.5, and 3.6). These preferences are expressed by parents of children at all grade levels, from preschool through high school, in diverse communities. Parents' requests require teachers to involve all families in new ways with their children in academic activities at home.

TIPS interactive homework was designed to fulfill this goal: Teachers at every grade level and subject can select or design one homework assignment a week or every other week that requires students to talk to someone at home about something interesting they are learning in class. If such activities were well designed and assigned on a regular schedule, all families would be able to follow their children's progress in learning; all children would be able to share ideas and information at home; and all teachers would have a realistic strategy for communicating with families about students' curriculum, homework, and academic choices and decisions.

TIPS activities recognize the central role of students as the main actors in their own education. Students—not parents—must study, complete homework, take tests, and learn as much as possible. Students also are active participants in school, family, and community partnerships. They are couriers of all kinds of information from school to home and from home to school, including information on homework. Students are the natural leaders of and participants in conversations and interactions about schoolwork and homework, academic decisions such as course choices, and plans for the future.

RESEARCH LEADING TO TIPS

TIPS interactive homework processes grew from early research that revealed that when elementary school teachers frequently involved families in reading activities at home, more parents conducted these activities with their children, and more of these students improved their reading test scores from fall to spring of the school year. The study suggested an important subject-specific link between parent involvement in reading and gains in student achievement in reading (see Readings 3.1 and 3.7).

The same studies revealed that although many teachers, particularly in the younger grades, asked parents to be involved with their children in reading, few teachers at any grade level asked parents to become involved in other subjects. Teachers did not have effective strategies to guide parental involvement in math, science, or other subjects and, therefore, did not feel comfortable about requesting involvement in these subjects. The research raised several questions:

- Could an interactive homework process be designed that would help teachers involve all families with their children at home in math, science, writing, and other subjects?
- Could interactive assignments be conducted successfully by students at different grade levels, with varying abilities, and in diverse communities?

- If teachers involved students in activities with family partners in math, science, or other subjects, would students increase their skills, improve attitudes, and complete more homework in these subjects?

To address these questions, my colleagues and I worked with educators, families, and students in the elementary and middle grades to design and study interactive homework and its effects (Van Voorhis and Epstein, 2002). Exploratory work also was conducted with high school educators, families, and students to learn if and how interactive homework might work in high schools.

TIPS prototype activities show teachers how to design research-based interactive homework assignments in math, science/health, and language arts. In TIPS activities, students may demonstrate their mastery of skills; conduct experiments; share ideas; obtain reactions and suggestions; conduct surveys or interviews; gather parents' memories of their own experiences as children, or memories of the students as young children; apply a skill to real life; or work with family members in other ways. The interactions are conducted by the students in ways that enable all parents to become involved in learning activities at home.

Different school subjects pose different challenges and require different designs for successful interactions. The next sections describe TIPS Math, TIPS Science, and TIPS Language Arts Interactive Homework. A few sample interactive homework assignments are included at the end of this reading to illustrate TIPS Math, Science, and Language Arts for the elementary and middle grades, and there is a high school activity in social studies.

TIPS MATH

In studying interactive homework in math, we learned that teachers worried that parents did not know how their children were being taught math in school. Parents worried that they might confuse their children about math. And children complained, cried, or argued, "You don't do it like my teacher does it."

The teachers knew that they could not teach all parents how to teach math, and that parents did not want to do this. Consequently, most families did not talk much about math with their children, and many did not approach math positively.

TIPS Math was designed to put parents, students, and teachers at ease in their interactions about math at home. TIPS Math:

- illustrates clearly how the teacher taught the skill in class;
- allows students to demonstrate, discuss, and celebrate their mastery of new math skills;
- enables parents to stay informed about their children's math work; and
- encourages parents to communicate with teachers about their observations, comments, or questions concerning their children's math homework and progress in math.

Math in the middle grades is more complex than is math in younger grades, making it even harder for most parents to monitor or assist their children. TIPS Math assignments in the middle grades guide early adolescents to review math skills and to talk with family partners about how each math skill is used in real-life situations.

Exploratory fieldwork with TIPS Math in elementary schools in a low-income community in Illinois suggested that interactive homework was easily implemented, and that just about all parents were able to participate. An early study of TIPS Math was conducted in three sixth grade classes in one middle school. The study compared levels of family involvement and math achievement of students completing TIPS Math interactive assignments with student completing noninteractive math assignments (i.e., without directions for the student to involve a family member in the assignment). Results indicated that parents appreciated the student-led interactions, students and parents reported more positive conversations with students about math. Most students believed that the interactions helped them be more prepared and successful in math class. In that study, students had the same math teacher, and all three math classes improved in achievement. However, students assigned TIPS Math interactive homework had significantly more interactions with parents and more positive attitudes about math than did students who were assigned traditional math homework (Balli, 1998; Balli, Demo, and Wedman, 1998).

Van Voorhis (in press) improved research on TIPS Math with a longitudinal study of students in the elementary grades. Van Voorhis followed 153 students and their families from grade 3 through grade 4 in schools in an urban system in a southern state (2009a; in press). Compared to students in control (non-TIPS) classes, students assigned TIPS assignments and their parents reported significantly more family involvement in math, more positive attitudes and "happy" emotions about math homework and about doing math together, and higher math achievement test scores, controlling on prior test scores.

Links to Curriculum

TIPS Math interactive homework should be an integral part of the math curriculum. (See Anderson and Gold, 2006; Remillard and Jackson, 2006, for related research on the connections of families and the math curriculum.) At each grade level, students can show family members that they are mastering major math skills. For example, TIPS Math prototype activities in grade 1 include more than 35 math skills, including counting from 1 to 100; writing numerals for sets of tens and ones; adding two-digit numbers without regrouping; and learning shapes, fractions, graphs, and other skills. TIPS Math in grade 5 includes more than 35 activities, such as estimating quotients, adding and subtracting mixed numerals, identifying line segments and rays, comparing unlike fractions, solving word problems requiring multiplication, creating graphs, and other skills. TIPS Math for the middle grades includes 20 prototype activities that help students review basic skills and focus on problem-solving and real-world applications.

From year to year, TIPS Math should help families see that their children's math skills are increasing and how new skills build on earlier activities. For example, graphing is introduced in grade 1 and 2 when students share picture graphs with their family partners. By grade 5, students demonstrate how they construct their own bar graphs and line graphs. Graphs also are included in TIPS Science activities in the middle grades to help students observe and classify information systematically. Graphing is a good interactive homework assignment at all grade levels across the curriculum because children enjoy the challenge of creating and interpreting graphs, as well as sharing information with their families.

Format

TIPS Math enables students to show parents or other family members what they learned in math class and how they practice new skills. The activities also guide student-parent discussions on how to apply specific skills in real-world problems. TIPS Math activities may include challenging games and problem-solving activities related to the specific skills in the assignments. TIPS Math enables teachers to obtain reactions from parents in home-to-school communications. Each interactive activity includes the following sections:

Look This Over shows an example of a skill that was taught in class, and allows the student to explain the skill to a parent or family partner. The answer to the example is given.

Now Try This presents another example for the student to demonstrate how to do the particular skill, with the answer on the back of the page.

Practice and *More Practice* are regular homework problems for the student to master the skill.

Let's Find Out or *In the Real World* may be added to help the student and family partner discover and discuss how the math skill is used at home or in common situations. Games or other interactions may be included to reinforce the math skill.

Home-to-School Communication invites the parent to record an observation, comment, or question for the math teacher about the skill the student demonstrated.

Parent Signature is requested on each activity.

Presentation and Schedule

Each activity must be prepared in readable type on two sides of one page and be printed on light colored paper to stand out in students' notebooks. TIPS Math should be assigned on a regular schedule (e.g., once a week or twice a month) to help students and families talk about math at home and to help parents see what their children are learning in math. In one school, a parent wrote about TIPS Math: "When I see that yellow paper, I know that is important homework for my son to complete with me." Another noted: "Send more of these. I forgot how to do this. It was fun for us."

Materials Available

TIPS Math interactive homework materials include over 200 prototype assignments for basic math skills from kindergarten through grade 5 and 20 prototype activities for functional math in the middle grades (Van Voorhis and Epstein, 2002). There also are teacher manuals for implementing TIPS in the elementary and middle grades (Epstein, Salinas, and Van Voorhis, 2001). Two examples of TIPS Math activities for the elementary and middle grades are included in the appendix to this reading:

Fractional Parts	Sample TIPS Math (elementary grades)
I Mean It!	Sample TIPS Math (middle grades)

TIPS SCIENCE

In studying interactive homework in science, we learned that most elementary school teachers did not have much time to teach science. After teaching math, reading, and language arts every day, many teachers had one block of time in which to fit social studies, science, art, music, physical education, and other subjects and activities. Because of the lack of class time, and, until recently, often a lack of attention to science on standardized tests, few elementary teachers ever assigned science homework. Teachers almost never expected family involvement except on science fair projects, which often were isolated from the regular science program.

In the mid-1980s, the National Science Foundation called for at least 30 minutes of science instruction per day in the elementary grades, but few schools met that standard. This was confirmed in a national study that reported that only 25 percent of states and 40 percent of school districts in the nation required even minimum amounts of time for math or science in the elementary grades (Resnick and Resnick, 1985). Specific requirements for class time usually referred to math, not science.

It was clear from national assessments and international comparisons that elementary and middle-grade students in the United States were not getting enough science instruction and had few opportunities to work as scientists with hands-on activities. In the 1990s, a national education goal called for the country to be "first in the world" in math and science by the year 2000. To begin to work toward that goal, science was added to national, state, and international lists of standards and assessments to make schools more accountable for science instruction. The goal for all students' science learning was not achieved by 2000. Indeed, according to statistics from the U.S. Department of Education, 82 percent of this nation's twelfth graders performed "below the proficient level" in science in 2000 (U.S. Department of Education, 2004).

The goal for advancing science teaching and learning was reset for 2014 in NCLB. Yet, unlike math and reading—required on state achievement tests every year for students in grades 3 to grade 8—NCLB required science tests only once per school level, starting in 2007. It is clear that although some students in some schools take advanced science courses and attain world-class science skills, most students in the U.S. receive relatively little science instruction and have few opportunities to gain or share science knowledge.

Very few schools have organized programs to involve all families with their children in regularly scheduled interactive science homework. Most parents have no idea what their children are learning in science in the elementary grades and rarely talk with their children about science at home. In the middle grades, most students have daily science classes, but most students and families still do not converse about science at home.

TIPS Science addresses some of these issues. TIPS activities require students to work as scientists, involve a family "assistant," discuss conclusions, and interview family members about how science affects them in everyday life. TIPS Science:

- encourages teachers to introduce science topics in class and follow up with discussions or demonstrations, after the TIPS interactive homework assignments are completed;
- guides students to conduct, discuss, and enjoy science activities at home;
- enables parents to stay informed about their children's science work and progress; and
- encourages parents to communicate with teachers about their observations and questions concerning their children's science homework and progress in science.

Exploratory studies in TIPS Science in the middle grades indicated that parents and students enjoyed their conversations about science, and they strongly recommended that the school continue to use TIPS Science activities from year to year. Teachers who introduced and discussed the homework assignments in class, before students took them home, and who followed up the assignments with some discussion, had students with higher rates of homework completion than did teachers who did not follow these implementation strategies. Knowledge gained from several years of field observations, interviews, and surveys of teachers, parents, and students was incorporated in the TIPS manuals for teachers (Epstein et al., 2001).

New questions about the effects of TIPS Science homework in the middle grades were explored by Van Voorhis (2003). She conducted a quasi-experimental study of the TIPS Science process with 250 sixth- and eighth-grade science students in ten classes of four teachers in a suburban middle school. Students in six classes received weekly TIPS Science activities with specific guidelines for students to interact with family partners in science experiments and activities. Students in four classes received the same homework but with no guidelines for family involvement (non-TIPS). Van Voorhis found that students who completed TIPS assignments reported significantly higher family involvement in science than did students in the non-TIPS classes. TIPS students also had higher science report card grades, even after accounting for the strong influence of students' prior science abilities, parent education, and the amount of homework completed.

Van Voorhis improved the early research on TIPS Science with a longitudinal study of students in the middle grades. She followed 309 students and their families from grade 7 through grade 8 in schools in a southern, suburban school district (Van Voorhis, 2008, 2009b). After statistically controlling for gender, socioeconomic status, students' prior ability, and other background variables, TIPS students had higher benchmark science test scores and report card grades than did students in control (non-TIPS) classes. Compared to students in control (non-TIPS) classes, students assigned TIPS Science assignments and their parents reported significantly more family involvement in science, and more positive attitudes about science homework and about doing science together. Nearly all (98 percent) of the students and families agreed that "TIPS science was a good idea."

These strong studies with control groups for comparisons indicate that TIPS Science added significantly and positively to students' learning science. They showed that even in the middle grades, interactive homework is one approach for students to engage family partners in experiments and discussions about science.

Links to Curriculum

TIPS Science interactive homework should be an integral part of the science curriculum. TIPS Science hands-on activities help students build science skills of observation, classification, hypothesizing, experimenting, graphing, recording data, interpreting data, drawing conclusions, and discussing ideas with others at home and in school. Prototype science activities emphasize writing across the curriculum as students record information and summarize results and conclusions from experiments and from interviews with family members.

Data collection in science becomes more complex across the grades. Simple charts or lists in the early elementary grades lead to longer systematic collections of data in the upper grades. Even young children, however, can keep track of data over time. For example, one TIPS activity asks third graders to draw the moon each night that it is visible for a month. An activity on osmosis asks seventh graders to chart changes in an egg that is set in vinegar over several days.

TIPS Science activities enable students to talk about science with family members at home and to see that science is all around us. For example, 12 prototype activities in grade 3 cover topics of living things, matter, and earth and space; and approximately 40 activities for grade 8 introduce topics in chemistry and physics. TIPS activities guide discussions on important issues as diverse as metric measures, pollution, digestion, and carbon dating to help students and families discuss and share opinions about the meaning of science in their lives at home and at school.

Some prototype science activities address health and mental health topics that require students to conduct conversations, gather reactions, or collect data from family members on good health and early adolescent development. Health may be covered in science, physical education, advisory periods, or separate health classes.

Regardless of their formal education, just about all parents have ideas to share about healthy development, such as good nutrition, the importance of exercise, or ideas for making good decisions. Sometimes, however, parents do not know how to begin to discuss sensitive topics with their children, such as adolescent sexual development, AIDS, or drug abuse prevention. TIPS interactive homework assignments on health topics give students opportunities and directions to start conversations with family members and exchange ideas and opinions on health issues. Prototype activities include such topics as physical changes in early adolescence; emotional development; personal strengths, weaknesses, plans, and values; and making tough decisions. Other sample activities include understanding sight/blindness; hearing; drugs; and organ systems of the body, including the circulatory, respiratory, digestive, excretory, nervous, reproductive, and endocrine systems.

Format

TIPS Science guides students to conduct and discuss hands-on "lab" activities at home. All activities include a brief letter to parents explaining the topic and outline the learning objectives, materials needed, directions for data collection, discussion questions, conclusions, and home-to-school communications. Each interactive activity includes the following sections:

> *Letter to parent, guardian, or family partner* explains briefly the topic and specific science skills involved in the activity. The student writes in the due date and signs the letter.
>
> *Objectives* explain the learning goal(s) of the activity. Materials are common, inexpensive, and immediately available at home or easily obtained. If they are not, the school should provide the materials.
>
> *Procedure* guides the student, step by step. Each assignment includes hands-on actions that require the student to think and act like a scientist. Teachers may change, simplify, or increase the difficulty of activities to meet the special needs of students.
>
> *Lab report or data chart* gives space for the student to report findings.
>
> *Conclusions* guide the student to discuss results and real-world applications of science or health with family partners.
>
> *Home-to-school communication* invites the parents to share comments and observations with science teachers about whether their child understood the homework, whether they all enjoyed the activity, and whether the parents gained information about the student's work in science and health.
>
> *Parent signature* is requested on each activity.

Presentation and Schedule

TIPS Science/Health activities must be prepared in readable type, on two sides of one page, and be printed on light colored paper to stand out in students' notebooks. TIPS Science interactive homework should be assigned on a regular schedule (e.g., once a week or twice a month) to help students discuss their work in science and health at home and to keep families aware of what their students are learning in science and health classes.

Typical comments from parents on TIPS Science include "His thought process was more mature than what I knew." And "I think she could have done a better job with the consequences." Family partners' comments on health activities include "I am glad we discussed working with blind people." And "This opened up an easier way of communicating."

Materials Available

TIPS Science prototypes are available for grade 3 and more than 100 examples are prepared for various science units in the middle grades (6–8) (Van Voorhis and Epstein, 2002). There also are teacher manuals for implementing TIPS Science in the elementary and middle grades (Epstein et al., 2001). Two examples of TIPS Science activities for the elementary and middle grades are included in the appendix to this reading:

Living Things: The Importance of Animals	Sample TIPS Science (elementary grades)
On Your Mark, Get Set, Go!	Sample TIPS Science (middle grades)

TIPS LANGUAGE ARTS

In studying TIPS Language Arts, we found that teachers in the middle grades were not as comfortable about guiding family involvement in reading, vocabulary, and writing as were teachers in the elementary grades. Middle school educators wanted assignments that went beyond asking parents to listen to their children read aloud or to give practice spelling tests. They wanted students to conduct conversations with family members about words, phrases, sentences, stories, speeches, themes, and ideas.

Language arts is an excellent interactive subject because families like to listen to what their children write; help children practice a speech; and share ideas and memories that make good topics for stories, poems, and essays. Data from students in elementary, middle, and high schools show that students like to interview parents, gather ideas, demonstrate skills, and share their work. TIPS Language Arts:

- encourages teachers to design homework that builds students' skills in reading, writing, speaking, and listening through communications with family partners;
- guides students to conduct, discuss, and enjoy language arts activities at home;
- enables parents to stay informed about their children's language arts work and progress; and
- encourages parents to communicate with teachers about their observations and questions concerning their children's homework and progress in language arts.

Research was conducted to study the influence of TIPS Language Arts on students' writing skills, language arts report card grades, and completion of TIPS interactive homework assignments (Epstein, Simon, and Salinas, 1997). The study included 683 students in grades 6 and 8 in two urban schools where over 70 percent of the students qualified for free or reduced-price lunch. Students completed writing samples in the fall, winter, and spring of the school year and provided their reactions to TIPS. Parents also were surveyed on their attitudes toward TIPS and their participation with their children in TIPS activities. Analyses statistically controlled for family socioeconomic status, grade level, attendance, fall report card grades, and fall writing sample scores, to identify the effects of TIPS on students' skills in the winter and spring and student and family attitudes at the end of the school year.

As might be expected, students with higher writing scores in the fall had higher scores in the winter and spring. However, there also were some important homework-related results. The more homework assignments students completed, the higher were their language arts report card grades. The more parents participated, the better they liked TIPS interactive homework, and the higher were their students' writing scores in the winter and spring.

Nearly 100 percent of the families surveyed agreed that TIPS gave them information about what their children were learning in class. Over 80 percent of the students reported that TIPS gave them a way to show their parents what they were learning. Students said that they liked TIPS because they did not have to copy the homework from the board, because it was not boring, and because they learned something from or about their parents or families that they did not know before. Most teachers reported that more children completed TIPS than other homework. TIPS goals and the results of the study of the effects of TIPS Language Arts in the middle grades are shown in Table 6.3.

Van Voorhis advanced research on TIPS Language Arts with a longitudinal study of students in the middle grades. She followed 263 students and their families for two years from grade 6 to 7 in schools in a southern, urban school district (Van Voorhis, 2009a, b). In this diverse community, over 60 percent of the middle grades students received free or reduced-price meals. Compared to non-TIPS students whose teachers assigned language arts "homework as usual," TIPS students and families reported greater family involvement. Parents reported more positive attitudes

Goals of Interactive Homework	Summary of Results
For families . . . To increase family awareness of their children's schoolwork To increase family involvement in children's learning activities at home linked to academic classes	**For families . . .** Nearly 100% of the parents agreed that TIPS gave them information about what their children were learning in class, and approximately 90% advised the school to continue TIPS next year. Over 80% of the families liked the TIPS process (44% a lot; 36% a little). Most were involved every week (40%) or every other week (23%). Parents who participated with their children in more TIPS activities liked TIPS better than did other parents, even after accounting for other parental monitoring of schoolwork.
For students . . . To increase students' ability to talk about schoolwork at home and the frequency of interactions with family members about homework To improve students' homework completion in specific subjects To improve students' skills in specific subjects	**For students . . .** About 60% of the students said TIPS activities are better than regular homework; 70% reported their parents liked TIPS; 82% believed TIPS "gives me a way to show my parent what I am learning in class"; and about 70% recommended that the school continue to use TIPS next year. Students' attitudes about TIPS were most influenced by their attitudes toward school and by their teachers' attitudes toward TIPS. Students' writing skills increased with more family involvement in TIPS, even after prior writing skills were taken into account. Students' language arts report card grades improved when more TIPS assignments were completed, even after prior report card grades and attendance were taken into account.
For teachers . . . To enable teachers to assign interactive homework designed to encourage students to share their ideas with family members To increase teachers' understanding of families' interest in their children's work	**For teachers . . .** Six of the eight teachers liked the TIPS process and reported that they could continue its use without assistance or supplies from the researchers. Seven of eight teachers agreed that TIPS "helps families see what their children are learning in class."

TABLE 6.3   Linking the Goals of TIPS Interactive Homework to Results of a Study of TIPS Writing in the Middle Grades

Source: Epstein, Simon, and Salinas (1997).

about talking and working with their middle school student on language arts homework. After statistically controlling background variables including prior test scores, students who had TIPS Language Arts assignments for two years had higher standardized achievement test scores than the comparison groups.

Links to Curriculum

TIPS Language Arts interactive homework should be an integral part of the language arts curriculum. TIPS Language Arts guides students to share a variety of skills in writing, reading, grammar, wordplay, and related language arts activities. The students do all of the reading and writing in the assignments, but students and family members may discuss, share, and exchange ideas. Parents or other family members may listen to students read their writing aloud; give reactions, ideas, memories, and experiences; and interact in other ways.

TIPS Language Arts interactive homework prototype assignments focus on skills such as writing descriptive sentences, letters, stories, tall tales, poems, and speeches; elaborating ideas and details; improving grammar; and studying words and meanings such as similes, homonyms, analogies, context clues, multiple meanings, and chronological order. TIPS sample writing activities show teachers how to design homework that guides students to plan their writing, discuss ideas, write a draft, read aloud, and edit and improve their work.

TIPS writing assignments should help students improve their skills from their own starting points. For example, the same assignment may help some students write a short paragraph while other students write a long essay. TIPS also helps students edit their work. When they read their writing aloud to someone at home, students are more likely to see and hear how their words and punctuation should be changed or corrected.

Format

TIPS Language Arts activities include the following sections:

Letter to parent, guardian, or family partner explains the purpose of the activity. The student writes in the due date and signs the letter.
Objectives explain the learning goal of the activity (if this is not clear from the title and letter).
Materials are listed if more than paper and pen are needed.

Writing activities include the following sections:

Prewriting gives the student space to plan a letter, essay, or story by outlining, brainstorming, listing, designing nets and webs, or other planning activities.

First draft gives the student space to write and edit. A student who needs more space may add paper. Some teachers ask the student to write a final copy on other paper at home or at school.

Interactions such as a family survey or interview guide students to interview someone for ideas or memories, read work aloud for reactions, edit their work based on responses, practice a speech, take turns with others in giving ideas, or other interactions.

Home-to-school communication invites the parents to share comments and observations with language arts teachers about whether their child understood the homework, whether they all enjoyed the activity, and whether the parents gained information about the student's work in language arts.

Parent signature is requested on each activity.

Presentation and Schedule

Each activity must be prepared in clear, readable type on two sides of one page and be printed on light colored paper so that it stands out in the students' notebooks. TIPS Language Arts homework should be assigned on a regular schedule (e.g., once a week or every other week) to help students share their work and to keep families aware of what their children are learning in language arts or English classes. One parent wrote in a home-to-school communication about TIPS Language Arts: "I can tell from Jenneaka relating the story to me that she really enjoyed reading it." Another wrote: "Very interesting assignment. I enjoyed this and it brought back good memories."

Materials Available

More than 100 TIPS Language Arts prototype assignments are available for the middle grades (6–8). There also are teacher manuals for implementing TIPS Language Arts in the middle grades (Epstein et al., 2001; Van Voorhis and Epstein, 2002). The process and activities can be adapted for use in other grades. Two examples of TIPS Language Arts are included in the appendix to this reading. Originally designed for the middle grades, one shows how an interactive assignment can be revised for an elementary grade (grade 4), and one illustrates the greater difficulty appropriate in the middle grades.

Hairy Tales	Sample TIPS Language Arts (elementary grades)
A Helping Hand	Sample TIPS Language Arts (middle grades)

GOALS OF TIPS INTERACTIVE HOMEWORK

The prototype activities in math, science, and language arts show that the content and goals of different subjects require different designs for interactive homework. Nevertheless, TIPS activities in all subjects have some common goals for students, parents, and teachers. TIPS activities aim to:

- increase students' ability and willingness to talk about schoolwork at home and increase the frequency of these interactions;
- increase students' knowledge about real-world applications and the usefulness of skills learned in school;
- improve students' skills and homework completion in specific subjects;
- increase parents' awareness of their children's schoolwork;
- increase parents' confidence about talking with their children about schoolwork and homework;
- increase parents' involvement in their children's learning activities at home that are linked to class work;
- enable teachers to design homework that encourages students to share their work with family members;
- increase teachers' positive attitudes about families' interest in their children's work;
- increase positive attitudes of students, parents, and teachers about homework; and
- increase opportunities for students and parents to celebrate the mastery of skills and progress in learning.

HOW TO DEVELOP A TIPS INTERACTIVE HOMEWORK PROGRAM FOR ANY SUBJECT

Because TIPS interactive homework must match the curriculum that is taught in class, it is necessary to review, select, or design homework assignments that will be used throughout the school year in each school or school district. The following steps guide the development of TIPS interactive homework in any school, in any grade level, and in any subject (Epstein and Van Voorhis, 2009).

1. Select the subject(s) for interactive homework. List or outline the major curriculum objectives, concepts, and skills that will be taught each week over one school year.
2. Select one skill for each week of the school year that would promote productive, family-friendly interactions. From the outline of learning objectives, identify one skill that will be taught or reviewed each week that lends itself well to an enjoyable and useful interaction between students and family members.

3. Select or design one interactive homework assignment for each of the weekly skills identified. Review the existing TIPS prototype activities to find those that match the selected skills or those that may be easily adapted. If appropriate prototype activities do not exist, design new interactive homework assignments to accompany the class lessons. Following are some helpful design elements:

   - Keep the activities short and focused. TIPS assignments should fit on two sides of one page. They should ask students to involve family partners for up to 20 minutes, even if the students have more work to do on TIPS or other assignments.
   - Require only inexpensive and readily available materials, or provide the students with the necessary materials.
   - Include enjoyable and thoughtful student-family interactions in every activity.
   - Draw on real-life experiences that are common to all families and that are not dependent on parents' formal education.
   - Include a place for "home-to-school" communications on every activity so that parents may send a message back to the teacher about their interactions with their children on the assignment.
   - Print the TIPS assignments on light colored paper so they do not get lost in students' notebooks. Use the same color for all assignments in particular subjects so that students and families become familiar, for example, with yellow TIPS Math or blue TIPS Science activities.

4. Work with other teachers. Teachers who teach the same subjects at the same grade level can share the work of designing interactive homework. Teachers from the same school or school district may work together to plan, discuss, write, edit, test, and revise the TIPS assignments, format for the computer, and add related graphics. Then, the resulting TIPS activities can be shared and used or adapted by all teachers who use the same or similar curricula.

5. Use the summer to plan, produce, revise, format, and computerize activities so that they will be easily accessible to teachers and ready for students and families for the next school year. Homework should be part of school plans for improving the curriculum, instruction, and family involvement. Federal, state, district, and school funds may be available for improving the curriculum and should support teachers' time during the summer to design, develop, and organize TIPS interactive homework assignments for the next school year.

HOW TO IMPLEMENT TIPS INTERACTIVE HOMEWORK

Once the TIPS assignments are selected, adapted, or designed, teachers must develop plans and set schedules to effectively implement, evaluate, and maintain TIPS. This begins with an orientation of students and parents to the new approach to homework. Following are some key implementation guidelines.

Orient Parents and Students to TIPS

Students and parents need to be well prepared to conduct TIPS interactive homework successfully. Students need to know that they are responsible for all homework, and that they will conduct the interactions with family members in TIPS assignments. Students also need to hear frequently from the teacher that their families are important; that students are essential for the success of connections between school and home; and that students are expected to show and share their work, ideas, and progress at home. This information must be shared at the start of the school year and reinforced periodically throughout the year.

Parents need to know the goals of TIPS assignments, their children's responsibilities to share their work, how parents should help, and the schedule for TIPS activities so that they can plan time for these interactions. Parents also need to hear frequently from the teacher that it is important for them to monitor their children's homework and to motivate and interact with their children.

To introduce parents to TIPS, teachers and principals may send a letter to all parents, announce the process in a newsletter, introduce and explain TIPS at parent-teacher meetings and conferences, and discuss the process with parents on other occasions. Teachers may conduct classroom or grade-level meetings to show parents examples of TIPS activities on an overhead projector and discuss with them how to proceed when their children bring TIPS activities home. Parents who cannot attend these meetings should be contacted by phone, paired with a "buddy" parent, or provided with easy-to-follow information from the orientation session.

Teachers must introduce each TIPS homework assignment in class and discuss each assignment with their students. By taking five minutes of class time to go over TIPS interactive homework, teachers will ensure that most or all students understand the sections that they will explain or share at home. Teachers should ask students if they have any questions about the directions or about their responsibilities for conducting interactions with family partners. This is the time for students to sign the short letter to parents in science or language arts assignments and to note when the assignment is due, so that they can plan when to complete the assignment when a parent or family member is available. This also is the time to reinforce the importance of students' interactions with family members at home. If teachers take five minutes in class to introduce the homework, point out the interactive sections, and discuss students' questions, all or most students will be able to conduct and complete the assignment at home.

Give Students Adequate Time to Complete Interactive Assignments

Some teachers give students two or more days to interact with family members and complete the homework. This ensures that even if parents are not available on one evening, they may be able to interact with students sometime the next day or evening. Some teachers assign TIPS homework over the weekend. In several studies, parents reported that they have time on the weekends to talk with their children about schoolwork.

Follow Up Each Assignment

Teachers should follow up the completed assignments with short, stimulating classroom discussions or demonstrations that reinforce or enrich the homework. Even a five-minute discussion reinforces the importance of completing homework on time and allows students to share some interactions they had with their families. Evaluations of TIPS indicate that teachers who regularly introduce and follow up the assignments have more students who complete their homework well.

Treat TIPS Assignments Like Other Homework

TIPS interactive homework should be collected, graded, and returned like other homework. Teachers are asked to specify points for completing each section of the TIPS assignment so that students understand that TIPS, like other homework, will be marked and will contribute to their report card grades.

Answer Parents' Questions

The home-to-school communication section at the end of every TIPS assignment gives parents a place for comments or questions and encourages two-way communication between school and home. Teachers must follow up parents' questions by phone, notes, e-mail, or other communication on a regular schedule that is known to parents. For example, parents may be told that if they ask a question on a TIPS activity, the teacher will respond within one week or other reasonable time period.

Recognize Good Work

Some teachers award Family-School Partnership Certificates of Merit (or other recognitions) after students complete a certain number of TIPS interactive homework activities with their families. This lets students and families know that the school recognizes and appreciates the time that parents or other family partners spend on interactive homework. This may be done once or twice a year or for each report card period.

Evaluate the Implementation and Effects of TIPS

There are two "built-in" evaluations in all TIPS assignments. First, students are expected to complete TIPS activities just as they do all homework assignments. Teachers should discuss, collect, grade, and return TIPS in the same way that they do other homework. Thus, students' homework completion and skills can be recorded for each assignment.

Second, every TIPS activity includes a section for home-to-school communications. In this section, parents report their observations of whether the child seemed to understand the assignment, whether it was enjoyable for everyone, and whether they have any questions about the assignment for the teacher. Teachers should monitor this section, record whether students shared their work with a family partner, and note whether they need to call or write to parents to respond to their questions. Parents' reactions to assignments should be noted to determine which activities should be edited or eliminated from year to year.

At the start of the school year when the first TIPS activities are assigned, educators should conduct a short, targeted assessment of whether students and parents understand the TIPS interactive homework process. Teachers or counselors should call parents who are not involved initially to see if they understand the TIPS process and to assure them that they do not have to "teach" their children school subjects—but simply encourage the student to conduct the interactions. This implementation-check will help maximize the number of students who are able to engage their family partners in conversations about schoolwork, as well as the number of parents who know how to encourage their children to take the lead in discussing the TIPS activities.

Formal evaluations of TIPS may be designed with school, district, or external researchers to determine the added value of homework to class lessons (Van Voorhis, 2003; in press).

For more information on what teachers, administrators, parents, and students do to successfully conduct interactive homework, see the TIPS implementation manuals (Epstein et al., 2001) and guidelines and examples at www.partnershipschools .org—follow links to "TIPS interactive homework." (Also see other research on homework in Reading 3.8, discussions in Chapter 3.)

REFERENCES

Anderson, D. D., and E. Gold. (2006). Home to school: Numeracy practices and mathematical identities. *Mathematical Thinking and Learning* 8: 261–286.

Balli, S. J. (1998). When mom and dad help: Student reflections on parent involvement with homework. *Journal of Research and Development in Education* 31: 142–146.

Balli, S. J., D. H. Demo, and J. F. Wedman. (1998). Family involvement with children's homework: An intervention in the middle grades. *Family Relations* 47: 149–157.

Epstein, J. L., K. C. Salinas, and F. L. Van Voorhis. (2001). *Manuals for Teachers Involve Parents in Schoolwork (TIPS)* (rev. ed.) (Elementary Grades for TIPS Math and Science; Middle grades for TIPS Language Arts, Science/Health, and Math). Baltimore: Center on School, Family, and Community Partnerships, Johns Hopkins University.

Epstein, J. L., B. S. Simon, and K. C. Salinas. (1997, September). Effects of Teachers Involve Parents in Schoolwork (TIPS) language arts interactive homework in the middle grades. *Research Bulletin* 18.

Epstein, J. L., and F. L. Van Voorhis. (2001). More than minutes: Teachers' roles in designing homework. *Educational Psychologist* 36: 181–193. (Reading 6.1).

———. (2009). How to implement teachers involve parents in schoolwork (TIPS) processes. In J. L. Epstein et al. (Eds.), *School, family, and community partnerships: Your handbook for action* (3rd ed; Chapter 8). Thousand Oaks, CA: Corwin.

Hoover-Dempsey, K. V., and H. M. Sandler. (1995). Parental involvement in children's education: Why does it make a difference? *Teachers College Record* 97: 310–331.

Remillard, J. T., and K. Jackson. (2006). Old math, new math: Parents' experiences with standards-based reform. *Mathematical Thinking and Learning* 8: 231–259.

Resnick, D. P., and L. B. Resnick. (1985). Standards, curriculum, and performance: A historical and comparative perspective. *Educational Researcher* 14: 5–8.

U. S. Department of Education. (2004). The facts about science achievement. www2.ed.gov/print/nclb/methods/science/science.html.

Van Voorhis, F. L. (2003). Interactive homework in middle school: Effects on family involvement and students' science achievement. *Journal of Educational Research* 96: 323–339.

———. (2008, March). *Stressful or successful? An intervention study of family involvement in secondary student science homework*. Paper presented at the Fourteenth International Roundtable on School, Family, and Community Partnerships (INET), New York.

———. (2009a). Does family involvement in homework make a difference? Investigating the longitudinal effects of math and language arts interventions. In R. Deslandes (Ed.), *Family-school-community partnerships: International perspectives* (pp. 141–156). New York: Routledge.

———. (2009b). *Costs and benefits of family involvement in homework: Investments and results of three longitudinal interventions*. Paper presented at the Annual Meeting of the American Educational Research Association (AERA), San Diego, CA.

———. (In press). Adding families to the homework equation: A longitudinal study of family involvement and mathematics achievement. *Education and Urban Society*.

Van Voorhis, F. L., and J. L. Epstein. (2002). *Teachers involve parents in schoolwork: Interactive Homework CD*. Baltimore: Center on School, Family, and Community Partnerships, Johns Hopkins University. Includes 500 prototype assignments in math (grades K–5 and middle grades review), and language arts and science (grades 6–8).

Xu, J. (2003). Purposes for doing homework reported by middle and high school students. *Journal of Education Research* 99: 46–55.

Xu, J., and L. Corno. (2003). Family help and homework management reported by middle school students. *Elementary School Journal* 103: 503–537.

APPENDIX

Sample Teachers Involve Parents in Schoolwork (TIPS) Activities in Math, Science, and Language Arts in the Elementary and Middle Grades, and High School Social Studies

Fractional Parts	Sample TIPS Math (elementary)
I Mean It!	Sample TIPS Math (middle grades)
Living Things—The Importance of Animals	Sample TIPS Science (elementary)
On Your Mark, Get Set, Go!	Sample TIPS Science (middle grades)
Hairy Tales	Sample TIPS Language Arts (elementary)
A Helping Hand	Sample TIPS Language Arts (middle grades)
Why Do We Need Government?	Sample TIPS Social Studies (high school)[*]

---

[*] An exploratory study with one high school showed that teachers in all departments (math, science, social studies, English, and family life) were able to develop interactive assignments that students enjoyed conducting with a family partner. TIPS materials have not been developed for full courses at the high school level. Teachers and curriculum leaders may use the guidelines for developing TIPS provided in this chapter, or contact the author to conduct a TIPS development project in specific subjects in high school.

TIPS: FRACTIONAL PARTS

Dear Family Partner,
My class is learning how to write fractions. This activity will let me show you what I know about
fractions. We can talk about how we use fractions at home. This assignment is due_____.
                                              Sincerely,

                                      _____
                                              Student's signature

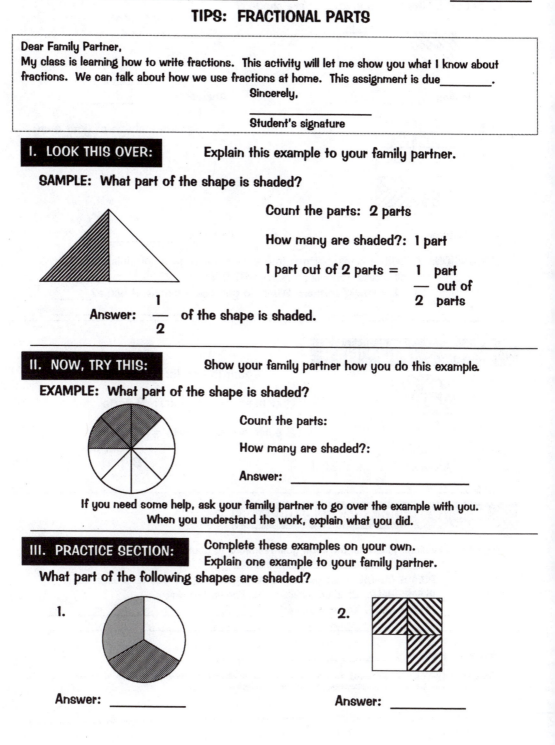

I. LOOK THIS OVER: Explain this example to your family partner.

SAMPLE: What part of the shape is shaded?

Count the parts: 2 parts

How many are shaded?: 1 part

1 part out of 2 parts =   1   part
                          —   out of
                          2   parts

Answer: $\dfrac{1}{2}$ of the shape is shaded.

II. NOW, TRY THIS: Show your family partner how you do this example.

EXAMPLE: What part of the shape is shaded?

Count the parts:

How many are shaded?:

Answer: _____

If you need some help, ask your family partner to go over the example with you.
When you understand the work, explain what you did.

III. PRACTICE SECTION: Complete these examples on your own.
                                 Explain one example to your family partner.

What part of the following shapes are shaded?

1.

Answer: _____

2.

Answer: _____

(continues)

What part of the following shapes are shaded?

3.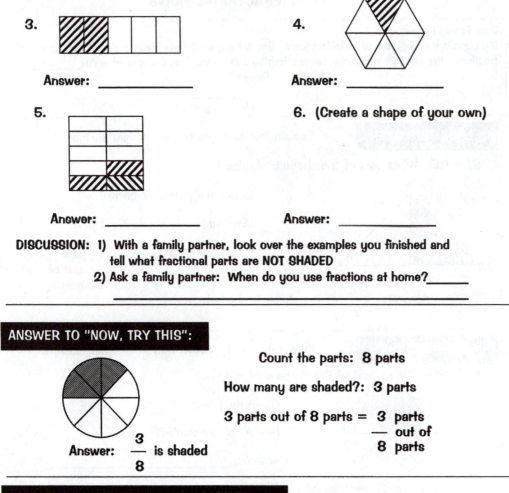

Answer: _____

4.

Answer: _____

5.

Answer: _____

6. (Create a shape of your own)

Answer: _____

DISCUSSION: 1) With a family partner, look over the examples you finished and tell what fractional parts are NOT SHADED
2) Ask a family partner: When do you use fractions at home?_____
_____

ANSWER TO "NOW, TRY THIS":

Count the parts: 8 parts

How many are shaded?: 3 parts

3 parts out of 8 parts = $\frac{3}{8}$ parts out of parts

Answer: $\frac{3}{8}$ is shaded

IV. HOME TO SCHOOL COMMUNICATION:

Parent Observation: Please let me know your reactions to your child's work on this activity.
____ O.K. Child seems to understand this skill
____ PLEASE CHECK. Child needed some help on this, but seems to understand.
____ PLEASE HELP. Child still needs instruction on this skill.
____ PLEASE NOTE. (other comments)_____
_____

Parent's signature: _____

Epstein, J.L., & Salinas, K.C. (revised 2000). Teachers Involve Parents in Schoolwork (TIPS) Interactive Homework for the Elementary Grades. Baltimore: Center on School, Family, and Community Partnerships, Johns Hopkins University.

Student's Name_____   Date_____

TIPS: I MEAN IT!

Dear Family Partner:
In math, we are finding and using averages to discuss some common facts. I hope you enjoy this activity with me. This assignment is due_____.

Sincerely,

_____
Student's signature

I. LOOK THIS OVER: Explain this example to your family partner.

Remember: To find the average (mean) for a set of data:
   1) add all of the data;
   2) divide by the number of pieces of data; and
   3) round to the nearest whole number if necessary.
DATA: 4, 9, 5, 6, 11
ADD: 4 + 9 + 5 + 6 + 11 = 35
         5 pieces of data
DIVIDE by Number of Items in Set: 35 ÷ 5 = 7
         AVERAGE (MEAN) = 7

II. NOW, TRY THIS: Show your family member how you do this example.

DATA: 7, 13, 23, 3, 17, 9, 12
ADD:
DIVIDE by Number of Items:
   AVERAGE (MEAN) =

III. PRACTICE SECTION: Complete these examples on your own. Show your work. Explain one example to your family partner.

1. List the ages of all your family and find the mean age.
   DATA:
   ADD:
   DIVIDE by Number of Items
   AVERAGE (MEAN) =   Is your age close to the mean?_____

2. Find the mean shoe size for all of your family (round half sizes up).
   DATA:
   ADD:
   DIVIDE by Number of Items
   AVERAGE (MEAN) =   Is your shoe size close to the mean?_____

3. Find the mean height (in inches) of all of your family.
   DATA:
   ADD:
   DIVIDE by Number of Items
   AVERAGE (MEAN) =   Is your height close to the mean?_____

(continues)

IN THE REAL WORLD...

People use averages or means to report survey results. Poll four family members or friends. Include at least one family member.

ASK: How many hours each day do you <u>work</u> (at school, at a job, or at home)?

How many hours each night do you <u>sleep</u>? (Fill in the chart below with your data)

Names of people you surveyed	Number of hours of <u>work</u> each day (at school, at a job, or at home)	Number of hours of sleep each day
1.		
2.		
3.		
4.		
————————	AVERAGE (MEAN) =	AVERAGE (MEAN) =

Find the average (mean) amount of time the people you selected work and sleep each day.

WORK SPACE:

Explain your results to a family member. Discuss with your family member:
Would I find the same means if I surveyed only friends my own age? Why or why not?

_____

_____

ANSWER TO "NOW, TRY THIS":

ADD: 7 + 13 + 23 + 3 + 17 + 9 + 12 = 84

DIVIDE by Number of Items: 84 ÷ 7 = 12

AVERAGE (MEAN) = 12

IV. HOME TO SCHOOL COMMUNICATION:

Dear Parent/Family Partner,

Please give me your reactions to your child's work on this activity.

Write YES or NO for each statement.

____My child understood the homework and was able to complete it.

____My child and I enjoyed the activity.

____This assignment helped me know what my child is learning in math.

Any other comments:_____

Parent's signature: _____

Epstein, J.L., Salinas, K.C., & Jackson, V. (revised 2000). Teachers Involve Parents in Schoolwork (TIPS) Interactive Homework for the Middle Grades. Baltimore: Center on School, Family, and Community Partnerships, Johns Hopkins University.

Student's Name_____   Date_____

TIPS: LIVING THINGS—THE IMPORTANCE OF ANIMALS

Dear Family Partner,
We are learning to identify useful products that come from animals. This activity will help build
science skills in observing, recording information, and drawing conclusions. I hope you enjoy this
activity with me. The assignment is due _____.

Sincerely,

_____

Student's signature

OBJECTIVE: To identify useful products from animals and to draw
conclusions about the importance of animals in our lives.

MATERIALS: Pen or pencil

PROCEDURE:

1. Discuss with your family partner different kinds of products that come from
   animals. Write a list of these products at the top of the Lab Report.

2. Observe objects in your living room, bedroom, and kitchen. In the kitchen,
   make sure to look in the refrigerator and cupboards for products that come
   from animals.

3. Record on the Lab Report the items that come from animals or animal
   products.

4. Next to each item on the Lab Report, write the animal the item is from.

5. Read your list of animal products to your family member. Add any other items
   that your family member suggests.

(continues)

DATA CHART:

Fill in the animal products you found and the animals the items come from:

ROOM	ITEMS FROM ANIMALS OR ANIMAL PRODUCTS	WHICH ANIMAL?
LIVING ROOM	1. 2. 3.	1. 2. 3.
BEDROOM	1. 2. 3.	1. 2. 3.
KITCHEN	1. 2. 3.	1. 2. 3.

CONCLUSIONS:

Discuss the following questions with your family member. Write complete sentences.

1. Which animal gave important food products to your home? _____

_____

2. Which animal gave important non-food items to your home? _____

_____

3. Which animal do you think is the most important to people? Why? _____

_____

HOME TO SCHOOL COMMUNICATION:

Dear Parent/Family Partner,

Please give me your reactions to your child's work on this activity.

Write YES or NO for each statement.

____My child understood the homework and was able to discuss it.

____My child and I enjoyed the activity.

____This assignment helped me know what my child is learning in science.

Any other comments: _____

Parent's Signature: _____

Epstein, J.L., & Salinas, K.C. (revised 2000). Teachers Involve Parents in Schoolwork (TIPS) Interactive Homework for the Elementary Grades. Baltimore: Center on School, Family, and Community Partnerships, Johns Hopkins University.

Student's Name_____ Date_____

TIPS: ON YOUR MARK, GET SET, GO!

Dear Family Partner,
In science we are studying the phases of matter. This activity focuses on liquids to help build
skills in observing, recording, and drawing conclusions. I hope you enjoy this activity with me.
This activity is due_____.

Sincerely,

_____
Student's signature

OBJECTIVE: To understand <u>viscosity</u>—a liquid's resistance to <u>flow</u>

MATERIALS: ONE TEASPOON of 3-5 liquids that have different
thicknesses—such as catsup, mustard, water,
syrup, honey, milk, or others that your family
partner will allow you to use.
Also, baking pan, teaspoon, clock with second hand
or count seconds.

PROCEDURE:

1. Explain the following to a family partner to share what we are learning in class:
   Who is working with you? _____
   Some liquids are thicker and <u>more viscous</u> than others. They <u>flow slowly</u>.
   Some liquids are thinner and <u>less viscous</u> than others. They <u>flow quickly</u>.

2. With your family partner decide: Which 3-5 liquids will you test?
   a._____   d._____

   b._____   e._____

   c._____

3. Tilt the pan and prop it up against something like a phone book so that it is at an
   angle (between 45° - 60°). At about what angle is your pan tilted?_____

   One of you will put each liquid in the pan and identify the finish line. The other will
   serve as the timer. You can check each other to get an accurate observation.

   Start each teaspoon of a new liquid <u>at the same level at the top of the pan</u> at least
   one inch away from the previous liquid. Make sure the pan remains tilted at the
   same angle for each test. When you are ready with all of the materials, do these
   steps:
   a. Place one teaspoon of liquid at the top of your pan.
   b. <u>Time the seconds</u> it takes for the liquid to reach the "finish line" at the bottom of the pan.
   c. Record the information on the Data Chart.
   d. Continue until you have tested each teaspoon of liquid.

(continues)

DATA CHART

LIQUID	SECONDS TO "FINISH" LINE	OBSERVATION HOW VISCOUS IS IT?
_____	_____	_____
_____	_____	_____
_____	_____	_____
_____	_____	_____
_____	_____	_____

CONCLUSIONS:

1. Which liquid finished
   first (fastest) _____
   midway _____
   last (slowest) _____
2. Which liquid has high viscosity? _____
3. Which liquid has low viscosity? _____
4. Why was it important that your pan remained at the same angle for each test?
   _____

FAMILY SURVEY:

ASK: Can you think of any foods or other products that use viscosity (how fast or slow the flow) as part of the advertising to get you to buy it?
Family member's idea _____
My idea _____
Why is high viscosity (slow flow) a good feature (or a bad feature) of a product you use?
_____
_____

Why is low viscosity (quick flow) a good feature (or a bad feature) of a product you use?
_____
_____

HOME TO SCHOOL COMMUNICATION:

Dear Parent/Family Partner,
Please give me your reactions to your child's work on this activity.
Write YES or NO for each statement.
____My child understood the homework and was able to discuss it.
____My child and I enjoyed the activity.
____This assignment helped me know what my child is learning in science.

Any other comments: _____
Parent's signature: _____

Epstein, J.L., Salinas, K.C., & Jackson, V. (revised 2000). Teachers Involve Parents in Schoolwork (TIPS) Interactive Homework for the Middle Grades. Baltimore: Center on School, Family, and Community Partnerships, Johns Hopkins University.

Student's Name_____   Date_____

TIPS: Hairy Tales

Dear Family Partner,
In language arts I am working on using information gathered from others to write explanations. For this assignment, I am comparing today's hairstyles with those of the past. I hope that you enjoy this activity with me. This assignment is due _____.

Sincerely,

_____
Student's signature

Family Interview

FIND A FAMILY MEMBER TO INTERVIEW.

Who is it?_____
Ask:

1) In what decade were you born? (1960s, 1970s, etc.)_____

2) What is one hairstyle that was popular when you were my age?

For boys:_____

For girls:_____

3) What hairstyle did you have when you were my age?_____

4) Did your family agree with your choice of hairstyle?_____

5) What is your favorite current hairstyle and why?_____

6) What is your least favorite current hairstyle and why?_____

Ask your family member to show you a picture of a hairstyle from the past. Draw a picture of the hairstyle here.

First Draft
Use the information from your interview to write a paragraph about hairstyles. Remember to:

- Give a paragraph a title.
- Be sure all of your sentences related to your topic.
- Use descriptive words to help explain the ideas.
- If you compare hairstyles, tell how they are alike and how they are different.

(continues)

Write your paragraph here

Title:_____

_____

_____

_____

_____

_____

_____

_____

Read your paragraph aloud to your family partner. Revise or add sentences, as needed.

Extension Activity

Select another topic for comparison—for example, clothing styles, ways to have fun, or rules at home or school.   What topic did you choose? _____

Next to each "Q" line, write a question about your topic. Use your questions to interview a family member. Write the family member's answer next to each "A" line.

1. Q: _____
   A: _____
2. Q: _____
   A: _____
3. Q: _____
   A: _____

Home-to-School Connection

Dear Parent/Guardian,

Your comments about your child's work in this activity are important.

Please write YES or NO for each statement:

____My child understood the homework and was able to discuss it.

____My child and I enjoyed this activity.

____This assignment helps me understand what my child is learning in language arts.

Other comments: _____

Epstein, J.L., Salinas, K.C., & Jackson, V. (revised 2000). Teachers Involve Parents in Schoolwork (TIPS) Interactive Homework for the Middle Grades. Baltimore: Center on School, Family, and Community Partnerships, Johns Hopkins University. (Adapted for the elementary grades.)

Student's Name_____   Date_____

TIPS: A HELPING HAND

Dear Family Partner,
We are writing narrative paragraphs that include the use of specific details. I hope you enjoy this activity with me. This assignment is due _____.

Sincerely,

_____
Student's signature

THINGS TO REMEMBER:

Narrative writing—
- Tells a story
- Includes a definite beginning, middle, and end
- Uses details to support the main ideas in a clear sequence of events

PROCEDURE:

1. Read the following prompt. You may discuss it with your family member.

PROMPT: A Helping Hand

Think of a time when you needed help and someone helped you. This person may have been a teacher, a neighbor, a classmate, a friend, or a family member. Write one paragraph or more to tell your teacher about a time when someone helped you.

Before you write, think about how the situation began. Think about who was involved and when and where it occurred. Think about what happened as it continued and how it ended. Think about your feelings toward the person who helped you.

2. Complete the pre-writing chart below.

Topic: _____   Purpose: _____
Audience: _____   Form: _____

QUESTIONS	ANSWERS	DETAILS
Who helped you?		
What happened first?		
Second?		
Next?		
Next?		
Last?		
Reactions?		

(continues)

551

3. Now, write the rough draft of your paragraph. Remember your title, topic sentence, and closing sentence.

Title: _____

_____
_____
_____
_____
_____
_____
_____
_____
_____
_____
_____

4. Read what you have written to your family member.
   Who is listening to you? _____
Add or delete details, or make other changes to improve your work.

FAMILY SURVEY—Ask: What experience do you remember when you were a teen and someone helped you? You write the example that your family partner shares. Use complete sentences.

_____
_____
_____
_____

HOME TO SCHOOL COMMUNICATION:

Dear Parent,
    Please give me your reactions to your child's work on this activity.
Write YES or NO for each statement.
____My child understood the homework and was able to discuss it.
____My child and I enjoyed this activity
____This assignment helped me know what my child is learning in language arts
Any other comments: _____
_____
Parent's Signature: _____

Epstein, J.L., Salinas, K.C., & Jackson, V. (revised 2000). Teachers Involve Parents in Schoolwork (TIPS) Interactive Homework for the Middle Grades. Baltimore: Center on School, Family, and Community Partnerships, Johns Hopkins University.

Student: _____   Class/Period: _____

Date Assigned: _____   Date Due: _____

TIPS: WHY DO WE NEED GOVERNMENT?
How have social conditions changed over time?

Interview a parent or other family partner who is at least 20 years older than you. Ask the following three questions. You record your family partner's opinions.

1. Compared to twenty years ago, have the following social conditions gotten better, stayed the same, or gotten worse? Please tell me <u>in what way</u>.

SOCIAL CONDITIONS	Got Better	Stayed the Same	Got Worse	IN WHAT WAY?
Education	___	___	___	_____
Environment	___	___	___	_____
Crime/violence	___	___	___	_____
Taxes	___	___	___	_____
Unemployment	___	___	___	_____
Poverty	___	___	___	_____
Health care	___	___	___	_____
Race relations	___	___	___	_____
Standard of living	___	___	___	_____
Individual freedom	___	___	___	_____
Family values	___	___	___	_____
Foreign Relations	___	___	___	_____

(continues)

2. Which TWO of the above topics do you think have been helped by governmental programs over the past 20 years, and IN WHAT WAY? You record your family partner's opinions .

TWO areas helped by government   IN WHAT WAY?

1. _____   _____
                                     _____

2. _____   _____
                                     _____

3. Which TWO of the above topics do you think could use MORE or LESS help from governmental programs over the next 5 or 10 years, and IN WHAT WAY? You record your family partner's opinions.

TWO areas that you think need
MORE OR LESS help from government   IN WHAT WAY?
(circle one)

MORE or LESS_____   _____
                                     _____

MORE or LESS_____   _____
                                     _____

STUDENT VIEW

Use a separate page to write your views, based on your interview of a family partner. Attach your work to this assignment.

    a. Write a short summary of your views on how social conditions have changed over the past 20 years.

    b. Choose TWO social conditions from the list on the first page. Discuss your views: Should there be more or less attention over the next 5-10 years from federal, state, or local government on the two social conditions you selected, and why?

Home-to-School Communication

Please ask your family partner for his/her views:

___Yes ___No   This assignment helped me know what my student is learning in Government/Social Studies.

Comments: _____

Family Partner's Signature: _____

Epstein, J.L. (2000). Teachers Involve Parents in Schoolwork (TIPS) Interactive Homework for High Schools. Baltimore: Center on School, Family, and Community Partnerships, Johns Hopkins University. (Assignment suggested by Chesapeake High School, Baltimore County.)

Organizing Productive Volunteers
in the Middle Grades

TEACHERS INVOLVE PARENTS IN SCHOOLWORK (TIPS)
VOLUNTEERS IN SOCIAL STUDIES AND ART

Studies consistently show a dramatic decline in parent volunteers at the school building in the middle grades (see Readings 3.3 and 3.6). Middle-grade educators report that they do not seek volunteers because they believe that students do not want their parents at the school. Parents report that they do not volunteer in their children's middle schools, in part because many are working during the school day and in part because they are not invited to volunteer. There are few programs or guidelines available to help educators engage parents productively as volunteers in the middle grades. This section introduces one process that organizes volunteers in new ways to support student learning in the middle grades.

OVERVIEW

The Teachers Involve Parents in Schoolwork (TIPS) Volunteers in Social Studies and Art process integrates art appreciation into the social studies curriculum in the middle grades and increases the number of productive volunteers in middle schools. The volunteers present prints of important artwork to increase students' knowledge and appreciation of art and to demonstrate connections of art with history, geography, and social issues. Over three years of monthly presentations (e.g., in grades 6–8 or 7–9), students are introduced to the work of at least 24 artists from different eras with varied artistic styles. The artists and their artwork are linked to specific social studies curricular units. For example, when students study American history, they see and learn about American artists; world history is linked to the work of artists from around the world; government and citizen participation is linked to artwork on themes of government and citizenship.

GOALS OF TIPS VOLUNTEERS IN SOCIAL STUDIES AND ART

The TIPS Volunteers in Social Studies and Art process helps solve three long-standing problems in the middle grades: a lack of easily implemented interdisciplinary curricula, a lack of productive family volunteers, and a lack of art appreciation education to develop students' cultural literacy (Catterall, 2009; Jackson, 1987).

Create an Integrated, Interdisciplinary Curriculum

Although most educators in the middle grades talk about the value of interdisciplinary curricula, relatively few schools have implemented such programs, in part because it requires a great deal of teachers' time to develop these connections. Teachers, administrators, and others must work together during common planning periods to develop and test lessons and materials. In most middle schools, students still study most subjects separately, without much awareness of their connections. TIPS Volunteers in Social Studies and Art infuses major social studies units with related art prints, discussions and critiques, writing across the curriculum, and art activities for homework or classwork.

Improve Family Involvement in the Middle Grades

Although parent volunteers are highly visible in the elementary grades, they all but disappear in the middle grades. TIPS Volunteers in Social Studies and Art creates productive partnerships of social studies teachers and parents or other volunteers. Volunteers research the selected artist and prints and develop presentations and discussions that integrate art with the social studies curriculum. Once a month, the same or other volunteers present the art prints and conduct discussions with students in their social studies classes. The process provides new, substantive roles for volunteers without requiring a great deal of the parents' or teachers' time. Parents and other family members may volunteer in any classroom, not necessarily their own child's class. Other community volunteers also may participate (e.g., museum staff or docents, high school or college art students, senior citizens). The presentations of art "masterpieces" require a minimum of 20 minutes of volunteer time each month.

Increase Art Appreciation in the Middle Grades

Art appreciation often is omitted from students' education in the middle grades. Required or elective art courses, if available at all, often are short-term, "exploratory" experiences in art techniques and media. These are important and necessary but insufficient experiences for students, because short courses do little to connect art with other subjects or to emphasize art history, criticism, and appreciation. The TIPS Volunteers in Social Studies and Art process organizes monthly presentations on artists and their work to extend all students' understanding about art in history and in the human experience.

Link with Curriculum

To show how the TIPS Volunteers in Social Studies and Art works, 40 prints were selected and prototype presentations were prepared that connect to three social studies units: American History, World Cultures, and Government and Citizen Participation (Epstein and Salinas, 1991). American History linkages are made in prototype presentations of prints of artwork by Frederic Remington, Currier and Ives, Edward Hicks, Horace Pippin, Georgia O'Keeffe, Romare Bearden, Robert Rauschenberg, Andy Warhol, and others representing a range of artists from different eras with diverse backgrounds and styles of painting. Similarly, prototype lessons for social studies units on World Cultures include presentations of work by artists from da Vinci to Picasso and the lessons on Government and Citizen Participation include prints by artists from Vermeer to Mondrian.

EVALUATION

A case study evaluating the effects on student learning about art was conducted in an urban middle school, serving approximately 80 percent African American students and 20 percent white students. At the time of the study, about 40 percent of the school's students were eligible for free or reduced-price lunch. The school scored higher in reading than most middle schools in the city, but did not meet the state's standards in math, writing, or student attendance. Approximately 400 students in grades 6 through 8 were included in the study of how students reacted to the TIPS Volunteers in Social Studies and Art program and what they learned (Epstein and Dauber, 1995).

Results indicated that students increased their awareness of art and developed attitudes and preferences for different styles of art. On their survey forms, about 80 percent of the students commented on an art print they liked, disliked, or would choose for their own living room. Students' comments reflected developmental changes from concrete to abstract thinking. The evaluation confirmed that the TIPS Volunteers process could be successfully implemented and that the results were notable for student learning about art and for helping students think critically about art.

Students recognized more artwork in the spring of the school year than they had the prior fall. It was easier for students to match paintings with their subjects or content than with their artists' names. Although students with higher report card grades knew more artists, students with Cs, Ds, and Fs also were able to recall paintings and their content. Report card grades did not influence whether students enjoyed the art presentations. Regardless of their school skills, students who enjoyed the art remembered more about the prints they saw. Students who had been in the program for at least two years also remembered more art prints. Most students preferred realistic art, but some, regardless of ability, preferred abstract art. Their preferences may have reflected students' different stages of development of abstract thinking, including the early adolescent stage of bridging concrete and abstract concepts.

The study indicated that the TIPS Volunteers in Social Studies and Art process helped students identify major artists and their work and describe and discuss art with greater insight and sophistication than they did before. When time for art appreciation is limited and teachers trained in art education are scarce, it is difficult for schools to include art in all students' education. The TIPS Volunteers in Social Studies and Art process is a useful tool for meeting the diverse goals of involving families, integrating subjects, and providing students with experiences in art awareness, appreciation, and criticism.

HOW TO DEVELOP AND IMPLEMENT TIPS VOLUNTEERS

The TIPS Volunteers in Social Studies and Art process links art prints to specific social studies units or topics. It is necessary to select the prints and develop presentations that match the social studies curriculum. Some of the prototype presentations for units of American History, World Cultures, or Government and Citizenship Participation may match units taught in a school or new prints and new presentations will be needed for other social studies units.

The TIPS Volunteers Social Studies and Art process can be implemented in any school with the following ten steps.

1. **Select a Teacher-Coordinator or Teacher Co-Coordinators.** This may be the chair of the Social Studies Department, a team leader, or a social studies teacher who is committed to implementing an interdisciplinary program and who supports family and community volunteers. The teacher may be a member of the Action Team for Partnerships or a designated leader for this program.

2. **Select a Parent-Coordinator or Parent Co-Coordinators.** This person will recruit volunteers, coordinate the schedules of the parent or other volunteers, and help train the volunteers. The assistant or co-coordinator may assume leadership for the volunteers in the next school year. The parents may be members of the Action Team for Partnerships (see Chapter 7), school council, PTA/PTO committee for this project, or designated leaders who are interested in art appreciation and willing to coordinate and work with parent volunteers and teachers.

3. **Select and order the prints that fit the social studies curriculum at each grade level.** Prints, dry mounted and laminated, may be ordered at a reasonable price from Shorewood Fine Art Reproductions/New York Graphics Society. Mailing address: Art Beats, 130 Scott Road, Waterbury, CT 06705. Telephone: (800) 677-6947. A catalogue of art prints, art reference guide, and art biographies guide can be ordered. These references will enable teachers and parents to select prints for the school's social studies units. Download order form at www.nygs.com.

Shorewood and other art reproduction collections also are online at www.liebermans.net. Click on "Publishers We Carry" and "Shorewood Fine Arts" for the museum collection.

Order enough prints for monthly rotations among participating teachers for eight months of the school year. A minimum of eight prints are needed per year per grade level. The maximum number of prints is determined by the number of teachers, their curricula, and the budget for the program. For example, a school with up to eight social studies teachers per grade level who teach different units in grades 6, 7, and 8, will need at least 8 prints per grade level to rotate over eight months of the school year, for a total of 24 art prints. If the same units are taught at the same time of the school year, then multiple copies of the selected prints will be needed so that teachers have the "right" prints for their classes each month. If the prints are dry mounted and laminated, the prints will last for several years. This is a thrifty investment in art appreciation for student learning.

4. Outline the schedule of art prints to be presented and discussed each month by the volunteers for each grade level.

5. Recruit volunteers to make classroom presentations. There should be one volunteer for each teacher or one volunteer for every social studies class. If there are not enough volunteers, then teachers must conduct the presentations in the classes without volunteers. The parents, other family members, or community volunteers who make classroom presentations need not be experts in art, but they must enjoy art and they must like talking with students in the middle grades.

If new art prints are selected, some volunteers will conduct research and prepare the presentations, following the style, content, and format of the prototypes. Additional information for presentations is available from the Getty Museum at www .artsednet@getty.edu. The research volunteers may or may not present the prints in class. Some parents who cannot come to school during the school day are happy to develop the presentations because they can do that work on their own schedule.

6. Train the volunteers so they are comfortable about making presentations to students in their assigned social studies class(es). The manual for TIPS Volunteers in Social Studies and Art describes, in detail, how to conduct an orientation session for volunteers in about an hour. The manual and prototype presentations may be ordered at www.partnershipschools.org in the TIPS section, under "Resources."

Duplicate training sessions should be offered during the day and in the evening, if needed, to meet the varied schedules of the volunteers. At the training workshop, the parent coordinators describe the program, schedule, and volunteers' responsibilities and demonstrate how to conduct a successful presentation with students in the middle grades.

If volunteers are employed during the school day, letters may be sent to employers requesting permission for the volunteers to assist the school for one hour once a month. Cooperating employers should be recognized as school business partners.

7. Schedule monthly presentations at times that are mutually convenient for the volunteers and the teachers. Volunteers will meet with the same class or classes each month for a 20-minute presentation and discussion. Each presentation includes information on the artist's life, style and technique, the specific artwork, and connections to social studies. Discussions include anecdotes and interesting information about the artist and artwork that should interest middle grade students. Time is allotted in each presentation for students' reactions, likes and dislikes, thoughts, and questions about the art and artists. The print remains on display in the classroom for one month, until the next presentation. Students are asked to examine the print and form their own opinions about the art. Teachers may use follow-up activities included in the manual or design their own social studies, art, and homework activities.

8. **Check in.** Parent coordinators will check in with volunteers and teachers after the first visit and periodically through the year to see that the program is working as planned. Each month, the parent coordinators remind volunteers about their schedules, serve as substitutes if needed, and address any questions that may arise as volunteers prepare their presentations.

9. **Evaluate results.** Teachers will evaluate the program to determine if students gain knowledge of the artists and artwork and develop an understanding and appreciation of art. Sample end-of-unit tests for students are included in the manual. Parent and teacher coordinators may conduct other annual or periodic evaluations of volunteers, teachers, and students to gather reactions to the program and suggestions for improvements.

10. **Make improvements in implementing the program, training volunteers, monitoring results, replacing prints, and continue the program.** These steps run smoothly as the parent coordinators and teacher coordinators become familiar with their roles and as the volunteers and teachers work together.

ADAPTING AND EXTENDING TIPS VOLUNTEERS

The guidelines for implementing TIPS Volunteers in Social Studies and Art may be used to develop other productive work by volunteers, such as interdisciplinary connections of art or music with English or science. The TIPS Volunteers process was designed for the middle grades, but it may be adapted for younger or older students. Indeed, TIPS Volunteers grew from an art appreciation activity called "Picture Parents" in the elementary grades. In that program, parent volunteers discussed artwork in elementary classes from kindergarten through grade 5, but mainly to expose young students to great art prints and to elicit reactions, not to help them link the art to social studies or other subjects. At the high school level, TIPS Volunteers may include parents, family members, community volunteers, or visiting artists. Also, high school students may be paired with volunteers to conduct research, prepare the presentations, or make the monthly presentations in their classes.

MATERIALS AVAILABLE AND PROGRAM COSTS

About forty prototype presentations, developed by researchers and volunteers and tested in grades 6, 7, and 8, are available for social studies units on American History, World Cultures, and Government and Citizenship Participation. Each presentation includes information on the artist's life, technique, specific artwork, connections to social studies, connections to other school subjects, connections among two or more artists and prints, where to see original work by the artist, and topics for class discussions and follow-up projects. The prototype presentations can be adapted to other social studies units, other grade levels, or other interdisciplinary combinations (e.g., art and English, music and social studies).

An implementation manual for TIPS Volunteers in Social Studies and Art includes ideas for written assignments and art activities that teachers may use as classwork or homework to extend the volunteers' presentations (Epstein and Salinas, 1991). The manual also includes guidelines for field trips to art museums; questionnaires to assess reactions to the program by teachers, students, and volunteers; and sample quizzes to assess students' knowledge and reactions to the program. The manual and packets of prototype presentations may be ordered at www.partnership schools.org in the TIPS section. This section also includes a sample presentation on the Mona Lisa by Leonardo da Vinci.

In most schools, the total cost of the art prints, implementation manuals, prototype presentations, training of volunteers, mailing reminders, recognition or celebration events at the end of the year, and other program costs will total under $2,500 in the first year and under $1,000 in subsequent years, depending on the size of the school and the need for replacement materials. Schools may decide to invest additional funds in art materials, trips to museums, and other enrichment activities.[*]

REFERENCES

Catterall, J. S. (2009). *Doing well and doing good by doing art: A 12-year longitudinal study of arts education.* Los Angeles: I-Group Books.

Epstein, J. L., and S. L. Dauber. (1995). Effects on students of an interdisciplinary program linking social studies, art, and family volunteers in the middle grades. *Journal of Early Adolescence* 15: 114–144.

Epstein, J. L., and K. C. Salinas. (1991). *TIPS social studies and art manual and prototype presentations.* Baltimore: Center on School, Family, and Community Partnerships, Johns Hopkins University.

Jackson, P. W. (1987). Mainstreaming art: An essay on discipline-based art education. *Educational Researcher* 16(6): 39–43.

---

[*] For more information, guidelines, and examples, see the TIPS *Social studies and art manual and prototype presentations* (Epstein and Salinas, 1991) and examples at www.partnershipschools.org (follow the links to "TIPS Social Studies and Art Volunteers").

The comments in this section extend and update the content of the readings in this chapter. Key concepts are summarized. Questions and activities are provided for class discussions, debates, and homework assignments. They may suggest other exercises, field activities, and research projects.

KEY CONCEPTS

Purposes of Homework. Ten purposes of homework influence the design and content of assignments. Homework may be designed to increase student learning, develop home and school connections, and improve school programs.

Interactive Homework. Interactive homework is a method of designing homework that enables students to share interesting things they are learning in class with family members, friends and peers, or members of the community. This kind of homework requires students to share ideas, gather information, or interact with someone in other ways to complete the assignments.

Teachers Involve Parents in Schoolwork (TIPS) Interactive Homework. TIPS is one approach for designing and implementing interactive homework. Used on a regular schedule, TIPS activities help parents remain aware of what their children are learning in school subjects. The activities encourage students and family members to engage in positive conversations about homework.

Teachers Involve Parents in Schoolwork (TIPS) Volunteers in Social Studies and Art. This process is one approach for organizing productive volunteers in the middle grades. Volunteers present and discuss art prints to increase students' art appreciation and awareness of interdisciplinary connections between art and history.

COMMENT

Key Components of Interactive Homework

Interactive homework is more interesting and effective when the following five features are built into the design.

Student-directed interactions. Students—not parents—must do the work of conducting interviews, gathering reactions, and completing the homework. Parents should not be required to teach school subjects, nor read or write for students. Homework is always the students' work.

Family input. Family members should be asked by students to share ideas, listen and react to something that the student reads aloud, recall experiences or memories, and participate in other kinds of conversations. The guided interactions should not depend on family members' formal education but rather on their care for and interest in their children.

Completed homework returned to class on time. Students and family members must do more than talk. Students must record something of the interactions in writing or in other forms. An activity sheet, data chart, or other papers or products must be completed and returned to class as regular homework. Interactive homework should be collected, reviewed, graded, discussed, or treated in the same way as other daily homework. If a parent cannot participate in a particular assignment, then another family member, neighbor, or peer may "substitute" for a parent to ensure that each student talks with someone about the work.

Positive, thoughtful, and enjoyable exchanges. Students and family partners should enjoy the interactive homework assignments. The activities should be important (linked to the class curriculum), challenging (not too hard or too easy for students to conduct), and enjoyable for students and parents.

Two-way communications. Interactive homework should include two-way communications. The assignment comes from school to home, but observations, questions, and reactions may come from home to school. Activities should include an easy-to-read checklist for parents' reactions, a place for a signature, and space for optional notes or questions.

QUESTIONS TO DISCUSS

The five features outlined above emerged from the analyses of data collected from parents about their children's homework.

1. From Reading 6.1 or Reading 6.2, add one feature to the above list that you think is another key element for successful interactive homework.
2. Give one reason why you think each of the six features of interactive homework (the five listed above and the one that you added) is important to each of the following:
   a. parents
   b. students
   c. teachers
3. Review the TIPS Math, TIPS Science, and TIPS Language Arts approaches in Reading 6.2.
   a. Identify two *similarities* in the approaches for interactive homework in different subjects, and explain why the similarities are important.
   b. Identify two *differences* in the approaches for interactive homework in different subjects, and explain why these differences are important.

    c.   What is one challenge that may arise in implementing TIPS interactive homework? What is one potential solution to that challenge?

4.   TIPS interactive homework activities are designed to be distributed once a week, twice a month, or on another regular schedule in conjunction with particular class lessons. Some teachers revised this approach and put many assignments together in a "homework packet" for students to take back and forth over the course of a unit of work or marking period. Controlled studies are needed on the effectiveness of alternative formats, but field experience suggests that packets of assignments are less successful in encouraging all families to become involved with their children than are individual weekly activities.

    a.   Identify a grade level and subject that interest you.

    b.   Fold a page in half. Label one half of the page (1) Weekly TIPS Activities and label the other half (2) Packet of many TIPS activities. For the grade level and subject you selected, give two pros and two cons for each of the two formats.

    c.   Discuss the pros and cons in class to hear others' ideas about these options.

ACTIVITY

How Many Ways Can Homework Be Interactive?

Using the information in Readings 6.1 and 6.2 and your own ideas, list some ways that students and parents may converse and interact on homework.

    A.   Select and identify a grade level that interests you and two school subjects in which teachers assign homework.

    B.   Label three columns: (1) Interactions, (2) What the Student Does, (3) What the Family Partner Does. For each subject:

        1.   In the first column, list at least five different kinds of interactions that students might conduct with family partners (e.g., show-and-tell, interviews).

        2.   In the second column, briefly explain what a student might do to engage a family partner in each kind of interaction (e.g., student reads sentences aloud; student demonstrates math skill).

        3.   In the third column, briefly explain what a family partner might do to assist or respond to the student (e.g., family partner shares ideas, listens to student).

        4.   Also, in the third column, put an X next to any interaction that requires a parent or family partner to read or write on the student's homework (other than for a home-to-school communication and

parent signature). For each X that you marked, explain whether all families could conduct the activity or which families would not be able to participate in that interaction.

5. Examine the interactions that you listed for the two subjects that you selected. Write a short summary of the similarities or differences in your lists that result from the nature or demands of the different subjects.

COMMENT

Helping All Parents Do What a Few Do on Their Own

Although some parents know how to help their children with homework because of their own school experiences, most parents say they do not know how to approach school subjects and topics across the grades. In the past, many teachers believed they should not try to involve parents in learning activities at home, because there always were a few parents who could not or would not participate. Studies indicate that about 20 percent of parents become involved with their children and the schools on their own, but over 70 percent of parents say they want to become involved and could do more if they were guided in how to do so.

TIPS interactive homework may help because it is assigned to *students* and asks them to show their skills and discuss ideas with a parent or other family partner. In the youngest grades, before students read with ease, parents are asked to guide their child to show what they are learning in school. In kindergarten and grade 1, most parents have no trouble in guiding their child and celebrating the learning that occurs from week to week. By grade 2, students can conduct the interactions with their family partner. With well-designed interactive assignments for students from kindergarten or first grade on, just about all parents would be able to continually monitor their children's work and progress and discuss ideas with their children.

QUESTIONS TO DISCUSS

1. Select and identify a grade level and subject that interest you.
2. List two reasons why the TIPS approach might help students and families conduct conversations about student work in the grade and subject you selected.
3. List two problems that might occur with interactive homework for students or for parents in the grade and subject you selected and a potential solution to each problem you listed.
4. If about 20 percent of parents already are involved with their children in learning activities at home and if about 70 percent would like to be so, which is more important:

a. guiding all parents' involvement, even if a few cannot become involved

or

b. leaving involvement up to parents to figure out on their own?

Explain why you think a or b is a better approach.

COMMENT

Common Questions about TIPS

Following are common questions that teachers raise about TIPS and answers based on TIPS studies and teachers' work.

1. What if a parent is not able to interact with the student about math (or any subject) on a particular night? It is highly recommended, based on data from parents, that teachers assign TIPS interactive homework over two or three days (e.g., assigned Tuesday, due Thursday or Friday, or assigned over the weekend). Research shows consistently that most parents (over 90 percent on several surveys) say they have time over the weekend to talk and work with their children on homework. This is the very time that some schools do not give homework.

Students should be guided to share their work with other family partners if a parent is not available. This includes older siblings, grandparents, other relatives, after-school teachers, child care providers, or a neighbor or friend. Most parents are available in the evening, in the morning, or on the weekend. Teachers' schedules for TIPS assignments should take into account when students' parents are available for interactions. An orientation for parents and follow-up calls should help all parents understand the TIPS process and their roles in encouraging their children to complete their homework and in motivating their children's interest in school.

2. What if a family does not have the materials needed for a science activity on a given night? TIPS Science materials must be common, inexpensive, and readily available at home. Unusual or costly items should be provided by the school. Students whose families cannot afford any extra expenses should be provided with the materials needed for each science activity. If the TIPS schedule is family-friendly, students and families will be able to find time and the common materials for TIPS Science activities.

3. What if a parent does not read English well? All homework is the *student's responsibility*. Parents do not have to read or write English to talk with their children or to listen to their children talk about schoolwork. Students complete TIPS, just as they complete all homework assignments. Their families can be involved speaking any language that is spoken at home. For example, teachers should explain that in TIPS Language Arts, the student will write their stories in English for homework, but may read them aloud to a parent by translating the work into whatever language is spoken at home. Students often serve as "interpreters" for a parent on the memos or notices that are sent home from school. In some schools, teachers or district leaders translate the letter to parents and home-to-school-communication section of TIPS into one or more languages spoken by large numbers of families served by the school.

One interesting application of TIPS was in a Japanese foreign language class for English-speaking students. The teacher knew that the students' parents did not know Japanese and could not "help" their children with their homework. She knew, however, that the children could show and share the new words and skills that they were learning in Japanese because TIPS guided students to conduct these interactions. The same would be true for students in homes where parents speak languages other than English. Students can demonstrate their skills and share ideas in the language that they speak with their parents at home.

4. Can you give the same TIPS activity to students who are slower learners and to those who have advanced skills? Like other homework, TIPS activities must match students' levels of ability. If homework is too hard, it will be frustrating and will not be completed. If homework is too easy, it will be boring, and students may disengage. TIPS activities should be written at an appropriate reading level for all students in a group or class. Teachers may assign struggling students some or all sections of an assignment, and advanced students may be assigned extra sections or sections for extra credit. Or groups within classes may be assigned different TIPS activities, if they are assigned different homework on other days.

QUESTIONS TO DISCUSS

The four topics discussed above are about equity.

1. What is the equity issue that underlies each of the four questions about TIPS homework?
2. Explain how the TIPS interactive homework process addresses each issue.

ACTIVITY

Design an Interactive Homework Assignment

A. Identify a grade level, a subject, and one specific skill in that subject that interest you.
B. Design one interactive homework activity using the TIPS format that requires children to talk with a family member to complete the assignment. Use your computer to store the assignment to permit easy editing.

1. For useful formats, see the samples of TIPS Math, Science/Health, and Language Arts in this chapter. For social studies, foreign language, family life, or other subjects, adapt one of the existing TIPS formats to fit the subject and skill that you selected.
2. Include a short and clear introductory letter to parents about the assignment. The letter would be signed by the student.
3. Develop the assignment using the information on the components of math, science, and language arts activities in this chapter.
4. End the assignment with a section for a home-to-school communication and for a parent's signature.

C. Class activity:
1. Share the draft designs of TIPS interactive homework in class. Work with a partner. Take the roles of student and parent as if the assignments were being conducted at home.
2. Exchange design and editing suggestions about how to make the assignments clear, family-friendly, and feasible for students to conduct at the grade levels selected for each design.
3. Edit the homework design to take into account your classmates' suggestions. Polish the assignment so that it is attractive, well spaced, and includes graphics, as needed.
4. Collect examples of good activities for a resource notebook or electronic file of ideas.

FIELD EXPERIENCE

Test a TIPS Assignment

A. Work with a cooperating teacher to develop and assign one TIPS interactive homework to match a specific class lesson or use an existing TIPS prototype activity that matches a specific class lesson.
B. Review with the cooperating teacher the steps needed to use a TIPS activity:
1. Provide more than one night to allow students and families to find time for their interactions.
2. Orient the students to the work they will do on the assignment at home. (Because this field experience involves just one class and one experimental assignment, it should not be necessary to conduct the full orientation process with parents that is needed when TIPS is used as a regularly scheduled approach to homework.)
C. The cooperating teacher will assign the TIPS activity to students in at least one class, after taking time to explain the sections where they will conduct conversations, demonstrations, or activities with a family partner.

D. The cooperating teacher will collect the TIPS interactive homework assignments when they are due.
E. Review the students' work with the cooperating teacher. Write a summary of your reactions to:
   - the rate and quality of students' completion of the homework
   - evidence of participation by family partners
   - parents' home-to-school communications and comments
   - other observations that you have about the clarity of the assignment, the student-family interactions, the teachers' views of the sample activity, and other issues.

COMMENT

Creating a Leadership Structure for Volunteers

To implement TIPS Volunteers in Social Studies and Art, one school created the position of parent coordinator for volunteers as one of its standing committees of its parent-teacher organization (PTO). Some schools that have Action Teams for Partnerships ask members to take leadership for the six types of involvement, resulting in a Type 3—Volunteering chair or co-chairs and related committee of volunteers for the school. These organizational approaches solve the problem of having to scramble to identify a parent coordinator for the TIPS Volunteers in Social Studies and Art program each year. Other schools solve the ongoing leadership problem by asking the parent co-coordinator to become the main parent coordinator the following year, with a new co-coordinator who follows in the same way. With ongoing and backup leaders, there is greater likelihood that the TIPS Volunteers in Social Studies and Art program will continue from year to year.

By creating a PTA/PTO committee for TIPS Volunteers in Social Studies and Art, a school also increases options for publicizing the program and for recruiting volunteers. This strategy also may encourage the parent association to contribute funds to purchase new or replacement art prints and other supplies or materials for the volunteers' presentation or for teachers' follow-up art activities. Similarly, a Type 3—Volunteering committee or specialist on an Action Team for Partnerships will strengthen and stabilize school volunteer programs and practices.

QUESTIONS TO DISCUSS

1. Imagine that a school principal asked you for advice about organizing a TIPS Volunteers in Social Studies and Art program. Select a school level that interests you (e.g., preschool or elementary, middle, or high school).
2. Identify a grade level that interests you, and specify the number of social studies teachers for that grade level in the hypothetical school.

3. Review the program components for TIPS Volunteers in Social Studies and Art in Reading 6.2.
4. List one idea to guide the teachers in the selected grade level to organize the following aspects of the TIPS Volunteers in Social Studies and Art program.

HOW COULD THIS SCHOOL: ONE IDEA:

A. Select a teacher coordinator?   _____
B. Select a parent coordinator and co-coordinator?   _____
C. Recruit parent volunteers?   _____
D. Train volunteers to present art prints to students
   in one teacher's class?   _____
E. Schedule volunteers for the teachers at the
   selected grade level?   _____
F. Monitor the work of the volunteers?   _____
G. Examine results for students?   _____

COMMENT

Reactions to TIPS Volunteers in Social Studies and Art

When we first developed TIPS Volunteers in Social Studies and Art, some teachers worried that middle school students would not want their parents to participate. Our studies indicated that middle-grade students did not want their parents to work with them and their teachers in the same ways as in elementary schools—that is no waving or hugging allowed! However, middle-grade students were positive in their evaluations of TIPS Volunteers in Social Studies and Art. The vast majority appreciated the mothers, fathers, grandparents, aunts, and other volunteers who brought art to their social studies classes. The students liked viewing art prints and discussing their likes and dislikes.

Most volunteers in the middle grades did not work in their own child's classroom but were assigned to work with any teacher who needed a volunteer. Initial evaluations revealed no systematic differences in the success of the program based on whether parents were in their own children's or other classrooms. Teachers appreciated the parents' contributions to the program. The parent volunteers were particularly enthusiastic, with some obtaining permission from their employers to participate once a month and others taking personal time off from work to participate.

Ideas and Interview about Volunteers in the Middle Grades

A. Should educators in the middle grades base their family involvement policies and practices on the belief that "students do not want their parents at school"? Explain your ideas.

B. Give two examples of how parents might be helpful volunteers in the middle grades.

C. 1. Identify two concerns that teachers or principals might have about volunteers who are asked to visit the same social studies class each month to share a new art print.

    2. List one idea to solve each of these concerns.

D. 1. Identify two concerns that parents or other volunteers might have about visiting the same social studies class each month to share a new art print.

    2. List one idea to solve each of these concerns.

E. Check your ideas and solutions (in A, B, C, and D above) with a middle school teacher, parent, or student.

    1. Identify your source, and report whether he or she believes your ideas in B are realistic.

    2. Ask your source for two more examples of how parents may be helpful and productive volunteers in the middle grades.

    3. Ask your source if the concerns in C1 and D1 are serious, and why.

    4. Ask your source if the solutions in C2 and D2 are realistic, and why.

    5. Record your questions and the responses you obtained.

Designing Other Interdisciplinary Connections for Volunteers

The TIPS Volunteers in Social Studies and Art process was designed to integrate art appreciation in social studies classes, but other interdisciplinary linkages may be made. Using parallel strategies with Social Studies and Art, how might volunteers be organized to link music and social studies, or art or music with English, a foreign language, or science?

A. Identify a grade level that interests you.

B. Select and identify one interdisciplinary connection (not art and social studies) that might productively use volunteers to help teachers enrich students' understanding and experiences in the grade level that you selected. You may use the above examples or one of your own.

C. Give two reasons why the interdisciplinary connection you selected is important for student learning.

D. Design one activity that a volunteer might conduct (e.g., a presentation, demonstration, or discussion) to make the interdisciplinary connection come alive for students in the grade you selected.

Note: Check the components of the TIPS Volunteers in Social Studies and Art process to guide your design. For example, an activity could highlight a musician who composed music when an early American writer was creating her work. The presentation might take about 20 minutes of class time with students at the grade level you selected. Include a suggestion for how the teacher could follow up and build on the volunteer's activity with a class discussion or homework assignment. The activity should develop or extend students' awareness, knowledge, and experiences about an important topic.

E. Share and critique the draft designs for interdisciplinary volunteer activities. For each one, consider:
1. Is the interdisciplinary connection important?
2. Is the topic of the activity compelling and appropriate for the grade level selected?
3. Would the activity engage all students at the grade level selected?
4. Is the activity using the time and talents of volunteers well?
5. Collect some of the best examples for a resource notebook or electronic file of ideas.

For other information about volunteers, see comments and activities on Type 3—Volunteering in Chapter 5.

Strategies for Action in Practice, Policy, and Research

THIS CHAPTER SERVES AS A SUMMARY and as a starting point. What have we learned about school, family, and community partnerships? What can we do with what we have learned? How should educators in schools, districts, and states develop policies and programs of partnership that improve schools, strengthen families, and help more students succeed? How might new teachers, principals, counselors, and others who work in schools and with families be prepared to conduct effective partnership practices? How could researchers contribute new knowledge that will help policy leaders and practitioners with their work?

One important question raised by all of the research and applications in this volume is: Who is responsible for developing and maintaining school, family, and community partnerships? The answer, of course, is that everyone with an interest or investment in children is responsible for producing and maintaining good schools, productive partnerships, and successful students. This includes state and district leaders whose policies and assistance support the development of excellent schools. It includes teachers, administrators, parents, and students who work together in each school to help students develop and learn. It includes members of the broader community, whose lives tomorrow depend on the skills of students today. And it includes researchers who conduct studies that contribute to wise policies and to research-based practices for excellent schools.

It is abundantly clear that one principal, teacher, or parent working alone cannot create a comprehensive and lasting program of partnership. Many partners in states, districts, schools, homes, communities, and research settings must work together to improve knowledge, policies, plans, and programs. It also is well known that if everyone is in charge of something, then no one is really responsible.

A crucial question, then, is: How can partnership programs be organized and sustained? Over the years, our work with educators and families in many communities has shown that state and district leaders for partnerships and school-based Action Teams for Partnerships are needed to develop and sustain successful programs.

Leaders must be identified; structures must be set; processes must be selected; budgets must be allocated; annual action plans must be written; and evaluations must be conducted to implement and continually improve programs of school, family, and community partnerships in schools, districts, and states.

Leadership, teamwork, written plans, implementation, evaluations, funding, internal and external support, and continuous improvement make a difference in whether, which, when, why, and how families and communities become involved in children's education. These "essential elements" have emerged from analyses of data from hundreds of schools, scores of districts, and many state departments of education whose actions have been evaluated to learn what it takes to establish and maintain programs of school, family, and community partnership. When these organizational components are well organized, educators and families develop the capacity and expertise to implement partnership programs as part of regular school practice.

This chapter builds on Reading 5.1 with a detailed discussion of the structure and activities of school-based Action Teams for Partnerships (ATP). The ATP is the "action arm," official committee, or work group of a school improvement team or school council. The members of an ATP—educators, parents, and others—work together to plan, implement, monitor, delegate leadership and tasks, evaluate, and continually improve school, family, and community partnership practices that will engage all families in ways that create a welcoming climate and help students reach school and classroom goals. The ATP turns partnership plans into actions and partnership goals into results.

Without an ATP, this teacher or that leader may conduct selected partnership projects or activities with some parents. With an ATP, every preschool and elementary, middle, and high school—and all teachers—could have a full and feasible plan for involving all families in their children's education at all grade levels. With well-functioning ATPs, programs of school, family, and community partnership should be as regular as reading, as expected as English, as methodical as math, and as standard as science or other subjects. Along with the school's curriculum, instruction, and assessments, a program of partnership should be viewed as an essential aspect of school organization—a regular part of school life.

This chapter also summarizes the central themes and major conclusions about school, family, and community partnerships that have been presented in the readings, discussions, and activities throughout the volume. Having a school-based action team or clear district and state leaders for partnerships to organize a partnership program is about structure. Program plans and practices must be based on key principles that get to the heart of the matter.

All of the studies, comments, and activities in this volume point to the need for mutual trust and respect by educators and parents for partnerships to succeed, the need for equity in partnership programs so that all families are informed about and involved in their children's education, and the simultaneous need for diversity in partnership programs to address the different situations and requirements of some families. Here, we explore these central themes. Finally, eight crosscutting conclusions not only summarize what has been learned from many studies but also raise new questions about how to effectively involve all families in their children's schools and education.

If you are a researcher, you are encouraged to establish connections with school, district, and/or state partners to bring research-based approaches to school, family, and community partnerships into education policy and practice and to study the results of these efforts. If you are an educator, this chapter should lead you from an understanding of the theory, research, and policies of partnership to the application of useful strategies in the real world. The fact is, all that you have learned about partnerships must be tailored to the goals and conditions of the specific school and classroom, district, and state in which you work. Thus, for researchers and for practitioners, the readings, discussions, debates, and projects in this volume are just the beginning of your work on school, family, and community partnerships.

This book is designed to lead educators and researchers to programs and research on the implementation of programs of school, family, and community partnerships in diverse communities. It is important to see how the research-based structures and processes discussed throughout the volume actually work in urban, suburban, and rural communities; at the preschool, elementary, middle, and high school levels; in schools that serve families with diverse backgrounds; and with students at all ability levels. This volume leads to a companion book for the implementation of effective programs of family and community involvement (Epstein et al., 2009) to enable educators and researchers put new knowledge to work in practice.

DISCUSSION AND ACTIVITIES

The comments in this section extend and update actions needed to organize partnership programs in schools. The comments also review the central themes and crosscutting conclusions from all readings and activities in this volume. Key concepts are summarized. Questions and activities are provided for class discussions, debates, and homework assignments. They may suggest other exercises, field activities, and research projects.

KEY CONCEPTS

1. Comprehensive program of school, family, and community partnerships. A full program of partnerships includes activities for all six types of involvement so that families and community members may be involved at home, at school, and in other locations. Partnership activities are selected and designed to focus on specific goals; meet key challenges; and produce results for students, families, teachers, schools, and the community. Comprehensive programs are ongoing. Teams in schools and leaders in districts and state departments of education plan and implement comprehensive programs of school, family, and community partnership as a regular part of their work every year.

2. Action Team for Partnerships (ATP). The Action Team for Partnerships is the basic school structure for implementing an ongoing, comprehensive partnership program tailored to school improvement goals. The ATP, including teachers, parents, administrators, and others, is the "action arm" or official committee of a school improvement team. The ATP is responsible for turning policies and expectations for family and community involvement into annual plans, implemented actions, and evaluated practices in a comprehensive program of school, family, and community partnerships.

3. Leadership for Partnerships. A dedicated, expert leader for partnerships is required in every school district and every state's Department of Education, with adjustments to time required in small districts (see Chapter 4). In all districts and states, leadership may be shared, and teamwork is required. A leader for partnerships will work with colleagues across departments who are responsible for various federal, state, and local programs that include family and community involvement in children's education.

District leaders for partnerships not only conduct activities for the district as a whole but also guide and support all elementary, middle, and high schools to create and maintain site-based partnership programs. This includes helping educators, parents, and others in every school gain the knowledge and skills they need to plan and implement partnership programs to meet school goals. State leaders not only establish their offices and guide work for the state but also encourage effective programs at the district and school levels.

4. Action plans. Written "One-Year Action Plans for Partnerships" are essential for making progress in involving families and communities in children's education. Written plans systematize "hopes" for partnerships by specifying activities for all six types of involvement that are linked to important academic, behavioral, and school-climate goals in school improvement plans. Action plans include detailed schedules and clear responsibilities to ensure that the activities will be successfully implemented.

5. Central themes. There are several crosscutting characteristics of strong programs of school, family, and community partnerships. High-quality partnership programs build trust and mutual respect among partners in children's education, attend to issues of equity, value diversity, and celebrate progress.

When partnership programs are equitable they inform and involve all families, not just a few. When programs are responsive to all families, they recognize and meet special needs of diverse families and students. The simultaneous, seemingly contradictory, goals of ensuring equity and responding to diversity can be met only if educators, parents, and community partners develop mutual respect for their individual and collaborative work with children. Thus, in addition to the instrumental structure of ATPs and detailed procedures of One-Year Action Plans for Partnerships, the expressive and humane qualities of trust, respect, equity, diversity, and celebration are at the heart of school, family, and community partnerships.

COMMENT

Program Versus Activities of School, Family, and Community Partnerships

What is a *program* of partnership? How does it differ from the parent involvement activities that most schools or individual teachers already conduct? Most principals and teachers communicate with families occasionally, not regularly, and in isolation from one another, not as part of a coherent and continuing schoolwide program. Typically, involvement activities are conducted by one teacher or a few, with some families but not with all.

By contrast, a comprehensive program of partnership is based on long-term goals to involve all families, and annual, detailed plans and schedules of activities for all six types of involvement that are linked to school improvement goals. In comprehensive partnership programs, each of the six types of involvement is represented by several activities, not just one. As programs develop, there should be many ways for parents, other family members, community groups, and other citizens to gain and share information about parenting (Type 1); communicate with educators and each other about school programs and children's progress (Type 2); volunteer at school, at home, or in the community (Type 3); interact with children in classwork, homework, and academic decisions such as course choices (Type 4); become informed about and involved in school decisions (Type 5); and connect with organizations, services, and other opportunities in the community (Type 6). In a comprehensive partnership program, the extent of outreach and the quality of the activities are reviewed and improved from year to year to involve all families of students at all grade levels and to incorporate community connections that promote student success in school.

QUESTIONS TO DISCUSS

1. What difference might a *program* of school, family, and community partnerships make to parents? In the chart in Figure 7.1, list two ways in which a typical parent might be differently informed or involved by a school with and without a comprehensive partnership program. Consider, as examples, a parent whose child is (a) entering kindergarten and (b) progressing from middle to high school.

Time in child's schooling	What might a typical parent expect from:	
	a school with a well-planned comprehensive program of partnerships?	a school without a planned program of partnerships?
A child is being enrolled in kindergarten	A 1. 2.	B 1. 2.
A student is moving from a middle school to a high school	C 1. 2.	D 1. 2.

FIGURE 7.1 Parent Expectations

2. Think of four hypothetical students represented in sections A, B, C, and D of Figure 7.1.
    a. Give each student a name.
    b. Explain how each student may be affected by the kinds of family-school connections that you listed.

COMMENT

Understanding Action Teams for Partnerships (ATP)

Many schools have school councils, school improvement teams, or other site-based advisory committees that oversee progress on all school improvement plans and goals. School councils usually identify changes that are needed in the curriculum, instruction, staffing, management, family involvement, community connections, and other areas of school and classroom organization. These decision-making or advisory bodies often set ambitious goals and write broad plans for school improvement, but do not often organize clear structures, processes, schedules, and responsibilities for turning plans into action.

In working with schools over many years, my colleagues and I have found that school councils, improvement teams, or other planning and advisory committees need an "action arm" (i.e., an official committee) to ensure that activities to involve all families and the community in students' education are planned, implemented, and improved from year to year. The team of teachers, parents, administrators, and others focus explicitly and exclusively on implementing partnership activities that contribute to the major goals in a school improvement agenda. For example, if teachers are working to help students improve their reading and math skills and scores, then the Action Team for Partnerships will involve families and the community with students on reading and math activities. Action teams are needed to turn plans into actions that will create a welcoming partnership climate and help all students reach major school improvement goals.

QUESTIONS TO DISCUSS

1. Give two reasons why a school improvement team needs an "action arm" or committee to take responsibility for implementing specific family and community involvement activities that support the goals of a school improvement plan.
2. Why must an ATP include both educators and parents, not only teachers and administrators?
3. List and explain three activities that are, typically, the responsibility of a school improvement team or council but should *not* be conducted by the action arm or committee that focuses on school, family, and community partnerships.

COMMENT

ATP Organization and Committee Structure

There are two main ways to organize the work of an ATP. The *goal-oriented approach* organizes plans and committees to conduct and improve involvement activities that are directly linked to school improvement goals. The *process-oriented approach* organizes plans and committees to conduct activities for the six types of involvement.

Focus on School Improvement Goals

The goal-oriented approach to school, family, and community partnerships creates ATPs dedicated to understanding, organizing, and conducting involvement activities that are directly linked to school improvement goals. In this approach, each member of the ATP becomes a chair, co-chair, or expert member in linking family and community involvement to one major school improvement goal for student success. This ensures that the school's partnership program will focus each year on involving families and the community in improving the school climate and in improving students' math, reading, writing, attendance, behavior, or other major goals in the school improvement plan.

Each ATP member may select whether they will lead, delegate, and oversee family and community involvement activities that help create a positive school climate or that improve students' reading skills, attendance, the school climate for partnerships, or another goal from the school improvement plan that is detailed in the One-Year Action Plan for Partnerships.

For example, some members of the ATP may form a subcommittee to engage families and the community in helping students improve attendance. The school's written Action Plan for Partnerships would include activities for some or all six types of involvement to reduce unexcused absences or improve on-time arrivals. Activities could guide families to conduct positive actions that get children to school on time every day, clarify report card statistics on attendance, train volunteers to telephone absent students' families, and help families pick up homework for students who are absent.

In the goal-oriented approach, the ATP will establish subcommittees to oversee plans and progress toward specific goals and will implement or coordinate activities that involve families and the community in all six types of involvement. The school's improvement goals are the basis for the action plan for partnerships, and the program is evaluated on whether progress is made toward those goals.

Focus on the Six Types of Involvement

The process-oriented approach to school, family, and community partnerships creates ATPs dedicated to understanding, organizing, and enacting the framework of six types of involvement (parenting, communicating, volunteering, learning at home, decision making, and collaborating with the community). In this approach, each member of the ATP becomes a chair, co-chair, or expert member for one of the six types of involvement.

For example, in a well-functioning, process-oriented ATP, one or two members will be the school's experts in Type 1—Parenting. These Type 1 co-chairs will plan, organize, or delegate leadership for parent workshops on child development, parent-to-parent connections, activities for families to inform the school about their children's needs or family goals, and other Type 1 activities. Other members of the ATP will become experts in Type 2—Communicating. The Type 2 co-chairs will plan, organize, monitor, or delegate leadership for activities that improve the clarity of communications, create two-way channels of communication, secure translators needed at parent-teacher conferences, develop new technologies for communicating, and other Type 2 activities. Still other ATP members will become the experts in organizing and assisting volunteers (Type 3 co-chairs), teachers' designs of interactive homework and curriculum-related involvement activities (Type 4 co-chairs), training parent representatives for committees and councils (Type 5 co-chairs), and identifying resources in the community (Type 6 co-chairs).

The process-oriented ATP evaluates its progress based on whether and how well activities for the six types of involvement effectively involve all families; whether the program is balanced with activities that are conducted at home, at school, and in the community; and whether various activities contribute to student success and other school goals.

In the process-oriented approach, the ATP will have subcommittees for each of the six types of involvement and implement or coordinate activities that involve families and the community in ways to contribute to school goals for student success. As the chairs or co-chairs for each type of involvement build their competencies, they will be better able to select and implement activities that link to school improvement goals. The types of involvement are the basis for the action plan for partnerships, and the program is evaluated on whether and how progress is made so that activities for all six types of involvement contribute to student success in school.

The Two Organizational Structures

The two approaches for organizing the work of ATPs are not mutually exclusive. A goal-oriented ATP that focuses on family and community involvement linked to school improvement goals still will select activities that cover the six types of involvement. A process-oriented ATP that focuses on the six types of involvement still will choose activities that help students reach important school goals. The main differences between the two approaches are in how the ATP's plans are written and evaluated each year and how the ATP members select their areas of expertise and describe how their work is linked to the overall school improvement plan. Tools for implementing the two approaches are included in an implementation guidebook (Epstein et al., 2009).

ACTIVITY

How Family and Community Involvement Helps Reach School Improvement Goals

Whether a school uses a goal-oriented approach or process-oriented approach, the activities to involve families and the community should contribute to the attainment of important school goals.

Suppose a school is working to meet the following goals:

- Improve attendance.
- Improve math skills.
- Improve attitudes toward science.
- Improve student behavior.
- Improve the school climate for partnerships.
- Add one common, important goal: _____

In the chart below:

A. List one family or community involvement activity that you think would directly contribute to reaching these goals.
B. Note the major type of involvement that the activity addresses.
C. Tell how the activity directly affects the listed goal.

Goal	Family or Community Involvement Activity	Type of Involvement	How Would the Activity Help Produce the Goal?
1. Improve attendance.			
2. Improve math skills.			
3. Improve students' attitudes toward science.			
4. Improve students' behavior.			
5. Improve the school climate for partnerships.			
6. Another goal that you select:_____			

COMMENT

Action Team Members and Leaders

Effective partnership programs cannot be developed by just one person or by an elite group. Every year, some school principals and teachers move, are promoted, or retire. Many active parents move or "graduate" with their children to new schools. Programs and practices that depend on just one leader may disappear completely if that person leaves the school. A small group of a few active parents may be viewed as a clique that makes other parents or teachers feel unwelcome, uncomfortable, and unlikely to participate in school activities. Sometimes programs that depend on one person or the same few leaders are viewed as *somebody's* program and not as the *school's* program of partnerships.

Action Team Members

An ATP should have a minimum of six members. Members include at least two teachers, at least two parents, an administrator, and other school and family leaders who have important connections with families and students (e.g., the nurse, social worker, Title I parent liaison, a PTA/PTO officer or representative, special education leader, or others). The ATP also may include representatives from the community. High school ATPs must include two students. The diverse members contribute many points of view to plans and activities for school, family, and community partnerships.

Many schools have larger teams, as parents or teachers elect to join the Action Team for Partnerships. Some schools have one parent and one teacher from each grade level on the team. Some add other key representatives to the ATP, including a teacher of students receiving special education services, or parents from major neighborhoods or language groups.

Very small schools may adapt these guidelines to create smaller ATPs. Very large middle and high schools may adapt these guidelines to create multiple ATPs for schools-within-the-school, grade levels, houses, career academies, or other large subdivisions. Indeed, other appropriate structural and procedural adaptations will be needed to accommodate the characteristics and constraints in diverse schools.

The ATP provides a stable structure that should endure even if some team members leave each year. New team members are selected to replace those who leave and then are oriented to the work of the ATP. Thus, teachers who leave the team are replaced by teachers, parents by parents, and so on.

Action Team Leaders

Many people play important leadership roles in organizing an ATP, implementing plans, conducting activities, and evaluating results of partnership programs.

The *principal* plays an essential role in supporting and maintaining the work of an ATP and in guiding the ATP's connections to the school improvement team or council. Ideally, the principal should not be the chair of the ATP but should be an active member and strong supporter of the action team. Principals should call all teachers' attention to the importance of planning and conducting school, family, and community partnerships with their students' families. Principals also should stress the importance of the participation of educators and families in schoolwide activities that help develop a welcoming school climate. The principal should evaluate each teacher's activities to involve families as part of the teacher's annual or periodic professional reviews of work and progress. Principals and other administrators also should recognize the various leaders, participants, and successful involvement activities that are conducted throughout the school year (Sanders and Sheldon, 2009).

Guidance counselors, school psychologists, school social workers, assistant principals, and *other social service professionals* may be members of an ATP and may serve as team chairs or co-chairs. Guidance counselors and assistant principals are particularly helpful team leaders or co-leaders in middle and high schools because their professional agendas link directly to students, families, and communities (Epstein and Van Voorhis, in press). These school professionals have time, training, and experience to plan and conduct meetings and to guide teachers, parents, students, and community members to work effectively together. Even if other administrators and counselors are on the ATP, the principal's leadership and support still are essential.

Master teachers, lead teachers, department chairs, or *classroom teachers* must be members of an ATP and may serve as team chairs or co-chairs. At least two or three teachers should be members of the ATP. The teachers on the ATP will work with all teachers in the school to reinforce the importance of their connections with students' families at all grade levels and to encourage teachers' participation in schoolwide partnership activities and events. In some schools, one teacher from each grade level serves on the ATP to ensure that family involvement activities are planned, implemented, and shared across the grades.

Paraprofessionals. Parent liaisons (also called parent coordinators, parent leaders, or family liaisons) are paid aides who help educators connect and communicate with parents and other family members. Parent liaisons must be members of the ATP. They may serve, with educators, as co-chairs of the ATP or as leaders of ATP committees (Sanders, 2008). They may have particular strengths for leading workshops or activities that directly assist families. Other paraprofessionals (e.g., instructional aides, assistants in school libraries, computer labs) and other school staff (e.g., secretarial, cafeteria, custodial, and transportation staff) also may serve as members of the ATP.

Parents, family members, and *community partners* must be members of the ATP and may serve as co-chairs of the team, along with an educator. They also may serve as chairs or co-chairs of ATP committees on the six types of involvement or specific school goals. Some schools match the number of educators and parents on an ATP, some include one parent from each grade level on the team, and some make sure that at least one parent has a child with special needs to ensure that an Action Plan for Partnerships includes the interests of and outreach to parents of children receiving special education services.

Parents on the ATP should come from different neighborhoods or groups served by the school. If the school has a PTA or PTO, one representative should be on the Action Team for Partnerships. With diverse representation, all parents in the school should see that they have a voice on the ATP and a contact with whom to share ideas and questions.

Business and other community partners may serve on an ATP. Some ATPs include a business partner, librarian, police officer, city council official, scientist, medical expert, and faith-based leader as team members. Community partners bring expert knowledge, useful connections, and various resources to ATP committees. Community members may take appropriate leadership roles, such as co-chairing an ATP committee or leading an involvement activity. If community partners are on the ATP, they, too, experience the one-day team training workshop as "professional development" to build their expertise on partnerships.

Students must serve on the ATP in high schools. Although they may not serve as ATP chairs or co-chairs, they may share leadership with an educator, parent, or community partner for specific activities in the One-Year Action Plan for Partnerships. Student members of the ATP communicate with other high school students in various ways to gather ideas about which school, family, and community partnerships are important and acceptable to students and their families. Only with student involvement and support will programs of school, family, and community partnerships succeed.

All members of a school's ATP receive "team training," help write the One-Year Action Plan for Partnerships, and share responsibilities for leading the activities that are scheduled in the annual plan for partnerships. This approach changes definitions of professional development and shared leadership to recognize and ensure parents' contributions to partnership programs.

District leaders play important roles in providing professional development and ongoing support for the work of schools' ATPs. Superintendents and school boards may officially evaluate progress on school, family, and community partnerships as part of principals' and teachers' annual or periodic professional reviews. This policy links the district's mission statements about the importance of partnerships with a high-stakes evaluation and encourages school leaders to work diligently on improving and maintaining their partnership programs.

In large school districts, district-level facilitators for school, family, and community partnerships are needed to guide from 15 to 30 elementary, middle, and high schools to organize their ATPs and partnership programs. The facilitators provide ongoing facilitation activities that enable all ATPs to develop their capacities in planning, implementing, and maintaining comprehensive programs of partnership. They also help all schools in the district share ideas with each other, evaluate their work, and continue to improve their programs from year to year. In small districts, part-time facilitators may work with fewer than 15 schools to help them develop and maintain their programs of school, family, and community partnerships.

State leaders also have important leadership roles in encouraging successful partnership programs in districts and in schools. State superintendents, state boards of education, and leaders of many departments, divisions, and programs that concern families and communities need to conduct activities that support schools and districts in understanding and developing partnership programs.

At the district and state levels, leaders for partnerships develop and implement policies and activities that support and advance school, family, and community connections. This includes two types of actions. Leaders conduct and coordinate state-level or district-level policies and programs that affect all schools, such as staff development workshops; state, regional, or district conferences; competitions for small grants to support partnership practices; dissemination of best practices; and other activities. District leaders also must facilitate individual schools' Action Teams for Partnerships on program development. (See Chapter 4 on state and district leadership and activities.)

Other organizations also have roles to play in leading and participating in school, family, and community partnership programs. For example, professional development providers, state and local PTAs, community organizations, teacher or administrator unions, chambers of commerce, business and labor leaders, and others may be part of leadership and action teams at the state, district, and school levels to improve programs of school, family, and community partnerships.

Chair or Co-Chairs of the Action Team for Partnerships

At the school level, there must be a chair or, better, co-chairs of the ATP. The chair must be someone whose leadership is recognized and accepted by all members and who communicates well with educators, parents, and community members. Most often, this is a teacher, counselor, or assistant principal who understands the importance of family involvement in children's education.

Some schools select an educator and a parent to serve as co-chairs of the ATP. Chairs and co-chairs also must be selected to lead the various ATP committees that conduct specific activities that are written in the One-Year Action Plan for Partnerships. Having educators and parents as co-chairs or co-leaders of the ATP and its committees sends an important message to everyone in the school community about teamwork. The co-chair structure also gives greater stability to the ATP in the event that one leader leaves the school. The chair or co-chairs of the ATP also may serve as "linking members" on the school council or school improvement team.

Linking ATP Members with the School Improvement Team

A common question about organizing partnerships is whether the school improvement team (sometimes called the SIT) should also *be* the ATP. If the school improvement team or council is very large or if its mission is unclear, it may be subdivided into "action teams," "work groups," or committees dedicated to particular topics, with one committee dedicated to school, family, and community partnerships.

In most schools, however, the school improvement team has a clear mission to oversee all areas of the school's program and progress and to serve as an advisor to the principal. Because educators and parents who serve on the school improvement team have limited time for meetings, it is best to recruit other teachers, parents, and community members to serve on the ATP—to meet, plan, implement, oversee, evaluate, and continually improve programs of family and community involvement.

With different people on the policy-advisory and action teams, a school will ensure that the same leaders are not trying to do too many things and that leadership skills are developed by many teachers, administrators, parents, and community partners. One "linking" member in addition to the principal may serve on both the school improvement team and the Action Team for Partnerships to ensure an on-going exchange of information between the policy group and its "action arm."

QUESTIONS TO DISCUSS

1. Select a policy level that interests you (i.e., school, district, or state level).
2. Identify two job titles at the level you selected that you believe are typically represented by people who could take leadership roles for improving school, family, and community partnerships.
3. Next to each job title that you listed, note (a) the professional training, (b) goals, and (c) one other characteristic that people in these positions typically have that would help them facilitate and support the work of teachers, parents, and administrators in developing programs of school, family, and community partnerships.

Policy Level of Interest: _____			
Two positions of leadership	Professional training?	Goals in this position?	How could these leaders support family and community involvement?
1.			
2.			

ACTIVITY

Ideal Members of an Action Team for Partnerships

Suppose that you are in a school that wants to create an ATP whose members will work together on all types of family and community involvement. Let us say that *you* are one member of a six- to twelve-person team. Who else would you want on an ideal ATP? How might the ATP divide responsibilities to develop expertise in partnerships among its teachers, parents, and administrator?

A. Select the level of schooling that interests you (preschool or elementary, middle, or high school).
B. Give your hypothetical school a name.

C. Give the ATP a name. You may call it "ATP" or a name of your choice that sends a message of partnerships.

School Name _____

Action Team for Partnerships		
Team Members' Names	Team Members' Positions	Team Members' Special Talents or Interests
1. You		
2.		
3.		
4.		
5.		
6.		
Add boxes as needed		

FIGURE 7.2 ATP Member Chart

D. In Figure 7.2, identify:
   1. Your own position on the ATP (e.g., teacher, principal, counselor, parent, or some other position).
   2. The other members of the ATP. Include at least two or three teachers, two or three parents, and an administrator. Give all members hypothetical names, and list their positions.
   3. For each team member, note one of his or her special talents or interests that may contribute to the work of the ATP.
E. Note: You may extend the table to include more than six members of your ideal ATP.
F. List three challenges that could prevent these team members from working well together to write and implement plans and activities for school, family, and community partnerships. For each challenge, provide one solution that might help the team succeed with its work on partnerships.

COMMENT

Action Team Responsibilities

In elementary, middle, and high schools, the ATP plans, implements, coordinates, and oversees action; monitors progress; solves problems; presents reports; and designs new directions for positive connections with families and communities to increase student success. Members of the ATP do not work alone on the planned activities; they work with other faculty, parents, community members, and the school council or improvement team (if one exists). The ATP gathers input from and presents ideas to the full faculty, school improvement team, and parent association for the school's one-year action plan. The ATP also recruits other teachers, parents, students, administrators, and community members, or delegates leadership to help design, conduct, and evaluate family and community activities for each type of involvement or for each major school goal.

Whether it uses the goal-oriented approach or the process-oriented approach to organize involvement activities, the ATP will do the following:

- Document present and new practices of partnership so that everyone knows how individual teachers and the school as a whole communicate and work with families.
- Develop a detailed One-Year Action Plan for Partnerships linked to school improvement plans, including activities for all six types of involvement that involve families in ways that help students reach school goals.
- Identify the budget(s) and resources that will support the activities in the One-Year Action Plan for Partnerships.
- Meet monthly as a whole team to ensure continuous progress in plans and activities and to evaluate activities that were implemented in the past month.
- Meet in smaller committees, as needed, to implement activities in the One-Year Action Plan for Partnerships.
- Publicize the partnership plans and practices to parents, students, and teachers, and, as appropriate, the broader community. All teachers, parents, school staff, community members, and students should know how they can help select, design, conduct, enjoy, benefit from, and evaluate partnership activities.
- Report its work and progress semiannually (or on a regular schedule) to the school improvement team (or council), parent organization, faculty, and broader community.
- Recognize and celebrate excellent participation from parents, other family members, students, and others in the community who contribute to the success of the planned partnership activities.
- Evaluate progress in improving the quality of implemented activities and the results of various involvement activities. This includes results for the school and teachers, results for parents and other family members, and results for students.
- Solve problems that impede progress on partnership activities.
- Gather ideas for new activities and solves problems that impede progress.

- Write a new One-Year Action Plan for Partnerships each year to ensure an ongoing program of partnerships in the life and work of the school.
- Replace teachers, parents, administrators, or other members who leave the ATP with new members so that a full team is always ready to conduct a planned program of partnerships at the school.
- Integrate new projects, grants, and activities for home, school, and community connections into a unified program of partnerships. Many activities that enrich and extend partnerships of home, school, and community come and go each year. These activities should be viewed as part of, not separate from, the school's ongoing, dynamic, comprehensive program of partnerships.

The ATP recognizes all of the family and community involvement activities that are conducted by individual teachers and other groups (e.g., PTA/PTO, after-school program, and business partners). The school's partnership program includes *all* family and community involvement activities that are conducted for the school as a whole, in specific grade levels, and by individual teachers each year.

If the ATP conducts its leadership activities well, then everyone in the school should know that the school has an active program of school, family, and community partnerships. All teachers, parents, school staff, community members, and students should know how they are contributing to the design, conduct, and evaluation of partnership activities. From year to year, the number and quality of activities in each One-Year Action Plan for Partnerships should improve, along with positive results of the activities. Details on organizing an effective ATP are in Epstein et al. (2009).

QUESTIONS TO DISCUSS

1. Which of the ATP actions listed above do you think is:
   a. easiest to accomplish, and why?
   b. most difficult to accomplish, and why?
2. Select three of the leadership actions of the ATP listed above that you believe are most important for a high-quality program of partnerships. Explain how each of the actions you selected would help make a school's program of school, family, and community partnerships permanent and a regular part of school life.

Using Tools to Take Action

To fulfill the responsibilities listed above and to develop and strengthen its program of partnerships from year to year, an ATP must address the following questions:

1. Where is this school starting from in its present practices at each grade level on each of the six major types of involvement? What do teachers do individually, and what does the school do as a whole, to involve families and communities?
2. What are this school's major goals for improving or maintaining student success?
3. What will be different about this school's program of family, school, and community partnerships three years from now?
4. Which partnership practices that are currently being conducted should be maintained or improved?
5. Which new practices should be added to involve families and the community in ways that help students attain specific learning goals? To activate all six types of involvement? To reach more families?
6. How is this school progressing? What indicators are used to measure the quality of partnerships and progress toward goals for student success? What activities should be monitored, documented, and formally evaluated to learn about the effects of school, family, and community partnerships?
7. How will the results of the assessments and evaluations be used to improve the next One-Year Action Plan for Partnerships?

Educators and researchers working together have developed several tools to help ATPs address these basic questions. The following tools are discussed in the implementation guidebook *School, Family, and Community Partnerships: Your Handbook for Action* (Epstein et al., 2009).

A. *Starting Points*. An inventory of present practices for the six types of involvement, accounting for the grade levels in which activities are presently implemented.
B. *One-Year Action Plan for Partnerships*. An annual, detailed plan that outlines activities, dates, and specific responsibilities for members of the ATP and others to implement the planned practices. Options include a goal-oriented or process-oriented action plan.
C. *Annual Evaluation of Activities*. A reflective assessment of quality of each activity that is implemented throughout the school year. The format matches the goal-oriented or process-oriented action plan so that plans and evaluations are parallel.

D. *Measure of School, Family, and Community Partnerships.* An inventory and rating system that extends Starting Points to assess how well the school is implementing partnership practices for the six types of involvement and how well the program is meeting key challenges for involving all families in their children's education.

E. *Annual Review of Team Processes.* Assess the quality of teamwork at the end of each year by rating 18 team processes to help an ATP become even more effective in the future.

Question	Which tool and why? A, B, C, D, and/or E?	What other information might be needed?
1. Where is this school starting from in its present practices of the six major types of involvement?		
2. What are this school's major goals for improving or maintaining student success?		
3. What will be different about this school's partnership program three years from now?		
4. Which partnership practices that are currently being conducted should be maintained or improved?		
5. Which new practices of family and community involvement should be added to help students attain specific learning goals?		
6. How is this school progressing in improving the quality of its partnership program?		
7. What should be included in the next *One-Year Action Plan for Partnerships*?		

FIGURE 7.3 Matching Tools to Tasks

Matching Tools to Tasks

A. Use the chart in Figure 7.3. Tell which of the above tools (A, B, C, D, or E) would help an ATP address the seven major questions listed above. (Tools may be used more than once.)
B. Fill in other school information that might be needed or helpful, whether the tools listed above are used or not.

Scheduling Meetings—Not Too Many, Not Too Few

In its *One-Year Action Plan for Partnerships*, an ATP must create a realistic schedule for full-team meetings, committee meetings, and periodic reports to other school groups so that all teachers, parents, students, and members of the community will know about the school's plans and activities for partnerships. A recommended schedule includes the following team meetings and reports:

- Team Meetings. The full ATP should meet on a regular, realistic schedule (at least monthly for at least one hour) to plan and schedule activities, coordinate actions, conduct events, evaluate results, identify problems, and celebrate progress. The meetings should be designed and conducted to keep the planned program moving forward.
- Committee Meetings. ATP committees should meet as needed to implement specific activities in the one-year action plan for which they are responsible. For teams using the process-oriented approach, six ATP committees on the six types of involvement will meet, as needed, throughout the year to implement their planned activities. For teams using the goal-oriented approach, ATP committees will meet to implement the activities planned on their specific goals.
- Reports or Presentations on Partnerships. The chair, co-chairs, or designated members of the ATP should report regularly (at least twice a year) to the school improvement team (school council), the full faculty, and the parent association on plans for and progress on school, family, and community partnerships. These also are occasions to gather information and ideas for needed changes and improvements and to recruit leaders and participants for various activities.
- Reports or Presentations on Partnerships. The chair, co-chairs, or designated members also should report the ATP's plans, activities, and progress to all families, students, and the community in school or community newsletters and in other forums where the work, plans, and goals of the school are discussed.

How Many Meetings?

A. Interview a teacher or administrator to discuss some of the challenges educators and parents might face in finding time to meet and work together on an ATP and some workable options. This activity may be conducted individually or invite an educator to discuss these issues with the class. First set the stage or scenario:

Suppose that the teachers, administrators, and parents in your school formed an Action Team for Partnerships—a committee that works together to improve the plans and practices of family and community involvement. The ATP wrote a One-Year Action Plan for Partnerships so that involvement activities, conducted throughout the school year, would contribute to goals for student success. Now the team is meeting to determine a reasonable schedule for team and committee meetings. They want to have just enough meetings—not too many, but not too few—to ensure that their work is well organized and that planned activities are well implemented.

Given the realities of school life in your school, what are your recommendations on the following?

1. Team Meetings: If your school had an ATP that included teachers, parents, and an administrator, how often should the whole team meet to plan, conduct, and monitor their work and progress? What might be a reasonable schedule, time, and place for whole-team meetings?

2. Committee Meetings: If your ATP had committees to conduct involvement activities to contribute to specific school goals (e.g., helping students improve attendance, math achievement, etc.), how often should each committee meet to plan, conduct, and monitor their specific activities? What might be a reasonable schedule, time, and place for committee meetings?

3. Reports on Partnerships: If your school had an ATP, how often should reports about partnership plans and progress be made to the following groups? What form should those reports take: oral report, computerized phone message, written summary, detailed written report, or some other form?

Action Team for Partnerships should report to:	How often?	In what form?
1. School improvement team or council		
2. PTA/PTO or parent organization		
3. All parents in the school		
4. All teachers in the school		
5. Students		
6. Community members		
7. Local media		
8. Any others?		

4. Assessments and New Plans: If your school had an ATP, how much time should be spent evaluating its work and writing new one-year action plans for the next school year? What might be a reasonable schedule, time, and place for these activities?

B. Summarize the questions and the interviewee's responses.

C. From the responses to the interview questions and from your readings in this chapter on the ATP, create and label a realistic meeting schedule over one school year (12 months) for ATP meetings and reports. Include in the calendar time for the ATP to:
- orient new members of the team
- write a one-year action plan
- meet as a whole team
- meet as committees on activities linked to school goals for student success
- report their work and progress to major stakeholder groups
- evaluate their work and progress
- write plans for the next school year
- conduct other meetings or responsibilities that you identify.

COMMENT

Establishing Permanent Partnership Programs— As Regular as Reading!

A school's partnership program should be organized to operate as efficiently, effectively, and predictably as a school's reading, math, science, and other curricula and testing programs. For example, a school's reading program accounts for all of the reading and literacy activities that are conducted with students at all grade levels. Reading skills are planned, taught, tested, reported, and continually improved. Every principal, teacher, student, and parent knows that the school has a reading program that students experience daily. If new reading activities or opportunities come along (such as a grant for improving reading instruction, for purchasing new books, or for teachers' professional development in linking reading and writing), the additions are woven into the fabric of the school's reading program.

Similarly, a well-organized, comprehensive program of school, family, and community partnerships accounts for all home-school-community connections that are planned and conducted with students and families. Some activities are conducted by classroom teachers, some activities are grade-level events, and other activities are schoolwide. Some are individual connections between a parent and teacher, administrator, or counselor; others are group activities; and still others involve all students, families, educators, and the community.

Like reading, partnership programs and practices must be planned, reviewed, and improved each year. If new partnership projects, grants, and activities are initiated, they should be integrated into the school's ongoing partnership program. This simple analogy—partnership programs must be planned and conducted "like reading"—is key to sustaining school, family, and community partnerships that inform and involve all families in their children's education every year.

ACTIVITY

How Are Partnerships Like and Unlike Reading?

A. Invite a school principal, or teacher, or school district or state education leader to discuss how one "regular" or "permanent" program (such as reading, math, science, other subject, or testing program) is organized to ensure that it continues and improves from year to year. Fill in the chart on page 597 to summarize the information about the selected, permanent program. Ask:
   1. What is one program in your school(s) that is permanent, regular, and expected from year to year?
   2. How do the following organizational features help make the selected program permanent? (Fill in column 1.)
   3. Do the same organizational features contribute to the development of a program of school, family, and community partnerships in your school(s)? If yes, how does each feature apply? If no, why not? (Fill in column 2.)
B. From what you learned in the interview, how permanent do you think the selected program is, and how permanent do you think the school, family, and community partnership program is in this educator's school(s)? Explain.

One permanent program in our school is: _____.

How does each feature help make the selected program "permanent"?	How does each feature presently apply to your school's program of family and community involvement?
a. A policy	
b. A written plan	
c. Funding	
d. Leadership and supervision	
e. Teamwork	
f. Materials and equipment	
g. Orientation of new participants	
h. Evaluations	
i. Any other feature? _____	

COMMENT

What's in a Name?

A school may call its team the (School Name) Action Team for Partnerships; or the (School Name) School, Family, and Community Partnership Team; or the Home, School, Community Partnership Team. Or a school may choose a unique name for its team, such as the Parent-Educator Network (PEN), Teachers Getting Involved with Families (TGIF), Partners in Education (PIE), Partners for Student Success (PASS), or Teachers and Parents for Students (TAPS).

Sometimes districts name their partnership initiatives to link all of the schools in their own local "network." For example, districts have called their initiatives the (District Name) School, Family, and Community Partnership Program; (District Name) Network of Partnership Schools; and Building Educational Success Together (BEST).

QUESTIONS TO DISCUSS

1. Give two reasons why a school or district might want to give its ATP or partnership program a unique name.
2. Why are the above names for school teams and district programs better than names that focus only on parents (such as Parent Network, Family Focus Group, or Parents Involved in Education), and better than names that focus only on community connections (such as Community Education Committee)? Give two reasons why names of ATPs or district initiatives should have a "partnership" focus.

How Effective Are School Improvement Committees?

A. Select a school level that interests you (i.e., preschool or elementary, middle, or high school).

B. Interview a teacher or administrator about the current and ideal committee structures in that person's school. Ask:
  1. About how many students are in this school?
  2. About how many teachers and administrators are in this school?
  3. What are four major goals or objectives that this school has for improving or maintaining the quality of the school's program and students' success?
     Goal 1: _____
     Goal 2: _____
     Goal 3: _____
     Goal 4: _____

C. Create a chart like the one below that outlines the interviewee's responses to the questions in this chart.

School conditions and committee structure	What is the current situation?	What is ideal for this school?
1. What advisory or grade level committees meet regularly with the principal? a. Who serves on these committees?		
2. What action-oriented committees are there that plan and implement activities? a. Who serves on these committees?		
3. How well do these committees link their work to the four goals or objectives listed in question B3, above?		
4. Add a question of your own:		

D. Look over the information from the interview. How would you describe the school's current committee structure? Is there evidence of teamwork? Is there broad representation of teachers, parents, other staff, and community members on the various committees?

E. Do you agree with the interviewee's ideas for the ideal committee structure for the school? Explain.

F. List two actions that you would recommend to help this school improve its committee structure and representation. Give one reason for each of your recommendations.

CENTRAL THEMES

The readings and discussions in this volume provide an understanding of the theory, research, policies, and implementation of programs and practices of school, family, and community partnerships. The next sections review the central themes and major conclusions that crosscut the readings and activities across chapters.

Central Theme Number 1: Building Mutual Trust and Respect of Teachers and Parents

Everyone agrees that mutual trust and mutual respect between parents and teachers are basic and required qualities of good partnerships. Programs of school, family, and community partnerships will not be sustained unless teachers, administrators, parents, and others who share an interest in children understand each other; respect the hard work they each do for children; convey their mutual respect to each other; and demonstrate their mutual trust in the way that they design and conduct programs of school, family, and community partnerships.

Trust and *respect* are not just words; it takes concerted action to establish these underlying qualities for successful partnerships. Trust and respect cannot be legislated or mandated but must be developed over time within school communities.

QUESTIONS TO DISCUSS

1. Discuss one way in which mutual respect and trust between parents and teachers are *prerequisites* for some practices of partnership.

2. Discuss one way that mutual respect and trust between parents and teachers *facilitate* good partnerships.

3. Discuss one way that mutual respect and trust between parents and teachers are the *result* of good practices of partnership.

4. Suppose that a school or district wanted to make sure that its work on school, family, and community partnerships increased parents' and teachers' mutual trust and respect for each other.

a.   Select a level of schooling that interests you (e.g., preschool or elementary, middle, or high school).
b.   Select one type of involvement that interests you.
c.   Describe one activity for the type of involvement you selected that you think would help build mutual respect and trust between parents and teachers at the school level you selected.
d.   Explain why you think this activity would produce trust and mutual respect between teachers and parents.
e.   Analyze the following features of the activity you described at the school level you selected:
   (1)   Would all families benefit from this activity—even parents who work during the school day or cannot come to the school building for other reasons?
      If yes, describe how the activity involves all parents.
      If no, add one idea about how to inform and include families, even if they were not able to participate.
   (2)   What is one way that the activity you described might involve or affect students, in addition to parents?

COMMENT

Resolving Conflicts and Concerns

Activities to inform and involve families in children's education at school and at home are not always successful on the first try. Some teachers and principals need practice in relating to and cooperating with parents. Some parents may not see eye-to-eye with their children's teachers. Sometimes good partners have honest disagreements and must work out their differences.

Parents may have different opinions from teachers and from each other about homework (e.g., too much or too little), student placements (e.g., the group or special program in which the child should be placed), improvements needed in school subjects and programs, and other topics. Some differences in opinions occur when educators are not aware of parents' views or when teachers or administrators are inflexible about responding to requests from families. Differences in opinions may occur if parents are not well informed and included in decisions about their children's education from preschool on. Without information and involvement every year that children are in school, gaps are created in parents' and educators' knowledge of and comfort with each other. Such gaps, if not addressed, become increasingly hard to bridge.

Even when parents and teachers share mutual respect and trust each other, problems may arise, but solutions should be easier to achieve. For example, by knowing and respecting the families of their students, many schools have redesigned winter holiday concerts and celebrations to prevent offending or excluding students of different cultures or religions. Some schools have "detracked" courses to offer challenging programs to all students, not just to a few who are labeled "gifted." One school in a large urban area served many families who, because of their religious beliefs, objected to some curricular topics. Instead of ignoring or criticizing the parents, teachers created alternative learning activities for students to select to develop the same important skills in reading, writing, or social studies. Schools in many communities now give parents and students choices of whether or not to attend classes or activities that counter family beliefs.

A well-functioning action team will design ways to review and discuss parents' concerns and opinions. Indeed, good communications help build an important base of trust and respect needed to address questions and resolve differences.

QUESTIONS TO DISCUSS

1. How might an ATP respond to the following parental concerns? Give one possible solution to each of the following issues:

Parental Concern	One Strategy That May Address This Concern
a. Parent complains that the family's religious beliefs are contradicted by the school program or policy (a Type 1 challenge).	
b. Parent wants to meet with the child's teacher but does not speak English (a Type 2 challenge).	
c. Parent feels unwelcome by other volunteers (a Type 3 challenge).	
d. Parent says that the child is being given too little homework (a Type 4 challenge).	
e. Parent thinks that children in the afternoon kindergarten class have fewer hours of school than in the morning class (a Type 5 challenge).	
f. Parent is worried that children are unsafe walking to and from school (a Type 6 challenge).	

2. Not all strategies will fully address parental concerns. Some actions may help a concerned parent understand and accept the school's point of view and some may help the school understand and accept the parent's point of view. Discuss the suggested strategies in class: Are the actions realistic? What is the likely result if the suggested strategy were enacted? Will the exchange build trust or distrust between parents and educators?

Central Theme Number 2:
Recognizing the Diversity of Families

1. **The diversity of family cultures and languages will continue in the nation's schools.** Students come to school from families with diverse cultural and linguistic backgrounds, religions, customs, talents, and experiences. Cultural and linguistic diversity will increase as the nation welcomes new groups of immigrants and as generations of immigrant children and families not only assimilate but also maintain pride in their heritage.

2. **The diversity of family structures will continue in the nation's schools.** Students come to school each day from one-parent and two-parent homes, blended families, extended families, foster families, same-sex parents, and other family arrangements. Some children are from large families, others from small families. Some have grandparents nearby; others do not. Families have diverse forms and members.

3. **The diversity of family work experiences will continue in the nation's schools.** In most families, one or both parents work full-time or part-time outside the home. Some parents are or may become unemployed, are in training for new jobs, have a disability, receive federal or state assistance, or are moving to a new location. Families have diverse work schedules and experiences.

4. **The diversity of family economic situations will continue in the nation's schools.** Some parents are wealthy, many are middle class, others are working hard and getting by, and still others are poor. Some children have economic advantages that facilitate educational experiences. Other children and their families need various kinds of assistance to participate fully in educational programs at school and in the community. Families have diverse resources even in seemingly homogeneous communities.

5. **Diverse families are similar in many ways.** Despite important cultural, structural, and economic differences, families are similar in profound ways. All families care about their children and want them to succeed in schools with excellent educational programs. All families want to feel welcome at their children's schools, respected by their children's teachers, and safe in their communities. All students are eager to succeed, want their families to be appreciated by their schools, and want their families as knowledgeable partners in their education.

QUESTIONS TO DISCUSS

1. Add to the list above one more way in which you believe families within a school are *different* from one another, and explain.

2. Add to the list above one more way in which you believe families within a school are *similar* to one another, and explain.
3. Identify one of the features of diversity from the list that interests you.
    a. Identify one type of family involvement and one grade level that interest you.
    b. Describe one activity for school, family, and community partnerships for the type of involvement and grade level you selected that you believe would:
        • help diverse families and students appreciate their differences;
        • help diverse families and students appreciate their similarities; and
        • help teachers or principals learn more about the strengths, interests, needs, or goals of diverse families.

FIELD EXPERIENCE

How Do Communities Address Diversity?

A. Identify a community that interests you.
B. Select a parent, educator, or other individual in that community to interview about whether and how the community recognizes similarities and differences of families and students. Ask:
    1. How diverse is this community's population, and in what ways?
    2. Are the students in the local schools more or less diverse than people in the surrounding community, or about the same? Explain.
    3. Are *similarities*, common goals, and interests of families in this community discussed and celebrated? If so, give one example of how this is done. If not, give one reason why this is not done.
    4. Are *differences* in the goals and interests of families in the community discussed and celebrated? If so, give one example of how this is done. If not, give one reason why this is not done.
C. Write one more question to ask the parent, educator, or other individual about similarities or differences in the community.
D. Summarize the questions and your interviewee's responses. From this interview, how would you describe the "sense of community" in this location? Provide one idea that you think would strengthen this community's understanding of its families.

Appreciating Family Diversity

Family histories, cultures, talents, values, and religions are rarely discussed in school. These topics are important, however, for increasing students' understanding and appreciation of others who are different from themselves. Comprehensive partnership programs include activities that illuminate family backgrounds and strengths to help students, families, and educators understand and appreciate each other's similarities and differences.

    A. Identify a grade level that interests you.

    B. Design a bulletin board for a classroom, school hallway, or community location for the grade level you selected that focuses attention on the strengths, similarities, or diversities of families. For example, consider displaying student drawings, stories, or photographs about aspects of family life that students may enjoy sharing (e.g., favorite foods, sports, holidays, sayings, histories, hopes and dreams, talents, hobbies and interests, stories of coming to America, or other topics of interest).

        1. Show a diagram of how you think the display will look.

        2. Explain the purpose and content of your design.

        3. Design one classroom or homework activity for students to plan, create, or react to the bulletin board.

    C. "Bulletin boards may celebrate the diversity of families in a school, but they are not enough to help students develop an understanding and appreciation of their similarities and differences."

        1. Do you agree or disagree with the above statement?

        2. Write or discuss at least two arguments to support or refute this statement for the grade level you selected.

        3. In addition to a bulletin board, what is one activity that might strengthen a school's focus on the similarities and differences of its students and families?

Website Exploration Diversity of Students and Families

Explore the annual collections of *Promising Partnership Practices* at www.partnershipschools.org in the section "Success Stories."

    A. Select one year's book, and click on "Multicultural Awareness."

    B. Select one activity reported by a school, district, state, or organization and critique it.

        1. What were two positive features of the activity that increased awareness of and interactions by diverse students and families in a school?

2. What were two weaknesses or limitations to the activity that could be corrected for even greater success? Tell how.

Central Theme Number 3: Equity in School, Family, and Community Partnerships

Can family involvement at home ever be equal for all children and families?

- Some parents have more formal schooling than other parents.
- Families have different skills to share, such as music, sports, arts, cooking, carpentry, car repair, sewing, and child care.
- Some parents have more time to spend with their children than others.
- Some families have more money to spend on tutoring, lessons, and summer experiences.
- Some communities have more free activities for families and for children than do other communities.
- Some families have older children who can help the younger ones with schoolwork.
- Some families have only one child, who receives all of the parents' attention.
- Add one or two other inevitable inequalities that exist for children and families at home that you believe have an impact on student success in school: _____

The inequalities listed above are not all associated with wealth or formal education. For example, some parents, though economically strapped, may spend more time with children than do other families. Some communities in distressed neighborhoods help students and families participate in enriching activities. All families, regardless of socioeconomic status, have useful skills and knowledge to share with children.

QUESTIONS TO DISCUSS

Almost all families want to do the best they can for and with their children, but many conditions and resources are different and unequal. What do these inequalities mean for producing greater equity in school, family, and community partnerships?

1. Select one of the inequalities in the list above.
2. Discuss the importance of the factor you selected for children's success in school.
3. Describe one activity in a program of school, family, and community partnerships that might help to increase equality on the factor you selected.

Choices That Respond to Diverse Students' Needs

From preschool on, decisions are made for, about, and with students and their families that affect students' experiences in school. Some states, districts, and schools offer families and students options in their education, including choice of:

- schools
- courses
- teachers
- special programs in schools
- activities in programs
- after-school activities
- summer school or enrichment programs
- ways to make up a failing grade
- add one more choice that may be made: _____

To make wise choices, families and students need good information in useful forms and understandable language. For example, some families prefer information in print form, while others prefer to talk with other parents, educators, or others in the community. Or a combination of verbal and written exchanges might be needed.

QUESTIONS TO DISCUSS

1. Identify one of the choices that interests you from the bulleted list above.
2. For the choice you selected:
   a. What do parents need to know to make an informed choice?
   b. Discuss at least one *equity issue* associated with this choice that determines whether all families or some families exercise their options.
   c. Describe two strategies that schools might use to provide the kinds of information that all families need to make good decisions for this choice. Describe each strategy and the results you anticipate.

Luck Versus Equity in Partnerships

Parents speak of involvement in their children's education in terms of "luck." A parent may say: "I'm really lucky this year. Paul's teacher is so open and encouraging.

I can call with my questions, and I know she will return the call." Or "We are so lucky. Adrienn's teacher is so helpful. He keeps us informed about how she is doing and how to help at home." These parents may not feel so lucky the next school year.

Families also talk about their children's schools in the same way. Parents may say: "We are so lucky that our school welcomes ideas from parents. In the last school our children attended, the principal was not interested in what we had to say." Families feel lucky if they are welcomed, informed, and involved.

Teachers also speak of luck. A teacher says: "I am so lucky this year. My students' parents are so easy to reach. They are eager to help me and my class at school, and they work with their children at home." Teachers appreciate parents' help. They talk about being lucky if they have good relationships with their students and families.

This volume suggests that it is possible to take school, family, and community partnerships out of the realm of luck and put them into regular teaching practice. This can be done by planning and implementing a comprehensive, permanent program of partnerships that involves all teachers, all families, and the community every year that students are in school.

FIELD EXPERIENCE

Do Parents Feel Lucky or Confident about Partnerships?

A. Select a parent whose child has been in the same school for more than one year. Identify the child's grade level and whether the school is public or private. Ask:
   1. This year, how do your child's school and teacher(s) inform and involve you in your child's education?
   2. How do you feel about the information and opportunities you receive?
   3. How did you feel last year about the information and opportunities for involvement that you received from the school or your child's teacher(s)?
B. Add one question of your own.
C. Record the questions and responses.
D. Summarize the parent's reports about contacts with the school to tell:
   1. Were the parent's experiences consistent or different from one year to the next?
   2. Were parents expecting information and opportunities for involvement, or did they feel "lucky" this year or last year?
E. Add other reflections.
F. *Optional class activity*. Compare responses with others in class for an overview of parents' reports of consistency of information from year to year.

Real or Imagined Families

We need to design and implement family involvement activities that meet the needs of today's families, not real or imagined families of the past. This means understanding families' conditions and constraints. Not all families can come to all workshops, meetings, or events on the school's schedule. Not all who are employed can leave work to come to parent-teacher conferences. Not all parents can volunteer at school during the day. Not all parents can help with homework on a specific evening. Not all parents want to serve on school committees. Not all parents can work in their communities at specifically scheduled times.

These are not new problems. There always were diverse situations and constraints on time that restricted family involvement. There always were one-parent and two-parent homes where parents were employed during the school day, or in one, two, or more jobs, who could not come often or easily to the school building. There always were immigrant parents and others who did not feel welcome at school. In the past, most parents had very limited knowledge of their children's schooling across the grades, and most had limited information about how to work with their children's schools to maximize student success.

The imagined "golden years" of parent involvement never existed in all or most schools for all or most families. Most parents have always needed more and better information than they were given, and more and different opportunities for involvement at school and at home. Because of advances in research, policy, and practice, we know more now than in the past about the organization of programs and practices that enable all families to be involved in their children's education across the grades.

Meeting the Needs of Twenty-first-Century Families

A. Figure 7.4 shows six of many crucial challenges to excellent progress on the six types of involvement. Give one example of an activity that would help meet each of the following challenges so that more of today's families might become more involved in their children's education.

B. Discuss ideas about the challenges and suggested solutions in class. How would each suggestion address the simultaneous challenges of equity in partnerships to involve all families and meeting the needs of diverse families?

Selected Challenges to Excellent Partnerships	One Strategy or Activity That Schools Could Use to Meet Each Challenge to Involve All (or Most) Families
Type 1 Challenge: Provide information to families who cannot come to a meeting at school.	
Type 2 Challenge: Schedule conferences so that employed parents can attend.	
Type 3 Challenge: Organize volunteer work that can be done at home or in the community.	
Type 4 Challenge: Keep families informed about what their children must learn and do to pass each subject, without requiring parents to "teach" school subjects.	
Type 5 Challenge: Organize committees so that parent leaders from the major recial, ethnic, socioeconomic, and other groups in the school are involved.	
Type 6 Challenge: Organize business and other community partnerships so that attention and resources focus on school improvement goals for student success	

FIGURE 7.4   Challenges to Partnerships

Conclusions and Looking Ahead

This volume takes readers on a journey from theory to research, to policy, and to the development of school, family, and community partnership programs in practice. From the collection of readings, activities, and other research, we draw eight conclusions to help you think about, talk about, and take action on school, family, and community partnerships as you proceed to use and build on what you have learned.

1. School, family, and community partnerships are about *children* and their success as students in school. In the past, parental involvement was, too often, about the parents. Because schools are responsible and accountable for students' success, it is necessary to redirect programs of family and community involvement to focus on helping all students succeed in school.

Teachers, parents, administrators, and community members care about their children and want them to succeed in school and in life. Indeed, children are the reason these partners communicate and work together. Research suggests that children who have multiple sources of support at home, at school, and in the community are more likely to succeed in school, graduate from high school, and make postsecondary plans for the future. Well-designed partnership programs and practices should help all of the people who care about children organize their interactions and mobilize their resources in ways that help youngsters define themselves and work as students. Some partnership activities also will benefit parents, educators, and others, but these results are the means to the main goal of promoting students' learning, development, and success.

2. School, family, and community partnerships are for all families. Partnerships are not just for families who are formally educated, easy to reach, or able to come often to school. They are not just for families whose children are doing well in school and not just for those whose children are in trouble, not just for families who live close to the school or only those who have telephones and computers with Internet access, not just for those who speak English or read it well, not just for those with two parents at home, and not just for families who always agree with school policies. Comprehensive programs of school, family, and community partnerships are designed to inform and involve families of all races, cultures, family structures, and educational backgrounds. Schools with excellent partnership programs reach out to mothers and fathers, foster parents and guardians, grandparents, and others who are raising children in all families.

When comprehensive programs of partnership are conducted, schools send powerful messages to students:

> Your school respects all families. Your school will communicate and collaborate with your family to help you succeed.

Partnership programs say to teachers:

> Involving families in children's education is part of educators' professional work. This school does not stereotype or dismiss any families as irrelevant to their children's learning and development.

Crucial messages also are sent to families:

> All students and all families are important in this school. We communicate with families, and we encourage families to communicate with educators to help students succeed.

3. School, family, and community partnerships are important at all grade levels, from preschool through high school. Families are important in their children's lives every year, not just in infancy, preschool, and the primary grades. Community services and programs assist families and their children from infancy on, not just in the upper grades.

Of course, practices of partnership change each year as children mature and assume more responsibilities for their own learning; school programs become more complex; and families accumulate information about their children's education, talents, and interests. Partnerships are particularly important at times of transition, when children and their families move to new schools or are promoted from one grade level to the next. To do their best for their children, families need good information about their children's development, school programs, community services, and how to help at home at every grade level.

4. Students are key to the success of school, family, and community partnerships. Not only are students the reason for partnerships, they also are essential partners. Students are important couriers, messengers, interpreters, negotiators, interviewers, decision makers, and discussants in school, family, and community partnership activities for all six types of involvement. Students help teachers, counselors, and administrators reach their families, and they help their families communicate with their schools. They often are the main source of information for families about school and community programs. Without students' participation in communications between school and home, there will be few successful partnerships of any type at any grade level. Most important, students are the main actors in their own education and, ultimately, in charge of their own success in school. Still, teachers, parents, and others in the community must work with students and with each other to help students succeed.

5. The community is important for the success of partnership programs. *Community* includes the family and the school, and it extends to the neighborhood, the city or township, and all of society. The vastness of the term means that every school, district, or state must identify its community and design productive connections that will strengthen the school programs, assist families and students, and advance the interests of the community.

Community resources include people, programs, policies, facilities, finances, and other less tangible norms, beliefs, and attitudes that can be targeted to help students succeed. Business partners; cultural, civic, religious, and educational groups; the media; and others in the community may contribute to comprehensive partnership programs in ways that help prevent students' academic and behavioral problems and that promote student success. All communities, not just wealthy ones, have traditions, talents, and opportunities that can be organized to enrich the lives of children.

Connections with the community do not take the place of connections with all students' families. Even when schools organize and use community programs, people, and resources well (e.g., mentors, tutors, educational programs, recreational opportunities), students' families need to be informed and involved. They must know about their children's opportunities, work, and progress. From year to year, families remain students' main support system.

Community is an attitude and feeling of connectedness. When educators, parents, other citizens, and organizations work together to help students succeed, they strengthen the sense of community in and beyond the school.

6. Developing and implementing programs and practices of school, family, and community partnerships are processes, not events. Programs of partnership are developed over time, not overnight. It takes time to plan, implement, evaluate, and improve school-level partnership programs. It takes time to develop insightful and facilitative district and state policies, organize staff, implement inservice education, award grants, and conduct conferences and other leadership activities that support and assist all schools. Planned programs make the difference in whether, which, and how families and communities become involved in children's education. At least three years are needed for schools, districts, and states to establish strong leadership for and effective processes and practices of school, family, and community partnerships. After that, annual plans, thoughtful evaluations, and continuous improvements are needed to sustain excellent programs of partnership.

7. School, family, and community partnerships focus on results to help students succeed in school. After establishing a welcoming school environment that sends messages of trust, respect, and welcome to all families, schools' programs of partnership must *focus on results* for student success in school. Annual plans for school, family, and community partnerships must include activities that involve families and communities in productive ways to help promote, improve, or maintain school goals and high standards for student success. Involvement activities must be balanced to include some conducted at school, at home through homework, and in community settings. It is no longer enough to count "bodies in the school building" to measure family involvement.

Involvement activities may be designed to help students increase skills in reading, math, writing, or other subjects. And productive partnerships may focus on improving student attendance, behavior, or attitudes toward school and learning so that students are in school, on time, and motivated to learn and do their best.

A focus on results requires schools, districts, and state departments of education to monitor the quality of partnership programs and to measure the impact of family and community involvement on student success. Clear measures are needed, first, of the quality of involvement activities to learn whether planned activities are implemented, who is involved and who is excluded, and how well the activities are conducted. Next, clear measures of results are needed to learn whether there are added benefits for all or some students or others as a result of participating in the activities that are implemented. This two-step approach to evaluation ensures that results cannot be expected unless involvement activities are effectively implemented. A focus on results affirms that school programs of family and community involvement must be periodically reviewed and continually improved.

8. School, family, and community partnerships do not substitute for other school improvements and innovations that are needed to increase student learning and success. The best way to ensure student success and high achievement is for all students to have excellent teachers every day, every year, in every subject. Schools must provide all students with talented teachers; challenging curriculum; effective instruction; up-to-date technology; equal opportunities to learn; responsive assessments; enriching educational resources and activities; *and* excellent school, family, and community partnerships.

In sum, school, family, and community partnerships are about children, include all families, at all grade levels, give key roles to students, involve the community, are planned and ongoing, and are evaluated for their quality and results. Along with all other aspects of excellent schools and excellent teaching, school, family, and community partnerships are necessary for increasing students' test scores, reducing dropout rates, improving attendance, or increasing other indicators of student success. The eight conclusions lead, full circle, back to the first chapter's list of facts and call for action for better professional preparation of educators about school, family, and community partnerships.

QUESTIONS TO DISCUSS

1. Based on the eight conclusions listed above and your other readings, in the chart below list one reason why each of the following is *important* in a comprehensive program of partnership. Then, list one reason why each focus is *not* enough for ensuring trust, respect, equity, and diversity in programs of partnership.

Focus	Why is this important?	Why is this *not enough* for a comprehensive partnership program?
A. Involve parents of young children.		
B. Involve families in workshops on parenting.		
C. Involve families with many years of formal education who understand schools.		
D. Involve families when students are in trouble.		
E. Involve families and the community in one big event at school each year.		
F. Have an active PTA/PTO or other parent organization.		

2. Discuss classmates' ideas of why each focus is necessary but not sufficient in excellent programs of partnership.

20/20 Vision of School, Family, and Community Partnerships

Today's students are tomorrow's parents. They are witnessing and experiencing how their schools treat their families and how their families treat the schools. They are learning by example how parents are involved at school and at home in their children's education.

In 10 years, some elementary school students (now 6–10 years old), more middle-grade students (now 11–14 years old), and many high school students (now 15–18 years old) will be parents. By 2020, many of their children will be in day care, preschool, and elementary school. Will tomorrow's parents be good partners with their children's schools? Will the schools be good partners with tomorrow's parents?

QUESTIONS TO DISCUSS

Based on the articles you read and the discussions and activities you conducted, how do you think school, family, and community partnerships should be conducted in the future?

1. Identify a school level that interests you (i.e., preschool or elementary, middle, or high).
2. For the school level you selected, write an essay on your vision of ideal school, family, and community partnerships in 2020.
   a. Address these questions:
      - In the year 2020, how should schools connect with families and communities?
      - How should parents connect with their children's schools, interact with educators, and influence their children's education?
   b. Include ideas about the policies and actions that will be needed to realize your vision. These may include school, district, state, and/or federal policies; educators' preparation; family factors and approaches; and other requirements.
   c. How likely is it that your vision of school, family, and community partnerships will be fulfilled by 2020? Explain.

Shaping the Future

We cannot change past patterns of school, family, and community partnerships, but we can shape the future. This includes improving preservice, advanced, and inservice education so that all teachers and administrators understand school, family, and community partnerships and can apply what they know.

From all of the studies, fieldwork, discussions, and activities discussed in this volume, one thing is very clear. It is unreasonable to expect parents, on their own, to create the knowledge needed every year to interact productively with their children as students or to connect with their children's schools and teachers. By contrast, it is reasonable to expect all schools, districts, and state departments of education to organize ongoing programs of school, family, and community partnerships so that all parents are well informed and productively involved every year with their children and schools.

This volume for preparing educators to understand school, family, and community partnerships takes readers one step toward improving policies and practices of involvement. When well-prepared teachers, administrators, counselors, and other professionals take positions in schools, districts, and state departments of education, the real work to organize, implement, and sustain programs of partnership begins.

REFERENCES

Epstein, J. L., and F. L. Van Voorhis. (In press). School counselors' roles in developing partnerships with families and communities for student success. *Professional School Counseling*.

Epstein, J. L., et al. (2009). *School, family, and community partnerships: Your handbook for action* (3rd ed.). Thousand Oaks, CA: Corwin.

Sanders, M. (2008). How parent liaisons can help bridge home and school. *Journal of Educational Research* 101: 287–297.

Sanders, M. G., and S. B. Sheldon. (2009). *Principals Matter: A Guide to School, Family, and Community Partnerships*. Thousand Oaks, CA: Corwin.

Index